COMPUTER AND COMMUNICATION
NETWORKS

Second Edition

COMPUTER AND COMMUNICATION NETWORKS

Second Edition

Nader F. Mir

PRENTICE
HALL

Upper Saddle River, NJ • Boston • Indianapolis • San Francisco
New York • Toronto • Montreal • London • Munich • Paris • Madrid
Capetown • Sydney • Tokyo • Singapore • Mexico City

Many of the designations used by manufacturers and sellers to distinguish their products are claimed as trademarks. Where those designations appear in this book, and the publisher was aware of a trademark claim, the designations have been printed with initial capital letters or in all capitals.

The author and publisher have taken care in the preparation of this book, but make no expressed or implied warranty of any kind and assume no responsibility for errors or omissions. No liability is assumed for incidental or consequential damages in connection with or arising out of the use of the information or programs contained herein.

For information about buying this title in bulk quantities, or for special sales opportunities (which may include electronic versions; custom cover designs; and content particular to your business, training goals, marketing focus, or branding interests), please contact our corporate sales department at corpsales@pearsoned.com or (800) 382-3419.

For government sales inquiries, please contact governmentsales@pearsoned.com.

For questions about sales outside the United States, please contact international@pearsoned.com.

Visit us on the Web: informit.com/ph

Library of Congress Catalog-in-Publication Data

Mir, Nader F.
  Computer and communication networks / Nader F. Mir.—Second edition.
    pages   cm
  Includes bibliographical references and index.
  ISBN 978-0-13-381474-3 (hardcover : alk. paper)—ISBN 0-13-381474-2 (hardcover : alk. paper)
  1. Computer networks. 2. Data transmission systems. I. Title.
  TK5105.5.M567 2015
  004.6—dc23
                                                      2014037209

ISBN-13: 978-0-13-381474-3
ISBN-10: 0-13-381474-2

Text printed in the United States on recycled paper at Courier in Westford, Massachusetts.
First printing, December 2014

Editor-in-Chief
Mark L. Taub

Senior Acquisitions Editor
Trina MacDonald

Development Editor
Songlin Qiu

Managing Editor
John Fuller

Full-Service Production Manager
Julie B. Nahil

Project Manager
Vicki Rowland

Indexer
Ted Laux

Proofreader
Andrea Fox

Publishing Coordinator
Olivia Basegio

Cover Designer
Chuti Prasertsith

Compositor
diacriTech, Inc.

To Shahrzad and Navid

Contents

PART II: Advanced Concepts   401

Preface

This textbook represents more than a decade of work. During this time, some material became obsolete and had to be deleted. In my days as a telecommunication engineer and then a university professor, much has changed in the fields of data communications and computer networks. Nonetheless, this text covers both the foundations and the latest advanced topics of computer communications and networking.

The Internet is a revolutionary communication vehicle by which we all conveniently communicate every day and do business with one another. Because of its complexities at both hardware and software levels, the Internet is a challenge to those who want to study this field. The growing number and variety of communication services introduces other challenges to experts of computer networks. Such experts are in need of effective references having in-depth balanced analysis, architecture, and description, and enabling them to better design emerging communication networks. This book fills the gaps in current available texts.

Objectives

This textbook offers a mix of theory, architecture, and applications in computer networking. The lack of computer communications books presenting moderate analysis with detailed figures covering both wireline and wireless communication technologies led me to write this book. The main objective of this book is to help readers learn the fundamentals and certain advanced concepts of computer and communication networks, using a unified set of symbols throughout a single textbook. The preparation of this book responds to the explosive demand for learning computer communication science and engineering.

This book targets two groups of people. For people in academia, at both the undergraduate and graduate levels, the book provides a thorough design and performance evaluation of communication networks. The book can also give researchers the ability to analyze and simulate complex communication networks. For engineers who want to work in the communication and networking industry and need a reference covering various angles of computer networks, this book provides a variety of learning techniques: exercises, case studies, and computer simulation projects. The book makes it easy and fun for an engineer to review and learn from a reliable networking reference covering all the necessary concepts and performance models.

Organization of This Book

The range of topics presented in this text allows instructors to choose the topics best suited for their classes. Besides the explanations provided in each chapter, readers will learn how to model a communication network and how to mathematically analyze it. Readers of this text will benefit from the combination of theory and applications presented in each chapter, with the more theoretical portions of each chapter challenging those readers who are more ambitious.

This book is organized into 22 chapters in two main parts, as follows. The ten chapters of Part I cover the fundamental topics in computer networking, with each chapter serving as a base for the following chapter. Part I of the book begins with an overview of networking, focusing on TCP/IP schemes, describing routing and multicasting in regular networks and wireless networks, and ending with a discussion of network applications, P2P networking, network management, and security. Part I is most appropriate for readers with no experience in computer communications. The 12 chapters in Part II cover detailed analytical aspects and offer a closer perspective of advanced networking protocols: architectures of switches and routers, delay and congestion analysis, label switching, virtual private networks, optical networks, cloud computing, SDN, data compression, voice over IP (VoIP), multimedia networking, ad-hoc networking, and sensor networks. An overview of the 22 chapters is as follows:

- **Chapter 1, Packet-Switched Networks**, introduces computer networks, touching on the need for networks, explaining relevant packet-switched networks, and giving an overview of today's Internet. Fundamental concepts, such as *messages*, *packets*, and *frames* and *packet switching* versus *circuit switching*, are defined. Various types of packet-switched networks are defined, and how a message can be handled by either *connection-oriented networks* or *connectionless networks* is explained. The second part of the chapter presents basics of the five- and seven-layer Internet Protocol reference models, as well as Internet and addressing scheme. Finally, this chapter presents a detailed analysis of packet size and optimization.

- **Chapter 2, Overview of Networking Devices**, introduces the overall architectures of regular and wireless networking devices. The chapter starts with introducing *network interface cards* (NICs), followed by switching and routing devices, such as hubs, bridges, switches, and routers. These devices are used to switch packets from one path to another. The devices include both wireline and wireless devices used as user, server, or network equipment. Networking modems are used for access to the Internet from remote and residential areas. Finally, multiplexers are used in all layers of a network and are utilized to combine data from multiple lines into one line.

- **Chapter 3, Data Links and Link Interfaces**, focuses on the links and transmission interfaces, the two basic components that networking starts with. This chapter presents both wired and wireless links and describes their characteristics, advantages, and channel access methods. This chapter also presents various *error-detection and correction* techniques at the link level and discusses the integrity of transmitted data. The chapter further presents link-layer *stop-and-wait* and *sliding-window* flow controls. We then proceed to presenting methods of link and then channel access by multiple users, both in regular and wireless environments. Finally, at the end of the chapter, the *link aggregation* method is described. The method combines multiple network links to increase throughput beyond what a single link can sustain. Link aggregation also has a second benefit of providing redundancy in case one of the links fails. We then introduce the well-known *Link Aggregation Control Protocol* (LACP).

- **Chapter 4, Local Area Networks and Networks of LANs**, explores the implementation of small networks, using the functional aspects of the fundamental knowledge gained in Chapters 1, 2, and 3 on basic protocols, devices, and links, respectively. The chapter provides some pointers for constructing a network with those devices and making connections, gives several examples of local area networks (LANs), and explains how such LANs are internetworked. Next, the chapter explores address conversion protocols by which addresses at layers 2 and 3 are converted to one another. The chapter at this point proceeds to the very important topic of the Spanning-Tree Protocol (STP). STP prevents frames or packets from the looping that causes infinite circulation of frames in a network. *Virtual LANs* (VLANs) are the next topic. A VLAN methodology allows a single LAN to be partitioned into several seemingly and virtually separate LANs. At the end of the chapter, a reader can see an overview of wireless local area networks including WiFi, and wireless LANs and associated standards such as IEEE 802.11.

- **Chapter 5, Wide-Area Routing and Internetworking**, focuses on routing in wide area networks (WANs) and introduces related routing algorithms and protocols. We begin the chapter with some IP packet format and basic routing policies such as the *Internet Control Message Protocol* (ICMP), *Dynamic Host Configuration Protocol* (DHCP), and *Network Address Translation* (NAT). We then proceed to explain path selection algorithms such as the *Open Shortest Path First* (OSPF) protocol, and the *Routing Information Protocol* (RIP) followed by the interdomain routing protocols with a focus on the *Border Gateway Protocol* (BGP) covering both internal BGP (iBGP) and external BGP (eBGP). The chapter then presents IPv6 and its packet format. The chapter finally covers congestion-control algorithms at the network layer: *network-congestion control* and *link-flow control*, and especially looks at *random early detection* for congestion control and describes a useful technique to estimate the link-blocking probability.

- **Chapter 6, Multicast Routing and Protocols**, covers the multicast extension of routing protocols in the Internet. First, the chapter defines basic terms and algorithms: multicast group, multicast addresses, and multicast tree algorithms, which form the next set of foundations for understanding packet multicast in the Internet. Two main classes of protocols are discussed: *intradomain* multicast routing protocols, by which packets are multicast within a domain; and *interdomain* routing protocol, by which packet multicast among domains is managed.

- **Chapter 7, Wireless Wide Area Networks and LTE Technology**, presents the basics of wireless wide area networking. The chapter discusses challenges in designing a wireless network: *management of mobility, network reliability,* and *frequency reuse*. The chapter then shifts to cellular networks, one of the main backbones of our wireless wide area networking infrastructure. The *mobile IP* in cellular networks is then presented, in which a mobile user can make a data connection while changing its location. The chapter then focuses on *wireless mesh networks* (WMNs). Finally, the chapter proceeds to the presentation of the fourth-generation wireless wide area networks called *Long-Term Evolution* (LTE).

- **Chapter 8, Transport and End-to-End Protocols**, first looks at the basics of the *transport layer* and demonstrates how a simple file is transferred. This layer handles the details of data transmission. Several techniques for Transmission Control Protocol (TCP) congestion control are discussed. Next, *congestion-avoidance* methods, which are methods of using precautionary algorithms to avoid a possible congestion in a TCP session, are presented. The chapter ends with a discussion of methods of congestion control.

- **Chapter 9, Basic Network Applications and Management**, presents the fundamentals of the *application layer*, which determines how a specific user application should use a network. Among the applications are the *Domain Name System* (DNS); *e-mail protocols*, such as SMTP and Webmail, the *World Wide Web* (WWW), remote login, File Transfer Protocol (FTP), and *peer-to-peer* (P2P) networking. Finally, the chapter proceeds to the presentation of network management techniques and protocol.

- **Chapter 10, Network Security**, focuses on security aspects of networks. After introducing network threats, hackers, and attacks, this chapter discusses *cryptography techniques: public- and symmetric-key protocols, encryption standards, key-exchange algorithms, authentication methods, digital signature* and secure connections, firewalls, IPsec, and security methods for virtual private networks. This chapter also covers some security aspects of wireless networks.

- **Chapter 11, Network Queues and Delay Analysis**, begins Part II of the book by discussing how packets are queued in buffers. Basic modeling theorems are presented such as *Little's theorem*, the *Markov chain theorem*, and *birth and death processes*. Queueing-node models are presented with several scenarios: finite versus infinite queueing capacity, one server versus several servers, and Markovian versus non-Markovian systems. Non-Markovian models are essential for many network applications, as multimedia traffic cannot be modeled by Markovian patterns. In addition, delay analysis, based on networks of queues, is discussed. *Burke's theorem* is applied in both serial and parallel queueing nodes. *Jackson's theorem* is presented for situations in which a packet visits a particular queue more than once, resulting in *loops* or *feedback*.

- **Chapter 12, Advanced Router and Switch Architectures**, looks inside structures of advanced Internet devices such as switches and routers. The chapter begins with general characteristics and block diagrams of switches and routers followed by basic features of *input port processors* (IPPs) and *output port processors* (OPPs) as the interfacing processors to central controllers and switch fabrics.

The details of IPPs and OPPs with several regular IP and IPv6 examples for building blocks such as routing tables, packet parsers, and packet partitioners are presented. A number of switch fabric structures are introduced starting with the building block of *crossbar* switch fabric. In particular, a case study at the end of chapter combines a number of buffered crosspoints to form a buffered crossbar. A number of other switch architectures—both blocking and nonblocking, as well as shared-memory, *concentration-based*, and *expansion-based* switching networks—are presented. The chapter also introduces packet multicast techniques and algorithms used within the hardware of switches and routers.

- **Chapter 13, Quality of Service and Scheduling in Routers**, covers quality-of-service issues in networking. The two broad categories of QoS discussed are the *integrated services approach*, for providing service quality to networks that require maintaining certain features in switching nodes; and the *differentiated services approach* (DiffServ), which is based on providing quality-of-service support to a broad class of applications. These two categories include a number of QoS protocols and architectures, such as *traffic shaping, admission control, packet scheduling, reservation methods*, the *Resource Reservation Protocol* (RSVP), and traffic conditioner and bandwidth broker methods. This chapter also explains fundamentals of resource allocation in data networks.

- **Chapter 14, Tunneling, VPNs, and MPLS Networks**, starts by introducing a useful Internet technique called *tunneling*, used in advanced, secured, and high-speed networking. The chapter explains how networks can be *tunneled* to result in *virtual private networks* (VPNs) by which a private-sector entity tunnels over the public networking infrastructure, maintaining private connections. Another related topic in this chapter is *multiprotocol label switching* (MPLS) networks, in which networks use labels and tunnels to expedite routing.

- **Chapter 15, All-Optical Networks, WDM, and GMPLS**, presents principles of fiber-optic communications and all-optical switching and networking. The optical communication technology uses principles of light emission in a glass medium, which can carry more information over longer distances than electrical signals can carry in a copper or coaxial medium. The discussion on optical networks starts with basic optical devices, such as *optical filters, wavelength-division multiplexers* (WDMs), *optical switches*, and *optical buffers* and *optical delay lines*. After detailing optical networks using routing devices, the chapter discusses *wavelength reuse and allocation* as a link in all-optical networks.

Generalized multiprotocol label switching (GMPLS) technology, which is similar to MPLS studied in the previous chapter, is applied to optical networks and is also studied in this chapter. The chapter ends with a case study on an optical switching network, presenting a new topology: the *spherical switching network* (SSN).

- **Chapter 16, Cloud Computing and Network Virtualization**, covers basics of cloud computing, large data centers, networking segments of data centers, and virtualization in networking. Data center and cloud computing architectures continue to target support for tens of thousands of servers, massive data storage, terabits per second of traffic, and tens of thousands of tenants. First, the chapter defines basic terms such as *virtualization*, *virtual machines*, and the structure of large data centers constructed from server racks and large data bases. The chapter also presents *data center networks* (DCNs). In a data center, server and storage resources are interconnected with packet switches and routers to construct the DCN.

- **Chapter 17, Software-Defined Networking (SDN) and Beyond,** covers primarily advanced paradigms in control and management of networks. Growth at the infrastructure and applications of the Internet causes profound changes in the technology ecosystems of Internet-related industries. *Software-Defined Networking* (SDN) is a networking paradigm by which a central software program known as "controller" (or SDN controller) determines and controls the overall network behavior resulting in potential improvement in the network performance. This chapter focuses on the fundamentals of SDN and a couple of other alternative innovative networking features, and describes the details of related topics such as OpenFlow switches and flow tables in switches. Protocols such as *network functions virtualization* (NFV) and *Information-Centric Networking* (ICN) are other advanced network control and management topics covered in this chapter. Finally, the chapter concludes with a section that presents network emulators such as the Mininet emulator.

- **Chapter 18, Voice over IP (VoIP) Signaling**, presents the signaling protocols used in voice over IP (VoIP) telephony and multimedia networking. The chapter starts with reviewing the basics of call control and signaling in the traditional Public Switched Telephone Network (PSTN). The chapter then presents two important voice over IP (VoIP) protocols designed to provide real-time service to the Internet, the *Session Initiation Protocol* (SIP) and the *H.323 series* *of protocols.* At the end of the chapter, a reader can find presentations on a series of internetworking examples between a set of callers, each supplied through a different Internet service provider and a different protocol.

- **Chapter 19, Media Exchange and Voice/Video Compression**, focuses on data-compression techniques for voice and video to prepare digital voice and video for multimedia networking. The chapter starts with the analysis of information-source fundamentals, source coding, and limits of data compression, and explains all the steps of the conversion from raw voice to compressed binary form, such as sampling, quantization, and encoding. The chapter also summarizes the limits of compression and explains typical processes of still-image and video-compression techniques, such as JPEG, MPEG, and MP3.

- **Chapter 20, Distributed and Cloud-Based Multimedia Networking**, presents the transport of real-time voice, video, and data in multimedia networking. The chapter first presents protocols designed to provide real-time transport, such as the *Real-time Transport Protocol* (RTP). Also discussed are the *HTTP-based streaming* which is a reliable TCP-based streaming, and the *Stream Control Transmission Protocol* (SCTP), which provides a general-purpose transport protocol for transporting stream traffic. The next topic is streaming video using *content distribution (delivery) networks* (CDNs). We then present *Internet Protocol television* (IPTV). IPTV is a system through which television services are delivered using the Internet. *Video on demand* (VoD) as a unique feature of IPTV is also described in this chapter. Next, cloud-based multimedia networking is introduced. This type of networking consists of distributed and networked services of voice, video, and data. For example, voice over IP (VoIP), video streaming, or *interactive voice response* (IVR) for recognizing human voice, can be distributed in various clouds of services. The chapter ends with detailed streaming source modeling using self-similarity analysis.

- **Chapter 21, Mobile Ad-Hoc Networks**, presents a special type of wireless network, known as a *mobile ad-hoc network* (MANET). Ad-hoc networks do not need any fixed infrastructure to operate and they support dynamic topology scenarios where no wired infrastructure exists. The chapter explains how a mobile user can act as a routing node and how a packet is routed from a source to its destination without having any static router in the network. The chapter also discusses *table-driven routing protocols* such as DSDV, CGSR, and WRP, and also *source-initiated routing protocols*, as well as DSR, ABR, TORA, and AODV. At the end of the chapter, we discuss the security of ad-hoc networks.

- **Chapter 22, Wireless Sensor Networks**, presents an overview of such sensor networks and describes intelligent sensor nodes, as well as an overview of a protocol stack for sensor networks. The chapter explains how the "power" factor distinguishes the routing protocols of sensor networks from those of computer networks and describes *clustering protocols* in sensor networks. These protocols specify the topology of the hierarchical network partitioned into nonoverlapping *clusters* of sensor nodes. The chapter also presents a typical routing protocol for sensor networks, leading to a detailed numerical case study on the implementation of a clustering protocol. This chapter ends with *ZigBee technology*, based on IEEE standard 802.15.4. This technology uses low-power nodes and is a well-known low-power standard.

Exercises and Computer Simulation Projects

A number of exercises are given at the end of each chapter. The exercises normally challenge readers to find the directions to solutions in that chapter. The answers to the exercises may be more elusive, but this is typical of real and applied problems in networking. These problems encourage the reader to go back through the text and pick out what the instructor believes is significant.

Besides typical exercises, there are numerous occasions for those who wish to incorporate projects into their courses. The computer simulation projects are normally meant to be a programming project but the reader can use a simulation tool of choice to complete a project. Projects listed at the end of a chapter range from computer simulations to partial incorporation of hardware design in a simulation.

Appendixes

The book's appendixes make it essentially self-sufficient. **Appendix A, Glossary of Acronyms**, defines acronyms. **Appendix B, RFCs**, encourages readers to delve more deeply into each protocol presented in the book by consulting the many requests for comments (RFCs) references. **Appendix C, Probabilities and Stochastic Processes**, reviews probabilities, random variables, and random processes. **Appendix D, Erlang-B Blocking Probability Table,** provides a numerically expanded version of the Erlang-B formula presented in Chapter 11. This table can be used in various chapters to estimate traffic blocking, which is one of the main factors in designing a computer network.

Instructions and Instructor Supplements

This textbook can be used in a variety of ways. An instructor can use Part I of the book for the first graduate or a senior undergraduate course in networking. Part II of the text is aimed at advanced graduate courses in computer networks. An instructor can choose the desired chapters, depending on the need and the content of the course. The following guidelines suggest the adoption of chapters for five different courses:

- *First undergraduate course in Computer Networking:* Chapters 1, 2, 3, 4, and 5 and another chapter such as part of Chapter 6, 7, 8, or 9.
- *First graduate course in Computer Networking:* Chapters 1 through 10 with less emphasis on Chapters 1 and 2.
- *Second graduate course in Advanced Computer Networking:* Chapters 11 through 17.
- *Graduate course in Convergent Data, Voice and Video over IP:* Chapters 7, 9, 16, 18, 19, and 20.
- *Graduate course in Wireless Networking:* Chapters 2, 3, 4, 7, 9, 16, 21, and 22, and other wireless network examples presented in various chapters such the wireless VoIP signaling covered in Chapter 18.

An instructor's solutions manual and other instructional material, such as PowerPoint presentations, will be available to instructors. Instructors should go to Pearson's Instructor Resource Center (http://www.pearsonhighered.com/educator/profile/ircHomeTab.page) for access to ancillary instructional materials.

Acknowledgments

Writing a text is rarely an individual effort. Many experts from industry and academia graciously provided help. I would like to thank them all very warmly for their support. Many of them have given me invaluable ideas and support during this project. I should acknowledge all those scientists, mathematicians, professors, engineers, authors, and publishers who helped me in this project.

I am honored to publish this book with the world's greatest publishing company, Prentice Hall. I wish to express my deep gratitude to everyone there who made an effort to make this project succeed. In particular, I would like to thank editor-in-chief Mark L. Taub and senior acquisitions editor Trina MacDonald for all their advice. Trina, with her outstanding professional talent, provided me with invaluable information and directed me toward the end of this great and challenging project. I would also like to thank managing editor John Fuller, full-service production manager Julie Nahil, development editor Songlin Qiu, freelance project manager Vicki Rowland, freelance copy editor/proofreader Andrea Fox, and all the other experts for their outstanding work but whom I did not get a chance to acknowledge by name in this section, including the marketing manager, the compositors, the indexer, and the cover designer; many thanks to all. Last but not least, I would like to thank Pearson sales representative Ellen Wynn, who enthusiastically introduced the first edition of my manuscript to the publisher.

I am deeply grateful to the technical editors, and all advisory board members of this book. In particular, I thank Professor George Scheets, Professor Zongming Fei, and Dr. Parviz Yegani for making constructive suggestions that helped me reshape the book to its present form. In addition, I would like to especially recognize the following people, who provided invaluable feedback from time to time during the writing phases of the first and second editions of the book. I took all their comments seriously and incorporated them into the manuscript. I greatly appreciate their time spent on this project.

Professor Nirwan Ansari (New Jersey Institute of Technology)

Professor Mohammed Atiquzzaman (University of Oklahoma)

Dr. Radu Balan (Siemens Corporate Research)

Dr. Greg Bernstein (Grotto Networking)

R. Bradley (About.com)

Deepak Biala (OnFiber Communications)

Dr. Robert Cane (VPP, United Kingdom)

Kevin Choy (Atmel, Colorado)

Dr. Kamran Eftekhari (University of California, San Diego)

Professor Zongming Fei (University of Kentucky)

Dr. Carlos Ferari (JTN-Network Solutions)

Dr. Jac Grolan (Alcatel)

Professor Jim Griffioen (University of Kentucky)

Ajay Kalambor (Cisco Systems)

Parviz Karandish (Softek, Inc.)

Aurna Ketaraju (Intel)

Dr. Hardeep Maldia (Sermons Communications)

Will Morse (Texas Safe-Computing)

Professor Sarhan Musa (P. V. Texas A&M University)

Professor Achille Pattavina (Politecnico di Milano TNG)

Dr. Robert J. Paul (NsIM Communications)

Bala Peddireddi (Intel)

Christopher H. Pham (Cisco Systems)

Jasmin Sahara (University of Southern California)

Dipti Sathe (Altera Corporation)

Dr. Simon Sazeman (Sierra Communications and Networks)

Professor George Scheets (Oklahoma State University)

Professor Mukesh Singhal (University of Kentucky)

Professor Kazem Sohraby (University of Arkansas)

Dr. Richard Stevensson (BoRo Comm)

Professor Jonathan Turner (Washington University)

Kavitha Venkatesan (Cisco Systems)

Dr. Belle Wei (California State University, Chico)

Dr. Steve Willmard (SIM Technology)

Dr. Parviz Yegani (Juniper Networks)

Dr. Hemeret Zokhil (JPLab)

I am thankful to my graduate students who helped me throughout the long phase of preparing the manuscript of this textbook. Over the past several years, more than 112 of my graduate students read various portions of this book and made constructive comments. I wish them all the best for their honest support and verbal comments on early versions of this book used in my class lectures. I am especially thankful to the following graduate students who voluntarily reviewed some sections of the book while taking my networking courses: Howard Chan, Robert Bergman, Eshetie Liku, Andrew Cole, Jonathan Hui, Lisa Wellington, and Sitthapon Pumpichet. Special thanks to Marzieh Veyseh for making all the information about sensor networks available for Chapter 22.

Last but not least, I am indebted to my parents who opened the door to the best education for me and supported me all my life; and above all, I want to thank my family who supported and encouraged me in spite of all the time it took me away from them to work on this book. It was a long and difficult journey for them.

How to Contact the Author

Please feel free to send me any feedback at the Department of Electrical Engineering, Charles W. Davidson College of Engineering, San Jose State University, San Jose, California 95192, U.S.A., or via e-mail at nader.mir@sjsu.edu. I would love to hear from you, especially if you have suggestions for improving this book. I will carefully read all review comments. You can find out more about me at www.engr.sjsu.edu/nmir. I hope that you enjoy the text and that you receive from it a little of my enthusiasm for computer communications and networks.

—Nader F. Mir
San Jose, California

About the Author

Nader F. Mir received the B.Sc. degree (with honors) in electrical engineering in 1985, and the M.Sc. and Ph.D. degrees, both in electrical engineering, from Washington University in St. Louis, Missouri, in 1990 and 1995, respectively.

He is currently a professor, and served as the associate chair, at the Department of Electrical Engineering, Charles W. Davidson College of Engineering, San Jose State University, California. He also serves as the academic coordinator of the university's special graduate programs offered at several Silicon Valley companies such as Lockheed-Martin Space Systems Company.

Dr. Mir is a well-known expert in patent and technology litigation cases in the areas of communications, telecommunications, and computer networks, and has worked as a patent consultant for leading companies in the field such as Google, Cisco, Netflix, Sony, Tekelec, and YouTube (Google).

Dr. Mir is internationally known through his research and scholarly work, and has been invited to speak at a number of major international conferences. He has published more than 100 refereed technical journal and conference articles, all in the field of communications and computer networking. This textbook is now a worldwide adopted university textbook and has been translated into several languages, such as Chinese.

He was granted a successful U.S. Patent (Patent 7,012,895 B1), claiming an invention related to hardware/protocol for use in high-speed computer communication networks.

Dr. Mir has received a number of prestigious national and university awards and research grants. He is the recipient of a university teaching award and also a university research excellence award. He is also the recipient of a number of outstanding presentation awards from leading international conferences.

He is currently the technical editor of *IEEE Communications Magazine.* He has held several other editorial positions such as editor of *Journal of Computing and Information Technology*, guest editor for computer networking at *CIT Journal*, and editorial board member of the *International Journal of Internet Technology and Secured Transactions.* He is a senior member of the IEEE and has also served as a member of the technical program committee and steering committee for a number of major IEEE communications and networking conferences such as WCNC, GLOBECOM, and ICC and ICCCN conferences.

The areas of his research are: Computer and Communication Networks, TCP/IP Internet, Client/Server, SDN, Cloud Computing, Web, Load Balancing, VoIP, Video and Streaming over IP, Multimedia Networks, Design of Networking Equipment, Modems, Switches and Routers, PSTN, SS7, Wireless and Mobile Networks, and Wireless Sensor Networks.

Prior to his current position, he was an associate professor at his current school, and assistant professor at University of Kentucky in Lexington. From 1994 to 1996, he was a research scientist at the Advanced Telecommunications Institute, Stevens Institute of Technology in New Jersey, working on the design of advanced communication systems and high-speed computer networks. From 1990 to 1994, he was with the Computer and Communications Research Center at Washington University in St. Louis and worked as a research assistant on the design and analysis of a high-speed switching systems project. From 1985 to 1988, he was with Telecommunication Research & Development Center (TRDC), Surrey, and as a telecommunications system research and development engineer, participated in the design of a high-speed digital telephone Private Branch Exchange (PBX), and received the best "design/ idea" award.

PART I

FUNDAMENTAL CONCEPTS

CHAPTER 1

Packet-Switched Networks

Computer and communication networks provide a wide range of services, from simple networks of computers to remote-file access to digital libraries, voice over IP (VoIP), Internet gaming, cloud computing, video streaming and conferencing, television over Internet, wireless data communication, and networking billions of users and devices. Before exploring the world of computer and communication networks, we need to study the fundamentals of *packet-switched networks* as the first step. Packet-switched networks are the backbone of the data communication infrastructure. Therefore, our focus in this chapter is on the big picture and the conceptual aspects of this backbone highlighted as:

- *Basic definitions in networks*
- *Types of packet-switched networks*
- *Packet size and optimizations*
- *Foundation of networking protocols*
- *Addressing scheme in the Internet*
- *Equal-sized packet model*

We start with the basic definitions and fundamental concepts, such as *messages*, *packets*, and *frames*, and *packet switching* versus *circuit switching*. We learn what the Internet is and how Internet service providers (ISPs) are formed. We then proceed to types of packet-switched networks and how a message can be handled by either *connection-oriented networks* or *connectionless networks*. Because readers must get a good understanding of *packets* as data units, packet size and optimizations are also discussed.

We next briefly describe specific type of networks used in the Internet. Users and networks are connected together by certain rules called *protocols*. The Internet Protocol (IP), for example, is responsible for using prevailing rules to establish paths for packets. Protocols are represented by either the TCP/IP model or the OSI model. The *five-layer TCP/IP model* is a widely accepted Internet backbone protocol structure. In this chapter, we give an overview of these five layers and leave any further details to be discussed in the remaining chapters. Among these five layers, the basics of IP *packets and network addressing* are designated a separate section in this chapter, entitled IP Packets and Addressing. We make this arrangement because basic definitions related to this layer are required in the following few chapters.

As numerous protocols can be combined to enable the movement of packets, the explanation of all other protocols will be spread over almost all upcoming chapters. In the meantime, the reader is cautiously reminded that getting a good grasp of the fundamental material discussed in this chapter is essential for following the details or extensions described in the remainder of the book. At the end of this chapter, the *equal-sized packet protocol model* is briefly introduced.

1.1 Basic Definitions in Networks

Communication networks have become essential media for homes and businesses. The design of modern computer and communication networks must meet all the requirements for new communication applications. A ubiquitous *broadband network* is the goal of the networking industry. Communication services need to be available anywhere and anytime. The broadband network is required to support the exchange of multiple types of information, such as voice, video, and data, among multiple types of users, while satisfying the performance requirement of each individual application. Consequently, the expanding diversity of high-bandwidth communication applications calls for a unified, flexible, and efficient network. The design goal of modern communication networks is to meet all the networking demands and to integrate capabilities of networks in a broadband network.

Packet-switched networks are the building blocks of computer communication systems in which data units known as *packets* flow across networks. The goal of a broadband packet-switched network is to provide flexible communication in handling all kinds of connections for a wide range of applications, such as telephone calls, data transfer, teleconferencing, video broadcasting, and distributed data processing. One obvious example for the form of traffic is *multi-rate* connections, whereby traffic containing several different bit rates flows to a communication node. The form of information in packet-switched networks is always digital bits. This kind of communication infrastructure is a significant improvement over the traditional telephone networks known as *circuit-switched networks*.

1.1.1 Packet Switching Versus Circuit Switching

Circuit-switched networks, as the basis of conventional telephone systems, were the only existing personal communication infrastructures prior to the invention of packet-switched networks. In the new communication structure, voice and computer data are treated the same, and both are handled in a unified network known as a packet-switched network, or simply an integrated data network. In conventional telephone networks, a circuit between two users must be established for communication to occur. Circuit-switched networks require resources to be reserved for each pair of end users. This implies that no other users can use the already dedicated resources for the duration of network use and thus the reservation of network resources for each user may result in inefficient use of available bandwidth.

Packet-switched networks with a unified, integrated data network infrastructure collectively known as the *Internet* can provide a variety of communication services requiring different bandwidths. The advantage of having a unified, integrated data network is the flexibility to handle existing and future services with remarkably better performance and higher economical resource utilizations. An integrated data network can also derive the benefits of central network management, operation, and maintenance. Numerous requirements for integrated packet-switched networks are explored in later chapters:

- Having robust routing protocols capable of adapting to dynamic changes in network topology
- Maximizing the utilization of network resources for the integration of all types of services

- Providing quality of service to users by means of priority and scheduling
- Enforcing effective congestion-control mechanisms that can minimize dropping packets

Circuit-switched networking is preferred for real-time applications. However, the use of packet-switched networks, especially for the integration and transmission of voice and data, results in the far more efficient utilization of available bandwidth. Network resources can be shared among other eligible users. Packet-switched networks can span a large geographical area and comprise a web of switching *nodes* interconnected through transmission links. A network provides links among multiple users facilitating the transfer of information. To make efficient use of available resources, packet-switched networks dynamically allocate resources only when required.

1.1.2 Data, Packets, and Frames

A packet-switched network is organized as a multilevel hierarchy. In such a network, digital data are fragmented into one or more smaller units of data, each appended with a *header* to specify control information, such as the source and the destination addresses, while the remaining portion carries the actual data, called the *payload*. This new unit of formatted message is called a *packet*, as shown in Figure 1.1. Packets are forwarded to a data network to be delivered to their destinations. In some circumstances, packets may also be required to be attached together or further partitioned, forming a new packet having a new header. One example of such a packet is referred to as *frame*. Sometimes, a frame may be required to have more than one header to carry out additional tasks in multiple layers of a network.

As shown in Figure 1.2, two packets, A and B, are being forwarded from one side of a network to the other side. Packet-switched networks can be viewed from

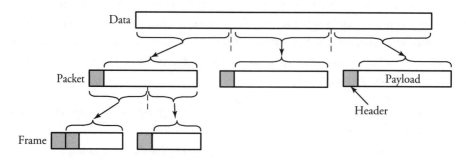

Figure 1.1 Creating packets and frames out of a raw digital data

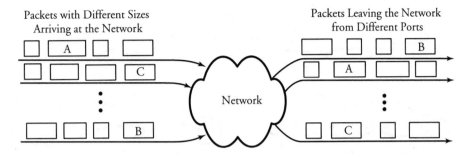

Figure 1.2   A packet-switched network receiving various-sized packets to route out

either an external or an internal perspective. The external perspective focuses on the network services provided to the upper layers; the internal perspective focuses on the fundamentals of *network topology*, the structure of communication protocols, and addressing schemes.

A single packet may even be split into multiple smaller packets before transmission. This well-known technique is called *packet fragmentation*. Apart from measuring the delay and ensuring that a packet is correctly sent to its destination, we also focus on delivering and receiving packets in a correct sequence when the data is fragmented. The primary function of a network is directing the flow of data among the users.

1.1.3   The Internet and ISPs

The *Internet* is the collection of hardware and software components that make up our global communication network. The Internet is indeed a collaboration of interconnected communication vehicles that can network all connected communicating devices and equipment and provide services to all distributed applications. It is almost impossible to plot an exact representation of the Internet, since it is continuously being expanded or altered. One way of imagining the Internet is shown in Figure 1.3, which illustrates a big-picture view of the worldwide computer network.

To connect to the Internet, users need the services of an *Internet service provider* (ISP). ISPs consist of various networking devices. One of the most essential networking devices is a *router*. Routers are network "nodes" that can operate to collectively form a network and to also connect ISPs together. Routers contain information about the network routes, and their tasks are to route packets to requested destinations.

Users, networking devices, and servers are connected together by communication *links*. Routers operate on the basis of one or more common *routing protocols*. In

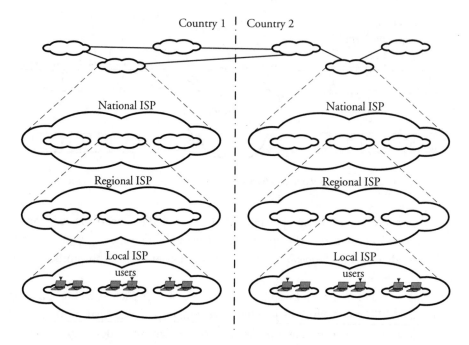

Figure 1.3   The Internet, a global interconnected network

computer networks, the entities must agree on a protocol, a set of rules governing data communications and defining when and how two users can communicate with each other. Each country has three types of ISPs:

- *National* ISPs
- *Regional* ISPs
- *Local* ISPs

At the top of the Internet hierarchy, national ISPs connect nations or provinces together. The traffic between each two national ISPs is very heavy. Two ISPs are connected together through complex switching nodes called *border routers* (or gateway routers). Each border router has its own system administrator. In contrast, *regional* ISPs are smaller ISPs connected to a national ISP in a hierarchical chart. Each regional ISP can give services to part of a province or a city. The lowest networking entity of the Internet is a local ISP. A local ISP is connected to a regional ISP or directly to a national service provider and provides a direct service to end users called *hosts*. An organization that supplies services to its own employees can also be a local ISP.

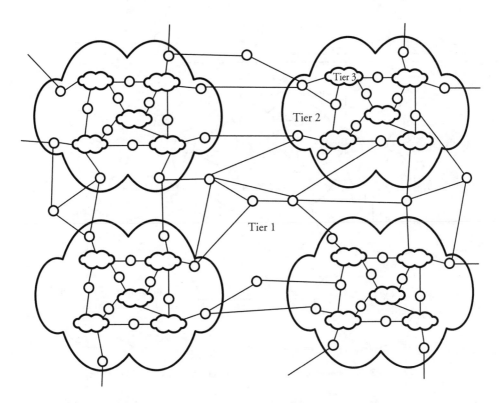

Figure 1.4   Hierarchy of networks from a different angle

Figure 1.4 illustrates a different perspective of the global interconnected network. Imagine the global network in a hierarchical structure. Each ISP of a certain hierarchy or tier manages a number of other network domains at its lower hierarchy. The structure of such networks resembles the hierarchy of nature from the universe to atoms and molecules. Here, Tier 1, Tier 2, and Tier 3 represent, respectively, a national ISP, a regional ISP, and a local ISP.

1.1.4   Classification of ISPs

In most cases, a separate network managed by a network administrator is known as a *domain*, or an *autonomous system*. A domain is shown by a cloud in this book. Figure 1.5 shows several domains. An autonomous system can be administered by an *Internet service provider* (ISP). An ISP provides Internet access to its users. Networks under management of ISPs can be classified into two main categories: *wide area networks* (WANs) and *local area networks* (LANs). A wide area network can be as large as the entire infrastructure of the data network access system known as the Internet.

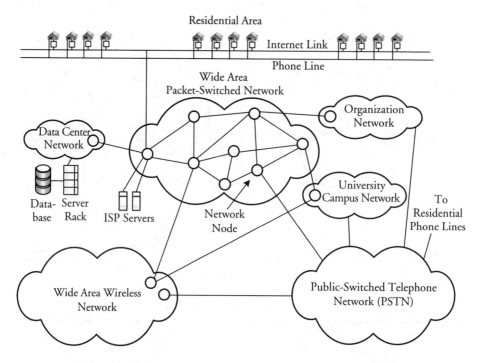

Figure 1.5   Overview of various types of Internet service providers (ISPs)

A communication network can also be of wireless type both at LAN or WAN scales. We refer to such networks as *wireless networks*.

Figure 1.5 shows several major WANs each connected to several smaller networks such as a university campus network. Depending on the size of the network, a smaller network can be classified as a LAN or as a WAN. The major WANs are somehow connected together to provide the best and fastest communication for customers. One of the WANs is a wide area wireless network that connects wireless or mobile users to destination users. We notice that aggregated traffic coming from wireless equipment such as smartphone and a mobile laptop in the wide area wireless network is forwarded to a link directed from a major node. The other WAN is the telephone network known as *public-switched telephone network* (PSTN) that provides telephone services.

As an example of the local area network, a university campus network is connected to the Internet via a router that connects the campus to an Internet service provider. ISP users from a residential area are also connected to an access point router of the wide area ISP, as seen in the figure. Service providers have varying policies to overcome the problem of bandwidth allocations on routers. An ISP's *routing server* is conversant with the policies of all other service providers. Therefore, the "ISP server" can direct the received routing information to an appropriate part of the ISP. Finally, on the left side of Figure 1.5, we see the *data center network* connected to the wide area packet-switched network. Cloud computing data centers contain databases and racks of servers that provide brilliant data processing services; these are discussed in detail in Chapter 16.

Network nodes (devices) such as *routers* are key components that allow the flow of information to be switched over other links. When a link failure occurs in a packet-switched network, the neighboring routers share the fault information with other nodes, resulting in updating of the routing tables. Thus, packets may get routed through alternative paths bypassing the fault. Building the *routing table* in a router is one of the principal challenges of packet-switched networks. Designing the routing table for large networks requires maintaining data pertaining to traffic patterns and network topology information.

1.2   Types of Packet-Switched Networks

Packet-switched networks are classified as *connectionless networks* and *connection-oriented networks*, depending on the technique used for transferring information. The simplest form of a network service is based on the connectionless protocol that does not require a call setup prior to transmission of packets. A related, though more complex, service is the connection-oriented protocol in which packets are transferred through an established virtual circuit between a source and a destination.

1.2.1   Connectionless Networks

Connectionless networks, or datagram networks, achieve high throughput at the cost of additional queuing delay. In this networking approach, a large piece of data is normally fragmented into smaller pieces, and then each piece of data is encapsulated into a certain "formatted" header, resulting in the basic Internet transmission packet, or *datagram*. We interchangeably use packets and datagrams for connectionless networks. Packets from a source are routed independently of one another. In this type of network, a user can transmit a packet anytime, without notifying the network layer. A packet is then sent over the network, with each router receiving the packet forwarding it to the best router it knows, until the packet reaches the destination.

The connectionless networking approach does not require a call setup to transfer packets, but it has error-detection capability. The main advantage of this scheme is its capability to route packets through an alternative path in case a fault is present on the desired transmission link. On the flip side, since packets belonging to the same source may be routed independently over different paths, the packets may arrive out of sequence; in such a case, the misordered packets are resequenced and delivered to the destination.

Figure 1.6 (a) shows the routing of three packets, packets 1, 2, and 3, in a connectionless network from point A to point B. The packets traverse the intermediate nodes in a *store-and-forward* fashion, whereby packets are received and stored at a node on a route; when the desired output port of the node is free for that packet, the output is forwarded to its next node. In other words, on receipt of a packet at a node, the packet must wait in a queue for its turn to be transmitted. Nevertheless, packet loss may still occur if a node's buffer becomes full. The node determines the next hop read from the packet header. In this figure, the first two packets are moving along the path A, D, C, and B, whereas the third packet moves on a separate path, owing to congestion on path A–D.

The delay model of the first three packets discussed earlier is shown in Figure 1.7. The total transmission delay for a message three packets long traversing from the source node A to the destination node B can be approximately determined. Let t_p be the propagation delay between each of the two nodes, t_f be the time it takes to inject a packet onto a link, and t_r be the total processing delay for all packets at each node. A packet is processed once it is received at a node. The total transmission delay, D_p for n_h nodes and n_p packets, in general is

$$D_p = [n_p + (n_h - 2)]t_f + (n_h - 1)t_p + n_h t_r. \tag{1.1}$$

In this equation, t_r includes a certain crucial delay component, primarily known as the *packet-queueing delay* plus some delay due to route finding for it. At this point,

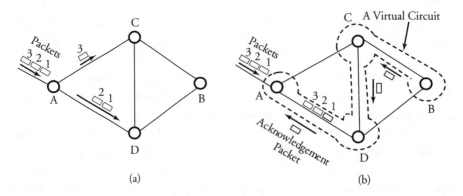

(a)   (b)

Figure 1.6 Two models of packet-switched networks: (a) a connectionless network and (b) a connection-oriented network

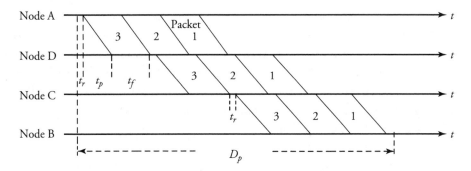

Figure 1.7   Signaling delay in a connectionless network

we focus only on t_p and t_f, assume t_r is known or given, and will discuss the queueing delay and all components of t_r in later chapters, especially in Chapter 11.

Example.   Figure 1.7 shows a timing diagram for the transmission of three (instead of two) packets on path A, D, C, B in Figure 1.6(a). Determine the total delay for transferring these three packets from node A to node B.

Solution.   Assume that the first packet is transmitted from the source, node A, to the next hop, node D. The total delay for this transfer is $t_p + t_f + t_r$. Next, the packet is similarly transferred from node D to the next node to ultimately reach node B. The delay for each of these jumps is also $t_p + t_f + t_r$. However, when all three packets are released from node A, multiple and simultaneous transmissions of packets become possible. This means, for example, while packet 2 is being processed at node A, packet 3 is processed at node D. Figure 1.7 clearly shows this parallel processing of packets. Thus, the total delay for all three packets to traverse the source and destination via two intermediate nodes is $D_p = 3t_p + 5t_f + 4t_r$.

Connectionless networks demonstrate the efficiency of transmitting a large message as a whole, especially in noisy environments, where the error rate is high. It is obvious that the large message should be split into packets. Doing so also helps reduce the maximum delay imposed by a single packet on other packets. In fact, this realization resulted in the advent of connectionless packet switching.

1.2.2   Connection-Oriented Networks

In *connection-oriented networks*, or *virtual-circuit networks*, a route setup between a source and a destination is required prior to data transfer, as in the case of conventional telephone networks. In this networking scheme, once a connection or a path is initially set up, network resources are reserved for the communication duration, and all packets belonging to the same source are routed over the established connection. After the communication between a source and a destination is finished, the connection is terminated using a connection-termination procedure. During the call setup, the network can offer a selection of options, such as best-effort service, reliable service, guaranteed delay service, and guaranteed bandwidth service, as explained in various sections of upcoming chapters.

Figure 1.6 (b) shows a connection-oriented - network. The connection set-up procedure shown in this figure requires three packets to move along path A, D, C, and B with a prior connection establishment. During the connection set-up process, a virtual path is dedicated, and the forwarding routing tables are updated at each node in the route. Figure 1.6 (b) also shows acknowledgement packets in connection-oriented networks initiated from destination node B to source node A to acknowledge the receipt of previously sent packets to source node. The acknowledgement mechanism is not typically used in connectionless networks. Connection-oriented packet switching typically reserves the network resources, such as the buffer capacity and the link bandwidth, to provide guaranteed quality of service and delay. The main disadvantage in connection-oriented packet-switched networks is that in case of a link or switch failure, the call set-up process has to be repeated for all the affected routes. Also, each switch needs to store information about all the flows routed through the switch.

The total delay in transmitting a packet in connection-oriented packet switching is the sum of the connection set-up time and the data-transfer time. The data-transfer time is the same as the delay obtained in connectionless packet switching. Figure 1.8 shows the overall delay for the three packets presented in the previous example. The transmission of the three packets starts with *connection request packets* and then

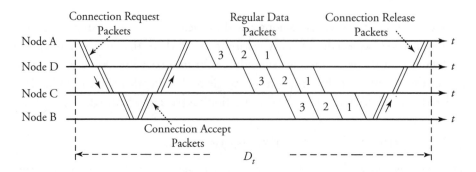

Figure 1.8   Signaling delay in a connection-oriented packet-switched network

connection accept packets. At this point, a circuit is established, and a partial path bandwidth is reserved for this connection. Then, the three packets are transmitted. At the end, a *connection release packet* clears and removes the established path.

The estimation of total delay time, D_t, to transmit n_p packets is similar to the one presented for connectionless networks. For connection-oriented networks, the total time consists of two components: D_p, which represents the time to transmit packets, and D_c, which represents the time for the control packets. The control packets' time includes the transmission delay for the connection request packet, the connection accept packet, and the connection release packet:

$$D_t = D_p + D_c. \tag{1.2}$$

Another feature, called *cut-through switching*, can significantly reduce the delay. In this scheme, the packet is forwarded to the next hop as soon as the header is received and the destination is parsed. We see that the delay is reduced to the aggregate of the propagation times for each hop and the transfer time of one hop. This scheme is used in applications in which retransmissions are not necessary. Optical fiber transmission has a very low loss rate and hence uses cut-through switching to reduce the delay in transmitting a packet. We will further explain the concept of cut-through switching and its associated devices in Chapters 2 and 12.

1.3   Packet Size and Optimizations

Packet size has a substantial impact on the performance of data transmission. Consider Figure 1.9, which compares the transmission of a 16-byte message from node A to node B through nodes D and C. Assume that for this transmission we would like to compare the transmission of the message with two different packet

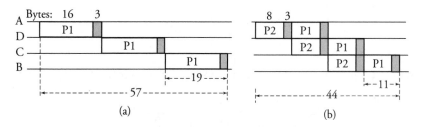

Figure 1.9   Comparison of two cases of transmitting data: (a) using three packets and (b) using six packets

sizes but each requiring the same-size packet header of 3 bytes. In the first scheme shown in part (a) of the figure, the message is converted to a packet, P1, with 16-byte payload and 3-byte header. When the packet is received by node B, a total of 57-byte units have elapsed. If the message is fragmented into two packets, P1 and P2, of 8 bytes each as shown in part (b) of the figure, the total elapsed time becomes 44-byte units of delay.

The reason for the time reduction in the second case is the parallel transmission of two packets at nodes D and C. The parallel transmission of multiple packets can be understood better by referring again to Figure 1.7 or 1.8 in which the times of packets 2 and 1 are coinciding on the times of packets 3 and 2 in nodes D or C. The trend of delay reduction using smaller packets, however, is reversed at a certain point, owing to the dominance of packet overhead when a packet becomes very small.

To analyze packet size optimization, consider a link with a speed of s b/s or a rate of μ packets per second. Assume that packets of size $d + h$ are sent over this link at the rate λ packets per second, where d and h are the sizes of the packet data and the packet header, respectively, in bits. Clearly,

$$\mu = \frac{s}{d + h}. \tag{1.3}$$

We define *link utilization* to be $\rho = \lambda/\mu$. Then the percentage of link utilization used by data, ρ_d, is obtained by

$$\rho_d = \rho \left(\frac{d}{d + h} \right). \tag{1.4}$$

The average delay per packet, D, can be calculated by using $\mu - \lambda$, where this term exhibits how close the offered load is to the link capacity:

$$D = \frac{1}{\mu - \lambda}. \tag{1.5}$$

Using Equations (1.3) and (1.4), we can rewrite the average delay per packet as

$$D = \frac{1}{\mu(1 - \rho)} = \frac{d + h}{s(1 - \rho)} = \frac{d + h}{s \left[1 - \frac{\rho_d}{d}(d + h) \right]}. \tag{1.6}$$

Apparently, the optimum size of a packet depends on several contributing factors. Here, we examine one of the factors by which the delay and the packet size become optimum. For optimality, consider d as one possible variable, where we want

$$\frac{\partial D}{\partial d} = 0. \tag{1.7}$$

This releases the two optimum values (we skip from the detail of derivation):

$$d_{opt} = h\left(\frac{\sqrt{\rho_d}}{1 - \sqrt{\rho_d}}\right) \tag{1.8}$$

and

$$D_{opt} = \frac{h}{s}\left(\frac{\sqrt{\rho_d}}{1 - \sqrt{\rho_d}}\right)^2. \tag{1.9}$$

Note that here, d_{opt} and D_{opt} are optimized values of d and D, respectively, given only the mentioned variables. The optimality of d and D can also be derived by using a number of other factors that will result in a more accurate approach.

1.4   Foundation of Networking Protocols

As discussed earlier in this chapter, users and networks are connected together by certain rules and regulations called *network communication protocols*. The Internet Protocol (IP), for example, is responsible for using prevailing rules to establish paths for packets. Communication protocols are the intelligence behind the driving force of packets and are tools by which a network designer can easily expand the capability of networks. One growth aspect of computer networking is clearly attributed to the ability to conveniently add new features to networks. New features can be added by connecting more hardware devices, thereby expanding networks. New features can also be added on top of existing hardware, allowing the network features to expand.

Protocols of communication networks are represented by either the TCP/IP model or its older version, the OSI model. The *five-layer TCP/IP model* is a widely accepted Internet backbone protocol structure. In this section, we describe the basics of these five layers and leave further details to be discussed in the remaining chapters.

However, among these five layers, the basics of IP *packets and network addressing* are designated a separate section, 1.5 IP Packets and Addressing. As stated before, we make this arrangement because basic definitions related to this layer are required in the following chapters, mostly in Part I of this book.

1.4.1   Five-Layer TCP/IP Protocol Model

The basic structure of communication networks is represented by the *Transmission Control Protocol/Internet Protocol* (TCP/IP) model. This model is structured in five layers. An end system, an intermediate network node, or each communicating user or program is equipped with devices to run all or some portions of these layers, depending on where the system operates. These five layers, shown in Figure 1.10, are as follows:

1. Physical layer
2. Link layer
3. Network layer
4. Transport layer
5. Application layer

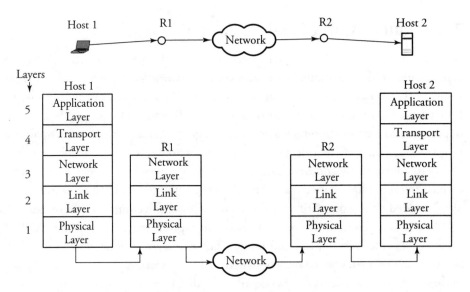

Figure 1.10   Hierarchy of the five-layer communication protocol model

Layer 1, known as the *physical layer*, defines electrical aspects of activating and maintaining physical links in networks. The physical layer represents the basic network hardware. The physical layer also specifies the type of medium used for transmission and the network topology. The details of this layer are explained in later chapters, especially in Chapters 3, 4, 6, 13, 15, 17, and 20.

Layer 2, the *link layer*, provides a reliable synchronization and transfer of information across the physical layer for accessing the transmission medium. Layer 2 specifies how packets access links and are attached to additional headers to form frames when entering a new networking environment, such as a LAN. Layer 2 also provides error detection and flow control. This layer is discussed further in Chapters 3 and 4 and the discussion is extended in almost all other chapters.

Layer 3, the *network layer* (IP) specifies the networking aspects. This layer handles the way that addresses are assigned to packets and the way that packets are supposed to be forwarded from one end point to another. Some related parts of this layer are described in Chapters 5, 6, and 7, and the discussion is extended in other chapters such as Chapters 10, 12, 13, 14, 15, 16, 21, and 22.

Layer 4, the *transport layer*, lies just above the network layer and handles the details of data transmission. Layer 4 is implemented in the end points but not in network routers and acts as an interface protocol between a communicating device and a network. Consequently, this layer provides logical communication between processes running on different hosts. The concept of the transport layer is discussed in Chapter 8, and the discussion is extended in other chapters such as Chapters 9, 14, 17, 18, 20, 21, and 22.

Layer 5, the *application layer*, determines how a specific user application should use a network. Among such applications are the *Simple Mail Transfer Protocol* (SMTP), *File Transfer Protocol* (FTP), and the *World Wide Web* (WWW). The details of layer 5 are described in Chapter 9, and descriptions of other advanced applications such as voice over IP (VoIP) are extended in other chapters such as Chapters 18, 19, and 20.

The transmission of a given message between two users is carried out by (1) flowing the data down through each and all layers of the transmitting end, (2) sending it to certain layers of protocols in the devices between two end points, and (3) when the message arrives at the other end, letting the data flow up through the layers of the receiving end until it reaches its destination.

Hosts

A network *host* is a computing device connected to a computer network and is assigned a network layer address. A host can offer information resources, services, and applications to users or other nodes on the network. Figure 1.10 illustrates a scenario in which different layers of protocols are used to establish a connection between two hosts. A message is transmitted from host 1 to host 2, and, as shown, all five layers of the protocol model participate in making this connection. The data being transmitted from host 1 is passed down through all five layers to reach router R1. Router R1 is located as a gateway to the operating regions of host 1 and therefore does not involve any tasks in layers 4 and 5. The same scenario is applied at the other end: router R2. Similarly, router R2, acting as a gateway to the operating regions of host 2, does not involve any tasks in layers 4 and 5. Finally at host 2, the data is transmitted upward from the physical layer to the application layer.

The main idea of the communication protocol stack is that the process of communication between two end points in a network can be partitioned into layers, with each layer adding its own set of special related functions. Figure 1.11 shows a different way of realizing protocol layers used for two hosts communicating through two routers. This figure illustrates a structural perspective of a communication setup and identifies the order of fundamental protocol layers involved.

1.4.2 Seven-Layer OSI Model

The *open systems interconnection* (OSI) model was the original standard description for how messages should be transmitted between any two points. To the five TCP/IP layers, OSI adds the following two layers below the application layer:

1. *Layer 5*, the *session layer*, which sets up and coordinates the applications at each end

2. *Layer 6* the *presentation layer*, which is the operating system part that converts incoming and outgoing data from one presentation format to another

The tasks of these two additional layers are dissolved into the application and transport layers in the newer five-layer TCP/IP model. The OSI model is becoming less popular. TCP/IP is gaining more attention, owing to its stability and its ability to offer better communication performance. Therefore, this book focuses on the five-layer model.

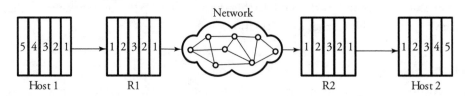

Figure 1.11 Structural view of protocol layers for two hosts communicating through two routers

1.5   Addressing Scheme in the Internet

An addressing scheme is clearly a requirement for communications in a computer network. With an addressing scheme, packets are forwarded from one location to another. Each of the three layers, 2, 3, and 4, of the TCP/IP protocol stack model produces a header, as indicated in Figure 1.12. In this figure, host 1 communicates with host 2 through a network of seven nodes, R1 through R7, and a payload of data encapsulated in a frame by the link layer header, the network layer header, and the transport layer header is carried over a link. Within any of these three headers, each source or destination is assigned an address as identification for the corresponding protocol layer. The three types of addresses are summarized as follows.

- *Link layer (layer 2) address.* A 6-byte (48-bit) field called Media Access Control (MAC) address that is represented by a 6-field hexadecimal number, such as 89-A1-33-2B-C3-84, in which each field is two bytes long. Every input or output of a networking device has an interface to its connected link, and every interface has a unique MAC address. A MAC address is known only locally at the link level. Normally, it is safe to assume that no two interfaces share the same MAC address. A link layer header contains both MAC addresses of a source interface and a destination interface, as seen in the figure.

- *Network layer (layer 3) address.* A 4-byte (32-bit) field called Internet Protocol (IP) address that is represented by a 4-field dot-separated number, such as 192.2.32.83, in which each field is one byte long. Every entity in a network must have an IP address in order to be identified in a communication. An IP address can be known globally at the network level. A network layer header contains both IP addresses of a source node and a destination node, as seen in the figure.

- *Transport layer (layer 4) address.* A 2-byte (16-bit) field called port number that is represented by a 16-bit number, such as 4,892. The port numbers identify the two end hosts' ports in a communication. Any host can be running several network applications at a time and thus each application needs to be identified by another host communicating to a targeted application. For example, source host 1 in Figure 1.12 requires a port number for communication to uniquely identify an application process running on the destination host 2. A transport layer header contains the port numbers of a source host and a destination host, as seen in the figure. Note that a transport-layer "port" is a logical port and not an actual or a physical one, and it serves as the end-point application identification in a host.

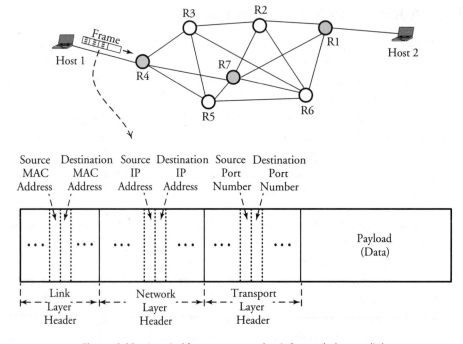

Figure 1.12   A typical frame structure that is forwarded over a link

The details of the link layer header, including the MAC addresses and all other of the header's fields are described in Chapter 4. The details of the network layer header fields, including the IP addresses and all other of the header's fields are presented in Chapter 5. Finally, the details of the transport layer header, including the port numbers and all other of the header's fields are explained in Chapter 8. In the meanwhile, some of the basic IP addressing schemes are presented in the next section, as understanding IP addressing will help us better understand the upcoming networking concepts.

1.5.1   IP Addressing Scheme

The IP header has 32 bits assigned for addressing a desired device on the network. An IP address is a unique identifier used to locate a device on the IP network. To make the system scalable, the address structure is subdivided into the *network* ID and the *host* ID. The network ID identifies the network the device belongs to; the host ID identifies the device. This implies that all devices belonging to the same network have a single network ID. Based on the bit positioning assigned to the network ID and the host ID, the IP address is further subdivided into classes A, B, C, D (multicast), and E (reserved), as shown in Figure 1.13.

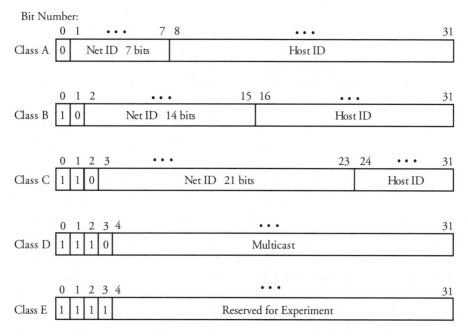

Figure 1.13 Classes of IP addresses

Consider the lengths of corresponding fields for each class shown in this figure:

- Class A starts with 0 followed by 7 bits of network ID and 24 bits of host ID.
- Class B starts with 10 followed by 14 bits of network ID and 16 bits of host ID.
- Class C starts with 110 followed by 21 bits of network ID and 8 bits of host ID.
- Class D starts with 1110 followed by 28 bits. Class D is used only for multicast addressing by which a group of hosts form a multicast group and each group requires a multicast address. Chapter 6 is entirely dedicated to multicast techniques and routing.
- Class E starts with 1111 followed by 28 bits. Class E is reserved for network experiments only.

For ease of use, the IP address is represented in *dot-decimal* notation. The address is grouped into four dot-separated bytes. For example, an IP address with 32 bits of all 0s can be shown by a dot-decimal form of 0.0.0.0 where each 0 is the representation of 00000000 in a logic bit format.

A detailed comparison of IP addressing is shown in the Table 1.1. Note that in this table, each of the "number of available network addresses" and the "number of available

Table 1.1   Comparison of IP addressing schemes

Class	Bits to Start	Size of Network ID Field	Size of Host ID Field	Number of Available Network Addresses	Number of Available Host Addresses per Network	Start Address	End Address
A	0	7	24	126	16,777,214	0.0.0.0	127.255.255.255
B	10	14	16	16,382	65,534	128.0.0.0	191.255.255.255
C	110	21	8	2,097,150	254	192.0.0.0	223.255.255.255
D	1110	N/A	N/A	N/A	N/A	224.0.0.0	239.255.255.255
E	1111	N/A	N/A	N/A	N/A	240.0.0.0	255.255.255.255

host addresses per network" has already been decreased by 2. For example, in class A, the size of the network ID field is indicated in the table to be $N = 7$; however, the number of available network addresses is presented as $2^N - 2 = 128 - 2 = 126$. The subtraction of 2 adjusts for the use of the all-bits-zero network ID (0 in decimal) and the all-bits-one network ID (127 in decimal). These two network IDs, 0 and 127, are reserved for management and cannot be available for any other use. The same argument is true for the number of available host addresses, where with the size of the host ID field indicated as $N = 24$, we can have $2^N - 2 = 16,777,216 - 2 = 16,777,214$ host addresses per network available for use. The last two columns of the table show the start address and the end address of each class, including the reserved addresses explained earlier.

Example.   A host has an IP address of 10001000 11100101 11001001 00010000. Find the class and decimal equivalence of the IP address.

Solution.   The host's IP address belongs to class B, since it starts with 10. Its decimal equivalence is 136.229.201.16.

1.5.2   Subnet Addressing and Masking

The concept of subnetting was introduced to overcome the shortcomings of IP addressing. Managing a large number of hosts is an enormous task. For example, a company that uses a class B addressing scheme can support up to 65,535 hosts on one network. If the company has more than one network, a multiple-network address scheme, or *subnet scheme*, is used. In this scheme, the host ID of the original IP address is subdivided into *subnet ID* and *host ID*, as shown in Figure 1.14.

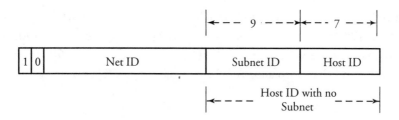

Figure 1.14   A subnet ID and host ID in class B addressing

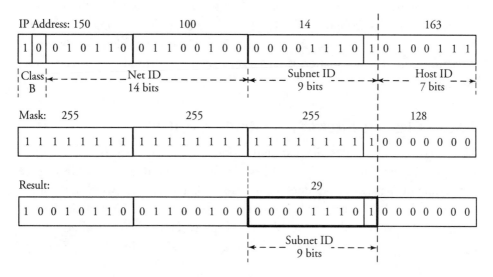

Figure 1.15   An example of subnet and masking

Depending on the network size, different values of subnet ID and host ID can be chosen. Doing so would prevent the outside world from being burdened by a shortage of new network addresses. To determine the subnetting number, a subnet *mask*—logic AND function—is used. The subnet mask has a field of all 0s for the host ID and a field of all 1s for the remaining field.

Example.   Given an IP address of 150.100.14.163 and a subnet mask of 255.255.255.128, determine the maximum number of hosts per subnet.

Solution.   Figure 1.15 shows the details of the solution. Masking 255.255.255.128 on the IP address results in 150.100.14.128. Clearly, the IP address 150.100.14.163 is a class B address. In a class B address, the lower 16 bits are assigned to the subnet and host fields. Applying the mask, we see that the maximum number of hosts is $2^7 = 128$.

Example.   A router attached to a network receives a packet with the destination IP address 190.155.16.16. The network is assigned an address of 190.155.0.0. Assume that the network has two subnets with addresses 190.155.16.0 and 190.155.15.0 and that both subnet ID fields have 8 bits. Demonstrate the details of routing the packet.

Solution.   When it receives the packet, the router determines to which subnet the packet needs to be routed, as follows: The destination IP address is 190.155.16.16, the subnet mask used in the router is 255.255.255.0, and the result is 190.155.16.0. The router looks up its routing table for the next subnet corresponding to the subnet 190.155.16.0, which is subnet 2. When the packet arrives at subnet 2, the router determines that the destination is on its own subnet and routes the packet to its destination.

1.5.3   Classless Interdomain Routing (CIDR)

The preceding section described an addressing scheme requiring that the address space be subdivided into five classes. However, giving a certain class C address space to a certain university campus does not guarantee that all addresses within the space can be used and therefore might waste some addresses. This kind of situation is inflexible and would exhaust the IP address space. Thus, the classful addressing scheme consisting of classes A, B, C, D, and E results in an inefficient use of the address space.

A new scheme, with no restriction on the classes, emerged. *Classless interdomain routing* (CIDR) is extremely flexible, allowing a variable-length *prefix* to represent the network ID and the remaining bits of the 32-field address to represent the hosts within the network. For example, one organization may choose a 20-bit network ID, whereas another organization may choose a 21-bit network ID, with the first 20 bits of these two network IDs being identical. This means that the address space of one organization contains that of another one.

CIDR results in a significant increase in the speed of routers and has greatly reduced the size of routing tables. A routing table of a router using the CIDR address space has entries that include a pair of network IP addresses and the mask. *Supernetting* is a CIDR technique whereby a single routing entry is sufficient to represent a group of adjacent addresses. Because of the use of a variable-length prefix, the routing table may have two entries with the same prefix. To route a packet that matches both of these entries, the router chooses between the two entries, using the longest-prefix-match technique.

Example.   Assume that a packet with destination IP address 205.101.0.1 is received by router R1, as shown in Figure 1.16. Find the final destination of the packet.

Solution.   In the table entries of router R1, two routes, L1 and L2, belonging to 205.101.8.0/20 and 205.101.0.0/21, respectively, are initially matched with the packet's IP address. CIDR protocol then dictates that the longer prefix must be the eligible match. As indicated at the bottom of this figure, link L1, with its 21-bit prefix, is selected, owing to a longer match. This link eventually routes the packet to the destination network, N3.

CIDR allows us to reduce the number of entries in a router's table by using an *aggregate technique*, whereby all entries that have some common partial prefix can be combined into one entry. For example, in Figure 1.16, the two entries 205.101.8.0/20 and 205.101.0.0/21 can be combined into 205.101.0.0/20, saving one entry in the table. Combining entries in routing tables not only saves space but also enhances the speed of the routers, as each time, routers need to search among fewer addresses.

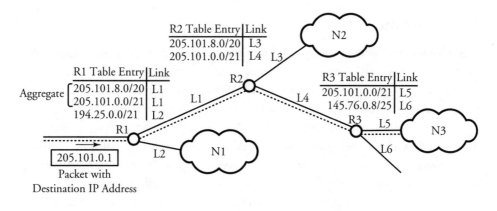

Packet Dest:	205.101.0.1	1100 1101 . 0110 0101 . 0000 0000 . 0000 0001
L1:	205.101.8.0/20	1100 1101 . 0110 0101 . 0000 1000 . 0000 0000
L1:	205.101.0.0/21	1100 1101 . 0110 0101 . 0000 0000 . 0000 0000

Figure 1.16   CIDR routing

1.6   Equal-Sized Packets Model

A networking model in which packets are of equal size can also be constructed. Equal-sized packets, or *cells*, bring a tremendous amount of simplicity to the networking hardware, since buffering, multiplexing, and switching of cells become extremely simple. However, a disadvantage of this kind of networking is the typically high overall ratio of header to data. This issue normally arises when the message size is large and the standard size of packets is small. As discussed in Section 1.3, the dominance of headers in a network can cause delay and congestion.

One of the networking technologies established using the equal-sized packets model is *asynchronous transfer mode* (ATM). The objective of ATM technology is to provide a homogeneous backbone network in which all types of traffic are transported with the same small fixed-sized *cells*. One of the key advantages of ATM systems is flexible processing of packets (cells) at each node. Regardless of traffic types and the speed of sources, the traffic is converted into 53-byte ATM cells. Each cell has a 48-byte data payload and a 5-byte header. The header identifies the virtual channel to which the cell belongs. However, because the high overall ratio of header to data in packets results in huge delays in wide area networks, ATM is rarely deployed in networking infrastructure and therefore we do not expand our discussion on ATM beyond this section.

1.7   Summary

This chapter established a conceptual foundation for realizing all upcoming chapters. First, we clearly identified and defined all basic key terms in networking. We showed a big-picture view of computer networks in which from one side, mainframe servers can be connected to a network backbone, and from the other side, home communication devices are connected to a backbone network over long-distance telephone lines. We illustrated how an Internet service provider (ISP) controls the functionality of networks. ISPs have become increasingly involved in supporting packet-switched networking services for carrying all sorts of data, not just voice, and the cable TV industry.

The transfer of data in packet-switched networks is organized as a multilevel hierarchy, with digital messages fragmented into units of formatted messages, or packets. In some circumstances, such as local area networks, packets must be modified further, forming a smaller or larger packet known as a frame. Two types of packet-switched networks are networks using connectionless protocol, in which no particular advanced connection is required, and networks using connection-oriented protocol, in which an advance dedication of a path is required.

A packet's size can be optimized. Using the percentage of link utilization by data, ρ_d, as a main variable, we showed that the optimized packet size and the optimized packet delay depend on ρ_d. The total delay of packet transfer in a connectionless network may be significantly smaller than the one for a connection-oriented network since if you have a huge file to transfer, the set-up and tear-down times may be small compared to the file transfer time.

This chapter also covered a tremendous amount of fundamental networking protocol material. We presented the basic structure of the Internet network protocols and an overview of the TCP/IP layered architecture. This architectural model provides a communication service for peers running on different machines and exchanging messages.

We also covered the basics of protocol layers: the *network layer* and the structure of IPv4 and IPv6. IP addressing is further subdivided as either *classful* or *classless*. Classless addressing is more practical for managing routing tables. Finally, we compared the equal-sized packet networking environment to IP networks. Although packet multiplexing is easy, the traffic management is quite challenging.

The next chapter focuses on the fundamental operations of networking devices and presents an overview of the hardware foundations of our networking infrastructure. Networking devices are used to construct a computer network.

1.8   Exercises

1. We transmit data directly between two servers 6,000 km apart through a geostationary satellite situated 10,000 km from Earth exactly between the two servers. The data enters this network at 100Mb/s.

   (a) Find the propagation delay if data travels at the speed of light (2.3×10^8 m/s).
   (b) Find the number of bits in transit during the propagation delay.
   (c) Determine how long it takes to send 10 bytes of data and to receive 2.5 bytes of acknowledgment back.

2. We would like to analyze a variation of Exercise 1 where servers are placed in substantially closer proximity to each other still using satellite for communication. We transmit data directly between two servers 60 m apart through a geostationary satellite situated 10,000 km from Earth exactly between the two servers. The data enters this network at 100Mb/s.

   (a) Find the propagation delay if data travels at the speed of light (2.3×10^8 m/s).
   (b) Find the number of bits in transit during the propagation delay.
   (c) Determine how long it takes to send 10 bytes of data and to receive 2.5 bytes of acknowledgment back.

3. Stored on a flash memory device is a 200 megabyte (MB) message to be transmitted by an e-mail from one server to another, passing three nodes of a *connectionless network*. This network forces packets to be of size 10KB, excluding a packet header of 40 bytes. Nodes are 400 miles apart, and servers are 50 miles away from their corresponding nodes. All transmission links are of type 100Mb/s. The processing time at each node is 0.2 seconds.

   (a) Find the propagation delays per packet between a server and a node and between nodes.

   (b) Find the total time required to send this message.

4. Equation (1.2) gives the total delay time for connection-oriented networks. Let t_p be the packet propagation delay between each two nodes, t_{f1} be the data packet transfer time to the next node, and t_{r1} be the data packet processing time. Also, let t_{f2} be the control-packet transfer time to the next node, and t_{r2} be the control-packet processing time. Give an expression for D in terms of all these variables.

5. Suppose that a 200MB message stored on a flash memory device attached to a server is to be uploaded to a destination server through a connection-oriented packet-switched network with three serially connected nodes. This network forces packets to be of size 10KB, including a packet header of 40 bytes. Nodes are 400 miles apart from each other and each server is 50 miles away from its corresponding node. All transmission links are of type 100Mb/s. The processing time at each node is 0.2 seconds. For this purpose, the signaling packet is 500 bits long.

   (a) Find the total connection request/accept process time.

   (b) Find the total connection release process time.

   (c) Find the total time required to send this message.

6. We want to deliver a 12KB message by uploading it to the destination's Web site through a 10-node path of a *virtual-circuit packet-switched network*. For this purpose, the signaling packet is 500 bits long. The network forces packets to be of size 10KB including a packet header of 40 bytes. Nodes are 500 miles apart. All transmission links are of type 1Gb/s. The processing time at each node is 100 ms per packet and the propagation speed is 2.3×10^8 m/s.

   (a) Find the total connection request/accept process time.

   (b) Find the total connection release process time.

   (c) Find the total time required to send this message.

7. Consider five serial connected nodes A, B, C, D, E and that 100 bytes of data are supposed to be transmitted from node A to E using a protocol that requires packet headers to be 20 bytes long.

   (a) Ignore t_p, t_r, and all control signals; and sketch and calculate total t_f in terms of byte-time to transmit the data for cases in which the data is converted into 1 packet, 2 packets, 5 packets, and 10 packets.

   (b) Put all the results obtained from part (a) together in one plot and estimate where the plot approximately shows the minimum delay (no mathematical work is needed, just indicate the location of the lowest delay transmission on the plot).

8. To analyze the transmission of a 10,000-bit-long packet, we want the percentage of link utilization used by the data portion of a packet to be 72 percent. We also want the ratio of the packet header, h, to packet data, d, to be 0.04. The transmission link speed is $s = 100$ Mb/s.

   (a) Find the link utilization, ρ.
   (b) Find the link capacity rate, μ, in terms of packets per second.
   (c) Find the average delay per packet.
   (d) Find the optimum average delay per packet.

9. Consider a digital link with a maximum capacity of $s = 100$ Mb/s facing a situation resulting in 80 percent utilization. Equal-sized packets arrive at 8,000 packets per second. The link utilization dedicated to headers of packets is 0.8 percent.

   (a) Find the total size of each packet.
   (b) Find the header and data sizes for each packet.
   (c) If the header size is not negotiable, what would the optimum size of packets be?
   (d) Find the delay for each optimally sized packet.

10. Develop a signaling delay chart, similar to Figures 1.7 and 1.8, for circuit-switched networks. From the mentioned steps, get an idea that would result in the establishment of a telephone call over circuit-switched networks.

11. In practice, the optimum size of a packet estimated in Equation (1.7) depends on several other contributing factors.

    (a) Derive the optimization analysis, this time also including the header size, h. In this case, you have two variables: d and h.

    (b) What other factors might also contribute to the optimization of the packet size?

12. Specify the class of address and the subnet ID for the following cases:

    (a) A packet with IP address 127.156.28.31 using mask pattern 255.255.255.0
    (b) A packet with IP address 150.156.23.14 using mask pattern 255.255.255.128
    (c) A packet with IP address 150.18.23.101 using mask pattern 255.255.255.128

13. Specify the class of address and the subnet ID for the following cases:

    (a) A packet with IP address 173.168.28.45 using mask pattern 255.255.255.0
    (b) A packet with IP address 188.145.23.1 using mask pattern 255.255.255.128
    (c) A packet with IP address 139.189.91.190 using mask pattern 255.255.255.128

14. Apply CIDR aggregation on the following IP addresses: 150.97.28.0/24, 150.97.29.0/24, and 150.97.30.0/24.

15. Apply CIDR aggregation on the following IP addresses: 141.33.11.0/22, 141.33.12.0/22, and 141.33.13.0/22.

16. Use the subnet mask 255.255.254.0 on the following IP addresses, and then convert them to CIDR forms:

    (a) 191.168.6.0
    (b) 173.168.28.45
    (c) 139.189.91.190

17. A certain organization owns a subnet with prefix 143.117.30.128/26.

    (a) Give an example of one of the organization's IP addresses.
    (b) Assume the organization needs to be downsized, and it wants to partition its block of addresses and create three new subnets, with each new block having the same number of IP addresses. Give the CIDR form of addresses for each of the three new subnets.

18. A packet with the destination IP address 180.19.18.3 arrives at a router. The router uses CIDR protocols, and its table contains three entries referring to the following connected networks: 180.19.0.0/18, 180.19.3.0/22, and 180.19.16.0/20, respectively.

    (a) From the information in the table, identify the exact network ID of each network in binary form.
    (b) Find the right entry that is a match with the packet.

19. Part of a networking infrastructure consists of three routers R1, R2, and R3 and six networks N1 through N6, as shown in Figure 1.17. All address entries of each router are also given as seen in the figure. A packet with the destination IP address 195.25.17.3 arrives at router R1.

    (a) Find the exact network ID field of each network in binary form.
    (b) Find the destination network for the packet (proof needed).
    (c) Specify how many hosts can be addressed in network N1.

R1 Table Entry	Link	R2 Table Entry	Link	R3 Table Entry	Link
195.25.0.0/21	L11	195.25.24.0/19	L21	111.5.0.0/21	L31
195.25.16.0/20	L12	195.25.16.0/20	L22	Else	L32
195.25.8.0/22	L13	195.25.8.0/22	L23	195.25.16.0/20	L33
135.11.2.0/22	L14				

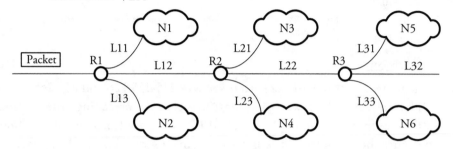

Figure 1.17   Exercise 19 network example

20. Consider an estimated population of 620 million people.
    (a) What is the maximum number of IP addresses that can be assigned per person using IPv4?
    (b) Design an appropriate CIDR to deliver the addressing in part (a).

21. A router with four output links L1, L2, L3, and L4 is set up based on the following routing table:

Mask Result	Link
192.5.150.16	L3
192.5.150.18	L2
129.95.38.0	L1
129.95.38.15	L3
129.95.39.0	L2
Unidentified	L4

The router has a masking pattern of 255.255.255.240 and examines each packet using the mask in order to find the right output link. For a packet addressed to each of the following destinations, specify which output link is found:
    (a) 192.5.150.18
    (b) 129.95.39.10
    (c) 129.95.38.15
    (d) 129.95.38.149

22. A router with four output links L1, L2, L3, and L4 is set up based on the following routing table:

Mask Result	Link
192.5.150.0	L1
129.95.39.0	L2
129.95.38.128	L3
Unidentified	L4

The router has two masking patterns of 255.255.255.128 and 255.255.255.1 and examines each packet using these masks in the preceding order to find a right output link among L1, L2, and L3. If a mask finds one of the three outputs, the second mask is not used. Link L4 is used for those packets for which none of the masks can determine an output link. For a packet addressed to a destination having each of the following IP addresses, specify which mask pattern finds a link for the packet and then which output port (link) is found:

(a) 129.95.39.10

(b) 129.95.38.16

(c) 129.95.38.149

1.9   Computer Simulation Project

1. **Simulation of Networking Packets.** Write a computer program in C or C++ to simulate a "packet." Each packet must have two distinct parts: header and data. The data is fixed on 10 bytes consisting of all logic 1s. The header is 9 bytes long and consists of three fields only: priority (1 byte), source address (4 bytes), and destination address (4 bytes).

   (a) For a Packet A, initialize the priority field to be 0, and source and destination addresses to be 10.0.0.1 and 192.0.1.0, respectively.

   (b) For a Packet B, initialize the priority field to be 1, and source and destination addresses to be 11.1.0.1 and 192.0.1.0, respectively.

   (c) For a Packet C, initialize the priority field to be 0, and source and destination addresses to be 11.1.0.1 and 192.0.1.0, respectively.

   (d) Demonstrate that your program can create the packets defined in parts (a), (b), and (c).

(e) Extend your program such that a comparator looks at the priority fields and destination addresses of any combination of two packets. If the destination addresses are the same, it chooses the packet with the highest priority and leaves the packet with lower priority in a register with incremented priority. Otherwise, it chooses randomly one of the packets and leaves the other one in the register with incremented priority. Show that your program is capable of choosing Packet B.

CHAPTER 2

Overview of Networking Devices

This chapter focuses on networking devices. Familiarity with networking hardware devices is essential for understanding how a local area or a wide area network operates. This chapter covers the following aspects of network component functionality:

- *Network interface cards* (NICs)
- *Switching and routing devices*
- *Wireless switching and routing devices*
- *Modems*
- *Multiplexers*

We start this chapter with discussion on the architecture of a *network interface card* (NIC). A NIC physically interfaces a networking device with its outside world such as a link that connects it to computer networks. We then proceed to the next topic of routing and switching devices by illustrating the block diagram setting for routing or switching functions. Our discussion in this chapter will also extend to the internal structure of wireless switching and routing devices.

The last topics of this chapter cover two other main categories of networking devices, *modems* that modulate data, and *multiplexers* that combine data from several links into one link. For multiplexers, we introduce some useful analytical methods.

Figure 2.1 shows a list of major computer networking and communication devices with their symbols that are used in this book. The devices include both wireline and wireless devices used as user host, server, or network equipment. Section (a) of Figure 2.1 presents switching and routing devices, wireless switching and routing devices, and some other networking devices such as network interface cards, multiplexers, and modems. Figure 2.1 (b) presents "computing" and "user" equipment and some miscellaneous symbols such as those for servers, laptops, and smartphones.

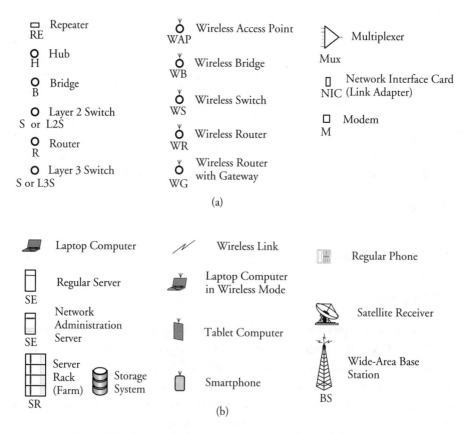

Figure 2.1   Communication and networking devices and their symbols

2.1 Network Interface Cards (NICs)

A *network interface card* (NIC), also known as a network interface controller, network adapter, link adapter, or LAN adapter, is an interfacing hardware component that connects a networking device to a computer network. A network interface card is normally built into the rest of the device circuitry and acts as a physical interface between the device and the link that connects it to the network.

A NIC implements all the functions required to communicate using specific data link layer standards such as Ethernet or WiFi, which are discussed in the next two chapters. Thus, the concept of network interfacing provides a base for implementation of the link layer portion of the network protocol stack, allowing communication among groups of computers and networking devices. Figure 2.2 shows an example of a simple communication between a routing device and a laptop host. In this example, the host is generating frames of a message through its NIC while having the control of the interconnecting link stay in contact with the other side's NIC.

A network interface card allows computers to communicate over a computer network using cables or a wireless medium. A NIC mainly implements layer 2 (data link layer) protocols as it engages a link addressing scheme; however, as it provides physical access to a networking medium, it may engage some aspects of layer 1 functions. A NIC may use these functions as shown in Figure 2.3. Note that a NIC has a bidirectional port (not shown in the figure), meaning that the process shown in the figure could also be reversed.

In Figure 2.3, incoming messages arrive at the *frame process* unit in which frames, and in particular, link level addresses are processed. We cover link level addresses in Chapter 4 in the section on MAC addresses. In summary, the frame process unit converts IP addresses to local link layer addresses or vice versa using a look-up table. In Chapter 4, we learn how *Address Resolution Protocol* (ARP) can manage this task.

Frames are temporarily stored in the *buffer* to provide time for the completion of other outstanding frames in the NIC. Arriving frames are inspected at the *error detection* unit to learn about any possible errors. This process is followed by the *frame*

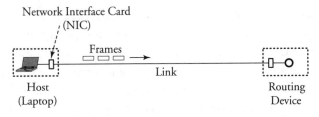

Figure 2.2   The role of a network interface card (NIC) in interfacing between devices and a link

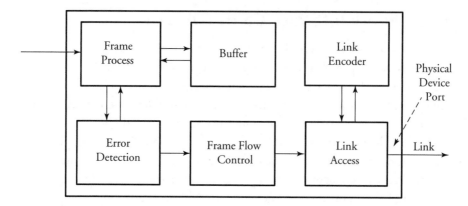

Figure 2.3   A block diagram of a network interface card (NIC)

flow control, which is responsible for control of frame transmission rate over the attached link. The *link encoder* process is required in NICs according to link standards. Finally, the *link access* module tries to access a free channel for a frame over its attached link. All four units—*link encoder, error detection, frame flow control,* and *link access*—are described in detail in Chapter 3.

2.2   Switching and Routing Devices

Switching and routing devices are designed to receive frames or packets, and then route or transmit them to a different part of a network based on a certain policy or protocol. They are categorized by their capabilities, functionality, and complexity. They are mainly classified in three categories as follows:

- *Layer 1 devices*
- *Layer 2 devices*
- *Layer 3 devices*

Figure 2.4 depicts interconnections and switching functions at layer 1, layer 2, and layer 3 of the five-layer protocol stack. Layer 1 devices are typically simple. *Repeaters* and *hubs* are examples of devices in this category. When a network deploys a layer 1 device in a certain part of a network, the physical layer of the protocol stack is the only layer that engages in communication with the device, as shown in Figure 2.4 (a).

When a layer 2 device is used in a network, the communication requires the engagement of both the physical and link layers at the bridge, and thus a bridge can

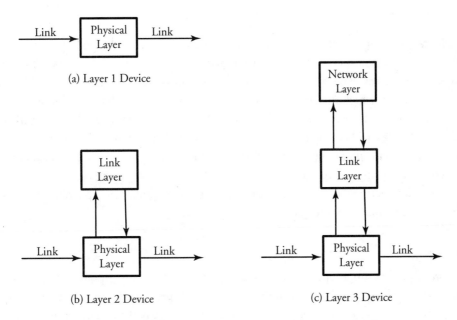

Figure 2.4 Connections in different layers of the protocol stack

also be called a layer 2 switch, as shown in Figure 2.4 (b). Layer 2 devices have more complexity compared to layer 1 devices, mainly due to their ability to route frames; however, the routing functionality of layer 2 devices is defined only for simple and small networks. Examples of devices in this category are *bridges* and *layer 2 switches*. Layer 2 switches are also known as LAN switches or simply switches.

Layer 3 devices are complex. Two types of layer 3 devices are *routers* and *layer 3 switches*. A layer 3 switch is a simpler version of a router and is often called a *switch*. Figure 2.4 (c) shows the functionality of a layer 3 device such as a router that requires the involvement of the physical, link, and network layers of the protocol stack.

2.2.1 Layer 1 Devices

Layer 1 of the protocol stack defines the electrical, procedural, and functional specifications for activating and maintaining the physical link between end points. As a result, we should not expect any routing functionality among the layer 1 devices. The physical interface on the NIC can be considered a part of layer 1 performance. Two well-known devices in this category are *repeaters* and *hubs*. Figure 2.4 (a) shows a point-to-point connection model for such layer 1 devices.

Repeaters

Repeaters are considered to be the simplest switching devices, designed primarily to interconnect two hosts or two LAN units without any involvement in the complex routing processes. The repeater's essential function is signal regeneration or signal strengthening, which differentiates it from other networking devices. Signal regeneration is needed when the transmission link length is extended. When a link is extended, bits can become decayed or corrupted if there is no signal amplification between the end points of transmission. As shown in Figure 2.4 (a), two links are interconnected using a repeater at the physical layer (layer 1). The repeater assumes that the connecting parts have the same protocol and it simply accepts bits from one host and transmits them to the other one.

Hubs

A *hub* is another simple device and is used to provide connections among multiple users in layer 1 of the protocol stack. A hub is similar to a repeater but connects several hosts or pieces of a LAN. Thus, a hub is a multipoint repeater. To perform multipoint connections using a hub, a copying element is installed in a hub to copy and forward a packet or a frame to all connected users. Figure 2.4 (a) shows only a point-to-point model of a hub. As a typical repeater, a hub has regeneration capability to strengthen incoming data to prevent any decay. Chapter 4 provides several examples of repeaters and hubs.

2.2.2   Layer 2 Devices

Unlike layer 1 devices that transmit frames to all associated users within a LAN, a layer 2 device does not forward a frame to all LAN users and thus can isolate traffic between two LANs. Layer 2 devices can make decisions about where to forward frames, and do not process IP addresses nor do they examine IP addresses. They perform data link functions, such as forwarding, formatting, and error detection. However, unlike a hub that just duplicates data and sends it out to all ports, a layer 2 device holds and updates a forwarding table that shows what layer 2 addresses (MAC addresses) have been detected and on what port. We review two main devices in this category: *bridges* and *layer 2 switches*. Layer 2 switches have some specific variations such as a *cut-through switch* and a fragment-free switch, which are also covered.

Bridges

A *bridge* is a device that normally connects two LANs; however, some manufacturers design bridges with more than two ports. A bridge operates in layer 2 of the protocol stack. Bridges or any other intelligent layer 2 switches are devices that use layer 2 data to forward or filter traffic. As it operates at layer 2, a bridge does more than simply extend the range of the network. A bridge checks the MAC address of any destination user and enhances the efficiency of networks by facilitating simultaneous transmissions within multiple LANs. The MAC address, as explained in Chapter 4, is the link layer address associated in the link adapters.

Layer 2 Switches

A *layer 2 switch*, often called a *LAN switch* or an *Ethernet switch*, or simply referred to as a *switch*, is essentially a bridge with more switching function capabilities. A *layer 2 switch* is an improved version of a bridge and typically has 32 to 128 ports. A switch is designed to operate in a larger LAN network, and is capable of minimizing traffic congestion to some extent. Bridges lack this traffic congestion control feature, but the trade-off is that they are less expensive than switches. Bridges also typically do not have the capability to filter frames. Switches may have the capability to filter frames, based on factors saved in their access control lists.

A layer 2 switch forwards frames from one part of a LAN to another, and extends connections to edge devices of a subnet such as a router. If a switch receives a frame for a destination that it does not have in its forwarding table, it floods that frame out to all ports, like a hub does ordinarily. However, the switch learns from the responses of the frame flood, and records the responses in its forwarding table for decision making the next time. Switches hold inbound frames by buffering them before switching them, so there are no frame collisions.

Cut-Through Switches

A special type of layer 2 switch is called a *cut-through switch*. Regular layer 2 switches can forward only one frame at a time in a store-and-forward fashion. This means a frame must be first stored in a buffer upon its arrival, and then the switch discovers the frame's destination before forwarding it to the desired output of the switch. However, more sophisticated layer 2 devices can forward multiple frames simultaneously through multiple parallel data paths. Layer 2 "cut-through" switches significantly enhance communication performance by forwarding a frame before the entire frame has been received, normally as soon as the destination address is processed. In terms of speed requirements, note that cut-through switching can only be done if the output line is of equal or lower speed than the input line.

Compared to regular layer 2 switches that store and forward frames, the cut-through technique reduces latency (delay) through the switch and relies on the destination devices for error handling. Certain layer 2 switches perform adaptive switching dynamically, in which case the switch selects between cut-through and store-and-forward behaviors based on current network conditions.

Fragment-Free Switches

A *fragment-free switch* is a variation of a cut-through switch. The speed advantage of cut-through switching comes with a price. When cut-through switching is used in a LAN environment, the switch is not able to verify the integrity of an incoming frame before forwarding it. This is because the frame check sequence field of a frame (discussed in Chapter 3) appears at the end of the frame. In such a case, the cut-through switch forwards any corrupted frame without checking it and possibly dropping it. A fragment-free switch is a variation of a cut-through switch that partially addresses this problem by ensuring that collision fragments are not forwarded.

A fragment-free switch holds a frame until the first several bytes, typically the first 64 bytes, are read from the source port to detect a collision before forwarding. This is useful only if there is a chance of a frame collision on the source port. When two frames from two different sources arrive to access a link at the same time, they collide and become damaged. The damaged frames are often shorter than the minimum valid standard frame size of 64 bytes. In this case, the buffer in a fragment-free switch holds the first 64 bytes of each frame, updates the source and port if necessary, reads the destination, and forwards the frame. But if the frame is less than 64 bytes, it discards the frame. Although the fragment-free switch is a faster switch compared to a regular switch that stores and forwards, because it discards some frames a risk of forwarding bad frames may still exist.

2.2.3   Layer 3 Devices

Layer 3 devices are designed essentially to support connectivity to the Internet. These devices have the capability to process IP addresses, but depending on their networking capability, they can make decisions on routing IP packets at various levels. A layer 3 device keeps and updates a routing table that shows which layer 3 addresses (IP addresses) are associated with which ports. Figure 2.5 shows an abstract model of layer 3 devices. Packets arrive at n input ports and are routed out from n output ports. A device consists of four main parts: *network interface card* (NIC), *input port processor* (IPP), *output port processor* (OPP), *switch fabric*, and *central controller*.

NICs were discussed at the beginning of this chapter. We describe all the details of the remaining four components of a switching and routing device in Chapter 12,

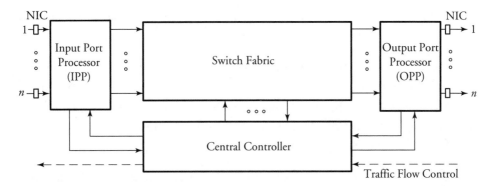

Figure 2.5   A block diagram of layer 3 devices such as layer 3 switches and routers

where the architecture of advanced routers is presented. But in summary, an IPP is mainly responsible for buffering, fragmenting large packets to smaller ones, and then finding a route for the incoming packets. In contrast, an OPP transmits them to the right output port. The switch fabric and the central controller ensure the packet switching function among various input and output ports.

Routers

A *router* is a layer 3 device that connects other routing nodes, providing a virtual or nonvirtual circuit. A router is dependent on protocols and establishes physical circuits for an individual node-pair connection. A router is designed to be a device that connects WANs, a LAN to a WAN, or a subnetted LAN to another subnetted LAN. A router routes IP packets between networks using an IP routing table. An IP routing table contains either static or dynamic routes. Static routes are set manually and are fixed until updated. Dynamic routes are dynamically updated based on the network condition. When an IP packet arrives at a physical port, the router looks up the destination address in the routing table. If the destination is not found in the table, the router drops the packet unless it has a default route.

In packet-switched networks, several pairs of communicating end points can share a circuit virtually, through their own dedicated channels, instead of occupying the entire physical circuit. Bandwidth in a packet-switched network is then dynamically released and shared as needed. A router has a routing look-up table for routing packets. If a communication is connectionless, packets of a message are sent individually but not necessarily in order. Owing to the presentation of more sophisticated input and output processors in routers, a router is not concerned about the order of the packets. Layer 3 devices are of two types:

- *Packet-by-packet routers*, by which packet forwarding is handled based on each individual packet.
- *Flow-based routers*, by which a number of packets having the same source and destination are identified and forwarded together. This scheme speeds up the forwarding process.

Depending on their size, complexity, and functionality, routers can be designed according to the following categories:

- *Small-size routers*, designed to be used in small networks such as in homes.
- *Medium-size routers*, designed for use inside or at the border of a building. These devices are normally called *gateway routers* (GRs) or simply *gateways*.
- *High-capacity routers*, designed to be used in the core networking structure of the Internet backbone. Sometimes these routers are sophisticated to connect to regional ISPs or even to counties; in such cases, they are called *border routers* (BRs) or edge routers (ERs).

Layer 3 Switches

We learned that layer 2 devices have been developed to replace costly routers when the devices are supposed to be attached to destination hosts. Typically, the general strategy of network management is to use the technology of layer 2 switching at or close to destination hosts to improve the quality and speed of forwarding packets and to let another layer of switching called *layer 3 switches* be responsible for the interface between routers and layer 2 switches. In light of this idea, a *layer 3 switch* or simply *switch* is a more sophisticated device compared to a layer 2 switch, and is capable of handling IP addresses. It is important to remember that if this device is used as a "switch," it should not be mistaken for the "switch" as a short form of the layer 2 switch.

A layer 3 switch is a less complex and expensive device compared to a router or an advanced router but it is capable of handling both MAC and IP addresses. Layer 3 switches can be deployed in places between hosts and the Internet quite often. A layer 3 switch is treated as a simple router that has a link interface, which thus it makes it both a router and a layer 2 switch. Truly, there is no need for a layer 3 switch in a subnet if a router of the same capacity can have packets exit the associated subnet.

Routers, though, seem to support more traffic monitoring features whereas switches do not seem to have that kind of support. Depending on the software version a switch is running, a layer 3 switch can also run a routing protocol.

A switch works much like a router because it has an IP routing table for lookups and it forms a broadcast domain. The layer 3 switch is similar to a layer 2 switch but with the router's IP routing intelligence built in. In other words, a switch is really like a high-speed router without the WAN connectivity. A switch does switching at layer 3 by preserving the source and destination MAC addresses and preserving the time to live (TTL) value of the IP header of the first routed packet, so the first packet is routed using normal routing lookup, but after that all packets are switched. Unlike routers, switches do not support many quality-of-service (QoS) features, mainly because they are not meant to perform at the level of core Internet routers. To some extent, a layer 3 switch integrates the abilities of both layer 2 switches and small size routers.

2.3   Wireless Switching and Routing Devices

Wireless communication is the transfer of information between two or more points that are not connected by physical links. *Wireless links* replace physical wireline links in wireless communication. The most common wireless link technologies use *radio waves*. Radio wavelengths can be short, such as a few meters for television, or as far as thousands or even millions of kilometers for deep-space radio communications. Radio communication encompasses various types of fixed, mobile, and portable applications, including two-way radios, cellular telephones, wireless networking, garage door openers, wireless computer mice or keyboards, headphones, radio receivers, satellite television, broadcast television, and cordless telephones.

In the following sections, we review some basic wireless networking devices, such as *wireless access point* (WAP), *base station* (BS), *wireless switches* (WS), *wireless router* (WR), and *wireless router with gateway* (WG)

2.3.1   Wireless Access Points and Base Stations

A *wireless access point* (WAP) is a local area network device that allows wireless devices to connect to a link that connects to a wired network using a related standard. A WAP usually connects to a router via a wireline link as a standalone device, but it can also be an integral component of the router itself. With a wireless access point, users are able to add devices to the associated wireless network for accessing the network with no cables.

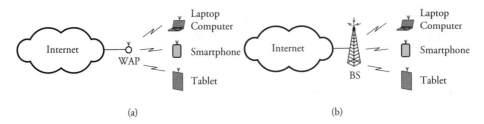

Figure 2.6   The use of (a) wireless access point (WAP) and (b) base station (BS) in wireless networks to connect users to the Internet

A WAP normally connects directly to a wired LAN connection and ultimately to the Internet. It provides wireless connections using radio frequency links for hosts and other devices with wireless connections. Most WAPs are designed to support IEEE 802.11 standards for sending and receiving data. WAPs are commonly used in home networks. Home networks generally use a certain type of WAP that is also a wireless router acting as a converged device that includes a WAP, a router, and often a layer 2 switch. Some WAPs even include a broadband modem.

The actual range of WAPs can vary significantly, depending on such variables and factors as the weather, operating radio frequency, indoor or outdoor placement, height above ground, nearby obstructions, other electronic devices that might actively interfere with the signal by transmitting in the same frequency range, type of antenna, and the power output of devices. The range of operability of WAPs can be extended through the use of repeaters, which can amplify radio signals.

In contrast, a *base station* (BS), normally referred to as a wide area network access point device, allows wireless devices in a wide area network to connect to a wired network using a related standard. Small-scale base stations can also be designed to act as WAPs, in which case a BS and WAP can be used interchangeably. Figure 2.6 shows example applications of WAP and BS units, where each unit connects a laptop, a smartphone, and a computer tablet to the Internet.

2.3.2   Wireless Routers and Switches

A *wireless router* (WR) is a networking device that performs similar functions to a router but also includes functions of a wireless access point via radio waves. Thus, the general big picture of routing and switching functions shown in Figure 2.6 can also be applied to wireless routers and switches. A wireless switch or router is commonly used to provide access to the Internet or a computer network wirelessly. Such a device does not require a wired link, as the connection is made wirelessly, via radio waves.

A wireless switch or router can be designed for a wired local area network (LAN), a wireless LAN (WLAN), or in a mixed wired/wireless LAN or WAN, depending on the need. A *wireless router with gateway* (WG) is a router that can provide radio communications to certain wireless access points and to wired Internet devices.

In contrast to a regular router or switch, one unique feature of wireless devices is *antennas* through which they can propagate and receive radio signals. These are discussed next.

2.3.3   Antennas in Wireless Devices

An *antenna* is an electrical device through which a wireless communication device can convert electric power into radio waves or vice versa, and propagates or receives radio waves. Thus an antenna is usually associated with a radio transmitter or radio receiver. When a device is in transmission mode, its radio transmitter supplies an electric current oscillating at radio frequency to the antenna's terminals, and the antenna radiates the energy from the current as electromagnetic waves called *radio waves*. If a device is in receiving mode, an antenna intercepts some of the power of an electromagnetic wave and produces electric current at its antenna terminals.

A good antenna in a wireless system can potentially enhance the signal-to-noise ratio. Antennas are classified in several ways. The two main types of antennas used in wireless systems are *isotropic antennas* and *directional antennas*.

Isotropic Antennas

Isotropic antennas transmit signals equally in all directions. Consider an isotropic transmitter that radiates P_t watts equally in all directions, forming a sphere of flux with radius d. Given that the surface area of the sphere is $4\pi d^2$, power-flux density measured on the surface of the sphere used by a receiver located at distance d is

$$\phi_r = \frac{P_t}{4\pi d^2}.$$

(2.1)

At the other end of communication systems, P_r, as the captured power, depends on the size and orientation of the antenna with respect to the transmitter. If we let a be the effective area of the receiving antenna, P_t and P_r are related by

$$P_r = \phi_r a = \left(\frac{P_t}{4\pi d^2} \right) a.$$

(2.2)

According to electromagnetic theory, the effective area of an isotropic antenna is obtained by $a = \frac{\lambda^2}{4\pi}$. Thus, Equation (2.2) can be rewritten as

$$P_r = \frac{P_t}{\left(\frac{4\pi d}{\lambda}\right)^2},$$
(2.3)

where λ is the wavelength of the signal. In most propagation media other than free space, the received signal power varies inversely with d^3 or d^4, compared to d^2 for free space.

Directional Antennas

Directional antennas are used to mitigate unwanted effects. Directional antennas amplify the signal in a small angular range but attenuate the signal at all other angles. This helps reduce the power in the various multipath components at the receiver. Directional antennas can be used to reduce the effects of interference from other users. The antenna must be accurately pointed to the correct user and must follow the user's path. This fact should lead to the development of smart antennas that can be used to track mobile users accurately by antenna steering.

MIMO Antennas

Multiple-input and multiple-output (MIMO) is a multiple-antenna unit that can be used at both the transmitter and receiver to improve communication performance. MIMO is one of several forms of smart antenna technologies. The terms "input" and "output" refer to the radio channel carrying the signal. MIMO technology offers significant enhancement in data throughput and link range without additional bandwidth or increased transmit power. It achieves this goal by spreading the same total transmit power over the antennas to achieve an array gain that improves the spectral efficiency. More spectral efficiency means more bits per second per hertz of bandwidth. MIMO also achieves a diversity gain that improves the link reliability resulting in reduced signal fading. Because of these properties, MIMO is an important part of modern wireless communication standards, wireless routers, and access points.

2.4 Modems

In order to reduce the bandwidth of digital signals, *digital modulation technique* is required before any transmission. In a modulation process, the amplitude, phase, or frequency of an analog "carrier signal," such as a sinusoidal carrier, varies with

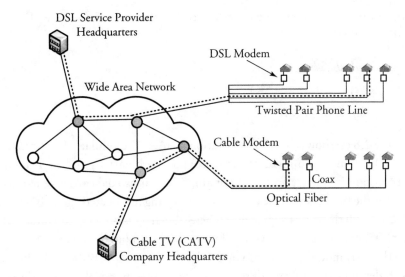

Figure 2.7 The choice of DSL modem or cable modem in residential areas for Internet access

the variations of an information signal. As a result of the modulation process, an information signal, such as a digital signal, is represented by an analog signal sent over cables, wireless links, or other transmission lines requiring significantly less bandwidth. The process of modulation is then reversed through the demodulation process at the other end of transmission lines.

Users access the Internet from residential areas primarily through *modems* (*modulation-demodulation*). A modem unit is a device that converts the digital data to a modulated form of signal making it appropriate for transmission. A modem is required to create an appropriate digital signal to access the Internet. A user can access the Internet by using either the existing telephone link infrastructure or the existing cable TV (CATV) infrastructure. As a result, an Internet user has choices of modems. Two commonly used ones are the *digital subscriber line* (DSL) *modem* and the *cable modem* as shown in Figure 2.7. A DSL company uses the existing twisted-pair copper lines to provide Internet access; a cable TV company uses optical fibers and coaxial cables to provide that access.

2.4.1 Basic Modulation: ASK, FSK, and PSK

The following three schemes are basic modulation techniques. In practice, these types of modulation are not used independently. However, since a combination of one or more of these techniques is used in advanced and practical communication systems, we would like to briefly study them here. These basic techniques are:

- *Amplitude shift keying* (ASK)
- *Frequency shift keying* (FSK)
- *Phase shift keying* (PSK)

Figure 2.8 (a) shows the implementation of an ASK modulation technique. In an ASK modulation, incoming data, $D(t)$, containing binary 0s and 1s, is modulated over a constant frequency and constant amplitude sinusoidal carrier signal, $\cos 2\pi ft$, where f is the frequency of the carrier. The resulting modulated signal is represented by a cosine with the same frequency f where a binary 1 is present, and no signal when a binary 0 is present. In other words, if we multiply our binary data by the cosine, we obtain the ASK-modulated version of our data, $M(t) = D(t) \cos(2\pi ft)$. At the receiver, the ASK demodulator only needs to determine the presence or absence of the sinusoid

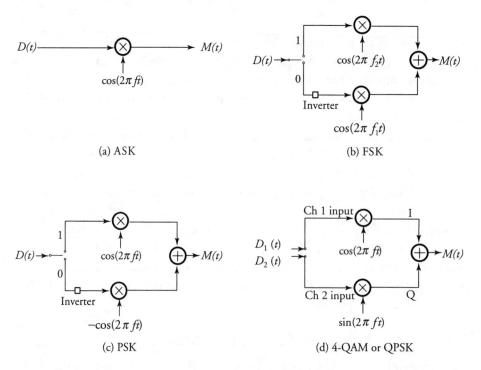

Figure 2.8   The three basic models of modulation techniques: (a) ASK, (b) FSK, and (c) PSK; and the two practical models of modulation techniques: (d) QPSK or 4-QAM

in a given time interval in order to detect 0s and 1s of the original data. In practice, $D(t)$ can be extracted at the receiver if $M(t)$ is multiplied by the same carrier signal but with doubled amplitude, $2\cos(2\pi ft)$, as follows:

$$[D(t)\cos(2\pi ft)][2\cos(2\pi ft)] = 2D(t)\cos^2(2\pi ft) = D(t)[1 + \cos(4\pi ft)] \qquad (2.4)$$

Note that the $\cos(4\pi ft)$ component can be easily filtered out. The FSK scheme is a bit more complicated compared to the ASK scheme. In an FSK modulation, there are two different sinusoidal carriers: f_1 to represent a binary 1 and f_2 to represent binary 0 as shown in Figure 2.8 (b). Therefore, FSK and ASK are similar in the sense that we multiply binary data by a constant sinusoid to obtain the modulated version of data, and they are different in the sense that there is a sinusoid in FSK when 0 appears. Clearly, in an FSK system, the frequency of the carrier varies according to the information such that we have $\cos(2\pi f_1 t)$ when a binary 1 is present and $\cos(2\pi f_2 t)$ when a binary 0 is present. Note that in order to implement the multiplication function of the modulation when a 0 arrives, an *inverter* changes 0 to 1. This allows $\cos(2\pi f_1 t)$ to be generated by being multiplied by 1 instead of 0.

In a PSK system, the phase of the sinusoidal carrier signal changes according to the information sequence as shown in Figure 2.8 (c). A binary 1 is represented by $\cos(2\pi ft)$ and a binary 0 by $\cos(2\pi ft + \pi)$. Similarly, we can rephrase the definition of a PSK system: In a PSK modulator we multiply the sinusoidal signal by $+1$ when the information is a 1, and by -1 when a 0 is present.

2.4.2   Practical Modulation: 4-QAM and QPSK

While ASK, FSK, and PSK are fundamental digital modulation schemes, in practice, other modulation techniques are used more and often consist of a combination of the three fundamental modulation techniques. For example, depending on the nature and objective of a modem, the two types of modems—*digital subscriber line (DSL) modems* and *cable modems*—require a special type of modulation. The following practical modulation schemes are prevalent for this purpose:

- *Quadrature phase shift keying* (QPSK)
- *Quadrature amplitude modulation* (QAM)

The common ground between QPSK and QAM is the concept of "quadrature." The term quadrature means the carrier signal shifts by 90 degrees. In quadrature-based modulation, amplitude and phase can be simultaneously but separately modulated to convey more information than either method alone. This is in essence a combined ASK and PSK scheme. A typical method of implementing quadrature technique is to separate the original signal $D(t)$ into a set of independent components: I (In-phase) and Q (Quadrature). The I and Q components are considered orthogonal (in quadrature) because they are separated by 90 degrees. The I and Q coordination system can be mapped to a *constellation diagram*. A constellation diagram is a two-dimensional I-Q plane representation of a modulated signal where I represents imaginary numbers and Q represents real numbers. The diagram displays possible symbols that may be selected by a given modulation scheme as points in the complex plane.

By representing a transmitted symbol as a complex number, and modulating cosine and sine carrier signals with the real and imaginary parts, respectively, a symbol can be sent with two carriers on the same frequency. They are often referred to as *quadrature carriers*. This principle of using two independently modulated carriers is the foundation of quadrature modulation. In a phase modulation, the phase of the modulating symbol is the phase of the carrier itself. As the symbols are represented as complex numbers, they can be visualized as points on the complex plane. The real and imaginary axes are often called the *in phase* or I-axis, and the *quadrature* or Q-axis, respectively. Plotting several symbols in a diagram produces the constellation diagram. The points in the I-Q constellation diagram are a set of *modulation symbols*.

In QPSK, quadrature means the carrier signal's phase shifts in increments of 90 degrees as 225°, 135°, 315°, and 45°. Incoming data in bits, $D(t)$, arriving at the modulator is separated into two channels called I and Q, symbolically referred to as $D_1(t)$, and $D_2(t)$, portions of $D(t)$, respectively. Two-bit symbols, 00, 01, 10, and 11, are transmitted simultaneously through each channel. Each channel modulates a carrier. The two carrier frequencies are identical except their phases are offset by 90 degrees. This creates four states for transmitted symbols 00, 01, 10, and 11 with carrier phases of 225°, 135°, 315°, and 45°, respectively.

As shown in Figure 2.8 (d), a single carrier generated by a local oscillator, cos $2\pi ft$, can be sent to a 90 degree phase shift to produce sin $2\pi ft$, as the second carrier. The two carriers are amplitude modulated, one with the I signal and the other one with the Q signal. The two carriers are then added together in a summing circuit. The output is a digitally modulated signal. QPSK uses four points on the constellation diagram, equispaced around a circle. With four phases, QPSK can encode two bits per symbol, with Gray coding to minimize the bit error rate (BER). The analytical research results show that QPSK can be utilized to double the data rate compared with a PSK system while maintaining the *same* bandwidth of the signal. However, the price to pay for this advantage is that QPSK transmitters and receivers are more complex than the ones for PSK.

Four-level QAM, or 4-QAM, can be realized as a combination of ASK and PSK, and is functionally the same as QPSK. Thus, Figure 2.8 (d) is also showing a brief block diagram of 4-QAM. The carrier phases for symbols 00, 01, 10, and 11 are 270°, 180°, 90°, and 0°, respectively. In terms of number of levels, there are different versions of QAM: 4-QAM, 16-QAM, 64-QAM, and so on, where the number of levels in QAM indicates the number of symbols created out of data. In 4-QAM, for example, we split the original information stream into two equal sequences, $D_1(t)$ and $D_2(t)$, consisting of the odd (01 and 11) and even (00 and 10) symbols, respectively. In 16-QAM, we create 16 different symbols 0000, 0001, all the way to 1111.

As shown in Figure 2.8 (d), we take $D_1(t)$ and produce a modulated signal by multiplying it by $\cos(2\pi ft)$ for a T-second interval. Similarly, we take $D_2(t)$ and produce a modulated signal by multiplying it by $\sin(2\pi ft)$ for a T-second interval. The first component $D_1(t)$ is known as the *in-phase component*, and the second component $D_2(t)$ is known as the *quadrature-phase component*. Therefore, at the output of the modulator we have:

$$M(t) = D_1(t) \cos(2\pi ft) + D_2(t) \sin(2\pi ft). \tag{2.5}$$

The QAM scheme can be realized as the simultaneous modulation of the amplitude and the phase of a carrier signal as Equation (2.5) can be rearranged as:

$$M(t) = \sqrt{D_1^2(t) + D_2^2(t)} \cos\left(2\pi ft + \tan^{-1}\frac{D_2(t)}{D_1(t)}\right). \tag{2.6}$$

Similar to what was explained for the ASK system, the original data, $D(t)$, can be extracted at the receiver if $M(t)$ is multiplied by the same carrier signal but with doubled amplitude. However, since $M(t)$ has two terms in this case, $D_1(t) \cos(2\pi ft)$ must be multiplied by $2\cos(2\pi ft)$, and $D_2(t) \sin(2\pi ft)$ must be multiplied by $2\sin(2\pi ft)$.

2.4.3 Digital Subscriber Line (DSL) Modems

Digital subscriber line (DSL) technology is a convenient option for home users to access the Internet. This technology offers various versions of DSL technology: ADSL, VDSL, HDSL, and SDSL, or, in general, xDSL.

Among the xDSL types, *asymmetric* DSL (ADSL) is popular and is designed for residential users and small businesses. A modem is designed to be connected to telephone links. These links are capable of handling bandwidths up to 1.1MHz. Out of this bandwidth, only 4KHz are used for a phone conversation. Consequently, the remaining bandwidth can become available to be allocated to data communication. However, other factors, such as the distance between a user and a switching office, and the condition and size of the link, might restrict this remaining bandwidth from being completely available.

The details of spectrum division for an ADSL modem are shown in Figure 2.9 (a). The standard modulation technique for ADSL is 4-QAM. The available bandwidth of 1.1MHz is divided into 256 channels, each using a bandwidth of approximately 4.312KHz. Voice communication uses channel 0. Channels 1–5 remain idle and together act as a guard band between voice and data communication. Because data communication bandwidth is split into two unequal bandwidths—*upstream* for communications from the user to the Internet and *downstream* for communications from the Internet to the user—the technique is said to be asymmetric. Channels 6–30 are allocated to the upstream bandwidth, with 1 channel dedicated to control and 24 channels assigned to data transfer. The total upstream bandwidth is thus 25×5 KHz = 100 KHz, spread over from 26KHz to 126KHz as indicated in Figure 2.9 (a). In terms of bit rate, 24 channels with 4-QAM offer 24×4 KHz $\times 15$ = 1.44 Mb/s bandwidth in the upstream direction, as 4-QAM requires 15-bit/Hz encoding. Channels 31–255 are assigned to the downstream bandwidth, with 1 channel for control and the remaining 224 channels for data. With 4-QAM, up to 224×4 KHz $\times 15$ = 13.4 Mb/s is achieved for the downstream bandwidth.

Another type of DSL technique is the *symmetric digital subscriber line* (SDSL). This technique divides the available bandwidth equally between downstream and

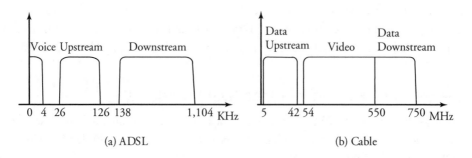

(a) ADSL   (b) Cable

Figure 2.9 The frequency bands of (a) ADSL modems and (b) cable modems

upstream data transfer. *High-bit-rate digital subscriber line* (HDSL), as another option, was designed to compete with T-l lines (1.544Mb/s). A T-l line is susceptible to attenuation at high frequencies and thus limits the length of the line to 1 km. HDSL uses two twisted-pair wires and 2B1Q, an encoding technique less susceptible to attenuation. As a result, HDSL can achieve a data rate of 2Mb/s without needing repeaters for up to 3.6 km. *Very high bit-rate digital subscriber line* (VDSL) is similar to ADSL but uses coaxial or fiber-optic cable for a bit rate of 50Mb/s to 55Mb/s downstream and 1.5Mb/s to 2.5Mb/s upstream data transfer.

2.4.4   Cable Modems

As mentioned in the previous section, the DSL modem uses the existing twisted-pair telephone cables to provide residential users with access to the Internet, as shown in Figure 2.7. This type of cable clearly has limited bandwidth and is susceptible to errors. An alternative is to use the cable TV network for Internet access. A cable company lays out very high-speed backbone optical fiber cables all the way to the residential buildings, each of which can then be connected to the optical infrastructure for TV, radio, and the Internet through either a coaxial (coax) cable or optical fiber, depending on its demand and budget. This network is called *hybrid fiber-coaxial* (HFC). Video signals are transmitted downstream from headquarters to users. Communication in an HFC cable TV network is bidirectional. The cable company divides the bandwidth into video/radio, downstream data, and upstream data. Coaxial cables can carry signals up to 750MHz.

The details of spectrum division for a cable modem are shown in Figure 2.9 (b). About 500MHz of this bandwidth is assigned to TV channels. As the bandwidth of each TV channel is 6MHz, the assigned bandwidth can accommodate more than 80 channels. Some technical methods allow this number to increase to 180 TV channels. About 200MHz of the coax bandwidth, from 550MHz to 750MHz, is allocated to the downstream data transfer, from the Internet side to a user. This bandwidth is also divided into about 33 channels, each with 6MHz bandwidth. The cable modem uses the 64-QAM or 256-QAM modulation technique for the downstream data transfer. These modulation techniques use 5-bit encoding, so the bandwidth of the downstream data channel can be 5 b/Hz $\times$ 6 MHz = 30 Mb/s.

The upstream data premises communicate to the Internet and occupy 37MHz, from 5MHz to 42MHz, including 6-MHz-wide channels. The upstream data is modulated using the quadrature PSK (QPSK) technique, which is less susceptible to noise in the lower frequency range. Using 2 bits per Hz offers the downstream data rate at 2 b/Hz × 6 MHz = 12 Mb/s. The protocol for upstream communication is summarized as follows.

Begin Upstream Communication Protocol

1. The cable modem checks the downstream channels to determine whether any packet periodically sent by the cable company seeks any new modems attached to the cable.

2. The cable company sends a packet to the cable modem, specifying the modem allocated downstream.

3. The cable modem sends a packet to the cable company, requesting the Internet address.

4. The modem and the cable company go through a handshaking process and exchange some packets.

5. The cable company delivers an identifier to the modem.

6. Internet access in the allocated upstream channel bandwidth can then be granted to the modem in the allocated upstream channel. ∎

Note that a user needs to use one 6-MHz-wide channel assigned by the cable company. To better use the optical-fiber bandwidth, all users of the same neighborhood need to timeshare a channel. Therefore, a user must contend for a channel with others and must wait if the channel is unavailable.

2.5 Multiplexers

Multiplexers are used in a network for maximum transmission capacity of a high-bandwidth line. Regardless of the type of multiplexer, multiplexing is a technique that allows many communication sources to transmit data over a single physical line. Multiplexing schemes can be divided into three basic categories: *frequency-division multiplexing, wavelength-division multiplexing,* and *time-division multiplexing.* The type of multiplexing called a *wavelength-division multiplexing* (WDM) transmission system divides the optical-fiber bandwidth into many nonoverlapping optical wavelengths: so-called WDM channels. A WDM mixes all incoming signals with different wavelengths and sends them to a common output port. The details of WDM are discussed in detail in Chapter 15. In the following sections, we give an overview of FDMs and TDMs.

2.5.1   Frequency-Division Multiplexing (FDM)

In *frequency-division multiplexing* (FDM), the frequency spectrum is divided into frequency bands, or *channels*, in which each user can be assigned a band. Figure 2.10 shows how *n* frequency channels are multiplexed using FDM. When many channels are multiplexed together, a certain guard band is allocated to keep the channels well separated.

To implement a multiplexer, the original frequencies at any of *n* inputs of the multiplexer are raised, each by a different constant amount. Then, the *n* new frequency bands are combined to let no two channels occupy the same portion of the spectrum. Despite the guard bands between the channels, any two adjacent channels have some overlap because channel spectra do not have sharp edges. This overlap normally creates spike noise at the edge of each channel. FDM is normally used over copper wires or microwave channels and is suitable for analog circuitry.

Orthogonal Frequency Division Multiplexing (OFDM)

Orthogonal frequency division multiplexing (OFDM) is a special form of FDM and designed for transmitting large amounts of data over a wireless links. It is especially popular because it is the core technique deployed in most wireless local area networks such as WiFi. The reason for adopting such a multiplexing system is that OFDM reduces the amount of crosstalk in signal transmissions.

OFDM works by splitting the radio signal into multiple smaller sub-signals that are then transmitted simultaneously at different frequencies to the receiver. In OFDM, a signal is split into several narrowband channels at different frequencies. The difference between FDM and OFDM lies in the way in which the signals are

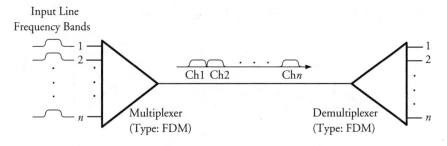

Figure 2.10   A frequency-division multiplexer (FDM) with *n* inputs

modulated and demodulated. In OFDM, a single channel utilizes multiple subcarriers on adjacent frequencies. Contrary to the traditional FDM technique, the spectra of channels in OFDM significantly overlap to maximize spectral efficiency. However, subcarriers of an OFDM system are orthogonal to one another. Thus, they are able to overlap without interfering. As a result, OFDM systems are able to maximize spectral efficiency without causing adjacent channel interference.

The process of an OFDM transmitter used in WiFi devices is shown in Figure 2.11. An OFDM transmitter starts with a *demultiplexer* typically called a *serial-to-parallel converter* that converts the serial bits of data to be transmitted into parallel format. The number of subcarriers and the type of digital communication technique used determine the typical number of bits in parallel. Normally, the incoming data is divided into a large number of carriers. Then, a mapping unit acts as digital *modulator*. Typically, *quadrature amplitude modulation* (QAM) or *quadrature phase shift keying* (QPSK), explained in the previous section, is used as modulator. The incoming spectrum of data is transmitted in parallel over a group of subcarriers. Since the carriers are orthogonal to one another, the nulls of one carrier coincide with the peak of another subcarrier, resulting in the possibility of extracting the subcarrier of interest.

The heart of this technique is an inverse *fast Fourier transform* (FFT). In FFT, a carrier frequency is generated based on the location of the stored value. This produces a set of time-domain samples. An FFT is an algorithm to compute the discrete Fourier transform (DFT). A DFT converts time (or space) to frequency and vice versa and rapidly computes such transformations by factorizing the DFT matrix into a product of sparse (mostly zero) factors.

At the receiver, the preceding process is reversed and the data is discovered. OFDM signal reception involves a challenging task of time-frequency domains, sampling, and clock synchronization, as well as channel estimations. Note that as the signal travels through the medium, the signal arrives at the receiver at different

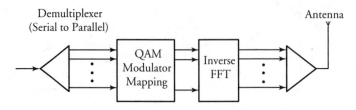

Figure 2.11   A block diagram of an OFDM transmitter

instances, owing to multipath propagation, resulting in a delay spread. A simple solution to overcome this issue is to widen the symbol duration. This can be achieved by increasing the number of carriers, causing the distortion to become insignificant.

2.5.2 Time-Division Multiplexing

With *time-division multiplexing* (TDM), users take turns in a predefined fashion, each one periodically getting the entire bandwidth for a portion of the total scanning time. Given n inputs, time is divided into frames, and each frame is further subdivided into time slots, or channels. Each channel is allocated to one input as shown in Figure 2.12. This type of multiplexing can be used only for digital data. Packets arrive on n lines, and the multiplexer scans them, forming a frame with n channels on its outgoing link. In practice, packet size is variable. Thus, to multiplex variable-sized packets, additional hardware is needed for efficient scanning and synchronization. TDM can be either *synchronous* or *statistical*.

Synchronous TDM

In *synchronous* TDM, the multiplexer scans all lines without exception. The scanning time for each line is preallocated; as long as this time for a particular line is not altered by the system control, the scanner should stay on that line, whether or not there is data for scanning within that time slot. Therefore, a synchronous multiplexer does not operate efficiently, though its complexity stays low.

Once a synchronous multiplexer is programmed to produce same-sized frames, the lack of data in any channel potentially creates changes to average bit rate on the ongoing link. In addition to this issue, the bit rates of analog and digital data being combined in a multiplexer sometimes need to be synchronized.

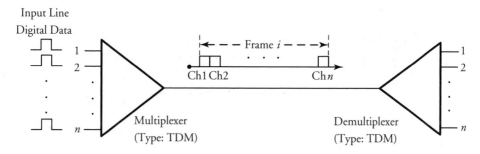

Figure 2.12 A time-division multiplexer with n inputs

Example. Consider the integration of three analog sources and four identical digital sources through a time-division multiplexer, as shown in Figure 2.13. The analog lines with bandwidths 5KHz, 2KHz, and 1KHz, respectively, are sampled, multiplexed, quantized, and 5-bit encoded. The digital lines are multiplexed, and each carries 8Kb/s. Find the output rate of the multiplexer.

Solution. Each analog input is sampled by a frequency two times greater than its corresponding bandwidth according to the Nyquist sampling rule. Therefore, we have $5 \times 2 + 2 \times 2 + 1 \times 2 = 16$ K samples per second. Once it is encoded, we get a total of $16,000 \times 5 = 80$ Kb/s on analog lines. The total share of digital lines is then is $4 \times 8 = 32$ Kb/s. Thus, the output rate of the multiplexer is $80 + 32 = 112$ Kb/s.

Consider a multiplexer with n available channels. If the number of requesting input sources, m, is greater than n channels, the multiplexer typically reacts by *blocking* where unassigned sources are not transmitted and therefore remain inactive. Let t_a and t_d be the two mean times during which a given input becomes active and idle, respectively. Assume that the transmission line has n channels available, where $m > n$.

If more than n inputs are active, we can choose only n out of m active sources and permanently block others. If one of the n chosen channels goes to idle, we can give service to one of the other requests. Typically, blocking is used when channels must be held for long time periods. The traditional telephone system is one example; channels are assigned at the start of a call, and other callers are blocked if no channel is available. Assuming that values of t_a and t_d are random and are exponentially distributed, the probability that a source is active, ρ, can be obtained by

$$\rho = \frac{t_a}{t_d + t_a}. \tag{2.7}$$

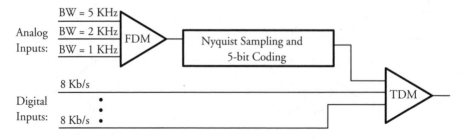

Figure 2.13   Integrated multiplexing on analog and digital signals

Let p_j be the probability that j out of m sources are active. Using Equation (C4) in Appendix C, for $0 \leq j \leq m$

$$p_j = \binom{m}{j} \rho^j (1 - \rho)^{m-j}. \tag{2.8}$$

Thus, the probability that j out of n channels on the transmission line are in use, P_j, can be expressed by normalizing p_j over n inputs as $P_j = p_j / \sum_{i=0}^{n} p_i$, or

$$P_j = \frac{\binom{m}{j} \rho^j (1 - \rho)^{m-j}}{\sum_{i=0}^{n} \binom{m}{i} \rho^i (1 - \rho)^{m-i}} \quad \text{for } 0 \leq j \leq n$$

$$= \frac{\binom{m}{j} \left(\frac{\rho}{1-\rho}\right)^j}{\sum_{i=0}^{n} \binom{m}{i} \left(\frac{\rho}{1-\rho}\right)^i} \quad \text{for } 0 \leq j \leq n. \tag{2.9}$$

The reason behind the normalization is that, as noted earlier, unassigned sources never become active. Hence, there will never be more than n active sources and n active output channels. Conditional probability requires the input probabilities be normalized in this instance to reflect that the maximum number of active sources, n, is less than the number of sources that may request services m. Note also that $\sum_{i=0}^{n} p_i$ can never be equal to 1, since $n \leq m$; but according to the rule of total probability, we can always say $\sum_{i=0}^{m} p_i = 1$. Equation (2.9) is known as the *Engset distribution*. The Engset distribution is used for computing lost calls cleared given a finite number of sources.

The blocking probability of such multiplexers, P_n, can be calculated by simply letting j be n in Equation (2.9), denoting that all n channels are occupied. If we also substitute $\rho = t_a/(t_d + t_a)$, the blocking probability can be obtained when $j = n$:

$$P_n = \frac{\binom{m}{n} \left(\frac{t_a}{t_d}\right)^n}{\sum_{i=0}^{n} \binom{m}{i} \left(\frac{t_a}{t_d}\right)^i}. \tag{2.10}$$

The preceding discussion can be concluded by using basic probability theory to find the average number of busy channels or the expected number of busy channels as

$$E[C] = \sum_{j=0}^{n} jP_j. \tag{2.11}$$

Example.   A 12-input TDM becomes an average of 2 μ s active and 1 μ s inactive on each input line. Frames can contain only five channels. Find the probability that a source is active, ρ, and the probability that five channels are in use.

Solution.   We know that $m = 12$ and $n = 5$; since $t_a = 2\ \mu$ s, and $t_d = 1\ \mu$ s:

$$\rho = \frac{t_a}{t_d + t_a} = 0.66,$$

and the probability that all five channels are in use is

$$P_{n=5} = \frac{\binom{12}{5}\left(\frac{2}{1}\right)^5}{\sum_{i=0}^{5}\binom{12}{i}\left(\frac{2}{1}\right)^i} = 0.72.$$

Statistical TDM

In *statistical* TDM, a frame's time slots are dynamically allocated, based on demand. This method removes all the empty slots on a frame and makes the multiplexer operate more efficiently. Meanwhile, the trade-off of such a technique is the requirement that additional overhead be attached to each outgoing channel. This additional data is needed because each channel must carry information about which line it belonged to. As a result, in the statistical multiplexer, the frame length is variable not only because of different channel sizes but also because of the possible absence of some channels.

Consider a multiplexer with n available channels. If the number of requesting input sources, m, is greater than n channels, the multiplexer typically reacts by *clipping*, whereby unassigned sources are partially transmitted, or clipped. Designing multiplexers with $m > n$ stems from the fact that all m sources may not be practically active simultaneously. In some multiplexing systems, *clipping* is exploited especially for applications in which sources do not transmit continuously, and the best usage of the multiplex output line is targeted. By assigning active sources to channels dynamically, the multiplex output can achieve more efficient channel usage. For example, some satellite or microwave systems detect information energy and assign a user to a channel only when a user is active.

Consider the same definitions as presented in the blocking case for t_a, t_d, m, n ($m > n$), and ρ. Similarly, assume that values of t_a and t_d are random and are exponentially distributed. Assume also that the outgoing transmission line has n channels available but the multiplexer has m input sources, where $m > n$. If more than n input sources are active, we can dynamically choose n out of m active sources and temporarily block other sources. With temporary blocking, the source is forced to lose, or clip, data for a short period of time, but the source may return to a scanning scenario if a channel becomes free. This method maximizes the use of the common transmission line and offers a method of using the multiplexer bandwidth in silence mode. Note that the amount of data lost from each source depends on t_a, t_d, m, and n. Similar to the blocking case, ρ can be defined by $\rho = t_d/(t_d + t_a)$, and the probability that exactly i out of m sources are active is

$$P_i = \binom{m}{k} (\rho)^i (1 - \rho)^{m-i}. \tag{2.12}$$

Therefore, P_C, the clipping probability, or the probability that an idle source finds at least n input sources active at the time it becomes active, can be obtained by considering all m minus 1 (the examining source) sources beyond n active sources

$$P_C = \sum_{i=n}^{m-1} \binom{(m-1)}{i} \rho^i (1 - \rho)^{m-1-i}. \tag{2.13}$$

Clearly, the average number of used channels is $\sum_{i=0}^{n} i p_i$. The average number of busy channels can then be derived by

$$E[C] = \sum_{i=0}^{n} i p_i + n \sum_{i=n+1}^{m} p_i. \tag{2.14}$$

Example.   For a multiplexer with ten inputs, six channels per frame, and $\rho = 0.67$, find the clipping probability.

Solution.   Since $m = 10$, and $n = 6$, $P_c \approx 0.65$.

2.6 Summary

This chapter introduced the hardware building blocks of computer networks. These building blocks or devices are directly connected by physical links and allow message exchange in communication networks.

We started this chapter with the *network interface card* (NIC), which was also known as a network interface controller, network adapter, link adapter, or LAN adapter. The NIC is the hardware component that connects a networking device to a link in a computer network.

Switching and *routing devices* were the next topic we studied in this chapter. Clearly, these devices are the most important ones among others as a computer network mainly consists of such devices. Switching and routing devices are organized according to the layer at which they are connected in networks. *Repeaters* are layer 1 switching devices that primarily extend the geographic distance spanned by a LAN protocol. A *hub* is a layer 1 device and supports more ports than a repeater does. A hub broadcasts any input data to all its output ports. A *bridge* and *layer 2 switch* make connections at layer 2 of the protocol stack model. The most important component of the Internet, a *router*, is treated as a layer 3 device. A router is made up of *input port processors*, *output port processors*, *switch fabric*, and a *switch controller*.

Networking *modems* were the next devices we studied. Modems are used to access the Internet from remote and residential areas. A *DSL modem* uses twisted-pair telephone lines to access the Internet, whereas a *cable modem* uses optical fiber cables to provide Internet access. We studied basic modulation techniques, such as ASK, FSK, PSK, as well as the practical modulation schemes, QPSK and QAM, that are used in modems.

The *multiplexer* was the last topic we covered. A multiplexer is a device that provides cost-effective connectivity by collecting data from multiple links and carrying that data on one link. Multiplexers are of various types such as FDM and TDM. We studied a special form of FDM, known as OFDM, that had a number of applications in wireless networks including WiFi networks. We learned some useful analytical methods for multiplexers.

In the next chapter, we look at issues related to data links. Data links can be evaluated the at the data link layer and in connection with physical and network layers.

2.7 Exercises

1. Human voice frequency ranges from 16Hz to about 20KHz. Telephone companies use the most significant 4,000Hz portion of this spectrum to deliver voice conversation between two users. This downgrade in the quality of conversation allows the transmission links to save bandwidth remarkably. Using a three-level hierarchy of multiplexing (12:1, 5:1, and 10:1):

   (a) How many voice conversations can this system carry?
   (b) What would be the final transmission capacity of this system?

2. Consider the integration of three analog sources and four identical digital sources through a time-division multiplexer that uses its entire 160Kb/s maximum capacity. The analog lines—with bandwidths of 5KHz, 2KHz, and 1KHz, respectively—are sampled, multiplexed, quantized, and 5-bit encoded.

   (a) For the analog sources, find the total bit rate.
   (b) For the digital sources, find each line's bit rate.
   (c) Find the frame rate if a frame carries eight sampled analog channels, four digital data channels, a control channel, and a guard bit.

3. Assume that two 600-b/s terminals, five 300-b/s terminals, and a number of 150-b/s terminals are to be time-multiplexed in a character-interleaved format over a 4,800-b/s digital line. The terminals send 10 bits/character, and one synchronization character is inserted for every 99 data characters. All the terminals are asynchronous.

   (a) Determine the number of 150-b/s terminals that can be accommodated.
   (b) Sketch a possible framing pattern for the multiplexer, assuming three characters per 150-b/s terminal.

4. Consider a time-division multiplexer having a frame time of 26 μs. Each user channel has 6 bits, and each frame has 10 bits of overhead information. Assume that the transmission line carries 2Mb/s of information.

   (a) How many user channels can be accommodated on the line?
   (b) Consider ten sources in this system, and assume a probability of 0.9 that a source is busy. What is the clipping probability?

5. Consider a 2-to-1 time-division multiplexer (TDM) in which the length of each data channel or any type of control channel is 8 bits long. On input Line 1, "A" indicates an existence of an 8-bit data unit to be scanned and "x" indicates no

data. Similarly on input Line 2, "B" indicates an existence of an 8-bit data unit to be scanned and "x" indicates no data. Show and compare the structure of all the produced frames using both types of synchronous and asynchronous multiplexers for each of the following two cases of inputs:

(a) Input Lines 1 and 2 contain respectively AxAx and xBxB.

(b) Input Lines 1 and 2 contain respectively AxAx and BxBx.

6. Consider two 4-to-1 TDMs, a synchronous TDM and an asynchronous TDM. Both multiplexers receive identical data in the same time on their input lines where the data arrives at a speed of 10Mb/s on each line. Let Y (4 bits long) and N (4 bits long) represent the presence and non-presence of data, respectively, so that the input lines' data patterns are: Line 1 (YNYN), Line 2 (NNYN), Line 3 (NYNY), and Line 4 (YNNY). The synchronous TDM requires only one 4-bit control channel on its frame while the asynchronous TDM requires one 4-bit control channel for each frame and an additional 4-bit control channel per channel.

(a) Sketch the output of these two multiplexers in one timing chart.

(b) Find the frame rate (for the synchronous case).

(c) Find the clock speed for each multiplexer assuming each bit is run by one clock cycle.

7. Consider a synchronous TDM with eight inputs, each becoming an average of 2 μs active and 6 μs inactive. Frames can receive four channels only.

(a) Find the probability that a source is active.

(b) Find the probability that three channels of the frame are in use.

(c) Find the blocking probability for this multiplexer.

(d) Find the average number of used channels in the frame.

8. For a four-input statistical TDM, consider two different frame sizes of 2 and 3. Sketch a set of plots, each plot showing the clipping probability versus $\rho = 0.2, 0.4, 0.6, 0.8$.

9. Consider a statistical TDM in which 11 sources and 10 channels are present. Find the clipping probability, assuming a probability of 0.9 that a given source is busy.

10. Find the *average clipping time* for each burst of information in statistical TDMs.

11. A string of 100101011 arrives at the modulation unit of a modem. Give the output signal if the modulator is designed by:

(a) ASK

(b) FSK

(c) PSK

12. We want to design the input port processor of a high-speed router and analyze the delay. Incoming packets to IPP are fragmented into smaller segments, with each segment consisting of d bits data plus 50 bits of header. The switch fabric requires segments to be transmitted at r b/s. To achieve the highest possible speed:

   (a) Is there any way to optimize the processing delay D of each segment in terms of d and r? How?

   (b) Is processing delay in the switch fabric significant compared to D? Why?

2.8   Computer Simulation Project

1. *Simulation of a Router's Routing Table.* To simulate the routing table of a router, write a computer program to construct a look-up routing table with ten entries. Each entry must contain a sequence number, time, destination address, cost of a destination node (given a certain network), and router port number. Your program should demonstrate the updating mechanism on a frequent basis.

CHAPTER **3**

Data Links and Link Interfaces

So far, we have discussed basic networking protocols and devices. This chapter focuses on data *links* and the functions of *link interfaces* to devices. The chapter especially concentrates on methods of data transmission, both wired and wireless. After introducing general properties of transmission media, we investigate issues in the link layer of the overall protocol stack. The highlights of this chapter are

- *Data links*
- *Link encoder*
- *Error detection and correction on links*
- *Flow control on links*
- *Link access by multiple users*
- *Wireless channel access by multiple users*
- *Link aggregation*

One of the main focuses of this chapter is link issues, which were descibed briefly in the last chapter in the section on *network interface cards* (NICs). We begin this chapter by discussing wired and wireless transmission media in the section on data links. We contrast guided and unguided link alternatives, briefly discuss their applications, and summarize key transmission characteristics.

Our next major topic is *error detection* and *error correction* on data links. We then study the *flow control* of frames over links, which guarantees that the control of link flows can be implemented. The topic of flow control includes *stop-and-wait* and *sliding-window* protocols. For both of these flow control techniques, we will also review the *automatic repeat request* (ARQ) protocol that guarantees the retransmission of lost frames.

Next, we describe methods of link access and also channel access when multiple users attempt to utilize a single link or single channel in both wireline and wireless environments. Finally, at the end of the chapter, we discuss methods of multiple link aggregation that results in increasing throughput and provides redundancy in case one of the links fails.

3.1   Data Links

A *data link* is the physical path between a data transmitter and data receiver. Figure 3.1 shows the range of electromagnetic-spectrum frequencies for various applications in data communications.

- The *low-frequency* subspectrum covers all the frequencies in the range 0 to approximately 15,000Hz, which is the range of human-voice frequencies generally used in *telephone systems*.

- The *radio* frequency (RF) subspectrum covers frequencies from several kilohertz to several gigahertz. RF applications in telecommunications includes *radio systems*, *television systems*, *Bluetooth communications*, and *cellphones*.

- The *microwave* frequency subspectrum ranges from several gigahertz up to more than 10^{11} Hz and is used for such applications as *microwave systems*, *radar*, and *satellite communications*.

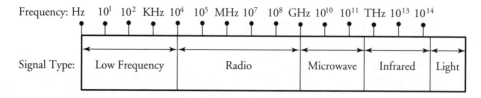

Figure 3.1   Frequency range for various data communications applications

- The *infrared* frequency subspectrum ranges from more than 10^{11} Hz to less than 10^{14} Hz. The infrared signal can be used for *remote controls, lasers,* and *guided missiles.*

- The *light* frequency subspectrum covers all the visible-light components and is used mainly for *fiber-optic communications.*

Data transmission may use either *wired links* or *wireless links*, depending on the application and the available bandwidth of the links. Transmission links can also be classified as *guided*, or directional, and *unguided*. A wired link is normally considered a guided medium for the propagation of data. A wireless medium can be designed to propagate signals in more than one direction, causing the medium to become unguided. Signals travel on the link in the form of electromagnetic waves. Let c be the speed of electromagnetic waves, f be the frequency of the traveling signal, and λ be the wavelength of the signal. Then:

$$\lambda = \frac{c}{f}. \tag{3.1}$$

A guided link, whether wired or wireless, can be *full-duplex*, whereby two bitstreams in opposite directions can be transmitted simultaneously, or *half-duplex*, whereby only one bitstream in one direction can be carried at any time. The following section explores the most commonly used data links.

3.1.1   Data Link Types

Data links provide a physical path for signals to propagate between two communication entities. Four types of common links used in computer networking are *twisted-pair links, coaxial cable links, fiber-optic links,* and *wireless links.*

Twisted-Pair Links

A *twisted-pair link* is the simplest form of guided medium used for data transmission. A twisted pair is normally manufactured using copper and consists of two insulated wires. The twisting action on wires reduces the crosstalk interference generated between each two pairs of transmission links. To increase the capacity of transmission cables, especially for long-distance applications, several pairs of such links are bundled together and wrapped in a protective sheath. One of the most common applications of the twisted-pair link is for telephone network transmission links. The frequency range of twisted-pair cables is approximately 0 to 1MHz.

Coaxial Cable Links

A higher data rate for longer-distance applications can be achieved with *coaxial cable*, a hollow outer cylindrical conductor surrounding an inner wire. The outer conductor is spaced tightly with inner wire by a solid dielectric material. The outer conductor is also shielded from outside. This concentric construction makes coaxial cables resistant to interference. Coaxial cables have a wide variety of applications, such as cable television distribution, long-distance telephone transmission, and local area networks. The frequency range that coaxial cables can carry is 0 to 750MHz.

Fiber-Optic Links

Remarkably higher-bandwidth communication links can be achieved using optical fibers. A *fiber-optic link* is a thin glass or plastic wire that can guide an optical ray. One of the best substances used to make optical fibers is *ultrapure fused silica*. These fibers are, however, more expensive than regular glass fibers. Plastic fibers are normally used for short-distance links where higher losses are tolerable.

Similar to coaxial cables, optical fiber cables have a cylindrical layout. The three concentrics are the *core*, the *cladding*, and the *jacket*. The core consists of several very thin fibers, each of which is surrounded by its own cladding. Each cladding also has a glass or plastic coating but different from that of the core. This difference is the key mechanism that confines the light in the cable. Basically, the boundary between the core and cladding reflects the light into the core and runs it through the cable.

The combined core and cladding are surrounded by a jacket. Jackets are made of materials that can protect the cable against interference and damage. Optical fibers are superior to coaxial cables mainly because of their higher bandwidths, lighter weights, lower signal attenuation, and lower impact by external interference. Optical fiber links are used in all types of data communication LAN and WAN applications. The frequency range of fiber optics is approximately 180THz to 330THz.

Wireless Links

Computer networks can take advantage of the wireless infrastructure where physical wires cannot be laid out. An obvious example is mobile data communication, whereby mobile users attempt to connect and stay connected to the Internet. Wireless classroom education is another example; an instructor teaches a class through wireless media, and students can follow the lecture with their portable computers from any location within a defined vicinity.

One of the key challenges in wireless networking is efficient utilization of the available transmission spectrum. Because the frequency spectrum available for wireless communication is normally limited, frequencies must be reused in different geographic areas. The spectrum used for wireless communication typically ranges up to several gigahertz. Security is also a concern in wireless networks. The open-air interface makes it difficult to prevent snooping.

Link-level design techniques involve making trade-offs among the various parameters relevant to the link layer. The optimum design would involve the use of minimum bandwidth and transmit power while maintaining a high data rate, low latency, and a low bit error rate (BER). These design challenges must be achieved in the presence of channel imperfections, such as flat fading, multipath effects, shadowing, and interference.

Wireless links, both guided and unguided, are used for data communication. Wireless links use a device as an antenna for transmitting signals through a *vacuum*, *space*, *air*, or *substances*. Electromagnetic waves can be propagated through the first three, as well as through water and wood. The frequency range depends on the type of substance. The two key challenges faced in overall design of efficient wireless links and transmission systems are the *choice of antenna* and *wireless channels*.

3.2   Link Encoder

Recall from the last chapter that one of the main functions of a network interface card (NIC) is *line encoding*. Before processing a raw signal for modulation, a *line coding process* is performed on binary signals for digital transmission. With line coding, a binary information sequence is converted into a digital code. This process is required to maximize bit rate in digital transmission. The encoding process is essential to also recover the bit timing information from the digital signal so that the receiving sample clock can synchronize with the transmitting clock. The timing synchronization is especially crucial in the performance of LANs. Other reasons for line coding are reduction in transmitted power and removal of DC voltage from transmission lines.

Typically, the cost and complexity of a line encoder are the main factors in the selection of an encoder for a given application. Figure 3.2 shows several practical line coding techniques for computer communications. Encoded signals are produced by the line codes for the binary sequence 1011 0100 1110 0010. The simplest form of line coding is the use of original bits where a binary 1 is represented by a $+V$ voltage level, and a 0 is represented by a 0 voltage. The average transmitted power in this method is $(1/2)V^2 + (1/2)0^2 = V^2/2$. This method creates an average of $V/2$ DC voltage on the transmission lines, which is not popular for LAN systems.

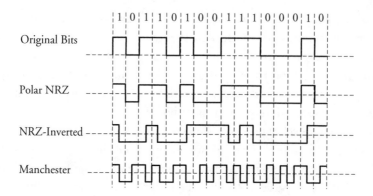

Figure 3.2 Typical line coding techniques for computer communications

A more power-efficient line coding method is known as *polar NRZ* where NRZ stands for *nonreturn to zero*. In this method, a binary 1 is mapped to $+V/2$ and a binary 0 is represented by $-V/2$. The average power is then given by $(1/2)(+V/2)^2 + (1/2)(-V/2)^2 = V^2/4$. On average, this method has no DC component and is suitable in most networking applications.

A problem with original bits and polar NRZ coding methods is that a polarity error can cause a sequence of 1s to be delivered as a weak 1 or even a 0. As a solution to this problem the *NRZ-inverted* method is introduced. With NRZ-inverted coding, a binary 1 is mapped into a transition in the middle of the bit interval. For example, if the the binary level has been 1 before a new binary 1 arrives, the new binary 1 is mapped to three parts: (1) 1 for half of the bit period, (2) a transition from 1 to 0, and (3) a 0 for the other half of the bit period. Similarly, if the the binary level has been 0 before a new binary 1 arrives, the new binary 1 is mapped to three parts: (1) 0 for half of the bit period, (2) a transition from 0 to 1, and (3) a 1 for the other half of the bit period. With NRZ-inverted coding, the code requires no transition for a binary 0, and the signal remains constant during the actual bit time. Notice that the NRZ-inverted coding creates a zero voltage on the avarage of the produced code. Errors in this method of encoding occur in pairs. This means that any error in one bit time generates a wrong basis for the next time leading to a new error in the next bit.

From the frequency standpoint, both the original bits and NRZ-inverted methods produce a spectrum starting from very low frequencies close to zero due to the existence of either DC components or less frequent transitions of 0s to 1s or vice versa. Although, the bipolar NRZ has a better spectrum distribution in this sense, the immunity to noise can still be an issue for all three types of NRZ coding. Low frequencies can also be a bottleneck in some communication systems, as telephone transmission systems do not pass the frequencies below 200Hz. To overcome this issue, the *Manchester encoding method* is introduced.

With the Manchester encoding method, a binary 1 is represented by a 1 plus a transition to 0 and then a 0; and a binary 0 is represented by a 0 plus a transition to 1 and then a 1. A great feature of the Manchester encoding method is that it is self-clocking. The fact that each binary bit contains a transition at the middle of its timing makes timing recovery very easy. From the frequency standpoint, the bit rate is doubled compared with NRZ methods, which significantly enhances the shape of its spectrum where lower frequencies are shifted up. This method of line encoding is suitable for LANs, especially for gigabit Ethernet, which isdiscussed in Chapter 4.

3.3   Error Detection and Correction on Links

Error sources are present when data is transmitted over a medium. Even if all possible error-reducing measures are used during the transmission, an error invariably creeps in and begins to disrupt data transmission. Any computer or communication network must deliver accurate messages.

Error detection is applied mostly in the data-link layer but is also performed in other layers. In some cases, the transport layer includes some sort of error-detection scheme. When a packet arrives at the destination, the destination may extract an error-checking code from the transport header and perform error detection. Sometimes, network-layer protocols apply an error-detection code in the network-layer header. In this case, the error detection is performed only on the IP header, not on the data field. At the application layer, some type of error check, such as detecting lost packets, may also be possible. But the most common place where errors occur is still the data-link layer. Possible and common forms of errors at this level are described here and are shown in Figure 3.3.

- *Noise* is continuous and is dependent on the temperature of the medium. Noise might change the content of data, as seen in the figure. Noise can be removed by passing the noisy signal through a set of filters.

- *Spike* is not continuous but may completely obliterate the data, so that it cannot be recovered.

- *Crosstalk* is a coupling action between two active links. Coupling can be electrical, as between two sets of twisted-pair wire, or electromagnetic, as when unwanted signals are picked up by an antenna.

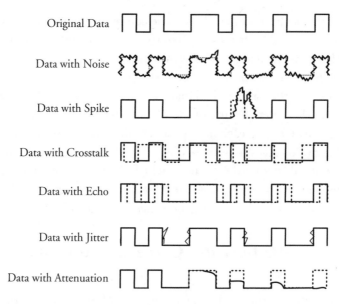

Figure 3.3   Common forms of data errors at the data-link level

- *Echo* is the reflecting impact of a transmitted signal. A signal can hit the end of a cable and bounce back through the wire, interfering with the original signal. This error occurs in bus-type LANs. A one-directional filter, known as an *echo canceler*, can be attached to a link to eliminate echo.

- *Jitter* is a timing irregularity that shows up at the rises and falls of a signal, causing errors. Jitter can result from electromagnetic interference or crosstalk and can be reduced by proper system shielding.

- *Bit attenuation* is the loss of a bit's strength as it travels though a medium. This type of error can be eliminated with the use of amplifiers and repeaters for digital systems.

No link is immune to errors. Twisted-pair copper-based media are plagued by many types of interference and noise. Satellite, microwave, and radio networks are also prone to noise, interference, and crosstalk. Fiber-optic cable, too, may receive errors, although the probability is very low.

3.3.1   Error Detection Methods

Most networking equipment at the data-link layer inserts some type of error-detection code. When a frame arrives at the next hop in the transmission sequence, the receiving hop extracts the error-detection code and applies it to the frame. When an error is detected, the message is normally discarded. In this case, the sender of the erroneous message is notified, and the message is sent again. However, in real-time applications, it is not possible to resend messages. The most common approaches to error detection are

- Parity check
- Cyclic redundancy check (CRC)

The *parity check* method involves counting all the 1 bits in the data and adding one extra bit, called the *parity bit*. This makes the total number of 1 bits even (even parity) or odd (odd parity). The parity-check method is the simplest error-detection technique but it is not effective. The *cyclic redundancy check* (CRC) method is one of the most elaborate and practical techniques but it is more complex, adding 8 to 32 check bits of error-detection code to a block of data. Our emphasis is on CRC.

At this point, we need to clarify that the *Internet checksum* is another error-detection method, though it is used at the network and transport layers and is discussed in Chapters 5 and 8.

3.3.2   Cyclic Redundancy Check (CRC) Algorithm

The *cyclic redundancy check* (CRC) method provides smart error checking and has been adopted in most computer and communication systems. Figure 3.4 shows the CRC unit of a transmitting network interface card (NIC) for error detection on links.

In any system, a standard and common value between transmitters and receivers is adopted for error processing. This g-bit-long common value, known as a checking *generator*, is denoted by G. At the transmitter, a partial or entire frame is treated as a block of data, and each block is processed individually.

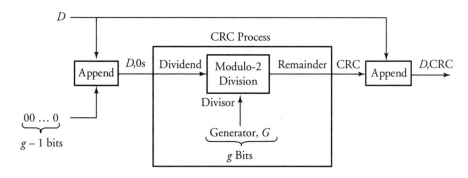

Figure 3.4   CRC unit at a transmitter to perform error detection on links

The CRC unit at the transmitter first combines data (D) with $g-1$ zeroes to generate a term called $D,0$s. The value of $D,0$s undergoes a CRC process consisting of modulo-2 division using G, as shown in the figure. This process creates the value CRC to be appended to D to generate $D,$CRC. The term $D,$CRC is the one sent over links with a guarantee that any error in $D,$CRC, which is basically our data frame, can be detected at the other end of the link using a reverse but similar process, to be discussed. The CRC algorithm at the transmitter part can be summarized as follows.

Begin CRC Algorithm at Transmitter

1. A string of $g-1$ zero bits is appended to the incoming data, D. We call this new block D,0s.

2. D,0s, as a dividend, is divided by the generator G acting as the divisor. The division is of type *modulo-2*.

3. The quotient of this division is discarded, but the remainder is called CRC.

4. The CRC value is appended to the data, producing D,CRC. ∎

At the other end point of the communication system, the receiver receives the value of D, CRC and performs an algorithm to detect errors. Figure 3.5 shows the CRC unit of a receiving network interface card (NIC) for error detection on links. The CRC unit at the receiver first performs a similar CRC process consisting of a modulo-2 division using G but this time the process is applied on the incoming $D,$CRC value. This process creates either 0 to indicate that the data has no error and can be accepted, or a nonzero value representing an error in the data (frame). The CRC algorithm at the receiving part can be summarized as follows.

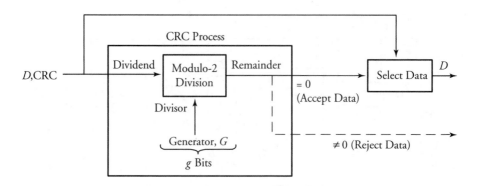

Figure 3.5 CRC unit at a receiver to perform error detection on links

Begin CRC Algorithm at Receiver

1. `D,CRC`, as a dividend, is divided by the same generator `G` acting as the divisor used by the transmitter. The division is of type `modulo-2`.

2. The quotient of this division is discarded, but if the remainder is 0, the receiver knows that the data has no errors; otherwise, the data is not accepted, as it contains one or more errors. ■

The modulo-2 division arithmetic is very simple. A modulo-2 division function is done without carries in *additions* or borrows in *subtractions*. Interestingly, the modulo-2 division function performs exactly like the Exclusive-OR logic. For example, with modulo-2 arithmetic, we get $1 + 1 = 0$ and $0 - 1 = 1$. Equivalently, with Exclusive-OR logic: $1 \oplus 1 = 0$, and $0 \oplus 1 = 1$.

Example.   Assume that 1010111 as a block of data (D) is going to be transmitted using the CRC error-checking method. Suppose that the common value of the generator, G, is 10010. Produce the final value that the transmitter sends on the link (D,CRC), and show the detail of the error-detection process at the receiver.

Solution.   At the transmitter, clearly, the number of 0s needed to be appended to D is four ($g - 1 = 4$), since the generator has 5 bits ($g = 5$). Figure 3.6 (a) shows the details of the CRC process at the transmitter side. Since $D = 1010111$, D,0s = 1010111,**0000**, the dividend. The divisor is $G = 10010$. Using modulo-2 arithmetic, the quotient turns out to be 1011100, and the remainder is CRC = 1000. Therefore, the transmitter transmits D,CRC = 1010111,1000. At the receiver, as shown in Figure 3.6 (b), D,CRC = 1010111,1000 is treated as the dividend and is divided by the same divisor, $G = 10010$. Since the remainder in this case is 0, the receiver learns that there is no error in the data and can extract the data.

The CRC algorithms are fairly straightforward. Consider again the example. A fact from the modulo-2 arithmetic states that the remainder is always ($g - 1$) bits long; therefore, for this example, the remainder is 4 bits long. Hence, if we make sure that $g - 1$ additional 0s, or four 0s in the example, are at the end of the dividend, the receiver can perform an identical arithmetic in terms of size of dividend. If the transmitter produces a remainder, let's say 1000, the addition of this value to the same data can indeed result in a 0 remainder, provided that the data is the same data used in the transmitter. Therefore, if there is any error during transmission, the remainder may not become 0 at the receiver, giving a notion of error. The reader may want to investigate that, even if there is an error during transmission, there is a small possibility that the remainder becomes 0 at the reciver.

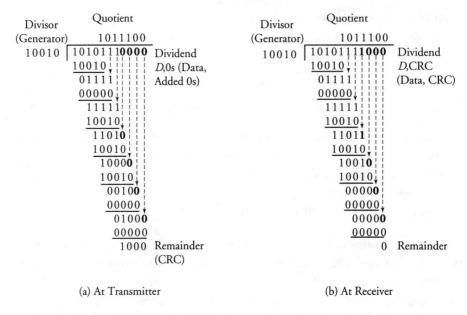

Figure 3.6 Modulo-2 division for the CRC process shown for a transmitter and a receiver

Equivalent Polynomial Interpretation

The preceding analogy can be restated such that the CRC error-detection method treats the data to be transmitted as a polynomial. In general, consider the bit string $a_{n-1}a_{n-2}a_{n-3} \cdots a_0$, which forms a generic polynomial:

$$a_{n-1}x^{n-1} + a_{n-2}x^{n-2} + a_{n-3}x^{n-3} + \cdots + a_0x^0,$$

where a_i can be 0 or 1. In other words, when a data bit is 1, the corresponding polynomial term is included. For example, the bit string $D = 1010111$ produces the string $a_6a_5a_4a_3a_2a_1a_0 = 1010111$, which is interpreted as

$$x^6 + x^4 + x^2 + x^1 + x^0.$$

The *generator* value, acting as the divisor, is known as the *generating polynomial* in this case. Some well-known and widespread industry-approved generating polynomials—common divisors between transmitters and receivers—used to create the cyclic checksum remainder are:

CRC-10: $x^{10} + x^9 + x^5 + x^4 + x + 1$

CRC-12: $x^{12} + x^{11} + x^3 + x^2 + x + 1$

CRC-16: $x^{16} + x^{15} + x^2 + 1$

CRC-CCITT: $x^{16} + x^{15} + x^5 + 1$

CRC-32-IEEE 802:

$$x^{32} + x^{26} + x^{23} + x^{22} + x^{10} + x^8 + x^7 + x^5 + x^4 + x^2 + x + 1$$

Note that the polynomial interpretation is simply a convenient method of explaining the CRC algorithm. In practice, the transmitter and the receiver perform divisions in bits, as described earlier.

Effectiveness of CRC

The CRC method is pretty goof-proof. However, an analysis is needed to answer whether the receiver is always able to detect a damaged frame. Consider the generating polynomial $x^{g-1} + x^{g-2} + \cdots + 1$ with g terms. Apparently, $g - 1$ is the highest power of the generating polynomial. Let n be the length of burst error occurring in a received message. If the size of the error burst is $n < g$, error detection is 100 percent. For all other cases, the terms between x^{g-1} and 1 define which bits are erroneous. Since there are $g - 2$ such terms, there are 2^{g-2} possible combinations of erroneous bits. Considering that all combinations can occur with equal probability, there is a chance of $\frac{1}{2^{g-2}}$ that a combination exactly matches the terms of the polynomial. This is the probability of a damaged bit becoming undetected. The probability of catching such error bursts through CRC for all cases is

$$p = \begin{cases} 1 & \text{if } n < g \\ 1 - \left(\dfrac{1}{2}\right)^{(g-2)} & \text{if } n = g. \\ 1 - \left(\dfrac{1}{2}\right)^{(g-1)} & \text{if } n > g \end{cases} \qquad (3.2)$$

Example.   Consider a computer communication standard based on CRC-CCITT, defined earlier. For this standard, the highest power of the polynomial is $g - 1 = 16$. If the error burst n is less than $g = 17$ bits in length, CRC detects it. Assuming that $n = g = 17$:

$$p = 1 - \left(\frac{1}{2}\right)^{(17-2)} = 0.999969,$$

which is close to 1.

Hardware Implementation of Modulo-2 Division in CRC Units

Hardware with a combination of software performs the process of division very quickly. An example of the basic hardware used to perform the CRC calculation is shown in Figure 3.7. The hardware includes a simple register that implements the CRC process-generating polynomial $x^4 + x$. Except for the first term (x^4), an Exclusive-OR is included for each power of the existing term, as shown. Note that the notion of the generator value 10010 is now appearing in the form of hardware shown by a combination of 1-bit shift registers and Exclusive-OR gates to represent each existing term (such as x) except the first term (such as x^4) and a register to request each nonexisting term (such as x^2 or x^3). Therefore, we can see from the figure where there is a term in the generating polynomial.

Initially, the registers contain 0s. All data bits of 1010111,**0000**, beginning from the most significant bit, arrive from the left, and a 1-bit shift register shifts the bits to the right every time a new bit is entered. The rightmost bit of shift registers feeds back around at select points. At these points, the value of this feedback bit is Exclusive-ORed with the bits in the register. Before a bit shifts right, if there is an Exclusive-OR to shift through, the rightmost bit currently stored in the shift register wraps around and is Exclusive-ORed with the moving bit. Once all data bits are fed through, the register's contents must be exactly the same as the remainder indicated in Figure 3.6 (a).

Example.   For the same $D,0 = 1010111,0000$ presented in the example of the CRC section, and with the same common divisor $G = 10010$, show directly the contents of modulo-2 shift registers. Prove that the final contents of the registers show the value of CRC.

Solution.   We need to shift $D,0 = 1010111,0000$ into shift registers constructed with $G = 10010$ ($x^4 + x$) while the contents of the shift registers are initialized with 0000. The contents of the shift registers after shifting the first and second bits of $D,0$ turned into 1000 and 0100, respectively, noting that the bit shifting starts at the MSB of $D,0$ as seen in Table 3.1. If we continue shifting all bits of $D, 0$ into the shift register step-by-step, the end result contents of the shift registers will be 0001 whose bits are the reverse of CRC = 1000.

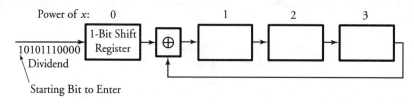

Figure 3.7   Implementation of modulo-2 division in CRC units: the most significant bit enters first

Table 3.1   The results of data in modulo-2 implementation of shift registers

Bits of $D,0$ left to shift	Contents of shift registers
1010111,0000	0000
010111,0000	1000
10111,0000	0100
0111,0000	1010
111,0000	0101
11,0000	1110
1,0000	1111
0000	1011
000	0001
00	0100
0	0010
-	**0001**

3.4   Flow Control on Links

Communication systems must use *flow-control techniques* on their transmission links to guarantee that a transmitter does not overwhelm a receiver with data. Several protocols guarantee the control of link flows. Two widely used flow-control protocols are *stop and wait* and *sliding window*.

3.4.1   Stop-and-Wait Flow Control

The *stop-and-wait* protocol is the simplest and the least expensive technique for link-overflow control. The idea behind this protocol is that the transmitter waits for an acknowledgment after transmitting one frame (see Figure 3.8). The essence of this protocol is that if the acknowledgment is not received by the transmitter after a certain agreed period of time, the transmitter retransmits the original frame.

In this figure, we assume two consecutive frames 1 and 2. Frame 1 is ready to enter the link and is transmitted at $t = 0$. Let t_f be the time required to transfer all the bits of a frame onto link, t_p, the propagation time of the frame between the transmitter (T) and the receiver (R), and t_r be the processing time of a frame at a node once received. It takes as long as $t = t_f + t_p$ to transmit a frame from a transmitter to a receiver. At the arrival of frame 1, the receiver processes the frame for as long as t_r and generates an acknowledgment, ACK 2, frame, so that the elapsed time turns into $t = (t_f + t_p + t_r) + t_{fa}$ where t_{fa} is assumed to be the time required to transfer an ACK

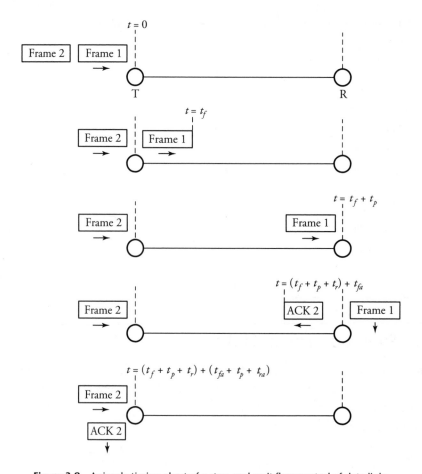

Figure 3.8   A simple timing chart of a stop-and-wait flow control of data links

frame onto link. Note that the protocol requires that the acknowledgment of a frame 1 must always hint to an expectation of the next frame (frame 2) and thus ACK 2 is returned by the receiver.

For the same reason, the ACK 2 frame takes $t = t_{fa} + t_p$ to be received by the transmitter and it takes t_{ra} to be processed. Therefore, the total time to transmit a frame and receive its acknowledgment frame is

$$t = (t_f + t_p + t_r) + (t_{fa} + t_p + t_{ra}) \tag{3.3}$$

Note here that with this technique, the receiver can stop or slow down the flow of data by withholding or delaying acknowledgment. Practically, t_r, t_{fa}, and t_{ra} are negligible compared to other components of the equation. Thus, this equation can be approximated as

$$t \approx t_f + 2t_p. \tag{3.4}$$

Therefore, the link efficiency is defined as

$$E_\ell = \frac{t_f}{t} = \frac{1}{1 + 2\left(\dfrac{t_p}{t_f}\right)}. \tag{3.5}$$

In this equation, $t_f = f/r$, where f is the length of the frame in bits; r is the data rate; and $t_p = \ell/c$, where ℓ is the length of the transmission line, and c is the speed of transmission. For wireless and wired transmissions, $c = 3 \times 10^8$ m/s where, except for fiber-optic links, $c \approx 2.3 \times 10^8$ m/s, owing to the fact that light travels zigzag over links, and thus overall speed is lower.

Example.   Two computers communicate directly on an $\ell = 1$ km fiber-optic link using frames of total size $f = 424$ b. Suppose data is transmitted at rate $r = 155.5$ Mb/s and speed of transmission is $c \approx 2.3 \times 10^8$ m/s. Find the link efficiency assuming that the stop-and-wait flow control protocol is used.

Solution.   We first obtain transmission time, $t_f = f/r$, to be $2.7 \mu s$ and propagation time, $t_p = \ell/c$, to be $4.3 \mu s$. Next, equation (3.5) will give us the link efficiency as

$$E_\ell = \frac{1}{1 + 2\left(\dfrac{4.3}{2.7}\right)} = 23\%.$$

We can find out about the link efficiency performance through a similar example when we study another kind of flow control called "sliding window," to be discussed next.

Automatic Repeat Request (ARQ) Protocol

The *automatic repeat request* (ARQ) protocol, also known as the automatic repeat query protocol, is a protocol that controls the timing of frames to achieve reliable data transmission over an unreliable service. ARQ can be used for any of the flow-control protocols such as the stop-and-wait protocol. With this protocol, an acknowledgment frame (ACK) sent by a receiver (R) indicates that the receiver has correctly received a data frame within a *timeout*. A timeout is a specified period of time allowed to elapse before an acknowledgment is to be received. If the transmitter (T) does not receive an acknowledgment for a frame before the timeout, it must retransmit the frame until the transmitter receives an acknowledgment or exceeds a predefined number of retransmissions.

Figure 3.9 illustrates five different time periods of a stop-and-wait link flow control between a transmitter (T) and a receiver (R), and includes the ARQ protocol in the link activities. The five periods are considered to be the five ARQ timeout periods, timeouts 1 through 5. During timeout 1, there is a normal situation in which an ACK for a frame 1 is received before the timer expires, implying successful transmission of frame 1 and receipt of its ACK 2. Note that the protocol requires that the acknowledgment of a frame 1 must always hint to an expectation of the next frame (frame 2) and thus ACK 2 is returned by the receiver. During timeout 2, the situation is that the next frame 2 has reached the receiver successfully, but for some reason ACK 3 is lost over the transmission link. For this, the transmitter realizes that it has not received the acknowledgment and hence it retransmits frame 2 during timeout 3. During timeout 4, there is a similar situation resulting in retransmission of the frame over timeout period 5, but this time frame 3 itself is lost during the transmission.

3.4.2 Sliding-Window Flow Control

The shortcoming of the stop-and-wait protocol is that only one frame at a time is allowed for transmission. This flow control can be significantly improved by letting multiple frames travel on a transmission link. However, allowing a sequence of frames to be in transit at the same time requires a more sophisticated protocol for the control of data overflow on links. The well-known *sliding-window* protocol is one technique that efficiently controls the flow of frames.

Figure 3.10 shows an example of sliding-window flow control with no congestion. Using this protocol, a transmitter (T) and a receiver (R) agree to form identical-size sequences of frames. Let the size of a sequence be w. Thus, a transmitter allocates buffer space for w frames, and the receiver can accept up to w frames. In this figure, $w = 5$.

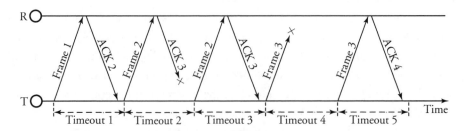

Figure 3.9 Automatic repeat request (ARQ) implemented for stop-and-wait flow control

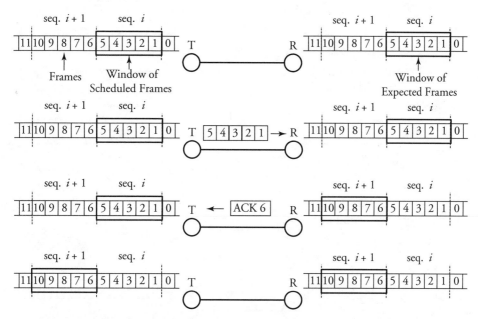

Figure 3.10 Timing chart of a sliding-window flow control for a sequence of five frames

The transmitter can then send up to $w = 5$ frames without waiting for any acknowledgment frames. Each frame in a sequence is labeled by a unique sequence number.

First, a transmitter opens a window of size $w = 5$, as the figure shows. The receiver also opens a window of size w to indicate how many frames it can expect. In the first attempt, let all five frames 1, 2, 3, 4, and 5 be part of sequence i to be transmitted. The transmitter then waits until it hears back from the receiver that the frames have been received by the receiver. Similar to the stop-and-wait control, ARQ protocol requires here that the acknowledgment of frames 1 through 5 must hint to an expectation of the next frame (frame 6), and thus, ACK 6 is returned by the receiver (and not ACK 1), as seen in the figure. At this point, both the transmitter and the receiver move their window over the next w frames to repeat the preceding process for transmission of frames 6 through 10.

Figure 3.11 shows an example of sliding-window flow control under a traffic congestion circumstance. First, a transmitter opens a window of size $w = 5$, as the figure shows. The receiver also opens a window of size w to indicate how many frames it can expect. In the first attempt, let's say that frames 1, 2, and 3 as part of sequence i are transmitted due to traffic congestion. The transmitter then shrinks its window to $w = 2$ but keeps the copy of these frames in its buffer just in case any of the frames is not received by the receiver. At the receipt of these three frames,

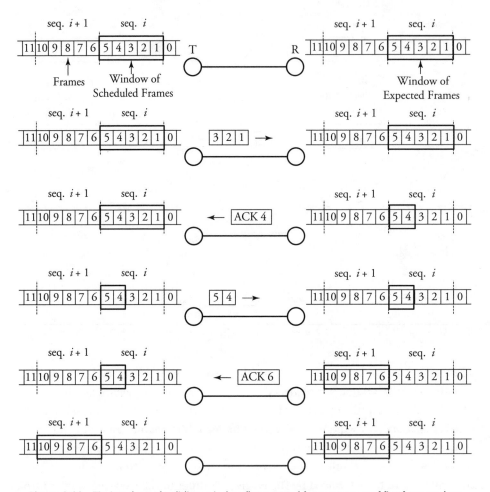

Figure 3.11   Timing chart of a sliding-window flow control for a sequence of five frames when there is congestion leading to shrinkage of window size

the receiver shrinks its expected window to $w = 2$ and acknowledges the receipt of frames by sending an acknowledgment ACK 4 frame to the transmitter telling it the next expected sequence must start with frame 4.

At the release of ACK 4, the receiver changes its expected window size back to $w = 5$. This acknowledgment also carries information about the sequence number of the next frame expected and informs the transmitter that the receiver is prepared to receive the next w frames. At the receipt of ACK 4, the transmitter maximizes its window back to $w = 5$, discards the copies of frames 1, 2, and 3, and continues the procedure. In this protocol, the window is imagined to be sliding on coming frames as shown in the figure.

Similarly, we can derive an expression for this protocol as we did for the stop-and-wait protocol. For the transmission of a frame as the integral portion of the w frames sequence, the total time, including all the acknowledgment processes, is obtained using Equation (3.3), with averaging over w and inclusion of wt_f as

$$t = \frac{1}{w}\left[(wt_f + t_p + t_r) + (t_{fa} + t_p + t_{ra})\right]. \tag{3.6}$$

Practically, t_r, t_{fa}, and t_{ra} are negligible compared to other components of the equation. Thus, this equation can be approximated as

$$t \approx t_f + 2\left(\frac{t_p}{w}\right). \tag{3.7}$$

Therefore, link efficiency is expressed as

$$E_\ell = \frac{t_f}{t} = \frac{w}{w + 2\left(\dfrac{t_p}{t_f}\right)}. \tag{3.8}$$

Link efficiency provides a network designer with a good understanding of the link utilization for network management purposes.

Example. Repeat the same example presented for the stop-and-wait flow-control protocol but this time use the sliding-window flow-control protocol where the window size is $w = 5$. We remember that in this example, two computers communicate directly on an $\ell = 1$ km fiber-optic link using frames of total size $f = 424$ b. Suppose data is transmitted at rate $r = 155.5$Mb/s and speed of transmission is $c \approx 2.3 \times 10^8$ m/s.

Solution. We obtain transmission time, $t_f = f/r$, to be $2.6\mu s$, and then propagation time, $t_p = \ell/c$, to be $11.3\mu s$. Next, equation (3.8) will give us the link efficiency as

$$E_\ell = \frac{5}{5 + 2\left(\dfrac{4.3}{2.7}\right)} = 61\%.$$

The better link performance using the sliding-window protocol compared to the stop-and-wait protocol makes the sliding window more popular, especially for cases in which the link traffic is heavy.

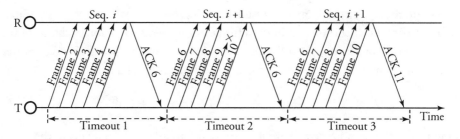

Figure 3.12   A "Go-back-N" type automatic repeat request (ARQ) implemented for sliding-window flow control

ARQ in Sliding Window

The automatic repeat request (ARQ) protocol is also implemented for the sliding-window flow control. Figure 3.12 illustrates three different time periods of a sliding-window link flow control between a transmitter (T) and a receiver (R), and includes the ARQ protocol in the link activities. The three time periods are considered to be the three ARQ timeout periods, timeouts 1 2, and 3. During timeout 1, there is a normal situation in which ACK 6 for a window of sequence i including frames 1 through 5 is received, before the timer expires, implying successful transmissions of frames 1 through 5 and receipt of its ACK 6. Note again that the protocol requires here that the acknowledgment of frames 1 through 5 must always hint to an expectation of the next frame (frame 6), and thus, ACK 6 is returned by the receiver (and not ACK 1). During timeout 2, the situation is that the next window of sequence $i + 1$ including frames 6 through 10 are sent, but one of the frames in the sequence, frame 9, for some reason is lost over the transmission link. For this, the receiver notices in the order of sequence $i + 1$ that there is a lost frame, and thus, it requests the retransmission of sequence $i + 1$ by sending again ACK 6. The receipt of ACK 6 by the transmitter indicates that the transmitter is required to retransmit the entire sequence $i + 1$. This technique is also known as *Go-back-N* ARQ.

3.5   Link Access by Multiple Users

Access methods for either wireline or wireless links can be broadly classified as three types:

- *Contention access method*, by which each user needing to transmit data must contend to access the medium.
- *Round-robin access method*, by which each user is given a fair chance to transmit data in a round-robin fashion.

- *Reservation access method* is used mainly for streaming traffic. With this method, as in synchronous time-division multiplexing, time slots are used to access the medium. A user can reserve time slots for transmission in advance. The control mechanism for the reservations can be either centralized or decentralized.

The reservation access method will be explained later in the chapters on multimedia and advanced networking throughout Part II of this book. Of the first two access methods, the round-robin method is not practical since it causes possible waste of link bandwidth; thus, we will not discuss it any further. The contention access method is the most popular method of link access, and is described next.

The *contention-access* method is stochastic, more suitable for bursty traffic, whereby the waste of shared-medium bandwidth cannot be tolerated. Unlike the round-robin and reservation schemes, no control is involved in the contention scheme. Rather, each user needing to transmit frames must contend to access the medium. This scheme is simple to implement and is an effective solution for light or moderate traffic.

When a user logs on to a LAN, a channel for the transmission of a frame can be demanded at any random instance, potentially resulting in frame collision. This serious issue can be resolved in a number of ways, as follows:

- *Permanent assignment of one channel to each user.* This method can clearly waste the system bandwidth.
- *Checking users regularly.* The system can poll each user on a regular basis to see whether it has anything to transmit. This method could result in a long delay for larger networks.
- *Random access of a channel.* The system can provide a mechanism whereby a user can gain access at any time. This method is efficient but faces the collision issue if two or more frames are transmitted at the same time.

Several random-access methods are provided for computer networks. Two commonly used ones are the *Aloha* method and *Carrier Sense Multiple Access* (CSMA). The CSMA scheme is explained in the next section.

3.5.1   Carrier Sense Multiple Access (CSMA)

Carrier Sense Multiple Access (CSMA) is a protocol that lets only one user at a time transmit data. A user needing to transmit data first listens to the medium and senses a carrier on the medium to determine whether other users are transmitting: the *carrier-sense* phase. If the medium is busy, the user has to wait until the medium is idle. The amount of time a user must wait depends on the particular type of the protocol. If no other users transmit data, the user proceeds to transmit its data onto the medium. However, when the medium is busy, a user can take one of the following three approaches:

1. *Nonpersistent CSMA.* The user waits for a random amount of time after a collision before sensing the channel again. The random delay is used to reduce the chance of collision. However, this scheme uses the transmission channel inefficiently: Even though another transmission is completed, the user rechecks the medium only after expiration of the random delay. The random wait time is normally 512 g bit times, where g is a number drawn randomly.

2. *1-persistent CSMA.* This scheme overcomes the disadvantage of the nonpersistent CSMA by continuing to sense the channel while it is busy. As soon as the medium is idle, the user transmits immediately. In this scheme, a collision occurs if more than one user is waiting to transmit.

3. *p-persistent CSMA.* This scheme is a compromise between the nonpersistent and the 1-persistent methods. When the medium is idle, the user can transmit with a probability p. If the medium is busy, the user can transmit for a time equal to the maximum propagation delay. Deciding on an appropriate value of p is crucial for efficient operation of the scheme.

If two or more users simultaneously try to transmit, a collision of frames occurs, and all data is corrupted. In such a case, all corresponding users stop transmitting. If the nonpersistent CSMA is adopted, after a collision, all the users involved will start contention, each after a randomly chosen amount of time. After finishing the transmission of data, a user waits for an acknowledgment from the destination user. If the acknowledgment does not arrive, the user retransmits the data.

The main disadvantage of CSMA when a collision occurs is that other users cannot use the medium until all corrupted frames finish transmission. This problem is worse in the case of long frames. However, this issue can be resolved with the use of CSMA/CD, whereby a user listens to the channel while transmitting data. In case of a collision, the transmission is halted, and a jamming signal is transmitted to inform the other users that a collision has occurred. The user enters into *back-off mode* and transmits after the back-off duration if the medium is idle. In Figure 3.13 (a), a frame that leaves user 4 destined for user 2 collides with another frame that leaves user 1 destined for user 3, as shown in Figure 3.13 (b). Immediately after the collision, user 2 finds the medium idle and transmits its frame destined to user 1, as shown in Figure 3.13 (c).

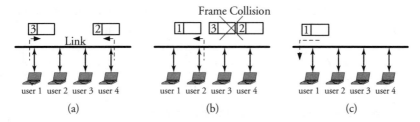

Figure 3.13   The movement and collision of frames in a contention-access process of CSMA

Consider n users to be connected onto a common cable so that when one user transmits a frame while others are silent, all other users sense that frame. When a user starts the transmission, no others start before the user has propagated a signal throughout the cable. This way, the user can finish its frame without collision. It is quite possible for a user to listen to the cable while transmitting; obviously, if two or more users start to transmit simultaneously, they find a collision in process and cease transmission. That is why this process is called CSMA with collision detection (CSMA/CD).

CSMA/CD requires the frame length to be long enough to permit collision detection before the completion of transmission. The maximum time to detect a collision is not greater than twice the end-to-end propagation delay. The process of CSMA/CD is viewed in terms of slots and minislots. Setting minislots is required for a signal to propagate from one end of the cable to the other. Minislots are used in a contention mode. If all users are synchronized in minislots and one user transmits during an empty slot, all the other users pick up the transmitted frame until the frame is transmitted completely. However, if more than one user transmits during that slot, each transmitting user senses the situation and ceases transmitting.

Analysis of Frame Delay

Consider once again the contention of the users shown in Figure 3.13. Let ℓ be the average distance between any two users. The maximum ℓ is the distance between user 1 and user 4, and the minimum ℓ is the distance between user 1 and user 2. Let c be the speed of propagation. The average propagation delay of a frame between any two users can be determined by

$$t_p = \frac{\ell}{c}. \tag{3.9}$$

Now, let f be the average frame size in bits and r be the data rate on the channel over the medium. The frame transmission time, t_f, can be calculated by

$$t_f = \frac{f}{r}.$$ (3.10)

Here, the *utilization* of the LAN bus can be obtained by

$$u = \frac{t_f}{t_f + t_p}.$$ (3.11)

Analysis of Contention

If a total of n users are attached to the medium, n_a of them are active each with probability p. Practically, this probability is different for each of the n_a users. In general, an empty time slot remains empty, is taken by a user, or undergoes a collision. Apparently, the probability that a time slot is available and only one of the n_a users successfully transmits without frame collision is

$$p_c = \binom{n_a}{1} p^1 (1-p)^{n_a-1} = n_a p (1-p)^{n_a-1}.$$ (3.12)

A different situation is that a user tries i times in i different empty slots to transmit its frame and is unsuccessful owing to collision, but it successfully sends its frame on time $i + 1$. The probability that this situation happens is obviously modeled by a geometric random variable, explained in Appendix C, and is obtained by

$$p_i = p_c (1 - p_c)^i.$$ (3.13)

Interestingly, the average number of contentions can be computed by knowing this behavioral model using the expected value, $E[C]$, explained in Appendix C:

$$
\begin{aligned}
E[C] &= \sum_{i=1}^{\infty} i p_i = \sum_{i=1}^{\infty} i p_c^{(1-p_c)i} \\
&= \frac{1 - p_c}{p_c}.
\end{aligned}
$$ (3.14)

Example.   Assume that seven host computers as users are connected to a cable. At a certain time, three of the hosts become active, each with probability 0.33 while there is only one time slot is available. Find p_8, that is, the probability that a frame from an active host tries eight times and finally succeeds to transmit on its ninth attempt. Also, find the average number of contentions per host.

Solution.   In this example, $n = 7$, $n_a = 3$, and $p = 0.33$. By using equation (3.12), we can get $p_c = 0.44$. The probability that a frame from an active host tries eight times and finally succeeds to transmit on its ninth attempt is calculated using equation (3.13), which results in $p_8 = 0.004$. The average number of contentions per host is obtained from equation (3.14) and can be computed to be $E[C] = 1.27$.

Figure 3.14 (a) shows frame arrivals with a frame duration of T seconds. The delay time caused by the last colliding frame is modeled by a random variable Y. In this case, the desired frame intended to be sent on a link indicated by frame 2 is colliding with frames 1 and 3. In contrast, Figure 3.14 (b) shows that frame 1 is transmitted without collision where Y is defined as a random variable representing time separation between frames 2 and 3.

3.6   Wireless Channel Access by Multiple Users

Voice and video applications that run on wireless networks could require continuous transmission, requiring dedicated allocation of available resources for that application. Similar to what was explained in the previous section for multiple user access over physical links, the sharing of the available bandwidth among wireless users also

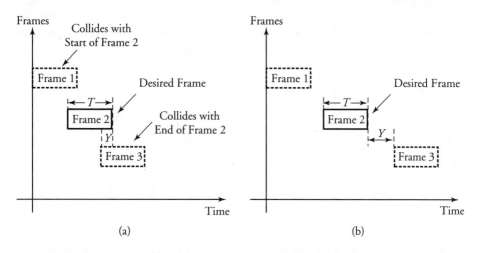

Figure 3.14   A timing illustration of CSMA/CD for a desired frame: (a) colliding with two other frames, (b) transmission with no collision

requires a dedicated *multiple-access* mechanism. Any wireless link has an available bandwidth, as is the case for any wireline links.

Figure 3.15 shows two scenarios for link access. In part (a) of the figure, three hosts 11, 12, and 13 are trying to access a certain channel over a common link (shown by a thicker line) to reach out from their network. According to what we learned in the previous section, if there is only one channel available over a common link, the dominating protocol, such as CSMA, lets one of the hosts access the link. In this case, host 13 is the winner, and the others lose the competition. In contrast to this scenario, in part (b) of the figure, we see three wireless hosts 21, 22, and 23 are similarly contending to access the common wireless link through their *wireless access point* (WAP). To resolve this competition, a number of special-purpose wireless protocols are available to identify a winning host such as host 23 shown in the figure.

Notice that wireless hosts are propagating their data over radio frequency waves, and assignment of channels over the common link is challenging. A wireless host must attempt to access a "channel" on a wireless link before the transmission can start. Thus, a wireless channel is a portion of transmission bandwidth through which communication can be established. Most wireless applications involve transmission of random data requiring some form of random "channel allocation," which does not guarantee resource availability. Multiple-access techniques assign bandwidth to users by allocating a portion of the available spectrum to each independent user.

Channels are susceptible to interference and noise. Most commercial wireless systems use radio waves in the ultrahigh frequency (UHF) band for communication. The UHF band ranges from 0.3GHz to about 3GHz. Satellite communication typically uses the super-high frequency (SHF) band ranging from 3GHz to 30GHz.

There are several wireless link channel access methods. The most prevelant methods are *frequency-division multiple access* (FDMA), *time-division multiple access*

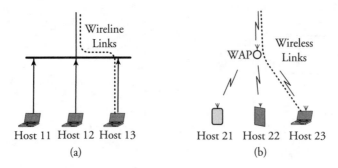

Figure 3.15   Link channel access, a comparison on (a) wireline links and (b) wireless links

(TDMA), *orthogonal frequency-division multiple access* (OFDMA), *single-carrier frequency-division multiple access* (SC-FDMA), and *code-division multiple access* (CDMA). The following sections discuss these channel access methods.

3.6.1 Frequency-Division Multiple Access

In *frequency-division multiple access* (FDMA), each user transmits with no limitations on time, but utilizing only a portion of the entire available frequency bandwidth, as seen in Figure 3.16 (a). Different users are separated in the frequency domain. Therefore, in FDMA, the available bandwidth is divided into nonoverlapping frequency slots, known as frequency channels, and each user is assigned a portion of the link's spectrum.

3.6.2 Time-Division Multiple Access

Time-division multiple access (TDMA) divides a given spectrum into channels in the frequency domain. Each user is then allocated one channel for the "entire" duration of its usage. As seen in Figure 3.16 (b), each user is allowed to transmit only within specified time intervals so that when a user transmits, it occupies the entire frequency bandwidth. The separation among users is performed in the time domain. These time slots are nonoverlapping.

TDMA techniques are more complex, as they require synchronization in timing among the users. TDMA divides each channel into orthogonal slots and hence limits the number of users, based on the available bandwidth. TDMA places a hard limit on the number of supported users and bandwidth available for each user. A practical version of TDMA is the *random-access technique, which* is mainly used in local area networks.

3.6.3 Orthogonal Frequency-Division Multiple Access

Orthogonal frequency-division multiple access (OFDMA) is a very popular multiple user link access method that is used in most fourth-generation (4G) wireless networks. We discuss the 4G network in Chapter 7. OFDMA can be realized as a multiuser version of the popular orthogonal frequency-division multiplexing (OFDM) digital modulation scheme explained in the previous chapter. Multiple access is achieved in OFDMA by assigning subsets of subcarriers to individual users as shown in Figure 3.16 (c). This method allows simultaneous low data rate transmission from several users.

OFDMA transmits a data stream by using several narrowband *subcarriers* simultaneously. Each subcarrier is transmitted on a different frequency. The number of subcarriers could reach 512, 1024, or even more depending on whether the overall available channel bandwidth is 5, 10, or 20MHz. As many bits are transported in parallel, the transmission speed on each subcarrier can be much lower than the overall resulting data rate. This is important in a practical radio environment in order to minimize the effect of multipath fading created by slightly different arrival times of the signal from different directions.

The modulation scheme in OFDMA is QAM, such as 16-QAM, and is used for constructing each subcarrier. In theory, each subcarrier signal could be generated by a separate transmission chain hardware block. The output of these blocks would then have to be summed up with the resulting signal to be transmitted over the air. As not all subcarriers are used by the mobile station, many of them are set to zero. These subcarriers may or may not be used by other mobile stations, as shown in the figure.

3.6.4   Single-Carrier Frequency-Division Multiple Access

Single-carrier frequency-division multiple access (SC-FDMA) is another frequency-division multiple access scheme that assigns multiple users to a shared communication resource. SC-FDMA has been given a lot of attention as an attractive alternative to OFDMA, especially in the uplink communications where a lower peak-to-average power ratio (PAPR) greatly benefits the mobile terminal as cellphones in terms of transmit power efficiency, which leads to reduced cost of the power amplifier. SC-FDMA has been adopted as the uplink multiple-access scheme in 4G *Long Term Evolution* (LTE) wireless networking, which is discussed in Chapter 7.

Similar to OFDMA, SC-FDMA also transmits data using numerous subcarriers but adds an additional processing step. The additional processing block in SC-FDMA spreads the information of each bit over all the subcarriers. This is done by having a number of bits, like the 4 bits representing a 16-QAM modulation, grouped together. In SC-FDMA, however, these bits are piped into a *fast Fourier transform* (FFT) function. The end result is shown in Figure 3.16 (d). The output of the process is the basis for the creation of the subcarriers. As with OFDMA, not all subcarriers are used by the mobile station.

3.6.5   Code-Division Multiple Access

In *code-division multiple access* (CDMA), a user is assigned a "unique code sequence," which is used to encode its data signal. Each receiver of a user knows its unique code sequence, and therefore, it can decode the received signal and recover the original data by applying its code. The bandwidth of the coded data signal is chosen to be much larger than the bandwidth of the original data signal, as shown in Figure 3.16 (e); that is, the encoding process spreads the spectrum of the data signal. CDMA is thus based on *spread-spectrum modulation*. If multiple users transmit a spread-spectrum signal at the same time, the receiver is still able to distinguish between users, due to the unique code assigned to each user.

With CDMA, each data bit being transmitted is encoded by multiplying the bit by a "unique code sequence." The code changes at a faster rate, called the *chipping rate,* than the data rate. Figure 3.17 illustrates a CDMA encoding and decoding scenario. In this figure, we assume that each user data bit 1 to be transmitted requires a one-bit time slot. Note that for simplification of the analysis, we use a -1 value instead of 0. During each data time slot, 1 or -1, we also assume that user 1 data is {1, -1}, and the code sequence of user 1 uniquely assigned to both receiver and transmitter is {-1, 1, -1, -1, 1, -1, 1, 1}.

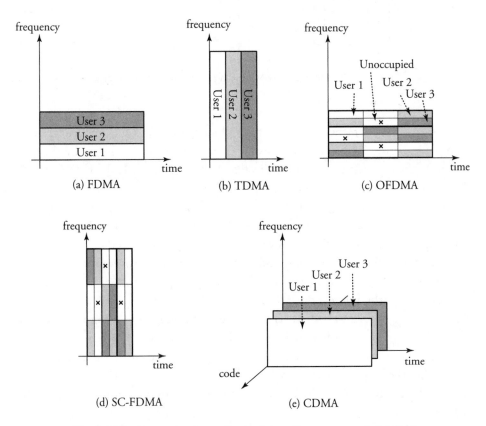

Figure 3.16   Comparing the methods of channel access over wireless links

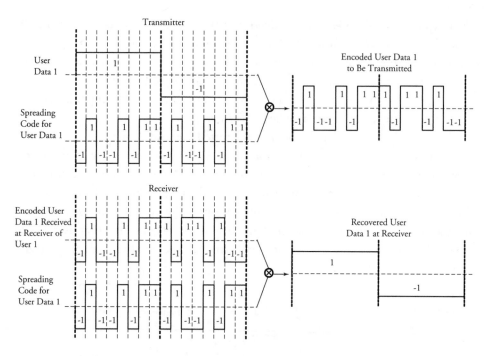

Figure 3.17   Method of CDMA coding at transmitter and receiver

In the transmitter, the user data is multiplied by the user's code sequence. In the example in Figure 3.17, once the transmitter multiplies the user's data by the code sequence, the encoded user data 1 indicated in the figure, {-1, 1, -1, -1, 1, -1, 1, 1, 1, -1, 1, 1, -1, 1, -1, -1}, results and is propagated to the receiver over radio frequency waves. The encoded user data 1 at the receiver of user 1 is once again multiplied by its same unique code to recover the original data of {1, -1} as seen in the figure. The amazing part of this encoding and decoding theory of CDMA is that no other users can recover user data 1, as the only code sequence that can recover user data 1 is the code sequence {-1, 1, -1, -1, 1, -1, 1, 1}, which is assigned only to user 1.

In practice, though, encoded data bits of other users can be transmitted with the encoded data bits of user 1. CDMA operates under the assumption that the interfering transmitted bit signals from others are additive. For example, if each of the five transmitters sends a 1 value, and a sixth sends a –1 value during the same time, then the received signal at all receivers during that time is a 4. This can still be easily resolved during decoding, but its discussion is outside of this chapter's scope.

Spread-Spectrum Technique

The fundamental superiority of CDMA over other channel-access method lies in the use of the *spread-spectrum technique*. The spread-spectrum technique involves spreading frequencies of a transmitted signal over a wider range. This technique reduces flat fading and intersymbol interference. The message signal is modulated by a *pseudonoise signal*, which encompasses a wider bandwidth. Hence, the resultant transmission signal obtains a much larger bandwidth.

Spread-spectrum techniques can be implemented in two ways. In the first one, *direct sequence spread spectrum* (DSSS), the message signal is Exclusive-ORed with the pseudonoise sequence, thereby spreading the frequency range. A pseudonoise sequence is a sequence of pulses that repeats itself after its period. The second technique, *frequency hopping*, involves using the "random" pseudonoise sequence to transmit over a range of frequencies.

In the DSSS shown in Figure 3.18, the multipath technique, in which a transmitter transmits multiple copies of the signal (binary data), each with different delay, is used, and hence the receiver can recover the signal from multiple transmissions. The binary data to be transmitted is first Exclusive-ORed with the transmitter's chipping code (a designated code with pulse speed faster than the one for 0s and 1s of the binary data) to spread the frequency range of the transmitted signal. The signal is then modulated for transmission over the wireless medium. The multipath effects in the wireless medium result in multiple copies of the signal, each with different delays of t_1, t_2, and t_3 and with different attenuations of α_1, α_2, and α_3. The receiver demodulates the combined signal and then feeds the result into its *rake receiver* unit, as shown in the figure. In the rake receiver, signals are first Ex-ORed with the recovered codes but delayed corresponding to the delays introduced at the transmitter. The resulting signals are then combined with different weighing factors—β_1, β_2, and β_3—to give the resultant signal with reduced multipath effects.

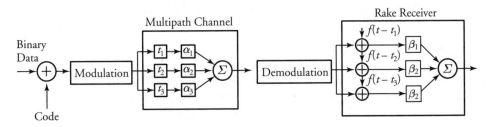

Figure 3.18   The transmitter (left) and the receiver (right) of the direct-sequence spread spectrum technique in CDMA

CDMA advantageously does not place any hard limit on the number of users supported. But owing to the impact of codes, the interference from other users increases as the number of users becomes large. However, the interference can be reduced by using steering antennas, interference equalization, and multiuser detection techniques.

In CDMA, the available frequency bandwidth for each cell is divided in half: one for forward transmission between the base station to the mobile unit and the other part for reverse transmission from the mobile unit to the base station. The transmission technique used is called *direct-sequence spread spectrum* (DSSS). Orthogonal chipping codes are used to increase the data rates and to support multiple users. The transmitted signal also has an increased bandwidth. Using CDMA for cellular systems has several advantages:

- *Diversity in frequency.* In CDMA, the transmitted signal occupies a wider range of frequencies. Therefore, the transmitted signal is not greatly affected by noise and selective fading.

- *Multipath effects.* The orthogonal chipping codes used in CDMA have low cross-correlation and autocorrelation. Hence, multipath signals delayed by more than one chip interval do not interfere with the dominant signal.

- *Privacy.* Since DSSS techniques use pseudorandom sequences, privacy is ensured.

- *Scalability.* FDMA or TDMA systems support only a fixed number of users. CDMA can support a larger number of users with an acceptable amount of degradation in performance. The error rate increases gradually as the number of users becomes larger.

CDMA also has certain disadvantages. In CDMA, the spreading sequence of different users is not orthogonal, and there is some overlap, which results in some cross-correlation, resulting is self-jamming. Also, signals, being at a greater distance from the receiver, experience significant attenuation compared to signals close to the receiver. Thus, signal strength is weak for remote mobile units.

3.6.6   Other Multiple-Access Methods

The three multiple-access techniques—FDMA, TDMA, and CDMA—are based on *isotropical antennas*. Recall that an isotropical antenna operates essentially in a uniform manner in all directions. Another method of multiple access in wireless systems is *space-division multiple access* (SDMA), which uses smart antennas. At one end of communication system, a directional antenna, typically known as a smart antenna, can focus directly on the other end of the system. This technique offers a number of advantages, such as reduction of transmission power, reduced amount of interference owing to reduced transmission power, and the strong signal received by the receiver, owing to the high-gain antenna.

An effective multiple-access scheme needs to be carefully chosen on the basis of application requirements. Practical wireless systems normally use two or more multiple-access techniques. This strategy provides a reasonable growth plan and compatibility with existing systems. Multiple-access methods can also be combined to better serve certain applications. The two most commonly used hybrid schemes are FDMA/TDMA and FDMA/CDMA. Other forms of CDMA are so-called W-CDMA and TD-CDMA. W-CDMA provides higher data rates and uses the spectrum in an efficient manner. TD-CDMA combines W-CDMA and TDMA.

Random-Access Techniques

Most wireless networks carry traffic in a bursty form. The dedicated resource allocation schemes, such as multiple-access techniques, prove to be inefficient for some types of systems under bursty traffic. With *random-access* schemes, channels are accessed at random. *Aloha-based* and *reservation-based* protocols are two well-known random-access techniques that require packets to be acknowledged. Distortions in the wireless channel of these schemes, however, may result in loss or delay of acknowledgments. In such cases, a packet retransmission is required, which in turn makes the process inefficient. One solution to this problem would be to use smarter link-layer techniques for the acknowledgment packets to increase their reliability. Common objectives of performing channel access are as follows:

- To minimize interference from other users, a transmitter listens before any transmission.

- To give fair access of the spectrum to all other users, a transmitter transmits for only a certain period of time.

- To minimize transmitter power, the same frequency could be reused in farther areas.

In the basic Aloha scheme, each transmitter sends data packets whenever it has data available to send. This naturally leads to a large number of collisions, and thus a number of data packets have to be retransmitted. Hence, the effective throughput of the Aloha channel is very low because the probability of packet collisions is high. The slotted Aloha scheme was developed to deal with the collision problem. In slotted

Aloha, the time is divided into slots, and packet transmission is restricted to these time slots. Thus, the number of collisions is reduced significantly. The throughput with slotted Aloha is double that with basic Aloha. Spread-spectrum techniques are used in combination with Aloha to support a large number of users.

Collision detection and carrier sensing are very difficult in a wireless environment. Shadow-fading effects impair collision detection, as objects obstruct the direct signal path between users. This difficulty of detecting collisions in a wireless environment is often referred to as the *hidden-terminal problem*. Path loss and shadow-fading effects result in signals being hidden between users. Thus, collision-avoidance schemes are normally used in wireless networks, especially in wireless LANs. In a collision-avoidance scheme, the receiver sends a busy tone on receiving a packet. This busy tone is broadcast to all the nearby transmitters. A transmitter that receives a busy tone from any receiver refrains from transmitting. Once the busy tone ends, the transmitter waits for a random amount of time before sending packets. This random back-off scheme is used to prevent all transmitters from transmitting at the same time when the busy signal ends. The collision-avoidance schemes help reduce the collisions in Aloha channels and thus significantly improve the throughput of Aloha.

Reservation-based schemes assign channels to users on demand. The effective channel bandwidth is divided between the data channel and the reservation channel. Users reserve channel bandwidth on the reservation channel and send the data packets on the data channel. Users send small packets along the reservation channel, requesting access to the data channel. If a data channel is available, the request is accepted, and a message is sent to the user. Thus, the overhead in reservation-based schemes is the assignment of the data channel. But these data channels are assigned only on demand. For networks on which only small messages are exchanged, the overhead may be tolerable. Also, when the traffic in the network increases rapidly, the reservation channel may get congested with request messages.

The *packet-reservation multiple-access* (PRMA) scheme combines the benefits of the Aloha and the reservation-based schemes. In PRMA, time is slotted and organized into frames, with N time slots per frame. A host that has data to transmit competes for an available time slot in each frame. Once a host successfully transmits a packet in a time slot, the slot is reserved for the user in each subsequent frame until the user has no more packets to transmit. When the user stops transmitting, the reservation is revoked, and the user has to compete for a time slot to send more packets. PRMA is used in multimedia applications.

3.7 Link Aggregation

Link aggregation, also known as *port trunking, link bundling, or NIC teaming,* is a method of combining multiple parallel links to increase throughput beyond what a single link can sustain. Link aggregation also has a second benefit of providing redundancy in case one of the links fails. Link aggregation can be implemented at any of the layers 2, and 3 of the protocol stack model. Our focus in this section is on layer 2 link aggregation, which is the most common resource aggregation method among all.

3.7.1 Link Aggregation Applications

Aggregating links can generally be done either through combining multiple NICs to share one address (IP address or link layer address), or it can be implemented such that each NIC has its own address. As a summary of what we discussed previously, link aggregation is applied on networks mainly to achieve two benefits: *increased total link bandwidth* and *link resiliency provisioning,* which is discussed in detail next.

Increased Total Link Bandwidth

Bandwidth shortage on links can typically occur when two or more users simultaneously try to transmit. Connection bandwidth can be increased by using a better integrated-circuit chip technology and a faster clocking system incorporated in a NIC. But clearly this is a solution that eventually faces a limit due to various factors of technology. An alternative solution to increase bandwidth independent of the circuit technology is link aggregation. This method requires that both ends of a link use the same aggregation method.

Figure 3.19 shows a situation in which switch S1 is connected to server SE1 through three links. The link aggregation protocol can virtually combine two or more physical links into one logical link as seen in the figure via a procedure called "channel bonding." With channel bonding, two or more NICs on a host or switching device are combined. Note that this solution requires manual configuration and identical equipment on both sides of the aggregation. Link aggregation at NICs requires cooperation from both the engaging switch or router at one end, and the host computer's operating system, which must stripe the delivery of frames across the network NICs at the other end.

Link Resiliency Provisioning

A second benefit of link aggregation is resiliency for a system in which a port at either side where the link is plugged in fails. Resiliency in this context introduces a ready-to-use redundant port or link in place of a failed port or link, respectively. Figure 3.19

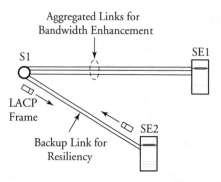

Figure 3.19   Link Aggregation Control Protocol (LACP)

shows a situation in which switch S1 is connected to server SE2 through two links. The link aggregation operation in this case can manually or automatically configure a replacement link for the failed link as long as there is at least a redundant link for resiliency purposes as seen in the figure.

We discuss resource redundancy and resiliency in networking in various levels of networks in this book. Several IEEE standards for link aggregation have been proposed. Among them, the *Link Aggregation Control Protocol* (LACP) offers a method to control the bundling of several physical ports together to form a single logical channel; this is presented next.

3.7.2   Link Aggregation Control Protocol (LACP)

The *Link Aggregation Control Protocol* (LACP) offers a method to control the bundling of several physical ports together to form a single logical channel. With LACP, a network device is allowed to negotiate an automatic bundling of links by sending LACP frames to its directly connected network devices that support this protocol, as seen in Figure 3.19. LACP, however, puts a limit on the number of bundled ports in switches and routers that are allowed in the port channel.

This protocol can be implemented in a device to generate LACP frames (LACPDUs) sent down from one end of a link to all other links whose NICs have the protocol enabled. This phase requires a multicast (copying) of an LACP frame to all related physical ports of a device. If the frames find out through a response message that a networking device on the other end of the link also has LACP already enabled, the device forwards frames along the same links. This action enables the two end devices to detect multiple links between themselves and then combine them into a single logical link.

During LACP detection period, LACP frames are transmitted every fixed period of time, typically every fraction of a second. LACP can generate a *link-ID* integer that identifies the "member link" among bundled links for load balancing purposes. Thus, links can be dynamically combined to a logical bundle of links by receiving a link-ID for the bundle. The link-ID is saved within NICs for implementation.

When implementing a dynamic LACP at all ports of a device such as a host, switch, and router, and a link fails, the system connecting such devices to the other side is able to perceive any connectivity problems. Hence, the device can confirm that the configuration at the other end can handle link aggregation, and therefore, the link-ID is immediately arranged for shuffling the links and replacing the failed link with a healthy one. LACP also allows static link aggregation for link failure resiliency, which can be done manually; however, as mentioned, with manual link aggregation, a configuration mistake can stay undetected and cause undesirable network reaction.

3.8 Summary

We started this chapter by discussing wired and wireless transmission media. Data can travel on guided links, such as optical fibers, and unguided links, such as certain types of wireless links. Link capacity is further partitioned into *channels*.

Methods of accessing link channels deal with how to mediate access to a shared link so that all users eventually have a chance to transmit their data. We examined frequency-division, time-division, code-division, and space-division multiple-access methods; in most cases, time-division multiple-access methods offer several benefits for channel access in local area networks.

We also looked at methods that determine whether transferred bits are in fact correct or whether they possibly were corrupted in transit. With the *cyclic redundancy check* (CRC) method, some frames arriving at the destination node contain errors and thus have to be discarded.

Two link-control schemes are *stop and wait* and *sliding window*. In the stop-and-wait method, a sender waits for an acknowledgment after transmitting one frame. This flow-control method is significantly improved in the *sliding-window* method, which lets multiple frames travel on a transmission link. We noticed that by including the *automatic repeat request* (ARQ) protocol in any of these flow-control techniques, a retransmission of lost frame(s) became possible.

Finally, at the end of the chapter, methods of link and then channel access by multiple users, both in regular and wireless environments, were discussed. The necessary discussion of multiple access over links was identified to be important, as voice and video applications that run on networks could require continuous and dedicated allocation of available resources for that application over links having limited resources. We covered the well-known multiuser link access method of CSMA for wired links that was clearly one of the most popular access protocols. However, its frame collision during high-usage periods was indeed a bottleneck.

We reviewed the most prevelant multiuser link access methods: *frequency-division multiple access* (FDMA), *time-division multiple access* (TDMA), *orthogonal frequency-division multiple access* (OFDMA), *single-carrier frequency-division multiple access* (SC-FDMA), and *code-division multiple access* (CDMA).

The last topic of this chapter was *link aggregation,* which combines multiple parallel links to increase throughput beyond what a single link can sustain. Link aggregation also has a second benefit of providing redundancy in case one of the links fails.

In the next chapter, we use our knowledge of data links from this chapter to form small local area networks (LANs) and networks of LANs.

3.9 Exercises

1. In order to transmit a 500-page book with an average of 1,000 characters per page between locations 5,000 km apart, we assume that each character uses 8 bits, that all signals travel at the speed of light, and that no link-control protocol is used.

   (a) How much time is required if a digital voice circuit operating at the speed of 64kb/s is used?

   (b) How much time is required if a 620Mb/s fiber-optic transmission system is used?

   (c) Repeat parts (a) and (b) for a library with 2 million volumes of books.

2. A string of 110011101 arrives at the line encoder of a link adapter. Give the output form if the line encoder is designed by:

   (a) Natural NRZ

   (b) Polar NRZ

   (c) Manchester

3. Calculate the total power consumed to transfer the data over the link for following cases:

   (a) Natural NRZ

   (b) Polar NRZ

   (c) Manchester

4. Design a CRC process unit for the following two standard generators of computer networking:

   (a) CRC-12

   (b) CRC-16

5. For the example presented in the CRC section, we had 1010111 as a block of data (*D*), and the common value of generator, *G*, 10010, as the divisor.

   (a) Show the dividend and the divisor in polynomial forms.
   (b) Divide the dividend and the divisor in polynomial forms.
   (c) Compare the results of part (b) to its binary form obtained in the example.

6. Consider a link layer error-checking system that sets the common value of generator, *G*, to value 10010. Sketch the implementation of the CRC process unit and the step-by-step development of the registers' content for any of the following data:

   (a) $D, \text{CRC} = 1010111, 0000$
   (b) $D, \text{CRC} = 1010111, 1000$

7. Assume that 101011010101111 is a block of data (*D*) to be transmitted using the CRC error-checking method. Suppose that the common value of generator, *G*, is 111010. Using modulo-2 arithmetic:

   (a) Produce the final value that the transmitter sends on the link (*D*,CRC).
   (b) Show the detail of the error-detection process at the receiver.

8. For exercise 6, part (a), show the implementation (shift register design) of the CRC process and the step-by-step development of the registers' content.

9. Consider a coaxial transmission link that uses the stop-and-wait protocol requiring a propagation time to transmission time ratio of 10. Data is transmitted at rate 10Mb/s, using 80-bit frames.

   (a) Calculate the efficiency of this link.
   (b) Find the length of this link.
   (c) Find the propagation time.
   (d) Sketch a plot of link efficiency when the ratio of propagation time to transmission time is reduced to 8, 6, 4, and 2.

10. Consider a 2Mb/s satellite transmission link through which 800-bit frames are transmitted. The propagation time is 200 ms.

    (a) Find the link efficiency, using the stop-and-wait protocol.
    (b) Find the link efficiency, using the sliding-window protocol if the window size is $w = 6$.

11. Consider the flow control of a link using sliding-window protocol with a window size of $w = 6$. Sketch the detail of timing for a scheduled window when instant congestion does not allow the transmission of more than 2 frames at time.

12. Consider the bidirectional control of links with the sliding-window method applied between two routers R2 and R3 (window size $w = 5$) and stop-and-wait control between routers R3 and R4. Assume that the distance between R2 and R3 is 1,800 km and is 800 km between R3 and R4. A total of 1,000 data frames with average size of 5,000 bits flow from R2 to R3 at a rate of 1Gb/s. Acknowledgment frames are small enough to be ignored in the calculations. All links generate 1 μs/km propagation delay.

   (a) Determine a condition on the data rate at the output port of R3 toward R4 so that R3 remains congestion-free.

   (b) Find the link efficiency for the R2–R3 link.

   (c) Find the link efficiency for the R3–R4 link.

13. Consider the bidirectional control of links with the sliding-window method applied between two routers R2 and R3 (window size $w = 50$) and stop-and-wait control between routers R3 and R4. Assume that the distance between R2 and R3 is 1,800 km and is 800 km between R3 and R4. A total of 1,000 data frames with average size of 5,000 bits flow from R2 to R3 at a rate of 1Gb/s. Acknowledgment frames are small enough to be ignored in the calculations. All links generate 1 μs/km propagation delay.

   (a) Assume that part of incoming traffic to R3 can be diverted to another path such that R3–R4 can intuitively be synchronized with R2–R3. Determine a condition on the data rate at the output port of R3 toward R4 so that R3 remains congestion-free.

   (b) Find the link efficiency for the R2–R3 link.

   (c) Find the link efficiency for the R3–R4 link.

14. A 10Gb/s link with 10 users attached to it uses CSMA/CD. The bus is about 10 meters, and users' frames are restricted to a maximum size 1,500 bytes. Based on the statistics, four users in average are active at the same time.

   (a) Find the frame propagation and transmission times.

   (b) Find the average utilization of the bus.

   (c) Find the probability that a user attempts to transmit frames in an empty time slot.

   (d) Find the probability that a user attempts seven different times in seven different empty slots to transmit its frame and is not successful, owing to collision, but is successful on the eighth attempt.

   (e) Find the average number of contentions.

15. Using the CSMA details discussed in this chapter, sketch a block diagram that represents the implementation of this algorithm for the following cases:

    (a) Nonpersistent CSMA
    (b) p-persistent CSMA

16. A 1Gb/s fiber-optic link having 12 directly attached users utilizes the CSMA/CD access scheme. The link is about 100 meters and frames are restricted to a maximum size 1500 bytes. On average, 3 users are active at the same time. In this system, the chance that a user is active is always 80 percent.

    (a) Find the frame propagation and transmission times.
    (b) Find the average utilization of the bus assuming the LAN adopts the *stop-and-wait* protocol.
    (c) Find the probability that an empty time slot on the bus is taken by one of the 3 users.
    (d) Find the probability that a user attempts five different times in five different empty slots to transmit its frame and is not successful due to collision, but is successful on the sixth attempt.
    (e) Find the average number of contentions.

17. Assume that a wireless system with 200 terminals uses TDMA for its channel access. The packet lengths are T in average and are considered short compared with the TDMA long channel length. Compare the efficiency of two strategies: *polling* and CSMA.

18. Consider two users of a CDMA system. Users 1 and 2 have data of {1, -1} and {1, 1}, respectively, and the spreading code sequences of users 1 and 2 uniquely assigned to associated receivers and transmitters are {1, 1, 1, -1, 1, -1, -1, 1} and {-1, -1, 1, -1, -1, 1, 1, -1}, respectively.

    (a) Show the timing diagram of CDMA encoding for each user independently.
    (b) Show the timing diagram of CDMA decoding for each user independently
    (c) Repeat part (a), but this time consider the impact of one user on the other user at the transmission that requires the addition of both users' encoded values. Show what values are practically propagated to users.
    (d) Repeat part (b) for user 1 when it receives the additive encoded result from the transmission explained in part (c). Do you think any extra operations on the decoded results need to be performed in order to extract the original data?

3.10   Computer Simulation Project

1. *Simulation of Link Random Access.* Write a program in C, C++, or Java to present the link access concept. Your program must define 10 channels representing a link, where each channel in turn represents a position for transmission of data over the link. A channel becomes available at random during each 1-second period. Define 20 different users, each requiring a channel every 3 seconds so that once a user becomes activated it looks for the first available channel and it uses it for 1 second.

   (a) Capture the link access performance by showing how often a channel is denied access to a link on average.

   (b) Accumulate the number of seconds a link has been accessed by more than its 50%, 70%, and 90% capacity.

CHAPTER 4

Local Area Networks and Networks of LANs

A *local area network* (LAN) is a small interconnection infrastructure that typically uses a shared transmission medium. Because of such factors as the volume of traffic, the level of security, and cost, the network structure in a local area network can be significantly different from that for a wide area network. This chapter focuses on the fundamentals of local area networks and describes the *internetworking* concept at the LAN level. Major topics are as follows:

- *LANs and basic topologies*
- *LAN protocols*
- *Networks of LANs*
- *Address conversion protocols*
- *Spanning-Tree Protocol* (STP)
- *Virtual LANs* (VLANs)
- *Wireless LANs*
- *IEEE 802.11 wireless LAN standard*
- *Case study: DOCSIS, a cable TV protocol*

First, we explore some simple topologies of local area networks and see how a LAN is formed. We then extend the discussion of the protocol stack presented in Chapter 1 to LAN protocols, focusing on *media access control* (MAC) and addressing.

Another important topic to be covered in this chapter is *internetworking* or *networking of LANs*. Some pointers toward interconnecting of LANs with basic networking devices such as, bridges, and switches followed by more advanced *internetworking* examples are provided. The focus of this chapter is primarily on layer 2 of the protocol stack reference model.

We then explore *address conversion protocols* by which addresses at layers 2 and 3 are converted to one another. The chapter at this point proceeds to the very important topic of the *Spanning-Tree Protocol* (STP). STP prevents frames or packets from the looping that causes infinite circulations of frames in a network.

Virtual LANs (VLANs) are the next topic. A VLAN methodology allows a single LAN to be partitioned into several seemingly and virtually separate LANs. The discussion of LANs is then be extended to wireless LANs followed by the IEEE 802.11 wireless LAN standard used for Ethernet networking. We examine a variety of wireless LANs, including the ones we are all using on a daily basis such as WiFi.

Finally, at the end of this chapter, a case study on a cable TV protocol called *Data over Cable Service Interface Specification* (DOCSIS) is presented. DOCSIS is an international telecommunications standard specifying cable data network architecture and its technology.

4.1   LANs and Basic Topologies

A LAN is used for communications in a small community in which resources, such as printers, software, and servers, are shared. Each device connected to a LAN has a unique address. Two or more LANs of the same type can also be connected to forward data frames among multiple users of other local area networks. In LANs, packets have additional headers appended for local routing. These new-looking packets are known as *frames*. Hosts in a local area network can be interconnected in several ways. The fundamental network topology in LANs can be categorized into *bus* and *star* as shown in Figure 4.1.

In Figure 4.1 (a), four hosts 1, 2, 3, and 4 are connected together by using a simple *bus*. Each host is directly connected to the bus through a bidirectional link. In the bus topology, all hosts are connected to a common transmission medium referred to as a bus. The hosts are connected to a common bus via a duplex link that allows both uplink and downlink operations, as seen in the figure. The transmission from

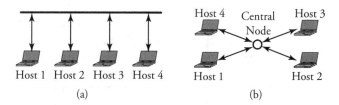

Figure 4.1   Two fundamental LAN configurations to connect hosts: (a) bus LAN topology and (b) star LAN topology

a host is propagated on the bus in both directions, and all hosts in the path receive its frame. However, only the destination host copies the frame into its computer; all other hosts discard the frame.

In the *star* topology shown in Figure 4.1 (b), each host is directly connected to a "central node" through a bidirectional link: one for uplink and the other for downlink. The central node can be selected from among the variety of layer 1, 2, or 3 devices. If the central node is chosen from among layer 1 devices, such as a hub, it functions as a *broadcast* node. In this case, when the node receives a frame from a host on the uplink, it retransmits the frame to "all" hosts on the downlinks. If the central node is chosen from among layer 2 or 3 devices, it allows only one host to transmit at a time. In this case, the central node functions in *frame-switched mode*, so that when it receives a frame it buffers first, and then retransmits the frame only to the destination.

The bus topology is agile to deploy and inexpensive. It is simply a piece of cable and connectors to computers. However, the lack of ability to control its LAN in terms of congestion, security, and even turning the network on and off makes the bus LAN unpopular for creating professionally designed networks. On the other hand, the star LAN can deploy a sophisticated networking device, such as a layer 2 switch, as a central node to create a secured and low-congested LAN.

4.2   LAN Protocols

Protocols designed for LANs are normally concerned with the data-link layer (layer 2) and the physical layer. Hence, protocols designed for layers 3 and above are independent of the underlying network topology. Organizations working on LAN standards comply with the specifications of the IEEE 802 reference model. The physical layer of a LAN implements such a reference model that functions for signal transmission and reception, encoding and decoding, and generation and removal of synchronization information. Figure 4.2 shows the position of the two LAN sublayers in the overall

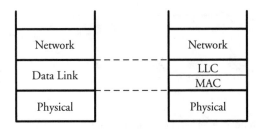

Figure 4.2   LAN sublayer protocols in the overall structure of the protocol stack

structure of the protocol stack. The IEEE 802 standard subdivides the *data-link layer* of the protocol model into the *logical-link control* (LLC) layer and the *media access control* (MAC) layer. These two sublayers are discussed next.

4.2.1   Logical-Link Control (LLC)

Data to be transmitted from the higher layers is passed down to the *logical-link control* (LLC) which determines the mechanism for addressing users across the medium. The LLC layer implements flow and error control apart from providing an interface to the network layer. The details of the flow and error control mechanisms were explained in Chapter 3. The LLC sublayer also controls the exchange of data between users. The LLC appends its header to form the LLC protocol data unit, which is then sent to the MAC layer, which appends the header and the frame check sequence to create the MAC frame.

4.2.2   Media Access Control (MAC)

The *media access control* (MAC) sublayer primarily controls access to the transmission medium and is responsible for framing. The LLC has the option of choosing from various types of MAC layers. When a LAN is required to provide shared access to the transmission medium. To ensure efficient access to a medium, users have to comply with some rules. The MAC protocol manages access to the medium. Figure 4.3 shows a generic frame format within frame formatting for the MAC protocol. This frame is commonly used in a connection-oriented network and includes all layer 2 (MAC and LLC), 3 (IP), and 4 (TCP) headers. The fields of the frame format are as follows:

- *MAC header* gives the MAC control information, such as the MAC address of the destination and the priority level.
- *LLC header* contains the data from the logical-link control layer.
- *IP header* specifies the IP header of the original packet.

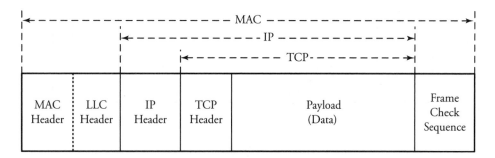

Figure 4.3   Generic frame format used in a connection-oriented network

- *TCP header* specifies the TCP header of the original packet.
- *Frame check sequence* is used for error checking.

MAC protocols can be broadly classified as *centralized* or *distributed* based on the type of network architecture. In the centralized scheme, a central controller controls the operation of the users, and users communicate only with the controller. Users adhere to the transmission schedule specified by the controller. In a distributed network, users talk to each other and dynamically determine the transmission schedule. Centralized schemes are used in applications that require a simple access scheme, quality of service (QoS), and guaranteed capacity. However, centralized schemes are vulnerable to a single point of failure. Distributed schemes have no single point of overall failure. Yet, coordinating access among devices is a complex process for distributed schemes, and the network cannot provide a QoS guarantee.

MAC protocols can also be characterized as *synchronous* or *asynchronous*. In the synchronous scheme, such as time-division multiplexing and frequency-division multiplexing, capacity is preassigned to each connection. The synchronous scheme is rarely used in LANs, as users' transmission requirements vary dynamically. Rather, it is optimal to assign capacity to users asynchronously, based on demand.

Ethernet LAN Standard 802.3, MAC, and MAC Address

The IEEE 802.3 standards committee developed a widely used LAN standard called *Ethernet*, which covers both the MAC layer and the physical layer. The IEEE 802.3 standard uses CSMA for controlling media access and the *1-persistent* algorithm explained earlier, although the lost time owing to collisions is very small. Also, IEEE 802.3 uses a back-off scheme known as *binary exponential backoff*. The use of random backoff minimizes subsequent collisions. This back-off scheme requires the interval

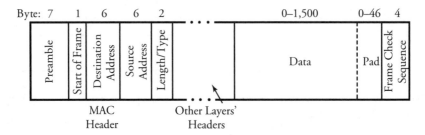

Figure 4.4   Details of Ethernet IEEE 802.3 MAC frame

from which the random delay is randomly chosen to be doubled. The user drops the frame after 16 retries. The combination of the 1-persistent scheme and binary exponential backoff results in an efficient scheme. A brief description of the frame fields follows and is shown in Figure 4.4.

- *Preamble* is 7 bytes and consists of a pattern of alternating 0s and 1s. This field is used to provide bit synchronization.
- *Start of frame* consists of a 10101011 pattern and indicates the start of the frame to the receiver.
- *Destination address* specifies the destination MAC address.
- *Source address* specifies the source MAC address.
- *Length/Type* specifies the frame size in bytes or type of packet. If the Length/Type field has a value less than 1,500 bytes, it implies the frame size, otherwise it denotes the type of packet being sent such as IP, ARP (discussed in the upcoming section), and so on.
- *Data* and *Pad*. Data (payload) can be 0–1,500 bytes and Pad can be 0–46 bytes. Thus, the total of the Data and Pad fields can be 1,546 bytes. However, the largest size for the combined Data and Pad parts is typically 1,500 bytes. This would correspond to a maximum Ethernet frame size of 1,518 bytes. *Pad* is used to increase the frame length to the value required for collision detection to work.
- *Frame check sequence* is 32-bit cyclic redundancy check (CRC) for error checking. We discussed CRC in detail in the previous chapters.

We mentioned earlier that a source or a destination address at the link layer is basically a MAC address. Now it is time to know what the MAC address is. A MAC address is a 48-bit long address presented by a 6-field hexadecimal number such as 89-A1-33-2B-C3-84. Every network interface card (NIC) of a device or host has a unique MAC address. A MAC address is stored in the NIC's memory. Every host or networking device must have at least one NIC depending on the number of input/output ports of the host or device. Normally, it is safe to assume that no two NICs share the same MAC address, because NIC vendors purchase blocks of addresses from the Institute of Electrical and Electronics Engineers (IEEE) and assign a unique address to each NIC at the time of manufacture.

The Ethernet versions have different data rates. Version 1000Base-SX, carrying 1Gb/s, and 10GBase-T, carrying 10Gb/s, hold the most promise for the future of high-speed LAN development.

4.3   Networks of LANs

Increasing the number of interconnected devices and the volume of traffic requires splitting a single large LAN into multiple smaller LANs. Doing so dramatically improves network performance and security but also introduces a new challenge: how to interconnect multiple LANs. LANs may be of different types or may have devices that are not compatible with one another. New protocols need to be developed that allow all partitions of a LAN to communicate with one another.

Multiple LANs can be connected to form a college campus network. The campus backbone serves as a channel between a department and the rest of the campus network and facilitates the connection of the department to the Internet via a gateway router. The campus backbone is an interconnection of routers and switches. Servers used by an entire organization are usually located in a data bank and organization dispatching center.

Devices known as *protocol converters* are used to interconnect multiple LANs. Depending on the level of interconnection required, layer 1, layer 2, and layer 3 protocol converters are available. Two LANs can be connected using layer 1 devices, *repeaters* or *hubs*. Layer 2 protocol converters have information about the layer 2 protocols on both interconnected LANs and can translate one to the other. At layer 2, *bridges* (LAN *switches*) and also *layer 2 switches* (switches) can carry out the task as layer 2 devices. At layer 3, *layer 3 switches* (switches) or *routers* can function as layer 3 devices.

4.3.1   LAN Networking with Layer 1 Devices

In Chapter 2, we explained the operations of layer 1 devices such as *repeaters* and *hubs*. A repeater is a device that is essentially made to amplify a signal. Normally, a repeater is placed between two users that are far apart and thus a repeater can relay the signal from one side to another so that the receiving user can receive the signal in its original form with minimal attenuation. Two LANs can be connected through hubs. A hub copies frames and forwards them to all connected LANs or users. As in the case of a bus LAN itself, collisions may occur if two or more users try to transmit at the same time. Hubs have the following limitations:

- Hubs forward frames to all hosts. This method of networking results in reduced LAN performance, owing to excess traffic.
- A large number of hosts are included in the collision domain.
- Security cannot be implemented, since a frame is forwarded to all hosts.

Figure 4.5 depicts an example of LAN networking using a hub. The network consists of Ethernet LANs 1, 2, and 3 with a connecting hub, H1, having ports 1, 2, and 3. In LAN 1, host 1 is a transmitting host whose MAC address is 89-A1-33-2B-C3-84. Note that MAC addresses are typically described in hexadecimal format. LAN 2 has three hosts, 2, 3, and 4, and LAN 3 has three hosts, 5, 6, and 7. Assume that host 7 with MAC Address 21-01-34-2D-C3-33 is the destination so that this MAC address is included in all frames heading to host 7. As shown in the figure, when H1 receives a frame from host 1 at its port 1, it "broadcasts" the frame on both its output ports 2 and 3 according to the functionality of hubs explained in Chapter 2.

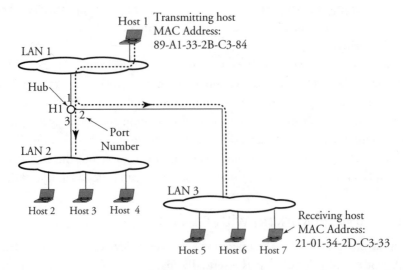

Figure 4.5 A hub interconnects three LANs; host 1 as the transmitting host communicates with host 7 as the receiving host.

As a result of this action, any frame being sent to LAN 3 is also sent to LAN 2, which is not intended. Hosts on LAN 2 must discard the frame as it is unwanted, but LAN 3 will eventually deliver the frame to the destination host 7.

Note here that, if LAN 3 has a simple broadcast structure, it also broadcasts the frame to all three hosts 5, 6, and 7. However, all unwanted frames are discarded by hosts. Any host reads all flowing frames sent by other hosts but accepts those frames that are specifically addressed to it. Thus, collisions may be possible throughout the network if two or more hosts try to transmit at the same time. The concluding remark here is that a hub does not isolate two connected networks.

4.3.2   LAN Networking with Layer 2 Devices

Clearly, using a *bridge,* also called LAN *switch,* for networking Ethernet LANs can reduce the possibility of collision compared to hubs. This is because bridges split a LAN system into different collision domains. Because they can selectively retransmit the frame, bridges also offer a greater level of security than repeaters can. Bridges also facilitate communication across multiple LANs and bridges. Sometimes, a bridge that connects two LANs with nonidentical bit rates must have a buffer. A buffer in a bridge holds frames that arrive from a faster LAN directed to a slower LAN. This introduces transmission delay and may have adverse effects on the network, causing the flow-control protocols to time out.

Figure 4.6 shows a similar scenario as described for a hub in the previous section but this time a bridge is used. Similarly, suppose the network consists of Ethernet LANs 1, 2, and 3 with a connecting bridge B1 having ports 1, 2, and 3. In LAN 1, host 1 is a transmitting host whose MAC address is 89-A1-33-2B-C3-84. LAN 2 has three hosts, 2, 3, and 4, and LAN 3 also has three hosts, 5, 6, and 7. Assume that host 7 with MAC Address 21-01-34-2D-C3-33 is the destination so that this MAC address is included in all frames heading to host 7.

In this case, when B1 receives a frame from host 1 at its port 1, it examines the destination address and determines whether the forwarded frame is to be delivered to any of the hosts on LAN 3. If host 7 is not the destination within its connected LANs, the frame can be dropped. Making such routing decisions is a bridge routing capability and depends on how well the routing table of the bridge is structured. Thus, the bridge decides whether to accept or reject a frame at any time. If the bridge identifies the right output port for the frame, it "routes" (instead of broadcasts) the frame on its intended output port 2 according to its forwarding table. As a result of this action, any frame being sent to LAN 3 will eventually be delivered to host 7.

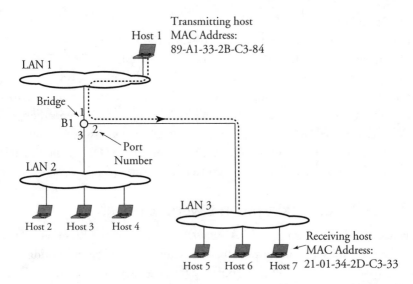

Figure 4.6 A bridge interconnects three LANs; host 1 as the transmitting host communicates with host 7 as the receiving host

Any host in LAN 3 reads all flowing frames sent by other hosts but accepts those frames that are specifically addressed to it. Thus, collisions may possibly be limited to bus LANs only, and the bridge has completely isolated the three LANs. This is considered as the most important advantage of a bridge over a hub. The concluding remark here is that a bridge does isolate two connected networks.

A *layer 2 switch* (or simply a *switch*) is an improved version of a bridge. A switch is designed to operate in a larger LAN network and is capable of minimizing traffic congestion to some extent. The inability of bridges to handle heavy traffic is a trade-off with the lower cost of bridges. As a result, a switch enables connections to edge devices of a subnet such as a router.

Figure 4.7 shows part of a campus network as an example in which LANs are interconnected through layer 2 switches. In the center of this partial campus network, a layer 3 switch, S5, brings in all the traffic heading to LANs 1 through 4 (we will learn about the layer 3 switch in the next section). The multiport switch S5 isolates the traffic between the two layer 2 switches S2 and S4 as well as the remaining part of the campus. LANs 1 and 2 are equipped with two switches S1 and S2 to isolate LANs 1 and 2. Similarly, LANs 3 and 4 are equipped with switches S3 and S4 for the same reason. We notice that every LAN in this network topology uses a switched star LAN topology.

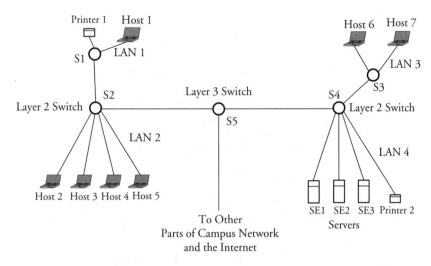

Figure 4.7   Using layer 2 switches in a campus network

Routing Table in Layer 2 Devices

A layer 2 device does not have a global view of its outside network but rather has knowledge of only its immediate neighbors. Layer-2-device routing is a process of deciding where to forward received frames within a LAN. Bridges or layer 2 switches have the routing information stored in a table called the *routing table*. There are multiple subrouting tables for corresponding to all its existing surrounding connected LANs. The routing table consists of the destination address and the destination LAN. As a layer 2 switch is an improved version of a bridge, our focus will be on the structure of a layer 2 switch. A bridge has a similar structure but a less complex routing table.

Figure 4.8 shows multiple LANs connected by layer 2 switches (switches). Each number at a port of a switch indicates the corresponding port number of the switch. Suppose that host 1 wants to transmit a frame to host 3. First, switch S1 examines the destination address and determines whether the forwarded frame is to be delivered to any of the hosts on LAN 2. If host 3 is not the destination within its connected LANs, the frame can be either dropped or forwarded on LAN 2. Making such decisions is a switch routing capability and depends on how well the routing table of the switch is structured. Thus, the switch decides whether to accept or reject a frame at any time.

If S1 decides to forward a frame on LAN 2, it also performs error detection to ensure that the frame is not corrupted. Next, the switch checks whether LAN 1 and LAN 2 have the same frame format. If they do, the switch forwards the frame as is.

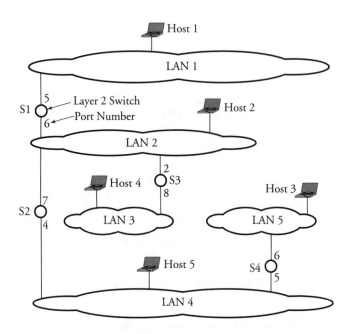

Figure 4.8 Connecting multiple Ethernet LANs through switches

If the frame format is different, it is reformatted to match the frame format of LAN 2. If a switch in such scenarios is connected to a bus Ethernet LAN, the switch has to conform to CSMA/CD while transmitting the frame. When a frame reaches switch S2 and S3, the same procedure as the one completed in S1 takes place. As a result, S3 rejects the frame, and S2 accepts the frame. The frame is now forwarded on LAN 4, and thereby ultimately reaches the destination at host 3 after passing safely over LAN 4, S4, and LAN 5.

Example.   Create a routing table for a layer 2 switch, S1, of Figure 4.8.

Solution.   Table 4.1 provides routing table for S1 that has one routing table for LAN 1 and another routing table for LAN 2. If a frame arrives on LAN 1, the switch parses the frame for the destination address and looks up the routing table for source LAN 1. If the destination is host 1, the LAN does not need to forward the frame. However, for destinations at host 2, host 4, and host 5, switch S1 forwards the frame to LAN 2. For the destination at host 5, switch S1 forwards the frame to LAN 4.

In a static network, connections are fixed, so the routing table entries can be programmed into switches under *fixed routing*. In case of any changes to the network,

Table 4.1   Routing table for switch S1 in Figure 4.8 with more detail

Destination from LAN 1	Destination MAC Address	Next LAN from LAN 1	Outgoing Port Number	Next LAN from LAN 2	Outgoing Port Number
Host 1	00-40-33-40-1B-2C	-	-	LAN 1	5
Host 2	00-40-33-25-85-BB	LAN 2	6	-	-
Host 3	00-40-33-25-85-BC	LAN 2	6	-	-
Host 4	00-61-97-44-45-5B	LAN 2	6	-	-
Host 5	00-C0-96-25-45-C7	LAN 2	6	-	-

the table entries need to be reprogrammed. This solution is not scalable for large, dynamic networks having frequent user addition and removal. Hence, such networks use an *automatic update* of the routing tables.

A switch initializes its routing tables by updates received from other switches. This updating mechanism is similar for bridges as well. Any switch in LAN, broadcasts its routing table to all switches if the LAN. When none of the switches in the LAN have routing table entries, the first frame flooded across the network to all switches initialize the entries of switches' routing tables. The flooded updates are sent from a switch to all others in a regular basis according to the layer 2 protocol. As more frames are flooded through the network, all switches will eventually have routing table entries updated.

Example.   Demonstrate the automatic update of a routing table for switch S2 in Figure 4.8.

Solution.   Suppose that frames containing routing information from S1 move across LAN 2 to LANs 3 and 4, updating S2 and S3, respectively. In the meantime, frames containing routing information from S4 move across LAN 4 to reach LAN 2, updating S2. A similar process can also happen when S3 sends updates to all switches including S2. At this point S2 can understand the topology of the LAN only at the scale of its surrounding switches. This information would be sufficient to process and route any incoming frame destined to any of the LAN's hosts.

For another scenario of layer 2 networking using bridges, consider Figure 4.9. The connecting functionality of bridges is similar to that for layer 2 switches, while we know that layer 2 switches are more sophisticated devices compared to bridges. In this figure, if host 1 on LAN 1 sends a frame to host 9 on LAN 4, bridge B1 can figure out that the frame with the destination MAC address of host 9 should be sent to the

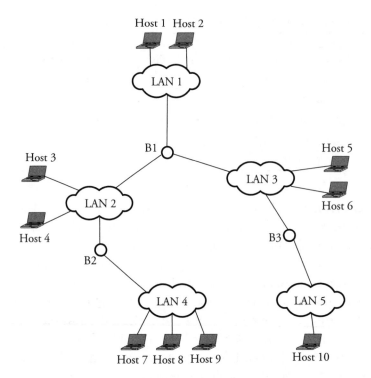

Figure 4.9   Bridging among LANs

path that connects it to LAN 2. Normally, a bridge can only have this type of limited knowledge about the network to which it is connected. Similarly, bridge B2 uses the MAC address of host 9 in its routing table and finds LAN 4 to be the destination.

Bridges that update their routing tables are called *transparent bridges* and are typically equipped with the IEEE 802.1d standard. These bridges act as *plug-and-play* devices and have the capability to rapidly build their own routing tables. A transparent bridge also has the intelligence to learn about any change in the topology and to update its routing table. This type of bridge can dynamically build the routing table, based on the information from arriving frames. By parsing the source address of a received frame, a bridge can determine how it can access the local area network of the arriving frame. Based on this information, the bridge updates its routing table.

4.3.3   Networking with Layer 2 and 3 Devices

As the complexity of the network system grows, layer 2 devices are not adequate to meet its needs. Users on LANs connected by layer 2 switches have a common MAC broadcast address. Hence, a frame with a broadcast MAC address is forwarded to all users on the network. In a large network, this is considered a large overhead and may result in network congestion. Another issue with layer 2 switches is that to avoid closed loops, there can be only one path between two users. This poses a significant limitation on the performance of large networks. The limitations are overcome by splitting the network into subnets.

Routers, or layer 3 switches, implement the switching and forwarding functions at the network layer of the protocol stack. The routers are capable of handling heavy traffic loads. Routers are also used to connect multiple subnets in LANs. Routers are sophisticated devices that permit access to multiple paths among users. A router uses software to forward packets or frames. However, the use of software significantly reduces the speed of forwarding frames. But high-speed LANs and high-performance LAN switches can operate on millions of frames per second, which mandates layer 3 devices to match the load.

Switching Tiers: Edge, Core, and Aggregate Switches

In practice, network designers lay out the networking of a typical organization based on a *switching tiers structure*. Figure 4.10 shows a typical network scenario in an organization located in a building. The network is split into subnet LANs, each having a number of desktop hosts, servers, and equipment such as printers.

The very first tier of the switching structure, directly connected to users' devices, is composed of *edge switches*. Edge switches are layer 2 switches indicated by S6, S7,

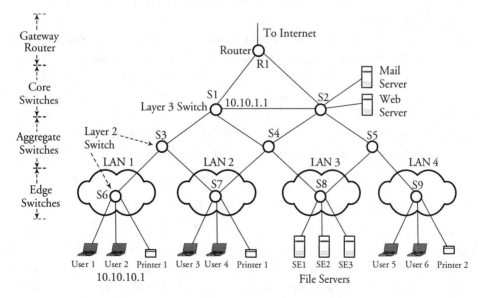

Figure 4.10   A network with layer 2 and 3 switches and routers

S8, and S9 and they utilize MAC addresses to route to end-users. These four switches are in turn connected to an *aggregate switches* tier. Having two tiers of layer 2 switches is a normal practice and provides a better flexibility of routing from outside to users. On top of these two tiers of switches, layer 3 switches, S1, and S2, act as the *core switches* or backbone while they are associated with IP addresses, as shown in the figure. S1 and S2 connect layer 2 switches, and other facilities in the organization such as the mail server and Web server, through higher-speed links and eventually to the main router, R1, to access the Internet.

4.4   MAC/IP Address Conversion Protocols

Each port of a node in a network has at least an IP address. Each node's NIC to its attached link has a link-layer address, which is in fact the *MAC address*. Recall that a MAC address is as wide as 6 bytes and is normally shown in hexadecimal notation, such as 00-40-33-25-85-BB. The MAC address is unique for each device and is permanently stored in the adapter's read-only memory. Consequently, networking manufacturers need to purchase MAC addresses for their products. Unlike an IP address, a MAC address is not hierarchical. The advantage of MAC addressing is that a device may not need to have an IP address in order to communicate with the surrounding devices in its own LAN.

Each node adapter that receives a frame checks whether the MAC address of the frame matches its own MAC address. If the addresses match, the adapter extracts the inner packet and passes it up the protocol stack. In summary, each destination address specified in an IP header is the logical address and is different from the physical or the link-layer address. For a packet from a source host to be delivered successfully to its destination, the host needs to identify both the IP address and the link-layer address.

We are now ready for a detailed discussion on the MAC addressing scheme and its interaction with IP addresses. A source host uses the *Address Resolution Protocol* (ARP) to find the link-layer address of a destination. Another protocol that performs the reverse function is called the *Reverse Address Resolution Protocol* (RARP). These two protocols are described next.

4.4.1   Address Resolution Protocol (ARP)

The *Address Resolution Protocol* (ARP) is designed to convert IP addresses to MAC addresses or vice versa. But it is noteworthy to mention here that ARP resolves IP addresses only for hosts on the same subnet. Suppose that a host wants to transmit a packet to its destination. If it does not know the link-layer address of the destination, the host broadcasts an ARP packet requesting the link-layer address given the IP address. ARP has dedicated packets that are formatted to request conversion of IP addresses to MAC addresses. An ARP packet has a sending and a receiving IP address as well as a sending and a receiving MAC address. An ARP query packet and response packet both have the same format.

An ARP query packet requests that all the other hosts and routers on the subnet determine the MAC address given the IP address. An ARP query is broadcast to all hosts of the subnet. To do this, the ARP query packet is encapsulated in a frame with a broadcast address. Each *network interface card* (NIC) of a host has an ARP module within part of its frame process unit (a block diagram of a NIC was presented in Chapter 2). The ARP module at each host checks to see if there is an IP address match. A host finding the IP address match returns a response ARP packet including the requested MAC address.

The source host then stores this address in the local ARP table for its subsequent use. Remember that each NIC has a table that keeps the MAC address of each device within the network (its subnet) it is attached to. MAC addresses are listed in the NIC's ARP table. The ARP process described here has a plug-and-play property so that an ARP table at each host's NIC gets built automatically without the need for a network administrator.

Example.   Figure 4.11 shows LANs 1, 2, 3, and 4 connected through a layer 3 switch S1. A source host with IP address 150.176.8.55 located in LAN 1 finds the MAC address of another host with IP address 150.176.8.5 in LAN 4. Give the details of how ARP packets are broadcast from the source host and eventually reach LAN 4.

Solution.   First we note that the source host with the IP address 150.176.8.55 (LAN 1) and the destination host with the IP address 150.176.8.5 (LAN 4) reside on the same subnet while switch S1 connects them. In this case, the NIC of the source host first converts the ARP query packet to frames and then broadcasts it to all hosts within the subnet hosts. The ARP packet is then broadcast to all hosts of LAN 1 and switch S1. Switch S1 is capable of operating in both layers 2 and 3 and thus can pass the ARP packets to LAN 4 hosts. Only the destination host with IP address 150.176.8.5 finds the match and replies to the ARP query, providing its NIC's MAC address of 76-A3-78-08-C1-6C. This new address is used by the router to forward the message of the sending host to the destination.

We did mention earlier that ARP resolves IP addresses only for hosts residing on the same subnet. In some rare circumstances, the only way to obtain the MAC address

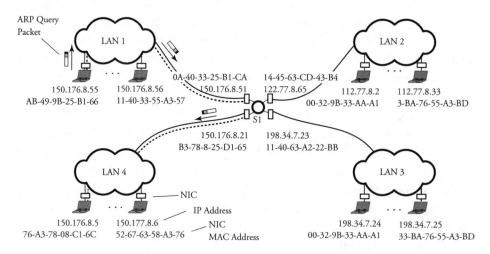

Figure 4.11 ARP packets and MAC and IP addresses

of a host situated outside the subnet is if the router between the subnets has the IP address of the port connecting it to the subnet of the desired host. This requires an advance configuration of the connecting router, such that a host should append the MAC address of the router and IP address of the second host, if it needs to move traffic out of its subnet. Otherwise, the ARP process would fail. In the previous example, switch S1 must have the information of all attached hosts' IP addresses in order to be able to also pass the ARP packets to destinations outside of 150.176.8 subnet.

4.4.2   Reverse Address Resolution Protocol (RARP)

Reverse Address Resolution Protocol (RARP) is also a protocol used to find a certain address. But in this case, RARP is used when the link-layer address, but not the IP address, of the destination is known and the IP address is requested. Using the RARP solution, the host first broadcasts the link-layer address of the destination and requests the IP address. But the destination responds to the RARP message by including and sending its IP address. Note that the application of RARP in computer networks has been mostly replaced by a more powerful protocol called DHCP, which is described in detail in Chapter 5.

Example.   Figure 4.12 shows a network of four subnet LANs 1, 2, 3, and 4 belonging to the same network. The network uses two layer 2 switches S1 and S2 and a gateway router. In this network, every component (link adapter) of the devices in the LANs is assigned an IP address (the link adapters are not shown for simplicity).

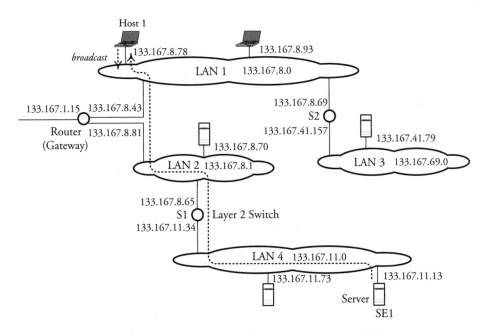

Figure 4.12 A LAN system and the implementation of RARP

In this network, the source host, host 1, with IP address 133.167.8.78 broadcasts the link-layer address of the destination host, server SE1, and requests the IP address. The destination host then responds by sending its IP address 133.167.11.13.

4.5 Spanning-Tree Protocol (STP)

The *Spanning-Tree Protocol* (STP) is used to overcome the problem of infinite loops in networks with bridges or switches. It ensures a loop-free topology for any bridged or switched local area network. The basic function of STP is to prevent bridge or switch from developing loops but it also allows a network design to include redundant links. Creation of redundant links provides automatic backup paths if an active link fails, without the danger of loops or the need for manual enabling/disabling of backup links.

STP is standardized as IEEE 802.1D. As the name suggests, it creates a "spanning tree" in a network of LANs and disables those links that are not part of the spanning tree, leaving a single active path between any two network nodes. The protocol includes an algorithm implemented in every LAN switching device that generates a subset of devices to be used in the network to avoid loops. The algorithm of the Spanning-Tree Protocol for a network of LANs using switches (or bridges) is as follows:

Begin Spanning-Tree Algorithm

1. **Assign a Root Switch.** All switches used to connect LANs in a network agree on a switch called the "root switch" whose ID number (normally a MAC address) is the smallest value:

   - **Initialize.** Any switch initially claims to be the root switch and broadcasts a frame to its neighbors containing: (a) its ID number and (b) its distance from the current claiming root switch (which is 0 at this initial stage).

   - **Analyze Frames.** A switch compares the received ID number of the original sender to its own ID number:

     - **If** the original sender's ID number is larger than its own, the switch knows that it is a better candidate to be the root switch than the sender, and thus stops passing the frame to its neighbors.

     - **Otherwise** the switch realizes that the original sender is the root switch so far and thus: (a) computes its distance from the claiming root switch by incrementing the number of hops (switches), (b) updates its database to indicate the ID and the distance to the root switch so far, and (c) passes the frame to its neighbors.

   - **Determine Root Switch.** Once this process is settled, the ID number of the root switch and its distance are known to all switches.

2. **Find the Shortest Paths.** Each switch determines the shortest path and its distance to the root switch. The port of the switch that connects to the root switch is called the "root port."

3. **Find a Designated Switch.** Each LAN determines a "designated switch" through which it can reach the root switch using the shortest path.

4. **Open All Loops.** Steps 2 and 3 form a shortest tree called a "spanning tree" from a root to all switches of the network. Each switch blocks any of its ports that do not participate in the spanning tree (loops are opened). ■

In step 1 of this algorithm, the switch with the lowest ID number is selected as the root. The ID number could be any number that the network administrator chooses including the MAC address. For simplicity, here we assume that the ID number of a switch is its label such as S1. A spanning tree is constructed originating from the root switch. To determine the root for a spanning tree, any switch sends a special control frame, called the *bridge protocol data unit* (BPDU) frame, comprising a switch ID and the aggregate cost. The cost in this process is usually referred to as the number of switches between a source and the current node. However, sometimes in cases in which the traffic is high in a network, each link is assigned a cost where the link cost is inversely proportional to the link's bit rate. A higher bit rate implies a lower cost.

A receiving switch then compares the sender's switch ID with its own ID. If the sender's switch ID is lower than its own ID, the BPDU is not forwarded. Thus, the switch determines that it is not the root switch and stops sending BPDU advertising for the lowest switch ID. If the sender's switch ID is higher, the BPDU is stored and forwarded to other users after incrementing the cost. Over a period of time, all switches, excluding the switch with the lowest ID, stop sending BPDUs. When a switch with the lowest ID number receives no other BPDUs, it declares itself the root switch. In step 2, based on the comparison of all the stored BPDUs, each of the involving switches determines the shortest path to the root switch with an identified port number. This port is called the root port, and any switch communicates with the root switch through the root port.

In step 3 of this algorithm, every LAN determines a designated switch through which it forwards frames. To determine the designated switch, each switch sends BPDUs to all LANs to which it is connected. Switches connected to a particular LAN compare the respective costs to reach the root switch. The switch with the lowest cost (shortest path) is designated the root switch. In case of a tie, the lowest switch ID determines the designated switch. This way, steps 2 and 3 form a shortest tree called a "spanning tree" from a root to all switches of the network. To create a network with no loops, any switch blocks those of its ports that do not participate in the spanning tree leading to opening all loops.

Example.   Figure 4.13 (a) shows a network of LANs. LANs 1 through 5 are interconnected using switches S1 through S5. We assume the ID number of each switch is the same as its label; for example, the ID number of switch S1 is S1. Assume

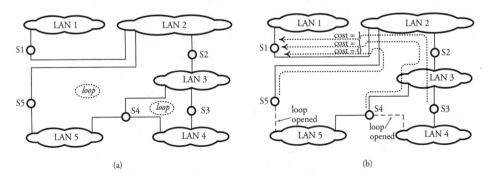

Figure 4.13   The Spanning-Tree Protocol applied on a network of LANs: (a) a network of LANs having two loops; (b) the network after implementation of the Spanning-Tree Protocol

LAN 4 and LAN 5 choose, respectively, S3 and S4 as a designated switch. Clearly, two loops are seen in this network. The existence of a loop causes any external frame with an unknown destination MAC address arriving at this network through any of the switches to circle around any of these loops indefinitely. Apply the spanning-tree algorithm to resolve the looping issue in this network.

Solution.   Figure 4.13 (b) shows the implementation of the Spanning-Tree Protocol to avoid looping. In step 1 of this protocol, switch S1 is assigned as the root switch clearly because the ID number, S1, is considered smaller than S2 through S5. For example, at switch S3, step 1 chooses S2 as the candidate for root among the neighboring switches, S2 and S4, and hence only the BPDU frame of S2 is allowed to be further propagated to others. In step 2, all other switches measure their costs to S1 as shown in the figure. For example, the cost from S4 to S1 is 1 since there is only one switch on the way (S2). In step 3, S5 opens its connection with LAN 5 as S4 is its designated switch, and the connection from S5 to LAN 5 does not participate in the spanning tree. For a similar reason, S4 opens its connection with LAN 4 as S3 is its designated switch, and the connection from S4 to LAN 4 does not participate in the spanning tree. The end result of this protocol is the creation of a shortest tree shown by the dotted lines and the removal of the two loops by opening the loops shown by dashed lines.

4.6   Virtual LANs (VLANs)

A *virtual local area network* (VLAN) is a group of hosts with a common set of requirements communicating as if they were attached to the same domain regardless of their physical locations. A VLAN allows a single LAN to be partitioned into several seemingly and virtually separate LANs. Each virtual LAN is assigned an identifier, and frames can only be forwarded from one segment to another if both segments have the same identifier. A VLAN has the same attributes as a physical LAN does, but it has the advantage that it enables users to be grouped together even if they are not located on the same network switch. Configuration of such a networking structure requires certain software instead of physically relocating the devices.

There are several advantages to using VLANs. First and foremost, a newly defined virtual local area network over a physical local area network can isolate the traffic of the virtual segment from the rest of physical network. VLANs also manage users more effectively. If a user physically moves within a network, the physical cabling need not be changed to connect the user to a different switch if a VLAN is used. Users within a VLAN communicate with one another as if they were the only ones connected to a switch.

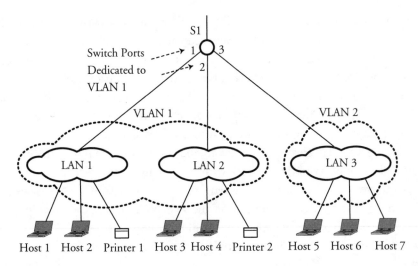

Figure 4.14 Creation of two virtual local area networks (VLANs) and dedication of switch ports

A virtual LAN can be formed through a "VLAN switch," which is a switch that allows multiple *virtual* local area networks to be defined over a single *physical* LAN. The ports of a VLAN switch are divided into several groups by its network manager. Each group of ports forms a VLAN domain. This way, each group is isolated from all other groups.

Figure 4.14 shows three LANs connected through switch S1. The issue in this network is broadcast communication privacy or security. For example, if a certain frame arriving at S1 from outside is intended to be broadcast to LAN 1 and LAN 2 only, switch S1 is not able to process it due to its limited multicast routing capability, and hence the switch has to broadcast the frame to all hosts including the users of LAN 3. This issue can be resolved by creating two virtual local area networks, VLAN 1, and VLAN 2, and dedicating two switch ports 1 and 2 to VLAN 1 and a third one to VLAN 2. Designating a certain number of switch ports to a VLAN is done by switch management software designed for this purpose at a switch. The network manager can declare any port to belong to a given VLAN utilizing the software. In this software, there is a table that maps a switch port to a VLAN.

4.6.1 VLAN Switches

Consider again Figure 4.14. To configure a VLAN in this figure, we need to configure a VLAN ID on each port of switch S1 using the software. Once a frame is transmitted by LAN 1, it arrives at switch S1. The switch observes that the frame comes in a port that was configured as being in VLAN 1. To avoid sending the frame to LAN 3, the switch inserts a "VLAN header" between the MAC header and its payload. In this case, the switch uses its normal routing for forwarding the frame while keeping it away from VLAN 2, which is LAN 3. Notice that any traffic within VLAN 1, for example, from LAN 1 to LAN 2, can also be forwarded through configuration of the switch acting as a router. The combination of a switch, a router, and the necessary software has been designed in one unit called a *VLAN switch*.

Including a VLAN switch in a network opens a door to the possibility of changing the logical topology of the network without moving or modifying any hardware, wires, or addresses. For example, if we wanted LAN 2 be part of VLAN 2, we could simply change the port configuration on the switch. As an another example, if we wanted printer 2 be part of VLAN 2, we would just need to replace a VLAN switch inside LAN 2 and configure it accordingly so that users in LAN 3 could have access to printer 2.

4.6.2   VLAN Trunking Protocol (VTP) and IEEE 802.1Q

VLAN Trunking Protocol (VTP) is a protocol that propagates the configuration of a defined VLAN in a network on the entire domain of connected LANs in the network. The VLAN Trunking Protocol carries VLAN information to all the switches in the network domain. To implement this protocol, typically a special port in each switch is configured as a "trunk port" for connecting VLAN switches.

All VLANs in the network then use the trunk port so that any frame sent to a VLAN in a domain is forwarded to the trunk port and thereby to the other switches. When a frame arrives at a trunk port, each switch finds out which particular VLAN it belongs to by examining an extended MAC frame format, standardized by IEEE 802.1Q. The 802.1Q frame is the same as the regular MAC frame except a 4-byte VLAN tag field included in the header carries the identity of the VLAN to which the frame belongs. The transmitting side of a VLAN includes the VLAN tag information in a frame and the receiving side of the VLAN removes it from the frame. It is worth mentioning here that VLANs can also be used based on network layer protocols.

VTP Switch Modes

There are three modes of switches for VTP configuration based on their behavior in the network domain. These modes are used for the VTP advertisements:

- *Server in server* mode. A switch can add, delete, or modify a VLAN. VLAN modification includes configuration revision, VTP version, and VTP parameters.

VTP parameters are advertised by the switches in the same network domain. If the domain is the same, the switches accept frames and change their stored parameters and update them.

- *Client in client* mode. A switch cannot modify a VLAN. In client mode, the switch only accepts advertisement packets from the server switch.

- *Transparent in transparent* mode. A switch behaves as a transparent switch and does not create or accept any advertisements. It just conveys these packets in the domain. The transparent mode switch does not add, delete, or modify a VLAN in the network domain.

Now we move on to wireless LANs and explain the functionality of networks in wireless mode. By the end of the chapter, we should be able to understand a number of interconnected LANs integrated from regular and wireless components.

4.7 Wireless LANs

Wireless technology helps wired data networks join wireless components. Local area networks can be constructed in a wireless fashion so that wireless users moving within a certain organization, such as a university campus, can access a backbone network.

The basic topology in wireless LANs is shown in Figure 4.15 (a). Each host in the wireless network communicates directly with all others, without a backbone network. An improvement to this scheme involves the use of *wireless access points* (WAPs), or transceivers that can also serve as an interface between the wired and the wireless LANs. Figure 4.15 (b) shows a typical setup with an wireless access point.

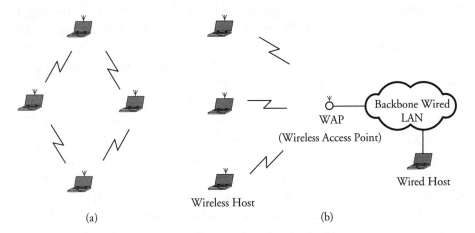

(a)   (b)

Figure 4.15 Basic wireless LANs: (a) basic topology; (b) typical setup with wireless access point

In this scheme, all wireless hosts transmit to the WAP to communicate with hosts on the wired or wireless LAN. The range of user mobility in a wireless LAN can be extended by using several wireless access points. A mobile host searches for a new wireless access point when the signal level from a nearby access point increases beyond that of its current one. Wireless LAN technologies can be classified into four types:

- *Infrared LANs*
- *Spread-spectrum LANs*
- *Narrowband RF LANs*
- *Home RF and Bluetooth LANs*

4.7.1 Infrared LANs

Each signal-covering cell in an *infrared LAN* is limited to one room. The coverage is small, because the infrared rays cannot penetrate through walls and other opaque obstacles. Infrared communication technology is used in several home devices, such as television remote controls. Three alternative transmission techniques are used for infrared data transmission: *directed beam, omnidirectional configuration*, and *diffused configuration*.

The *directed beam* involves point-to-point connections. The range of communications is limited by the transmitted power and the direction of focus. With proper focusing, ranges up to a kilometer can be achieved. This technology can be used in token-ring LANs and interconnections between buildings. The *omnidirectional configuration* consists of a single base station that is normally used on ceilings. The base station sends an omnidirectional signal, which can be picked up by all transceivers. The transceivers in turn use a directional beam focused directly at the base-station unit. In the *diffused-configuration* method, the infrared transmitters direct the transmitted signal to a diffused reflecting ceiling. The signal is reflected in all directions from this ceiling. The receivers can then pick up the transmitted signal.

The use of infrared has several advantages. For example, the bandwidth for infrared communication is large and can therefore achieve high data rates. Also, because infrared rays are reflected by lightly colored objects, it is possible to cover the entire area of the room with reflections from objects. Since infrared cannot penetrate through walls and other opaque obstacles, it becomes very difficult for any adversary to carry out a passive attack or to eavesdrop. Hence, communication with infrared technology is more secure. Also, separate infrared networks can be used in adjacent rooms without any interference effects. Finally, equipment for infrared communication is much cheaper than microwave communication equipment. The one major disadvantage of infrared technology is that background radiation from sunlight and indoor lighting can cause interference at the infrared receivers.

4.7.2   Spread-Spectrum LANs

Spread-spectrum LANs operate in industrial, scientific, and medical applications, making use of multiple adjacent cells, each having a different center frequency within a single band to avoid any interference. Within each of these cells, a star or *peer-to-peer* topology can be deployed. If a star topology is used, a hub as the network center is mounted on the ceiling. This hub, serving as an interface between wired and wireless LANs, can be connected to other wired LANs. All hosts in the wireless LAN transmit and receive signals from the hub. Thus, the traffic flowing among hosts moves through the central hub. Each cell can also deploy a peer-to-peer topology. The spread-spectrum techniques use three different frequency bands: 902–928 MHz, 2.4–2.4835 GHz, and 5.725–5.825 GHz. Higher-frequency ranges offer greater bandwidth capability. However, the higher-frequency equipment is more expensive.

4.7.3   Narrowband RF LANs

Narrowband radio frequency (RF) LANs use a very narrow bandwidth. Narrowband RF LANs can be either licensed or unlicensed. In licensed narrowband RF, a licensed authority assigns the radio frequency band. Most geographic areas are limited to a few licenses. Adjacent cells use different frequency bands. Transmissions are encrypted to prevent attacks. The licensed narrowband LANs guarantee communication without any interference. The unlicensed narrowband RF LANs use the unlicensed spectrum and peer-to-peer LAN topology.

4.7.4   Home RF and Bluetooth LANs

Home RF is a wireless networking standard that operates in the 2GHz frequency band. Home RF is used to interconnect various home electronic devices, such as desktops, laptops, and appliances. Home RF supports data rates of about 2Mb/s for both voice and data and has a range of about 50 meters. *Bluetooth* is a technology that replaces the cables necessary for short-range communication within 10 meters, such as between monitors and CPUs, printers and personal computers, and so on. Bluetooth technology also eliminates the need for cables in laptops and printers. Bluetooth operates at the 2.4GHz frequency band and supports data rates of 700Kb/s.

4.8   IEEE 802.11 Wireless LAN Standard

The IEEE 802.11 wireless LAN standard defines services for physical, MAC layer, and MAC management protocols of wireless local area networks such as WiFi networks. The physical layer is responsible for transmitting raw data over RF or infrared media. The MAC layer resolves access control issues and ensures privacy of transmitted data and reliability of data services. The management protocols ensure authentication and data delivery.

Each wireless LAN host in Figure 4.15 (b) has a wireless LAN adapter for communication over the wireless medium. This adapter is responsible for authentication, confidentiality, and data delivery. To send data to a host in the wired LAN, a host in the wireless LAN first sends the data packet to the access point. The access point recognizes the wireless host through a unique ID called the *service-set identification* (SSID). SSID is like a password-protection system that enables any wireless client to join the wireless LAN. Once the wireless host is authenticated, the access point forwards data packets to the desired wired host through the switch or hub.

Access points build a table of association that contains the MAC addresses of all hosts in the wireless network. The access point uses this information for forwarding data packets in the wireless network. Figure 4.16 shows a setup whereby LANs 1 and 2, residing in two different rooms of a building, are interconnected by *wireless bridges* WB1 and WB2. A wireless bridge is basically the same as a regular bridge but is equipped with a wireless transceiver. The most common medium for wireless networks is radio waves at a frequency of 2.4GHz. Wireless bridges are also used to interconnect LANs in different buildings. The access range of wireless LANs can be extended by deploying a greater number of access points.

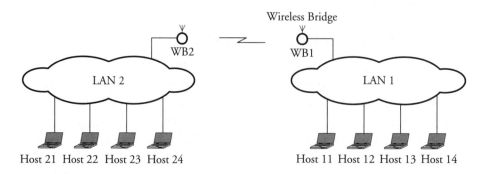

Figure 4.16   Connecting two LANs through wireless bridges

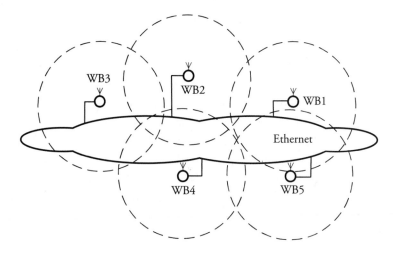

Figure 4.17   Use of multiple access points to extend the range of wireless access

Figure 4.17 shows multiple access points being used to extend the connectivity range of the wireless network. The area of coverage of each access point can be overlapped to adjacent ones to provide seamless host mobility without interruption. Radio signal levels in a wireless LAN must be maintained at an optimum value. Normally, a site survey must be conducted for these requirements. Site surveys can include both indoor and outdoor sites. The surveys are normally needed for power requirements, placement of access points, RF coverage range, and available bandwidth.

The transmission media used in high-speed LANs are twisted-pair and fiber-optic cables. The use of wireless media presents a few advantages, such as host mobility and reduced cost of transmission media. Host mobility enables hosts to access the network resources from any point in the geographic area. Wireless LANs must be reliable and secure in order to be widely deployed. The standards for wireless LANs include 802.11 and its family: 802.11a, 802.11b, and 802.11g.

Standard 802.11 typically uses the *Carrier Sense Multiple Access* with *collision avoidance* (CSMA/CA) method. With this method, each host listens for traffic coming from other hosts and transmits data if the channel is idle. If the channel is busy, the host waits until the channel becomes idle. The host then transmits data after a random *back-off time*. This is done to prevent all hosts from transmitting at the same time when the channel becomes idle. The details of the 802.11 standards are explained further in the next two sections.

4.8.1   IEEE 802.11 Physical Layer

IEEE 802.11 operates in the 2.4GHz band and supports data rates of 1Mb/s to 2Mb/s. IEEE 802.11a operates in the 5GHz band and supports data rates of up to 54Mb/s. IEEE 802.11b operates in the 2.4GHz band and supports data rates of 5.5Mb/s to 11Mb/s. IEEE 802.11g operates at 2.4GHz and supports even higher data rates.

Two other popular IEEE physical layer standards are IEEE 802.11n and IEEE 802.11ad. IEEE 802.11n uses multiple-input multiple-output (MIMO) antennas, explained in Chapter 2, to improve network throughput over the two previous standards, 802.11a and 802.11g. As a result of such a hardware improvement, the data rate may even reach up to 600Mb/s. This standard can be used in the 2.4GHz or 5GHz frequency bands.

The IEEE 802.11 physical layer is of four types:

1. *Direct-sequence spread spectrum* (DSSS) uses seven channels, each supporting data rates of 1Mb/s to 2Mb/s. The operating frequency range is the 2.4GHz ISM band. DSSS uses three nonoverlapping channels in the 2.4GHz ISM band. The 2.4GHz frequency band used by 802.11 results in interference by certain home appliances, such as microwave ovens and cordless telephones, which operate in the same band.

2. *Frequency-hopping spread spectrum* (FHSS) uses a pseudonoise sequence and signal hopping from one channel to another. This technique makes use of 79 channels. FHSS operates in the 2.4GHz ISM band and supports data rates of 1Mb/s to 2Mb/s.

3. *Infrared* with an operating range of about 20 meters operates on a broadcast communication paradigm. A *pulse position modulation* (PPM) scheme is used.

4. *Orthogonal frequency division multiplexing* (OFDM), explained in Chapter 2, is a multicarrier modulation/multiplexing scheme whereby the carrier spacing is carefully selected so that each subcarrier is orthogonal to the other subcarriers. Two signals are *orthogonal* if they are multiplied together and their integral over an interval is 0. Orthogonality can be achieved by letting the carrier spacing be equal to the reciprocal of the useful symbol period. As the subcarriers are orthogonal, the spectrum of each carrier has a null at the center frequency of each of the other carriers in the system. This results in no interference between the carriers, allowing them to be spaced as closely as possible.

IEEE 802.11a uses OFDM, which uses 12 orthogonal channels in the 5GHz range. This reduces the interference from other home appliances, unlike the case with 802.11b. The two standards 802.11a and 802.11b can operate next to each other without any interference: 802.11a equipment is more expensive and consumes more power, as it uses OFDM. The frequency channels are nonoverlapping. IEEE 802.11a operates in the 5GHz band. The achievable Mb/s data rates are 6, 9, 12, 18, 24, 36, 48, and 54. Convolution coding is used for forward error correction.

IEEE 802.11b uses DSSS but supports data rates of up to 11Mb/s. The modulation scheme employed is called *complementary code keying* (CCK). The operating frequency range is 2.4GHz and hence it can interfere with some home appliances. *IEEE 802.11g* achieves very high data rates compared to 802.11b and uses the 2.4GHz frequency band. A combination of encoding schemes is being used in 802.11g. An 802.11g client can operate with an 802.11b access point; similarly, an 802.11b client can operate with an 802.11g access point.

4.8.2   802.11 MAC Layer

IEEE 802.11 provides several key functionalities: reliable data delivery, media access control, and security features. *Reliable data delivery* is a key feature available in the MAC layer of IEEE 802.11. The imperfections of the wireless medium, such as noise, interference, and multipath effects, may lead to frame loss. IEEE 802.11 uses acknowledgment (ACK) to ensure reliable data delivery. When a source sends a data frame, the destination responds with an ACK to acknowledge receipt of the frame. If the source does not receive an ACK for a certain period of time, it times out the process and retransmits the frame.

The *request-to-send/clear-to-send* (RTS/CTS) scheme also can be used to further enhance reliability. When it has data to send, a source sends an RTS signal in the form of a frame to the destination. The destination sends a CTS signal if it is ready to receive data. The source sends the data frame after receiving the CTS signal from the destination. The destination then responds with an ACK to indicate successful receipt of data. This four-way handshake leads to a greater reliability of data delivery. When a source sends an RTS frame and accordingly the hosts within the reception range of the source receive the RTS frame, the hosts refrain from sending frames during this interval, to reduce the risk of collisions. For the same reason, when the destination sends a CTS frame and accordingly the hosts within the reception range of the destination receive the CTS frame, the hosts refrain from sending any frames during this interval.

Another key functionality is *media access control* (MAC). Media-access algorithms are of two types: *distributed access* and *centralized access*. In distributed-access protocols, media access control is distributed among all the nodes. Nodes use a carrier-sense mechanism to sense the channel and then transmit. Distributed-access protocols are used in ad-hoc networks with highly bursty traffic. In centralized-access protocols, the media-access issues are resolved by a central authority. Central-access protocols are used in some wireless LANs that have a base-station backbone structure and in applications that involve sensitive data. The IEEE 802.11 MAC algorithm provides both distributed- and centralized-access features. Centralized access is built on top of distributed access and is optional.

The MAC layer consists of two sublayers: the *distributed-coordination function* (DCF) algorithm and the *point-coordination function* (PCF) algorithm.

Distributed-Coordination Function (DCF) Algorithm

The DCF algorithm uses contention resolution, and its sublayer implements the CSMA scheme for media access control and contention resolution. As explained in Chapter 3, a CSMA sender listens for traffic on the medium. If it senses that the medium is idle, it transmits; otherwise, if the medium is busy, the sender defers transmission until the medium becomes idle. DCF has no provisions for collision detection, which is difficult in wireless networks because of the hidden-node problem. To overcome this problem, the interframe space (IFS) technique is used. IFS is a delay whose length is based on frame priority. IFS has three timing levels. The steps in the algorithm follow.

DCF Algorithm for Wireless 802.11 MAC

1. The sender senses the medium for any ongoing traffic.

2. If the medium is idle, the sender waits for a time interval equal to IFS. Then the sender senses the medium again. If the medium is still idle, the sender transmits the frame immediately.

   If the medium is busy, the sender continues to sense the medium until the medium becomes idle.

3. Once the medium becomes idle, the sender delays its activity by a time interval equal to IFS and senses the medium again.

4. If the medium is still idle, the sender backs off for an exponential time interval and senses the medium again after that interval.

   If the medium continues to be idle, the sender transmits immediately.

   If the medium becomes busy, the sender stops the back-off timing and restarts the process once the medium becomes idle. ■

The IFS time-interval technique is based on the priority of the data. The three timing intervals used for IFS are:

1. *Short IFS* (SIFS). This timing interval is used if immediate response is required. A sender using a SIFS has highest priority. SIFS is used to send ACK frames. A host receiving a frame directed to only itself responds with an ACK after a time interval equal to SIFS. The SIFS time interval compensates for the lack of a collision-detection system in wireless networks.

2. *Point IFS coordination function* (PIFS). This timing interval is used by the central authority or controller in the PCF scheme.

3. *Distributed IFS coordination function* (DIFS). This timing interval is used for the normal asynchronous frames. Senders waiting for the DIFS interval have the least priority.

Point-Coordination Function

The *point-coordination function* (PCF) provides a contention-free service. PCF is an optional feature in IEEE 802.11 and is built on top of the DCF layer to provide centralized media access. PCF includes a *polling feature* implemented at the centralized polling master (point coordinator). The point coordinator uses the PIFS interval to issue polls. Since this interval is greater than the DIFS interval, the coordinator effectively restrains all asynchronous traffic when issuing a poll. The protocol defines an interval called the *superframe interval*, which consists of a contention-free period that the point coordinator used to issue polls. The other interval is the contention period used for stations to send normal asynchronous data. The next superframe interval begins only after the medium becomes idle. The point coordinator has to wait during this period to gain access.

802.11 MAC Frame

The frame header format for the 802.11 MAC is shown in Figure 4.18 and is described as follows.

- The *frame control* (FC) field provides information on the type of frame: control frame, data frame, or management frame.

- *Duration/connection* ID (D/I) refers to the time allotted for the successful transmission of the frame.

- *Addresses* fields denote four 6-byte addresses: source address, destination address, receiver address, and transmitter address.

- The *sequence control* (SC) field consists of 4 bits reserved for fragmentation and reassembly and 12 bits for a sequence number of frames between a particular transmitter and receiver.
- The *frame body* field contains a MAC service data unit or control information.
- The *cyclic redundancy check* (CRC) field is used for error detection.

The three frame types in IEEE 802.11 are *control frames*, *data-carrying frames*, and *management frames*. Control frames ensure reliable data delivery. The types of control frames are:

- *Power save–poll* (PS–Poll). A sender sends this request frame to the access point. The sender requests from the access point a frame that had been buffered by the access-point because the sender was in power-saving mode.
- *Request to send* (RTS). The sender sends an RTS frame to the destination before the data is sent. This is the first frame sent in the four-way handshake implemented in IEEE 802.11 for reliable data delivery.
- *Clear to send* (CTS). The destination sends a CTS frame to indicate that it is ready to accept data frames.
- ACK *frame*. The destination uses this frame to indicate to the sender a successful frame receipt.
- *Contention-free end* (CFE). The PCF uses this frame to signal the end of the contention-free period.
- *CFE/End + CFE/ACK*. PCF uses this frame to acknowledge the CFE end frame.

The data-carrying frames are of the following types:

- *Data*. This is the regular data frame and can be used in both the contention and contention-free periods.

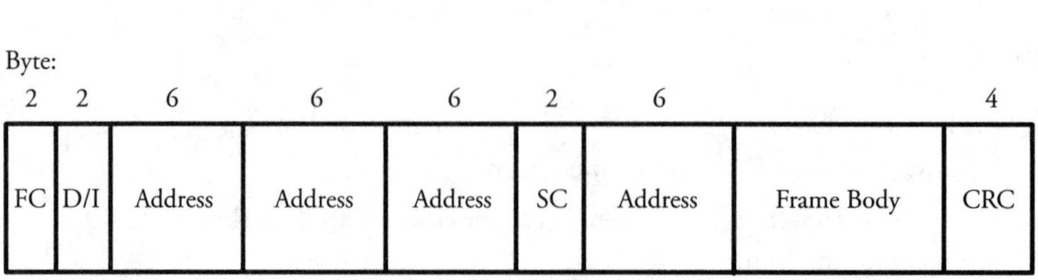

Byte:

2	2	6	6	6	2	6		4
FC	D/I	Address	Address	Address	SC	Address	Frame Body	CRC

Figure 4.18   IEEE 802.11 MAC frame header

- *Data/CFE-ACK.* This is used for carrying data in the contention-free period and is used to acknowledge received data.
- *Data/CFE-Poll.* PFC uses this frame to deliver data to destinations and to request data frames from hosts.
- *Data/CFE ACK/CFE-Poll.* This frame combines the functionalities of the previous three frames into one frame.

Management frames are used to monitor and manage communication among various hosts in the IEEE 802.11 LAN through access points.

4.8.3   WiFi Networks

Wireless fidelity (WiFi)—a term trademarked by the WiFi Alliance technology—is a set of standards for wireless local area networks (WLANs). WiFi is based on 802.11 standards and allows mobile devices, such as laptop computers, digital cameras, and tablet computers to connect to wireless local area networks. WiFi is also intended for Internet access and wireless voice over IP (VoIP) phones. Any host can have built-in WiFi, allowing offices and homes to be networked without expensive wiring.

Routing in WiFi Networks

Figure 4.19 shows three WiFi networks 1, 2, and 3 connected somehow to the Internet. Network 1 uses a *wireless router with gateway,* WG1, and thus it can establish communication with its four hosts 11, 12, 13, and 14 wirelessly while its gateway provides a wireline access to the Internet. Network 2 is equipped with a *wireless access point*, WAP1, to communicate with its hosts 21, 22, 23, and 24 while, due to lack of access to wireline, it requires WG2 to access the Internet. The two routers with gateway, WG1 and WG2, can also communicate with one another while, due to the assumption of long distance between the two routers, the communication is assumed to be through wireline and the Internet.

Network 3 is similar to network 2, and uses a *wireless access point*, WAP2, to communicate with its hosts 31, 32, 33, and 34 but since it does not have access to wireline Internet, a *wireless router,* WR1, has been set up to access the Internet through neighboring WG2. In Figure 4.19, host 13 and host 21 are communicating through the Internet to establish a connection. Also host 24 and host 34 are communicating to establish a connection without needing to access the Internet.

Several routing protocols are used to set up WiFi devices. One of these protocols is the *Optimized Link State Routing* (OLSR) protocol developed for mobile

WAP = Wireless Access Point
WR = Wireless Router
WG = Wireless Router with Gateway

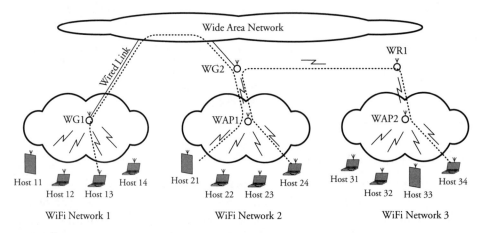

Figure 4.19 Connectivity of wireless hosts to WiFi access points to reach the Internet and direct wireless connections

networks. OLSR operates as a table-driven and proactive protocol. Thus, it regularly exchanges topology information with other nodes of the network. Nodes are selected as multipoint relays by some neighboring nodes. They exchange this information periodically in their control messages.

Physical and Link Layers of WiFi

A connection in WiFi networks is made by radio link signals. A *hotspot* is defined as an access point in a geographical region covered by WiFi. The range of an access point built into a typical WiFi home router is about 50 meters indoors and 90 meters outdoors. WiFi is based on the IEEE 802.11 standard. The most widespread version of WiFi is based on IEEE 802.11b/g operating over 11 channels (5MHz each), centered on Channel 1 at 2,412MHz all the way to Channel 11 at 2,462MHz. In the United States, maximum transmitter power is 1 watt, and maximum effective radiated power is 4 watts. Newer WiFi standards use *orthogonal frequency division multiplexing* (OFDM), explained in Chapter 2, for its users to be managed over the wireless link. OFDM is a multicarrier modulation and multiplexing scheme whereby the carrier spacing is carefully selected so that each subcarrier is orthogonal to the other subcarriers.

WiFi allows LANs to be deployed without cabling, thereby lowering the cost of network deployment and expansion. WiFi may be used in places where cables cannot be laid. However, the use of the 2.4GHz WiFi band does not require a license in most of the world, provided that one stays below the local regulatory limits and accepts interference from other sources, including interference that causes devices to no longer function.

The 802.11b and 802.11g standards over the 2.4GHz spectrum used for WiFi are crowded with other equipment, such as Bluetooth devices, microwave ovens, and cordless phones. This may cause degradation in performance, preventing the use of open access points by others. In addition, the power consumption is fairly high compared to that for other standards, making battery life and heat a concern.

4.9   Case Study: DOCSIS, a Cable TV Protocol

As a case study, let's learn about one of our popular systems, cable TV (CATV) systems. In Chapter 2, we reviewed cable modems followed by modulation techniques used in them. A cable modem is used in homes to access the Internet. A cable TV company may be both the Internet and television service provider. A cable access network connects residential cable modems to a *cable modem termination system* (CMTS) as the end-system at the cable network headquarters.

Cable TV companies use the *Data over Cable Service Interface Specification* (DOCSIS) protocol, which is an international telecommunications standard specifying cable data network architecture and its technology. DOCSIS allows the addition of high-speed Internet access to an existing cable TV system. The protocol is employed by many cable TV operators to provide Internet access over their existing hybrid fiber-coaxial cable infrastructure. To explain DOCSIS, we base our discussion on downstream transmissions, which are CMTS to home modem transmissions, and on upstream transmissions, which are home modem to CMTS transmissions.

At the physical layer, DOCSIS utilizes 6MHz channels for downstream transmission and 6.4MHz channels for the upstream. Any of the upstream and downstream channels is a broadcast channel. Typical versions of DOCSIS specify that 64-level or 256-level QAM (64-QAM or 256-QAM) be used for modulation of downstream data, and the QPSK or 16-level QAM (16-QAM) modulation scheme be used for upstream transmission (both reviewed in Chapter 3). A downstream channel bandwidth is 6MHz, with a maximum of 40Mb/s data rate per channel. An upstream channel bandwidth is 6.4MHz, with a maximum of 30Mb/s data rate per channel.

The data-link layer of DOCSIS employs a mixture of deterministic access methods for upstream transmissions, TDMA (reviewed in Chapter 3) and synchronous CDMA, with a limited use of contention for bandwidth requests. For frames transmitted on downstream channels by the CMTS received by all home cable modems, there is no multiple access issue. For frames on the upstream direction, as multiple cable modems share the same upstream channel to the CMTS, collisions can potentially occur. DOCSIS systems experience relatively few collisions compared to the pure contention-based MAC CSMA/CD employed in older Ethernet systems. With TDMA, an upstream channel is divided into time intervals, each containing a sequence of smaller slots during which a cable modem can transmit to the CMTS. The CMTS assigns permission to a cable modem for such a transmission by forwarding a control message known as a MAP message on a downstream channel to specify which cable modem can transmit during which data slot for the interval of time mentioned in the control message.

For DOCSIS, the MAC layer also includes extensive quality-of-service (QoS) features that help efficiently support applications such as voice over IP. The newer version, DOCSIS 3.0, includes channel bonding, which enables multiple downstream and upstream channels to be used together at the same time by a single subscriber. The network layer of DOCSIS supports modems managed via an IP address. DOCSIS 3.0 adds management over IPv6 (discussed in Chapter 5).

4.10   Summary

A local area network is a communication network that interconnects a variety of data communication devices to serve within a small community. The primary feature of a LAN is its ability to share data and software to provide common services, such as file serving, print serving, support for electronic mail, and process control and monitoring in office and industrial environments. We explored the two basic topologies of LANs, bus and star, using fundamental knowledge on devices covered in Chapter 2 and on links covered in Chapter 3. The simplicity of bus LANs is an advantage when a cable can connect hosts through its taps. The star topology is a variation on the bus topology, whereby a hub provides connection capability. Star topology has the advantage of easier installation than bus topology.

This chapter also presented basics of wireless networking without focus on the large-scale routing issues. Starting with the fundamental concepts at the LAN level, we analyzed several IEEE 802.11 standards. The basic versions—802.11a, 802.11b, and 802.11g—typically use *Carrier Sense Multiple Access* with *collision avoidance* (CSMA/CA).

For a host to be able to place data onto a local area network, the network must be equipped with a MAC protocol to find ways of sharing its medium. The *Address Resolution Protocol* (ARP) is designed to convert an IP address to a MAC address or vice versa.

We also covered important topics of *internetworking* and the use of repeaters, hubs, bridges, and switches. A bridge operates at layer 2 and typically separates hosts into two collision domains. Routers, known as layer 3 switches, are also used to connect multiple subnets in larger LANs. Routers are typically designed to handle heavy traffic loads.

We then explored two *address conversion protocols* by which addresses at layers 2 and 3 are converted to one another. The *Address Resolution Protocol* (ARP) is one of the address conversion protocols designed to convert IP addresses to MAC addresses or vice versa. Our discussion also covered the very important topic of Spanning-Tree Protocol (STP). STP prevents frames or packets from the looping that causes infinite circulations of frames in a network.

Virtual LANs (VLANs) was also topic of interest. We learned that VLAN methodology allows a single LAN to be partitioned into several seemingly and virtually separate LANs. Finally, at the end of the chapter, we covered a variety of wireless LANs including the ones we are all using on a daily basis such as WiFi. Specifically, we targeted several IEEE standards for wireless LANs including 802.11 and its family: 802.11a, 802.11b, and 802.11g.

In the next chapter, we study wide-area routing and internetworking topics. We explore how routing algorithms and protocols are performed both within and beyond a single wide area network.

4.11   Exercises

1. Consider the transfer of a file containing 1 million characters from one computer to another. Transfer consists of a sequence of cycles. For one cycle, $a =$ (time for data frame + propagation) + (time for ACK frame + propagation). The throughput refers to the number of sequences required to transfer 1 million characters. Each character in its digital form requires 8 bits. The two computers are $D = 1\,$km apart, and each generates a data rate of $b = 1$Mb/s, with a frame size $s = 256$ bits, which includes 80 bits of header. The propagation speed on the bus is 200 m/μ sec. Find the total elapsed time using throughput for the following two cases:

    (a) A bus topology, with each frame acknowledged with an 88-bit frame before the next frame is sent.

    (b) A ring topology having a total circular length of $2D$, with the two computers D distance apart. Acknowledgment is achieved by allowing a frame to circulate past the destination host back to the source host. The ring has $N = 100$ repeaters, each of which introduces a delay of 1 bit time.

2. We would like to see how likely it is that any two MAC addresses in the same Ethernet network of an organization are the same, assuming that Ethernet MAC addresses are chosen at random.

   (a) What is the probability that, on a 500-host Ethernet network of an organization, two MAC addresses become the same?

   (b) What is the probability that a same MAC address occurs on one of the 1,000,000 Ethernet networks of 500 hosts worldwide?

3. Consider a LAN consisting of a 200Mb/s ring cable. Data travels over the cable at the speed of light (2.3×10^8 m/s). On the ring, n repeaters are interconnected in equal distance to form a closed loop, and each host is connected to one repeater. When a host transmits a frame, its associated repeater forwards the frame to the ring. The ring is unidirectional, so a frame can flow in one direction. During the circulation of the frame in the ring, the destination host copies the frame into its buffer. Once copied by the destination, the frame continues its circulation until the sender receives it and removes it from the system. To avoid collision, only one host can transmit at a given time.

   (a) Ignoring delay at repeaters, find the circumference of the ring to exactly contain a 1,400-byte frame.

   (b) Find the circumference of the ring to exactly contain a 1,400-byte frame if n is supposed to be 12 and each repeater and its host combined introduce a 5-bit delay.

4. We want to design a coaxial LAN for 12 offices arranged on three similar floors, each floor having two rows with two offices and the rows separated by a hallway. Each office is 5 m $\times$ 5 m with a height of 3 m. The LAN center is in the center of the ground floor beneath the three office floors. Assume that each office requires two IP telephone lines and retrieves two Web pages per minute at the average rate of 22 KB per page.

   (a) Estimate the distance from each office to the LAN center.

   (b) Estimate the required available bit rate for the LAN.

5. Consider a 1,000 m bus LAN with a number of equally spaced computers with a data rate of 100Mb/s.

   (a) Assume a propagation speed of 200 m/μ s. What is the mean time to send a frame of 1,000 bits to another computer, measured from the beginning of transmission to the end of reception? Assume a mean distance between pairs of computers to be 0.375 km, an approximation based on the following observation: For a computer on one end, the average distance is 0.5 km. For a computer in the center, the average distance is 0.25 km. With this assumption, the time to send is transmission time plus propagation time.

(b) If two computers with a mean distance of 0.375 km start transmitting at the same time, their frames interfere with each other. If each transmitting computer monitors the bus during transmission, how long does it take before it notices a collision? Show your answer in terms of both time and bit time.

6. Consider a 100Mb/s 100Base-T Ethernet LAN with four attached hosts, as shown in Figure 4.1 (a). In a nonpersistent CSMA/CD algorithm, a host normally waits 512 g bit times after a collision before sending its frame, where g is drawn randomly. Assume that a 96 bit times of waiting period are needed for clearing the link from the jammed signal in the 100Base-T Ethernet LAN. Assume that only host 1 and host 4 are active and that the propagation delay between them is 180 bit times. Suppose that these two hosts try to send frames to each other and that their frames collide at the halfway LAN link. Host 1 then chooses $g = 2$, whereas host 4 picks $g = 1$, and both retransmit.

(a) How long does it take for host 1 to start its retransmission?

(b) How long does it take for host 4 to start its retransmission?

(c) How long does it take the frame from host 4 to reach host 1?

7. Consider the interconnected LAN structure shown in Figure 4.8. Assume that hosts 1 through 5, respectively, are assigned the following MAC addresses: 00-40-33-40-1B-2C, 00-40-33-25-85-BB, 00-40-33-25-85-BC, 00-61-97-44-45-5B, and 00-C0-96-25-45-C7. Show the organization of the switch S3 routing table for which the input entry is: Destination (Host, MAC Address); and the two types of output entries are: From LAN 2 (Next LAN, Switch Port Number) and From LAN 3 (Next LAN, Switch Port Number).

8. Consider the interconnected LAN structure shown in Figure 4.8, and assume there is another switch in the network that connects LAN 3 to LAN 5 through switch S5. The ID of each switch is indicated by a number next to the letter S. We would like to implement the *Spanning-Tree Protocol* to have a loop-free structure.

(a) Find the "root switch" for this network.

(b) Show the shortest tree for switches.

(c) Determine the "designated switch" for each LAN.

(d) Show the result of the Spanning-Tree Protocol applied on the network.

9. Suppose the interconnected LAN structure shown in Figure 4.20 is part of a building network. Assume that hosts 1 through 6, respectively, are assigned the following MAC addresses: 11-24-C2-25-78-90, DD-34-93-1D-CC-BC, 00-40-33-40-1B-2C, 00-40-33-25-85-BB, 00-40-33-25-85-BC, and 00-C0-96-25-45-C7. Show the organization of the switch S2 routing table for which the input entry is: Destination (Host, MAC Address); and the two types of output entries are: From LAN 1 (Next LAN, Switch Port Number) and From LAN 4 (Next LAN, Switch Port Number).

10. Suppose the interconnected LAN structure shown in Figure 4.20 is part of a building network. The ID of each switch is indicated by a number next to the letter S. We would like to implement the *Spanning-Tree Protocol* to have a loop-free structure.

    (a) Find the "root switch" for this network.
    (b) Show the shortest tree for switches.
    (c) Determine the "designated switch" for each LAN.
    (d) Show the result of the Spanning-Tree Protocol applied on the network.

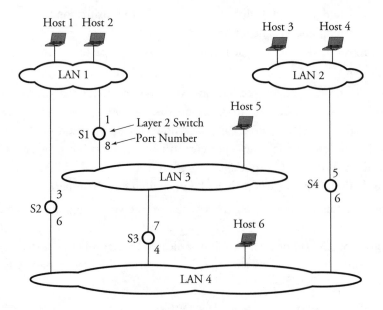

Figure 4.20 Exercises 9 and 10 network of LANs using bridges

11. Design (show only the network) a LAN system for a small five-story building. One floor is dedicated to two mail servers and three separate database servers. Each remaining floor has four computers with broadband access. Your design should meet the following restrictions and conditions: three input hubs, one bridge, and unlimited Ethernet buses. The incoming broadband Internet access must be connected to a six-repeater ring, no bus LAN is allowed outside of a floor, and a traffic analyzer must be attached to the network.

12. We would like to apply the VLAN Trunking Protocol on five switches supporting ten VLANs. Each VLAN covers two physical LANs.

    (a) Find the number of ports needed to connect the switches.
    (b) Find the number of ports per switch needed to connect the LANs to the network.
    (c) Show a rough sketch for the network configuration.

4.12 Computer Simulation Project

1. *Simulation of Virtual Local Area Networks (VLANs).* Use a computer network simulator such as the ns-3 tool to simulate a virtual local area network (VLAN). The simulator must be capable of VLAN implementation. The primary objective of this project is to evaluate the performance of VLANs that play a pivotal role in computer networking. The topology that is used in this project must contain 50 switching nodes including hosts and local switches. Ten nodes are placed in each VLAN. Thus, the project contains five VLANs. Frames are sent both from nodes in the same VLAN and from nodes in the VLAN.

    (a) Create a VLAN "install function." In ns-3, create a new function that can add a VLAN ID in a switch. This can be done by creating a new install_vlan function in ns-3. This function iterates through the switch adding all the required ports. It then returns to the switch the added VLAN. Note that in VLANs, during the configuration of hosts, the assignment of IP addresses in the same subnet as their respective VLAN ID is required. Thus, the switch takes the forwarding decision based on the virtual local area network ID that the host belongs to. The most significant part of the switch logic is the restriction of traffic. The restriction is done for both unicast and broadcast packets.

    (b) Add traffic restriction logic to the switch. The code you write must iterate through all the ports of the switch. During the forwarding decision of a frame, the VLAN ID of the incoming port is compared with the virtual local area network ID of the outgoing port. The frame is only forwarded out of those ports that have the same VLAN ID as the incoming port. The restriction of traffic happens here where the frames are restricted to a segmented VLAN broadcast domain. After adding the traffic restriction logic to the switch, it is necessary to access the individual ports of the switch and assign the respective VLAN ID to its ports.

(c) Access ports of the switch. If you use the ns-3 tool, you must get: `n0 = switch -> GetBridgePort(0); … n10 = switch -> GetBridgePort(0).`

(d) Assign VLAN IDs to the switch ports. To access the ports, it is necessary to first access the switch. Random VLAN IDs are to be assigned to the ports. If you use the ns-3 tool, you will create port assignments as: `n0->vlanid = 1,… n10->vlanid = 1.`

(e) Capture packets. All the nodes are connected to a bridge-net-device that is working as a switch in ns-3. Packet captures: Packets are sent from nodes in the same VLAN and between nodes in different VLANs. When the frames are sent between nodes belonging to the same VLAN, show the communication using Wireshark capture.

(f) Collect performance evaluation results. The performance evaluation of VLANs can be done using the flow monitor class in ns-3. This class has the flow stats function that can be used to collect parameters such as bandwidth, jitter, throughput, and efficiency.

CHAPTER 5

Wide-Area Routing and Internetworking

This chapter focuses on the networking structure of larger networks. One of the most important functions in computer networking, especially in wide area networks, is *routing* packets. In packet-switched networks, this function includes procedures through which a packet uses certain algorithms to find all the necessary paths from its source to its destination. In this chapter, we look at routing algorithms and protocols both within one WAN (*intradomain networking*, or *intranetworking*) and beyond it (*interdomain networking*, or *internetworking*). This chapter covers the following main topics:

- *IP packets and basic routing policies*
- *Path selection algorithms*
- *Intradomain routing protocols*
- *Interdomain routing protocols*
- *Internet Protocol version 6* (IPv6)
- *Congestion control at the network layer*

We begin with some basic routing policies such as the *Internet Control Message Protocol* (ICMP), *Dynamic Host Configuration Protocol* (DHCP), and *network address translation* (NAT). We then proceed to explain *path selection algorithms* that teach us how a path in a wide area network is selected for routing. In this section, we first start with the definition of path cost and the classification of path selection algorithms.

A networking infrastructure deploys a variety of algorithms for routing packets, classified as those using optimal routes and those using nonoptimal routes. We also classify routing protocols by whether they are applied within a domain (*intradomain*) or beyond a domain (*interdomain*). An intradomain *routing protocol* routes packets within a defined domain. A number of protocols in this category such as the *Open Shortest Path First* (OSPF) *protocol*, and the *Routing Information Protocol* (RIP) are presented. By contrast, an interdomain routing protocol is a procedure for routing packets on networks of domains. Our focus in this category of protocols will be on the *Border Gateway Protocol* (BGP) that utilizes two primary modes of data exchange, *internal* BGP (iBGP) and *external* BGP (eBGP).

Next, we look at the overview of the Internet Protocol version 6 (IPv6). This is newer than the IPv4 version of the Internet Protocol. Various aspects of IPv6 are covered in the upcoming chapters.

At the end of this chapter, congestion-control mechanisms that can be implemented either unidirectionally or bidirectionally among nodes at the network layer are presented. At the end of the discussion on congestion control, an approximation method for calculating *link blocking* is introduced. This method provides a quick approximation solution for the performance evaluation of links.

5.1   IP Packets and Basic Routing Policies

The packet header format of IP version 4 (IPv4) is shown in Figure 5.1 (a). The size of the header is variable, with 20 bytes of fixed-length header and an *options* field whose size is variable up to 40 bytes. Detailed descriptions of the fields appear throughout this chapter, and a brief description of each follows.

- *Version* specifies the IP version.
- *Header length* (HL) specifies the length of the header (including options and padding) in terms of 4-byte blocks. For example, if the total header of a packet (including options and padding) is 60B, HL=60B/4B=15, which is 1111 in binary.
- *Type of service* specifies the quality-of-service (QoS) requirements of the packet, such as priority level, delay, reliability, throughput, and cost.

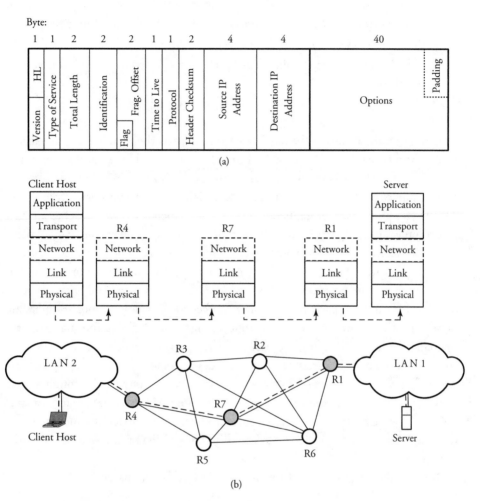

Figure 5.1   (a) IP packet header format (b) communication between a client host and a server at the network layer

- *Total length* specifies the total length of the packet in bytes, including the header and data. A total of 16 bits are assigned to this field.

- *Identification, flags,* and *fragment offset* are used for packet fragmentation and reassembly.

- *Time to live* specifies the maximum number of hops after which a packet must be discarded.

- *Protocol* specifies the protocol used at the destination.

- *Header checksum* is a method of error detection and is described in Chapter 3.

- *Source address* and *destination address* are 32-bit fields specifying the source address and the destination address, respectively.
- *Options* is a rarely used variable-length field to specify security level, timestamp, and type of route.
- *Padding* is used to ensure that the header is a multiple of 32 bits.

Recall that the 16 bits in the *total length* field express the total length of a packet. Hence, the total length of the packet is limited to 2^{16} bytes. However, the maximum packet size of 2^{16} bytes is rarely used, since the packet size is limited by the physical network capacity. The real physical network capacity per packet is normally less than 10,000 bytes and gets even smaller, to 1,500 bytes, when the packet reaches a LAN. To accomplish packet partitioning, the *identification*, *flags*, and *fragment offset* fields perform and keep track of the packet-fragmentation process when needed.

Before we dive into the topic of internetworking and routing, the principal policies and protocols are presented in this section. *Routing algorithms* and *protocols* create procedures for routing packets from their sources to their destinations. Routers are responsible mainly for implementing routing algorithms. These routing tasks are essentially methods of finding the best paths for packet transfer in a network. The choice of routing protocol determines the best algorithm for a specific routing task. As seen in Figure 5.1(b), a host and a server are two end points connected through routers R4, R7, and R1. Each end point belongs to a separate LAN. In such scenarios, a layer 3 (network) route must be set up for IP packets (datagrams); all devices, including end users and routers, process the route at the third layer of the protocol stack, as shown in the figure.

Routing algorithms can be differentiated on several key characteristics:

- *Accuracy.* An algorithm must operate correctly so that it can find the destination in an appropriate amount of time.
- *Simplicity.* Low complexity of algorithms is particularly important where routers with limited physical resources involve software.
- *Optimality.* This refers to the ability of the routing algorithm to select the best route.
- *Stability.* Routing algorithms must perform correctly in the face of unforeseen circumstances, such as node failure and routing table corruption.
- *Adaptability.* When a failure happens in a network, an algorithm should be able to adapt load increases or decreases.

- *Convergence.* Routing algorithms must converge rapidly when a network distributes routing update messages.

- *Load balancing.* A good routing algorithm balances load over eligible links to avoid having a heavily and temporarily congested link.

In practice, this list is used to determine how efficiently a route is selected. The first factor to consider in determining the best path to a destination is the volume of traffic ahead.

Before we start the topic of routing, in the next few sections, we learn a number of principal policies in the form of protocols used in layer 3 of the protocol stack such as *packet fragmentation and reassembly*, the *Internet Control Message Protocol* (ICMP), *obtaining and assigning IP addresses*, *Dynamic Host Configuration Protocol* (DHCP), *network address translation* (NAT), and *Universal Plug and Play* (UPnP).

5.1.1   Packet Fragmentation and Reassembly

The physical capacity of networks enforces an upper bound on the size of packets. The *maximum transmission unit* (MTU) represents this restriction. For example, as a LAN standard, Ethernet limits the size of flowing frames to 1,500 bytes. The objective of inducing this method is that we need a mechanism that avoids requiring large buffers at intermediate routers to store the fragments. This restriction requires the Internet Protocol to break up large messages into fragments. The fragment sizes are limited to the MTU of the underlying physical network. The fragments could in turn be split into smaller fragments, depending on the physical network being used. Each fragment is routed independently through the network. Once all the fragments are received, they are reassembled at the final destination to form the original packet.

The identification, flag, and offset fields of the IP header help with the fragmentation and reassembly process. The identification field is used to distinguish between various fragments of different packets. The flag field has a more-fragment (MF) bit. When the MF bit is set, it implies that more fragments are on their way. The offset field indicates the position of a fragment in the sequence of fragments making up the packet. The lengths of all the fragments, with the exception of the last one, must be divisible by 8.

To be successfully reassembled, all fragments making up a packet must arrive at the destination. In the case of a missing fragment, the rest of the fragments have to be discarded, and thus the packet needs to be retransmitted. In such cases, the retransmission of packets results in an inefficient use of the network bandwidth.

Example. Suppose that a host application needs to transmit a packet of 3,500 bytes. The physical layer requires an MTU of 1,500 bytes. The packet has an IP header of 20 bytes plus a combined options and padding (explained in Section 5.1) header of 20 bytes. Fragment the packet, and specify the ID, MF, and offset fields of all fragments.

Solution. The allowable data length $= 1,500 - 20 - 20 = 1,460$ bytes. Because the 1,460-byte portion is not divisible by 8, the allowable data length is limited to 1,456 bytes. Thus, including the headers, the data to be transmitted of 3,540 bytes has to be split into fragments of 1,456, 1,456, and 628 bytes. Here, fragment 1 = total length 1,456, MF 1, offset 0; fragment 2 = total length 1,456, MF 1, offset 182; and fragment 3 = total length 628, MF 0, and offset 364.

5.1.2   Internet Control Message Protocol (ICMP)

The *Internet Control Message Protocol* (ICMP) is used by hosts or routers to transmit management and routing information to each other at the network layer. One of the most typical applications of ICMP is for reporting errors in networks. For example, in wide area networks, the Internet Protocol may not be able to deliver a packet to its destination, resulting in possible failures to connect to a destination. This issue is also typical in connectionless routing when routers operate autonomously. They forward and deliver packets without requiring any coordination with the source. Another issue—related and equally important—is that a sender cannot know whether a delivery failure is a result of a local or a remote technical difficulty.

An ICMP message is encapsulated in the data portion of an IP packet (datagram). Although ICMP is considered part of the layer 3 protocol, we need to understand that ICMP messages are carried inside IP packets as payload. When an error occurs, ICMP reports it to the originating source of the connection. This is compatible with the fact that an IP datagram header itself specifies only the original source and not any routers. ICMP messages carry the header and the first 8 bytes of the IP packet that caused the ICMP message to be generated. This way, the source of the ICMP message can determine the original IP packet that caused the error. The source must interpret the error.

Table 5.1 shows a typical ICMP message. An ICMP message is identified by two fields: *type* and *code*. Let's look at some examples of ICMP messages. A common error in the Internet happens when a destination network is unreachable and a router is unable to find a path to the destination host specified in application. In this case, an ICMP message is generated containing the two fields: type=3 and code=1.

Table 5.1 Typical ICMP messages

Type	Code	Function
0	0	ping, echo reply
3	0	destination network unreachable
3	1	destination host unreachable
3	2	destination protocol unreachable
3	3	destination port unreachable
3	6	destination network unknown
9	0	router advertisement
10	0	router discovery
11	0	time-to-live (TTL) expired
12	0	Internet Protocol header bad

Besides hardware failure, other factors may be present to create this problem. For example, as noted in Section 5.1, the *time-to-live* (TTL) field in an IP packet header specifies the maximum number of hops after which a packet must be discarded. If the counter of this field expires, packet delivery can become impossible. An ICMP message in this case is generated containing the two fields: type=11 and code=0.

Example.   In Figure 5.2, a source host tries to send a packet to a destination host. But router R1 incorrectly sends the packet to a wrong path (R1-R3-R4-R5) instead of to the correct one (R1-R2-R6).

Solution.   When the packet is forwarded far from the source, an action eventually is required to correct the routing error. In this case, if a router, such as R5, finds out about this error in the middle of routing, it cannot issue an ICMP message to R1 to correct the routing. The ICMP message that is able to resolve such routing errors is the *destination host unreachable* message, which is used in this case. However, as R5 does not know the address of R1, instead, the ICMP message is issued as a redirect ICMP message to the source host.

5.1.3   Obtaining and Assigning IP Addresses

IP addresses are organized by a nonprofit organization known as the *Internet Corporation for Assigned Names and Numbers* (ICANN). An ISP can request a block of addresses from ICANN. Then, a network administrator of an organization can also request a block of addresses from its ISP. A block of addresses obtained from an ISP can be assigned over hosts, servers, and router interfaces by a network manager.

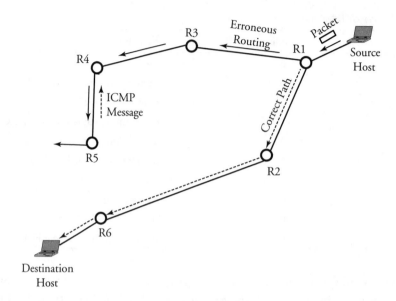

Figure 5.2   With ICMP, a redirect message cannot be sent to R1, since R6 does not know the address of R1.

Note that a unique IP address must always be assigned to each host as a client or server or router interface (input port or output port). However, under some circumstances, a globally unique IP address assignment can be avoided.

Example.   Suppose an ISP owns the address block 188.32.8.0/21. Show how organizations A, B, and C each requesting 256 IP addresses are allocated address blocks by the ISP. (Recall from Chapter 1 the CIDR IP addressing scheme being used here.)

Solution.   The ISP can divide its address block into several contiguous address blocks and give each of the address blocks to each of the three organizations requesting address blocks. The distribution of address blocks is shown below. The third byte (.8.) is 0000,1000 in binary, and /21 indicates the first 5 bits of the third byte (i.e., 00001xxx). Thus, 188.32.8.0/21 would give the ISP all addresses from 188.32.8.0 to 188.32.15.255. The ISP can then continue assigning the remaining address blocks to other organizations, companies, or private entities.

   Address block of ISP: 188.32.8.0/21

   Allocated address block to organization A: 188.32.8.0/24

   Allocated address block to organization B: 188.32.9.0/24

   Allocated address block to organization C: 188.32.10.0/24

Merging the allocated IP addresses is also possible. Suppose that ISP 1 operating in a city handles the networking tasks of two organizations with IP address blocks 188.32.8.0/24 and 188.32.9.0/24, respectively. In this scenario, ISP 1 clearly advertises to its outside domains through its gateway router that it can process any datagram (IP packet) whose first 23 address bits exactly match 188.32.8.0/23. Notice here that we merged the two CIDR IP address blocks of 188.32.8.0/24 and 188.32.9.0/24 resulting in 188.32.8.0/23. Also note that the outside domains need not know the contents of these two address blocks, as the internal routing within each organization is handled by an internal server.

Similarly, merging allocated IP addresses at the ISP level can also be possible. For example, assume that ISP 2 operating in a city handles the networking tasks of two other organizations in the same city with IP address blocks 145.76.8.0/24 and 145.76.9.0/24, respectively. ISP 2 advertises to its outside domains through router R4 that it can process any datagram (packet) whose first 23 address bits exactly match 145.76.8.0/23. Now, if for any reason ISP 1 and ISP 2 merge, the least costly solution to avoid changing the address blocks of the ISPs is to keep all address blocks unchanged and to have the organizations' gateway routers advertise to their outside domains that each can process any datagram whose first 23 address bits exactly match 188.32.8.0/23 or whose first 23 address bits exactly match 145.76.8.0/23.

5.1.4   Dynamic Host Configuration Protocol (DHCP)

Automatically assigning an IP address to a host is handled through a protocol called *Dynamic Host Configuration Protocol* (DHCP). DHCP allows a host to learn its subnet mask, the address of its first-hop router, or even the addresses of other major local servers. Because this addressing automation lets a host learn several key pieces of information in a network, DHCP is sometimes called a *plug-and-play* protocol, whereby hosts can join or leave a network without requiring configuration by network managers.

Process of Dynamic IP Address Allocation

Operating hosts and routers of an organization require IP addresses at all times in order to stay connected to the Internet. After an organization has obtained its block of addresses from its ISP, it can assign individual IP addresses to the host and router interfaces in its organization. The network administrators of organizations manually and remotely configure the IP addresses in the router interfaces using a network management tool. However, host addresses can be done using DHCP. DHCP allows a host be allocated an IP address automatically.

DHCP operates in such a way that a given host is allocated the same IP address each time it connects to the network. A new host joining the network may be assigned a temporary IP address that will be different each time the host connects to the network. The convenience of this method of address assignment gives DHCP multiple uses of IP addresses. If any network administrator does not have a sufficient number of IP addresses, DHCP is used to assign each of its connecting hosts a temporary IP address. When a host joins or leaves, the management server must update its list of available IP addresses. If a host joins the network, the server assigns an available and arbitrary IP address; each time a host leaves, its address is included in the pool of available addresses.

Once a host is assigned an IP address, it can be given a chance to learn its subnet mask, the address of its gateway router, and the address of its local *Domain Name System* (DNS) server. DHCP is especially useful in *mobile* IP, with mobile hosts joining and leaving an ISP frequently. In practice, a mobile Internet user requires a new subnet and thus a new IP address for only a limited amount of time at each location it enters. The process of assigning IP address allocations is called *dynamic address allocation*.

Dynamic address allocation can also be utilized in larger residential areas when a limited number of IP addresses should be managed to cover the Internet services in a large area. An ISP can use the available statistics of the Internet usage and decides how many IP addresses are really needed in a certain area.

For example, consider a certain part of a city where 10,000 customers are subscribed to the Internet service, but customers' hosts join and leave during a certain period of the day. The ISP may estimate that there is a need to provide only 3,000 IP addresses for that period of time and for that area of the city, as not all customers are active at all times. Therefore, the DHCP server of the ISP can assign IP addresses "dynamically." Similar to an organization's dynamic address allocation, dynamic address allocation in residential areas requires the DHCP server to update its lists of used and available IP addresses. The DHCP process is summarized as follows:

Begin DHCP Steps

1. **Discover**

   The arriving host inserts in a discover packet:
   - Source address: 0.0.0.0
   - Destination multicast address: 255.255.255.255

   The arriving host multicasts the discover packet to discover a DHCP server.

2. **Offer**

   The DHCP server replies with a DHCP offer packet.

   Offer: transaction ID + proposed IP address + network mask + lease time

3. **Request**

   The arriving host sends the DHCP request.

4. **AKC/NAK**

   If the DHCP server acknowledges the request, it replies with ACK. **Otherwise** it denies the request and sends NAK.   ■

In step 1 of the preceding process, the arriving host needs to discover a DHCP server in its vicinity. This process is performed by broadcasting a "discover" packet to port 67. This "port" is a fourth-layer parameter, and UDP is a protocol defined in the fourth layer of the protocol stack. Since the host does not have an IP address yet, the source address 0.0.0.0 is inserted into the packet's header by default. The destination multicast address is 255.255.255.255.

In step 2, any DHCP server receiving the discover packet responds to the host with an "offer" packet that is also broadcast to all nodes on the subnet, again using the IP broadcast address of 255.255.255.255. The offer packet contains a transaction ID, a proposed IP address for the host, a network mask, and a lease time of up to several hours or days for which the IP address is valid. In step 3, the arriving host chooses from among one or more DHCP server offers and responds to its selected offer with a DHCP request packet. This step is also done by multicasting the request packet with a destination multicast address of 255.255.255.255.

In step 4, the DHCP server responds by either confirming the requested parameters of the host (ACK) or denying them (NAK). This method of dynamic address allocation is similar to a plug-and-play action where a mobile Internet user who moves from one building to another actually joins a new subnet and receives a new IP address. Figure 5.3 shows an example of address allocation by a DHCP server to a newly arriving host. Two networks are connected through router R1 while the DHCP server is attached to network 2. In WiFi network 1, host 1 is the newly arrived host going through the four steps of the DHCP process.

5.1.5   Network Address Translation (NAT)

Any IP-type device requires a unique IP address. Because of the growing number of Internet users and devices, each requiring a unique IP address, the issue is critical, especially when new hosts and LANs need to be added to a community network

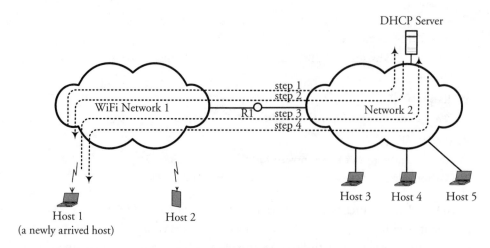

Figure 5.3   An example of address allocation to a newly arrived host by a DHCP server

despite a limited number of IP addresses available for that community. Even in very small residential networks, the issue arises when new devices are added to the network. Although the numbers of users, servers, or subnets expands over time, the total allocated IP addresses are still limited to a certain level by the associated ISP.

Besides the popular IPv6, explained later in this chapter, an alternative solution, called *network address translation* (NAT), can be used to overcome the challenge presented by this issue. The idea behind NAT is that all the users and hosts of a private network do not need to have globally unique addresses. Instead, they can be assigned private unique IP addresses within their own private networks, and a NAT-enabled router or server that connects the private network to the outside world can translate these addresses to globally unique addresses. The NAT-enabled router hides from the outside world the details of the private network. The router acts as a single networking device with a single IP address to the outside world. NAT protocol recommends three IP address ranges to be reserved for NAT applications. These IP address ranges are:

- 10.x.x.x
- 172.16.x.x and 172.31.x.x
- 192.168.x.x

Assume that a private network with a NAT-enabled router is connecting to the outside world. Suppose that all the machines in this network are internally assigned 10.0.0.0/9 and that the output port of the router is assigned an IP address of 197.36.32.4. Now, this network has the advantage that additional machines or even

LANs can be added to it and that each can use an address in the block 10.0.0.0/9. Therefore, users and servers within the network can easily use 10.0.0.0/9 addressing to transmit packets to each other, but packets forwarded beyond the network into the Internet clearly do not use these addresses. This way, the NAT-enabled router does not act as a router to outside world; instead, it is presented to the outside world as a single device with a single IP address. With this technique, thousands of other networks, communities, or domains can use the same block of addresses internally.

Private IP addresses are assigned to hosts in a private network of an ISP using the DHCP technique explained in the previous section. The associated NAT-enabled router of the ISP can get a host private address from the DHCP server of the ISP, and runs the DHCP server to provide addresses to hosts.

Given a datagram received by the NAT-enabled router, we now need to know how the router knows to which internal (private) host it should deliver the datagram. The answer lies in the use of a *port number* for the hidden host along with a private *IP address* included in a NAT translation table in the router. Recall from Chapter 1 that a port number is another identification of a networking device or host defined at the fourth layer of the protocol stack, or "transport layer," and is discussed in detail in Chapter 8. For simplicity, the combination of an IP address and a port number is shown by "IP address-port number."

Example. Assume that host 1 in Figure 5.4 belongs to a private network. It has an internal IP address and port number combination of 10.0.0.2-4527. Host 1 requests a connection to server 1 with IP address 144.55.34.2 and port number 3843, housed in a public network in a different country. Suppose that the outside port of the connecting NAT-enabled router is assigned IP address 197.36.32.4. The router has dedicated 5557 to host 1 to act as a public port number. Show the details of the NAT operation.

Solution. Figure 5.4 shows the detail of NAT operation. To set up this connection, host 1 sends its request with source address 10.0.0.2-4527 to the NAT-enabled router R1. The router "translates" this address in its NAT routing table by changing the arbitrary port number from 4527 to an official one of 5557 and changing the internal IP address 10.0.0.2 to its own port IP address, 197.36.32.4. The router then makes the connection request to site 144.55.34.2-3843, using address 197.36.32.4-5557. When the router receives the response from the remote site, the router does the reverse translation and delivers the response to host 10.0.0.2. Although the NAT protocol solves the shortage of IP addresses in small communities, it has a major drawback of avoiding the assignment of a unique IP address to every networking component.

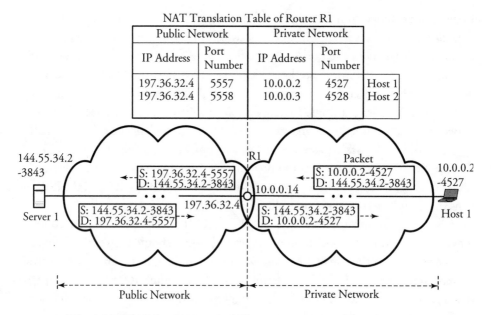

Figure 5.4   An example of the NAT protocol in a network

5.1.6   Universal Plug and Play (UPnP)

Universal Plug and Play (UPnP) is a protocol that uses the Internet to enable client hosts such as laptops and wireless computers to be plugged into a network and
automatically know about each other. UPnP has an objective that makes the task of
joining and leaving a network simple and agile. UPnP also allows a host to discover
and configure a nearby NAT device. When a host is plugged into the network, it
configures itself, acquires a TCP/IP address, and utilizes a discovery protocol to
announce its presence on the network to other networking devices. The discovery
protocol is based on the *Hypertext Transfer Protocol* (HTTP), which is covered in
Chapter 9.

    When a host plugs into a private network, an application program running in the
host requests a NAT mapping between its private IP address and port number and the
public IP address and port number. At this point, the host depends on NAT to accept
the request. If the request is accepted, the NAT device produces the mapping by
which outside users can initiate connections to the public IP address and port number.

    For example, if a laptop and a printer are connected to a network, one can initiate
printing a file in the laptop and have the laptop send a discover request asking if

there were any printers on the network. The printer would identify itself using UPnP protocol, and send its location in the form of a *universal resource locator* (URL). Once a common language between the laptop and the printer is established, the laptop would control the printer and print the file.

5.2   Path Selection Algorithms

Now we can proceed to *path selection algorithms*. The path selection process is the first step of a routing protocol and determines a path from a source host to a destination host. Path selection algorithms can be classified in several ways. One way is to classify them as either *least-cost path*, whereby the lowest-cost path must be determined for routing, or *non-least-cost path*, whereby the determination of a route is not based on the cost of a path.

A packet-switched network consists of nodes—routers or switches—that are connected by links. A *link cost* between a pair of source and destination nodes mainly refers to the number of packets currently waiting ahead in the destination node, although other less important factors may contribute to link cost. The goal is to choose a routing based on the *minimum number of hops*, or *least-cost path*. For example, Figure 5.5 shows a network in which the lines between each two nodes represent a link and its cost in its corresponding direction.

The *least-cost path* between each pair of nodes is the minimum cost of the routing between the two nodes, taking into account all possible links between the two nodes. For example, the least-cost path in Figure 5.5 between nodes

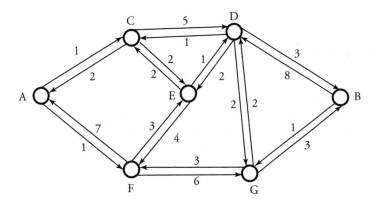

Figure 5.5   A packet-switched network and all link costs

A and D is not A-C-D. The calculated cost of this path is $1 + 5 = 6$. The better path is A-C-E-D, with a calculated cost of $1 + 2 + 1 = 4$. Thus, the second case has more hops, but it has a lower cost than the first case, which has a shorter path but a higher cost.

In practice, the majority of Internet routing methods are based on least-cost algorithms. In such algorithms, a link cost is proportional to the link's current traffic load. However, the link cost may not always be proportional to the current load. The link cost is defined on both directions between each pair of nodes. Several least-cost-path algorithms have been developed for packet-switched networks. In particular, *Dijkstra's algorithm* and the *Bellman-Ford algorithm* are the most effective and widely used algorithms.

Our networking infrastructure deploys a variety of procedures, algorithms, and protocols for routing packets, depending on the applications, their significance, and the budget for building a network. Besides the least-cost-path algorithms that effectively identify the best possible paths, some nonoptimal algorithms can be used for applications that may not need complex and expensive routing protocols. Two examples of such *non-least-cost routing algorithms* are the *packet flooding algorithm* and *deflection routing*.

5.2.1 Dijkstra's Algorithm

Dijkstra's algorithm is a centralized routing algorithm that maintains information in a central location. The objective is to find the least-cost path from a given source node to all other nodes. This algorithm determines least-cost paths from a source node to a destination node by optimizing the cost in multiple iterations. Dijkstra's algorithm is as follows.

Begin Dijkstra's Algorithm

Define

> s = Source node
> k = Set of visited nodes by the algorithm
> α_{ij} = Cost of the link from node i to node j
> β_{ij} = Cost of the least-cost path from node i to node j

1. **Initialize**

   > $k = \{s\}$
   > **For** any $j \neq s$, $\beta_{sj} = \alpha_{sj}$

2. Next node

> **For** all *j*s where $j \notin k$,
>> **find** $x \notin k$ that $\beta_{sx} = \min \beta_{sj}$ for $j \notin k$
>> **add** x to k.

3. Least-cost paths

> **For** all *j*s where $j \notin k$,
>
> $\beta_{sj} = \min(\beta_{sj}, \beta_{sx} + \alpha_{xj})$ ∎

If any two nodes *i* and *j* are not connected directly, the cost for that link is infinity, indicated by $\beta_{ij} = \infty$. At step 1, *k* represents *s*, and β_{sj} computes the cost of the least-cost path from *s* to node *j*. At step 2, we want to find *x* among the neighboring nodes but not in *k* such that the cost is minimized. At step 3, we simply update the least-cost path by minimizing the route cost among the route options. The algorithm ends when all nodes have been visited and included in the algorithm. Steps 2 and 3 are repeated until paths are assigned to all nodes.

Example.   Using Dijkstra's algorithm, find the least-cost path from node A to node B in Figure 5.5.

Solution.   The detailed operation is shown in the Table 5.2. The first step is to find a path from the source node A to all other nodes. Thus, at the first row, $k = \{A\}$. It is obvious that there are direct links from A to nodes C and F. Therefore, the cost of the least-cost path for either node is 1, as shown in Figure 5.5. We then fill the table with AC(1) and AF(1), respectively. Given $k = \{A\}$, there are no connections between A and nodes D, E, G, and B. The

Table 5.2   Use of Dijkstra's algorithm

k	β_{AC}	β_{AF}	β_{AE}	β_{AD}	β_{AG}	β_{AB}
{A}	AC(1)	AF(1)	∞	∞	∞	∞
{A,C}	AC(1)	AF(1)	ACE(3)	ACD(6)	∞	∞
{A,C,F}	AC(1)	AF(1)	ACE(3)	ACD(6)	AFG(7)	∞
{A,C,F,E}	AC(1)	AF(1)	ACE(3)	ACED(4)	AFG(7)	∞
{A,C,F,E,D}	AC(1)	AF(1)	ACE(3)	ACED(4)	ACEDG(6)	ACEDB(7)
{A,C,F,E,D,G}	AC(1)	AF(1)	ACE(3)	ACED(4)	ACEDG(6)	ACEDB(7)
{A,C,F,E,D,G,B}	AC(1)	AF(1)	ACE(3)	ACED(4)	ACEDG(6)	ACEDB(7)

algorithm continues until all nodes have been included as $k = \{A,C,F,E,D,G,B\}$ and we obtain the least-cost path of ACEDB(7).

5.2.2 Bellman-Ford Algorithm

The *Bellman-Ford algorithm* finds the least-cost path from a source to a destination by passing through no more than ℓ links. The essence of the algorithm consists of the following steps.

Begin Bellman-Ford Algorithm

Define

s = Source node

α_{ij} = Cost of the link from node i to node j

$\beta_{ij}(\ell)$ = Cost of the least-cost path from i to j with no more than ℓ links

1. **Initialize**

   For all js where $j \neq s$

   $\beta_{ij}(0) = \infty$,

   For all ℓs

   $\beta_{ss}(\ell) = 0$,

2. **Least-cost path**

   For any node $j \neq s$ with predecessor node i:

   $\beta_{ij}(\ell + 1) = i$

If any two nodes i and j are not connected directly, the cost is infinity and thus $\beta_{ij}(\ell) = \infty$. At step 1, every value of β is initialized. At step 2, we increase the number of links ℓ in a sequence of iterations. During each iteration, we find the least-cost path, given the value of ℓ. The algorithm ends when all nodes have been visited and included in the algorithm.

Example.   Use the Bellman-Ford algorithm to find the least-cost path from node A to node B in Figure 5.5.

Solution.   Table 5.3 shows the details of the least-cost-path iterations. For iteration $\ell = 1$, only AC with cost 1 and AF with cost 1 exist, owing to the restriction enforced

Table 5.3   Use of the Bellman-Ford algorithm

ℓ	β_{AC}	β_{AF}	β_{AE}	β_{AD}	β_{AG}	β_{AB}
0	∞	∞	∞	∞	∞	∞
1	AC(1)	AF(1)	∞	∞	∞	∞
2	AC(1)	AF(1)	ACE(3)	ACD(6)	AFG(7)	∞
3	AC(1)	AF(1)	ACE(3)	ACED(4)	AFG(7)	ACDB(9)
4	AC(1)	AF(1)	ACE(3)	ACED(4)	ACEDG(6)	ACEDB(7)

by $\ell = 1$. This trend changes at iteration $\ell = 2$, when ACE with cost 3 can be added to the set of least-cost paths. As seen, the result of the final least-cost path is identical to the one obtained by Dijkstra's algorithm.

We can now compare these two algorithms. In step 2 of Bellman-Ford, the calculation of the link cost to any node j requires knowledge of the link cost to all neighboring nodes. In step 3 of Dijkstra's algorithm, each node requires knowledge of the network topology at each time of iteration. The performance of each algorithm varies network to network and depends on the topology and size of a particular network. The comparison of these two algorithms, therefore, depends on the speed of each to achieve its objective at its corresponding step given a network under routing. A simulation can clarify the efficiency of each algorithm given a certain network topology.

5.2.3   Packet Flooding Algorithm

The *packet flooding algorithm* is a very simple routing strategy involving less hardware setup. The essence of this routing method is that a packet received from a node is copied and transmitted on all outgoing links of that node except for the link that the packet arrived from. After the first transmission, all the routers within one hop receive the packet. After the second transmission, all the routers within two hops receive the packet, and so on. Unless a mechanism stops the transmission, the process continues; as a result, the volume of traffic increases with time, as shown in Figure 5.6.

In this figure, three packets arrive at node A from a source. The first packet is copied to both nodes B and E. At nodes B and E, the copies of the packet are copied to their neighboring nodes. This method has the deficiency of packet reflection: a node can receive an unwanted copy of a packet. Although this problem can be fixed by dropping unwanted packets at any time, the network does not function effectively,

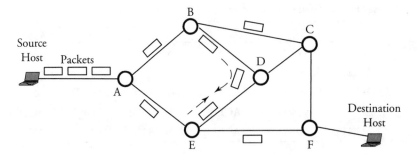

Figure 5.6   Packet flooding algorithm

owing to increased unnecessary traffic. One way to prevent packet duplication is to set up memory for each node so it remembers the identity of those packets that have already been retransmitted and blocks them.

5.2.4   Deflection Routing Algorithm

In the *deflection routing algorithm*, sometimes referred to as the *hot-potato routing algorithm*, a packet is sent to a destination determined at each router. At each step of the routing, a packet is examined with respect to its destination. If the requested link is free, the packet is sent on that link; otherwise, the packet is *deflected* onto another link, selected at random. The deflected packet is given an increment on its priority field. This increment gives the packet a better chance to win the contention with others in future contentions. For the deflected packet, if a new contention occurs with another packet in its next hop, the packet with the higher priority gets the desired link, and the other one is deflected with, of course, an increment in its priority field. In Figure 5.7, a packet is deflected at node B but eventually gets to node C, with a total of one additional hop and a total cost difference of 3, using node B.

5.3   Intradomain Routing Protocols

There are two classes of routing protocols: *intradomain routing protocol* or *intranetwork routing protocol* or *intranet*, and *interdomain routing protocol* or *internetwork routing protocol* or *extranet*. An intradomain routing protocol routes packets within a defined domain, such as for routing e-mail or Web browsing within an institutional network.

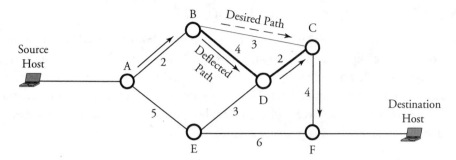

Figure 5.7 Deflection routing algorithm

One way of classifying the intradomain routing protocols is based on whether a routing protocol is *distributed* or *centralized*. In distributed routing, all nodes contribute in making the routing decision for each packet. In other words, an algorithm in distributed routing allows a node to gain information from all the nodes, but the least-cost path is determined locally. In centralized routing, only a designated node can make a decision. This central node uses the information gained from all nodes, but if the central node fails, the routing function in the network may be interrupted. A special case of centralized routing is *source routing*, whereby the routing decision is made only by the source server rather than by a network node. The outcome is then communicated to other nodes.

Intradomain routing protocols can also be classified as either *static* or *dynamic*. In static routing, a network establishes an initial topology of paths. Addresses of initial paths are loaded onto routing tables at each node for a certain period of time. The main disadvantage of static routing is that the size of the network has to be small enough to be controllable. Also, if a failure happens in the network, it is unable to react immediately. In dynamic routing, the state of the network is learned through the communication of each router with its neighbors. Thus, the state of each region in the network is propagated throughout the network after all nodes finally update their routing tables. Each router can find the best path to a destination by receiving updated information from surrounding nodes.

Figure 5.5 shows an example of an intradomain routing platform, where each point-to-point link connects an associated pair of routers and indicates the corresponding cost of the connection. A *host* is an end system that can be directly connected to the router. A *cost* is considered with the output side of each router interface. The most widely used intranetworking routing protocols are the two unicast routing protocols RIP and OSPF, explained next.

5.3.1   Open Shortest Path First (OSPF) Protocol

The *Open Shortest Path First* (OSPF) *protocol* is a better choice of intradomain routing protocols, especially for TCP/IP applications. OSPF is based on Dijkstra's algorithm, using a tree that describes the network topology to define the shortest path from each router to each destination address. Since it keeps track of all paths of a route, the OSPF protocol has more overhead than RIP, but provides more stability and useful options. The essence of this protocol is as follows.

Begin OSPF Protocol Steps

1. **Identify the Neighboring Node Cost Table.** For each router, obtain the cost to neighboring routers and list them in a table.

2. **Apply Dijkstra's algorithm.** Apply Dijkstra's algorithm for each host and router to calculate the least-cost path.

3. **Form a Routing Table.** Using step 2, form a routing table at each router.

4. **Update the Network's Routing Tables.** Using OSPF packets, each router sends the information containing "the neighboring (attached) router cost table" to "all" routers and hosts in the network (link-state routing process). ∎

Before focusing on the details of OSPF, we need to understand the essence of the *link-state routing* process that is used in step 4 of these protocol steps.

Link-State Process

In the *link-state process*, routers collaborate by exchanging packets carrying status information about their adjacent links. A router collects all the packets and determines the network topology, thereby executing its own shortest-route algorithm.

As explained in the section on RIP, with distance vector routing, each router must send a distance vector to all its neighbors. If a link cost changes, it may take a significant amount of time to spread the change throughout the network. The *link-state routing process* is designed to resolve this issue; each router sends routing information to all routers, not only to the neighbors. That way, the transmitting router discovers link-cost changes, so a new link cost is formed. Since each router receives all link costs from all routers, it is able to calculate the least-cost path to each destination of the network. The router can use any efficient routing algorithm, such as Dijkstra's algorithm, to find the shortest path.

The core function of the link-state process is the packet flooding algorithm, which requires no network topology information. Let us review the three important properties of packet flooding used in the link-state process. First, a packet always traverses completely between a source and a destination, given at least one path between these two nodes. This property makes this routing technique robust. Second, at least one copy of the packet arriving at the destination must possess the minimum delay, since all routers in the network are tried. This property makes the flooded information propagate to all routers very quickly. Third, all nodes in the network are visited whether they are directly or indirectly connected to the source node. This property makes every router receive all the information needed to update its routing table.

Details of OSPF Operation

To return to the OSPF protocol: Every router using OSPF is aware of its local link-cost status and periodically sends updates to all routers. After receiving update packets, each router is responsible for informing its sending router of receipt of the update. These communications, though, result in additional traffic, potentially leading to congestion. OSPF can provide a flexible link-cost rule based on type of service (TOS). The TOS information allows OSPF to select different routes for IP packets, based on the value of the TOS field. Therefore, instead of assigning a cost to a link, it is possible to assign different values of cost to a link, depending on the TOS value for each block of data.

TOS has five levels of values: *level 1* TOS, with the highest value to act by default, through *level 5* TOS, with the lowest value for minimized delay. By looking at these five categories, it is obvious that a router can build up to five routing tables for each TOS. For example, if a link looks good for delay-sensitive traffic, a router gives it a low, level 5 TOS value for low delay and a high, level 2 TOS value for all other traffic types. Thus, OSPF selects a different shortest path if the incoming packet is normal and does not require an optimal route.

OSPF Packet Format

An IP packet that contains OSPF has a standard broadcast IP address of 224.0.0.5 for the packet flooding algorithm. All OSPF packets use a 24-byte header as shown in Figure 5.8 that includes the following details:

- *Version number* indicates the version of OSPF.
- *Type* is one of the five types of packets for OSPF to choose from: *hello, database description, link-state request, link-state update,* and *link-state acknowledgment.*

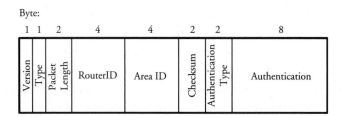

Figure 5.8   Open Shortest Path First (OSPF) header format

- *Packet length* specifies the length of the OSPF packet.
- *Router ID* specifies the packet's source router ID.
- *Area ID* refers to the area that the source router belongs to.
- *Checksum* specifies the standard IP checksum of the packet contents (see Chapter 3).
- *Authentication type* identifies which authentication method to choose (see Section 10.5).
- *Authentication* specifies the authentication method (see Section 10.5).

The *hello* packet specified in the *Type* field is used to detect each router's active neighbors. Each router periodically sends out *hello* packets to its neighbors to discover its active neighboring routers. Each packet contains the identity of the neighboring router interface taken from the *hello* packet already received from it. The *database description* packets are used for database structure exchange between two adjacent routers to synchronize their knowledge of network topology. The *link-state request* packet is transmitted to request a specific portion of the link-state database from a neighboring router. The *link-state update* packet transfers the link-state information to all neighboring routers. Finally, the *link-state acknowledgment* packet acknowledges the update of a link-state packet.

In summary, when a router is turned on, it transmits *hello* packets to all neighboring routers and then establishes routing connections by synchronizing databases. Periodically, each router sends a link-state update message describing its routing database to all other routers. Therefore, all routers have the same description of the topology of the local network. Every router calculates a shortest-path tree that describes the shortest path to each destination address, thereby indicating the closest router for communications.

Example.   Apply OSPF protocol on router A located in the network of Figure 5.5. Assume that each of gateway routers C, F, D, G, and B is further attached to a destination with IP addresses respectively 152.1.2.45, 178.3.3.2, 123.45.1.1, 148.11.58.2, and 165.2.2.33. Also assume router A uses 255.255.255.0 as a mask to determine subnets if there is a need for it.

Solution. In step 1 of the OSPF protocol, router A obtains costs of its neighboring routers: cost=1 from router C, and cost=1 from router F. In step 2 of the protocol, router A creates a Dijkstra least-cost table such as the one in Table 5.2. Notice here that the table in the first iteration may not look as complete as the one shown in Table 5.2, but it will ultimately match Table 5.2 after several iterations of updating. In step 3, a routing table is constructed as shown in Table 5.4. The first column of the table shows destination IP addresses that the associated gateway routers further process for routing beyond their domain. These IP addresses are reached using the associated gateway routers, and as a result router E, which is not a gateway router, is not associated with any IP address. Note that a routing table might include other parameters such as quality of service (QoS), type of service (TOS), gateway NAT router address, and so on. In step 4 of the protocol, router A sends the information containing "the neighboring (attached) router cost table" (routers C and F) to all routers C, F, E, D, G, and B in the network (link-state process). These four steps are updated periodically.

5.3.2 Routing Information Protocol (RIP)

The *Routing Information Protocol* (RIP) is a simple intradomain routing protocol. RIP is one of the most widely used routing protocols in the Internet infrastructure but is also appropriate for routing in smaller domains. In RIP, routers exchange information about reachable networks and the number of hops and associated costs required to reach a destination. This protocol is summarized as follows.

Table 5.4 Routing table constrcuted by router A in Figure 5.5, using the OSPF protocol

Destination IP Address	Designated Mask (If Needed)	Destination Router	Next Hop	Cost	Path	Updated Total Cost
152.1.2.45	255.255.255.0	C	C	1	AC	1
178.3.3.2	255.255.255.0	F	F	1	AF	1
-	-	E	C	1	ACE	3
123.45.1.1	255.255.255.0	D	C	1	ACED	4
148.11.58.2	255.255.255.0	G	C	1	ACEDG	6
165.2.2.33	255.255.255.0	B	C	1	ACEDB	7

Begin RIP Protocol Steps

1. **Identify the Neighboring Node Cost Table.** For each router, obtain the
   cost to neighboring routers and list them in a table.

2. **Apply the Bellman-Ford algorithm.** Apply the Bellman-Ford algorithm
   for each host and router to calculate the least-cost path.

3. **Form a Routing Table.** Using step 2, form a routing table at each
   router or host.

4. **Update the Network's Routing Tables.** Using RIP packets, send
   the information containing "entire routing table" to only
   "neighboring" routers and hosts in the network (distance vector
   process).

Before focusing on the details of RIP, we need to understand the essence of the
distance vector process (discussed next).

Distance Vector Process

The *distance vector process* was designed mainly for small network topologies.
The term *distance vector* derives from the fact that the protocol includes its routing
updates with a vector of distances, or hop counts. In distance vector routing, all
nodes exchange information only with their neighboring nodes. Nodes participating
in the same local network are considered neighboring nodes. In this protocol, each
individual node i maintains three vectors:

$$\mathbf{B_i} = [b_{i,1}, \ldots, b_{i,n}] = \textit{link-cost vector}$$
$$\mathbf{D_i} = [d_{i,1}, \ldots, d_{i,m}] = \textit{distance vector}$$
$$\mathbf{H_i} = [h_{i,1}, \ldots, h_{i,m}] = \textit{next-hop vector}$$

For the calculation of the link-cost vector, we consider node i to be directly connected to n networks out of the total of m existing networks. The link-cost vector $\mathbf{B_i}$ is
a vector containing the costs of node i to its directly connected network. For example,
$b_{i,1}$ refers to the cost of node i to network 1. Distance vector $\mathbf{D_i}$ contains the estimated
minimum delays from node i to all networks within its domain. For example, $d_{i,1}$ is
the estimated minimum delay from node i to network 1. Finally, the next-hop vector
$\mathbf{H_i}$ is a matrix vector containing the next node in the minimum-delay path from node
i to its directly connected network. As an example of this vector, $h_{i,1}$ refers to the next
node in the minimum-delay path from node i to network 1. Each node exchanges

its distance every r seconds with all its neighbors. Node i is responsible for updating both of its vectors by:

$$d_{i,j} = \min_{k \in \{1, \cdots, n\}} \left[d_{k,j} + b_{i,\, g(x,y)} \right] \qquad (5.1)$$

and

$$h_{i,j} = k, \qquad (5.2)$$

where $\{1, \ldots, n\}$ is the set of network nodes for node i, and $g(x, y)$ is a network that connects node x to node y; thus, $b_{i,\,g(x,y)}$ is the cost of node i to network $g(x,y)$. Equations (5.1) and (5.2) are a distributed version of the Bellman-Ford algorithm, which is used in RIP. Each router i begins with $d_{i,j} = b_{i,j}$ if it is directly connected to network j. All routers concurrently replace the distance vectors and compute Equation (5.1). Routers repeat this process again. Each iteration is equal to one iteration of step 2 in the Bellman-Ford algorithm, processed in parallel at each node of the graph. The shortest-length paths with a distance of at most one hop are considered after the first iteration. Then, the second iteration takes place, with the least-cost paths with at most two hops; this continues until all least-cost paths have been discovered.

Updating Routing Tables in RIP

Since RIP depends on distance vector routing, each router transmits its distance vector to its neighbors. Normally, updates are sent as replies whether or not requested. When a router broadcasts an RIP request packet, each router in the corresponding domain receiving the request immediately transmits a reply. A node within a short window of time receives distance-vectors from all its neighbors, and the total update occurs, based on incoming vectors. But this process is not practical, since the algorithm is asynchronous, implying that updates may not be received within any specified window of time.

RIP packets are sent typically in UDP fashion, so packet loss is always possible. In such environments, RIP is used to update routing tables after processing each distance vector. To update a routing table, if an incoming distance vector contains a new destination network, this information is added to the routing table. A node receiving a route with a smaller delay immediately replaces the previous route. Under certain conditions, such as the one after a router reset, the router can receive all the entries of its next hop to reproduce its new table.

The RIP *split-horizon* rule asserts that it is not practical to send information about a route back in the direction from which it was received. The split-horizon advantage is increased speed and removal of the incorrect route within a timeout. The RIP *poisoned-reverse* rule has a faster response and bigger message size. Despite the original split horizon, a node sends updates to neighbors with a hop count of 16 for routing information that arrived from those neighbors.

RIP Packet Format

Figure 5.9 shows the packet format of a version 1 RIP header. Each packet consists of several address distances. The RIP packet header contains the following specifications for the first address distance.

- *Command* indicates a request with value 1 or a reply with value 2.
- *Version number* specifies the version: RIP-1 or RIP-2.
- *Address family identifier* shows the type of address, such as an IP address.
- *IP address* provides the IP address in a particular network.
- *Metric* identifies the distance from a router to a specified network.

As seen in Figure 5.9, four additional fields containing all 0 bits in the version 1 RIP header are considered to be unused. In version 2 of RIP, three of these four fields have been attributed to three metrics defined as follows: the first 4-byte 0 field starting from right to left is dedicated to the *next hop* where packets for this entry should be forwarded; the next 4-byte 0 is dedicated to the *subnet mask,* which can be applied to the IP address to resolve the network portion of the address; and the next 2-byte 0 field is dedicated to the *route tag,* which is used for readvertising routes such that routes for networks within the RIP routing domain can be separated from routes imported from other protocols.

If a link cost is set to 1, the *metric* field acts as a hop count. But if link costs have larger values, the number of hops becomes smaller. Each packet consists of several

Byte:

1	1	2	2	2	4	4	4	4
Command	Version Number	0	Address Family Identifier	0	IP Address	0	0	Metric

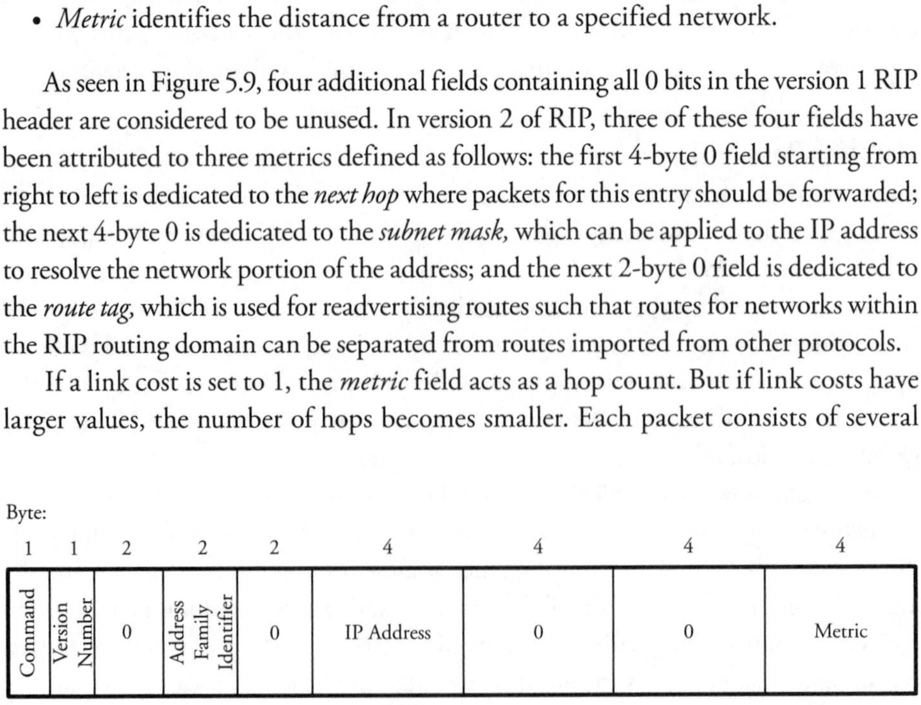

Figure 5.9   Routing Information Protocol (RIP) version 1 header

address distances. If more than one address distance is needed, the header shown in Figure 5.9 can be extended to as many address distances as are requested, except for the *command* and *version number* and its 2 bytes of 0s; the remaining field structure can be repeated for each address distance.

Example.   Apply RIP on router A located in the network in Figure 5.5. Assume that each of gateway routers C, F, D, G, and B is further attached to a destination with IP addresses respectively 152.1.2.45, 178.3.3.2, 123.45.1.1, 148.11.58.2, and 165.2.2.33. Also assume router A uses 255.255.255.0 as a mask to determine subnets if there is a need for it.

Solution.   In step 1 of the RIP protocol, router A obtains costs of its neighboring routers: cost=1 from router C, and cost=1 from router F. In step 2 of the protocol, router A creates a Bellman-Ford least-cost table such as the one in Table 5.3. Notice here that the table in the first iteration may not look as complete as the one shown in Table 5.3, but it will ultimately match Table 5.3 after several iterations of updating. In step 3, a routing table is constructed as shown in Table 5.4 (this is similar to the one developed for the OSPF case). The first column of the table shows destination IP addresses that the associated gateway routers further process for routing beyond their domain. These IP addresses are reached using the associated gateway routers, and as a result router E, which is not a gateway router, is not associated with any IP address. Note that a routing table might include other parameters such as quality of service (QoS), gateway NAT router address, and so on. In step 4 of the protocol, router A sends the information containing the "entire routing table" to only "neighboring" (attached) routers C and F (distance vector process). These four steps are updated periodically.

Issues and Limitations of RIP

One of the disadvantages of RIP is its slow convergence in response to a change in topology. *Convergence* refers to the point in time at which the entire network becomes updated. In large networks, a routing table exchanged between routers becomes very large and difficult to maintain, which may lead to an even slower convergence. Also, RIP might lead to suboptimal routes, since its decision is based on hop counts. Thus, low-speed links are treated equally or sometimes preferred over high-speed links. Another issue with RIP is the *count-to-infinity* restriction. Distance vector protocols have a limit on the number of hops after which a route is considered inaccessible. This restriction would cause issues for large networks.

Other issues with RIP stem from the distance vector algorithm. First, reliance on hop counts is one deficiency, as is the fact that routers exchange all the network values via periodic broadcasts of the entire routing table. Also, the distance vector algorithm may cause loops and delays, since they are based on periodic updates. For example, a route may go into a *hold* state if the corresponding update information is not received in a certain amount of time. This situation can translate into a significant amount of delay in update convergence in the network before the network discovers that route information has been lost.

Another major deficiency is the lack of support for variable-length subnet masks. RIP does not exchange mask information when it sends routing updates. A router receiving a routing update uses its locally defined subnet mask for the update, which would lead to complications and misinterpretation in a variably subnetted network. Distance vector networks do not have hierarchies, which makes them incapable of integrating with larger networks.

5.4   Interdomain Routing Protocols

Unlike intradomain routing protocols, *interdomain routing protocols* create a network of networks, or an *internetwork*. Interdomain routing protocols route packets outside of a defined domain. Each domain consists of several networks and routers that can be accessed publicly. Figure 5.10 shows an example of internetworking, in which a packet at router R_1 faces two defined larger service provider domains, A and B. Each service domain is shown by a number of interconnected circles, each representing a network or a router. Obviously, at router R_1, finding the best path for a packet to go to a particular domain is a challenge. The *Border Gateway Protocol* (BGP) as one of the widely

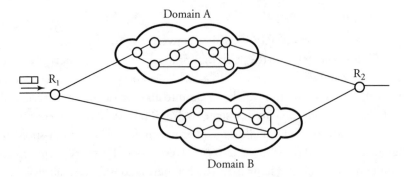

Figure 5.10   Internetworking, in which routing a packet faces two defined service domains

used interdomain protocols helps meet this challenge, and is discussed in the upcoming section. In order to understand the essence of BGP, we first need to learn the hierarchy of the routing structure under the *autonomous system* (AS) model, discussed next.

5.4.1   Autonomous System (AS)

An *autonomous system* (AS) in the Internet is defined as a collection of connected IP routing devices under the control of one network administrative entity that presents a common defined routing policy to the Internet. An autonomous system can also be called a *domain* with the company operating the domain called the *Internet service provider* (ISP). Domains A and B in Figure 5.10 can be treated as autonomous systems A and B, respectively, if each is controlled autonomously under an independent ISP. The need to see the Internet from the angle of autonomous systems makes it easier to view its administration. Storing routing information at each of the hosts and routers would require enormous amounts of memory and increases the complexity of route computation in networks as large as the Internet.

One can view the big picture of the Internet organized as a collection of autonomous systems, each of which is under the control of a single administrative entity or ISP. For example, a corporation's internal network can be a single AS. The need for autonomous systems is attributed to the increasing number of routers leading to large overhead involved in computing, storing, and communicating routing information. There is also a definition in some references that came into use that multiple organizations can run BGP using private AS numbers to an ISP connecting the organizations to the Internet. We should note that even though there may be multiple autonomous systems supported by a single ISP, the Internet only recognizes the routing policy of the ISP. In such a case, the ISP must have an officially registered *autonomous system number* (ASN). Luckily, a unique ASN is designated for each AS that identifies each autonomous network in the Internet.

5.4.2   Border Gateway Protocol (BGP)

The *Border Gateway Protocol* (BGP) is a preferred routing protocol for interdomain (among autonomous systems) communications. BGP is involved in making routing decisions based on network policies, a network's path status, and rule sets configured by a network administrator. With BGP, routers exchange comprehensive information about routes to a certain destination instead of simply costs and the best link. Before we learn the details of this protocol, let us first get familiar with the BGP packets to be discussed next.

BGP Packets

There are four different BGP packets as shown in Figure 5.11 (a), (b), (c), and (d), respectively, as follows:

(a) *Open packet*. This packet requests establishment of a relationship between two routers; it has the following header fields: *Optional Parameters* is a variable-length field containing a list of optional parameters used to advertise the support for optional capabilities, such as multiprotocol extensions, route refresh, and so on. *Optional Parameters Length* is a 1-byte field expressing the total length of the Optional Parameters field. *BGP Identifier* is a 4-byte field indicating the IP address assigned to an originating BGP router. *Hold Time* is a 2-byte field indicating the number of seconds proposed by the originator for the hold time of a BGP session. *My Autonomous System* is a 2-byte field to indicate the AS number of the originator. *Version* is a 1-byte field indicating the BGP version. *Type* is a 1-byte field specifying one of the four packet types. *Length* is a 2-byte field specifying the total length of the packet, including the header. *Marker* is a 16-byte field used to detect the loss of synchronization between BGP peers and to authenticate the packet.

(b) *Update packet*. This packet conveys update information about routes and advertises a single feasible route, or withdrawn multiple unfeasible routes, or both. The packet header has the following header fields: *Network Layer Reachability Information* (NLRI) is a variable-length field containing a list of IP prefixes that can be reached via this path using [Length – Prefix]. A Length value of 0 indicates a prefix that matches all IP prefixes. *Path Attributes* is a variable-length field listing the attributes associated with the Network Layer Reachability Information field. Each path attribute is a variable-length field of [Attribute Type, Attribute Length, Attribute Value]. *Total Path Attribute Length* is a 2-byte field that indicates the total length of the Path Attributes field, in bytes. *Withdrawn Routes* is a variable-length field containing a list of unreachable routes that are to be withdrawn from service. *Unfeasible Routes Length* is a 2-byte field indicating the total length of the Withdrawn Routes field, in bytes. *Type, Length,* and *Marker* fields are similar to the same fields in *Open packet*.

(c) *Keep-alive packet*. Once a relationship between two routers is established, this packet confirms its neighbor relationship frequently. The packet header has the following header fields: *Type, Length,* and *Marker, which are also* similar to the same fields in *Open packet*.

(d) *Notification packet.* This packet is used when an error occurs. The packet header has the following header fields: *Error Code* is a 1-byte field indicating the error code, such as 1 for "message header error" or 4 for "Hold Timer Expired." Each *Error Code* may have one or more *Error Subcodes* associated with it. *Error Subcode* is 1-byte field providing more specific information about the nature of the reported error. The *Type, Length,* and *Marker* fields are similar to the same fields in *Open packet.*

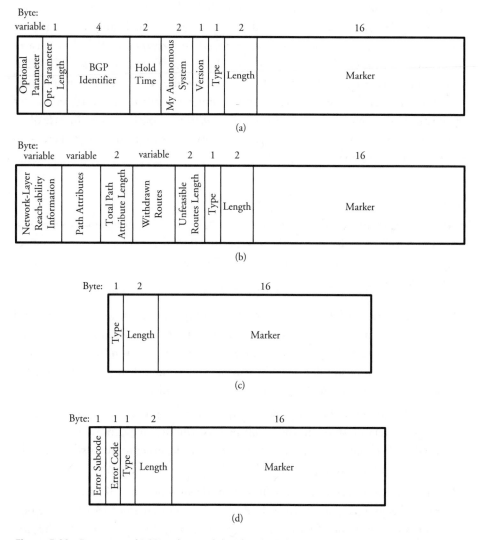

Figure 5.11   Four types of BGP packets and their header fields: (a) open packet, (b) update packet, (c) keep-alive packet, and (d) notification packet

In BGP, two contributing routers can exchange routing information even if they are located in two different autonomous systems. When an external destination is chosen, a router sends the information to all internal neighbors. Then, a network entity decides with the help of all other routers whether a selected route is possible, and if so, the route is added to the router's database. Thus, the new update packet is propagated.

The update packet can include the information of a single route that passes through a network. This information can be divided into three fields: the *network-layer reach-ability information* field, the *path attributes* field, and the *total path attributes length* field. *The network-layer reach-ability information* field has a list of subnetwork identifiers that can be found by the router. The *path attributes* field has a list of attributes that can be referred to a specific route. The second type of update information is used to remove one or more routes identified by the IP address of the destination subnetwork. In this case, the *notification* packet is sent in case of an error, which may be authentication errors, validity errors in the update packet, or an expired hold-time error.

BGP Details

BGP was created to find a solution to interdomain routing among autonomous systems and is used to perform interdomain routing. It works well for making a connection when a long-haul TCP session must be established. BGP has three functional components:

1. *Neighbor relationship.* The neighbor relationship refers to an agreement between two routers in two different autonomous systems to exchange routing information on a regular basis. A router may reject its participation in establishing a neighbor relationship for several reasons, such as the rule of the domain, overload, or a temporary malfunctioning of external links.

2. *Neighbor maintenance.* Neighbor maintenance is a process of maintaining the neighbor relationship already established. Normally, each corresponding router needs to find out whether the relationship with the other router is still available. For this reason, two routers send *keep-alive* packet to each other.

3. *Network maintenance.* The last BGP component is network maintenance. Each router keeps a database of the subnets that it can reach and tries to get the best route for each subnet. One of the most important techniques in BGP is the *path vector routing protocol.*

RIP and OSPF are not suitable for interdomain routing protocols. As discussed earlier, distance vector routing is used to send information to each of a router's neighbors, and then each router builds up a routing database. However, a router is not aware of the identity of routers on any particular path. Two problems arise here. First, if different routers give different information to an assigned cost, it is impossible to have stable and loop-free routes. Second, an autonomous system can have limitations about which specific autonomous system should be used. This is true while the distance vector algorithm has no information about the autonomous systems. Each router sends its link cost to all other routers and then starts routing calculations. Two issues can arise in link-state routing:

1. Different independent systems can use different costs and have different limitations. The link-state protocol allows a router to make the topology, and its metrics may be different for each independent system. In this case, it is impossible to create a reliable routing algorithm.

2. When flood routing occurs, the use of an interdomain routing protocol across the independent system can be unstable.

To resolve these issues, BGP considers an alternative solution: the *path vector routing protocol*, which provides information about how to reach a network given a certain router and identifies which autonomous system should be visited. The path vector routing protocol is different from the distance vector algorithm, in which each path has information about cost and distance. In the path vector routing protocol, these packages of information are not included, and all visited autonomous systems and all components of a domain reaching the destination network are listed in each routing information package. Thus, a router can be programmed to refuse the acceptance of a particular path if the information about the path is not included in the package it receives.

Figure 5.12 shows the implementation of BGP in handling a long-haul TCP connection. Assume that host 1 in autonomous system 1 (domain 1) under the control of ISP 1 tries to establish a TCP connection to host 2 located in autonomous system 3 (domain 3) under the control of ISP 3. Autonomous systems 1 and 3 are connected via autonomous system 2 (domain 2). Each two autonomous systems can be connected through one or more pairs of border routers; for example, [R13 and R21], [R13 and R24], and [R15 and R24] act as paired border routers for autonomous systems 1 and 2. These pairs of routers can exchange routing information and are often referred to as BGP *peers* when they engage a long-haul TCP connection.

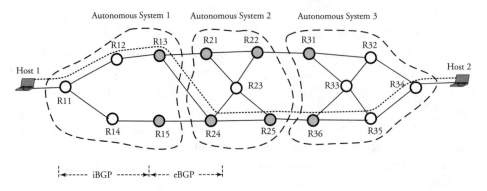

Figure 5.12 Use of BGP in an interdomain routing

As a result, TCP connections can be made through one of the paired border routers [R13 and R21], [R13 and R24], and [R15 and R24]. In addition, each pair of internal routers creates a mesh of TCP connections within each autonomous system. In this case we can also define internal BGP peers as border routers residing in the same autonomous system.

With BGP routing, each autonomous system learns which destinations are reachable via its neighboring autonomous systems. Note that a destination in BGP is the *prefix* of a CIDR address representing one or more subnets. For example, if a subnet with CIDR address 188.32.8.0/24 is attached to an autonomous system, the autonomous system uses BGP to advertise the prefix 188.32.8.0/24 (the first 24 bits of 188.32.8.0). In an ISP, every border router learns about all routes experienced by all the other border routers. For example, when a border router in an ISP learns about an address prefix, all other routers in the ISP learn of this prefix. This makes it possible for any router of the ISP to reach the prefix.

BGP utilizes two primary modes of data exchange, *internal* BGP (iBGP) and *external* BGP (eBGP). The *My Autonomous System* field of the *Open packet* indicates the AS number of the originator, and determines whether the BGP session is iBGP if eBGP. The iBGP mode may be used for routing within an autonomous system to communicate with internal peers, and runs between two BGP routers in the same autonomous system. A BGP session between two BGP peers is said to be an iBGP session if the BGP peers are in the same autonomous system. To avoid loops within an autonomous system, an iBGP peer does not advertise the prefix it learned from a pair of other iBGP peers. Thus, BGP is not set up to propagate routes throughout the autonomous system; however, internal peers are configured to advertise any route advertised by one router to all peers within the autonomous system. To advertise routes to internal peers, iBGP mode is used.

In contrast, eBGP can be used for routing beyond an autonomous system to communicate with external peers and runs between two BGP routers in different autonomous systems. In other words, in eBGP, peering occurs in two different autonomous systems. With eBGP, the time-to-live (TTL) field of a packet is set to 1, implying that peers are directly connected. An eBGP peer advertises all the best routes it knows or that it has learned from its peers. External peers are configured to advertise routes experienced from eBGP peers to other peers. For example, in Figure 5.12, applying the eBGP mode session between the border routers R13 and R24, autonomous system 1 forwards a list of prefixes that are reachable from autonomous system 1 to autonomous system 2; autonomous system 2 forwards a list of prefixes that are reachable from autonomous system 2 to autonomous system 1. Autonomous systems 2 and 3 also exchange similar related information via one of the border router pairs such as R22 and R31.

Route Selection Policy in BGP

So far, we learned that with BGP, the information learned by a border router of an autonomous system can be shared with another attached autonomous system. For this, BGP uses eBGP and iBGP to share routes with all the routers of an autonomous system. If there is more than one route to a prefix address, the selection of the best route by a router requires the implementation of a policy. The following list presents some of the important policies used in BGP:

- Route selection based on the highest preference of the associated autonomous system, set locally by a router and learned by another router, and implemented by a network administrator.
- Route selection based on the least number of autonomous systems. This policy is applied when there are multiple routes from a source to a destination crossing other autonomous systems.
- Route selection based on the least-cost path determined within the autonomous system.
- Route selection based on a learning process so that each router in an autonomous system may learn a route from the router it is connected to.

For example, in Figure 5.12, host 1 starts a TCP connection to host 2. The details of TCP connections will be described in Chapter 8, but for now just consider this as a connection between the two hosts. Assume host 1 finds from the BGP learning process that the exiting point where its border router R13 connects to R24 is the best choice to reach host 2. According to BGP, host 1 opens a TCP connection to the destination host 2, for which router R13 sends an *open* packet to R24. The TCP packets are identified by R24, telling it which domain the sender belongs to.

Any of the engaging border routers in each autonomous system sends a *keep-alive* packet to its neighbors to prevent an agreed hold time from expiring. Router R13 learns that it can reach host 2 via either router R21 or router R24. Border routers R25 and R36 are similarly engaging in the TCP connection. Each router in turn decides which route in the set of routes is the best one to use taking into account some strategies or policies. Additionally, in this case, choosing a path is based on the least number of autonomous systems, of which there is only one intermediating autonomous system in this example (autonomous system 2).

5.5   Internet Protocol Version 6 (IPv6)

The use of IPv4 has resulted in the exhaustion of the 32-bit address space to the extent that IPv4 has run out of addressing spaces. Therefore, 128-bit address spaces were introduced with *Internet Protocol version 6* (IPv6). It enjoys tremendous popularity because of its simplicity and flexibility in adapting to diverse network technologies. Compatible with IPv4, IPv6 also supports real-time applications, including those that require guaranteed QoS. Figure 5.13 shows the IPv6 header. A brief description of the fields in the header follows.

- *Version* is the same as in IPv4, indicating the version number of the protocol. Therefore, IPv6 carries a value of 6 for this field

- *Traffic class* is an 8-bit field and specifies the priority level assigned to a packet, and its functionality is similar to ToS in IPv4.

- *Flow label* is a 20-bit field and indicates a certain flow of datagrams (packets).

- *Payload length* is a 16-bit field that specifies the number of data (payload) bytes of the datagram.

- *Next header* specifies the protocol, such as TCP or UDP, to which the data field of the datagram is delivered.

- *Hop limit* is the same as the time-to-live field in IPv4.

- *Source address* and *destination address* are each identified by a 128-bit field address.

Byte:

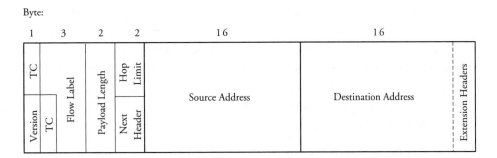

Figure 5.13   An IPv6 packet format

The IPv4 and IPv6 header formats have some notable differences. First, IPv6 uses a 128-bit address field rather than the 32-bit field in IPv4. The 128-bit field can support a maximum of 3.4×10^{38} IP addresses. IPv6 has a simpler header format, eliminating the fragmentation, the checksum, and header length fields. The removal of the checksum field in IPv6 allows for faster processing at the routers without sacrificing functionality. In IPv6, *error detection* and *correction* are handled at the data link and the TCP layers. Note also that IPv6 can accommodate the QoS requirements for some applications. Besides all these significant advantages, IPv6 can provide built-in security features such as confidentiality and authentication. These features are discussed in Chapter 10.

5.5.1   IPv6 Addressing Format

With its large address spacing, IPv6 network addressing is very flexible. To efficiently represent the 128-bit address of IPv6 in a compact form, hexadecimal digits are used. A colon separates each of the four hexadecimal digits. For example, 2FB4:10 AB:4123:CEBF:54CD:3912:AE7B:0932 can be a source address. In practice, IPv6 addresses contain a lot of bits that are zero. The address is commonly denoted in a more compact form. For example, an address denoted by 2FB4:0000:0000:0000:54 CD:3912:000B:0932 can be compressed to 2FB4::::54CD:3912:B:932.

Similar to CODER, in IPv6, the size of a block of addresses is determined by adding a slash (/) followed by a number in decimal whose value is the length of the network prefix in bits. For example, the address block 1::DB8:0:1:1/34 has 34 bits in the prefix and such a block contains $2^{128-34} = 2^{94}$ addresses.

The network address space is classified into various types, each of which is assigned a binary prefix. Currently, only a small portion of the address space has been assigned, with the remaining reserved for future use. One of the address types with a leading byte of 1s is assigned for multicast; the rest of the currently assigned types are used for unicast applications. Apart from the unicast and multicast addresses, IPv6 introduces *anycast* addresses. An anycast address is similar to a multicast address and identifies a group of network devices for making connections. However, unlike with multicast addressing, a packet needs to be forwarded to any one device in the group. Anycast addresses share the address space with unicast address types. IPv6 reserves some addresses for special purposes.

5.5.2   Extension Header

Extension headers are positioned between the header and the payload. The functionality of the options field in IPv4 is specified in the extension header, while the extension header is more flexible than the options field. Figure 5.14, top, shows a single extension header to a TCP segment (TCP is a layer 4 protocol). If multiple extension headers are used, they are concatenated, as shown in Figure 5.14, making it mandatory for them to be processed in the sequence in which they are listed. Figure 5.14 specifies the sequence in which the extension headers are to be listed where the next header can be routing, fragment, authentication, and TCP.

5.5.3   Packet Fragmentation

In IPv6, fragmentation is permitted only at the source. The result of this restriction is faster processing of packets at routers. Before transmitting a packet, a host performs a *maximum transmission unit* (MTU) discovery in the route of the packet. The minimum MTU obtained determines the packet size and thus requires the route from the host to the destination to remain steady. If this minimum value of the physical network is less than the packet size to be transmitted, the intermediate router

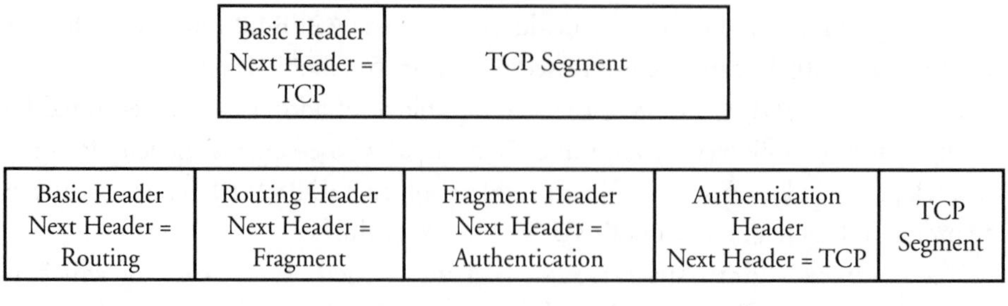

Basic Header Next Header = TCP	TCP Segment

Basic Header Next Header = Routing	Routing Header Next Header = Fragment	Fragment Header Next Header = Authentication	Authentication Header Next Header = TCP	TCP Segment

Figure 5.14 Concatenated IPv6 extension header

discards the packet and sends an error message back to the source. In rare cases, the packet needs to be fragmented, and the extension header contains the fragmentation information.

5.5.4   Other Features of IPv6

Other features of IPv6 will be covered in various upcoming chapters. For example, the routing table based on IPv6 will be presented in Chapter 12, and tunneling of IPv4 through IPv6 will be covered in Chapter 14.

5.6   Congestion Control at the Network Layer

Congestion represents an overloaded condition in a network. Congestion control can be achieved by optimum usage of the available resources in the network. Figure 5.15 shows a set of performance graphs for networks in which three possible cases are compared: no congestion, moderate congestion, and severe congestion. These plots indicate that if a network has no congestion control, the consequence may be a severe performance degradation, even to the extent that the carried load starts to fall with increasing offered load. The ideal situation is the one with no loss of data, as a result of no congestion, as shown in the figure. Normally, a significant amount of engineering effort is required to design a network with no congestion.

Congestion can be either *logical* or *physical*, as shown in Figure 5.16. In this figure, host A and host B, each located in a different LAN, try to communicate,

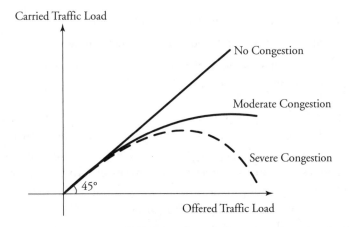

Figure 5.15   Comparison among networks in which no congestion, moderate congestion, and severe congestion exist

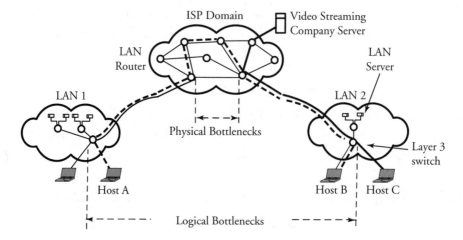

Figure 5.16   Forms of bottleneck along a round-trip path between two users

passing through their connected ISP domain. The queueing feature in the two remote devices, such as the LAN's layer 3 switches shown in the figure, can create a logical bottleneck between host A and host B. This issue may have a cause rooted in the exhaustive bandwidth usage at the LAN 2 layer 3 switch by host C as it performs video streaming at a server.

Meanwhile, insufficient bandwidth—a resource shortage—on physical links between routers and the network can also be a bottleneck, resulting in congestion. Resource shortage can occur

- At the *link layer*, where the link bandwidth runs out
- At the *network layer*, where the queues of packets at nodes go out of control
- At the *transport layer*, where logical links between two routers within a communication session go out of control

One key way to avoid congestion is to carefully allocate network resources to users and applications. Network resources, such as bandwidth and buffer space, can be allocated to competing applications. Devising optimum and fair resource-allocation schemes can control congestion to some extent. In particular, congestion control applies to controlling data flow among a group of senders and receivers, whereas flow control is specifically related to the arrangement of traffic flows on links. Both resource allocation and congestion control are not limited to any single level of the protocol hierarchy. Resource allocation occurs at switches, routers, and end hosts. A router can send information on its available resources so that an end host can reserve resources at the router to use for various applications.

General methods of congestion control are either *unidirectional* or *bidirectional*. These two schemes are described next.

5.6.1   Unidirectional Congestion Control

A network can be controlled unidirectionally through *back-pressure signaling, transmission of choke packets*, and *traffic policing*. Figure 5.17 shows a wide area network of eight routers: R1 through R8. These routers connect a variety of servicing companies: wireless cellular, residential, and corporate networks. In such a configuration, congestion among routing nodes may occur at certain hours of the day.

The first type of congestion control is achieved by generating a *back-pressure signal* between two routers. The back-pressure scheme is similar to fluid flow in pipes. When one end of a pipe is closed, the pressure propagates backward to slow the flow of water at the source. The same concept can be applied to networks. When a node becomes congested, it slows down the traffic on its incoming links until the congestion is relieved. For example, in the figure, router R4 senses overloading traffic and consequently sends signals in the form of back-pressure packets to router R3 and thereby to router R2, which is assumed to be the source of overwhelming the path. Packet

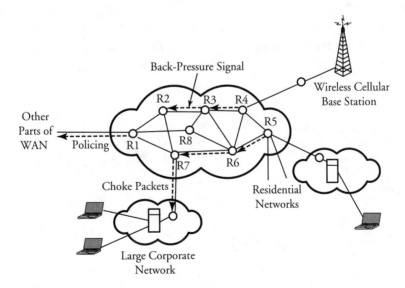

Figure 5.17   Unidirectional congestion control

flow can be controlled on a hop-by-hop basis. Back-pressure signaling is propagated backward to each node along the path until the source node is reached. Accordingly, the source node restricts its packet flow, thereby reducing the congestion.

Choke-packet transmission is another solution to congestion. In this scheme, choke packets are sent to the source node by a congested node to restrict the flow of packets from the source node. A router or even an end host can send these packets when it is near full capacity, in anticipation of a condition leading to congestion at the router. The choke packets are sent periodically until congestion is relieved. On receipt of the choke packets, the source host reduces its traffic-generation rate until it stops receiving them.

The third method of congestion control is *policing* and is quite simple. An edge router, such as R1 in the figure, acts as a "traffic police" and directly monitors and controls its immediate connected consumers. In the figure, R1 is policing traffic coming from "other parts of WAN" flowing into the network, and may prohibit or slow down certain patterns of traffic to keep the network available bandwidth and functionality in good shape.

5.6.2 Bidirectional Congestion Control

Figure 5.18 illustrates *bidirectional congestion control*, a host-based resource-allocation technique. Suppose at one side of an Internet service provider (ISP) a major Web server serves substantial queries while at the other side of the ISP a large corporate file server is the destination for numerous file queries. Assuming these two servers have interactions, the ISP in this case needs to balance the traffic bidirectionally between these two hot traffic spots and control the rate at which these spots receive

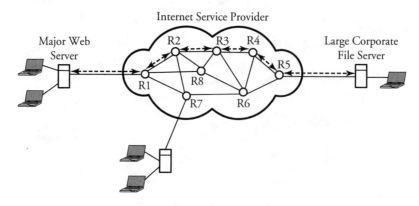

Figure 5.18   Bidirectional congestion control

traffic. This traffic control has to be based on observable network conditions, such as delay and packet loss. If a source detects long delays and packet losses, it slows down its packet flow rate. All sources in the network adjust their packet-generation rate similarly; thus, congestion comes under control. Implicit signaling is widely used in packet-switched networks, such as the Internet.

In bidirectional signaling, network routing nodes alert the source of congested resources by setting bits in the header of a packet intended for the source. An alternative mechanism for signaling is to send control packets as choke packets to the source, alerting it of any congested resources in the network. The source then slows down its rate of packet flow, and when it receives a packet, the source checks for the bit that indicates congestion. If the bit is set along the path of packet flow, the source slows down its sending rate.

5.6.3   Random Early Detection (RED)

Random early detection (RED) avoids congestion by detecting and taking appropriate measures early. When packet queues in a router's buffer experience congestion, they discard all incoming packets that could not be kept in the buffer. This *tail-drop policy* leads to two serious problems: global synchronization of TCP sessions and prolonged congestion in the network. RED overcomes the disadvantages of the tail-drop policy in queues by randomly dropping the packets when the average queue size exceeds a given minimum threshold.

From the statistical standpoint, when a queueing buffer is full, the policy of random packet drop is better than multiple-packet drop all at once. RED works as a feedback mechanism to inform TCP sessions that the source anticipates congestion and must reduce its transmission rate. The packet-drop probability is calculated based on the weight allocation on its flow. For example, heavy flows experience a larger number of dropped packets. The average queue size is computed, using an exponentially weighted moving average so that RED does not react to spontaneous transitions caused by bursty Internet traffic. When the average queue size exceeds the maximum threshold, all further incoming packets are discarded.

RED Setup at Routers

With RED, a router continually monitors its own queue length and available buffer space. When the buffer space begins to fill up and the router detects the possibility of congestion, it notifies the source implicitly by dropping a few packets from the source. The source detects this through a time-out period or a duplicate ACK. Consequently, the router drops packets earlier than it has to and thus implicitly notifies the source to reduce its congestion window size. The "random" part of the RED method suggests that the router drops an arriving packet with some drop probability when the queue length exceeds a threshold. This scheme computes the average queue length, $E[N_q]$, recursively by

$$E[N_q] = (1 - \alpha)E[N_q] + \alpha N_i, \tag{5.3}$$

where N_i is the instantaneous queue length, and $0 < \alpha < 1$ is the weight factor. The average queue length is used as a measure of load. Every time a new packet arrives at the gateway of a network, N_i is measured. With having N_i, the average queue length, $E[N_q]$, is obtained. The reason for obtaining the average queue length is that the Internet has bursty traffic, and the instantaneous queue length may not be an accurate measure of the queue length.

RED sets minimum and maximum thresholds on the queue length, N_{min} and N_{max}, respectively. A router applies the following scheme for deciding whether to service or drop a new packet. If $E[N_q] \geq N_{max}$, any new arriving packet is dropped. If $E[N_q] \leq N_{min}$, the packet is queued. If $N_{min} < E[N_q] < N_{max}$, the arriving packet is dropped with probability P given by

$$P = \frac{\delta}{1 - c\delta}, \tag{5.4}$$

where coefficient c is set by the router to determine how quickly it wants to reach a desired P.

The probability of packet drop, P, increases slowly when $N_{min} < E[N_q] < N_{max}$, reaching a maximum packet drop probability, P_{max}, at the upper threshold. In fact, c can be figured to be the number of arriving packets that have been queued. We can then obtain δ from

$$\delta = \left(\frac{E[N_q] - N_{min}}{N_{max} - N_{min}} \right) P_{max}. \tag{5.5}$$

In essence, when the queue length is below the minimum threshold, the packet is admitted into the queue. Figure 5.19 shows the variable setup in RED congestion avoidance. When the queue length is between the two thresholds, the packet-drop probability increases as the queue length increases. When the queue length is above the maximum threshold, the packet is always dropped. Also, shown in Equation (5.4), the packet-drop probability depends on a variable that represents the number of arriving packets from a flow that has been queued. When the queue length increases, all that is needed is to drop one packet from the source. The source then halves its congestion window size.

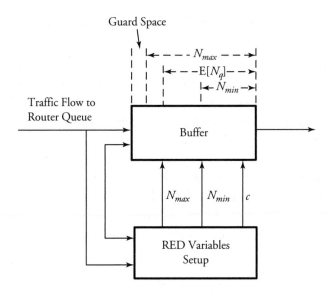

Figure 5.19 Variables setup in the RED congestion-avoidance method

Once a small number of packets are dropped, the associated sources reduce their congestion windows if the average queue length exceeds the minimum threshold, and therefore the traffic to the router drops. With this method, any congestion is avoided by an early dropping of packets.

RED also has a certain amount of fairness associated with it; for larger flows, more packets are dropped, since P for these flows could become large. One of the challenges in RED is to set the optimum values for N_{min}, N_{max}, and c. Typically, N_{min} has to be set large enough to keep the throughput at a reasonably high level but low enough to avoid congestion. In practice, for most networks on the Internet, the N_{max} is set to twice the minimum threshold value. Also, as shown by *guard space* in Figure 5.19, there has to be enough buffer space beyond N_{max}, as Internet traffic is bursty.

5.6.4   A Quick Estimation of Link Blocking

A number of techniques can be used to evaluate a communication network's blocking probabilities. These techniques can vary according to accuracy and to network architectures. One of the most interesting and relatively simple approaches to calculating the level of blocking involves the use of Lee's probability graphs. Although Lee's technique requires approximations, it nonetheless provides reasonably accurate results.

5.6.5   Lee's Serial and Parallel Connection Rules

Lee's method is based on two fundamental rules of *serial* and *parallel* connections. Each link is represented by its blocking probability, and the entire network of links is evaluated, based on blocking probabilities represented on each link, using one or both of the rules. This approach is easy to formulate, and the formula directly relates to the underlying network structures, without requiring any other detailed parameters. Thus, Lee's approach provides insight into the network structures, giving a remarkable solution for performance evaluations.

Let p be the probability that a link is busy, or the percentage of link utilization. Thus, the probability that a link is idle is denoted by $q = 1 - p$. Now, consider a simple case of two links in parallel to complete a connection with probabilities p_1 and p_2. The composite blocking probability, B_p, is the probability that both links are in use, or

$$B_p = p_1p_2. \tag{5.6}$$

If these two links are in series to complete a connection, the blocking probability, B_s, is determined as 1 minus the probability that both links are available:

$$B_s = 1 - (1 - p_1)(1 - p_2). \tag{5.7}$$

We can generalize the estimation of a network of links by two fundamental rules.

Rule 1: For a parallel connection of links, the blocking probability is estimated by forming the product of the blocking probabilities for the subnetworks, as shown in Figure 5.20. Let a source and a destination be connected in general through n links with probabilities p_1 through p_n, respectively, as shown in Figure 5.20. Therefore, if the source and the destination are linked through parallel connections, the probability of blocking B_p is obtained from a product form as follows:

$$B_p = p_1p_2 \cdots p_n. \tag{5.8}$$

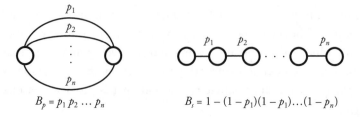

$$B_p = p_1 p_2 \cdots p_n \qquad\qquad B_s = 1 - (1 - p_1)(1 - p_1)...(1 - p_n)$$

Figure 5.20   Models for serial and parallel connection rules

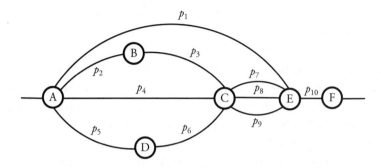

Figure 5.21   A network of links and their blocking probabilities

Rule 2: For a serial connection of links, the probability of blocking is estimated by forming the product of the probabilities of no blocking for the network. This method makes the assumption that the probability that a given link is busy is independent from link to link. Although this independence assumption is not strictly correct, the resulting estimates are sufficiently accurate. If links are in series, the probability of blocking is obtained from

$$B_s = 1 - (1 - p_1)(1 - p_2) \ldots (1 - p_n). \tag{5.9}$$

Example.   The network in Figure 5.21 has six nodes, A through F, interconnected with ten links. The corresponding blocking probabilities of links, p_1 through p_{10}, are indicated on the corresponding links. For this network, find the overall blocking probability from A to F.

Solution.   This network consists of a number of serial and parallel connections: for example, $p_{ADC} = 1 - (1 - p_5)(1 - p_6)$, $p_{ABC} = 1 - (1 - p_2)(1 - p_3)$, and $p_{CE} = p_7 p_8 p_9$. Thus:

$$B = p_{AF} = 1 - \{1 - [1 - (1 - p_4 \cdot p_{ABC} \cdot p_{ADC})(1 - p_{CE})]p_1\}(1 - p_{10}).$$

5.7   Summary

This chapter focused on layer 3 of the protocol stack reference model and routing among layer 3 devices. The chapter started with basic routing policies such as the *Internet Control Message Protocol* (ICMP), *network address translation* (NAT), *universal plug and play* (UPnP), and *Dynamic Host Configuration Protocol* (DHCP).

Path selection algorithms were discussed next. In this section, we saw how a path in a wide area network is selected for routing. We first defined a path cost and then classified path selection algorithms. Two least-cost-path algorithms were Dijkstra's algorithm—a centralized least-cost algorithm designed to find the best path from a source to a destination through the optimization of path costs; and the Bellman-Ford algorithm—a distributed least-cost approach by which each node retrieves information from reachable nodes to each of its neighbors. Non-least-cost algorithms—*deflection routing*, and *packet flood routing algorithms*—are not optimal but they have their own useful applications.

This chapter further introduced a number of existing practical routing protocols. One category is intradomain routing protocols, such as OSPF and RIP. A router equipped with OSPF is aware of its local link-cost status and periodically sends updates to all surrounding routers. OSPF is based on *link-state routing*, by which routers exchange packets carrying status information of their adjacent links. A router collects all packets at its input ports and determines the network topology, thereby executing its own best-route algorithm. RIP is one of the most widely used routing protocols in the Internet infrastructure in which routers exchange information about reachable routers and the number of hops. RIP uses the Bellman-Ford algorithm.

By contrast, *interdomain routing protocols*, such as BGP, let two contributing routers exchange routing information even if they are located in two different autonomous systems. Each router sends information to all internal neighbors and decides whether the new route is possible. We learned that BGP utilizes two primary modes of data exchange, *internal* BGP (iBGP) and *external* BGP (eBGP). The iBGP mode may be used for routing within an autonomous system to communicate with internal peers, and eBGP can be used for routing beyond an autonomous system to communicate with external peers.

We also learned about IP version 6 (IPv6) in this chapter. The protocol requires a 128-bit long network addressing field. This improvement in addressing scheme solved all the issues in connections with the shortage of addresses in IPv4. Various examples of IPv6 will be presented in upcoming chapters.

Congestion control at the network layer is a major issue. In computer networks, congestion represents some form of overload, generally resulting from resource shortage at links and devices. *Unidirectional congestion control* can take several forms: *back-pressure signaling, transmission of choke packets*, and *traffic policing. Bidirectional congestion control* is a host-based resource-allocation scheme. In this category, *random early detection* is one congestion-avoidance technique. An approximation method to calculate *link blocking* follows two simple rules: two links in series and two links in parallel. These two rules can be used to estimate the blocking in any complex combination of links.

The next chapter discusses multicast routing and protocols, which is an advanced topic of routing in computer networking.

5.8   Exercises

1. Consider a packet-switching network for server communications with n nodes. For each of the following topologies, sketch the network, and give the average number of hops between a pair of servers (include the server-to-node link as a hop).

   (a) *Star*: one central node with all servers attached to the central node

   (b) *Bidirectional ring*: each node connects to two other nodes to form a loop, with each node connected to one server

   (c) *Fully connected*: each node is directly connected to all other nodes, with each node connected to one server

   (d) *A ring with $n - 1$ nodes connected to a central node*, with each node in the ring connected to one server

2. A NAT-enabled router, R1, interfaces a private network with a public network. The private side of the router has used the 192.168.0.0 IP address. There are 20 hosts in the private network. The 20 hosts are classified into 5 different categories, each handling a certain application for which a same port number needs to be dedicated. Suppose that the public port of the connecting NAT-enabled router is assigned IP address 136.2.2.2.

   (a) Present a proposed structure of a NAT translation table for the NAT-enabled router.

   (b) Assume host 6 requests a connection to server 1 housed in a public network with IP address 205.1.1.1 and port number 8001. Show the source and destination IP addresses and port numbers for a packet moving in each of the following cases: from host 6 to R1, from R1 to server 1, from server 1 to R1, and from R1 to host 6.

3. Figure 5.22 shows a network.

   (a) Find the least-cost path between the two servers, using Dijkstra's algorithm.

   (b) Show an iteration graph as the least-cost path is developed.

4. In exercise 3, give the information that node A provides through an OSPF packet to:

   (a) node C.

   (b) node D.

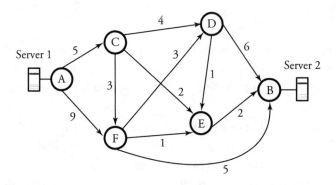

Figure 5.22   Exercises 3–7 network example

5. For the network shown in Figure 5.22:
   (a) Find the least-cost path between the two servers, using the Bellman-Ford algorithm.
   (b) Show an iteration graph as the least-cost path is developed.

6. In exercise 4, give the information that node A provides through an RIP packet to:
   (a) node C.
   (b) node D.

7. Consider again the network in Figure 5.22. Assume that each link is bidirectional and that the cost of either direction is identical.
   (a) Find the least-cost path between the two servers, using Dijkstra's algorithm.
   (b) Show an iteration graph as the least-cost path is developed.

8. The network shown in Figure 5.23 is a snapshot of a practical network consisting of seven routers. The load on each link is normalized to a number indicated on that link.
   (a) Find the least-cost path between the two routers R1 and R7, using Dijkstra's algorithm.
   (b) Show an iteration graph as the least-cost path is developed.

9. In exercise 8, give the information that node R1 provides through an OSPF packet to:
   (a) node R2.
   (b) node R7.

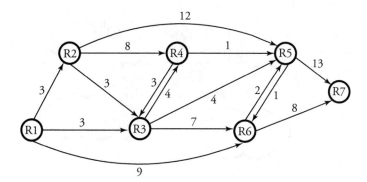

Figure 5.23   Exercises 8–11 network example

10. For the network shown in Figure 5.20:
    (a) Find the least-cost path between R1 and R7, using the Bellman-Ford algorithm.
    (b) Show an iteration graph as the least-cost path is developed.

11. In exercise 10, give the information that node R1 provides through an RIP packet to:
    (a) node *R2*.
    (b) node R7.

12. The practical network shown in Figure 5.24 is a WAN consisting of seven routers R1 through R7 interconnecting four LANs. The load on each link is normalized to a number indicated on that link. Assume that all links are bidirectional with equal indicated load.
    (a) Find the least-cost path between the two routers R1 and R4 connecting users A and B, using Dijkstra's algorithm.
    (b) Show an iteration graph as the least-cost path is developed.

13. The practical network shown in Figure 5.24 is a WAN consisting of seven routers R1 through R7 interconnecting four LANs. The load on each link is normalized to a number indicated on that link. Assume that all links are bidirectional with equal indicated load.
    (a) Find the least-cost path between the two routers R1 and R4 connecting hosts A and B, using the Bellman-Ford algorithm.
    (b) Show an iteration graph as the least-cost path is developed.

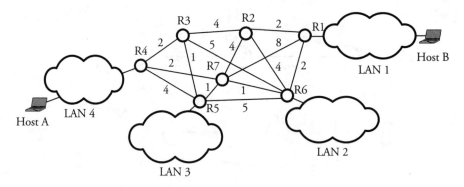

Figure 5.24   Exercises 12 and 13 network example

14. A large corporation owning IP address range of 192.168.2.0/25 has its own ISP. Assume that an office building within the corporation using address range of 192.168.2.0/28 desires a connection with its own autonomous ISP in addition to the connection with its corporation. The building is connected to corporation edge router R1 through its edge router R2, and is also connected to its own ISP through R3. We would like to configure connecting routers according to BGP.

   (a) Show the configuration of R1 and R2 and specifically demonstrate what R1 and R2 should advertise.

   (b) Repeat part (a) when the building management decides to have its own independent network IP addresses.

   (c) Show how routers should be configured if the corporation decides to use the building's ISP when it experiences slow bit rates during the peak traffic times.

15. Consider an estimated population of 3 million people.

   (a) What is the maximum number of IP addresses that can be assigned per person using IPv4?

   (b) What is the maximum number of IP addresses that can be assigned per person using IPv6?

16. For each of the following IPv6 addresses, give an abbreviated form and then convert the result to binary form:

   (a) 1111:2A52:A123:0111:73C2:A123:56F4:1B3C

   (b) 2532:0000:0000:0000:FB58:909A:ABCD:0010

   (c) 2222:3333:AB01:1010:CD78:290B:0000:1111

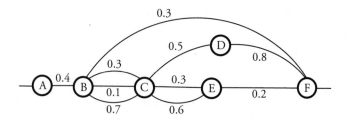

Figure 5.25 Exercise 18 network of links

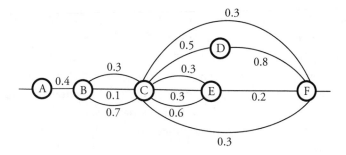

Figure 5.26 Exercise 19 network of links

17. Research why IPv6 allows fragmentation only at the source.

18. The network in Figure 5.25 has six interconnected nodes, A through F. The corresponding blocking probabilities of links are indicated on the corresponding links. For this network, find the overall blocking probability from A to F.

19. Figure 5.26 shows a large communication network of six interconnected nodes, A through F. The corresponding blocking probabilities of links are indicated on the corresponding links. For this network, find the overall blocking probability from A to F.

5.9 Computer Simulation Project

1. *Simulation of Dijkstra's Algorithm.* Write a computer program to simulate Dijkstra's algorithm for the seven-node network shown in Figure 5.24. Your program must

(a) Use a scheme that runs for any hypothetical link cost. Users A and B use Dijkstra's algorithm.

(b) Compute the least-cost path between any two routers.

2. **Simulation of the Bellman-Ford Algorithm.** Write a computer program to simulate the Bellman-Ford algorithm for the seven-node network shown in Figure 5.24. Your program must

(a) Use a scheme that runs for any hypothetical link cost. Users A and B use the Bellman-Ford algorithm.

(b) Compute the least-cost path between any two routers.

3. **Simulation of Network Address Translation (NAT) Protocol.** Use the C or C++ program language to simulate a NAT operation. Assign to a number of private hosts one of the private addresses in the range 192.168.2.0/28 with corresponding port numbers (layer 4 parameter) selected from number 2000 or higher. Log these data in a database and name it NAT1 database. Create another database, NAT2, in which pairs of IP addresses and port numbers each consisting of IP address 158.1.1.2 and a public port number randomly selected from range 3000 or higher exist.

(a) Link NAT1 and NAT2 in your simulation.

(b) Show the detail of address translation for a connection set up from a device with ID 192.168.2.1-2000 to a hypothetical public destination host 200.1.1.1-5000

(c) Show the detail of address translation for a connection set up from the hypothetical public destination host with ID 200.1.1.1-5000 to the private device 192.168.2.1-2000.

CHAPTER **6**

Multicast Routing and Protocols

The capability of *multicasting* traffic has become a fundamental factor in the design of computer communications. Multicasting is the transmission of data from one source to a group of destinations. Data networks must be able to support multimedia applications by multicasting data, voice, and video. Multicasting has led to the development of such applications as teleconferencing, multipoint data dissemination, educational distance learning, and Internet TV. In such applications, audio and video streaming technologies are needed to implement multicasting, owing to the real-time component of multimedia applications. In this chapter, we focus on several advanced multicast protocols used in the Internet. The following topics are covered:

- *Basic definitions and techniques*
- *Local and membership multicast protocols*
- *Intradomain multicast protocols*
- *Interdomain multicast protocols*

This chapter begins with some basic definitions and techniques: multicast group, multicast addresses, and multicast tree algorithms. Tree algorithms must be explored, as they are a set of foundations for understanding Internet packet multicasting. Next, the category of *local and membership multicast protocols* are described. This category of protocols is used in local area networks and for creation of multicast groups of hosts.

Next, two main classes of protocols at the wide area network level are presented: *intradomain multicast protocols,* by which packets are multicast within a single networking domain, and *interdomain multicast protocols,* by which packets are multicast among two or more networking domains.

Note that the packet copying techniques and algorithms used within a router alone are introduced in Chapter 12 where the detailed architecture of advanced routers is presented.

6.1   Basic Definitions and Techniques

A simple operation of data multicasting can be viewed through a transmitting host and several receiving hosts. Instead of forcing the source host to send a separate packet to each destination host or user, the source needs to be able to forward a single packet to multiple addresses, and the network must be able to deliver a copy of that packet to each *group* of receiving hosts or users. Hosts can then choose to join or leave this group without synchronizing with other members.

A host may also belong to more than one group at a time. Figure 6.1 shows a typical packet multicasting and its position among the different protocol layers. As shown, while multicasting a packet is primarily a task of the network layer protocol, but it can still involve all protocol layers of a communication network. A multicast task can be performed at the application layer, where two hosts can directly connect through a copy of the source. Meanwhile, a message can be multicast systematically through the physical, link, and network layers.

With the use of a robust multicasting protocol, a network reduces traffic load by simultaneously delivering a single stream of information to potentially thousands of recipients. An example is the distribution of real-time stock quotes and news. In such cases, the application source traffic is delivered to multiple receivers without burdening the source or the receivers and using a minimum amount of network bandwidth. Among the challenges of implementing data multicasting are the following two, which are especially relevant in large networks:

1. *Manageability.* As a data network becomes larger, constructing a central management system for distributed multicast tasks can become increasingly challenging.

2. *Scalability.* In practice, large networks that lack mechanisms for extending or adding equipment can experience substantial scalability problems, especially in constructing multicast trees.

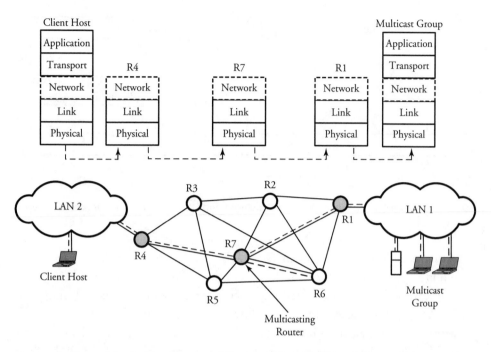

Figure 6.1 An IP multicast model presented at router R7 and also at LAN 1

Tight real-time components require a constant flow of data and have a very low jitter tolerance. To this end, corrupted data frames are often dropped rather than retransmitted. In this context, one would like to see a dynamic multicast system that adapts to deletions and additions of ongoing data over time. In the multicast service, we want to make copies of data at or near a source with only one access to the transport media. But having copied packets floating around raises issues of congestion. However, copying packets near destinations has a risk of losing all copies of packets if the original packet is lost at that location.

6.1.1 IP Multicast Addresses

Chapter 1 discussed IP addressing, noting that multicast packets are of class D. The first four bits a class D IP address identify the class of the address, where 1110 represents a multicast address. The remaining 28 bits identify a particular multicast group. Thus, multicast addresses can range from 224.0.0.1 through 239.255.255.255, and 2^{28} is the maximum number of multicast groups that can be formed simultaneously.

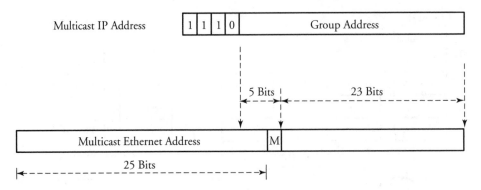

Figure 6.2 Mapping between IP multicast and Ethernet multicast addresses

Multicast addressing is an open issue at both the network and the link layers. As shown in Figure 6.2, a multicast address from the network layer needs to be mapped to multicast addresses of the data-link layer when mapping between IP multicast and an Ethernet multicast address is performed. Note that the first 23 bits of the IP multicast address are placed into the first 23 bits of the Ethernet multicast address field. The 26 bits left in the Ethernet multicast address are assigned a 25-bit-long fixed value followed by a 1-bit field, M, representing the two cases: the Internet multicast with 0 and any other applications with 1.

6.1.2   Basic Multicast Tree Algorithms

Multicast group membership is a dynamic function, so any host can join or leave an IP multicast group at any time. Multicast packets are also subject to loss, delay, duplication, and out-of-order delivery. In WANs, data multicast transmission requires routers capable of managing multicast trees. A main difference between a regular unicast communication and a multicast communication is the nature of their routing. Unicast routing uses the shortest path, whereby two nodes communicate by means of a minimum-weight path.

The challenge in multicast routing is to identify the multicast group of nodes and then to find in the multicast group the minimum-weight tree that spans all members of the group. The multicast tree must also have low end-to-end delay, be scalable and survivable, and support dynamic membership. In a multicast transmission, a single copy of the packet is sent to a router with multicast capability, and the router makes copies and forwards them to all receivers. This is an efficient use of the bandwidth, as there is only one copy of a message over a link. The standard multicast model for

IP networks expresses the way end systems send and receive multicast packets. This model is summarized as follows:

- A source can use either TCP or UDP as a transport protocol when multicasting, although UDP is a more common transport protocol as compared with TCP. If TCP is selected, reliable connections from one to multiple hosts are established. If UDP is used, multicast packets are delivered using a best-effort algorithm anytime, with no need to register or to schedule transmission.

- Sources need to consider only the multicast address; they need not be a member of the multicast group to which they are sending.

- Multicast group members do not need to negotiate within the central group manager. Thus, they can join or leave a group at any time.

A *multicast tree algorithm* is the heart of multicast protocols and implements the fundamental task of packet copying and distribution in networks. Note that unicast routing uses the destination address to make its forwarding decision, whereas multicast routing normally uses the source address to make its forwarding decision. Tree algorithms form a triangle, or a tree, whereby the top vertex is represented by the source, and all recipients of the packet reside on the bottom line. During construction of a distribution tree, a *group* membership has to be formed, with copying nodes as members of the group. Updated information has to be maintained in a router if it is a member of the group. Two types of methods are used to construct a multicast tree: *dense-mode* trees and *sparse-mode* trees as seen in Figure 6.3.

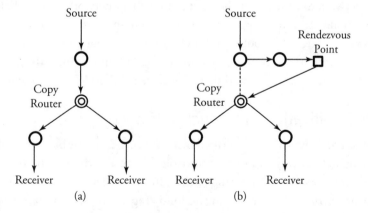

Figure 6.3   Two methods of constructing multicast algorithms: (a) dense mode, using a source-based tree; (b) sparse-mode, using a shared tree

Dense-Mode Algorithm

With the *dense-mode*, or *broadcast-and-prune*, algorithm, a multicast tree technique called a *source-based tree* is used. This technique requires the determination of a shortest-path tree to all destinations and uses a reverse shortest-path tree rooted at a source. The tree starts at the source; for every source, there is always a corresponding shortest-path tree. As a result, the spanning tree guarantees the lowest cost from a source to all leaves of the tree. Packets are forwarded on the best (shortest-path or least-cost path depending on the policy of the network) tree according to: (1) the source address they originated from, and (2) the group address they are addressed to. The source-based tree in a network provides the shortest distance and the least delay from a source to all receivers.

Sparse-Mode Algorithm

The *sparse-mode algorithm* uses a *shared-tree* technique. Relatively short distances are selected, and no effort is made to find the best paths to destinations. First, some shared trees are formed. These trees consider multiple senders and receivers and use some nodes acting as *rendezvous points* (RPs) to connect sources and receivers. A rendezvous point—known as the *core*, or *root*—is considered a point in the network where roots of distribution subtrees are shared and the multicast data flows down to reach the receivers in the network. The sparse-mode algorithm uses a rendezvous point to coordinate forwarding packets from source to receivers and to prevent the initial flooding of datagrams. However, this may introduce extra delay from the source to all receivers but requires less hardware complexity for finding the shortest path. All routers in the network must discover the information about network routers that become rendezvous points and the mappings of multicast groups to rendezvous points.

The sparse mode has a couple of drawbacks. One is that a rendezvous point can be a hotspot for multicast traffic and a point of failure in routing. Also, forwarding traffic to the rendezvous point and then to receivers causes delay and longer paths.

6.1.3   Classification of Multicast Protocols

The fundamental algorithms described in Section 6.1.2 are the basic procedures for constructing networking multicast protocols. These algorithms are used as foundations of protocols for multicasting packets in the Internet. Three main classes of multicast protocols are described in the following sections: *local and membership multicast protocols*, for local multicasting and joining a host to a group; *intradomain multicast protocols*, by which packets are multicast within a domain; and *interdomain multicast protocols*, by which packets are multicast among domains.

6.2 Local and Membership Multicast Protocols

Local and membership multicast protocols are primarily designed for joining a host to a group and for simple multicasting in a small network such a local area network. The most popular protocol in this category is the *Internet Group Management Protocol* (IGMP) described next.

6.2.1 Internet Group Management Protocol (IGMP)

The *Internet Group Management Protocol* (IGMP) is used in a computer network between a potential multicast group member and its immediate multicast-enabled routers reporting multicast group information. The immediate multicast-enabled router (or layer-3 switch) of a multicast group is called a *designated router* (DR). This protocol has several versions and is required on all hosts that receive IP multicasts. Equivalent IGMP multicast management in IPv6 networks is handled by *Multicast Listener Discovery* (MLD) messaging.

As the name suggests, IGMP is a group-oriented management protocol that provides a dynamic service to registered individual hosts in a multicast group. The protocol operates between multicast clients and a local multicast router, and is implemented on hosts and their associated designated routers. Figure 6.4 illustrates an overview of IGMP packet multicasting over a partial local area network (LAN) that is attached to a wide area network (WAN). In this figure, router R9 acts as a DR for the multicast group consisting of hosts 1, 2, and 3 residing on the LAN. A DR is responsible for coordination between multicast groups and their ISPs.

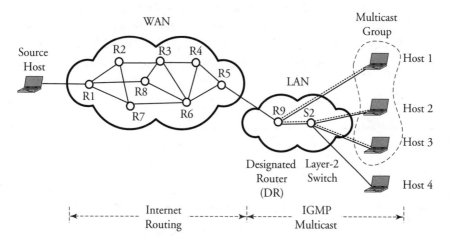

Figure 6.4 Overview of IGMP

Any host running an application and wanting to join a multicast group requests membership through its DR. The DR listens for these requests and periodically sends out subscription queries. When a source host sends an IGMP message to its DR, the host in fact identifies the group membership. DRs are usually sensitive to these types of messages and periodically send out queries to discover which subnet groups are active. When a host wants to join a group, the group's multicast address is inserted in an IGMP message stating the group membership. The DR receives this message and constructs all routes by propagating the group membership information to other multicast routers throughout the network.

The IGMP packet header format has several versions; Figure 6.5 shows version 3 of the IGMP packet header. The first 8 bits indicate the message *Type*. The *Type* field may be one of the following: *membership query*, sent to a host to ask whether the host wants to join a group; *membership report*, used to respond to a membership query; or *leave group*, sent by a host to leave a group. A host can also send a *membership report*, expressing an interest in joining that group without being asked by a *membership query*.

IGMP is compatible with TCP/IP, so the TCP/IP stack running on a host forwards the IGMP membership report when an application opens a multicast socket. A router periodically transmits an IGMP *membership query* to verify that at least one host on the subnet is still interested in receiving traffic directed to that group. In this case, if no response to three consecutive IGMP membership queries is received, the router times out the group and stops forwarding traffic directed to that group.

IGMP version 3 supports *include* and *exclude* modes. In *include* mode, a receiver announces the membership to a host group and provides a list of source addresses from which it wants to receive traffic. With *exclude mode*, a receiver expresses the membership to a multicast group and provides a list of source addresses from which it does not want to receive traffic. With the *leave_group* message, hosts can report to

Byte:					
1	1	2	4	4	
Type	Maximum Response Time	Checksum	Group Address	Resv S QRV QQIC N	Source Addresses [1] ... [N]

Figure 6.5 IGPM packet header format

the local multicast router that they intend to leave the group. If any remaining hosts are interested in receiving the traffic, the router transmits a group-specific query. In this case, if the router receives no response, the router times out the group and stops forwarding the traffic.

The next 8 bits, *maximum response time*, are used to indicate the time before sending a response report (the default is 10 seconds). The *Resv* field is set to 0 and is reserved for future development. The next field is the *S* flag, to suppress router-side processing. *QRV* (*querier's robustness variable*) indicates a performance factor. *QQIC* is the querier's query interval code. *N* shows the number of sources, and *Source Address* [*i*] provides a vector of *N* individual IP addresses.

Example.   Reconsider Figure 6.4 and suppose the three hosts 1, 2, and 3 attached to the local area network (LAN) try to join a multicast group with an address of 239.255.255.255 in order to collectively communicate with the source host located at the wide area network (WAN). Host 2 leaves right after joining the instance. Present the details of membership and routing.

Solution.   First, router R9 sends the *membership query* message to all hosts including hosts 1, 2, 3, and 4 to determine the existence of a multicast group with address 239.255.255.255 in the LAN. Hosts 1, 2, and 3 respond to the *membership query* message with a *membership report* message confirming their membership. At this time, host 2 sends a *leave group* message to R9 to indicate that it wants to leave the group. Router R9 updates its database accordingly. Now, the source host can use multicast address 239.255.255.255 to communicate with the group.

6.3   Intradomain Multicast Protocols

Intradomain multicast protocols carry out the multicast function within domains. The implementation of multicast routing faces the following particular challenges:

- Dynamic change in the group membership
- Minimizing network load and avoiding routing loops
- Finding concentration points of traffic

In practice, several protocols play major roles in establishing multicast connections. The *Distance Vector Multicast Routing Protocol* (DVMRP) is an original protocol forming the early version of the *multicast backbone* (MBone) protocol. Other protocols, such as *Multicast Open Shortest Path First* (MOSPF), *core-based tree* (CBT), and *protocol-independent multicast* (PIM) are playing a significant role in the Internet. We describe these protocols next.

6.3.1   Multicast Backbone (MBone)

The first milestone in the creation of a practical multicast platform was the development of the *multicast backbone* (MBone), which carried its first worldwide event when several sites received audio simultaneously. The multicast routing function was implemented using unicast-encapsulated multicast packets. The connectivity among certain receivers was provided using point-to-point IP-encapsulated *tunnels*. Figure 6.6 shows an example of tunneling among routers in the early version of MBone. Each tunnel connects two end points via one logical link and crosses several routers. In this scenario, once a packet is received, it can be sent to other tunnel end points or broadcast to local members. The routing in earlier version of MBone was based on DVMRP and IGMP.

For example, a tunnel initiated from border router R1 is extended over routers R2 and R3, where R3 makes two branches of the tunnel one toward R4 and the other one toward R5. Each of these two branches constructs a tunnel extension. This trend of making new tunnel extensions can occur again before any tunnel ends.

6.3.2   Distance Vector Multicast Routing Protocol (DVMRP)

The Distance Vector Multicast Routing Protocol (DVMRP) is one of the oldest multicast protocols. It is based on a concept of exchanging routing table information

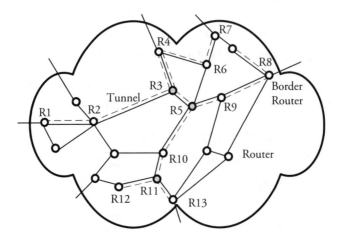

Figure 6.6   Tunneling in the multicast backbone

among directly connected neighboring routers. The MBone topology can enable multiple tunnels to run over a common physical link. Each participating router maintains information about all the destinations within the system. DVMRP creates multicast trees, using the dense-mode algorithm. A multicast router typically implements several other independent routing protocols besides DVMRP for multicast routing, such as RIP or OSPF for unicast routing.

This protocol is not designed for WANs with a large number of nodes, since it can support only a limited number of hops for a packet. This is clearly considered a drawback of this protocol, as it causes packet discarding if a packet does not reach its destination within the maximum number of hops set. Another constraint in this protocol is the periodic expansion of a multicast tree, leading to periodic broadcasting of multicast data. This constraint in turn causes the issue of periodic broadcast of routing tables, which consumes a large amount of available bandwidth. DVMRP supports only the source-based multicast tree. Thus, this protocol is appropriate for multicasting data among a limited number of distributed receivers located close to the source.

6.3.3   Multicast OSPF (MOSPF) Protocol

The *Multicast Open Shortest Path First* (MOSPF) protocol, an extension to the unicast model of OSPF discussed in Chapter 5, constructs a link-state database with an advertisement mechanism. Let's explore what new features a link-state router requires to become capable of multicast functions.

Link-State Multicast

As explained in Chapter 5, *link-state routing* occurs when a node in a network has to obtain the state of its connected links and then send an update to all the other routers once the state changes. On receipt of the routing information, each router reconfigures the entire topology of the network. The link-state routing algorithm uses Dijkstra's algorithm to compute the least-cost path.

The multicast feature can be added to a router using the link-state routing algorithm by placing the spanning tree root at the router. The router uses the tree to identify the best next node. To include the capability of multicast support, the link-state router needs the set of groups that have members on a particular link added to the *state* for that link. Therefore, each LAN attached to the network must have its host periodically announce all groups it belongs to. This way, a router simply detects such announcements from LANs and updates its routing table.

Details of MOSPF

With OSPF, a router uses the flooding technique to send a packet to all routers within the same hierarchical area and to all other network routers. This simply allows all MOSPF routers in an area to have the same view of group membership. Once a link-state table is created, the router computes the shortest path to each multicast member by using Dijkstra's algorithm. The core algorithm of this protocol is summarized as follows.

Begin MOSPF Protocol

Define:

j = Multicast group number (a class D IP address)

i = Recipient (device, host, LAN, etc.) identification in multicast group j among the n recipients of the group, where $i \in \{1, 2, \cdots, n\}$

$DR_j(i)$ = The designated router (DR) attached to recipient i in multicast group j

1. **Multicast groups:** Ri maintains all N_j group memberships.

2. **Update Membership:** Each recipient device i floods its multicast group membership to all its $DR_j(i)$s (there can be more than one DR for a group).

3. **Least-Cost Tree:** Each router constructs a least-cost tree for every destination group using the link-state multicast.

4. When a multicast packet arrives at a router, the router finds the right tree, makes the necessary number of copies of the packet, and routes the copies. ∎

In step 1, MOSPF adds a link-state field, containing mainly multicast group membership information about the group of hosts or LANs needing to receive the multicast packet. In step 2, each device in a network with a group number registers its group with the attached designated router $DR_j(i)$ enabling the router to share the group membership with other network routers. In step 3, MOSPF uses Dijkstra's algorithm, as was the case for OSPF, and calculates a least-cost multicast tree. Dijkstra's algorithm must be rerun when group membership changes. MOSPF does not support the sparse-mode tree (shared-tree) algorithm. Each OSPF router builds the unicast routing topology, and each MOSPF router can build the shortest-path tree for each source and group. Group-membership reports are broadcast throughout the OSPF area. MOSPF is a dense-mode protocol, and the membership information is broadcast to all MOSPF routers. Note that frequent broadcasting of membership information degrades network performance.

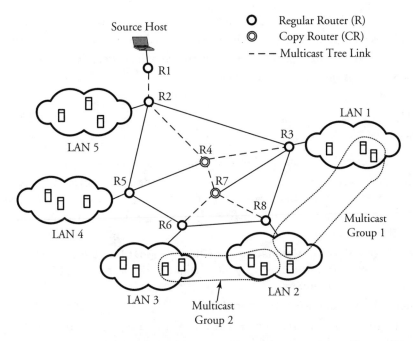

Figure 6.7   Use of MOSPF to multicast from router R1 to seven servers located in two different multicast groups spread over three LANs

Example.   In Figure 6.7, each of the five LANs in a certain domain has an associated router. Show an example of MOSPF for multicasting from source host to the seven servers located in LANs 1, 2, and 3.

Solution.   Multicast groups $j = 1$ and $j = 2$ are formed. For group 1, the best tree is implemented using copying root R4. For group 2, the best tree is implemented using copying root R7.

6.3.4   Protocol-Independent Multicast (PIM)

Protocol-independent multicast (PIM) is an effective multicast protocol for networks, regardless of size and membership density. PIM is "independent" because it implements multicasting independently of any routing protocol entering into the multicast routing information database. PIM can operate in both *dense mode* and *sparse mode*. Dense mode is a flood-and-prune protocol and is best suited for networks densely populated by receivers and with enough bandwidth. This version of PIM is comparable to DVMRP.

Sparse-mode PIM typically offers better stability because of the way it establishes trees. This version assumes that systems can be located far away from one another and that group members are "sparsely" distributed across the system. The core algorithm of this protocol is summarized as follows.

Begin PIM

Define:

j = Multicast group number (a class D IP address)

i = Recipient (device, host, LAN, etc.) identification in multicast group j among the n recipients of the group, where $i \in \{1, 2, \cdots, n\}$

$DR_j(i)$ = The designated router (DR) attached to recipient i in multicast group j

1. **Register with the designated router (DR):** Any multicast recipient i registers with its $DR_j(i)$ by sending a join message. DR maintains group j memberships.

2. **Rendezvous point (RP) and shared tree:**
   - $DR_j(i)$s of all multicast recipients in group j decide on the location of an RP.
   - Each $DR_j(i)$ constructs a path to the RP. The collection of paths from other $DR_j(i)$s form a shared tree for group j with its root at RP.

3. **Multicast communication:**
   - Source host finds the IP address of the RP for which a multicast communication to group j is prepared.
   - Source host sends its multicast packets to RP.
   - RP finds the right shared tree for group j and forwards a Class D multicast packet to all recipients using the shared tree. ∎

Any multicast recipient i can join or leave a multicast group j by sending *Join* or *Prune* protocol messages, respectively. A multicast recipient host i joining group j is associated with a designated router $DR_j(i)$, which is the immediate router attached to the network. In step 1, the multicast group membership information about the group j from any recipient i is sent to the recipient's designated router, $DR_j(i)$. This way, $DR_j(i)$ collects all the information about the group members.

In step 2, a *rendezvous point* (RP) is chosen by all designated routers of a group. The location of an RP is considered to be the least crowded spot in the network, as RP acts as a meeting place for multicast sources and recipients. This way, other routers do not need to be aware of the source's address for every multicast group. All they need to know is the IP address of the RP router. An RP discovers the source for all corresponding multicast groups. The rendezvous point setup shifts the burden of finding sources of multicasting from each router.

Now, suppose a $DR_j(i)$ router learns that a multicast recipient in one of its directly connected subnet devices is interested in forming a multicast group j. The router then decides to create a *shared tree* for this group. $DR_j(i)$ first determines the IP address of the RP for group j and sends a unicast join message to RP. A shared tree is typically a least-cost tree, but it need not be, since, as mentioned previously, the location of an RP must be the best spot for its group in the network. Note that at this point the source of the multicast does not play any role, and thus, this join message lacks the IP address of the source host of the multicast. Each router on the path over which the join message traverses to reach its RP makes a "forwarding table," indicating from which input interface in the multicast the join message arrives and from which output interface it leaves. This is carried out to ensure that any router on a shared tree has a detailed record of the tree structure.

Once the message reaches the designated RP, one segment of a shared tree with its root at RP has been constructed. The shared tree can be expanded later with more branches as new DRs join the associated multicast group. At this point, the IP address of the RP for this multicast group needs to be public knowledge and must be inserted into the database of major routers. Note that the least-cost path algorithm made by unicast routing is used in this protocol for the construction of individual paths of a shared tree. Ironically and interestingly, we notice that the multicast shared tree in this protocol is constructed from bottom to top.

At step 3, when a source host wants to send a multicast message to group j, it first finds the IP address of the RP for which the multicast group j has been formed. It then encapsulates the multicast IP packet with a class D address into a regular unicast IP packet called a *Register* message and sends it to the associated RP for the group. Now, RP has received the multicast packet from the source host and is well aware of the exact shared-tree paths to the members of the multicast group. The RP router now acts as the source of the message and sends the message over the shared tree and thereby to every group member.

Example.   In Figure 6.8, the five LANs in a certain domain each has its own designated router. Show an example of sparse-mode PIM for multicasting from the source host to four servers located in a multicast group spread over LANs 2 and 3 as shown.

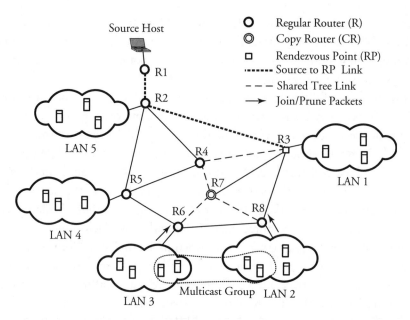

Figure 6.8   Sparse-mode PIM for multicasting from router R1 to four servers in a multicast group
spread over LANs 1 and 2

Solution.   Multicasting is formed with R3 as the associated rendezvous point (RP)
for this group. Thus, the group uses a reverse unicast path as shown to update the
rendezvous point of any joins and leaves. For this group, the multicast shared tree is
implemented including a copying root CR.

6.3.5   Core-Based Trees (CBT) Protocol

In sparse mode, forwarding traffic to the rendezvous point and then to receivers
causes delay and longer paths. This issue can be partially solved in the *core-based trees*
(CBT) protocol, which uses bidirectional trees. Sparse-mode PIM is comparable to
CBT but with two differences. First, CBT uses bidirectional shared trees, whereas
sparse-mode PIM uses unidirectional shared trees. Clearly, bidirectional shared trees
are more efficient when packets move from a source to the root of the multicast tree;
as a result, packets can be sent up and down in the tree. Second, CBT uses only a
shared tree and does not use shortest-path trees.

CBT uses the basic sparse-mode paradigm to create a single shared tree used by all
sources. As with the shared-trees algorithm, the tree must be rooted at a *core* point. All
sources send their data to the core point, and all receivers send explicit join messages

to the core. In contrast, DVMRP is costly, since it broadcasts packets, causing each participating router to become overwhelmed and thereby require keeping track of every source-group pair. CBT's bidirectional routing takes into account the current group membership when it is being established.

When broadcasting occurs, it results in traffic concentration on a single link, since CBT has a single delivery tree for each group. Although it is designed for intradomain multicast routing, this protocol is appropriate for interdomain applications as well. However, it can suffer from latency issues, as in most cases the traffic must flow through the core router. This type of router is a bottleneck if its location is not carefully selected, especially when transmitters and receivers are far apart.

6.4   Interdomain Multicast Protocols

Interdomain multicast protocols are designed for hierarchical and Internet-wide multicast purposes. Within a domain, a network manager can implement any routing protocol desired. The challenge in interdomain multicast administration is choosing the best external link to route to hosts in an external domain. Among the protocols in this category are *Multiprotocol Border Gateway Protocol* (MBGP), *Multicast Source Discovery Protocol* (MSDP), and *Border Gateway Multicast Protocol* (BGMP).

6.4.1   Multiprotocol BGP (MBGP)

Multiprotocol BGP (MBGP) is an extension to its unicast version, *Border Gateway Protocol* (BGP), discussed in Chapter 5. MBGP adds capabilities to BGP to enable multicast routing policy beyond an autonomous system (domain) and to connect multicast topologies between BGP autonomous systems. Since MBGP is an extension to the BGP protocol, the same basic rules of BGP studied in Chapter 5 apply to path selection and path validation. The main task of interdomain multicasting with this protocol is carried out by designated border routers called *MBGP routers*. Let us first learn the overview of the protocol steps:

Begin MBGP

Update: Each border MBGP router applies routing policy to multicast routes and updates MBGP routers of neighboring autonomous systems. MBGP routers also receive updates from regular routers in their own domains.

1. **MBGP Capability Negotiation:** Each MBGP router extends the "Open packet" format to include new parameters in the Capability Option Negotiation field and negotiates with its MBGP peers. An MBGP router routes the lowest common set of capabilities using Capability Option field.

2. **Interdomain Multicast:** Any MBGP router makes the necessary number of copies for intended domains.

3. **Intradomain Multicast:** Once a copy of the copied packet reaches the intended domain, an MBGP router uses the prevailing intradomain multicast protocol to implement multicasting within that domain. ∎

Figure 6.9 depicts an example of interdomain multicasting using MBGP in which three autonomous systems (domains), AS1, AS2, and AS3, are connected through MBGP routers, MR1, MR2, and MR3. The three MBGP routers are considered border router peers, each enabled to handle both unicast and multicast traffic, and they are connected through MBGP links on which peers update each other using the *MBGP Update packets*. These packets are similar to the *BGP Update packets* presented in the BGP section of Chapter 5. Recall that the Update packet

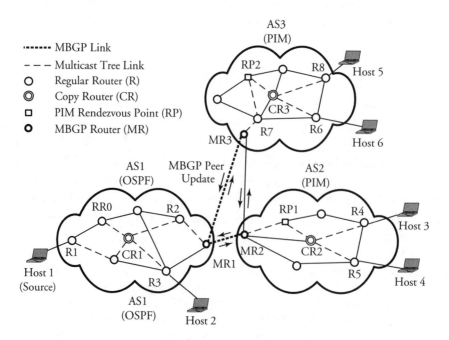

Figure 6.9   MBGP: interdomain multicast routing

uses the *Network Layer Reachability Information* (NLRI) field in its header, which contains a list of IP prefixes that can be reached via a selected path.

In any of the autonomous systems, routers are classified into two types: unicast routers (BGP routers) and multicast routers (MBGP routers). Similar to what we learned for unicast BGP, any MBGP router advertises the multicast routes to its other domains' counterpart peers. Thus, an MBGP router learns MBGP routes from its neighbors housed in other autonomous systems. Each MBGP router extends the *Open packet* (see BGP in Chapter 5) header to include new parameters in the *Capability Option Negotiation* field in the packet header. An MBGP router routes the lowest common set of capabilities using the "Capability Option" fields. If two MBGP peers are unable to agree on the capabilities supported, the MBGP session is terminated and an Error packet is generated.

Each domain-management system advertises the set of routes that can reach a particular destination. Packets are routed on a hop-by-hop basis. Thus, MBGP can determine the next hop but cannot provide multicast tree-construction functions. Sources within a domain register with a rendezvous point, when PIM is used as intradomain multicast protocol, and receivers send joins to this router. This join message is required to find the best reverse path to the source.

With MBGP, the multicast routing hierarchy operates the same way as multiple unicast routing does. Between each pair of adjacent domains, the two corresponding MBGP border routers compute the set of domain parameters that should be traversed to reach any network. Typically, the parameters in one domain are not known or trusted by the others. This protocol can handle multiprotocol paths, and each participating router needs to know only the topology of its own domain and the paths to reach each of the other domains. Since MBGP is an interdomain protocol, a class D address is not carried in an MBGP message, and it does not carry information about multicast groups. Because the time and frequency of join message transmissions are not determined in this protocol, and multicast trees in various domains are not connected, other multicast protocol choices are more attractive.

In Figure 6.9, host 1, as a source host, intends to multicast its data to hosts 2 through 6. In AS1, OSPF is the dominating intradomain protocol, and CR1, as a copy router, makes two copies of the multicast packets, one for destination host 2 and one for the MBGP router of its domain, MR1. It is needless to mention that all nodes in AS1 have updated one another through BGP Update packets on tasks including the MBGP tasks, and hence MR1 is well aware of its tasks. MR1 makes two identical copies of the source packets and send them to its peers MR2 and MR3. Both AS2 and AS3 domains use PIM in this example for their intradomain functions, and thus the multicast packets from the MBGP routers are sent first to rendezvous points RP1 and RP2, respectively. The rendezvous point of each domain finds the assigned copy router of the domain, in this case CR2 and CR3, respectively, thereby the necessary numbers of copies are made for the intended recipients.

6.4.2   Multicast Source Discovery Protocol (MSDP)

One of the main issues in interdomain multicasting is how to inform a rendezvous point in one domain while there are sources in other domains. In other words, rendezvous points of two adjacent domains are not able to communicate with each other when one receives a source register message. In practice, only one rendezvous point is in each domain. This issue becomes more critical when group members should be spread over multiple domains. In this case, multicast trees among domains are not connected. As a result, the traffic can reach all receivers of a domain, but any sources outside the domain stay disjoint.

The *Multicast Source Discovery Protocol* (MSDP) has potential solutions to these issues. A unique feature of this protocol is that it assigns representatives in each domain. A representative reports to other domains the existence of active sources. A new source for a group must first register with the domain's rendezvous point. The main task of interdomain multicasting with this protocol is carried out by designated border routers called *MSDP routers* and *MSDP representative routers*. Let us first learn the overview of the protocol steps:

Begin MSDP

1. **Registration with MSDP Representative:** Each router as a source in an autonomous system (AS) registers with an MSDP representative router of its own AS by sending Register packets and receiving Join packets.

2. **Updates among MSDP Representatives:** Each MSDP representative router exchanges information with other adjacent MSDP representative routers by sending Source-Active (SA) packets and receiving Join packets.

3. **Interdomain Multicast:** Any MSDP router makes the necessary number of copies for intended domains using Class D IP addressing.

4. **Intradomain Multicast:** Once a copy of the copied packet reaches the intended domain, the corresponding AS uses its prevailing intradomain multicast protocol to implement the necessary copies within that domain. ∎

Figure 6.10 depicts an example of interdomain multicasting using MSDP in which three autonomous systems, AS1, AS2, and AS3, are connected through MSDP routers, MR1, MR2, and MR3. With MSDP, all routers in an autonomous system register with a router called the *MSDP representative router* (RR). This can be done by sending a *Register packet* containing the information about the multicast group and receiving a *Join packet*. In the figure, router R1 registers with RR0.

An MSDP representative also communicates with all of its surrounding MSDP representatives belonging to adjacent domains and updates them on multicast routing. This can be done by sending a *Source-Active* (SA) *packet* and receiving a *Join packet*. The SA packet identifies the source, the group the source is sending to, and the address or the originator ID of the MSDP representative, which can also be an RP in the case of a PIM. In the figure, RR0 updates RR1 and RR2. Such packet exchange immediately updates all the passing border MSDP routers, as is the case for MSR1, MR2, and MR3.

Each MSDP representative router in a domain also detects the existence of any new sources and updates all other MSDP representative routers. If the MSDP representative is an RP and has a member of that multicast group, the data packet is

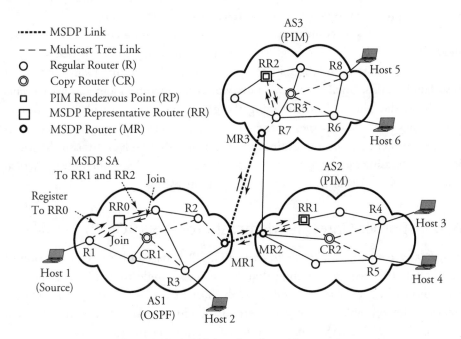

Figure 6.10   MSDP: interdomain multicast routing

decapsulated and forwarded down the shared tree in the remote domain. An MSDP representative checks whether the broadcasting representative has sent the message through the correct path to prevent possible message looping. Once this process is complete and the message is on the correct router interface, the message is forwarded to all remaining associated representatives.

An MSDP representative router (RR) and a PIM rendezvous point of the same domain have a peering relationship with the MSDP representative router in another domain. The peering relationship occurs over a TCP connection, where primarily a list of sources sending to multicast groups is exchanged. The TCP connections between RRs are achieved by the underlying routing system. The receiving RR uses the source lists to establish a source path. Therefore, an MSDP representative router and the rendezvous point within a domain can be the same point; this is the check-point where the state of group membership is checked. If it has the correct state, the router sends a join message to the source address mentioned in the message.

Here, we assume that the intradomain multicast is performed using PIM, whereby a join message is generated and processed. The message is then forwarded on the multicast tree by the rendezvous point; once all group members receive the data attached to the message, they may use a shortest-path tree, using sparse-mode PIM. This process ends when all the representatives finish the process.

This multicast procedure uses a combination of three protocols: MOSPF, sparse-mode PIM, and MSDP. Although this multicast procedure has been well accepted as a practical multicast method, its complexity results in a timing issue. One aspect is scalability. Also, when sources are bursty or group members join and leave events frequently, the overhead of managing the group can be noticeable. This fact in turn creates the timeout issue, whereby the period of silence between packet bursts becomes greater than the forwarding-state timeout. MSDP solves this issue by selecting and processing every n packets in burst. However, this trick is not quite a practical solution when a fairly large network is under multicasting.

6.4.3   Border Gateway Multicast Protocol (BGMP)

The *Border Gateway Multicast Protocol* (BGMP) is based on the construction of bidirectional shared trees among domains using a single root. Finding the best domain in which to place the root of such shared trees is a challenge, but several solutions are available. One of the methods of address resolution is the *Multicast Address-Set Claim* (MASC) protocol, which guarantees the immediate resolution of address collisions.

Another method of resolving this issue is to use *root-addressed multicast architecture* (RAMA) by which a source is selected as the root of the tree. This way, the complexity of root placement in other multicast routing protocols can be eliminated. RAMA is of two types. The first type is *express multicast*: The root of the tree is placed at the source, and group members send join messages on the reverse path back to the source. This protocol is aimed at systems that use logical channels, such as single-source multimedia applications, TV broadcast, and file distribution. The second type is *simple multicast*: Multiple sources per group are allowed. In this case, one source must be selected, and the root of the tree is put at this node as a primary and first-hop router. Then, all receivers send join messages to the source. The next step is to construct a bidirectional tree through which additional sources send packets to the root. Since a bidirectional tree is constructed, packets arrive at a router in the tree and are forwarded both downstream to receivers and upstream to the root.

6.5   Summary

Communication systems must be able to multicast a message to many users and even route many messages to one user. In a multipoint environment, traditional networks are subject to severe blocking, since they are not typically designed for high-bandwidth communications. Under both multirate and multipoint conditions, the performance of switching networks is closely related to the network architecture.

This chapter focused on multicast algorithms and protocols. After defining some basic terms and techniques—including dense-mode and sparse-mode multicast tree algorithms—we presented a category of *local and membership multicast protocols*. This category of protocols was only used in local area networks and for creation of multicast groups of hosts. The most popular protocol in this category is the *Internet Group Management Protocol* (IGMP), used to communicate with local hosts for joining and leaving a multicast group. IGMP itself could also be used for multicasting purposes but at the local area network level.

We then discussed two main classes of wide area network multicast protocols: *intradomain multicast protocols* that teach how to multicast packets within a domain, and *interdomain multicast protocols* that present how to multicast packets among domains. Among the intradomain protocols, two protocols were particularly popular: MOSPF as an extension to the unicast OSPF protocol, which is based on the dense-mode tree algorithm, and PIM, which typically uses the sparse-mode tree algorithm. Among the interdomain protocols, MSDP is the most commonly used in the structure of the Internet.

In the next chapter, we explore wide area wireless networks. We analyze such wireless networks with a main focus on cellular structures and the *Long-Term Evolution* (LTE) technology.

6.6   Exercises

1. For sending a message from a point to multiple points, compare the trade-offs of using multiple unicast connections, and using any multicast approach, such as DVMRP, explained in this chapter.

2. Discuss the efficiency of MOSPF if the sparse-mode algorithm is used.

3. Consider Figure 6.7, and assume that we want to implement MOSPF from a server in LAN 1 to a multicast group of five members, three group members in LAN 3 and the two others in LAN 4. Also assume that the cost of each link is indicated by the sum of two ending routers' subscripts. For example, the cost of link R3 to R8 is 11. If a router ends a LAN, the cost of its associated link is assumed to be 1.

   (a) Show the cost of all links on the network.
   (b) Form the least-cost tree for this multicast action, and find the root of copy-ing routers.

4. Suppose that in an ISP there are two hosts with IP addresses 192.1.12.1 and 192.1.12.2 in LAN 1 trying to group with a host with IP address 192.3.3.3 in LAN 2. A source host with IP address 178.5.12.6 tries to make a multicast connection with the group. The multicast group address assigned by the ISP is 224.1.1.1. Show the messaging activity to form this multicast group and include the addressing fields of the packets exchanged among the source, the three hosts, and their designated routers (DRs) specifically for communications on:

   (a) The source to DRs (non-IGMP packets)
   (b) DRs to the three hosts (IGMP packets)
   (c) Hosts to DRs (IGMP packets)
   (d) DRs to the source (non-IGMP packets)

5. To optimize the routing delay in a sparse-mode PIM:

   (a) Find the optimal place for the rendezvous point.
   (b) Give an example of a spanning tree, and justify your answer.

6. Consider Figure 6.8, and assume that we want to implement sparse-mode PIM from a server in LAN 1 to a multicast group of five members, with three group members in LAN 3 and the two others in LAN 4. Also assume that the cost of each link is indicated by the sum of two ending routers' subscripts. For example,

the cost of link R3 to R8 is 11. If a router ends a LAN, the cost of its associated link is assumed to be 1.

(a) Propose a reasonably good location for the rendezvous point for this multicast action.

(b) Form a shared tree, and find the root of copying routers.

7. Consider Figure 6.8, and assume that we want to implement sparse-mode CBT from a server in LAN 1 to a multicast group of five members, with three group members in LAN 3 and the two others in LAN 4. Also assume that the cost of each link is indicated by the sum of two ending routers' subscripts. For example, the cost of link R3 to R8 is 11. If a router ends a LAN, the cost of its associated link is assumed to be 1.

(a) Find a reasonably good location for the rendezvous point for this multicast action.

(b) Form the least-cost tree for this multicast action, and find the root of copying routers.

8. In Figure 6.11 five LANs, 1 through 5, are networked through their associated routers, R3, R8, R6, R5 and R1. The cost of each link is indicated in the figure. A server in LAN 1 wants to send messages to the indicated multicast group.

(a) For deploying the MOSPF protocol, find the multicast tree.

(b) For deploying the sparse-mode PIM protocol and using the same tree you obtained in part (a), propose a location of the rendezvous point and its associated costs to each multicast group member.

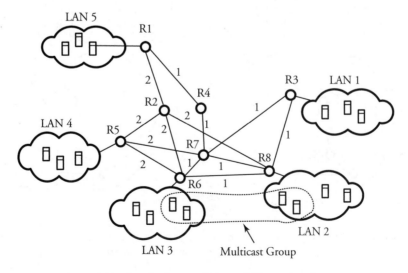

Figure 6.11   Exercise 8 example for multicast protocols

9. Three major Internet service provider domains—ISP 1, ISP 2, and ISP 3—are connected through three border routers: R10, R20, and R30, respectively, as shown in Figure 6.12. All three ISPs agree to use MSDP for interdomain multicasting. Each domain has selected a router as its ISP MSDP representative, which can also be used as a rendezvous point, if needed. A source in ISP 1 wants to multicast messages to three groups located in various geographical locations, as shown. ISP 1 uses MOSPF, and ISP 2 and ISP 3 use sparse-mode PIM for intradomain multicasting. The cost of each link (equal in both directions) is indicated in the figure.

(a) Indicate all involved routers in ISP 1, and find the total multicast cost to LAN 1 and LAN 2.

(b) Indicate all involved routers in ISP 2, and find the total multicast cost to LAN 3 and LAN 4.

(c) Indicate all involved routers in ISP 3, and find the total multicast cost to LAN 5.

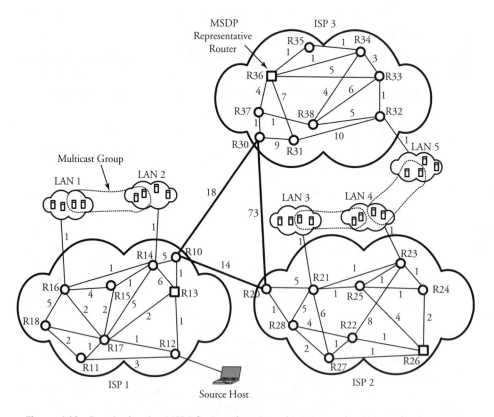

Figure 6.12   Exercise 9: using MSDP for interdomain multicasting and MOSPF and sparse-mode PIM protocols for intradomain multicasting

6.7   Computer Simulation Project

1. *Simulation of Sparse-Mode PIM.* Use the computer program you developed for the simulation of the seven-node network in Chapter 5 and modify it to model the network shown in Figure 6.8. Simulate a sparse-mode PIM for multicasting from router R1 to four recipients located in a multicast group spread over a wide geographic area.

   (a) Construct a multicast group and assign a class D IP address to it.
   (b) Write a computer program to do a sparse-mode multicast tree.
   (c) Assign a rendezvous point.
   (d) Demonstrate the formation of four packet copies made for the multicast group.

CHAPTER **7**

Wireless Wide Area Networks and LTE Technology

Wireless networks are designed for all home and business networking applications and are used in both local area networks (LANs) and wide area networks (WANs). In Chapters 2, 3, and 4, we reviewed some fundamentals of wireless communication media at the link layer and at the LAN scale. In this chapter, we explore the concept of wireless networks at the WAN scale. The main topics of the chapter are:

- *Infrastructure of wireless networks*
- *Cellular networks*
- *Mobile IP management in cellular networks*
- *Long-Term Evolution* (LTE) *technology*
- *Wireless mesh networks* (WMNs) *with LTE*
- *Characterization of wireless channels*

We start with an overview of wireless communication systems at all levels, from satellite to LANs. We then focus on *cellular networks*, one of the main backbones of our wireless networking infrastructure. We review the protocols and topologies of wide area networks in the wireless environment, as well as the mobility issue in wireless networks. The *mobile IP* in cellular networks is then presented, where a mobile user needs to place a data communication connection while changing its location. After discussing mobile IP cellular networks, we proceed with an overview of wireless wide area network generations and families.

We then devote a complete section to focusing on the fourth-generation wireless wide area networks called *Long-Term Evolution* (LTE). LTE has become the first truly global mobile phone and data standard. The discussion on LTE is extended to the study of hybrid wireless structures called *wireless mesh networks* (WMNs), through which various types of networking infrastructures such as WiFi and LTE can be connected together. The chapter ends with a discussion on *characterization of wireless channels*.

7.1   Infrastructure of Wireless Networks

Similar to wired networks, wireless networks are hierarchical. Figure 7.1 shows wireless communication network system hierarchies at all levels. Satellites can provide widespread global coverage for voice, data, and video applications. A satellite orbits

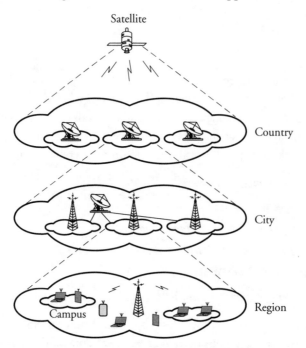

Figure 7.1   Wireless communication system hierarchies from satellite to campuses

the earth while interfacing between a receiver and transmitter pair. The interfacing facilitates the transmission of data to long-distance destinations. Satellite systems are classified according to their orbit distance from the earth:

- *Low-earth orbit.* These satellites orbit the earth at distances between 500 km and 2,000 km and can provide global roaming.
- *Medium-earth orbit.* These satellites orbit the earth at distances of about 10,000 km.
- *Geosynchronous orbit.* These satellites orbit the earth at distances of about 35,800 km. They have a large coverage area and can handle large amounts of data.

Wireless networks are characterized by limited resources from the perspective of frequency range and available bandwidth. The available bandwidth often varies with time. Wireless networks must be able to adapt to the changing network topology. Wireless wide area network topologies are classified into three main groups:

1. *Cellular networks*
2. *Wireless mesh networks* (WMNs)
3. *Mobile ad-hoc networks*

In a *cellular network,* a *base station* as the central device of a star topology in a region called a *cell* interfaces all the wireless communication of the cell. As we explained in Chapter 4, users' hosts in a star topology are connected through a central device. Thus, all traffic from users flows through this central device. Star networks are normally used in cellular and paging systems.

The *wireless mesh networks* (WMNs) are *hybrid networks* that act as a spanning tree of multiple smaller base stations to cover a region. WMN is normally set up to cover a large geographic area. The lowest layer of the hierarchy in a WMN typically represents indoor systems that cover very small areas. The next layer in the hierarchy consists of cellular systems. This hierarchy can be extended to global coverage. The *hybrid* topology is ideally suited for large networks.

The general concept of *mobile ad-hoc networks* will be deeply discussed in Chapter 21. In summary, in an ad-hoc network, two hosts independently communicate without needing a third-party server to assist in setting up connections. Ad-hoc networks are characterized by multiple pairs of nodes. In these networks, nodes are self-configuring, and various tasks are evenly distributed among nodes. Mobile ad-hoc networks are multi-hop networks where a node may use multiple hops to communicate with another node. These networks normally have multiple paths between each two nodes to route, bypassing link failures.

7.2   Cellular Networks

A *cellular network* is a wireless network consisting of multiple wireless networking areas called *cells*. Each cell is a star topology network equipped with a major *base station* (BS) as the central transceiver device located in the center of the cell. Each base station interfaces all the wireless communications of the cell. Mobile communication devices of users in a cell are connected through the cell's base station. Thus, all traffic from mobile users flows through the central base station. A cellular network is formed by a networked array of base stations, each located in a cell to cover the networking services in a certain area.

Each cell is assigned a small frequency band and is served by a base station. Neighboring cells are assigned different frequencies to avoid interference. However, the transmitted power is low, and frequencies can be reused over cells separated by large distances.

For convenience in network modelling, each cell within a cellular network is modelled by a hexagon, which is not far from reality as shown in Figure 7.2. The base station of each cell is typically considered to be located at the heart of the hexagon. The hexagonal pattern of a cell is chosen so that the distance d between the centers of any two adjacent cells becomes the same. Distance d is given by

$$d = \sqrt{3}r, \tag{7.1}$$

where r is the cell radius. A typical practical value for the cell radius is 3 km to 5 km. With the advent of current generation cellular networks, multimedia and voice applications are supported over wireless networks.

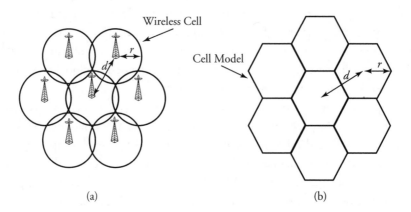

(a)   (b)

Figure 7.2   Cellular partitions: (a) real areas; (b) modeled areas

7.2.1   Cellular Network Devices and Operation

In this section, we introduce a generic set of devices a cellular network requires for its operation. Without loss of generality, we use the most common terms and names for devices in this section. A user's *mobile unit* (user's mobile equipment) in a cellular network can be a mobile host or a cell phone (also referred to as mobile phone or smartphone). At the center of a cell, there is a *base station* (BS) that consists of an antenna tower and a transceiver for transmitting and receiving radio waves. A cellular wireless service provider requires the following additional "control nodes" for its operation as shown in Figure 7.3:

- *Base station controller* (BSC). A base station controller is a router/processor that is responsible for connecting calls among mobile units and managing mobility within a cellular area. A base station controller can serve multiple base stations. The link between a base station and a BSC can be wireline or wireless.

- *Mobile switching center* (MSC). An MSC is a gateway router that can serve multiple base stations. The MSC provides a connection to the public-switched telephone network (PSTN).

- *Serving General* packet radio service *Support Node* (SGSN). SGSN handles packet routing to the public packet-switched network, IP-based device mobility management, authentication, and registration of users. SGSN performs the

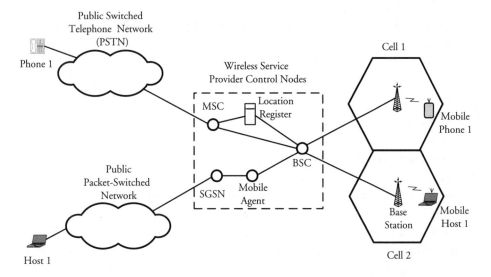

Figure 7.3   Two cells of a cellular network and wireless service provider control nodes

same functions as MSC does for voice traffic. SGSN also handles the protocol conversion from IP to link layer protocols used between the SGSN and the mobile users when needed.

- *Location register.* Location register is the main database of permanent mobile units' information for an area of a cellular network. *Home location register* (HLR) is maintained by the mobile unit's home ISP and contains the pertinent user's address, account status, and preferences. The HLR interacts with the MSC used for call control and processing. When a mobile unit enters a new cellular network the *visiting location register* (VLR) maintains temporary user information, including current location, to manage requests from users who are out of the area covered by their home system.

- *Mobile agent.* A home agent is a router that maintains information about the current location of a user's IP equipment. A *home agent* stores information about mobile units (hosts) whose permanent home address is in the home agent's network. A *foreign agent* stores temporary information provided in the visited (foreign) network and information about a mobile unit's permanent home address.

Figure 7.3 shows all the required links among phone 1 (located in the PSTN), mobile phone 1 (located in cell 1), host 1 (located in the public packet-switched network), and mobile host 1 (located in cell 2). Each base station at the center of a cell is connected to a common base station controller (BSC). An MSC is an intermediating interface between the cellular domain and the public-switched telephone network (PSTN) for connections between a mobile user and a fixed telephone subscriber. In this figure, the MSC is connected to a *location register* and also to a BSC. The BSC supervises the base stations under its coverage. SGSN acts as an interface between a *mobile agent* and the public packet-switched network (the rest of the Internet) to enable communication between a mobile unit and the rest of the Internet.

In terms of channelization on wireless links, cellular networks use two types of channels for communication between a mobile unit and a base station, depending on the application of an operation. These two types of channels are *control channel* and *traffic channel*. Control channels are used for call setup and maintenance. This channel carries control and signaling information. Traffic channels carry the data between the users. Calls between fixed and mobile subscribers are also possible. In the next sections, we discuss more detailed operation of mobile units and base stations in cellular networks. This discussion will be followed by the operation of mobile IP.

Registration and IMSI Assignment

When a mobile unit such as a smartphone is switched on in its home network, it first searches for the strongest radio control channel that is normally associated with the nearest base station. The mobile unit is then assigned the base station associated with the cell in which the mobile unit tries to operate. A handshake of messages takes place between the mobile unit and the associated base station controller (BSC) as shown by step 1 between mobile phone 1 and the base station in Figure 7.4. As a result of this step, the mobile unit is registered with the *home location register* (HLR) portion of the *location register* and thereby with the MSC of the network. The base station and MSC register and authenticate the mobile device through the base station.

Upon the registration of a mobile unit, an *international mobile subscriber identity* (IMSI) is assigned to the mobile unit. An IMSI is a unique identification associated with all cellular networks used by cellular network service providers to identify the user of a cellular network. IMSI is a 64-bit field sent by the phone to the network and is also used for acquiring other details of the mobile unit in the home location register.

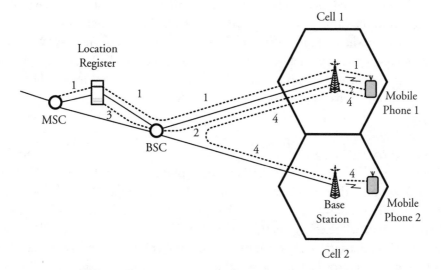

Figure 7.4   Connectivity of mobile users in a cellular network.

If the mobile unit moves to a new cell in the same cellular network, the preceding step of the registration repeats in the new cell using IMSI while the location of the mobile unit needs to be updated in the home portion of the location register. Location updating is used to determine the location of a mobile unit in the idle state. The idle state is a mode in which a mobile unit is connected to the network but has no active call.

Call Establishment and Termination

When a mobile unit originates a call, the called number is sent to the base station of the associated cell, and thereby it is forwarded to the base station controller (BSC). For example, after the step 1 handshake of messages takes place between the mobile unit and the associated base station controller (BSC) as shown in Figure 7.4 between mobile phone 1 and the base station, mobile phone 1 sends the dialed number to the base station of its cell shown at step 2. The base station forwards the dialed number to the BSC in continuation of step 2. The BSC finds the location of mobile phone 2 through the database of the *home location register* (HLR) portion of the *location register* at step 3. Finally at step 4, a wireless connection is established between mobile phones 1 and 2.

Once the connection is established, the exchange of voice occurs between the two communicating mobile units through the base stations and the BSC of the cellular network. If the called mobile phone is busy, the call is either blocked and a busy tone is returned to the calling mobile unit, or a voice mail is activated for the call. This is also the case when all the traffic channels to the base station are busy. When one of the mobile units in a mobile conversation hangs up, the base station controller is informed of the call termination, and the traffic channels are reset at both base stations for other calls. When a base station cannot maintain a minimum signal level during a call, the call is dropped. Weak signals may occur because of interference or channel distortions.

Figure 7.5 shows two other examples of cellular call connections. In the first example, regular phone 1 places a call to mobile phone 1 situated in cell 1 of cellular network 1. Notice that the steps of the call establishment are similar to the preceding example. At step 1 of routing shown in the figure, phone 1 dials the number through the public-switched telephone network (PSTN). The PSTN checks the called phone number within its database to see if the dialed number is any of the mobile numbers associated with its attached mobile switching centers (MSCs). In this case, MSC 1 is identified to be the intermediating node to the destination cellular network.

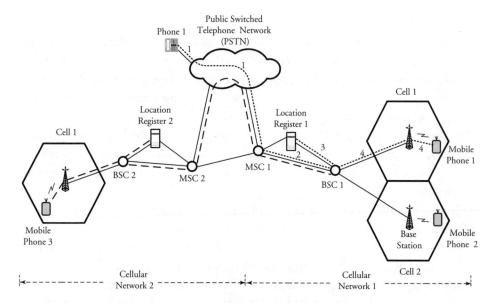

Figure 7.5   Connectivity between a phone and mobile phone, and a failed connection attempt between two mobile phones in cellular networks illustrating steps 1 through 4

Since each MSC can provide services to multiple cellular networks, at this point MSC 1 needs to make a decision as to which cellular network is the home network of the called mobile phone 1. This can be done through its database. Once the decision is made, in this case, BSC 1 is identified as the base station controller of the destination cellular network, and the request is forwarded to the appropriated BSC (in this case BSC 1 at step 2). The procedure of routing to mobile phone 1 from BSC 1, at steps 3 and 4, is similar to the previous case.

In the second example shown by the dashed line in Figure 7.5, mobile phone 3 from cell 1 of cellular network 2 tries to place a call to mobile phone 2 in cell 2 of cellular network 1 while mobile phone 2 is turned off. In this case, a similar routing search as in the previous example is completed in cellular network 2, illustrated by a dashed line track in the figure. Once the call request has reached MSC 2, this center has an option of either directing the connection to MSC 1, or routing the call request to the PSTN through which the call request reaches MSC 1 and thereby BSC 1. Normally the second option happens if MSC 2 does not have sufficient information in its database to find MSC 1. In this case, suppose BSC 1 is aware that mobile phone 2 is unavailable and it thus denies the call request.

Roaming

Roaming refers to the ability of a mobile unit to automatically access communication services, including voice and data communication, when travelling in a visited network located outside the geographic coverage area of the home network. If there is no roaming agreement between the two networks, communication service maintenance is impossible, and service is denied by the visited network. Roaming helps ensure that a traveling mobile unit is continues to receive wireless communication services in the visited network without breaking the connection. Roaming is supported by several factors such as mobility management, authentication, authorization, and billing procedures.

When a mobile unit is turned on in a new visited network managed under a different service provider, the visited network identifies the new arriving mobile unit in its area through receiving a service request from the mobile unit. If the visiting mobile unit has no entry in the home location register (HLR) of the visited network's location register, the visited network accordingly attempts to identify the mobile unit's home network. The required mobile unit information must first be requested by the visited network and any authorization for using the visited network services should be checked.

In summary, a visited network contacts the home network and makes a request for service information about the roaming mobile unit. If this process turns out to be successful, the visited network begins to maintain a temporary subscriber record for the device. Likewise, the home network must update its database to indicate that the mobile unit subscribed with it is on the visited network, and any calls sent to that mobile unit can be routed to the unit's new location. The mobile unit acquires an entry in the database located in the visited location register (VLR) portion of the location register in the visited network, and the authorized network services are enabled. For this, HLR forwards information to its own MSC, which in turn relays the information to the visited MSC and thereby to the VLR. The VLR forwards the routing information back to the MSC, which allows it to find the base station and thereby the mobile unit where the call originated.

Suppose a phone or mobile phone dials the mobile unit's telephone number while the mobile unit is roaming. The following signaling steps resolve the roaming function. The signaling messages such as IAM, SRI, and PRN in the following steps are based on *Mobile Application Part* (MAP) defined in the Signaling System 7 (SS7) standard, which is explained in detail in Chapter 18:

Signaling Steps to Establish a Call While Roaming

1. The call is routed to the MSC based on the phone number by applying an *initial address message* (IAM).

2. The MSC forwards a *send routing information* (SRI) message to the HLR in order to locate the mobile unit in the visited network.

3. The HLR now knows its current VLR based on the past location updates. The HLR then sends a *provide roaming number* (PRN) message to the VLR in order to obtain the phone number of the roaming mobile unit. This is similar to the HLR being able to route the call to the correct MSC.

4. The VLR assigns a temporary phone number to the roaming mobile unit. This number is copied to the HLR in a *routing information acknowledgement* (RIA) message.

5. The home MSC routes the call to reach the roaming mobile unit using the IAM message and treating the phone number as the called party number. The phone number and the IMSI of the mobile unit are now known to the visited network.

6. The MSC sends a *send information* (SI) message to the VLR to acquire other information of the visiting mobile unit capabilities and services subscribed to. If the called mobile unit turns out to be authorized and capable of taking the call, the VLR issues a *complete call* (CC) message back to the MSC. ∎

Paging

The base station controller (BSC) in a cellular network can *page* a specific mobile unit through base stations, based on the called number. The base stations in turn send a paging message on their set-up channel to locate the called unit, as shown in Figure 7.6. Paging is necessary in several cases. For instance, when a mobile unit is in the roaming status when a call arrives for it, the cellular network must page all the mobile units of the cells since the subscribed mobile user does not report its location unless it leaves the zone.

7.2.2   Handoff

A *handoff* in wide area wireless networks is the act of handing over a resource to another, and occurs under the following three circumstances: (1) when a mobile host needs to change its channel to another (*channel handoff*), (2) in a move from one cell

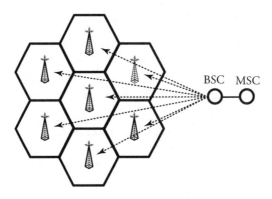

Figure 7.6 Paging operation in a cellular network consisting of multiple cells

to another (*cellular handoff*), or (3) in a move from one region to another (*regional handoff*).

Channel handoff involves transferring a call between channels in a cell. This is normally a task of the base station when the performance of an active channel becomes poor for reasons such as increased noise. In such cases, the wireless unit first initializes a request for a channel change to the base station in a cell, if necessary. If no channels are idle in the cell, the request is rejected, and the wireless terminal has to keep the old channel.

Cellular handoff occurs between two adjacent cells when a mobile host moves from one cell to another. When a cellular handoff request is initialized, the traffic channel needs to be switched to the new base station, using the MSC, as shown in Figure 7.7. This switch of base station requires a seamless handover to the mobile host, without any interruption of the traffic. If no channels are available in the new cell, the handoff call has to be rejected or terminated.

A base station controller with the support of its associated mobile switching center (MSC) can be viewed as an entity for call, routing, and mobility management in a cellular network. Mobility management consists of three functions: *location management with user tracking*, *user authentication*, and *call routing*. Location management involves keeping track of the physical locations of users and directing calls to correct locations. Before a user's call is routed to the desired location, the user must be authenticated. Routing involves setting up a path for the data directed to the user and updating this path as the user location changes. In cellular networks, MSCs in conjunction with base stations coordinate the routing and location-management functions.

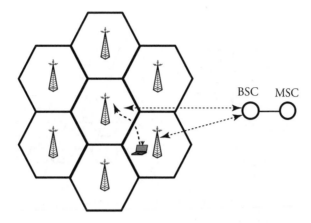

Figure 7.7   Cellular handoff operation from a mobile unit

When a mobile host moves to a new cell, the device requests a handoff for a new channel in the new cell. A successful handoff operation requires certain criteria to be achieved. When a wireless device moves from one base-station cell to another, handoff protocols reroute the existing active connections in the new cell. The challenges in wireless networks are to minimize the packet loss and to provide efficient use of network resources while maintaining quality-of-service (QoS) guarantees. Robustness and stability must also be taken into consideration for handoff protocol design. Robustness and stability are especially important when interference or fading in the radio channel results in a request-handoff operation by a wireless device.

Regional handoff occurs when the mobile user moves from one region to another. From a theoretical standpoint, we can model a handoff process between any two regions, using stochastic models. Consider several hexagonal-shaped regions that consist of a group of hexagonal-shaped cells, as illustrated in Figure 7.8. Typically, the assumption in regional handoff is that only the boundary cells in a region as labeled in Figure 7.8 are involved in the regional handoff model. Similarly, when all channels in the new region are in use, all handoff requests have to be rejected.

Cellular Handoff Modeling

Cellular handoffs can be modeled using different approaches. One of the approaches is called the *stop-and-go* model in which the speed of the mobile host is taken into account. The requirement for handoff is dependent on the speed of the mobile

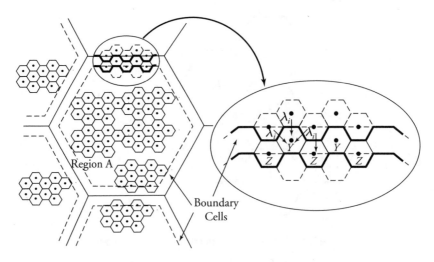

Figure 7.8　Cellular networks and a regional handoff

terminals and the distance between a mobile user and its cell boundaries. The alternation of states for a mobile unit—whether it is still or mobile while carrying a call in progress—also has to be considered for handoff analysis. In reality, a hand-off is needed in two situations: (1) the signal strength within the cell site is low or (2) when a vehicle reaches the cell boundary. We assume that the handoff model is free of signal-strength obstructions. Our second assumption prior to reaching a cell boundary is that a vehicle with a call in progress alternates between still (stop state) and moving (go state).

The stop-and-go states can be presented using a simple state machine. In state 0 (stop), a vehicle is at rest but it has a call in progress. In state 1 (go), the vehicle moves with an average speed of k mph and has a call in progress. Let $\alpha_{i,j}$ be the rate at which a system moves from state i to state j. For example, $\alpha_{0,1}$ is the rate at which state 0 leaves for state 1, and $\alpha_{1,0}$ is the rate at which state 1 leaves for state 0.

The time in the stop state is an exponential random variable with mean $1/\alpha_{0,1}$ (see Appendix C). The time in the go state also is an exponential random variable, with mean $1/\alpha_{1,0}$. Let $P_i(t)$ be the probability that a vehicle having a call in progress is in state i at time t. According to the *Chapman-Kolmogorov* theory on continuous-time Markov chain (explained in Section C.5.1), we can derive

$$P_j^{'}(t) = \sum_i \alpha_{i,j} P_i(t),\qquad(7.2)$$

where $P_j'(t)$ is the time differential of relative state j probability. Applying Equation (7.2) for a system with two states, 0 and 1, we have

$$P_0'(t) = \alpha_{0,0}P_0(t) + \alpha_{1,0}P_1(t), \tag{7.3}$$

and

$$P_1'(t) = \alpha_{0,1}P_0(t) + \alpha_{1,1}P_1(t), \tag{7.4}$$

where $P_0(t)$ and $P_1(t)$ are the probability that a vehicle having a call in progress is in states 0 and 1, respectively, at time t. Knowing that the sum of probabilities is always 1, we get $P_0(t) + P_1(t) = 1$. Now we can use $P_0(t) + P_1(t) = 1$ and also its derivative $P_0'(t) + P_1'(t) = 0$, and combine it with Equation (7.3) to form a first-order differential equation:

$$P_0'(t) + (\alpha_{0,1} - \alpha_{1,1})P_0(t) = -\alpha_{1,1}. \tag{7.5}$$

The total solution to the differential equation consists of a homogeneous solution, $P_{0h}(t)$, plus a particular solution, $P_{0p}(t)$. For a homogeneous solution, we know that $P_0'(t) + (\alpha_{0,1} - \alpha_{1,1})P_0(t) = 0$, with the initial condition $P_{0h}(0) = P_0(0)$, and thus we can obtain the general solution for Equation (7.5) by

$$P_0(t) = P_{0p}(t) + P_{0h}(t)$$

$$= \frac{\alpha_{1,0}}{\alpha_{0,1} - \alpha_{1,1}} + \left(P_0(0) - \frac{\alpha_{1,0}}{\alpha_{0,1} - \alpha_{1,1}}\right)e^{-(\alpha_{0,1}-\alpha_{1,1})t}, \tag{7.6}$$

where $P_0(t)$ is the probability that a vehicle with a call in progress is in state 0 at time t. Similarly, we obtain the general solution for Equation (7.4) by

$$P_1(t) = P_{1p}(t) + P_{1h}(t)$$

$$= \frac{\alpha_{0,1}}{-\alpha_{0,0} + \alpha_{1,0}} + \left(P_1(0) - \frac{\alpha_{0,1}}{-\alpha_{0,0} + \alpha_{1,0}}\right)e^{-(-\alpha_{0,0}+\alpha_{1,0})t}, \tag{7.7}$$

where $P_1(t)$ is the probability that a vehicle with a call in progress is in state 1 at time t. There are four cases for a vehicle to change states:

1. A vehicle is resting permanently but has a call in progress; thus, $P_0(0) = 1$ and $P_1(0) = 0$.

2. A vehicle is moving at an average speed k until it reaches a cell boundary; thus, $P_0(0) = 0$ and $P_1(0) = 1$.

3. A vehicle stops at the initial state and moves on a congested path until reaching a cell boundary, so $P_0(0) = 1$ and $P_1(0) = 0$.

4. A vehicle moves and stops on a congested path until reaching a cell boundary; thus, $P_0(0) = 0$ and $P_1(0) = 1$.

Now, consider the mobilized model shown in Figure 7.9. To show the probability of a call to reach a cell boundary with an average speed k m/h with stop and go or the probability of requiring a handoff, let s be the average speed of the vehicle, where $s = 0$ in state 0 and $s = k$ in state 1. Let $x(t)$ be the vehicle's position at time t, assuming $x(0) = 0$, and let d_b be the distance a vehicle takes to reach a cell boundary. Suppose that t is a random variable representing a channel holding time, or the time a vehicle takes to reach a cell boundary. Let $P_i(t, d_b)$ be the probability that a vehicle in state i with a call in progress is at the cell boundary at time t, where $i \in \{0, 1\}$. Consequently, the probability that a vehicle reaches a cell boundary with speed s undergoing stop-and-go states is

$$P[x(t) \geq d_b] = P_0(d_b/s, d_b)\big|_{s=0} + P_1(d_b/s, d_b)\big|_{s=k}, \tag{7.8}$$

where

$$P_0(d_b/s, d_b)\big|_{s=0} = \frac{\alpha_{1,0}}{\alpha_{0,1} - \alpha_{1,1}} \tag{7.9}$$

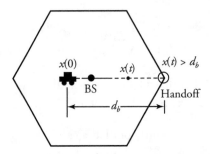

Figure 7.9 Cellular handoff model with mobility

and

$$P_1(d_b/s, d_b)\big|_{s=k} = \frac{\alpha_{0,1}}{-\alpha_{0,0} + \alpha_{1,0}}$$

$$+ \left(P_1(0) - \frac{\alpha_{0,1}}{-\alpha_{0,0} + \alpha_{1,0}} \right) e^{-(-\alpha_{0,0} + \alpha_{1,0})d_b/k}. \quad (7.10)$$

In case 1, since a vehicle is resting all the time, with an average speed of 0 m/h, the probability of reaching a cell boundary is clearly 0 percent. In contrast, for a vehicle moving with an average speed (k) (case 2), the chance of reaching a cell boundary is always 100 percent. Thus, when a vehicle is either at rest or moving, the probability of requiring a handoff is independent of d_b.

7.3 Mobile IP Management in Cellular Networks

The *mobile IP* scheme is a protocol responsible for handling the mobility of users attached to the Internet. *Mobile computing* allows computing devices, such as computers, to move about while functioning routinely. In a mobile IP network, it is essential for both mobile and wired users to interoperate seamlessly. In some mobile IP cases, TCP cannot be used, as the congestion-control scheme would greatly reduce the throughput, and the inherent delays and error bursts may result in a large number of retransmissions. In such cases, some changes have to be made to TCP to use it for internetworking wired and wireless networks. The major challenges with mobile IP are

- *Quality mobile connection.* A quality connection is desired for a user while it is mobile with different speeds.
- *Registration.* A mobile user's address must be identified and registered in different areas.
- *Interoperability.* A mobile user must interact with other stationary and mobile users.
- *Connection reliability.* TCP connections must survive in mobility cases.
- *Security.* A connection must be secured, especially since a wireless connection is less immune to intrusions.

A mobile user requires the same level of reliability for a TCP connection as he/she receives in a wired connection. Note that typical Internet congestion-control schemes cannot be used in wireless networks, because packet drop is caused mainly by poor link quality and channel distortions rather than by congestion. The channel imperfections make it difficult to implement a quality-of-service model other than the best-effort model. The varying data rates and delays make it challenging to implement high-speed and real-time applications, such as voice and video, over wireless networks.

7.3.1   Home Agents and Foreign Agents

In a mobile IP network, the permanent home of a mobile unit is referred to as the *home network*, and the network device in a home network that carries out the function of mobility management is called the *home agent*. A mobile host is allowed to hold two addresses simultaneously. One of the two addresses is permanent and the other is temporary. The permanent address of a host is the conventional IP address. Note that similar to regular networks, there are still MAC addresses (at the link layer) in wireless networks that identify the physical end points of links. In this case, the MSC is actually the home agent.

A mobile host must have a permanent IP address in its home network. A home network is defined as the wireless network in which a mobile host is permanently registered to the service provider of the network. This address is called the home address. A home address is an IP address and is assigned to a mobile host for an extended period of time. The home address remains unchanged even if the host moves out of its home area. In such cases, a host needs to be registered by the home agent.

When a mobile host leaves its home network and enters a *foreign network*, the host must also be registered by the new network and obtain a temporary address. Changing the network typically happens when a mobile host roams in a certain city or changes the city. Once a mobile host leaves its home network for a foreign network, it is assigned a *foreign address* reflecting the mobile host's current point of attachment when away from its home network. In such a case, its messages from the corresponding Internet servers are still sent to the mobile host's home address. Similarly, a *foreign agent* is a router in the mobile host's foreign network that informs a host's home agent of its current foreign address. The home agent always forwards messages to the mobile host's current location. Figure 7.10 shows two wireless networks attached to the Internet in which mobile host B has moved from its home network to a foreign network.

Generally, agent routers in a network are connected through high-speed links to all access points (base stations) in a network. An agent router maintains two

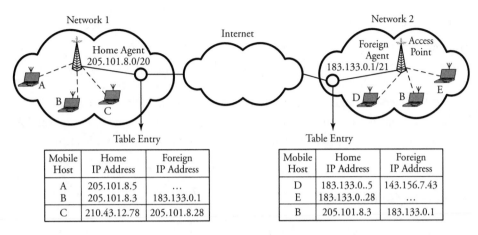

Mobile Host	Home IP Address	Foreign IP Address
A	205.101.8.5	...
B	205.101.8.3	183.133.0.1
C	210.43.12.78	205.101.8.28

Mobile Host	Home IP Address	Foreign IP Address
D	183.133.0..5	143.156.7.43
E	183.133.0..28	...
B	205.101.8.3	183.133.0.1

Figure 7.10   A mobile host moves from its home network to a foreign network

databases: a *home-location database* and a *foreign-location database*. When a mobile host moves to its home network, a signal is sent to the local base station, which forwards this signal to its MSC. The MSC router in turn authenticates the user and registers the user in its home-location database.

7.3.2   Agent Discovery Phase

A home agent maintains a database containing the mobile host's home address. When a mobile host moves to a foreign network, its home and foreign agents establish an association for updating registration with its home agent through the foreign agent. This association is made possible by sending agent advertisement messages. Upon receiving an agent advertisement, the mobile host can learn if it is located in its home network or in a foreign network depending on the type of message. A mobile host can detect whether it is connected to its home link or a foreign link. Once the host moves to a new network, it can determine whether it has changed its point of attachment to obtain a foreign address.

Advertisement messages are propagated periodically in a broadcast manner by all agents. It is always possible that a mobile host does not receive the advertisement due to restricted timing. In such a case, the mobile host needs to send a request message to the agent that it is attached to. If the agent to which the host is attached is a home agent, the registration process is the same as that of a traditional host in a fixed place. But, if the agent is a foreign one, the agent replies with a message containing a foreign address for the agent.

7.3.3 Registration

Mobile IP acts as an interface between the home network and the foreign network where the mobile host currently resides. Mobile IP keeps track of the mobile host's locations, and maps a home address to a current foreign address. The mobile IP interface delivers messages from the home network to the mobile host in its current foreign location in a seamless fashion after a registration process with the foreign agent is completed. The procedure of registration with a new network is summarized as follows:

Mobile IP Registration Steps

  1. Register with an agent on the new network.

  2. On the home network, register with an agent to request call forwarding.

  3. If any registration is about to expire, renew it.

  4. When returning to the home network, cancel the registration with the new network. ∎

A registration phase involves an exchange of two messages between the mobile host and its home agent: the *registration request* and *registration response*. Once a mobile host enters a foreign network, it listens for agent advertisements and then obtains a foreign address from the foreign network it has moved to. The host's home-network agent then adds the foreign network address agent to its home-location database. This is done after the agent authenticates the host through the host's home-network agent. The host's home-network agent now forwards all calls to the host in the foreign network. On the Internet, the location management and routing are done through mobile IP.

A mobile host can also register using a *collocated foreign address*. A collocated foreign address is a local IP address temporarily assigned to a mobile host without using a foreign agent. In collocated foreign addressing, a mobile host receives an assigned temporary foreign address through its own home network. In the meanwhile, as soon as the mobile host leaves the foreign network, it also needs to deregister.

Example.   Reconsider Figure 7.10 showing two wireless networks connected to the Internet. Network 1 is assigned a CIDR IP address (for CIDR addressing, see Chapter 1) 205.101.8.0/20 and it has three active mobile hosts A, B, and C. Suppose that this network is the home network for hosts A and B and but not for host C as it appears from the home IP addresses of the agent routing entry.

Consider a situation in a different time in which host A stays in this network (thus there is no foreign address for it), and host B moves out of this network (thus it obtains a foreign address). Particularly, host B has moved to network 2. Network 2 is also assigned a CIDR IP address 183.133.0.1/21 and it has three active mobile hosts D, E, and B. Present the addressing of network 2 and the relationship of host B and network 2.

Solution. Network 2 in this case is considered a foreign network for host B and is therefore assigned a foreign address of 183.133.0.1. This address appears in both its associated home and foreign agents as seen in Figure 7.10.

7.3.4 Mobile IP Routing

In mobile IP systems, datagrams are encapsulated by a mobile IP header. Figure 7.11 shows the header format of mobile IP registration. The *type* field determines whether the registration is a request or a reply. The *flags/code* field is used in the reply message to specify forwarding details. The *lifetime* field gives the permitted time (in seconds) a registration is valid. The home address and *temporary address* fields are the two addresses explained. The *home address* field specifies the home-agent address of the host. The *identification* field helps a mobile host prevent repeated messages.

Each datagram forwarded to the mobile host's home address is received by its home agent, and then it is forwarded to the mobile host's foreign address. In this case, the mobile host's foreign agent receives the datagram and forwards it to the mobile host. If a mobile host residing in a foreign network wants to send a message to a host outside of its new network, the message does not need to pass through its home agent. In such a case, the message is handled by the foreign agent.

Mobile IP has two routing schemes: *Delta routing* and *direct routing*. In Delta routing, a triangular path is established among the host's home agent, the host's foreign agent, and a corresponding machine. Suppose that the mobile host belonging

Byte:	1	1	2	4	4		
	Type	Flags/Code	Lifetime	Home Address	Temporary Address (Only for Request)	Identification	Extensions

Figure 7.11 Header format of mobile IP registration

to wireless network 1 moves to foreign network 2. While in the foreign network, the mobile host is contacted for communication by a server (as a corresponding machine) fixed in a residential area network. In this case, a datagram (IP packet) from the server is first sent to the mobile host's home network using standard IP routing. The host's home agent detects the message, finds the host's foreign address, and forwards the message to the host's foreign agent. The foreign agent delivers the message to the mobile host. In response, the mobile host can send its reply directly to the server through the foreign agent. This routing process forms a triangular-shape path routing, which is why it is called Delta routing.

Now, consider a case in which a mobile host is the one that wants to initiate the transmission of a message with a server in the same scenario as just explained. In the first step, the mobile host informs the server of its foreign address. Then, the mobile host can send the message directly to the server through its foreign agent bypassing its home agent. This way a chunk of signaling due to routing to the home agent is eliminated. We remember that the corresponding server should initiate communication with a mobile host by first contacting the mobile host's home agent, since the server does not have real-time knowledge of the mobile host's whereabouts.

As we see, the routing of mobile users may involve many different challenges. For example, using the previous scenario, consider that the mobile host moves to yet another new foreign network, say network 3. In this case, the mobile host can inform its previous foreign agent about its new foreign address, so that datagrams (IP packets) routed to the old location can now be routed to the new foreign location.

Virtual Registration and Routing

In order to reduce the cost and the amount of registration with the home agent, mobile Internet Protocol also offers a facility called *virtual registration*. In each region, *virtual agents* instead of just a home agent can be defined. Virtual regions are then defined based on statistics and the density of traffic. Each virtual agent covers service over a local virtual region. When a mobile host enters the virtual region, it registers with the virtual agent. Thus, in a scenario of routing messages between a mobile host and a corresponding server, as described in the previous section, datagrams from the corresponding server are sent to the mobile host's home address, and then routed to the mobile host's foreign address. Datagrams are then sent from the home agent to the virtual agent first and, from there, to the foreign agent. In such cases, the mobile host typically has no knowledge of the network for routing decision making.

Tree-Based Routing

The amount of registration between a home network and a foreign network can also be reduced by a carefully designed hierarchy of foreign agents. In a hierarchical structure, multiple foreign agents are advertised in the agent advertisement. With this scheme, a mobile host has to configure which upper level in the tree its new registration has to go. The mobile host should then transmit the registration to each level of the hierarchy between itself and the closest common parent between its new and previous foreign addresses. If a mobile host currently using the services of one foreign agent moves to a different foreign agent, it may not involve a direct registration with its home agent.

Figure 7.12 shows a tree-based hierarchy of foreign agents. Suppose that a mobile host is currently using the service of foreign agent A16 while at location L1. The mobile host receives agent advertisements from foreign agents A1, A2,

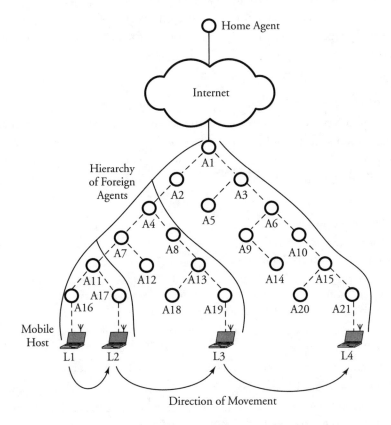

Figure 7.12   Routing in a tree-based structure of foreign agents

A4, A7, A11, and A16. Registration messages are sent to each of these foreign agents and its home agent. However, the home agent of the mobile host can only identify foreign agents in its outside world as far as foreign agent A1. This means that the topology of the hierarchy beyond A1 may stay unknown for the home agent even though it receives messages from other agents. The same thing is true for agent A1, which can see only up to its nearest neighbors A2 and A3, and so on for others. In fact, no agent knows exactly where the mobile host is located except for foreign agent A16.

When the mobile host moves to the vicinity of foreign agent A17 at location L2, the host needs a new registration valid to travel up to the vicinity of A11. If the mobile host moves to the vicinity of foreign agent A19 at location L3, the situation is different, as A17 and A19 are linked directly to a common node as was the case for A16 and A17. In this case, the mobile host receives advertisements specifying the hierarchy of A4, A8, A13, and A19. The mobile host then compares the previous hierarchy and this new one and determines that it has caused the registration to move to as high as level A4 in the tree-based scheme. The same procedure occurs when the mobile host decides to move to location L4.

Mobile Routing with IPv6

Mobile IPv6 offers a simpler mobile routing scheme. With IPv6, no foreign agent is required. A mobile host should use the *address autoconfiguration procedure* embedded in IPv6 to obtain a foreign address on a foreign network. The procedure for routing with mobile IPv6 is summarized as follows:

Mobile IPv6 Routing Steps

1. A host informs its home agent and also corresponding machines about its foreign address.

2. **If** a corresponding machine knows the mobile host's current foreign address, it can send packets directly to the mobile host by using the IPv6 routing header;

   Otherwise the corresponding machine sends packets without the IPv6 routing header.

3. Packets are routed to the mobile host's home agent.

4. Packets are forwarded to the mobile host's foreign address.

5. **If** the mobile host moves back to its home network, the host notifies its home agent. ■

It is clear that the routing steps are similar to those for IPv4 except for the elimination of the foreign agent in IPv6. Overall, routing with IPv6 is simpler and the option of source routing is also available.

7.3.5   Generations of Cellular Networks

First-generation (1G) cellular networks were mostly analog. Channels were allotted to a single user, and each user had dedicated access to the channel. This led to underutilization of resources. Second-generation (2G) cellular networks were digital and supported higher data rates, providing digital traffic channels and digitized voice before transmission over the channel. Data digitization made it simple to implement an encryption scheme. The digital traffic also made it possible to deploy better error detection and correction. Finally, multiple users shared a channel by using multiple-access schemes, such as TDMA or CDMA (see Chapter 3 for more about these schemes). Third-generation (3G) cellular networks provided high data rates and support for multimedia communications, in addition to voice communications. The main objectives of these cellular networks are to achieve quality voice communications, higher data rates for stationary and mobile users, support for a wide variety of mobile hosts, and ability to adapt to new services and technology usable in a wide variety of environments, such as offices, cities, and airplanes.

WiMAX Technology and IEEE 802.16

Worldwide interoperability for microwave access (WiMAX) is another wireless wide area network technology and belongs to a generation believed to be between 3G and 4G. WiMAX is a certification mark for the IEEE 802.16 standard. This standard is implemented for point-to-multipoint broadband wireless access. WiMAX is a wireless WAN technology that can connect IEEE 802.11 WiFi hotspots with one another and to other parts of the Internet. WiMAX also provides a wireless alternative to cable and DSL for broadband access. WiMAX devices are capable of forming wireless connections to allow Internet packets to be carried across a network.

The IEEE 802.16 standard offers a significant improvement for communications, as it defines a MAC layer that supports multiple physical-layer specifications, potentially making WiMAX a great framework for wireless broadband communications. The 802.16 MAC is a scheduling MAC whereby the user mobile unit competes once for initial entry into the network. After accessing the network, the base station allocates a time slot to the mobile unit. This time slot can be enlarged or constricted, and no other users can use it. Unlike 802.11, the 802.16 scheduling algorithm exhibits stability given overload and offers better bandwidth efficiency. Another advantage is that the 802.16 standard allows a base station to offer quality of service (QoS) by balancing the assignments of users.

The IEEE 802.16 standard has determined that the frequency range of 10GHz to 66GHz. WiMAX makes excellent use of multipath signals. IEEE 802.16 dictates up to 50 km of connectivity services between users without a direct line of sight. This does not mean that a user 50 km away with no line of sight has connectivity, and practically, this distance is 5 km to 8 km. The data rate with WiMAX is up to 70Mb/s, which is sufficient to simultaneously support more than 60 businesses with T-1-type connectivity. The line of sight is about 1,000 homes at 1Mb/s DSL-level connectivity.

WiMAX antennas can share a cell tower without impacting the normal operations of the cellular network. A WiMAX antenna can even be connected to an Internet backbone via optical fibers or a directional microwave link. WiMAX may be considered for cities or countries willing to skip a wired infrastructure, establishing a wireless infrastructure in an inexpensive, decentralized, deployment-friendly, and effective manner.

LTE and Beyond 4G

Telecommunications companies have made enormous investments on providing packet-switched wireless wide area services. These investments have led to fourth-generation (4G) wireless wide area networks called *Long-Term Evolution* (LTE). LTE is a cellular-oriented standard for wireless high-speed data for mobile phones and data terminals and achieves data rates in excess of 10Mb/s. Yet, fifth-generation (5G) mobile networks denote the next major phase of wireless networking standards beyond the current 4G. The 5G technology includes updated standards that define capabilities beyond those defined in the current 4G standards. Those new capabilities are being grouped under the current ITU-T 4G standards. Our focus at this point is LTE technology, which is discussed next.

7.4 Long-Term Evolution (LTE) Technology

Long-Term Evolution (LTE) has become the first truly global mobile phone and data standard. LTE is desigend for integrated wireless voice, video, and data communications with a goal of increased capacity and speed in wireless data networks. This technology also targets simplification in the structure of the network to furnish IP-based services with significantly reduced data transfer latency. By its nature, LTE is a cellular system and supports cell sizes from tens of meters radius, forming smaller cells called *femtocells* and *picocells*, up to 100 km (62 miles) radius *macrocells*. In the lower frequency bands used in rural areas, a cell with radius 5 km (3.1 miles) is the optimal cell size while cells of size 30 km (19 miles) have reasonable performance.

LTE has a set of standards defined under *Evolved Packet Core* (EPC). EPC unifies the separate cellular voice-based network and the cellular packet-switched network in an all-IP network where both voice and data are carried in IP packets. In Chapter 18, we will learn how voice can be converted to IP packets and used in packet-switched networks. The voice over LTE (VoLTE) scheme results in the voice service being delivered and treated as data flows. In this scheme, when a voice call is to be set up or received, the EPC manages network resources to provide quality of service for such applications.

7.4.1   LTE Networking Devices

In this section, we introduce specific devices used in LTE environments. The mobile user device in LTE is called *user equipment* (UE). A UE is an access device for a user, but it further provides measurements that indicate channel conditions to the network. At the center of an LTE cell, there is a base station called *evolved node B* (eNodeB). This base station is responsible for enforcing all rules and protocols such as the ones in the physical, media access control (MAC), radio link control (RLC), and Packet Data Convergence Protocol (PDCP) layers. The central eNodeB also carries out compression and encryption processes and does admission control, scheduling, and enforcement of negotiated uplink QoS. An LTE cellular network additionally requires the following networking nodes collectively called the *Evolved Packet Core* (EPC) for its operation as shown in Figure 7.13:

- *Packet* data network *Gateway* (PGW). The PGW is a router that provides connectivity between a UE and external packet data networks by being the point of exit and entry for UE traffic. It performs policy enforcement, packet filtering for mobile users, charging support, lawful interception, and packet screening. It also acts as the interface for mobility between LTE and non-LTE technologies.

- *Serving Gateway* (SGW). The SGW is a router for forwarding user data packets and also acting as the mobility anchor for the user plane during eNodeB-to-eNodeB handoffs. All the routing information within each cell is stored at this gateway router. One of other main tasks of the SGW is to terminate the

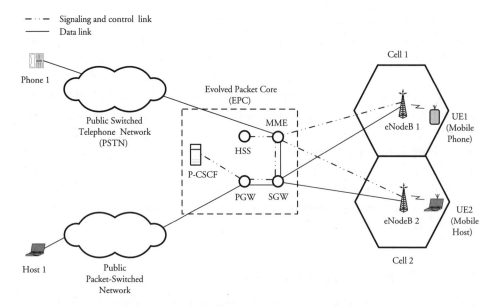

Figure 7.13   An overview of LTE cellular networks

downlink data path for idle state UEs and initiate paging when downlink data arrives for a UE.

- *Home Subscriber Server* (HSS). The HSS is a major database server containing user-related and subscription-related information. The HSS performs mobility management, call and session establishment support, user authentication, and access authorization.

- *Mobility Management Entity* (MME). The MME is an LTE control center responsible for idle mode UE tracking and paging procedures. When it comes to the choice of SGW for a user equipment unit at its initial attachment to a cell and at the time of intra-LTE handoff, the MME can choose an SGW for the user. It also authenticates the user by interacting with the HSS and handles security key management. The MME serves as the termination point for cases in which generation and allocation of temporary identities to UEs are needed. Finally, the MME is an interface between the LTE cellular network and the PSTN.

- *Proxy Call Session Control Function* (P-CSCF). The P-CSCF is a server specified to handle the signaling portion of a certain voice over IP protocol that will be discussed in Chapter 18.

7.4.2   Call Establishment in LTE Cells

Figure 7.14 shows an example of an LTE cellular data connection through the public packet-switched network. Assume mobile host UE 1 tries to connect to the Internet and upload a file from host 1. At step 1 of the routing shown in the figure, UE 1 starts a connection to its base station eNodeB 1, and then the base station sends the request to the MME at step 2. The role of the MME at this point is to ensure that the mobility status of UE 1 is in fine shape, and to obtain the authorization for UE 1 from the HSS at step 3. Once all parameters for a connection are approved, the MME tells the SGW at step 4 that the connection can be established. The SGW intermediates the connection to eNodeB 1 at step 5 and thereby to UE 1 at step 6. Meanwhile, the SGW coordinates the connection to the interfacing node PGW at step 7 and thereby to host 1 at step 8.

7.4.3   Handoff in LTE

As we saw in the previous section, LTE is equipped with a truly IP-based network architecture, called the *Evolved Packet Core* (EPC). The EPC has been designed to support seamless handoffs for both voice and data. The support for seamless handoff is exemplified by support for mobile units moving at up to 350 km/h (220 mph) or 500 km/h (310 mph) depending on the frequency band. Figure 7.15 shows a handoff scenario for a mobile host in cell 1 having a connection in the Internet moving to host 2. In Figure 7.15 (a), the mobile host is connected to the Internet through the SGW and MME while its control channel is associated with the MME. While moving toward cell 2, the mobile host continues to run signal strength measurement of the neighboring cell.

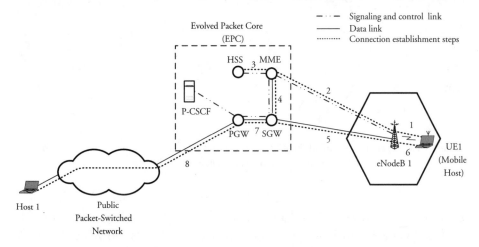

Figure 7.14   Connectivity between a mobile host in an LTE cellular network and a host in the wireline portion of the Internet using steps 1 through 8

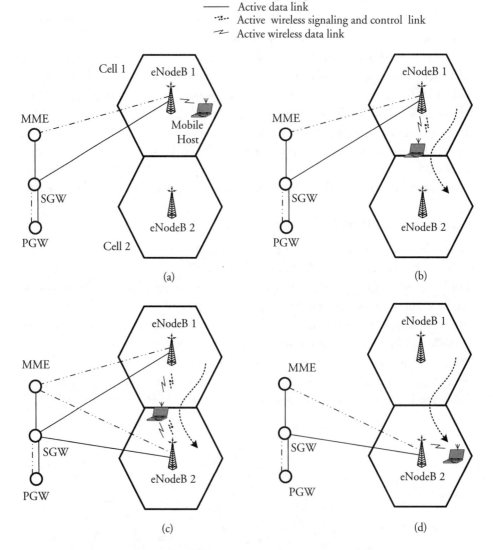

Figure 7.15 Operation of handoff in LTE cellular networks: (a) before handoff, (b) preparation of handoff, (c) handoff of radio channels, and (d) after handoff

Once the mobile host reaches the border zone between cell 1 and cell 2, the report on the signal strength of the data channels is sent through the signaling and control link to eNodeB 1 and then to the MME as shown in Figure 7.15 (b). The MME understands that the host is trying to pass the border from cell 1 to cell 2, and as soon as the report of signal strength measurement shows that cell 2 is dominating, the *handoff* happens.

With handoff, the radio data channel of the mobile host is handed over from eNodeB 1 to eNodeB 2 by providing a new channel that eNodeB 2 can identify as shown in Figure 7.15 (c). Finally, as indicated in Figure 7.15 (d), when the mobile unit enters cell 2's territory, the MME discontinues the wireless channel of the mobile host on eNodeB 1 and thus eNodeB 2 will be the base station of the mobile host.

7.4.4   Downlink and Uplink Schemes in LTE

For *downlink* communication, defined as a communication from eNodeB to a UE, LTE uses the OFDMA multiple access scheme; and for the *uplink* communication, defined as a communication from a UE to eNodeB, LTE uses the SC-FDMA multiple access scheme. Both of these schemes are multi-carrier schemes that allocate radio resources to multiple users as explained in Chapter 3. In order to conserve power, OFDMA splits the carrier frequency bandwidth into many small subcarriers spaced at 15kHz, and then modulates each individual subcarrier using the QPSK, 16-QAM, or 64-QAM digital modulation as explained in the modulation techniques in Chapter 2. OFDMA assigns each mobile user the bandwidth needed for their transmission. The interesting part of the downlink scheme with OFDMA is that any unassigned subcarrier becomes off, and thus reducing power consumption and interference becomes feasible. Each active mobile unit is assigned one or more 0.5 ms time slots in one or more of the channel frequencies such that a mobile unit is able to achieve increasingly higher transmission rates. In the uplink scheme, SC-FDMA, data spreads across multiple subcarriers.

7.4.5   Frequency Reuse

The basic idea of *frequency reuse* in cellular networks is that if a channel of a certain frequency covers an area, the same frequency can be reused to cover another area. The transmission power of the antenna in a cell is limited to keep energy from escaping into neighboring cells. We define a *reuse cluster of cells* as N cells in which no frequencies are identical. Two *cochannel cells* are then referred to as two cells in which a frequency in one cell is reused in the other one. Figure 7.16 shows a frequency-reuse pattern in a cellular network. In this example, each cluster has seven cells, and those cells with the same numbers are cochannel cells.

Let F be the total number of frequencies allotted to a cluster with N cells. Assuming that all cluster cells share an equal number of frequencies, the number of channels (frequencies) each cell can accommodate is

$$c = \frac{F}{N}. \qquad (7.11)$$

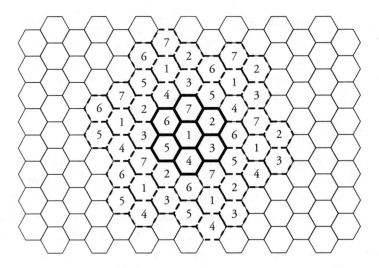

Figure 7.16   Cell clusters and frequency reuse among seven-cell clusters

A cluster can be replicated many times. If k is the number of times a cell is replicated, the total number of channels in the cellular system—so-called *system capacity*—is derived by

$$C = kF = kcN. \tag{7.12}$$

Let d be the distance between the centers of any two adjacent cells, and r be the radius of a cell as shown in Figure 7.17. In order to determine the location of a cochannel cell, we start from the center of a cell and move m cells or md km in any direction, then turn 60 degrees counterclockwise, and, finally, move n cells or nd km until we reach a cell with the same frequency. As shown in Figure 7.17, we have a case with $m = 2$ and $n = 1$. Using a simple geometric manipulation of this situation, we can calculate the distance between the center of the nearest neighboring cochannel cell, $D = \sqrt{A^2 + (md + x)^2}$:

$$\begin{aligned} D &= \sqrt{(nd\cos 30)^2 + (md + nd\sin 30)^2} \\ &= d\sqrt{m^2 + n^2 + mn}. \end{aligned} \tag{7.13}$$

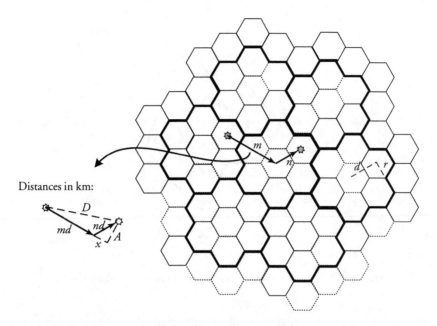

Figure 7.17   Nearest cochannel cells

As the distance between the centers of any two adjacent cells is $d = \sqrt{3}r$ according to Equation (7.1), we can rewrite Equation (7.13) as

$$D = r\sqrt{3(m^2 + n^2 + mn)}. \tag{7.14}$$

If we connect all the centers of all hexagons for the cochannel cells labeled 1 as shown in Figure 7.18 —the same arguments can be made for 2, 3, … cochannel cells—we make a larger hexagon, covering N cells with radius D. Knowing that the area of a hexagon is approximately $2.598 \times$ (square of its radius), we can derive the ratio of the areas of the r-radius hexagon, A_r, and D-radius hexagon A_D as

$$\frac{A_r}{A_D} = \frac{2.598r^2}{2.598D^2}. \tag{7.15}$$

Combining Equations (7.14) and (7.15), we calculate the area ratio as

$$\frac{A_r}{A_D} = \frac{1}{3(m^2 + n^2 + mn)}. \tag{7.16}$$

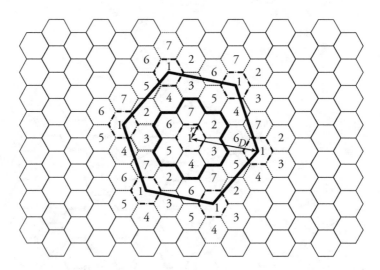

Figure 7.18   Forming a *D*-radius cluster by connecting all cell 1 centers

From the geometry, we can easily verify that the *D*-radius hexagon can enclose *N* cells plus 1/3 of the cells from each six overlapping peripheral *D*-radius hexagons. Consequently, the total number of cells covered in a *D*-radius hexagon is $N + 6(1/3)N = 3N$. Then, $\frac{A_r}{A_D} = \frac{1}{3N}$, and Equation (7.16) can be simplified to

$$N = m^2 + n^2 + mn. \tag{7.17}$$

This important result gives an expression for the size of the cluster in terms of *m* and *n*. As the number of users in a cellular network increases, frequencies allotted to each cell may not be sufficient to properly serve all its users. Several techniques can be used to overcome these problems, as follows:

- *Adding new channels.* As networks grow in size and cells expand, channels can be added to accommodate a large number of users.

- *Frequency borrowing.* When a cell becomes congested, it can borrow frequencies from adjacent cells to handle the increased load.

- *Cell splitting.* In areas with a high volume of usage, cells are split into smaller cells. The power level of the transceiver is reduced to enable frequency reuse. But smaller cells increase the number of handoffs that take place as the user moves from one cell to another more often.

- *Cell sectoring*: A cell can be partitioned into sectors, with each sector containing its own subchannel.

- *Microcells*. In congested areas, such as city streets and highways, microcells can be formed. In a smaller cell, the power levels of the base station and mobile units are low.

Example.   Consider a cellular network with 64 cells and a cell radius of $r = 2$ km. Let F be 336 traffic radio channels and $N = 7$. Find the area of each cell and the total channel capacity.

Solution.   Each hexagon has an area of $1.5\sqrt{3}r^2 = 10.39$ km². The total area covered by the hexagonal cells is $10.39 \times 64 = 664.69^2$. For $N = 7$, the number of channels per cell is $336/7 = 48$. Therefore, the total channel capacity is equal to $48 \times 64 = 3,072$ channels.

7.5   Wireless Mesh Networks (WMNs) with LTE

A *wireless mesh network* (WMN) is an alternative to a cellular network. A WMN is a dynamically self-organized wireless network that maintains "mesh" connectivity. WMNs utilize multiple base stations but each can be smaller than the one used in a cellular network. The base stations in a covered region cooperate with each other to help users stay online anywhere, anytime, for an unlimited time. One key component that makes this happen is the utilization of wireless nodes of routers and base stations in mesh infrastructures where each node acts both as a router and a base station. We look at applications of WMNs and WiMax networks, and the connectivity of P2P networks with backbone wireless mesh networks.

7.5.1   Applications of Mesh Networks

In WMNs, two types of nodes perform the routing: *mesh routers* and *mesh users*. Figure 7.19 shows the detailed connectivity of a backbone mesh network to WiFi and LTE wireless cellular networks. In this figure, a WiFi network and an LTE cellular network are connected through mesh-based *wireless routers with gateway*. A wireless router with gateway capability enables the integration of the WMN backbone with other types of networks.

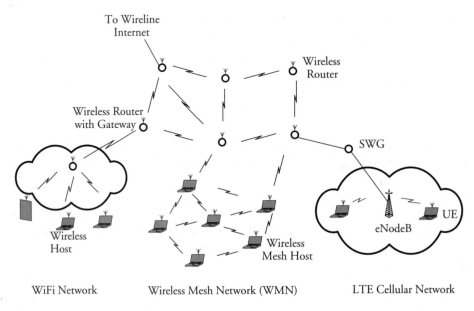

Figure 7.19 Overview of a wireless mesh network (WMN) serving as a backbone network to other networking environments

Wireless mesh hosts can also operate as wireless routers as part of the WMN, making the connectivity simpler than in conventional wireless networks with base stations. Figure 7.19 shows a scenario in which part of the wireless mesh network backbone consists of wireless mesh hosts. Wireless mesh hosts communicate in an ad-hoc fashion. Mobile ad-hoc networks are self-organizing with each individual host acting as a router; we will discuss them in Chapter 21. In WMNs, wired links can also be used in the structure of networks where there is a need for it. The WMN subnetwork consisting of wireless mesh hosts can alternatively be viewed as a *peer-to-peer* (P2P) network similar to the ones explained in Chapter 9.

Wireless mesh networks are designed for metropolitan and enterprise networking, and most of the standards, such as IEEE 802.11, IEEE 802.15, and IEEE 802.16, are accepted in WMN infrastructures. A widely accepted radio technology is the series of IEEE 802.11 standards. The inclusion of multiple wireless interfaces in mesh routers potentially enhances the flexibility of mesh networks. WMNs offer advantages of low cost, easy network maintenance, and more reliable service coverage than conventional ad-hoc networks. Other benefits of a wireless mesh network are as follows:

- *Mobility support of end nodes.* End nodes are supported through the wireless infrastructure.
- *Connectivity to wired infrastructure.* Gateway mesh routers may integrate heterogeneous networks in both a wired and wireless fashion.
- *Scalability.* The WMN infrastructure is designed to be scalable as the need for network access increases.
- *Ad-hoc networking support.* WMNs have the capability to self-organize and be connected to certain points of ad-hoc networks for a short period of time.

To achieve scalability in WMNs, all protocols—from the MAC layer to the application layer—must be scalable. "Topology-" and "routing-aware" MAC can substantially improve the performance of WMNs.

The QoS provisioning in wireless mesh networks is different from that of classical ad-hoc networks. Several applications are broadband services with heterogeneous QoS requirements. Consequently, additional performance metrics, such as delay jitter and aggregate and per node throughput, must be considered in establishing a route. Application-specific security protocols must also be designed for WMNs. Security protocols for ad-hoc networks cannot provide any reliability, as the traffic in such networks can resemble the one flowing in the wired Internet.

7.5.2 Physical and MAC Layers of WMNs

The *physical layer* of wireless mesh networks benefits from existing modulation and coding rates. *Orthogonal frequency multiple access* (OFDM) and *ultrawide band* (UWB) techniques are used to support high-speed wireless communications.

Physical Layer

WMN communication quality and system capacity have been improved through the use of multiantenna systems, such as antenna diversity, smart antenna, and MIMO (*multiple-input multiple-output*) systems. MIMO algorithms send information over two or more antennas. The radio signals reflect objects, making multiple paths that in conventional radios cause interference and fading. A MIMO system uses these paths to carry more information. Another improvement in WMNs includes the use of *cognitive radios*, which dynamically capture unoccupied spectrum. One of the unique features of this technology is that all components of its radio, including RF bands, channel-access modes, and even channel modulation, are programmable.

MAC Layer

The WMN MAC layer is different from that in classical wireless networks. In WMNs, the MAC layer is designed to face more than one-hop communication and has a self-organization feature. This makes WMN nodes somehow different from regular base stations. WMNs support moderately lower mobility than classical wireless networks. Wireless mesh MAC protocols can be designed for both a single channel and multiple channels or to even operate simultaneously. A multiple-channel MAC setup improves network performance significantly by increasing network capacity. Because of the poor scalability of CSMA/CA schemes, these techniques are not efficient solutions for single-channel MAC protocols. The best solution for WMNs is the enhanced versions of TDMA or CDMA, owing to their low complexity and cost.

Multichannel MAC can be deployed in various ways. With *multichannel single-transceiver* MAC, only one channel can be active at a time in each network node, as only one transceiver is available. With *multichannel multi-transceiver* MAC, several channels can be active simultaneously and only one MAC-layer module is assigned to coordinate all channels. With *multi-radio* MAC, each node has multiple radios, and each radio has its own MAC layer and physical layer.

7.6 Characterization of Wireless Channels

Wireless communication is characterized by several channel impediments. Channels are susceptible to interference and noise. The characteristics of a wireless channel vary with time and user movement. The transmitted signal reaches a receiver via three different paths: *direct, scattering,* and *reflection.* Signals arriving at a receiver through scattering and reflection are normally shifted in amplitude and phase. Wireless channels are characterized by *path loss, shadow fading, flat and deep fading, Doppler frequency shift,* and *interference.* We discuss each of these factors briefly.

Path Loss

Path loss is a measure of degradation in the received signal power. The path loss depends on the transmitted power and the propagation distance. An important measure of the strength of the received signal is the *signal-to-noise ratio* (*SNR*). If the average noise power at the receiver is P_n, the signal-to-noise ratio is given by

$$SNR = \frac{P_r}{P_n}, \tag{7.18}$$

where we define P_r to be the received power. The received signal power decreases for higher frequencies, since such signals attenuate more rapidly. Thus, the path loss increases with higher frequencies. The error rate in the channel is reduced when the signal-to-noise ratio is maintained at a high level. The path loss, L_p, is defined as the ratio of transmitted power to received power and obtained from:

$$L_p = \frac{P_t}{P_r} = \left(\frac{4\pi d}{\lambda}\right)^2. \tag{7.19}$$

where P_t is the transmitted power. For the detailed explanation of why the ratio of transmitted power to received power can also be expressed in terms in λ and d, see Equation (2.3) in Chapter 2.

Example.   Consider a commercial wireless mobile telephone system. Assume a transmitter operating at a frequency of 850MHz and with a power of 100 milliwatts communicates with a mobile receiver with received power of 10^{-6} microwatts. Find the distance between the transmitter and the receiver.

Solution.   We can first find the path loss by

$$L_p = \frac{P_t}{P_r} = \frac{100 \times 10^{-3}}{10^{-6} \times 10^{-6}} = 10^{11}. \tag{7.20}$$

Knowing that $\lambda = c/f$, where f is the operating frequency of 850MHz and c is the speed of light in free space estimated at 3×10^8 m/s, we can use Equation (7.19) to obtain d. The answer is $d = 8.8$ km.

Shadow Fading

A wireless signal may encounter various obstructions, such as buildings, walls, mountains, and other objects as it propagates through the wireless medium. Physical obstructions cause attenuation in the transmitted signal. The variation of the received signal power due to these obstructions is called *shadow fading*. In typical cases, the variation in the received signal power because of shadow fading follows a Gaussian distribution. From Equation (2.3), the received signal power seems to be the same at equal distance from the transmitter. However, even when d is the same in Equation (2.3), the received signal power varies, since some locations face greater shadow fading than do others. Normally, the transmit power P_t should be increased to compensate for the shadow-fading effect. Figure 7.20 shows the shadow-fading effect of a received signal.

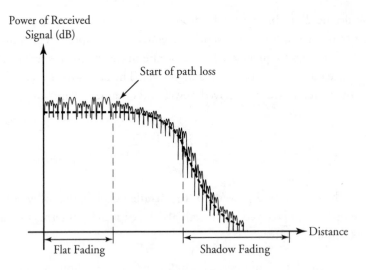

Figure 7.20   Flat fading, path loss, and shadow fading

Flat and Deep Fading

At each wireless receiver, the received signal power fluctuates rapidly with time and slightly with distance, a phenomenon called *flat fading*. Figure 7.20 shows a received signal power that varies with distance. The figure shows that the received signal power falls from its average value. This phenomenon, whereby the received signal power falls below the value required to meet link-performance constraints, is called *deep fading*.

Doppler Frequency Shift

Let v_r be the relative velocity between a transmitter and a receiver. The shift in the frequency of the transmitted signal caused by the relative velocity is called *Doppler shift* and is expressed by f_D:

$$f_D = \frac{v_r}{\lambda}, \tag{7.21}$$

where λ is the wavelength of the transmitted signal. As the relative velocity changes with time, the Doppler shift also varies. In frequency modulation, this shift could result in an increase in the bandwidth of the signal. In most scenarios, the Doppler shift can be of the order of several hertz, whereas the signal bandwidth is of the order of several kilohertz. Thus, the effect of Doppler shift is negligible in these cases.

Interference

The limited frequency spectrum in wireless channels leads to frequency reuse at spatially separated locations. Frequency reuse can lead to *interference*. The interference can be reduced by using more complex systems, such as dynamic channel allocation, multiuser detection, and directional antennas. Interference can also result from adjacent channels if they occupy frequencies outside their allocated frequency bands, although interference can be reduced by having a guard band between channels. Interference can also result from other users and other systems operating in the same frequency band. Certain filters and spread-spectrum techniques are used to eliminate this type of interference.

7.6.1   Capacity Limits of Wireless Channels

Claude Shannon derived an analytical formula for the capacity of communication channels. The capacity of a channel in bits per second is given by

$$C = B \log_2 (1 + SNR), \tag{7.22}$$

where B is the channel bandwidth, and SNR is the signal-to-noise ratio at the receiver. Shannon's formula gives only a theoretical estimate and assumes a channel without shadowing, fading, and intersymbol interference effects. For wired networks, Shannon's formula gives a good estimate of the maximum achievable data rates. For wireless channels, the achievable data rate is much lower than the one suggested by Shannon's formula. The reason is that the channel characteristics vary with time, owing to shadowing, fading, and intersymbol interference.

7.6.2   Channel Coding

Channel coding is a mechanism used to make channels immune to noise and to correct errors introduced by the channel. This process involves adding some redundant bits to the transmitted information. These redundant bits can be used for error detection and correction. The use of channel coding can eliminate the need for retransmission when channel-errors occur. The redundant bits can be used to correct the errors and thereby reduce the transmit power and achieve a lower BER.

   Forward error correction (FEC) is a commonly used scheme for channel coding. FEC schemes normally increase the signal bandwidth and lower the data rate. The *automatic repeat request* (ARQ) is data link error control technique through which transmission of data is carried out when an error is discovered. ARQ is normally used along with FEC, as FEC is not sufficient for implementing channel coding. *Turbo codes* have also been successful in achieving data rates near Shannon's capacity. Turbo codes, however, are very complex and have large delays.

7.6.3 Flat-Fading Countermeasures

The common techniques used to combat flat fading are *diversity, coding and interleaving*, and *adaptive modulation*. With *diversity* multiple independent fading paths are combined at the receiver to reduce power variations. These independent fading paths can be obtained by separating the signal in time, frequency, or space. Space diversity is one of the most commonly used and effective diversity techniques. An antenna array is used to achieve independent fading paths. Antenna elements in the array are spaced at least one-half wavelength apart.

Coding and interleaving is another technique used to counter flat fading. In general, flat fading causes errors to occur in bursts. With coding and interleaving, these burst errors are spread over multiple code words. The adjacent bits from a single code word are spread among other code words to reduce the burst of errors, because burst errors affect adjacent bits. The code words passed to the decoder of the interleaving process ideally contain at most one bit error. FEC channel coding can be used to correct these errors.

Adaptive modulation schemes adjust to channel variations. The transmission scheme adapts to the varying channel conditions, based on an estimate that is sent back to the transmitter. The data rate, transmit power, and coding scheme are tailored, based on the received channel estimate. The channel estimate varies, depending on the amount of flat fading. These adaptive schemes help reduce BER and increase efficiency. The adaptive schemes do not function properly if a channel cannot be estimated or if the channel characteristics change very rapidly. It should be noted that the feedback scheme for conveying the channel estimate to the transmitter requires additional bandwidth.

7.6.4 Intersymbol Interference Countermeasures

The techniques used to combat *intersymbol interference* (ISI) can be classified into signal-processing techniques and antenna solutions. The signal-processing techniques, which attempt to compensate for ISI or reduce the influence of ISI on the transmitted signal, include equalization, multicarrier modulation, and spread-spectrum techniques. The antenna solutions attempt to reduce ISI by reducing the delay between the multipath components and include directive beams and smart antennas.

The equalization method compensates for ISI at the receiver through channel inversion. The received signal is passed through a linear filter with inverse frequency response, making ISI zero. The noise has to be reduced before passing the signal through the inverse filter. This is done by a linear equalizer called the minimum mean square equalizer. Given a large variation in the channel frequency response, a nonlinear *decision-feedback equalizer* (DFE) is used. DFE uses the ISI information from the previously detected symbols to achieve equalization.

DFE is more complex and achieves a much lower BER. Other equalization techniques are the maximum-likelihood sequence and turbo equalization. These schemes perform better than DFE but are much more complex. The equalizer techniques require an accurate channel estimate to compensate correctly for ISI. As a result, equalizer techniques may not work well for channels in which the characteristics change rapidly.

Multi-carrier modulation is another technique used to reduce the effect of ISI. The transmission bandwidth is divided into a number of narrow slots called sub-channels. The message signal containing the information to be transmitted is also divided into an equal number of slots. Each of these slots is modulated on one of the subchannels. The resulting sequence is transmitted in parallel. The subchannel bandwidth is maintained less than the coherent bandwidth of the channel. This results in a flat fading instead of a frequency-selective fading in each channel, thereby helping to eliminate ISI. The subchannels can be either nonoverlapping or overlapping. The overlapping subchannels are referred to as *orthogonal frequency division multiplexing* (OFDM). This technique improves the spectral efficiency but results in a greater frequency-selective fading, thereby decreasing the signal-to-noise ratio.

7.7 Summary

This chapter presented the basics of wireless networking without focusing on large-scale routing issues. We introduced the fundamental concept of wireless wide area networking, starting with *cellular networks* including a networked array of *base stations*, each located in a hexagonal *cell* to cover networking services. Each mobile user should register with the regional *mobile switching center*. Because of unexpected interference whenever a user works with radio frequencies, we looked at known interference and *frequency reuse*. Frequency reuse in a certain region of a wireless network occurs when the same frequency used in one area could be reused to cover another area.

We also studied *mobile IP*. We learned that this protocol is responsible for handling the mobility of users attached to the Internet. A mobile host is allowed to hold two addresses simultaneously: a home address and a foreign address. One of the main elements of mobile IP is registration in a foreign network.

We next covered the fourth-generation cellular networks called *Long Term Evolution* (LTE). We saw that one of the outstanding features of LTE is that it is a wireless broadband technology designed to support roaming with Internet access through mobile equipment. This is a significant improvement over older cellular communication standards. Connection to the Internet is possible through a standard base station called eNodeB, a signaling router called the MME, and two gateway routers known as the SGW and PGW.

We then introduced *wireless mesh networks* (WMNs) constructed with distributed smaller base stations to collectively form a wireless network backbone for several applications. WMNs can connect to WiFi and LTE technologies. At the end of the chapter, we reviewed some issues related to wireless channels. We noticed that wireless channels have several weaknesses, such as shadow fading, path loss, and interference.

The next chapter presents fundamentals of the transport layer and end-to-end protocols. The transport layer is responsible for signaling and file transfer.

7.8 Exercises

1. Consider a commercial wireless mobile telephone system whose transmitter and receiver are located 9.2 km apart. Both use isotropic antennas. The medium through which the communication occurs is not a free space, and it creates conditions such that the path loss is a function of d^3 and not d^2. Assume that the transmitter operating at the frequency of 800MHz communicates with a mobile receiver with the received power of 10^{-6} microwatts.

   (a) Find the effective area of the receiving antenna.
   (b) Find the required transmission power.

2. Assume that cellular networks are modeled with square cells.

   (a) Find the cell coverage area, and compare it to the one using hexagonal cells. Assume that the distance between the cell centers are identical in these two models.
   (b) What are the disadvantages of this model compared to the one with hexagonal cells?

3. A cellular network over 1,800 km² supports a total of 800 radio channels. Each cell has an area of 8 km²

   (a) If the cluster size is 7, find the system capacity.
   (b) Find the number of times a cluster of size 7 must be replicated to approximately cover the entire area.
   (c) What is the impact of the cluster size on system capacity?

4. Consider a cellular network with 128 cells and a cell radius $r=3$ km. Let g be 420 traffic channels for an $N = 7$-channel cluster system.

   (a) Find the area of each hexagonal cell.
   (b) Find the total channel capacity.
   (c) Find the distance between the centers of nearest neighboring cochannel cells.

5. If cells split into smaller cells in high-traffic areas, the capacity of the cellular networks for that region increases.

   (a) What would be the trade-off when the capacity of the system in a region increases as a result of cell splitting?
   (b) Consider a network with 7-cell frequency reuse clustering. Each cell must preserve its base station in its center. Construct the cell-splitting pattern in a cluster performed from the center of the cluster.

6. We would like to simulate the mobility and handoff in cellular networks described in this chapter. Assume 25mph $\leq k \leq$ 45mph within the city and 45mph $\leq k \leq$ 75mph for the highway. Let d_b be the distance a vehicle takes to reach a cell boundary, ranging from -10 miles to 10 miles.

   (a) Plot the probability of reaching a cell boundary for which a handoff is required. Discuss why the probability of reaching a boundary decreases in an exponential manner.
   (b) Show that the probability of reaching a cell boundary for a vehicle that has a call in progress is dependent on d_b.
   (c) Show the probability of reaching a cell boundary as a function of a vehicle's speed.
   (d) Discuss why the probability of reaching a cell boundary is proportional to the vehicle's speed.

7. Consider an LTE cellular network of 32 cells with a cell radius of 5 km, a total frequency bandwidth of 343 channels. The channel reuse occurs every 7 channels.

   (a) Present an approximate geographical sketch for the cellular hexagons.

(b) Find the total number concurrent calls that can be handled in this cellular network.

(c) Repeat parts (a) and (b) with a cell radius of 2 km.

8. Suppose that a host attached to ISP1 utilizing sparse mode PIM (see Chapter 6) for its multicasting policy intends to open a multicast connection with a host in ISP2 also using sparse mode PIM, and a smartphone in an LTE cellular network. For interdomain multicasting, MSDP is used.

(a) Sketch the networking scenario of this multicasting connection and identify all the engaging nodes, including MSDP representative, PIM rendezvous point, and eNodeB, etc.

(b) Repeat part (a), this time consider that the connection to the cellular network has to pass through another ISP.

7.9   Computer Simulation Project

1. *Experimental Simulation of File Transfer in Wireless Cellular Networks.* Consider the mobility in cellular networks described in this chapter, but this time, we want to simulate it. Set up two laptop computers, one as a sending host connected wirelessly to your area's cellular network with mobility capability, and the other one as a fixed receiving host connected to the Internet. Send a large file from the sending host to the receiving host

(a) Try to identify the IP address of each host and the devices in between. Can the IP address of the eNodeB base station be guessed from the results?

(b) Run Wireshark on the live network connection to obtain a packet trace of the file transfer from the sending host to the receiving host. Capture 20 packets.

(c) How long did it take to transfer file? Can the time of file transfer from the eNodeB base station be estimated from the results?

CHAPTER 8

Transport and End-to-End Protocols

So far, we have covered networking activities at the physical, link, and network layers of the Internet Protocol stack. This chapter focuses on foundations of layer 4, the transport layer. We study several techniques for *Transmission Control Protocol* (TCP) congestion control. These techniques use a form of end-to-end congestion control in a TCP session when a sender sends a packet (segment) and a receiver acknowledges receipt of the packet. This chapter covers the following topics:

- *Overview of the transport layer*
- *User Datagram Protocol* (UDP)
- *Transmission Control Protocol* (TCP)
- *Mobile transport protocols*
- *TCP congestion control*

We first take a close look at *layer 4, the transport layer*, and explain how a file is transferred. Layer 4 handles the details of data transmission and acts as an interface protocol between a communicating host and a server through a network. We then explain the *User Datagram Protocol* (UDP), which is a connectionless transport-layer protocol that is placed on top of the network layer.

Next, the reliable end-to-end connection establishment under the *Transmission Control Protocol* (TCP) is presented. We will learn about both the connection request and connection termination signaling that are needed to start a connection and terminate a connection, respectively. Several modes of data transfer with TCP are also presented.

Mobility at the transport layer is another important topic to discuss at this point. In wireless mobile networks, both UDP and TCP have their own applications. One obvious case for the application of a wireless transport protocol is when a user (host) moves to a remote or cellular area and wants to maintain a seamless connection. We discuss some mobility aspects of transport protocols.

Finally, TCP congestion control is described near the end of the chapter. Normally, it would take a significant amount of engineering effort to design a network with low or no congestion. *Congestion* in communication networks represents a state in which the traffic flow exceeds the availability of network resources to service the flow. Generally, network congestion occurs due to lack of resources at links and devices. We distinguish between these two categories of resource deficits and explore precautionary solutions: *flow control* and *congestion control*, respectively. We end the chapter with a discussion of TCP and UDP applications.

8.1 Overview of the Transport Layer

The *transport layer*, as the layer 4 protocol in the TCP/IP protocol stack model, handles the details of data transmission. Transport-layer protocols are implemented in the end points but not in network routers. The transport layer ensures a complete data transfer for an application process, free from any networking issue or detail of physical infrastructure. This layer clearly acts as an interface protocol between an "application" of a communicating host and a network as seen in Figure 8.1.

The transport layer provides a "logical" communication between application processes. As seen in the figure, a client host in LAN 2 is running an application in connection with an application on a server in LAN 1 through a *logical,* but not physical, link between the two end points. By *logical link*, we mean that it is as if two end points, such as a client and a server, running their application processes were directly connected, while end points may be distant from each other and connected via physical links, switches, and routers. For example, the client host and the server shown in

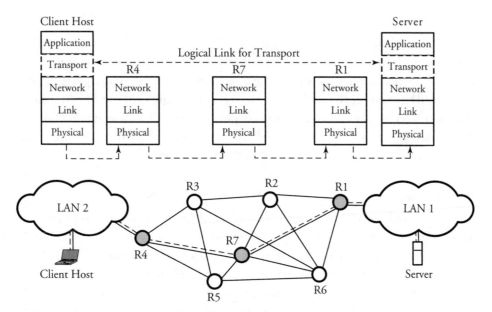

Figure 8.1 Demonstrating a "logical" end-to-end communication link at the transport layer between a client host and a server

the figure are located on opposite sides of the network and connected via routers R4, R7, and R1. This way, an application process sends messages to another application process using a logical link provided by the transport layer while disregarding the details of how handling these messages is carried out.

8.1.1 Interaction of Transport Layer and Adjacent Layers

The direct logical link shown in Figure 8.1 reflects the fact that three routers—R4, R7, and R1—act only on the network-layer fields of a traveling packet (datagram) and never inspect the fields of the transport-layer segment. This resembles a direct logical link between the two end points. Once the segment is received by the end server, the network layer extracts the transport-layer segment from the datagram and makes it available to the transport layer. At the receiving end, the transport layer processes the segment by extracting the application data in the segment.

Transport protocols can generally offer reliable data transfer service to a certain application in spite of the fact that the underlying network protocol can be unreliable owing to losing packets. A transport protocol can also use its own security procedures to guarantee that application messages are not intruded on by unknowns.

Segments

The transport layer converts application messages into transport-layer packets known as *segments*. This layer manages all end-to-end communication details, such as packet segmentation, packet reassembly, and error checking. The segmentation is performed by breaking the application messages into smaller chunks and attaching a transport-layer header to each chunk to create a segment. Once a segment is formed, it is passed to the network layer, where it is encapsulated within a network-layer packet—a datagram—and transmitted to the destination.

Port Numbers

Any host could be running several network applications at a time and thus each application needs to be identified by another host communicating to a targeted application. A *port number* is defined at the transport layer for this purpose and included in the header of each segment. A transport-layer port is a logical port and not an actual or a physical one, and serves as the end point application identification in a host. On the other hand, a source host requires a port number for communication to uniquely identify an application process running on the destination host. The concept of assigning a port to an application process within a host enables a single physical link connected to the host to be shared with other communicating applications, similar to time-division multiplexing.

Each port in a host is associated with the IP address of the host, and the type of protocol used for communication. When a connection is established between two hosts requiring the engagement of a layer 4 protocol, a *port number* is part of the addressing information used to identify a sending host and receiving host of messages. Thus, a point-to-point connection requires a *source port* and a *destination port* specifying the port number of the source that sends packets, and the port number of the destination that receives packets, respectively. Port numbers are associated with a network addressing scheme. A transport layer connection utilizes its own set of ports that work together with IP addresses.

One can imagine the IP address of a host as a telephone number, and its port number as a telephone extension number. A host with an IP address can possess multiple port numbers as a telephone number can be given multiple extension numbers. A port number consists of two bytes (16 bits). With 16 bits, 65,536 port numbers can be created starting at 0 and ending at 65,535. Table 8.1 presents a few well-known port number assignments for popular applications such as e-mail and the Web.

Table 8.1   Popular port numbers

Port Number	Protocol	Location of Port Assignment	Chapter That Covers the Description of the Protocol
25	SMTP	e-mail sever	Chapter 9
80	HTTP	Web server	Chapter 9
110	POP3	e-mail server	Chapter 9
143	IMAP	e-mail server	Chapter 9
443	HTTPS	secure Web server	Chapter 10

Socket

A network *socket* is an intermediary end point gateway of an application process through which a message passes from the network to the application process, and through which the message passes from the application process to the network. Note that by gateway we mean a virtual or logical gateway and not an actual or a physical gateway. A socket is simply a software interface gateway between the transport and application layers. The transport layer in the receiving host delivers data to a socket and thereby to an application process.

Each socket has a unique identifier. A socket identifier is the combination of an IP address of the associated host and a port number associated with a specific application. The Internet sockets deliver incoming packets to the appropriate application process. Any application process can have one or more sockets. When a segment is received by a host, the transport layer examines the header of the segment and identifies the receiving socket. Once the socket identifier of the segment is known, the segment is delivered to the intended socket. When a client host is assigned a local port number, it immediately binds a *socket* to it. The client interacts with the destination host by writing to the socket, and receives information from the destination host by reading from it.

As an example of ports and sockets, suppose a user is downloading a file from the Internet while receiving an e-mail from a friend. In this case, the user's computer must have two ports and subsequently two sockets through which the Web and e-mail applications communicate at the transport layer. Figure 8.2 details this situation in which a client is communicating with two servers A and B. Server A sends segments A and server B sends segments B to the client as a result of the communications. Segments arriving at layer 4 at the client host are demultiplexed over the two sockets using associated port numbers A and B identified in the segments. This way

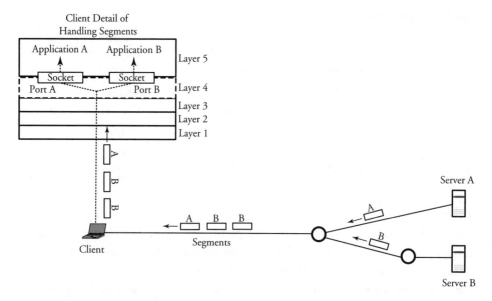

Figure 8.2 Illustration of segments being delivered to a client through sockets using port numbers

segments A and B are sorted and each type is delivered to its associated sockets and in turn delivered to the appropriate application processes in layer 5. The opposite act, called multiplexing, is made possible when a source host needs to transmit data from several of its application processes. In such a case, data from the application processes must be gathered from different sockets, converted to segments, and passed to the network layer. The act of multiplexing is the same as the one we discussed in Chapter 2 as time-division multiplexing (TDM).

8.1.2 Transport Layer Protocols

The two most important forms of transport in TCP/IP networking are governed by two protocols:

- User Datagram Protocol (UDP)
- Transmission Control Protocol (TCP)

UDP is a *connectionless* service and is unreliable to the invoking application. TCP is a *connection-oriented* service and is therefore a reliable service to an invoking application. A network application design involves making a careful choice between these two transport protocols, as each protocol acts differently to any invoking application.

8.2   User Datagram Protocol (UDP)

The *User Datagram Protocol* (UDP) is transport-layer protocol that is placed on top of the network layer. UDP is a connectionless protocol, as no handshaking between sending and receiving points occurs before sending a segment. UDP does not provide a reliable service mainly due to the lack of any acknowledgements to transmission of packets; however, it can perform error detection to a certain extent once the segments arrive at the destination.

When a host attempts to send packets (datagrams) to another host, IP is capable of delivering packets to the destination but it is not capable of delivering them to a specific application. UDP fills this gap by providing a mechanism to differentiate among multiple applications and deliver a packet to the desired application. When an application selects UDP in the source host instead of choosing TCP, the application interacts with IP. UDP takes application messages from the application process, attaches source and destination port number fields and other fields to the segment, and passes the resulting segment to the network layer. The network layer encapsulates the transport-layer segment into an IP datagram and then tries to deliver the segment to the destination host. At the destination host, UDP processes the arriving segment, identifies the destination port number, and delivers the data attached to the segment to the correct application process.

8.2.1   UDP Segments

The format of the UDP segment's header is shown in Figure 8.3. Note that other headers such as an IP header (layer 3 protocol) and a data link header (layer 2 protocol)

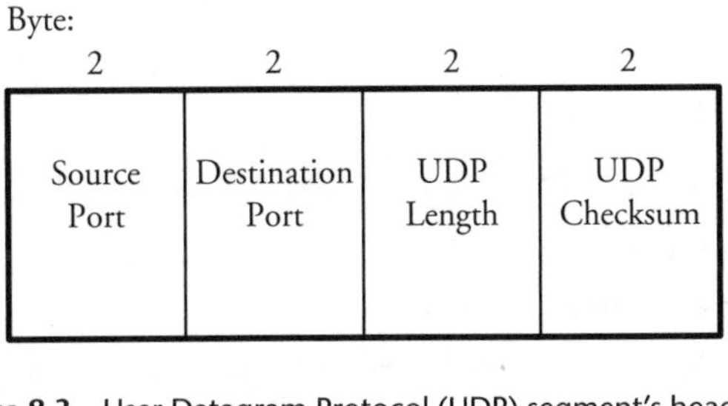

Byte:

2	2	2	2
Source Port	Destination Port	UDP Length	UDP Checksum

Figure 8.3   User Datagram Protocol (UDP) segment's header

are added to this header to form a packet having a complete set of information for routing and delivery of the packet.

The UDP segment header starts with the *source port*, followed by the *destination port*. These port numbers are used to identify the ports of applications at the source or the destination, respectively. The source port identifies the application that is sending the data. The destination port helps UDP demultiplex the packet and directs it to the right application. The *UDP length* field indicates the length of the UDP header and its associated data, where the length may be up to almost 2^{16} bytes long. The last field in the segment is *UDP checksum* that is explained in the next section.

UDP Checksum

UDP checksum is a 2-byte field for error detection. Although the data link layer protocol does provide error checking (as we learned in Chapter 3), the transport layer protocol performs error checking again at layer 4 as a safety measure. There are two reasons for this additional error checking. First, there is no guarantee that all individual links between a source and a destination perform error checking. Second, the source of errors—varying from noise to packet storage glitches—can occur within a router or switch and not necessarily on links. Hence, even if a segment is correctly transferred across a link, it is always likely for the segment to get a bit error when it is stored in a switch's or router's memory. Let us first learn the algorithm of the checksum implemented in the transport layer.

Begin Checksum Algorithm

Initialize:

- Partition the segment into n 2-byte (16-bit) words, where a word number is $i \in \{1, 2, \cdots, n\}$
- Set Sum = 0 and Checksum = 0

Checksum at source

1. **For** $1 \le i \le n$:

   Do Sum = word i + Sum

   If Sum has a carry, Sum = Sum + carry

2. **1's complement:** Checksum = Converted bits of Sum /* flipped bits */

Check for error at destination

3. Apply Step 1 of the "checksum at source" on the received segment and create "destination" Sum.

4. If the result of: Sum (made at destination) + Checksum (received)
= all 1s, **then** the received packet has no error,

Otherwise, the received packet has error(s).   ∎

Example.   Consider a hypothetical source segment as small as the following bit stream: 1000,1111,0000,1110,1000,0000,0110,0000 and create a checksum for it. Then check to see if the segment has any errors at a destination.

Solution.   In the initialization phase, we partition the bit stream into $n = 2$ words: word 1 = 1000,1111,0000,1110 and word 2 = 1000,0000,0110,0000. Also, we set Sum = 0000,0000,0000,0000. In step 1, for $i = 1$, Sum = word 1 + Sum = 1000,1111,0000,1110 + 0000,0000,0000,0000 = 1000,1111,0000,1110. This summation does not create any carry. For $i = 2$, Sum = word 2 + Sum = 1000,1111,0000,1110 + 1000,0000,0110,0000 = 0000,1111,0110,1110. This summation does create a binary carry, 1, and thus: Sum = Sum + carry = 0000,1111,0110,1110 + 1 = 0000,1111,0110,1111. In step 2, applying the 1's complement (converting 0s to 1s and 1s to 0s) on the resulting Sum results in Checksum = 1111,0000,1001,0000, which is inserted into the *checksum* field of the UDP segment. To check whether the segment received at the destination has any errors, at step 3, we create Sum at the destination the same way we did at source and obtain Sum = 0000,1111,0110,1111. Now, adding this Sum to the received Checksum results in 0000,1111,0110,1111 + 1111,0000,1001,0000 = 1111,1111,1111,1111, which indicates that no errors were introduced in the segment.

Note that even though UDP provides error checking, it does not apply any procedure to recover from an error. In most cases, UDP simply discards the damaged segment or passes the damaged segment to the application layer with a warning.

8.2.2   Applications of UDP

Although TCP provides a reliable service and UDP does not, many applications fit better in the communication system by using UDP, for the following reasons:

- *Faster delivery of the application object.* TCP is equipped with a congestion-control mechanism and requires the guarantee of data delivery at any timing cost. This may not be well suited for real-time applications.

- *Support for a larger number of active clients.* TCP maintains connection state and does track connection parameters. Therefore, a server designated to a particular application supports fewer active clients when the application runs over TCP rather than over UDP.

- *Smaller segment header overhead.* UDP has only 8 bytes of overhead, whereas the TCP segment has 20 bytes of header.

Applications such as routing table updates of RIP and OSPF (discussed in Chapter 5), Domain Name System (DNS), and SNMP network management run over UDP. For example, RIP updates are transmitted periodically, and reliability may not be an issue, as a more recent update can always replace a lost one. We discuss DNS and SNMP in detail in Chapter 9.

8.3   Transmission Control Protocol (TCP)

The *Transmission Control Protocol* (TCP) is another transport-layer protocol that provides a reliable service by using an *automatic repeat request* (ARQ). In addition, TCP provides flow control using a *sliding-window scheme* that was introduced in Chapter 3. TCP is built over IP services by facilitating a two-way connection between the host application and the destination application.

As a connection-oriented protocol, TCP requires a connection to be established between each of two applications. A connection is set up by defining variables that the protocol requires and storing them in the *transmission control block*. After establishing the connection, TCP delivers packets in sequence and in *bytestream*. TCP can either send the data received from the application layer as a single segment, or split it into multiple segments and transmit them if an underlying physical network poses a limitation.

The requisites of layer 4 are to transfer data without errors to make sure that packets follow the same sequence. A host application that needs to send a certain sort of data stores it in a send buffer. The data is then transmitted as a bytestream. The transmitting host creates a segment that contains a sequence of bytes. The segment is appended to a TCP header that specifies the destination application port and a *sequence number*. When it arrives at the destination, the segment is verified for its integrity. After making sure that the packet is not a duplicate and that the segment number lies in the range of the local buffer, the receiver accepts the packet. The receiver can accept segments out of order. In that case, the receiver simply repositions them in the buffer to obtain an in-order sequence before making the data available to the application. Acknowledgments are cumulative and traverse in the reverse direction.

8.3.1   TCP Segment

As defined earlier, a TCP *segment* is defined as a TCP session packet containing part of a TCP bytestream in transit. The fields of the TCP header segment are shown in Figure 8.4. As we noted for the UDP segment, other headers such as an IP header (layer 3 protocol) and a data link header (layer 2 protocol) are added to this header to form a packet having a complete set of information for routing and delivery of the packet. The TCP segment contains a minimum of 20 bytes of fixed fields and a variable-length options field. The details of the fields are as follows:

- *Source port* and *destination port* specify the user's port number at source, which sends packets, and the user's port number at destination, which receives packets, respectively.

- *Sequence number* is a 32-bit field that TCP assigns to each first data byte in the segment. The sequence number restarts from 0 after the number reaches $2^{32} - 1$.

- *Acknowledgment number* specifies the sequence number of the next byte that a receiver waits for and acknowledges receipt of bytes up to this sequence number. If the SYN field is set, the acknowledgment number refers to the *initial sequence number* (ISN).

- *Header length* (HL) is a 4-bit field indicating the length of the header in 32-bit words.

- *Urgent* (URG) is a 1-bit field implying that the urgent-pointer field is applicable.

- *Acknowledgment* (ACK) shows the validity of an acknowledgment.

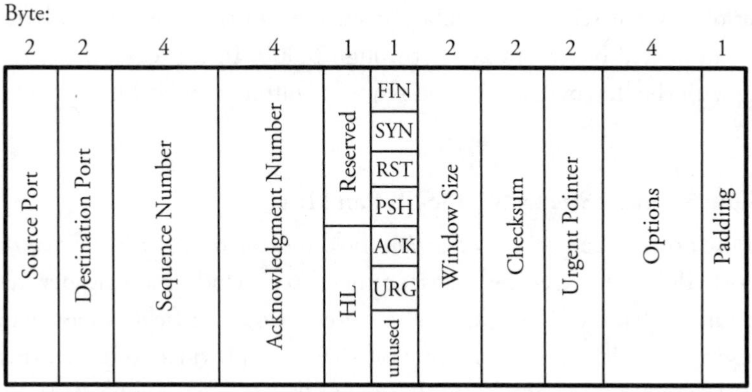

Figure 8.4   Transport Control Protocol (TCP) segment's header

- *Push* (PSH), if set, directs the receiver to immediately forward the data to the destination application.

- *Reset* (RST), if set, directs the receiver to abort the connection.

- *Synchronize* (SYN) is a 1-bit field used as a connection request to synchronize the sequence numbers.

- *Finished* (FIN) is a 1-bit field indicating that the sender has finished sending the data.

- *Window size* specifies the advertised window size.

- *Checksum* is used to find errors and check the validity of the received segment. The TCP checksum algorithm is identical to the one explained for UDP checksum in Section 8.2.1.

- *Urgent pointer* (URG), if set, directs the receiver to add up the values in the urgent-pointer field and the sequence number field to specify the last byte number of the data to be delivered urgently to the destination application.

- *Options* is a variable-length field that specifies the functions that are not available as part of the basic header.

As indicated in the segment fields, each segment in a TCP connection is assigned a *sequence number i,* which is shown in our upcoming discussions by seq(i). The sequence number of a segment is in fact the segment's bytestream number of the first byte in the segment. The sequence number assigned is randomly chosen from 0 to $(2^{32} - 1)$.

Example.   We would like to transmit 4,000 bytes of data using TCP. If a starting number of 2,001 is selected for data transmission in this connection, bytes should then be numbered by i from 2,001 through 6,000. In this case, the first segment starting with the first byte of data has sequence number seq(2,001).

Maximum Segment Size (MSS) for IPv4 and IPv6
One of the possible choices in the *options* field indicated earlier is the *maximum segment size* (MSS), defined as the largest segment size excluding any header that a TCP connection can handle. A destination host uses the options field to specify the maximum segment size it can receive. A total of 16 bits are provided to specify this option. Thus, the maximum segment size is limited to 65,535 bytes minus 20 bytes of TCP header and minus 20 bytes of IP header, resulting in 65,495 bytes. The typical TCP

segment size is between 576 bytes and 1,500 bytes, and therefore, the typical MSS for a TCP connection is 536 ($576 - 20 - 20=536$) bytes to 1,460 ($1500 - 20 - 20 =1,460$) bytes where in each case, 20 bytes of TCP header and 20 bytes of IP header are subtracted. Nevertheless, the default MSS is 536 bytes for typical hosts. One other fact about MSS is that each direction of data flow in a bidirectional TCP connection can use a different MSS. Also, note that IPv6 hosts are typically required to be able to handle an MSS of 1,220 ($1, 280 - 40 - 20=1,220$) bytes.

Another possible selection in the *options* field is the *window scale*. This option is used to increase the size of the advertised window beyond the specified $2^{16} - 1$ in the header. The advertised window can additionally be scaled to a maximum of 2^{14}.

8.3.2   A TCP Connection

As a connection-oriented protocol, TCP requires an explicit *connection set-up* phase, a *data transfer* phase, and a *connection termination* phase. In the following three subsections, these three phases are described.

Connection Setup Phase

A connection is set up using a three-way handshake process, as shown in Figure 8.5 (a). Assume that host A is a source and host B is a destination. In step 1 of this process, the source sends the first segment, which is called "connection request" to the destination. This segment carries no real data and it acts as an initialization of the connection. The connection request comprises a random number as an initial sequence number indicated by seq(i), with the SYN bit set (SYN=1). The sequence number seq(i) indicates that when the data starts to be transferred, the expected sequence number for it should be seq($i + 1$).

In step 2 of this three-way handshake process, on the receipt of the connection request, destination host B sends an acknowledgment segment with an acknowledgment number indicated by ack($i + 1$) back to the source with the ACK bit set (ACK=1). Again, by incrementing i to $i + 1$ in this step, the destination indicates that when the data transfer starts after the three-way handshake process, it is expecting the first data segment to have a sequence number of seq($i + 1$). The destination host also indicates here that it has started its own beginning sequence number seq(j) and hence sets the SYN bit (SYN=1).

Finally, in step 3 of this three-way handshake process, source host A returns an acknowledgment segment, ack($j + 1$) with the ACK bit set (ACK=1) specifying that it is waiting for the next byte. The sequence number of this third segment is still

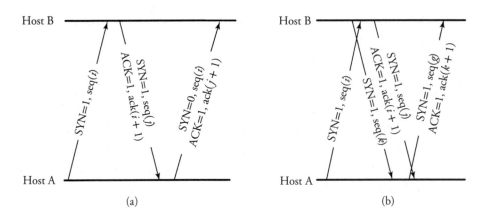

Figure 8.5   TCP signaling: (a) three-way handshake process of establishing a connection;
(b) collision of two simultaneous connection requests

seq(i) with SYN=0 since this segment still has no data and is merely a confirmative step to step 2. This process establishes a connection between the sender and the receiver and data transfer at this point can start with the first byte to have a sequence number of seq($i + 1$).

Example.   Use the three-way handshake process for the connection establishment procedure, to transmit 4,000 bytes of data using a TCP connection with a *maximum segment size* (MSS) of 1,000 bytes. Suppose the source host starts step 1 of the connection establishment with the first byte numbered with $i = 2,000$, and the destination host starts step 2 of the connection establishment with $j = 12,000$. Present the detailed segment numbers for this process.

Solution.   In step 1, the source host sends a connection request segment with sequence number seq(2,000) and the SYN bit set (SYN=1). In step 2, the destination host sends an acknowledgment segment with an acknowledgment number indicated by ack(2,001) back to the source with the ACK bit set (ACK=1). Here, by incrementing 2,000 to 2,001, the destination host indicates that when the data transfer begins, it is expecting the first data segment to have a sequence number of seq(2,001). We notice here that the destination host also includes its own sequence number seq(12,000) and with the SYN bit set (SYN=1). In step 3, the source host responds to the destination with an acknowledgment segment numbered ack(12,001) and with the ACK bit set (ACK=1) specifying that it is waiting for the next byte. The sequence number of this third segment is still seq(2,000) with SYN=0. When the data transfer begins, the first segment starting with the first byte of data has sequence number seq(2,001). For this connection, four (4,000/1,000 = 4) segments are created with sequence numbers seq(2,001), seq(3,001), seq(4,001), and seq(5,001), respectively, covering all bytes of data from 2,001 through 6,000.

There may be some circumstances in the phase of connection establishment that can result in special arrangements being made by the engaging hosts. For example, in Figure 8.5 (b), there is a situation in which both end-point hosts simultaneously try to establish a connection, one starting with seq(i) and the oposite request with seq(k). In this case, since both hosts recognize the connection requests coming from each other, only one connection is established. The connection process for this case uses different initial sequence numbers between the source host and the destination host to distinguish between the old and new segments and to avoid the duplication and subsequent deletion of one of the segments.

Two other examples of special cases requiring an arrangement on the initial sequence numbers are as follows. In a connection request phase, if one of the segments from a previous connection arrives late, the receiving host accepts the segment, presuming that it belongs to the new connection. The second special case may occur when the segment from a current connection with the same sequence number arrives and hence it is considered a duplicate and is dropped. Therefore, it is important to make sure that the initial sequence numbers are different.

Data Transfer Phase

Once the three-way handshake process is completed, the TCP connection is considered as established and consequently the source is allowed to send its data to the destination. Figure 8.6 shows an example of a data transfer. In this example, the source, host A, has data that is equivalent to twice the maximum segment size (MSS), and thus, it is broken up into two segments each with a data size of 1 MSS byte long. Assume that the first segment is assigned sequence number seq($i + 1$). This segment has the PSH flag set (PSH=1) so that the destination host knows to deliver data to the host application process as soon as it is received. TCP implementations have the option to set or not set the PSH flag. The data in the first segment has a length of MSS bytes and its bytes are numbered from $i + 1$ to $i + MSS$. The destination host buffers the data when it arrives, and then delivers it to the application program when the application program is prepared. Once the data of the first segment is buffered,

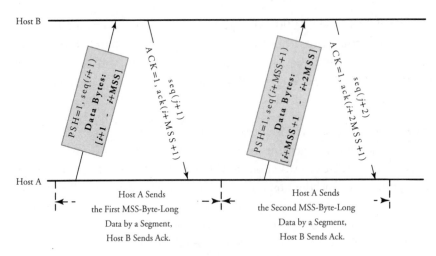

Figure 8.6   Data transfer in a TCP connection

the destination sends an acknowledgment with a randomly chosen sequence number, assuming seq($j + 1$), and an acknowledgment number ack($i + MSS + 1$), hinting to the seouce host that it is expecting the next segment to arrive with the segment number seq($i + MSS + 1$). As seen in the figure, the process of the second segment of this connection is similar to the first one starting with segment number seq($i + MSS + 1$).

Connection Termination Phase

When one of the end points decides to abort the connection, another three-way hand-shake process, called connection termination, between the two end hosts must be arranged. Figure 8.7 shows an example of a connection termination process. Assume that host A wants to terminate the TCP connection. In this case, in step 1 of this process, host A sends a segment that is called "termination request" to host B. The termination request contains a sequence number indicated by seq(i), with the FIN bit set (FIN=1). In step 2 of this process, on the receipt of the termination request, host B sends an acknowledgment segment with an acknowledgment number indicated by ack($i + 1$) back to the source with the ACK bit set (ACK=1). Host B also indicates here that it has started its own beginning sequence number seq(j) and hence it sets the FIN bit (FIN=1). Finally, in step 3 of this three-way handshake process, host A returns an acknowledgment segment, ack($j + 1$) with the ACK bit set (ACK=1). The sequence number of this third segment is still seq(i) with FIN=0 since this segment has no data and is merely a confirmative step to step 2.

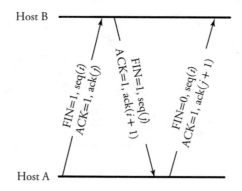

Figure 8.7 TCP signaling: connection termination

8.3.3 Window-Based Transmission and Sliding Window in TCP

Similar to the link layer, TCP at the transport layer of the protocol stack also has the capability to send more than one segment during a predetermined window of time. The choice of window size is based on the destination's buffer capacity allocated to a certain connection. This task is accomplished using the *window size* (*w*) field in the TCP header. Because of this, the source host is restricted to having no more than a window size of unacknowledged segments at any given time. As a result, the destination host must determine an appropriate window size value according to its buffering capacity to keep the source host from overrunning its buffering capacity.

Figure 8.8 shows a scenario in which host A starts a TCP data transfer process by sending one MSS-byte-long data through a segment and receiving its acknowledgment. In this figure, host B then allows the regular transmission of one segment at a time to a transmission with $w=2$ segments so that the two segments $\text{seq}(i + \text{MSS} + 1)$ and $\text{seq}(i + 2\text{MSS} + 1)$ are transmitted followed by one acknowledgment generated by the destination host B for both. Notice that in this figure it is shown as a bidirectional connection where host B also transmits its one MSS-byte-long data through a segment along with this acknowledgment segment for which it receives an acknowledgment from host A.

The *sliding-window protocol* as one of the effective methods of flow control at layer 2 of protocol stack (link layer) was described in Chapter 3. In summary, the sliding-window protocol guarantees the reliable delivery of frames, and ensures

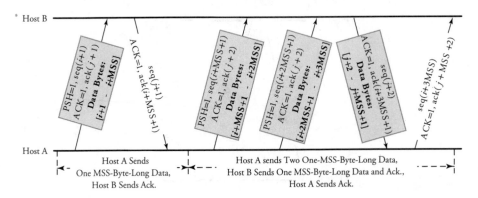

Figure 8.8   Creation of a window with window size of two

the delivered frames are in the same order in which they are transmitted. This is done mainly through an enforcement of acknowledgment for each window of received frames.

At layer 4 of the protocol stack, TCP also uses the sliding-window protocol to guarantee the reliable delivery of segments and ensure the delivered segments are in the same order in which they are transmitted. The only difference between the sliding-window protocol of the link layer and the one used for TCP is that the destination (receiving) host at the link layer advertises for a fixed-size sliding window, while the destination host in a TCP connection advertises a window size of choice to the sender.

To execute the sliding-window protocol, the source host must maintain a buffer for storing segments that have been sent but not yet acknowledged and also for those segments that have been produced by the source application but not transmitted. Similarly, the destination host must maintain a buffer for keeping segments that arrive out of order and also those segments that are in the correct order but not used yet by the application layer.

8.3.4   Applications of TCP

TCP provides a reliable service, as it is equipped with a congestion-control mechanism and requires the guarantee of data delivery at any timing cost. The most commonly used category of applications includes *e-mail, the Web, remote terminal access,* and *file transfer protocol.* These applications run over TCP, as they all require reliable data-transfer service. In Chapter 9, we describe these applications in depth.

8.4   Mobile Transport Protocols

In wireless mobile networks, both UDP and TCP have their own applications. However, some modifications are needed in these protocols so they are appropriate for wireless networks. One obvious reason for the modification requirement is the fact that a user (host) may move to a remote area and a seamless connection still is desirable.

8.4.1   UDP for Mobility

UDP is used in wireless mobile IP networks for several reasons. We learned in Chapter 7 that a mobile host needs to register with a foreign agent. The registration with an agent on a foreign network is done using UDP. This process starts with a foreign agent propagating advertisements using a UDP connection. Since traditional UDP does not use acknowledgments and does not perform flow control, it is not a preferred choice of transport protocol. One way of handling this situation is to stop sending datagrams to a mobile host once it reports fading. But this method cannot be practical due to its poor quality of connection.

8.4.2   TCP for Mobility

TCP provides reliable data delivery owing to its connection-oriented nature. The most challenging aspect of providing TCP services to a mobile host is the prevention of disruption caused by poor wireless link quality. A poor link quality typically causes the loss of TCP data segments, leading to a possible timeout. If the poor quality wireless channel is persistent for even a short period, the window remains small, causing a low throughput.

One option to solve this problem is to disallow a sender to shrink its congestion window when packets are lost for any reason. If a wireless channel soon recovers from disconnection, the mobile host begins to receive data immediately. A few other protocols are used for this purpose, among which the *Indirect Transmission Control Protocol* (I-TCP) and the *fast retransmit protocol* will be the focus of our discussion.

Indirect TCP

Assume a mobile host in a mobile IP network such as a cellular network is trying to establish an I-TCP connection to a fixed host in a fixed network, as shown in Figure 8.9. The I-TCP scheme first splits the connection into two separate connections. One connection is established between the mobile host and the base station (BS), and the other connection is between the BS and the fixed host. Note here that the details of

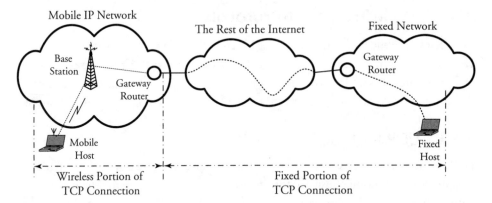

Figure 8.9   Indirect TCP for mobile hosts

networking between the BS and the gateway router, and the gateway router and the fixed host, are not shown in the figure. The connection between the two hosts consists of two linkage portions: the wireless link and the fixed link. At this point, the wireless and wired links' characteristics remain hidden from the transport layer. The separation of connections into two distinct portions is advantageous to the base station to better manage the communication overhead for a mobile host. This way the throughput of the connection is enhanced since the mobile host may be near the base station.

A TCP connection on the wireless portion can support disconnections and user mobility in addition to wired TCP features such as notification to higher layers on changes in the available bandwidth. Also, the flow control and congestion control mechanisms on the wireless link remain separated from those on the wired link. In the I-TCP scheme, the TCP acknowledgments are separate for the wireless and the wired links of the connection. This resembles two different TCP connections linked together. Note that, if for any reason the mobile host disconnects the communication on the wireless portion, the sender may not become aware of the disconnection as the wired portion is still intact, and the base station still delivers the TCP segments to the mobile host. Consequently, the sender of segments may not know of segments being delivered to the mobile host.

Fast Retransmit Protocol

The *fast retransmit protocol* is another TCP scheme for mobility. Fast retransmit protocol improves the connection throughput especially during a cell handoff. This scheme does not split the TCP connection to wireless and wired connections. As soon as the two wireless base stations hand off the switching function for a mobile host, the mobile host stops receiving TCP segments. This may be interpreted by the sender as a situation of congestion, and thereby a congestion control scheme such as window size reduction or retransmitting may begin to be implemented. This may also result in a long timeout causing the mobile host to wait a long period of time. With the fast retransmit protocol, the last old acknowledgment is triplicated and retransmitted by the mobile host as soon as it finishes a handoff. This results in significant reduction of the congestion window.

8.5   TCP Congestion Control

TCP uses a form of end-to-end flow control. In TCP, when a sender sends a segment, the receiver acknowledges receipt of the segment. A sending source can use the acknowledgment arrival rate as a measure of network congestion. When it successfully receives an acknowledgment, a sender knows that the packet has reached its desired destination. The sender can then send new segments on the network. Both the sender and the receiver agree on a common *window size* for segment flow. The window size represents the number of bytes that the source can send at a time. The window size varies according to the condition of traffic in the network to avoid congestion. Generally, a file of size f with a total transfer time of Δ on a TCP connection results in a *TCP transfer throughput* denoted by r and obtained from

$$r = \frac{f}{\Delta}.$$

(8.1)

We can also derive the *bandwidth utilization*, ρ_u, assuming that the link bandwidth is B, by

$$\rho_u = \frac{r}{B}.$$

(8.2)

TCP has three congestion-control methods: *additive increase*, *slow start*, and *fast retransmit*. The following subsections describe these three mechanisms, which are sometimes combined to form the TCP congestion-control scheme.

8.5.1   Additive Increase, Multiplicative Decrease Control

An important variable in TCP congestion control is the value of the *congestion window*. Each connection has a congestion window size, w_g. The congestion window represents the amount of data, in bytes, that a sending source is allowed to have in transit at a particular instant of time in a network. *Additive increase, multiplicative decrease* (AIMD) *control* performs a slow increase in the congestion window size when the congestion in the network decreases and a fast drop in the window size when congestion increases. Let w_m be the *maximum window size*, in bytes, representing the maximum amount of unacknowledged data that a sender is allowed to send. Let w_a be the advertised window sent by the destination, based on its buffer size. Thus,

$$w_m = \min(w_g, w_a). \tag{8.3}$$

By having w_m replace w_a, a TCP source is not permitted to transmit faster than the network or the destination. The challenge in TCP congestion control is for the source node to find a right value for the congestion window. The congestion window size varies, based on the traffic conditions in the network. TCP watches for a timeout as a sign of congestion. One can arrange timeouts to be used as acknowledgments to find the best size for the congestion window. This is done because the implications of having too large a window are much worse than having too small a window. This TCP technique requires that the timeout values be set properly. Two important factors in setting timeouts are

1. Average *round-trip times* (RTTs) and RTT standard deviations are based on set timeouts.

2. RTTs are sampled once every RTT is completed.

Figure 8.10 depicts the additive-increase method. The congestion window is interpreted in terms of packets rather than bytes. Initially, the source congestion window is set to one segment. Once it receives an acknowledgment for the segment, the source increments its congestion window by one segment. So the source transmits two segments at that point. On successful receipt of both acknowledgments,

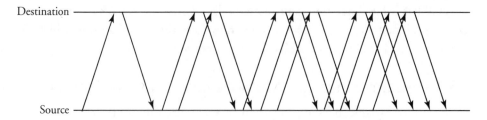

Figure 8.10   Additive increase control for TCP congestion control

the source once again increases the congestion window by one segment (additive increase).

In practice, the source increases its congestion window by a small amount for each acknowledgment instead of waiting for both acknowledgments to arrive. If a timeout occurs, the source assumes that congestion is developing and therefore sets the congestion window size to half its previous value (multiplicative decrease). The minimum congestion window size is the *maximum segment* size (MSS), which represents one segment. In general, a TCP segment is defined as a TCP session segment containing part of a TCP bytestream in transit.

8.5.2 Slow-Start Method

Additive increase is ideally suited for when the network operates near capacity. Initially, it would take a considerable amount of time to increase the congestion window. The *slow-start method* increases the congestion window size nonlinearly and in most cases exponentially, as compared to the linear increase in additive increase. Figure 8.11 shows the slow-start mechanism. In this case, the congestion window is again interpreted in segments instead of bytes.

A source initially sets the congestion window to one segment. When its corresponding acknowledgment arrives, the source sets the congestion window to two segments. Now, the source sends two segments. On receiving the two corresponding acknowledgments, TCP sets the congestion window size to 4. Thus, the number of segments in transit doubles for each round-trip time. This nonlinear trend of increase in the window size continues as seen in the figure. With this method of congestion control, routers on a path may not be able to service the flow of traffic, as the volume of segments increases nonlinearly. This congestion-control

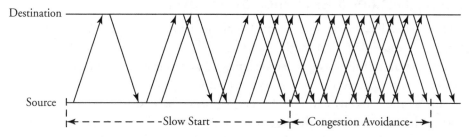

Figure 8.11 Slow-start timing between a source and a destination

scheme by itself may lead to a new type of congestion. The slow-start method is normally used

1. just after a TCP connection is set up, or
2. when a source is blocked waiting for a timeout, or after a timeout has happened.

A new variable, *congestion threshold*, is defined. This variable is a saved size of the congestion window when a timeout happens. When a timeout occurs, the threshold is set to half the congestion window size. Then the congestion window is reset to one segment and ramped up all the way to the congestion threshold, using the slow-start method. Once the connection is established, a burst of segments is sent during a slow start. In the meantime, a number of segments may be lost while the source admits no waiting time for acknowledgments. Accordingly, a timeout occurs, and the congestion window is reduced. Thus, a timeout results in the reduction of the congestion window, as in the previous scheme. Finally, the congestion threshold and the congestion window are reset.

After the congestion threshold is reached, an "additive increase" is used. At this point, as segments may be lost for a while, the source removes the waiting time for acknowledgments. Then, a timeout occurs immediately, and the congestion window size is reduced. The congestion threshold is reset, and the congestion window is reset to one segment. Now, the source uses slow start to ramp up, and then additive increase is used. After reaching the congestion threshold, additive increase is used. This pattern continues, creating a pulse-type plot. The reason for the large segment loss initially with slow start is that it is more aggressive in the beginning in order to learn about the network. This may result in a few segment losses, but it seems to be better than the conservative approach, in which the throughput is very small.

8.5.3 Fast Retransmit and Fast Recovery Methods

Fast retransmit is based on the concept of duplicate acknowledgment (ACK). The additive-increase and slow-start mechanisms have idle periods, during which the source admits no waiting time for an acknowledgment. Fast retransmit of segments sometimes leads to a retransmission of the lost segment before the associated timeout periods.

Each time it receives an out-of-order segment, the destination should respond with a duplicate ACK of the last successful in-order segment that has arrived. This must be done even if the destination has already acknowledged the segment. Figure 8.12 illustrates the process. The first three segments are transmitted, and their acknowledgments are received.

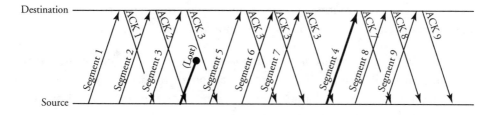

Figure 8.12   Timing of retransmit method between a source and a destination

Now, assume that segment 4 is lost. Since the source is not aware of this lost segment, it continues to transmit segment 5 and beyond. However, the destination sends a duplicate acknowledgment of segment 3 to let the source know that it has not received segment 4. In practice, once the source receives three duplicate acknowledgments, it retransmits the lost segment. In this case, ACK 3 is sent to the destination in response to the receipt for any of segments 5, 6, and 7. But notice that, once the third ACK 3 as the acknowledgment to segment 6 is received by the source, the source learns that it needs to retransmit segment 4. In response to segment 4, the destination initiates ACK 7 to indicate that it has received all segments up to segment 8.

Fast recovery is another improvement to TCP congestion control. It potentially removes the slow-start process that occurs between when fast retransmit detects a lost segment and additive increase resumes. When congestion occurs, instead of dropping the congestion window to one segment, the congestion window size is dropped to half, and additive increase is used. Thus, the slow-start method is used only during the initial connection phase and when a timeout occurs. Otherwise, additive increase is used.

Network congestion is a traffic bottleneck between a source and a destination. *Congestion avoidance* uses precautionary algorithms to avoid possible congestion in a network. Otherwise, TCP congestion control is applied once congestion occurs in a network. TCP increases the traffic rate to a point where congestion occurs and then gradually reduces the rate. It would be better if congestion could be avoided. This would involve sending some precautionary information to the source just before segments are discarded. The source would then reduce its sending rate, and congestion could be avoided to some extent.

Source-Based Congestion Avoidance

Source-based congestion avoidance detects congestion early from end hosts. An end host estimates congestion in the network by using the round-trip time (RTT) and throughput as its measures. An increase in round-trip time can indicate that routers'

queues on the selected routing path are increasing and that congestion may happen. The source-based schemes can be classified into four basic algorithms:

1. *Use of RTT as a measure of congestion in the network.* As queues in the routers build up, the RTT for each new segment sent out on the network increases. If the current RTT is greater than the average of the minimum and maximum RTTs measured so far, the congestion window size is reduced.

2. *Use of RTT and window size to set the current window size.* Let w be the current window size, w_o be the old window size, r be the current RTT, and r_o be the old RTT. A window RTT product is computed based on $(w - w_o)(r - r_o)$. If the product is positive, the window size is decreased by a fraction of its old value. If the product is negative or 0, the window size is increased by one segment.

3. *Use of throughput as a measure to avoid congestion.* During every RTT, the window size is increased by one segment. The achieved throughput is then compared with the throughput when the window size was one segment smaller. If the difference is less than half the throughput at the beginning of the connection when the window size was one segment, the window size is reduced by one segment.

4. *Use of expected throughput as a measure to avoid congestion.* This method is similar to method 3 but in this case, the algorithm uses two parameters, the current throughput and the expected throughput, to avoid congestion.

The *TCP normalized method* is presented next, as an example of the fourth algorithm.

TCP Normalized Method

In the *TCP normalized method*, the congestion window size is increased in the first few seconds, but the throughput remains constant, because the capacity of the network has been reached, resulting in an increase in the queue length at the router. Thus, an increase in the window size results in any increase in the throughput. This traffic over and above available bandwidth of the network is called *extra data*. The idea behind the TCP normalized method is to maintain this extra data at a nominal level. Too much extra data may lead to longer delays and congestion. Too little extra data may lead to an underutilization of resources, because the available bandwidth changes owing to the bursty nature of Internet traffic. The algorithm defines the expected value of the rate $E[r]$ as

$$E[r] = \frac{w_g}{r_m}, \tag{8.4}$$

where r_m is the minimum of all the measured round-trip times, and w_g is the conges-tion window size. We define A_r as the actual rate and $(E[r] - A_r)$ as the rate differ-ence. We also denote the maximum and minimum threshold to be ρ_{max} and ρ_{min}, respectively. When the rate difference is very small—less than ρ_{min}—the method increases the congestion window size to keep the amount of extra data at a nominal level. If the rate difference is between ρ_{min} and ρ_{max}, the congestion window size is unaltered. When the rate difference is greater than ρ_{max}, there is too much extra data, and the congestion window size is reduced. The decrease in the congestion window size is linear. The TCP normalized method attempts to maintain the traffic flow such that the difference between expected and actual rates lies in this range.

8.6 Summary

All end-to-end communications, such as packet segmentation, packet reassembly, and error checking, are managed through the *transport layer*. The transport layer is responsible for connection signaling and file transfer. The two most important forms of transport are the *User Datagram Protocol* (UDP) and the *Transmission Control Protocol* (TCP).

UDP is a transport-layer protocol described in this chapter. UDP is placed on top of the network layer and is a connectionless protocol, as there is no handshaking between sending and receiving points before sending a segment.

Transmission Control Protocol (TCP) is another transport-layer protocol that provides reliable service. We learned that TCP is a reliable end-to-end connection establishment protocol. We saw that there is a need for three-way handshake signal-ing for both the connection request and the connection termination. Several modes of data transfer with TCP were also presented. One of ways in which TCP provides reliability is through the use of the *automatic repeat request* (ARQ) protocol.

Next, we learned about mobility at the transport layer. One obvious case for the application of a wireless transport protocol is when a user (host) moves to a remote or cellular area and a seamless connection still is desirable. The *fast retransmit* protocol is one of the TCP schemes for mobility. Fast retransmit protocol does not split the TCP connection to wireless and wired connections. As soon as the two wireless base stations hand off the switching function for a mobile host, the mobile host stops receiving TCP segments.

TCP also provides flow control using a sliding-window scheme, as well as conges-tion control. *Additive increase, multiplicative decrease control* performs a slow increase in the congestion window size when network congestion decreases and a fast drop in the window size when congestion increases. A better technique is the *slow-start method*, which increases the congestion window size nonlinearly. The *fast retransmit* of segments sometimes leads to a retransmission of the lost segment before the associated timeout periods. We looked at various congestion-avoidance mechanisms, including the TCP normalized mechanism.

The next chapter presents the application layer in the protocol stack. This layer is responsible for networking applications such as the *File TransferPprotocol, e-mail,* the *World Wide Web* (WWW), and peer-to-peer (P2P) networking. The chapter ends with a discussion of network management.

8.7   Exercises

1. Consider a wide area network in which two hosts, A and B, are connected through a 100 km communication link with a data speed of 1Gb/s. Host A wants to transfer the contents of flash memory with 200KB of music data while host B reserves portions of its ten parallel buffers, each with a capacity of 10,000 bits. Use Figure 8.5 and assume that host A sends a SYN segment, where the initial sequence number is 2,000 and MSS = 2,000, and that host B sends an initial sequence number of 4,000 and MSS = 1,000. Sketch the sequence of segment exchange, starting with host A sending data at time $t = 0$. Assume host B sends ACK every five segments.

2. Consider a hypothetical source segment in a UDP communication to be as small as 1001,1001,0100,1010,1011,0100,0110,0100,1000,1101,0010,0010,1000,0110, 0100,1110.

   (a) Create a checksum for this segment.
   (b) Check to see if the segment has any errors at a destination.
   (c) Research to see how the network treats a segment content that is not a multiple of 2-byte words and hence a checksum algorithm cannot be implemented.

3. Consider that host 1 transfers a large file of size f to host 2 with MSS = 2,000 bytes over a 100Mb/s link.

   (a) Knowing that the TCP sequence number field has 4 bytes, find f such that TCP sequence numbers are not exhausted.
   (b) Find the time it takes to transmit f. Include the link, network, and transport headers attached to each segment.

4. Consider a reliable bytestream protocol that uses a sliding window used in a TCP communication. The TCP communication runs over a 1.5Gb/s connection. The RTT of the network is 98 ms, and the maximum segment lifetime is 2 minutes.

   (a) Suggest the number of bits you would include in the *window size* field.

   (b) Suggest the number of bits would you include in the *sequence number* field.

5. Assume that a TCP connection is established. Find the number of round-trip times (RTTs) the connection takes before it can transmit n segments, using

   (a) Slow-start congestion control

   (b) Additive increase congestion control

6. Assume that a TCP connection is established over a moderately congested link. The connection loses one segment every five segments.

   (a) Can the connection survive at the beginning with the linear portion of congestion avoidance?

   (b) Assume that the sender knows that the congestion remains in the network for a long time. Would it be possible for the sender to have a window size greater than five segments? Why?

7. A TCP connection is established over a 1.2Gb/s link with a round-trip time (RTT) of 3.3 ms. To transmit a file of size 2MB, we start sending it, using 1KB segments.

   (a) How long does the transmission take if an additive increase, multiplicative decrease control with a window size of $w_g = 500$KB is used?

   (b) Repeat part (a), using slow-start control.

   (c) Find the throughput of this file transfer.

   (d) Find the bandwidth utilization for this transfer.

8. Consider that an established TCP connection has a round-trip time (RTT) of approximately 0.5 second and forms a window size of $w_g = 6$KB. The sending source transmits segments every 50 ms, and the destination acknowledges each segment every 50 ms. Now, assume that a congestion state develops in this connection such that the destination does not receive a segment. This loss of segment is detected by the fast-retransmit method at the fourth receipt of duplicate ACKs.

(a) Find the amount of time the sending source has lost if the source uses the arrival of duplicate ACKs as a sign for moving the window forward one segment.

(b) Repeat part (a), this time under a condition in which the sending source waits to receive the ACK of the retransmitted segment before moving the window forward one segment.

9. Assume that server A sends 10KB of a document to host B using a TCP connection. TCP uses *slow-start* congestion control while the congestion control is a linier increase without having a possibility of fast transmission. Segments are all 1KB long and the link bandwidth is 150Mb/s. Suppose that the round-trip time (RTT) is 60 seconds.

   (a) Determine the maximum window size of the TCP connection.

   (b) Find the number of RTTs to accomplish the task of document delivery to host A. Sketch a timing diagram for this case.

   (c) Assuming the fifth segment is lost, repeat part (b), and comment as to whether the congestion window size can reach its maximum.

10. Consider a TCP connection that uses the *additive increase, multiplicative decrease* (AIMD) congestion-control method. The congestion window increases by 1 maximum size segment (MSS) every time an ACK is received. The round-trip time (RTT) is constant at 20 ms.

    (a) Sketch the timing diagram corresponding to this connection and label segments (MSSs) and ACKs until after the congestion window reaches $w_g = 5$ MSSs, and its data is transferred.

    (b) How long does it take for the congestion window to increase from 1 to 5?

11. Consider a 20KB file on the Web that must be downloaded through a TCP connection that uses the *additive increase, multiplicative decrease* (AIMD) congestion-control method. The connection starts with a congestion window of 1 MSS and increases by 1 every time an ACK is received. The maximum size segment (MSS) is set at 1,000 bytes. The average round-trip time (RTT) of a segment and its ACK is about 8 ms. (Ignore the process time between each segment and its immediate ACK.)

    (a) Sketch the timing diagram corresponding to this connection and label segments (MSSs) and ACKs until after the congestion window reaches $w_g = 7$ MSSs, and its data is transferred.

    (b) How long does it take for the congestion window to increase from 1 to 7?

(c) Find the *transfer throughput*, r, for downloading this file

(d) Repeat part (a), this time considering the *slow-start* congestion-control method being applied while there is a loss of segments due to loss of ACKs exactly in the middle of timing.

8.8 Computer Simulation Project

1. *Simulation of Transport Layer on Demultiplexing Segments Through Sockets.* Write a computer program to simulate the implementation of demultiplexing service at a socket transport layer. Your program must show the assignment of IP address 192.2.2.2 and two port numbers, 3500 and 3501, to socket 1 and socket 2, respectively, at a host. Create random 1,000-byte-long segments whose headers indicate the destination port number 3500 or 3501. When a segment arrives at the host, examine the destination port number in the segment and direct the segment to the corresponding socket. Then, the segment's data passes through the socket into the attached process.

(a) Capture a snapshot of segment delivery at each port.

(b) Find the average segment delay.

CHAPTER 9

Basic Network Applications and Management

Having presented basic concepts and definitions in networking to the point that an end-to-end connection can be established, we now look at the last layer of the protocol stack—the *application layer*—and certain network-management issues. This chapter examines fundamental network applications, such as e-mail and the Web, and their supporting protocols and services. These services demonstrate how users perceive a computer network and express the power of Internet technology. More advanced applications of the Internet, such as voice over IP (VoIP), video streaming, and multimedia applications will be presented in Part II of the book. This chapter focuses on the following topics:

- *Overview of the application layer*
- *Domain Name System* (DNS)
- *Electronic mail (e-mail)*
- *World Wide Web* (WWW)

- *Remote login protocols*
- *File transfer and FTP*
- *Peer-to-peer* (P2P) *networking*
- *Network management*

Layer 5, the *application layer,* determines how a specific user application should use a network. The *Domain Name System* (DNS) server is an essential entity for translating machine or domain names into numerical IP addresses.

In the following two sections, we cover the two most widely used Internet applications: *electronic mail* (e-mail) and the *World Wide Web* (WWW) or simply the *Web.* For each topic, several protocols are presented. For example, we describe the *Simple Mail Transfer Protocol* (SMTP), one of the protocols for sending an e-mail from the mail server of a source to the mail servers of destination. The *Web* is a global network of servers linked together by protocols allowing access to connected resources. For this application, we will cover the *Hypertext Transfer Protocol* (HTTP) that transfers Web pages at the application layer.

Remote login protocols allow applications to run at a remote site, with results transferred back to their local sites. Two remote login protocols covered in this chapter are TELNET and SSH. This chapter also presents the methods and protocols for file transfer such as FTP.

Peer-to-peer (P2P) networking is the next topic of this chapter. P2P is a networking approach where all hosts share responsibility for processing data such as uploading and downloading files without needing a third-party server. A couple of popular P2P protocols such as BitTorrent are presented.

Finally, this chapter discusses network management. ASN.1 is a formal language for each managed device to be defined in a network under management. MIB is another management tool for accommodating a database of information and characteristics of devices. The *Simple Network Management Protocol* (SNMP) enables a network manager to find the location of a fault. SNMP runs on top of UDP and uses client/server configurations. SNMP commands define how to query information from a server and forward information to a server or a client.

9.1 Overview of the Application Layer

The *application layer* is built on the transport layer and provides network services to user applications. The application layer defines and performs such applications as electronic mail (e-mail), remote access to computers, file transfers, newsgroups, and the Web, as well as streaming video, Internet radio and telephony, peer-to-peer (P2P) file sharing, multiuser networked games, streaming stored video clips, and real-time video conferencing. The application layer has its own software dependencies. When a new application is developed, its software must be able to run on multiple machines, so that it does not need to be rewritten for networking devices, such as routers that function at the network layer.

9.1.1   Client/Server Model

In a *client/server* architecture, for example, a *client* end host requests services from a *server* host. A client host can be on sometimes or all the time. Figure 9.1 shows an example of application-layer communication. In this figure, an application in a client host is communicating over a "logical" link (virtual link) with another application in a server. The "actual" communication between the two requires the engagement of all physical, link, network, and transport protocols as shown in the figure.

A client/server model provides specific computational services, such as part-time usage services, to multiple machines. Reliable communication protocols, such as TCP, allow interactive use of remote servers as well. For example, we can build a

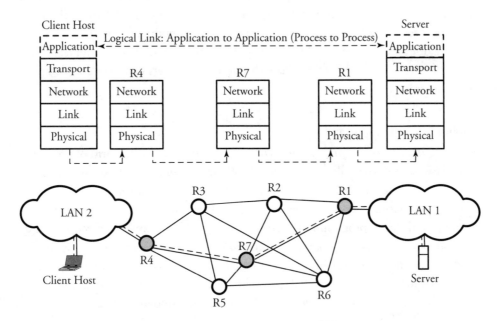

Figure 9.1   Logical communication between applications in two end systems

server that provides remote image-processing services to clients. Implementing such a communication service requires a server loaded with an application protocol to accept requests and a client to make such requests. To invoke remote image processing, a user first executes a client program establishing a TCP connection to a server. Then, the client begins transmitting pieces of a raw image to the server. The server processes the received objects and sends the results back.

9.1.2   Graphical User Interface (GUI)

A *graphical user interface* (GUI) is another element associated with the application layer. GUIs are interfaces to users of computing devices or any other electronic devices that allow users to interact with the devices through graphical visual indicators. The general concept of the "user interface" is not separable from the application layer protocols, as user interfaces are naturally designed for interactions between human and host using an application. Graphical user interfaces typically use a combination of icons, text, and visual indicia to control a given system. GUIs permit displaying and manipulating information in a manner that is intuitive and tailored to a particular task.

The simplest examples of GUI-based systems are the GUIs in operating systems such as Windows and Mac. GUIs have been firmly developed for use in fundamental and advanced network applications as well. Any of the network applications discussed in the next sections of this chapter can have a specific user interface of their own. For example, for an electronic mail (e-mail) application, network design engineers have created a specific e-mail user interface through which users can read and compose e-mail messages.

Application Programming Interface (API)

An *application programming interface* (API) is a set of rules in the form of programs and software tools that allow application programs to control and use network *sockets*. Recall from Chapter 8 that sockets are gateways from the application layer to the transport layer. A host attached to a network has an API that specifies how its running application program must request the network to transfer a piece of data to a destination application program running on another attached host. This can be conceived as an API interfacing in the process by which two application components interact with each other. An API can also be treated as a simple *graphical user interface* (GUI) that hides the complexity and details of the underlying infrastructure of engaged technology from users.

Furthermore, an API can be utilized to simplify the operation of programming GUI components. It can even be used in operating systems; for example, APIs allow users to copy and paste text from one application to another. In practice, an API often comes in the form of a database that includes specifications for data structures, variables, and computer programs.

9.2 Domain Name System (DNS)

A *domain name* is an identification string of a certain network domain or network entity in the Internet. Each domain name is identified by one or more IP addresses depending on the size of the domain. One of the most important components of the application layer is the *Domain Name System* (DNS), which is a distributed hierarchical and global directory server system that translates host or domain names to IP addresses. DNS can be thought as a distributed database system used to map host names or network domain names to IP addresses, and vice versa.

DNS can run over either UDP or TCP. However, running over UDP is usually preferred, since the fast response for a transaction provided by UDP is required. DNS routinely constructs a query message and passes it to the UDP transport layer without any handshaking with the UDP entity running on the destination end system. Then, a UDP header field is attached to the message, and the resulting segment is passed to the network layer. The network layer always encapsulates the UDP segment into a *datagram*. The datagram, or packet, is then sent to a DNS server. If the DNS server does not respond, the fault may be UDP's unreliability.

9.2.1 Domain Name Space

Any entity in the TCP/IP environment is identified by an IP address, which thereby identifies the connection of the corresponding host to the Internet. An IP address can also be assigned a *domain name*. Unique domain names assigned to hosts must be selected from a *name space* and are generally organized in a hierarchical fashion. Domain names are defined in a tree-based structure with the root at the top, as shown in Figure 9.2. A tree is structured with a maximum of 128 levels, starting at level 0 (root). Each level consists of nodes. A node on a tree is identified by a *label*, with a string of up to 63 characters, except for the root label, which has an empty string.

The last label of a domain name expresses the type of organization; other parts of the domain name indicate the hierarchy of the departments within the organization.

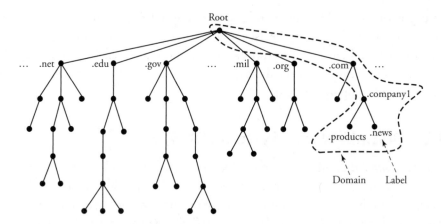

Figure 9.2　Hierarchy of a domain name space, labels, and domain names

Thus, an organization can add any suffix or prefix to its name to define its host or resources. A domain name is a sequence of labels separated by dots and is read from the node up to the root. For example, moving from right to left, we can parse a domain name as follows: news.company1.com, a commercial organization (.com) and the "news" section of "company1" (news.company1). Domain names can also be partial. For example, company1.com is a partial domain name.

DNS Servers

DNS is a critical infrastructure, and any host that is not aware of its destination IP address contacts a DNS server for resolution before it initiates connections. DNS is an application-layer protocol and every Internet service provider—whether for an organization, a university campus, or even a residence—has a DNS server. In the normal mode of operation, a host sends UDP queries to a DNS server. The DNS server either replies or directs the queries to other servers. The DNS server also stores information other than host addresses.

Some of the information-processing functions a DNS server handles are:

- Finding the address of a particular host
- Delegating a subtree of server names to another server
- Denoting the start of the subtree that contains cache and configuration parameters, and giving corresponding addresses
- Naming a host that processes incoming mail for the designated target
- Finding the host type and the operating system information

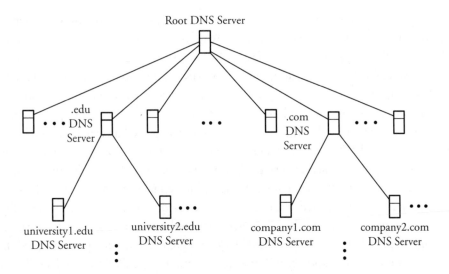

Figure 9.3   Hierarchy of DNS domain name servers

- Finding an alias for the real name of a host
- Mapping IP addresses to host names

The domain name space is divided into subdomains, and each domain or subdomain is assigned a *domain name server*. This way, we can form a hierarchy of servers, as shown in Figure 9.3, just as we did for the hierarchy of domain names. A domain name server has a database consisting of all the information for every node under that domain. Each server at any location in the hierarchy can partition part of its domain and delegate some responsibility to another server. The *root server* supervises the entire domain name space. A root server typically does not store any information about domains and keeps references only to servers over which it has authority. Root servers are distributed around the world.

9.2.2   Name/Address Mapping

DNS operates based on the client/server model. Any client host can send an IP address to a domain name server to be mapped to a domain name. Each host that needs to map an address to a name or vice versa should access the closest DNS server with its request. The server finds and releases the requested information to the host. If the requested information is not found, the server either delegates the request to other servers or asks them to provide the information. After receiving the mapping information, the requesting host examines it for correctness and delivers it to the requesting process.

Mapping can be either *recursive* or *iterative*. In recursive mapping, shown in Figure 9.4, the client host makes the request to its corresponding local DNS server. The local DNS server is responsible for finding the answer recursively. In step 1, requesting client host news.company1.com asks for the answer through its local DNS server, dns.company1.com. Assume that this server cannot find any answer to this request and therefore it has to contact the root DNS server at step 2. Further assume that the root DNS server is also lacking the requested information and hence informs the local DNS server at step 3. This time, the root DNS server sends the query to the .com DNS server at step 4 but the transaction still remains unsuccessful leading to step 5. Finally, the .com DNS server at step 6 sends the query to the local DNS server of the requested place, dns.company2.com, and finds the answer. The answer to a query in this method is routed back to the origin, as shown in the figure through steps 7, 8, 9, and 10. The local DNS server of the requested place is called the *authoritative server* and adds information to the mapping, called time to live (TTL).

In the iterative approach, the mapping function is as shown in Figure 9.5. In this case, if the server does not provide the name, the server returns to the client host. The host must then repeat the query to the next DNS server that may be able to provide the name. This continues until the host succeeds in obtaining the name. In Figure 9.5, the news.company1.com host sends the query to its own local DNS server, dns.company1.com—thus trying the root DNS server first (steps 2 and 3)—and then tries the .com DNS server (steps 4, and 5), finally ending up with the local DNS server of the requested place: dns.company2.com (steps 6, 7, and 8).

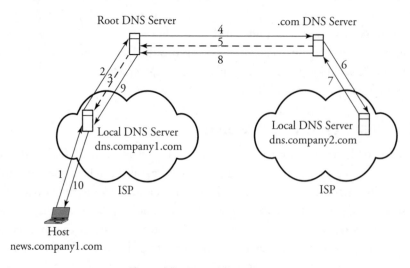

Figure 9.4 Recursive mapping

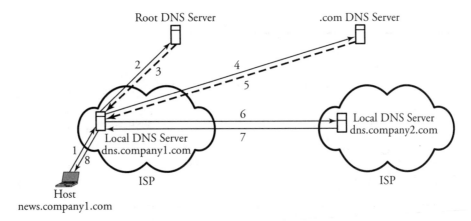

Figure 9.5 Iterative mapping

9.2.3 DNS Message Format

DNS communication is made possible through *query* and *reply* messages. Both message types have the 12-byte header format shown in Figure 9.6. The query message consists of a header and a question message only. The reply message consists of a header and four message fields: *question, answer, authority,* and *additional information.*

The header has six fields as follows. A client uses the *identification* field to match the reply with the query. This field may appear with a different number each time a client transmits a query. The server copies this number in its reply. The *flags* field contains subfields that represent the type of the message, such as the type of answer requested or requested DNS recursive or iterative mapping. The *number of questions* field indicates how many queries are in the *question* portion of the message. The *number of answers* field shows how many answers are in the *answer* field of the message. For the query message, this field contains all zeros. The *number of authoritative records* field consists of the number of authoritative records in the *authority* portion of a reply message. Similarly, this field is filled by zeros for a query message. Finally, the *number of additional records* field is in the additional information portion of a reply message and is similarly filled by zeros in a query message.

The *questions* field can contain one or more questions. The *answers* field belongs only to a reply message and consists of one or more replies from a DNS server to the corresponding client. The *authority* field is present only in reply messages and provides the domain name information about one or more authoritative servers. Finally, the *additional information* field is present only in reply messages and contains

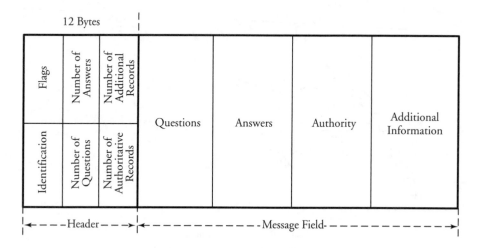

Figure 9.6 DNS message format

other information, such as the IP address of the authoritative server. This additional information helps a client further identify an answer to a question.

New information and names are included in a DNS database through a *registrar*. On a request for inclusion of a new domain name, a DNS registrar must verify the uniqueness of the name and then enter it into its database.

9.3   Electronic Mail (E-Mail)

Electronic mail or *e-mail* is a method of forwarding digital messages electronically from a sending host to one or more receiving hosts. E-mail systems are based on the store-and-forward model where an e-mail is composed by a sending host and sent to the host's *mail server*. Each network organization typically has a mail server. The mail server then stores the message in its buffer, finds the route to the destination, and forwards it onto the correct path. When the e-mail reaches the destination mail server, the store-and-forward action happens again; this time the end result is forwarding the e-mail to the destination host from its mail server. Thus, a mail server can act as either a receiving server or a sending server. In newer e-mail transmission systems, neither of the hosts are required to be online.

9.3.1   Basic E-Mail Structure and Definitions

An e-mail address has a structure including three components: user name, @ sign, and the domain name of the e-mail service provider. For example, the e-mail address user1@isp.com indicates a user name "user1" utilizing the e-mail service from the

Internet service provider domain with name "isp.com." Before we introduce the e-mail protocols, let us have a quick review of basic e-mail definitions such as *mailbox* and *user agent*.

Mailbox and Mail User Agent

Each e-mail user has a *mailbox* located in the user's associated mail server. The mailbox of a user is a storage area on a mail server where e-mails are placed and saved for the user. In any ISP's mail server, each user has a private mailbox. When the user receives an e-mail, the mail server automatically saves it in the mailbox of the user. In order to see and use an e-mail, an e-mail program called a *mail user agent* (MUA) must be installed on a user's host. A mail user agent is a user interface, which can be a graphical user interface (GUI), that allows a user to retrieve and send e-mails through the mail server. A mail user agent can further allow the user to download and store e-mail messages to hosts and read or write them offline.

General E-Mail Message Structure

An e-mail message within a packet consists of a *header* and a *body*. Both parts of the message are composed in ASCII text format. ASCII stands for *American Standard Code for Information Interchange* and is a character-encoding scheme based on the English alphabet that encodes 128 specified characters into 7-bit binary integers. The 128 specified ASCII characters are the numbers 0–9, the letters a–z and A–Z, some basic punctuation symbols, some control codes, and a blank space. The details of ASCII standard are outside the scope of this book.

The *message header* contains several pieces of control information including the sender's e-mail address (starting with From:), and recipient address(es) (starting with To:), a Subject header, and the Message-Id. The *message body* field contains the data portion of the e-mail a user wants to send. The message body carries all sorts of data and as explained, the data must be converted to ASCII text. The header and body fields are separated by a blank line.

Example.   The following practical example shows the contents of an e-mail header sent to user2@organization.com from user1@isp.com with a subject "technical inquiry." The example shows the sender e-mail address (at From) and when the message was transmitted, the received host name with a local ID of LAA35654, and time when the message was received (at Received), followed by the received server name of organization.com and IP address 128.12.1.2, the recipient of the e-mail address (at To), followed by a message-ID (at Message-Id) generated by the server, and a subject (at Subject).

```
From user1@isp.com Mon, Dec 5 2015 23:46:19
Received: (from user1@localhost)
        by isp.com (8.9.3/8.9.3) id LAA35654;
        Mon, 5 Dec 2015 23:46:18 -0500
Received: from organization.com (organization.com [128.12.1.2])
        by isp.com (8.9.3/8.9.3) id XAA35654;
        Mon, 5 Dec 2015 23:46:25 -0500
Date: Mon, 5 Dec 2015 23:46:18 -0500
From: user1 < user1@isp.com >
To: user2 < user2@organization.com >
Message-Id: <201512052346.LAA35654@isp.com >
Subject: technical inquiry

This sentence is an example of the message body separated by a
blank line from its header shown above
```

The Message-Id is a globally unique identifier of an e-mail message used in e-mail protocols. A Message-Id is required in e-mail exchanges to have a specific format and to be globally unique. No two different messages can have the same Message-Id. Its uniqueness is for the purpose of convenience in tracking an e-mail in the public mailing lists. Typically, a time and a date stamp along with the local host's domain name make up the Message-Id such as in the one shown: 201512052346.LAA35654@isp.com, which indicates the year, 2015, followed by a detailed time, and a host name, isp.com.

Classification of E-Mail Protocols

There are a number of protocols developed for e-mail communications between two servers. They are of two types, each responsible for a certain function. The first type of protocol is responsible for forwarding e-mail to the destination's mail server. The reason for not sending the e-mail all the way to the destination host is that the sending host of the mail server may not know the exact address of the receiving host. Thus, the e-mails are forwarded to the destination server only. One of the most practical protocols in this category used heavily in the Internet is the *Simple Mail Transfer Protocol* (SMTP), which is discussed next. The second type of protocol is responsible for retrieving e-mail from mail servers, and includes *Post Office Protocol, version 3* (POP3), the *Internet Mail Access Protocol* (IMAP), and *Webmail*. These protocols are presented in the next sections, except Webmail, which is presented in Section 9.4 World Wide Web (WWW).

9.3.2 Simple Mail Transfer Protocol (SMTP)

The *Simple Mail Transfer Protocol* (SMTP) plays a major role in transferring Internet *electronic mail* (*e-mail*). This protocol transfers e-mail from a sending host to the mail server of a host and thereby to the mail servers of destinations. SMTP imposes certain restrictions, such as limits on the size of e-mail content, and as discussed in the previous section it is a "push protocol," meaning that it only forwards e-mail. This implies a need for another type of protocol to retrieve the e-mail at the receiving host.

In Figure 9.7, user 1 is in a residential area, has an Internet service provider (ISP), and is sending an e-mail to user 2, who works in an organization. Suppose that the mail servers are isp.com and organization.com, respectively. Thus, user 1 and user 2 have e-mail addresses of user1@isp.com and user2@organization.com, respectively. SMTP uses the reliable data transfer service of TCP to transfer e-mail from the source mail server to the destination mail server. The port number at the SMTP server for this purpose is well known as 25. The procedure for an e-mail exchange between user 1 and user 2 is as follows.

Begin SMTP Steps Between User 1 and User 2

1. User 1 provides user 2's e-mail address (e.g., user2@organization. com) and composes its message.
2. User 1 sends the message to its mail server (e.g., isp.com).
3. User 1's mail server places the message in its queue.

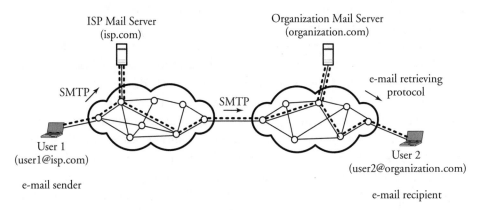

Figure 9.7 User 1 sends an e-mail to user 2 located in a different domain using SMTP, and user 2 obtains the e-mail using an e-mail retrieving protocol such as POP3, IMAP, or Webmail.

4. SMTP on user 1's mail server notices the message in the queue and opens a TCP connection with the organization mail server (e.g., organization.com).

5. Initial SMTP handshaking takes place between the two servers.

6. The e-mail message is sent to user 2's mail server, using the established TCP connection.

7. User 2's mail server receives the message and then puts it in user 2's mailbox, ready to be retrieved by user 2. ■

A *user mailbox* has been generally defined in the previous subsection, and it is a space in the SMTP mail server allocated to a user to keep its e-mails. SMTP is designed to connect the two mail servers of the associated parties, regardless of the distance between the two users. Consequently, this protocol involves only the two mail servers of the communicating users. For users to be able to retrieve their e-mail from their mail servers, other types of "retrieving protocols" such as POP3, IMAP, or Webmail are used. In the following two sections, we present POP3 and IMAP; Webmail will be described in Section 9.4 World Wide Web (WWW).

9.3.3   Post Office Protocol, Version 3 (POP3)

We already learned that once e-mail is saved in a mail server by SMTP, a receiving client uses a "retrieving protocol" to access its e-mail deposited in the mail server. *Post Office Protocol, version 3* (POP3) is one of these protocols for obtaining e-mail from a mail server. POP3 is a simple retrieving protocol having a limited functionality. When first implementing this protocol, the user agent of a host client must open a TCP connection to its mail server. The port number at the POP3 server for this purpose is well known as 110.

Upon establishment of the TCP connection, POP3 first gives permission to the e-mail user to access his or her e-mail after the user undergoes a "username and password" authorization step. Once this step is completed, the user agent of the user can access and retrieve its e-mail messages. At this point, any change in the deposited e-mail such as deleting e-mail can be reflected in the mailbox of the server. POP3 commands are simple; for example, `dele 2` means delete e-mail number 2 and `retr 3` means retrieve e-mail number 3. The POP3 server keeps track of users' messages marked as deleted but it does not keep any other state information in POP3 sessions. Figure 9.7 shows user 2 obtaining e-mail using one of retrieving e-mail protocols such as POP3.

9.3.4 Internet Mail Access Protocol (IMAP)

Although POP3 is simple and easy to deploy and maintain, it does not allow a user to create an e-mail folder hierarchy on a remote server that can be accessed from any host including a mobile host. The *Internet Mail Access Protocol* (IMAP), another "retrieving" e-mail protocol, has been designed to overcome this shortcoming of POP3. IMAP is more complex than POP3. With IMAP, e-mail is deposited in the Inbox folder of the user. The user can create a folder hierarchy in his or her host user agent and sort e-mails by keeping them in various folders.

The significant useful feature of this option is that as soon as e-mails are moved to a folder from the Inbox folder at the user agent side, IMAP will replicate the function immediately at its server. Another improvement with IMAP is that it allows a user to partially download a long e-mail to avoid wasting of time and space if viewing the entire e-mail is not desired. Figure 9.7 shows user 2 obtaining e-mail using one of retrieving e-mail protocols such as IMAP. An IMAP server typically listens on well-known port number 143. The port number is the parameter of transport protocol.

9.4 World Wide Web (WWW)

Application-layer software is the intelligence built for end servers. The *World Wide Web* (WWW), or simply the *Web*, is a global network of servers linked by a common protocol allowing access to all connected resources. The communication in the Web context is carried out through the *Hypertext Transfer Protocol* (HTTP). When a client host requests an object such as a file, the corresponding Web server responds by sending the requested object through browsing tools. The HTTP transfers that page at the application layer. There is also an alternative Internet Web protocol called *Gopher*, which is designed for distributing, searching, and retrieving documents over the Internet. The Gopher protocol is strongly oriented toward a menu-document design. The Gopher ecosystem is often regarded as the effective predecessor of the WWW. Before diving deeply into the details of the Web concept and protocol, let us first review the basic definitions in connection with the Web:

- *Hypertext* and *hyperlink*. *Hypertext* is a type of text with references or links to other more detailed text or additional descriptions that a reader can immediately access by using an available "link." In the context of HTTP, a link is called *hyperlink*.

- *Web page.* A *Web page* is a web document consisting of files or images. A Web page is created by using a markup language. The standard markup language is *Hypertext Markup Language* (HTML).

- *Web client* or *browser.* A *Web browser* is a *user agent* displaying the requested Web page. Web browsers coordinate the Web page's styles, scripts, and images to present the Web page. A Web browser is also called an HTTP *client.*

- *Web server.* A Web server refers to either the hardware or the software that implements the server side of Web protocols and contains Web objects to be accessed by clients. A Web server typically has a fixed IP address.

- *Uniform resource locator* (URL). A URL is the global address of a Web page, document, object, or resource on the Web. A URL is merely an application layer address.

A URL has three parts. The first part indicates which "application protocol" is used (e.g., HTTP or FTP), the second part is the "host name" of the server in which the object (such as a document) has been deposited, and the third part is the "path name" of the object. Although a URL is an address defined in networks, it cannot be used by itself for routing purposes. If a URL is the only address a host has for routing, the host must first resolve the URL via an address resolver database such as a DNS server to obtain the IP address so that routing becomes possible.

Example. The URL http://www.domain1.com/directory1/file1 consists of the following parts: the first part, http://, indicates that the type of application protocol is HTTP; the second part, www.domain1.com, specifies the hostname; and third part, /directory1/file1, expresses the path name of the object in the server. This domain name must be resolved to an IP address by a DNS server for routers.

9.4.1   Hypertext Transfer Protocol (HTTP)

The *Hypertext Transfer Protocol* (HTTP) is the main Web protocol designed to operate at the application layer. We can say HTTP is a distributed and collaborative protocol to exchange or transfer objects and hypertext using hyperlinks. HTTP is based on the client/server model, and is designed for communication between a client program and a server program by exchanging HTTP messages. The protocol has a footprint in both client programs and server programs. For example, HTTP defines how a pair of client/server hosts should exchange messages. Let us first look at an overview of how HTTP works in the following step-by-step algorithm:

Begin HTTP Steps to Download an Object to a Client from a Server

A. Establish a Three-Way Handshaking Connection—TCP:

1. The client (browser) initiates a TCP connection to the server by sending a request TCP segment, leading to the creation of a socket at the client. For this:
   - The client uses the server's IP address, and
   - The client uses server's default TCP port number 80 to create a socket.

2. The server sends an acknowledgment segment (ACK), leading to the creation of a socket at the server.

3. The client sends an HTTP request message including the URL to the server through the socket.

B. Transmit the Requested Object—by Server: The server process receives the request message at its socket, and
   - The server extracts the path name of the requested object.
   - The server attaches the requested object to an HTTP response message.
   - The server forwards the HTTP response message to the client through its socket.

C. Terminate the Connection—TCP: The client receives the requested object via the response message.
   - TCP gets ready to terminate the connection.
   - The server tells TCP to terminate the connection.
   - TCP terminates the connection. ■

Figure 9.8 illustrates downloading a simple file from the Web based on the the HTTP protocol steps just described. HTTP uses TCP, since reliability of delivery

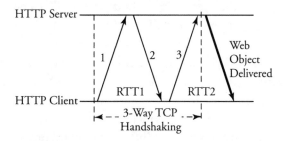

Figure 9.8   The three-way handshaking for a TCP connection in the process of Web downloading

is important for Web pages with text. The TCP connection-establishment delay in HTTP, though, is one of the main contributing delay factors associated with downloading Web documents. In part A of the preceding protocol steps, a three-way handshaking process for the TCP connection first needs to be completed. As seen in Figure 9.8, and the preceding step-by-step protocol description, the client or browser initiates a TCP connection to the server by sending a request TCP segment. This segment, as we discussed in Chapter 8, leads to the creation of a socket at the client. Notice here that the client must have the IP address and port number in order to establish the connection. The Web server default TCP port number is always 80. The server sends an acknowledgment segment (ACK) through its newly created socket for this connection. Finally, the client sends its HTTP request message including the URL to the server through its socket. At this point, the three-way handshaking process has been completed and the TCP connection has been established.

Upon establishing a TCP connection in part B of the protocol, both the client and the server processes are connected. Note that this connection establishment process is arranged automatically once the user selects the hyperlink of a Web page. The server in turn responds with an HTTP response messages that contain the contents of the requested Web page sent through server's socket and the TCP connection. Typically, this process takes two round-trip times (RTTs) to complete the transmission of the requested objects as shown in the figure.

Keep-Alive Connections and the SPDY Protocol

The protocol steps of the HTTP connection are collectively called a *non-persistent connection*. A *non-persistent connection* suffices for a single TCP connection. There are, however, cases in which a user can exercise multiple and parallel TCP connections where each of these connections furnishes one request response. Such cases are classified under a method called *HTTP keep-alive*, or *persistent connection*, or *HTTP connection reuse*. In the keep-alive method, a single TCP connection is expanded for sending and receiving multiple HTTP requests and responses, instead of opening a new connection for every single request and response pair. The idea of the keep-alive connection method was significantly improved on with regard to security and speed and resulted in the *SPDY protocol*. The SPDY protocol was developed by Google and allows multiple request and response pairs to be "multiplexed" over a single connection. The goal of this method was to reduce Web page load latency and improve Web security through the inclusion of data compression and prioritization in the protocol.

HTTP Messages

HTTP has two types of messages, a *request message* and a *response message,* as we realized from the description of the protocol in the previous section. Both types of messages are written in ASCII format. Recall that e-mail messages are also written in the ASCII format, as explained in Section 9.3.1.

The *request message* consists of a request line, a number of *header lines* followed by a blank line, and the message *entity body* as seen in Figure 9.9 (a). Any of the request line, header lines, and the blank line ends with a carriage return and a line feed. The request line consists of three fields: *method* (followed by a space), *URL* (followed by a space), and *version*. The method field acts as an instructional command telling the server what the browser wants it to do. The most common method fields are:

- GET retrieves information from a server when a browser requests an object indicated in the URL.

- POST is also a Web page request but it is used when a browser requests that a Web server accept the data included in the request message's body for storage purposes.

- HEAD is similar to GET but the response arrives without the response body. This is used for management.

- PUT is used by a browser to upload an object to a Web server.

- DELETE deletes the specified resource from a server.

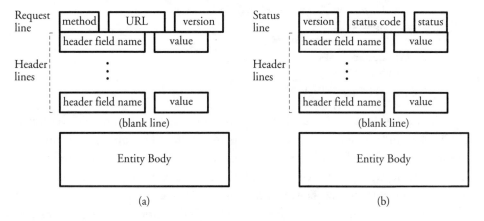

Figure 9.9   HTTP message format

The response message consists of a *status line*, a number of *header lines* followed by a blank line, and the message *entity body* as seen in Figure 9.9 (b). Similarly, any of the status line, header lines, and the blank line ends with a carriage return and a line feed. The status line consists of three fields: *version* (followed by a space), *status code* (followed by a space), and *status*. The status code and status fields report the status of the message, one in the form of a code and the other one in the form of a command.

Example.   Assume a user equipped with the Mozilla/4.0 browser requests file1 located in directory1 in the domain1 server. In this case, the browser uses the URL http://www.domain1.com/directory1/file1 and translates it to the following GET message:

```
GET /directory1/file1 HTTP/1.1
Host: www.domain1.com
Accept: image/jpeg, */*
Accept-Language: en-us
User-Agent: Mozilla/4.0 (compatible; MSIE 6.0; Windows 8)
```

This is the entity body. (Note that the request line consists of the GET *method,* a space, the path name of the *URL* (/directory1/file1), a space, and the *version* (HTTP/1.1). The subsequent lines are header lines. For example, the header field name and value combination of Accept-Language: en-us indicates the language, which is U.S. English)

An example of the HTTP response message is as follows:

```
HTTP/1.1 200 OK
Date: Fri, 9 Jan 2015 08:56:53 GMT
Server: Apache/2.2.14 (Win32)
Last-Modified: Sat, 10 Jan 2015 07:16:26 GMT
Content-Length: 44
Connection: close
Content-Type: text/html
```

This is the entity body. (Note that the status line reports the protocol version is HTTP/1.1, and the status code of the response is 200. This means everything in the response is OK. The header lines report other information. For example, the header field name and value combination of Last-Modified: Sat, 10 Jan 2015 07:16:26 GMT indicates the date and time when the requested object was created and last modified. Also, Content-Length: 44 indicates the number of bytes, in this case 44 bytes are contained in the object).

HTTPS Protocol

Anytime that a connection in the Web needs to be secure, such as for online financial transactions, the secure version of HTTP called HTTPS is used. For security purposes, the transport layer port number of HTTPS is 443, which is different from the one allocated to HTTP, port 80. The use of HTTPS in place of HTTP is expressed by the requested server and its usage is automatically rendered. The details of network security are described in Chapter 10.

9.4.2   Web Caching (Proxy Server)

An HTTP request from a user is first directed to the network *proxy server*, or *Web cache*. Once configured by the network, a browser's request for an object is directed to the Web cache, which must contain updated copies of all objects in its defined proximity. The main reason for Web caching is to reduce the response time for a user request. This benefit is much more obvious when the bandwidth to a requested server is limited because of traffic at certain hours of the day. Normally, each organization or ISP should have its own cache providing a high-speed link to its users. Consequently, it is to users' advantage that this rapid method of finding objects be available. This method of Internet access also reduces traffic on an organization's access link to the Internet. The details of Web caching are as follows:

Begin Web Caching Algorithm

1. The source user browser makes a TCP connection to the Web cache.
2. The user browser transmits its HTTP request to the Web cache.
3. **If** the Web cache has a copy of the requested object, the Web cache forwards the object to the user browser.

   Otherwise the Web cache establishes a TCP connection to the requested server and asks for the object. Once it receives the requested object, the Web cache stores a copy of it and forwards another copy to the requesting user browser over the existing TCP connection. ■

Figure 9.10 shows three Internet service providers (ISPs). A host in ISP domain 3 is browsing to find and watch an object named http://www.filmmaker.com in ISP domain 1. The request for this object is directed to the Web cache, shown by dashed lines. In this example, the Web cache has no record of the requested object and therefore is establishing another TCP connection to update its record.

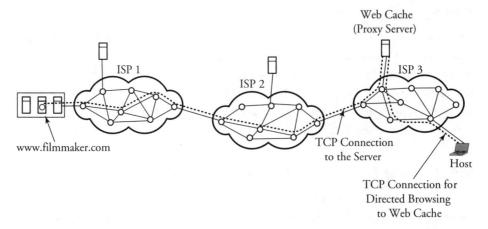

Figure 9.10   A user's browser requesting an object through the Web cache

9.4.3 Webmail

Webmail or *Web-based e-mail* is an e-mail client installed on a host implemented as a Web application to access a Web-based mailbox via a Web browser. Webmail is an alternative to the non-Web e-mail systems explained in Section 9.3. With Webmail, a mail user agent, as explained earlier, is an ordinary Web browser and thus a user must connect its mailbox through HTTP. Some Internet service providers (ISPs) include a Webmail client as part of the e-mail service in their Internet service package. To send and access an e-mail in a fully Web-operated e-mail system, both the sending and receiving users must use Webmail protocol via their browsers. These two processes substitute POP3, IMAP, or SMTP protocols. However, the transmission of e-mail from a sending mail server to a destination mail server must still be carried out using SMTP as seen in Figure 9.11.

9.5   Remote Login Protocols

A client/server model can create a mechanism that allows a user to establish a session on the remote machine and then run its applications. This application is known as *remote login*. A user may want to run such applications at a remote site, with results to be transferred back to its local site. For example, an employee working at home can log in to his or her work server to access application programs for doing a project. This can be done using a client/server application program for the desired service. Two remote login protocols are TELNET and SSH.

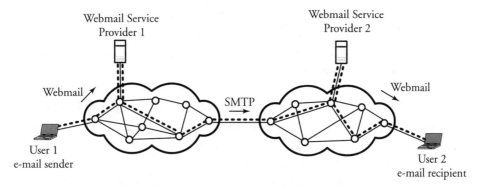

Figure 9.11   User 1 sends an e-mail to user 2 located in a different domain using Webmail and user 2 obtains the e-mail using Webmail.

9.5.1   TELNET Protocol

TELNET (teletype network) is a TCP/IP standard for establishing a connection to a remote system. TELNET allows a user to log in to a remote machine across the Internet by first making a TCP connection and then passing the detail of the application from the user to the remote machine. This application can be interpreted as if the text being transferred had been typed on a keyboard attached to the remote machine.

Logging In to Remote Servers

With TELNET, an application program on the user's machine becomes the client. The user's keyboard and its monitor also attach directly to the remote server. The remote-logging operation is based on timesharing, whereby an authorized user has a login name and a password. TELNET has the following properties:

- Client programs are built to use the standard client/server interfaces without knowing the details of server programs.
- A client and a server can negotiate data format options.
- Once a connection is established through TELNET, both ends of the connection are treated symmetrically.

When a user logs in to a remote server, the client's terminal driver accepts the keystrokes and interprets them as characters through its operating system. Characters are typically transformed to a universal character set called *network virtual terminal*

(NVT), which uses the 7-bit US-ASCII representation for data. The client then establishes a TCP connection to the server. Text in the NVT format are transmitted using a TCP session and are delivered to the operating system of the remote server. The server converts the characters back from NVT to the local client machine's format.

The NVT process is necessary because computers to be remotely logged in to differ. In such cases, a specific terminal emulator must also be used by the TELNET client and servers. The client accepts keystrokes from the user's keyboard while accepting characters that the server sends back. On the server side, data moves up through the server's operating system to the server application program. The remote operating system then delivers characters to the application program the user is running. In the meantime, remote character echo is transmitted back from the remote server to the client over the same path. If the application at the server's site stops reading input for any reason, the associated operating system and, therefore, the server are overwhelmed.

TELNET also offers several options that allow clients and servers to negotiate on nonroutine transactions. For example, one option allows the client and the server to pass 8-bit data. In that case, both the client and server must agree to pass 8-bit data before any transmission.

9.5.2   Secure Shell (SSH) Protocol

Secure Shell (SSH), another remote login protocol, is based on UNIX programs. SSH uses TCP for communications but is more powerful and flexible than TELNET and allows the user to more easily execute a single command on a remote client. SSH has the following advantages over TELNET:

- SSH provides a secure communication by encrypting and authenticating messages (discussed in Chapter 10).

- SSH provides several additional data transfers over the same connection by multiplexing multiple channels that are used for remote login.

SSH security is implemented by using *public-key encryption* between the client and remote servers. When a user establishes a connection to a remote server, the data being transmitted remains confidential even if an intruder obtains a copy of the packets sent over an SSH connection. SSH also implements an authentication process on messages so that a server can find out and verify the host attempting to form a connection. Normally, SSH requires users to enter a private password.

A simple SSH interactive session starts with the server's listening on its port specifically designated for secure transmissions. After a password is submitted, SSH starts a shell for the session. SSH can handle several data transfers simultaneously in the same session. This type of remote login service is multiplexed over an SSH connection. SSH can also be used between two machines to carry out *port forwarding* by establishing a secure tunnel. In the SSH remote login utility, a user can allow SSH to automatically splice an incoming TCP connection to a new connection across a tunnel. The details of tunneling and its applications are explained in Chapter 14. Data sent over the Internet is ensured to be delivered safe from snooping and alteration.

SSH resembles a tunneling function. For example, when it forms an SSH connection for its port k_1 to a remote server, a client can determine that an incoming TCP connection for this port be automatically forwarded across the tunnel to the server and then spliced to another connection to port k_2 of a second server. This way, the client has a TCP connection established on its machine, and the second server makes a TCP connection to the first server. The advantage of port forwarding is that application data can be passed between two sites—the client and the second server—without requiring a second client and server—the first server as a client and the second server. Figure 9.12 shows the format of an SSH packet.

- *Length* indicates the size of the packet, not including the *length* field or the variable-length *random padding* field that follows it.
- *Padding* causes an intrusion to be more difficult.
- *Type* identifies the type of message.
- *CRC*, or cyclic redundancy check, is an error-detection field (see Chapter 3).

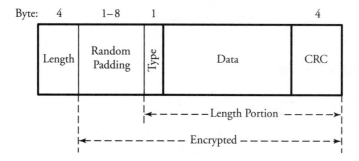

Figure 9.12   SSH packet format

When encryption is enabled, all fields except *length* are encrypted. SSH also permits optional compression of the data, which is useful when SSH is used in low-bandwidth situations. In such cases, the client and the server negotiate compression, and only the *type* and *data* fields are compressed.

9.6   File Transfer and FTP

File transfer is another computer networking application. It is always essential that files and information geographically distributed over different locations can be shared among the members of a work group. In a certain application, files are typically saved in a server. A user then uses a file transfer protocol to access the server and transfer the desired file. Two file transfer protocols are FTP and SCP.

9.6.1   File Transfer Protocol (FTP)

File Transfer Protocol (FTP) is part of the TCP/IP suite and is very similar to TELNET. Both FTP and TELNET are built on the client/server paradigm, and both allow a user to establish a remote connection. However, TELNET provides a broader access to a user, whereas FTP allows access only to certain files. The essence of this protocol is as follows.

Begin File Transfer Protocol

1. A user requests a connection to a remote server.
2. The user waits for an acknowledgment.
3. Once connected, the user must enter a user ID, followed by a password.
4. The connection is established over a TCP session.
5. The desired file is transferred.
6. The user closes the FTP connection. ∎

FTP can also run through a Web browser.

9.6.2   Secure Copy Protocol (SCP)

The *Secure Copy Protocol* (SCP) is similar to TELNET but is secure. Incorporated in the SCP structure are a number of encryption and authentication features that are similar to those in SSH. Also similar is the exchange of commands between local and remote hosts. SCP commands automatically prompt the user for the password information when it is time to access a remote machine. SCP cannot handle file transfer between machines of significantly different architectures.

9.7 Peer-to-Peer (P2P) Networking

Peer-to-peer (P2P) networking is a method of communication in the Internet that allows a group of hosts, called peers, to connect with each other, and directly access files or databases from one another. In a general sense, P2P ascribes to decentralization and self-organizing of data file or database locations where individual hosts organize themselves into a network without any centralized server coordination.

Remember that the client/server model described in Section 9.1.1 may look like a simple example of peer-to-peer communications where each host can have the privilege of becoming either a server or a client. However, the reliance of the client/server model on network resources makes it distinguishable from P2P models. The P2P scheme can also resemble a set of tunnels that interconnect resources and users in the absence of any major assisting server. This way, both the process of locating a file and the process of downloading that file onto a peer's host can happen without the peer having to contact a centralized server. P2P networking protocols can be classified into categories as follows:

- *P2P file sharing protocols* where a file can be shared among multiple peers.
- *P2P database sharing protocols* where a database can be shared among multiple peers.
- *P2P social networking protocols* where multiple peers can establish independent networking.

Figure 9.13 shows an abstract example of P2P networking. In this example, peer 2 attached to a wide area network (WAN) is connecting directly to peer 3, and the same networking scheme occurs between peer 4 attached to the WAN and peer 7 located in a local area network (LAN). We can also see that peer 5 belonging to a WiFi network is sending flooding queries to peers 1, 2, and 6 in search of a certain file or database. In the next section, we start our discussion with *P2P file sharing protocols*.

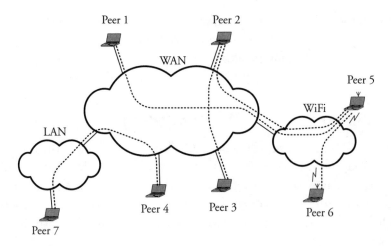

Figure 9.13   An overview example of peer-to-peer (P2P) networking

9.7.1   P2P File Sharing Protocols

One of the applications of P2P networking is *file sharing* through which *file distribution* from a server to a large number of peers can be carried out. The file for distribution can be as small as a simple text file and as large as a video file located in a server. P2P appears to be a convenient method when it comes to the context of sharing files, such as sharing music files, without needing to download them from a central site. With peer-to-peer networking, any peer can obtain the copy of the file from any other peer who has the file without needing to access a central server.

The advantage of P2P file sharing is apparent for large corporations because any peer receiving all or a portion of the file can redistribute it to other peers instead of needing the server to distribute the file to every peer. For example, with P2P file sharing, businesses and organizations are able to share files without the expense involved in maintaining a centralized server.

In a peer-to-peer scheme, the source host as a peer must first download and execute a peer-to-peer networking application program. The application program typically has a graphical user interface (GUI) allowing the host user to efficiently connect the respondent peer. Once the program is launched in the host, the host user should enter the IP address of the second peer in the allocated window of the P2P user interface. With the IP address, the source peer can find the destination peer and connect to it.

In peer-to-peer file sharing, the network of peers can be considered as "structured" where the networked peers follows a structured rule; otherwise, it is classified as "unstructured." One example of file sharing is application software that peer hosts use to arrange themselves into an unstructured P2P network. The application software running on each peer is aware of other peers also running the application. When a peer wants to find a file, the application software floods a query message to its neighboring peers. Any peer that has the requested file responds with the location of the file. The detail of the unstructured P2P file sharing protocol is as follows:

Begin Unstructured P2P File Sharing Protocol

1. The requesting peer floods a QUERY message with a unique QUERY identifier to neighboring peers with the inclusion of a time to live (TTL) in the QUERY to avoid an indefinite search time.

2. Any neighboring peer having the requested file responds with a QUERY RESPONSE.

3. A neighboring peer having or knowing about the requested file forwards to the requesting peer:
   - IP address of the file location, and
   - TCP port number of the file location.

4. The requesting peer uses GET or PUT messages to access the file.

5. **If** the requesting peer was unsuccessful in step 4

   Go to step 1 and exclude the location of the neighboring node that had already failed. ∎

In this protocol, it is important for each peer to maintain a history of the QUERY messages using unique QUERY identifiers to avoid forwarding the same messages to others. Next, one of the most important unstructured P2P file sharing protocols called BitTorrent protocol is presented next.

BitTorrent Protocol

The *BitTorrent* file sharing protocol was developed by Bram Cohen and is an "unstructured" P2P protocol. The BitTorrent protocol is commonly used to share large files over the Internet but it potentially reduces the impact of distributing large files on servers and networks. In the BitTorrent protocol, individual computers efficiently distribute files to many recipients in a peer-to-peer fashion. This approach clearly reduces bandwidth usage of the network and can also prevent sudden large traffic flows in a given area of a network. Let us first get familiar with the terminology of this protocol, as follows:

- *Client.* A *client* is defined as the program that implements the BitTorrent protocol, and thus a *peer* is defined as any computing device running an instance of a client.

- *Chunks.* Peers can download equal-size pieces of a file called *chunks* from one another.

- *Swarm.* A *swarm* refers to the collection of all peers participating in the distribution of a particular file. Each swarm receives a *swarm ID*.

- *Seeds* and *leechers*. Swarm peers are divided into two groups: *seeds* who have the complete version of a requested file, and *leechers* who have not yet downloaded the compete file.

- *Tracker.* A *tracker* is an individual server dedicated to the BitTorrent protocol that maintains and tracks the list of active client members in a swarm. The protocol also presents an alternative decentralized tracking approach in which every peer can act as a tracker. The BitTorrent protocol allows clients to join a *swarm* of hosts to download or upload from each other simultaneously. This can be compared to the traditional approach of downloading a file from a single source server. For this, a chunk is replicated and downloaded from multiple peers. The file replication in this protocol is natural part of the downloading process, as once a peer downloads a particular chunk it becomes a new source for that piece. In order to understand the operation of the BitTorrent protocol, let us first look at a summarized step-by-step algorithmic presentation of the protocol as follows:

Begin BitTorrent P2P File Sharing Protocol

1. **A computing device wants to join a swarm becoming a peer:**
   - The BitTorrent client is installed on the device.
   - The client registers with a tracker.

2. **A peer wants to share a file:**
   - The peer generates the corresponding "torrent file."
   - The torrent file is sent to the tracker to start file sharing.

3. A peer wants to download a file:
 - The peer downloads the corresponding torrent file of the
   requested file.
 - The client opens the corresponding torrent file in order to
   connect to the tracker.
 - The tracker forwards to the requesting peer a list of *seeds*
   and their IP addresses in the targeted swarm including the
   swarm ID.
 - The peer communicates with those swarm peers to download the
   chunks of the desired file using TCP. ∎

As seen in step 1 of the protocol, in order for a peer to join a swarm, it must have the BitTorrent software installed on its machine, and then register with a tracker. When a peer wants to share a file in step 2, it must first generate a small file called a *torrent file* such as file1.torrent. A torrent file contains information about the tracker, the files to be shared, and the peer that coordinates the file distribution. A torrent file has an *announce* field that specifies the URL of the associated tracker, and an *info* field that carries file names, file lengths, the chunk length used, and a security code called the *SHA-1 hash code* for each chunk. The SHA-1 hash is a security algorithm and is explained in Chapter 10. The collection of this information is then verified by the clients.

Downloading or uploading a file with BitTorrent is different from traditional methods using HTTP or FTP. With BitTorrent, numerous chunks of a file are transferred over several different TCP connections to different peers instead of one TCP connection to the source of file. This distributed format of handling a large file is actually faster than downloading a large file from a single source. Moreover, a TCP connection with the BitTorrent download ensures the download of data chunks in a random fashion instead of a traditional sequential TCP download. This strategy allows the download traffic to become evenly distributed over geographical areas of networking.

Any peer that wants to download a file must first download the corresponding torrent file of the targeted file as indicated in step 3 of the protocol. Next, when the torrent file is opened with the BitTorrent client, the client automatically connects to the tracker suggested in the torrent file. The tracker forwards a list of peers, called *seeds,* who can transfer chunks of the desired files, the seeds' IP addresses, and the corresponding swarm ID. The client then communicates with those peers to download the chunks in random order. Whenever a downloading peer finishes downloading a chunk, it sends a message identifying that chunk to each of its neighboring peers. A neighboring peer is a peer that is directly connected.

Each peer in a swarm can download chunks from the other, and send the other a report of which chunks it has, so that each peer in a swarm becomes aware of which peers have a certain chunk. When a peer joins a swarm for the first time, it has no chunks. But it accumulates chunks over time, and downloads chunks to and uploads chunks from other peers. Peers perform "fair trading" by sending chunks to those peers that return chunks to them except in the cases of newly joined peers. A client program uses a mechanism called *optimistic unchoking* by which the client reserves a portion of its available bandwidth for sending chunks to random peers. This can facilitate discovering more favorable partners for a peer.

As we discussed, the BitTorrent protocol can also support trackerless swarms. In this case, any peer client program is capable of being a peer and also a tracker using UDP.

Example.   Figure 9.14 shows an example of BitTorrent peer-to-peer (P2P) networking in which a new arriving peer is downloading a file consisting of a 3 chunks from various peers. Peer 5 is just joining the P2P network and thus first needs to register with the tracker. The tracker provides the list of those peers who have the file peer 5 wants to download. The list includes a swarm of seed peers 1, 2, and 4. Peer 3 remains a leecher as it does not yet have any part of the requested file. Peer 4 downloads chunk1 of the file from peer 1, chunk 2 of the file from peer 4, and chunk 3 of the file from peer 2. At this point, the swarm list is updated to include peer 5.

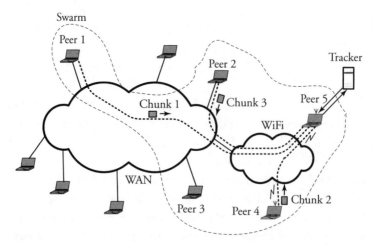

Figure 9.14   In this example of BitTorrent peer-to-peer (P2P) networking, a peer is downloading chunks of a file from various peers.

9.7.2 P2P Database Sharing Protocols

The second P2P application we examine is the category of P2P *database sharing protocols* by which databases of objects, such as video content, music, and books, can be distributed over a large community of peers. One of the key issues in database sharing is how to locate which peers have the specific object that is being sought. For example, an Internet user might have one or more objects such as songs, videos, and files, while other users might want to have them but finding these objects is a challenge. A straightforward solution to this challenge is to create one database of all the objects, but this approach is centralized and may not be appealing to the public. Having every peer keep its own database is not favorable either, as this approach requires a significant amount of effort to keep the databases of all peers updated. The solution to this challenge is to build a shared and distributed database so that each peer holds a small portion of the database contents while associating with other peers to access and update the contents. An examples of such a distributed database is a *distributed hash table* (DHT), described next.

Distributed Hash Tables (DHTs)

A *distributed hash table* (DHT) is a "structured" P2P network and operates as a database that contains (*object name, address of object*) pairs. An *object name* can be a music title, video clip name, or a book title, and an *address of object* can be an address of a peer that holds the object such as an IP address of a peer. Clearly, a database held by a peer can store multiple (object name, address of object) pairs and an object may be stored by multiple peers.

The challenge in such a P2P networking is how to build a "distributed" database of (*object name, address of object*) pairs where each peer can store only a subset of all pairs. In such an environment, a peer must query a significantly large distributed database using a particular key. The DHT must then be able to locate those peers who have the (*object name, address of object*) pairs where the targeted key in this pair is contained, and then return the (key, value) pairs to the requesting peer. This type of distributed database is referred to as a *distributed hash table* (DHT).

In order to build such a distributed database of objects for P2P applications, a *hash function* is used. The details of hash functions are presented in Section 10.5.1. Briefly, a hash function indicated by h is utilized to expose deliberate corruption of a message when any *message* is mapped to data of a fixed size called a *hash,* or a *message digest.* A hash function that operates in a computer network allows a host to easily verify that some input data is authenticated. Hash functions are typically used in *hash tables*, to agilely find a data record by mapping a search key to an index. The index in a hash table provides the location in the hash table where the corresponding record is stored.

One of the DHT networking topologies is called a *chord,* in which the overall database is distributed over peers joined a circular network. The hash function must be available to all peers and that is why the term *hash* is used in "distributed hash function." DHT networking uses the following rules:

- For any object, use the hash function to convert an *object name* to an $n-$ bit identifier integer called a "*key.*" The key is thus in the range 0 to $2^n - 1$.

- For any participating peer, use the hash function to convert an $n-$ bit identifier integer called a "*value.*" The value is thus in the range 0 to $2^n - 1$. The integer n depends on the number of peers.

- The hashed version of the (*object name, address of object*) pair is shown by (*key, value*) pair, which is associated with the object whose identifier is the *key* in the pair.

- The (*key, value*) pair associated with its object is stored in a peer with the closest successor for the key in a clockwise direction around the chord.

Example. Consider the participation of five active peers in a chord DHT shown in Figure 9.15. Suppose in the circular P2P network shown in the figure, n is selected to be 3. Thus, it can be understood that with $n = 3$, both object name and the address of object must be hashed to produce identifiers each in the range of 0 to $2^3 - 1 = 7$. Assume that the five active peers in this network are hashed to have identifiers 0, 1, 3, 4, and 6, respectively. In this case, consider that a music title as the name of an object is hashed to have a key whose identifier turns out to be 5. Since the closest successor to 5 among the peer values around the circle is peer 6, then the (*key, value*) pair of (5, 6) is formed and then saved in peer 6. Note that, if a key becomes larger than all the peer identifiers, DHT uses a modulo-2^n rule keeping the (*key, value*) pair in a peer with the smallest identifier.

Now, let us learn how a peer finds the peer that stores the object it looks for. Recall that in DHT, each peer must only keep track of its immediate successor, and its immediate predecessor, as in the case of the modulo-2^n rule. Hence, when a peer wants to find an object, it must first hash the object title to find the object's key. It then sends a query packet to find the (*key, value*) pair of the object clockwise

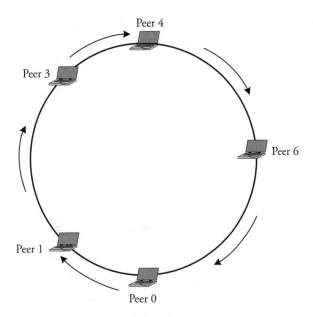

Figure 9.15 A chord (circular) DHT peer-to-peer (P2P) network

around the chord network. Any peer in the chord that receives the message knows the identifier of its successor and predecessor. Any peer receiving the query examines the key in the query and passes the query to the next peer (its successor) unless (1) the identity (value) of the peer is larger than the key and (2) the key is closer to the peer's identity than to its successor's identity.

In a chord network with m active peers, all m *peers* in the DHT have to forward a query around the circle in order to find the peer responsible for a key, and $m/2$ queries are sent on average. This is a fairly large amount of traffic and thus a solution called peer churn has been developed to overcome this traffic issue. In the peer churn approach, shortcuts are allowed to be implemented in the chord so that each peer not only keeps track of its immediate successor and predecessor, but also of a relatively small number of shortcut peers. In particular, when a peer receives a key query packet, it forwards it to the neighbor that is either its successor or one of the shortcut peers that is the closet to the key.

9.7.3 Estimation of Peer Connection Efficiency

Let us do a quick performance evaluation of P2P networking. Let t_e be the time required to establish a connection to a peer, and t_f be the time to complete the service after the connection is established. Assuming that connection requests to the peer arrive at random and with rate λ, the service time S is

$$S = \begin{cases} t_f & \text{if the peer is already connected} \\ t_f + t_e & \text{if the peer is not connected} \end{cases}. \tag{9.1}$$

When a request arrives, a peer can be connected with probability p and not connected with probability $1 - p$. Realizing that S is generally a continuous random variable (see Appendix C) and is discrete for the two cases discussed in Equation (9.1), the average or expected service time is derived by

$$E[S] = pt_f + (1 - p)(t_f + t_e) = t_f + (1 - p)t_e. \tag{9.2}$$

Let $\rho = \dfrac{\lambda}{\mu}$ be the utilization of the peer, where λ is the connection request arrival rate, and μ is the average peer service rate. Thus, a fraction ρ of any given time Δ, that either "the peer uses for connecting" or "the connection is used for service" is expressed by

$$\delta_s = p\rho\Delta. \tag{9.3}$$

Similarly, the fraction $1 - \rho$ of the same mentioned given time that the peer is idle can be derived by

$$\delta_i = (1 - p)(1 - \rho)\Delta, \tag{9.4}$$

where the idle time occurs when the peer is either disconnected or connected but not using the connection. We can now derive an expression for the peer connection efficiency, u, as follows:

$$u = 1 - [p\rho + (1 - p)(1 - \rho)]. \tag{9.5}$$

The connection efficiency of the peer can be used to determine the overall efficiency of the P2P connection.

9.8   Network Management

The main purpose of *network management* is to monitor, manage, and control a network. A network can be structured with many links, routers, servers, and other physical-layer devices, which can be equipped with many network protocols that coordinate them. Imagine when thousands of such devices or protocols are tied together by an ISP and how drastic their management can become to avoid any interruptions in routine services. In this context the purpose of network management is to monitor, test, and analyze the hardware, software, and human elements of a network and then to configure and control those elements to meet the operational performance requirements of the network.

Figure 9.16 illustrates a simple network management scenario in which LANs connect to the Internet. LAN 1 is dedicated to the network administrator facilities. The network administrator can periodically send management packets to communicate with a certain network entity. A malfunctioning component in a network can also initiate communication of its problem to the network administrator.

Network management tasks can be characterized as follows:

- *QoS and performance management.* A network administrator periodically monitors and analyzes routers, hosts, and utilization of links and then redirects traffic flow to avoid any overloaded spots. Certain tools are available to detect rapid changes in traffic flow.

- *Network failure management.* Any fault in a network, such as link, host, or router hardware or software outages, must be detected, located, and responded to by the network. Typically, any increase in checksum errors in frames is an

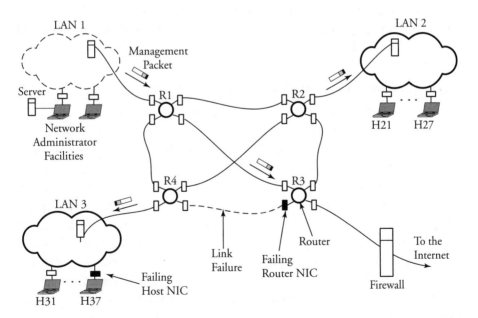

Figure 9.16   Simple network management in a scenario of LANs connecting to the Internet

indication of possible error. Figure 9.16 shows network interface card (NIC) failures at router R3 and host H37; these failures can be detected through network management.

- *Configuration management.* This task involves tracking all the devices under management and ensuring that all devices are connected and operate properly. If there is an unexpected change in routing tables, a network administrator wants to discover the misconfigured spot and reconfigure the network before the error affects the network substantially.

- *Security management.* A network administrator is responsible for the security of his or her network. This task is handled mainly through firewalls, as discussed in Chapter 10. A firewall can monitor and control access points. In such cases, the network administrator wants to know about any intrusion from a suspicious source to the network. For example, a host in a network can be attacked by receiving a large number of SYN packets (segments).

- *Billing and accounting management.* The network administrator specifies user access or restrictions to network resources and issues all billing and charges, if any, to users.

Locating a failing point, such as a network interface card (NIC) failure at a host or a router can be implemented by utilizing appropriate network management tools. Normally, a standard packet format is specified for network management.

9.8.1 Elements of Network Management

Network management has three main components: a *managing center,* a *managed device,* and a *network management protocol.* The managing center consists of the network administrator and his or her facilities. Typically, the managing center comprises a substantial human network. A managed device is the network equipment, including its software, that is controlled by the managing center. Any hub, bridge, router, server, printer, or modem can be a managed device. The network management protocol is a policy between the managing center and the managed devices. The protocol in this context allows the managing center to obtain the status of managed devices. In network management, an *agent* is a managed device, such as a router, hub, or bridge. A *manager* is a network administrative device, such as a management host. An agent can use the network management protocol to inform the managing center of an unexpected event.

9.8.2 Structure of Management Information (SMI)

The *Structure of Management Information* (SMI) language is used to define the rules for naming objects and to encode contents in a managed network center. In other words, SMI is a language by which a specific instance of the data in a managed network center is defined. For example, Integer32 means a 32-bit integer with a value between -2^{31} and $-2^{31} - 1$. The SMI language also provides higher-level language constructs, which typically specify the data type, status, and semantics of managed objects containing the management data. For example, the STATUS clause specifies whether the object definition is current or obsolete, and ipInDelivers defines a 32-bit counter to trace the number of IP datagrams received at a managed device and then received at an upper-layer protocol.

9.8.3 Management Information Base (MIB)

A *Management information base* (MIB) is an information storage medium that contains managed objects reflecting the current status of the network. Because managed objects have associated pieces of information that are stored in an MIB, the MIB forms a collection of named objects, including their relationships to one another in a management center. The information pieces can be obtained by directing the managing center to do so.

Objects are organized in a hierarchical manner and are identified by the *Abstract Syntax Notation One* (ASN.1) object definition language. The hierarchy of object names, known as *ASN.1 object identifier*, is an object identifier tree in which each branch has both a name and a number, as shown in Figure 9.17. Network management can then identify an object by a sequence of names or numbers from the root to that object.

At the root of the object identifier hierarchy are three entries: ISO (International Organization for Standardization), ITU-T (International Telecommunication Union–Telecommunication) standardization sector, and ISO-ITU-T, the joint branch of these two organizations. Figure 9.17 shows only part of the hierarchy. Under the ISO entry are other branches. For example, the *organization (3)* branch is labeled sequentially from the root as 1.3. If we continue to follow the entries on this branch, we see a path over *dod (6)*, *Internet (1)*, *management (2)*, *mib-2(1)*, and *ip (4)*. This path is identified by (1.3.6.1.2.1.4) to indicate all the labeled numbers from the root to the *ip (4)* entry. Besides that entry, MIB module represents a number of network interfaces and well-known Internet protocols at the bottom of this tree. This

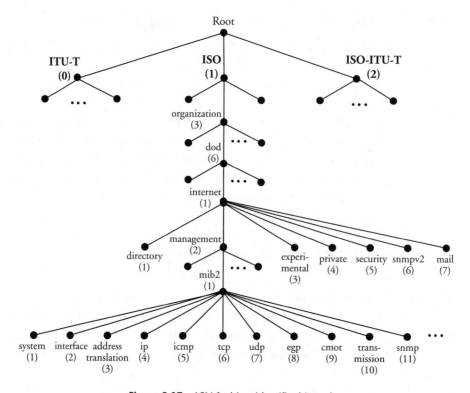

Figure 9.17   ASN.1 object identifier hierarchy

path clearly shows all the standards of "IP" associated with the "MIB-2" computer networking "management."

9.8.4   Simple Network Management Protocol (SNMP)

The *Simple Network Management Protocol* (SNMP) is designed to monitor the performance of network protocols and devices. SNMP protocol data units (PDUs) can be carried in the payload of a UDP datagram, and so its delivery to a destination is not guaranteed. Managed devices, such as routers and hosts, are objects, and each object has a formal ASN.1 definition. For each object, MIB accommodates a database of information that describes its characteristics. With this protocol, a network manager can find the location of a fault. SNMP runs on top of UDP and uses client/server configurations. The commands of this protocol define how to query information from a server and forward information to a server or a client.

The task of SNMP is to transport MIB information among managing centers and agents executing on behalf of managing centers. For each managed MIB object, an SNMP request is used to retrieve or change its associated value. If an unsolicited message is received by an agent, or when an interface or device goes down, the protocol can also inform the managing center. The second version of this protocol, SNMPv2, runs on top of more protocols and has more messaging options, resulting in more effective network management. SNMPv3 has more security options. SNMPv2 has seven PDUs, or messages, as follows:

1. GetRequest is used to obtain an MIB object value.

2. GetNextRequest is used to obtain the next value of an MIB object.

3. GetBulkRequest gets multiple values, equivalent to multiple GetRequests but without using multiple overheads.

4. InformRequest is a manager-to-manager message that two communicating management centers are remote to each other.

5. SetRequest is used by a managing center to initiate the value of an MIB object.

6. Response is a reply message to a request-type PDU.

7. Trap notifies a managing center that an unexpected event has occurred.

Figure 9.18 shows the format of SNMP PDUs. Two types of PDUs are depicted: Get or Set and Trap. The Get or Set PDU format is as follows:

- *PDU type* indicates one of the seven PDU types.

- *Request ID* is an ID used to verify the response of a request. Thus, a managing center can detect lost requests or replies.

- *Error status* is used only by Response PDUs to indicate types of errors reported by an agent.

- *Error index* is a parameter indicating to a network administrator which *name* has caused an error.

If requests or replies are lost, SNMP does not mandate any method for retransmission. The *Error status* and *Error index* fields are all zeros except for the one in a GetBulkRequest PDU. Figure 9.18 also shows the format of the Trap PDU, in which the *enterprise* field is for use in multiple networks; the *timestamp* field, for measuring uptime; and the *agent address* field, for indicating that the address of the managed agent is included in the PDU header.

Get or Set PDU

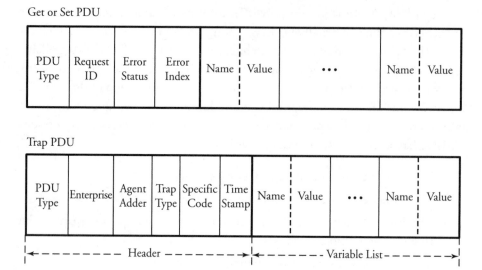

Trap PDU

Figure 9.18   SNMP PDU format

9.9 Summary

The top layer of the networking protocol stack is known as the application layer. Services in this category allow users and programs to interact with services on remote machines and with remote users. The *application layer* offers network services and applications to users and runs certain applications. The *Domain Name System* (DNS) is a distributed hierarchical and global directory that translates machine or domain names to numerical IP addresses. An IP address can be assigned a *domain name*. Unique domain names assigned to hosts must be selected from a *name space* and are generally organized in a hierarchical fashion.

The *Simple Mail Transfer Protocol* (SMTP) can transfer *e-mail* from the mail server of a source to mail servers of destinations. A user mailbox is a certain space the mail server allocates to the user to keep its e-mail. SMTP is designed to connect only the two mail servers of the associated parties, regardless of the distance between the two users. Consequently, this protocol involves only the two mail servers of the communicating users.

File transfer allows geographically distributed files and information to be shared among the members of a work group and for information sharing. A user can use a file transfer protocol to access a server and transfer the desired file. Two such protocols are FTP and SCP. The *World Wide Web* (WWW), or simply the *Web*, is a global network of servers linked together by a common protocol allowing access to all connected hypertext resources. HTTP requests are first directed to the network *proxy server* called the *Web cache*. Once configured by the network, a browser's request for an object is directed to the Web cache.

The TELNET remote login protocol uses a negotiation method to allow clients and servers to reconfigure the parameters controlling their interaction. The *Secure Shell* (SSH) remote login protocol is implemented on TCP for communications. SSH is more powerful and flexible than TELNET and allows the user to more easily execute a single command on a remote client.

We also covered *peer-to-peer* (P2P) networking in this chapter. We learned that P2P is a decentralized networking approach where hosts share responsibility for processing data such as uploading and downloading files without the need for a third-party server. One of the most important factors that makes P2P networking different from traditional networking is the fact that certain hosts have responsibility for providing or serving data while other others consume data or otherwise act as clients of those serving hosts. We noticed that in the popular BitTorrent protocol, a requested file can be partitioned to smaller-size pieces, called *chunks*, and each chunk can be saved in one of the peers for downloading by another peer.

The chapter ended with management aspects of computer networks. Managed devices, such as routers and hosts, are managed objects, and each object has a formal ASN.1 definition. Another tool through which a database of information and characteristics for objects can be accommodated is MIB. With SNMP, a network manager can find the location of a fault. SNMP runs on top of UDP and uses client/server configurations. SNMP commands define how to query information from a server and forward information to a server or a client.

The next chapter discusses the security aspects of computer networking. Types of network attacks, message encryption protocols, and message authentication techniques are covered.

9.10   Exercises

1. Find out about an IP address that is well known to you, such as that of your college or your work server. Set up an experiment in which you look up the domain name for this IP address.

2. Consider DNS servers.

   (a) Compare two approaches, obtaining a name from a file in a remote machine and from a DNS server of the local ISP.

(b) Describe the relationship between a domain name taken from a DNS server and an IP address subnet.

(c) In part (b), do all hosts on 3the same subnet need to be identified by the same DNS server? Why?

3. Suppose a Web browser starts a process of downloading n different but related files, each located in a different Web site. The Web browser must contact an avarage of m DNS servers to find the IP address for each of the Web servers. Find the total number of RTTs to receive the Web page using a non-persistent connection

(a) If iterative DNS mapping is used.

(b) If recursive DNS mapping is used.

4. Suppose a Web browser starts a process of downloading ten different files, file 1 through file 10, respectively, located on a Web site. Once the three-way handshaking of HTTP is completed, file 1 through file 10 requiring, respectively, 10, 20, ... 100 ms for delivery to the client are transferred. The Web server disconnects any server usage transaction taking longer than 110 ms. Assume also that each way of the three-way handshaking process takes 10 ms. Find the total time for downloading these files

(a) If a non-persistent connection is used.

(b) If a keep-alive connection is used.

5. Do research on which letters, such as A, B, C, ⋯, or signs, such as #, *, •, ⋯, are not allowed to be sent in a URL to a Web server.

6. Read all the RFCs associated with HTTP listed in Appendix B.

(a) What is the purpose of the GET command?

(b) What is the purpose of the PUT command?

(c) Following part (a), explain why a GET command needs to use the name of the contacted server when it is applied.

7. Read all the RFCs associated with TELNET and SSH listed in Appendix B.

(a) What are the most significant differences between these two protocols?

(b) Compare the two protocols on the functionality given by "rlogin."

8. Read all the RFCs associated with FTP listed in Appendix B.

(a) Does FTP compute any checksum for files it transfers? Why?

(b) FTP is based on TCP. Explain the status of a file transfer if the TCP connection is shut down, and compare it with the same situation in which its control connection remains active.

(c) Find all the commands from RFCs set for clients.

9. Set up an experiment in which two computers across a defined network exchange the same defined file through FTP. Measure the file transfer delay

   (a) On both directions when the network is in its best traffic state.
   (b) On both directions when the network is in its worst traffic state.
   (c) On one direction when you try FTP from one of the computers to itself.

10. Assume that a peer joins a BitTorrent P2P network without wanting to upload any object to any of the network's peers. Can the peer receive a copy of an object that is shared by the swarm?

11. Consider a BitTorrent P2P network.

    (a) Discuss the impact of the number of peers in a swarm on the performance of sharing a file.
    (b) Discuss the impact of chunk size on the performance of sharing a file.

12. Suppose that in a DHT P2P chord network $n = 4$ and hence the identifiers are in the range $[0, 31]$. Assume that there are nine active peers with identifiers 2, 7, 17, 18, 20, 25, 27, 28, and 30.

    (a) Identify the keys that each peer is responsible for if there are the following five keys in the network: 3, 8, 15, 16, and 29.
    (b) Find all the peers to which a query for key 29 is forwarded.

13. Consider a DHT P2P chord network where there are m active peers and k keys. Find an upper bound on the number keys each peer is responsible for.

14. Three peers numbered 0, 1, and 2 in a chord P2P network are in standby mode waiting to be activated. The average times required to establish a connection to the next peer and to complete the service after a connection on the ring is established are 200 ms and 300 ms, respectively. Let the connection request arrival rate for peers 0, 1, and 2 be 2, 3, and 4 inquiries per minute, respectively, while the average peer service rate is 7 inquiries per minute. When an inquiry arrives at any time, peers 0, 1, and 2 can be connected to the network with probability 0.2, 0.3, and 0.5, respectively.

    (a) Find the service time for each peer.
    (b) Find the utilization of each peer.
    (c) Calculate the average service time for each peer.
    (d) Calculate the average service time for all peers.
    (e) For each peer, estimate the fraction of any two hours that either the peer uses for connecting or the connection is used for service.
    (f) Calculate connection efficiency for each peer.

15. Figure 9.17 shows the hierarchical ASN.1 object identifier of network management.

    (a) Explain the role of ASN.1 in the protocol reference model, discussing it on either the five- or seven-layer protocol model.

    (b) Find the impact of constructing a grand set of unique global ASN.1 names for MIB variables.

    (c) Do research in the related RFCs listed in Appendix B, and find out where in the ASN.1 hierarchy a U.S.-based organization must register its own developed MIB.

16. Consider the SNMP network management environment.

    (a) Justify why UDP is preferable to TCP for this environment.

    (b) MIB variables can be read in a local router the MIB belongs to. What would be the pros and cons if we let all managing centers access MIBs in all routers?

    (a) Should MIB variables be organized in the local router memory the same way they are in SNMP? Why?

9.11   Computer Simulation Projects

1. *Simulation of Client/Server TCP Connections.* Write a computer program to simulate a TCP connection for a client/server combination. The server receives a small file from the client. Set up another machine as the proxy server, and try to send messages from the proxy server to the main server. Display all possible messages in the server.

2. *Experimental Analysis of HTTP Commands through a Software Tool.* Use Wireshark packet analyzer software to investigate several aspects of an HTTP application while requesting a Web page through your browser from any Website of your choice.

    (a) Load the trace file; filter out all the non-HTTP packets and focus on the HTTP header information in the packet-header detail window.

    (b) How many HTTP GET Request messages did your browser send?

    (c) Look into the information in the HTTP GET Request and its Response messages. Inspect the contents of the first HTTP GET Request from the browser to the server. Then inspect the contents of the server response. Justify if the server explicitly returns the contents of the file.

    (d) Inspect the contents of the second HTTP GET Request from the browser to the server. Present what information is contained in the "IF-MODIFIED-SINCE:" header.

3. ***Simulation of Streaming Content in a Peer-to-Peer* (P2P) *Network.*** Use a simulation tool to simulate streaming of content such as a video clip from one peer to another. You may simulate the P2P network with any of the available network simulator tools such as NS2, NS3, or GNS3. Set up a peer-to-peer connection under load balancing conditions. Create a video clip to be streamed from one peer to another, either bit by bit or packet by packet using a streaming protocol. You may need to install a TV tuner card on one of the peers, and convert the bitstream into packets of bits.

  (a) Measure the *playback delay,* which is the delay time between the generation of a particular packet of data and its playback on the screen.

  (b) Measure *playout loss,* which is the ratio of the number of packets of data that have not been received at the destination peer to the total amount of packets that have been transferred by the stream originator in the live video content delivery. The packet rate and the load on each node can be analyzed using network-analyzing tools such as Wireshark or NCTUns.

  (c) Measure the *startup delay,* which is the delay between the requests sent from a user to the streaming server and the time at which the content is displayed on the screen. Channel setup time and buffering delay are two parameters of startup delay. Channel setup is the time taken by a peer to search for a transmitting peer. The buffering delay is the time taken by the receiving peer to gather enough packets from the transmitting peer to play back the video content seamlessly.

  (d) Measure *playback lag,* which is the time difference existing during the playback of the same packet on two different nodes on the same P2P overlay.

4. ***Experimental Setup for Streaming of Video in Peer-to-Peer* (P2P) *Networking.*** Repeat project 2, but this time try to experimentally implement the streaming of content such as a video clip from one peer to another. You can implement this project by using protocols such as VP8, BitTorrent Live, or PPLive for streaming the video from one host to another. You should have a peer on your network called the signal originator. The stream originator should have the capability to transmit live video streams and then simultaneously facilitate an upload of the stream to another peer in a P2P network. This is done packet by packet; once a packet of data is downloaded from the live stream of the video, it is converted into data packets, which are then transmitted to the other peer. This simultaneous download and upload can create a live stream.

CHAPTER 10

Network Security

The invention of computers made the need for security of digital information a critical issue. Advances in the field of computer networks have made information security even more important. Computer systems have to be equipped with mechanisms for securing data. Computer networks need provisions that secure data from possible intrusions. Security is especially crucial in wireless networks, as a wireless medium, by its nature, is vulnerable to intrusions and attacks. This chapter focuses on *network security*. The following major topics in network security are covered:

- *Overview of network security*
- *Security methods*
- *Symmetric-key cryptography*
- *Public-key cryptography*
- *Authentication*
- *Digital signatures*
- *Security of IP and wireless networks*
- *Firewalls and packet filtering*

We begin by identifying and classifying types of network threats, hackers, and attacks, including DNS hacking attacks and router attacks. Network security can be divided into three broad categories: *cryptography, authentication*, and *digital signatures*. On *cryptography,* both symmetric-key and public-key encryption protocols are presented. We discuss message authentication and digital signature methods, through which a receiver can be assured that an incoming message is from whom it says it is.

We then consider several standardized security techniques, such as IPsec, and the security of wireless networks and IEEE 802.11 standards. At the end of this chapter, we learn about *firewalls* and *packet filtering*. Firewalls are programs or devices designed to protect a network by using predefined rule sets. Packet filtering is performed by firewalls.

10.1   Overview of Network Security

Network security is a top-priority issue in data networks. As communication networks are growing rapidly, security issues have pushed to the forefront of concern for end users, administrators, and equipment suppliers. Despite enormous joint efforts by various groups to develop effective security solutions for networks, hackers continue to pose new, serious threats by taking advantage of weaknesses present in the Internet infrastructure.

10.1.1   Elements of Network Security

Network security is concerned mainly with the following two elements:

1. *Confidentiality.* Information should be available only to those who have rightful access to it.

2. *Authenticity and integrity.* The sender of a message and the message itself should be verified at the receiving point.

In Figure 10.1, user 1 sends a message ("I am user 1") to user 2. In part (a) of the figure, the network lacks any security system, so an intruder can receive the message, change its content to a different message ("Hi! I am user 1") and send it to user 2. User 2 may not know that this falsified message is really from user 1 (authentication) and that the content of the message is what user 1 has created and sent (confidentiality). In part (b) of the figure, a security block is added to each side of the communication, and a secret key that only users 1 and 2 would know about is included. Therefore, the message is

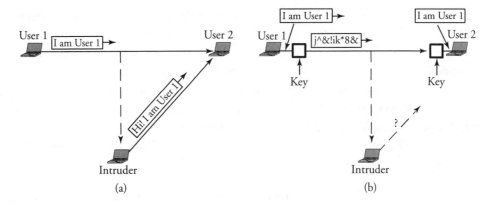

Figure 10.1   (a) Message content and sender identity falsified by an intruder;
(b) a method of applied security

changed to a form that cannot be altered by the intruder, who would be disabled in this communication transaction.

In general, no protocol or network architecture can ensure full security. Internet routing is based on a distributed system of many routers, switches, and protocols. These protocols have a number of points of vulnerability that can be exploited to cause such problems as misdelivery or nondelivery of user traffic, misuse of network resources, network congestion and packet delays, and the violation of local routing policies.

10.1.2   Classification of Network Attacks

Internet infrastructure *attacks* are broadly classified into four categories, as follows:

1. DNS hacking
2. Routing table poisoning
3. Packet mistreatment
4. Denial of service

Among these threats, the first three attacks are related to network infrastructure; *denial-of-service attacks* are related to end systems.

DNS Hacking Attacks

As mentioned in Chapter 9, the *Domain Name System* (DNS) server is a distributed hierarchical and global directory that translates domain names into numerical IP address. DNS is a critical infrastructure, and all hosts contact DNS to access servers and start connections. In the normal mode of operation, hosts send UDP queries to the DNS server. Servers reply with a proper answer, or direct the queries to smarter servers. A DNS server also stores information other than host addresses.

Name-resolution services in the modern Internet environment are essential for e-mail transmission, navigation to Web sites, and data transfer. Thus, an attack on DNS can potentially affect a large portion of the Internet. A DNS *hacking attack* may result in the lack of data authenticity and integrity and can appear in any of the following forms:

- An *information-level attack* forces a server to respond with something other than the correct answer. With cache poisoning, a hacker tricks a remote name server into caching the answer for a third-party domain by providing malicious information for the domain's authorized servers. Hackers can then redirect traffic to a preselected site.

- In a *masquerading attack*, the adversary poses as a trusted entity to obtain secret information. In this guise, the attacker can stop any message from being transmitted further or can change the content or redirect the packet to bogus servers. This action is also known as a *man-in-the-middle attack*.

- The attacker normally sends queries to each host and receives in reply the DNS host name. In an *information leakage attack*, the attacker sends queries to all hosts and identifies which IP addresses are not used. Later on, the intruder can use those IP addresses to make other types of attacks.

- Once a domain name is selected, it has to be registered. Various tools are available to register domain names over the Internet. If the tools are not smart enough, an invader might obtain secure information and use it to highjack the domain later. In the *domain highjacking* attack, whenever a user enters a domain address, he or she is forced to enter the attacker's Web site. This can be very irritating and can cause a great loss of Internet usage ability.

Routing Table Poisoning Attacks

A *routing table poisoning attack* is the undesired modification of routing tables. An attacker can do this by maliciously modifying the routing information update packets sent by routers. This is a challenging and important problem, as a routing table is the basis of routing in the Internet. Any false entry in a routing table could lead to significant consequences, such as congestion, an overwhelmed host, looping, illegal access to data, and network partition. Two types of routing table poisoning attacks are the *link attack* and the *router attack*.

A *link attack* occurs when a hacker gets access to a link and thereby intercepts, interrupts, or modifies routing messages on packets. Link attacks act similarly on both the link-state and the distance-vector protocols discussed in Chapter 5. If an attacker succeeds in placing an attack in a link-state routing protocol, a router may send incorrect updates about its neighbors or remain silent even if the link state of its neighbor has changed. The attack through a link can be so severe that the attacker can program a router to either drop packets from a victim or readdress packets to a victim, resulting in a lower throughput of the network. Sometimes, a router can stop an intended packet from being forwarded further. However, since more than one path to any destination exists, the packet ultimately reaches its destination.

Router attacks may affect the link-state protocol or even the distance-vector protocol. If link-state protocol routers are attacked, they become malicious. They may add a nonexisting link to a routing table, delete an existing link, or even change the cost of a link. This attack may cause a router to simply ignore the updates sent by its neighbors, leading to a serious impact on the operability of the network traffic flow.

In the distance-vector protocol, an attacker may cause routers to send wrong updates about any node in the network, thereby misleading a router and resulting in network problems.

Most unprotected routers have no way to validate updates. Therefore, both link-state and distance-vector router attacks are very effective. In the distance-vector protocol, for example, a malicious router can send wrong information in the form of a distance vector to all its neighbors. A neighbor may not be able to detect this kind of attack and thus proceeds to update its routing table, based on wrong distance vectors. The error can in turn be propagated to a great portion of the network before being detected.

Packet-Mistreatment Attacks

A *packet-mistreatment attack* can occur during any data transmission. A hacker may capture certain data packets and mistreat them. This type of attack is very difficult to detect. The attack may result in congestion, lower throughput, and denial-of-service attacks. Similar to routing table poisoning attacks, packet-mistreatment attacks can also be subclassified into *link attacks* and *router attacks*. The link attack causes interruption, modification, or replication of data packets. A router attack can misroute all packets, which may result in congestion or denial of service. Following are some examples of a packet-mistreatment attack:

- *Interruption.* If an attacker intercepts packets, they may not be allowed to be propagated to their destinations, resulting in a lower throughput of the network. This kind of attack cannot be detected easily, as even in normal operations, routers can drop some packets for various reasons.

- *Modification.* Attackers may succeed in accessing the content of a packet while in transit and change its content. They can then change the address of the packet or even change its data. To solve this kind of problem, a digital signature mechanism, discussed later in this chapter, can be used.

- *Replication.* An attacker might trap a packet and replay it. This kind of attack can be detected by using the sequence number for each packet.

- *Ping of death.* An attacker may send a *ping message*, which is large and therefore must be fragmented for transport. The receiver then starts to reassemble the fragments as the ping fragments arrive. The total packet length becomes too large and might cause a system crash.

- *Malicious misrouting of packets.* A hacker may attack a router and change its routing table, resulting in misrouting of data packets, causing a denial of service.

Denial-of-Service Attacks

A *denial-of-service attack* is a type of security breach that prohibits a user from accessing normally provided services. The denial of service does not result in information theft or any kind of information loss but can nonetheless be very dangerous, as it can cost the target person a large amount of time and money. Denial-of-service attacks affect the destination rather than a data packet or router.

Usually, a denial-of-service attack affects a specific network service, such as e-mail or DNS. For example, such an attack may overwhelm the DNS server in various ways and make it inoperable. One way of initiating this attack is by causing buffer overflow. Inserting an executable code inside memory can potentially cause a buffer overflow. Or, an adversary may use various tools to send large numbers of queries to a DNS server, which then is not able to provide services in a timely manner.

Denial-of-service attacks are easy to generate but may be difficult to detect. They take important servers out of action for few hours, thereby denying service to all users. Several other situations can also cause this kind of attack, such as UDP flood, TCP flood, and ICMP flood. In all these attacks, the hacker's main aim is to overwhelm victims and disrupt services provided to them.

Denial-of-service attacks are of two types:

1. *Single-source.* An attacker sends a large number of packets to a target system to overwhelm and disable it. These packets are designed such that their real sources cannot be identified.

2. *Distributed.* In this type of attack, a large number of hosts are used to flood unwanted traffic to a single target. The target cannot then be accessible to other users in the network, as it is processing the flood of traffic.

The flood may be either a UDP flood or a TCP SYN flood. UDP flooding is used against two target systems and can stop the services offered by either system. Hackers link the UDP character-generating services of a system to another one by sending UDP packets with spoofed return addresses. This may create an infinite looping between the two systems, leading to system uselessness.

Normally, a SYN packet is sent by a host to a user who intends to establish a connection. The user then sends back an acknowledgment. In the TCP SYN flood, a hacker sends a large number of SYN packets to a target user. Since the return addresses are spoofed, the target user queues up a SYN/ACK packet and never processes it. Therefore, the target system keeps on waiting. The result may be a hard disk crash or reboot.

10.2   Security Methods

Common solutions that can protect computer communication networks from attacks are classified as (a) *cryptography,* (b) *authentication,* and (c) *digital signatures.*

Cryptography has a long and fascinating history. Centuries ago, cryptography was used as a tool to protect national secrets and strategies. Today, network engineers focus on *cryptography* methods for computer communication networks. Cryptography is the process of transforming a piece of information or message shared by two parties into some sort of code. The message is scrambled before transmission so that it is undetectable by outside watchers. This kind of message needs to be decoded at the receiving end before any further processing.

The main tool that network security experts use to encrypt a message M is a secret key K; the fundamental operation often used to encrypt a message is the Exclusive-OR ($\oplus$). Suppose that we have one bit, M, and a secret bit, K. A simple encryption is carried out using $M \oplus K$. To decrypt this message, the second party—if he or she has the key, K—can easily detect M by performing the following:

$$(M \oplus K) \oplus K = M. \qquad (10.1)$$

In computer communication networks, data can travel between two users while it is encrypted. In Figure 10.2, two servers are exchanging data while two types of encryption devices are installed in their communication network. The first encryption device is *end-to-end encryption*, whereby secret coding is carried out at both end systems. In this figure, server A encodes its data, which can be decoded only by the server at the other end. The second phase of encryption is *link encryption*, which secures all the traffic passing over that link.

The two types of cryptography techniques are *symmetric-key cryptography* or *secret-key cryptography* and *public-key cryptography*. In a secret-key model, both sender and receiver conventionally use the same key for an encryption process. In a public-key model, a sender and a receiver each use a different key. The public-key system can be more powerful than the symmetric-key system and may provide better security and message privacy. But the biggest drawback of public-key encryption is speed. The public-key system is significantly more complex computationally and may not be practical in many cases. Hence, the public-key system is used only to establish a session to exchange a session key. Then, this session key is used in a secret-key system for encrypting messages for the duration of the session.

Encryption methods offer the assurance of message confidentiality. However, a networking system must be able to verify the authenticity of the message and the sender of the message. These forms of security techniques in computer networks

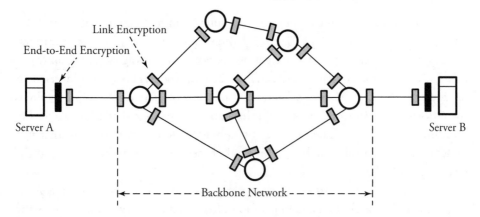

Figure 10.2 Overview of encryption points in a communication network

are known as *authentication techniques* and are categorized as *authentication with message digest* and *authentication with digital signature*. Message authentication protects a user in a network against data falsification and ensures data integrity. These methods do not necessarily use keys.

A *digital signature* is another important security measures. Much like a person's signature on a document, a digital signature on a message is required for the authentication and identification of the right sender. In the following sections, the mentioned three main categories of security methods are presented. The first topic is the *symmetric-key cryptography* protocol which is one of the two methods of cryptography.

10.3 Symmetric-Key Cryptography

Symmetric-key cryptography, sometimes known as *secret-key cryptography* or *single-key cryptography*, is a conventional encryption model. This type of message encryption method typically consists of an encryption algorithm, a key, and a decryption algorithm. At the end point, the encrypted message is called *ciphertext*. Several standard mechanisms can be used to implement a symmetric-key encryption algorithm. Here, we focus on two widely used protocols: *Data Encryption Standard* (DES) and *Advanced Encryption Standard* (AES).

In these algorithms, a shared secret key between a transmitter and a receiver is assigned at the transmitter and receiver points. The encryption algorithm produces a different key at any time for a specific transmission. Changing the key changes the output of the algorithm. At the receiving end, the encrypted information can be transformed back to the original data by using a decryption algorithm and the same key that was used for encryption. The security of conventional encryption depends on the secrecy of the key, not on the secrecy of the encryption algorithm. Consequently, the algorithm need not be kept secret; only the key has to be secret.

10.3.1 Data Encryption Standard (DES)

With the *Data Encryption Standard* (DES), plaintext messages are converted into 64-bit blocks, each encrypted using a key. The key length is 64 bits but contains only 56 usable bits; thus, the last bit of each 8 bytes in the key is a parity bit for the corresponding byte. DES consists of 16 identical rounds of an operation, as shown in Figure 10.3. The details of the algorithm on each 64-bit block of a message at each round *i* of operation are as follows.

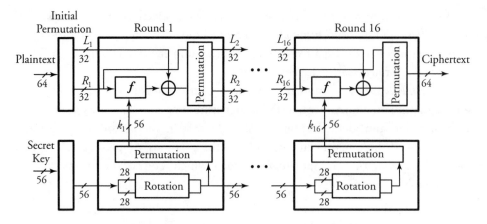

Figure 10.3   The Data Encryption Standard (DES)

Begin DES Algorithm

1. **Initialize.** Before round 1 begins, all 64 bits of an incoming message and all 56 bits of the secret key are separately permuted (shuffled).

2. Each incoming 64-bit message is broken into two 32-bit halves denoted by L_i and R_i, respectively.

3. The 56 bits of the key are also broken into two 28-bit halves, and each half is rotated one or two bit positions, depending on the round.

4. All 56 bits of the key are permuted, producing version k_i of the key on round i

5. In this step, $\oplus$ is a logic Exclusive-OR, and the description of function f appears next. Then, L_i and R_i are determined by

$$L_i = R_{i-1} \qquad\qquad (10.2)$$

and

$$R_i = L_{i-1} \oplus F(R_{i-1}, k_i). \qquad\qquad (10.3)$$

6. All 64 bits of a message are permuted. ∎

The operation of function f at any round i of DES is as follows.

1. Out of 56 bits of k_i, function f chooses 48 bits.

2. The 32-bit R_{i-1} is expanded from 32 bits to 48 bits so that it can be combined with 48-bit k_i. The expansion of R_{i-1} is carried out by first breaking R_{i-1} into

eight 4-bit chunks and then expanding each chunk by copying the leftmost bit and the rightmost bit from right and left adjacent chunks, respectively.

3. Function f also partitions the 48 bits of k_i into eight 6-bit chunks.

4. The corresponding eight chunks of R_{i-1} and eight chunks of k_i are combined as follows:

$$R_{i-1} = R_{i-1} \oplus k_i. \tag{10.4}$$

At the receiver, the same steps and the same key are used to reverse the encryption. It is now apparent that the 56-bit key length may not be sufficient to provide full security. This argument is still controversial. Triple DES provides a solution for this controversy: three keys are used, for a total of 168 bits. It should also be mentioned that DES can be implemented more efficiently in hardware than in software.

10.3.2   Advanced Encryption Standard (AES)

The *Advanced Encryption Standard* (AES) protocol has a better security strength than DES. AES supports 128-bit symmetric block messages and uses 128-, 192-, or 256-bit keys. The number of rounds in AES is variable from 10 to 14 rounds, depending on the key and block sizes. Figure 10.4 illustrates the encryption overview of this protocol, using a 128-bit key. There are ten rounds of encryptions for the key size of 128 bits. All rounds are identical except for the last round, which has no mix-column stage.

A single block of 128-bit plaintext (16 bytes) as an input arrives from the left. The plaintext is formed as 16 bytes m_0 through m_{15} and is fed into round 1 after an initialization stage. In this round, substitute units—indicated by S in the

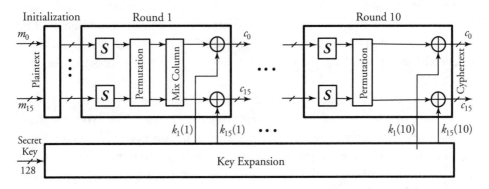

Figure 10.4   Overview of the Advanced Encryption Standard (AES) protocol

figure—perform a byte-by-byte substitution of blocks. The ciphers, in the form of rows and columns, move through a *permutation stage* to shift rows to mix columns. At the end of this round, all 16 blocks of ciphers are Exclusive-ORed with the 16 bytes of round 1 key $k_0(1)$ through $k_{15}(1)$. The 128-bit key is expanded for ten rounds. The AES *decryption algorithm* is fairly simple and is basically the reverse of the encryption algorithm at each stage of a round. All stages of each round are reversible.

10.4 Public-Key Cryptography

The introduction of *public-key cryptography* brought a revolution to the field of message encryption in computer networking. This model is sometimes known as *asymmetric cryptograpgy*, or *two-key cryptograpgy*. The public-key cryptography provides a very clever method for key exchange. In the public-key encryption model, a sender and a receiver of a message use different keys.

The public-key algorithm is based on mathematical functions rather than on substitution or permutation, although the security of any encryption scheme indeed depends on the length of the key and the computational work involved in breaking an encrypted message. Several public-key encryption protocols can be implemented. Among them, the following two protocols are the focus of our study:

- *Rivest, Shamir, and Adleman* (RSA) protocol
- *Diffie-Hellman key-exchange* protocol

In the public-key encryption methods, either of the two related keys can be used for encryption; the other one, for decryption. It is computationally infeasible to determine the decryption key given only the algorithm and the encryption key. Each system using this encryption method generates a pair of keys to be used for encryption and decryption of a message that it will receive. Each system publishes its encryption key by placing it in a public register or file and sorts out the key as a public one.

The companion key is kept private. If A wishes to send a message to B, A encrypts the message by using B's public key. On receiving the message, B decrypts it with the private B key. No other recipients can decrypt the message, since only B knows its private key. This way, public-key encryption secures an incoming communication as long as a system controls its private key. However, public-key encryption has extra computational overhead and is more complex than the conventional one.

10.4.1   RSA Algorithm

Rivest, Shamir, and Adleman (RSA) developed the RSA public-key encryption and signature scheme. This was the first practical public-key encryption algorithm. RSA is based on the intractability of factoring large integers. Assume that a plaintext m must be encrypted to a ciphertext c. The RSA algorithm has three phases for this: *key generation*, *encryption*, and *decryption*.

Key Generation

In the RSA scheme, the key length is typically 512 bits, which requires an enormous computational power. A plaintext is encrypted in blocks, with each block having a binary value less than some number n. Encryption and decryption are done as follows, beginning with the generation of a public key and a private key.

Begin Key Generation Algorithm

1. Choose two roughly prime numbers, a and b, and derive $n = ab$. (A number is prime if it has factors of 1 and itself.)
2. **Find** x. Select encryption key x such that x and $(a-1)(b-1)$ are relatively prime. (Two numbers are relatively prime if they have no common factor greater than 1.)
3. **Find** y. Calculate decryption key y:

$$xy \; mod \; (a-1)(b-1) = 1. \tag{10.5}$$

4. At this point, a and b can be discarded.
5. The public key = $\{x, n\}$.
6. The private key = $\{y, n\}$. ■

In this algorithm, x and n are known to both the sender (owner) and the receiver (non-owner), but only the receiver must know y. Also, a and b must be large and about the same size and both greater than 1,024 bits. The larger these two values, the more secure the encryption.

Encryption

Both the sender (owner) and the receiver (non-owner) must know the value of n. The sender knows the value of x, and only the receiver knows the value of y. Thus, this is a public-key encryption, with the public key $\{x, n\}$ and the private key $\{y, n\}$. Given $m < n$, ciphertext c is constructed by:

$$c = m^x \bmod n. \tag{10.6}$$

Note here that if a and b are chosen to be on the order of 1,024 bits, $n \approx 2,048$. Thus, we are not able to encrypt a message longer than 256 characters.

Decryption

Given the ciphertext, c, the plaintext, m, is extracted by

$$m = c^y \bmod n. \tag{10.7}$$

In reality, the calculations require a math library, as numbers are typically huge. One can see easily how Equations (10.6) and (10.7) work.

Example.   For an RSA encryption of a 4-bit message of 1,001, or $m = 9$, we choose $a = 3$ and $b = 11$. Find the public and the private keys for this security action, and show the ciphertext.

Solution.   Clearly, $n = ab = 33$. We select $x = 3$, which is relatively prime to $(a - 1)(b - 1) = 20$. Then, from $xy \bmod (a - 1)(b - 1) = 3y \bmod 20 = 1$, we can get $y = 7$. Consequently, the public key and the private key should be $\{3, 33\}$ and $\{7, 33\}$, respectively. If we encrypt the message, we get $c = m^x \bmod n = 9^3 \bmod 33 = 3$. The decryption process is the reverse of this action, as $m = c^y \bmod n = 3^7 \bmod 33 = 9$.

10.4.2   Diffie-Hellman Key-Exchange Protocol

In the *Diffie-Hellman key-exchange* protocol, two end users can agree on a shared secret code without any information shared in advance. Thus, intruders would not be able to access the transmitted communication between the two users or discover the shared secret code. This protocol is normally used for *virtual private networks* (VPNs), explained in Chapter 14. The essence of this protocol for two users, 1 and 2, is as follows. Suppose that user 1 selects a prime a, a random integer number x_1, and a generator g and creates $y_1 \in \{1, 2, \cdots, a - 1\}$ such that

$$y_1 = g^{x_1} \bmod a. \tag{10.8}$$

In practice, the two end users agree on a and g ahead of time. User 2 performs the same function and creates y_2:

$$y_2 = g^{x_2} \bmod a. \tag{10.9}$$

User 1 then sends y_1 to user 2. Now, user 1 forms its key, k_1, using the information its partner sent as

$$k_1 = y_2^{x_1} \bmod a, \qquad (10.10)$$

and user 2 forms its key, k_2, using the information its partner sent as

$$k_2 = y_1^{x_2} \bmod a. \qquad (10.11)$$

It can easily be proved that the two keys k_1 and k_2 are equal. Therefore, the two users can now encrypt their messages, each using its own key created by the other one's information.

10.5   Authentication

Authentication techniques are used to verify identity. Message authentication verifies the authenticity of both the message content and the message sender. Message content is authenticated through the implementation of a function referred to as a *hash function* and the encryption of the resulting message digest. The sender's authenticity can be implemented by use of a digital signature. A hash function is a function that creates sufficient redundant information about a message to expose any tampering.

10.5.1   Hash Function

A common technique for authenticating a message is to implement a *hash function* (also known as a *cryptographic checksum*). A hash function indicated by h is used to produce a fingerprint of a message and is meant to expose deliberate corruption of the message. By using a hash function, any arbitrary size *message,* as an input, is mapped to fixed-size data. The value returned by a hash function is called a *hash value, hash,* or *message digest.* A hash function that operates in a computer network allows a host to easily verify that some input data is authenticated.

Hash functions have several applications in network security, especially in forming digital signatures, message authentication codes, and other forms of authentication. Hash functions are typically used in *hash tables,* to agilely find a data record by mapping a search key to an index. The index in a hash table provides the location in the hash table where the corresponding record should be stored. Normally, the set of possible keys is much larger than the number of different table indexes, and thus several different keys to the same index may be used.

The process of a hash function starts with a hash value added at the end of a message before transmission. The receiver recomputes the hash value from the received message and compares it to the received hash value. If the two hash values are the same, the message is not altered during transmission. Once a hash function is applied to a message, m, the result is known as a message digest, or $h(m)$. The hash function has the following properties:

- Unlike the encryption algorithm, the authentication algorithm is not required to be reversible.
- It The process to compute a hash value for any given message is straightforward.
- Given a message digest $h(m)$, it is computationally infeasible to find m.
- It is computationally infeasible to modify a message without changing the hash.
- It is computationally infeasible to find two different messages m_1 and m_2 such that $h(m_1) = h(m_2)$.

Message authentication can be implemented as shown in Figure 10.5. A hash function is applied on a message m and then a process of encryption is carried out. The authenticity of a message in this method is assured only if the sender and the receiver share a secret *authentication key* shown as k. The shared authentication key is a string of bits. Assume that the sending host creates message m. The first step of authentication is to apply the hash function on the combination of m and k to produce a message digest known as the *message authentication code* (MAC) indicated by $h(m + k)$. The sending host then appends the MAC to the message m, where the result, m and $h(m + k)$, is forwarded to the receiving host via the Internet.

The receiving host has to decrypt the received message and the message authentication code m and $h(m + k)$ knowing the shared authentication key k. It first produces the $h(m + k)$ locally using the same hash function, and then compares it with the one received from the Internet. If the two $h(m + k)$ values are identical, the receiving host makes a positive judgment on the integrity of the message and accepts the message.

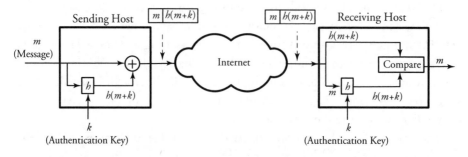

Figure 10.5 Message authentication using a hash function combined with encryption

Among the message authentication protocols are the MD5 *hash algorithm* and the *Secure Hash Algorithm* (SHA). SHA is the focus of our discussion.

10.5.2   Secure Hash Algorithm (SHA)

The *Secure Hash Algorithm* (SHA) was proposed as part of the digital signature standard. SHA-1, the first version of this standard, takes messages with a maximum length of 2^{24} and produces a 160-bit digest. With this algorithm, SHA-1 uses five registers, R_1 through R_5, to maintain a "state" of 20 bytes.

The first step is to pad a message m with length ℓ_m. The message length is forced to $\ell_m = 448 \mod 512$. In other words, the length of the padded message becomes 64 bits less than the multiple of 512 bits. The number of padding bits can be as low as 1 bit and as high as 512 bits. The padding includes a 1 bit and as many 0 bits as required. Therefore, the least-significant 64 bits of the message length are appended to convert the padded message to a word with a multiple of 512 bits.

After padding, the second step is to expand each block of 512-bit (16 32 bits) words $\{m_0, m_1, \cdots, m_{15}\}$ to words of 80 32 bits using:

$$w_i = m_i \text{ for } 0 \leq i \leq 15 \tag{10.12}$$

and

$$w_i = w_{i-3} \oplus w_{i-8} \oplus w_{i-14} \oplus w_{i-16} \pm 1 \text{ for } 16 \leq i \leq 79, \tag{10.13}$$

where $\pm j$ means left rotation by j bits. This way, bits are shifted several times if the incoming block is mixed with the state. Next, bits from each block of w_i are mixed into the state in four steps, each maintaining 20 rounds. For any values of a, b, and c, and bit number i, we define a function $F_i(a, b, c)$ as follows:

$$F_i(a, b, c) = \begin{cases} (a \cap b) \cup (\bar{a} \cap c) & 0 \leq i \leq 19 \\ a \oplus b \oplus c & 20 \leq i \leq 39 \\ (a \cap b) \cup (a \cap c) \cup (b \cap c) & 40 \leq i \leq 59 \\ a \oplus b \oplus c & 60 \leq i \leq 79 \end{cases} . \tag{10.14}$$

Then, the 80 steps ($i = 0, 1, 2, \cdots, 79$) of the four rounds are described as follows:

$$\delta = (R_1 \pm 5) + F_i(R_2, R_3, R_4) + R_5 + w_i + C_i \tag{10.15}$$

$$R_5 = R_4 \tag{10.16}$$

$$R_4 = R_3 \tag{10.17}$$

$$R_3 = R_2 \pm 30 \qquad (10.18)$$

$$R_2 = R_1 \qquad (10.19)$$

$$R_1 = \delta, \qquad (10.20)$$

where C_i is a constant value specified by the standard for round i. The message digest is produced by concatenation of the values in R_1 through R_5.

HTTPS, a Secure Web Protocol

In Chapter 9, we looked at an overview of the *Hypertext Transfer Protocol* (HTTP). Anytime that a connection in the Web needs to be secure, such as connections for online financial transactions, the secure version of HTTP called HTTPS must be used. For secure Web connections, the transport layer port number of HTTPS is 443. Remember from Chapter 9 that this port number is different from the one allocated to HTTP, port 80. The use of HTTPS in place of HTTP is expressed by the requested server and its usage is automatically rendered. The following protocol steps summarize the HTTPS:

Begin HTTPS Steps

1. The client authenticates the server through a process called the server's "digital certificate."
2. The client and server interact and negotiate on a set of security rules called a "ciphersuite" for their connection.
3. The client and server generate keys for encrypting and decrypting data.
4. The client and server establish a secure encrypted HTTPS connection. ∎

The digital certificate of a Web server mentioned in the preceding HTTPS steps establishes the user's credentials on the Web. It is issued by a certificate authority (CA) and contains the user's name, a serial number, an expiration date, a copy of the certificate user's public key used for encrypting messages, a digital signature (to be discussed next), and the digital signature of the certificate-issuing authority so that a recipient can verify that the certificate is real. Typically, digital certificates can be kept in registries.

The *ciphersuite* mentioned in the preceding HTTPS steps can be based on any of the security protocols we learned so far in this chapter such as the Secure Hash

Algorithm 1 (SHA-1), public key encryption, RSA encryption/decryption, Diffie-Hellman, or the *digital signature* to be discussed next.

10.6   Digital Signatures

A *digital signature* is one of the most important required security measures. Although message authentication code (MAC) described in the preceding section can provide message integrity, the destination of a message needs an assurance that any incoming message is indeed sent by the expected source. In such circummstances, an electronic kind of signature included in the message as proof of authenticity is referred to as the digital signature. Much like a person's signature on a document, a digital signature on a message is required for the authentication and identification of the right sender. The digital signature is document dependent, and hence different documents signed by the same individual will have different signatures. However, a digital signature is supposed to be unique to an individual and serves as a means of identifying the sender. An electronic signature is not as easy as it was with the paper-based system. The digital signature requires a great deal of study, research, and skill. Even if these requirements are met, there is no guarantee that all the security requirements have been met.

The digital signature method for providing a sender's authentication is also performed through cryptography. Among the cryptographic mechanisms developed, the RSA public-key algorithm implements both encryption and digital signature. When RSA is applied, the hashed message is encrypted with the sender's private key. Thus, the entire encrypted message serves as a digital signature. This means that at the receiving end, the receiver can decrypt it, using the public key. This authenticates that the packet comes from the right user.

10.7   Security of IP and Wireless Networks

This section presents a case study on some of the security policies adopted for the Internet Protocol (IP) and basic wireless technologies. We start with IPsec, a standard for the IP layer.

10.7.1   IP Security and IPsec

Between any two users with a TCP/IP connection are multiple layers of security. A number of fields are appended to an IP packet when it is ready to undergo the security implementation. *IP security* (IPsec) is a set of protocols developed by the *Internet Engineering Task Force* (IETF) to support the secure exchange of packets at the IP layer. Figure 10.6 illustrates an encrypted and authenticated IP packet. An IPsec authentication header has the following fields:

- *Security parameters index* (SPI) expresses an identification tag included in the IP packet header carrying IPsec. SPI is used for tunneling IP traffic, and is typically a one-way relationship between any two communicating end users where either of the end users can accept a security feature from the other one. The SPI tag is an essential part of an IPsec set of rules referred to as *Security Association* (SA) as the tag enables a receiving host to select the appropriate SA under which a received packet is processed. There can be different SAs used to provide security to one connection. SPI has only local significance, since it is initiated by the creator of the SA while the creator is still analyzing an SPI to facilitate local processing.

- *Sequence number* is an increasing counter number.

- *Payload data* is an encryption-protected upper-layer segment.

- *Padding* is used if the plaintext is required by the encryption algorithm to be a certain multiple of 1 byte.

- *Pad length* specifies the number of bytes for the padding.

- *Next header* indicates the type of next header attached.

- *Authentication data* provides the integrity check value.

IPsec provides enhanced security features, such as better encryption algorithms and more comprehensive authentication. In order for IPsec to work, both the sender

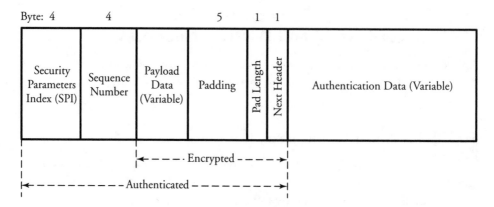

Figure 10.6 IPsec authentication header format

and receiver must exchange public encryption keys. IPsec has two encryption modes: tunnel and transport. Tunnel mode encrypts the header and the payload of each packet; the transport mode encrypts the payload. IPsec can encrypt data between devices: router to router, security device to router, PC to router, and PC to server.

Most IPsec implementations comprise of an *Internet Key Exchange* (IKE) *daemon* that runs in user space and an IPsec stack that processes the actual IP packets. A daemon is a program that runs as a background process, rather than being under the direct control of an interactive user. Daemon names typically end with the letter "d." for example, sshd is a daemon that services an SSH connection. IKE (or IKEv2) is indeed a protocol for setting up a security association (SA) in the IPsec protocol suite. It utilizes certain DNS and Diffie–Hellman key exchange explained in the previous section to set up a shared session from which cryptographic keys are derived.

IKE uses UDP for communication, and its packets arrive at port 500. The negotiated key material is created after a number of turn-around times and is then given to the IPsec stack. For example, in the case of AES, an AES key is created to identify (1) IP end points, (2) ports to be protected, and (3) the type of IPsec tunnel. In response, IPsec intercepts the relevant IP packets if required and performs encryption and decryption.

10.7.2   Security of Wireless Networks and IEEE 802.11

Wireless networks are particularly vulnerable because of their nonwired infrastructure. Wireless links are especially susceptible to eavesdropping or passive traffic monitoring. The inherent broadcast paradigm in wireless networks makes them more susceptible to various attacks. The security for these networks involves:

- Network security
- Radio link security
- Hardware security

Radio link security involves preventing the interception of radio signals, defense against jamming attacks, and encrypting traffic to ensure privacy of user location. The security portion of a wireless network must prevent the misuse of mobile units by making them tamper resistant. The hardware component of wireless security is especially complex. Intruders can access wireless networks by receiving radio waves carrying packets and frames propagated beyond the needed range of the network's base station and hosts. Our focus here is the security mechanisms for the wireless 802.11 standards known as *Wired Equivalent Privacy* (WEP).

This section also describes types of security features desired for IEEE 802.11a, b, and i. WEP provides a level of security similar to that found in wired networks. It is a standard of security for IEEE 802.11a and b and offers authentication and data encryption between a host and a wireless base station, using a secret shared key. The essence of this protocol between a host and a base station (wireless access point) is as follows.

1. The host requests authentication from the base station.

2. The base station responds.

3. The host encrypts data by using secret-key encryption.

4. The base station decrypts the received encrypted data. If the decrypted data matches the original data sent to the host, the host is authenticated by the base station.

Figure 10.7 shows how data is encrypted. First, a 40-bit secret key, k, known by both the host and the base station, is created. A 24-bit initialization field to be used to encrypt a single frame is appended to this key. The initialization field is different for each frame.

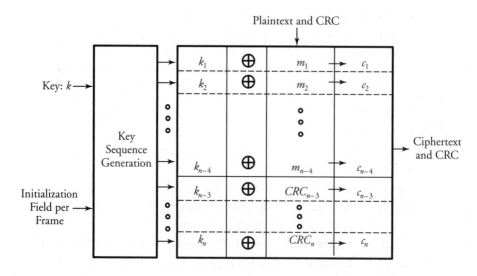

Figure 10.7   Security implementation in wireless IEEE 802.11

As shown in the figure, a 4-byte CRC field is computed for the data payload. The payload and the CRC bytes are then encrypted. The encryption algorithm produces a stream of key values: k_1, k_2, $\cdots$, k_i, $\cdots$, k_{n-1}, k_n. Assume that the plaintext is partitioned into i bytes. Let c_i be the ith byte of the ciphertext and m_i be the ith byte of the plaintext; the encryption is done by using k_i, as follows:

$$c_i = m_i \oplus k_i. \tag{10.21}$$

To decrypt the ciphertext, the receiver uses the same secret key as the sender used, appends the initialization field to it, and calculates

$$m_i = c_i \oplus k_i. \tag{10.22}$$

WEP is simple and relatively weak. The procedure for security of IEEE 802.11i is different because of its more sophisticated characteristics. This standard specifies an authentication server for the base-station communication. The separation of the authentication server from the base station means that the authentication server can serve many base stations. A new protocol, called *Extensible Authentication Protocol* (EAP), specifies the interaction between a user and an authentication server (IEEE 802.11i).

To summarize the IEEE 802.11i security mechanism: A base station first announces its presence and the types of security services it can provide to the wireless users. This way, users can request the appropriate type and level of encryption or authentication. EAP frames are encapsulated and sent over the wireless link. After decapsulation at the base station, the frames are encapsulated again, this time using a protocol called RADIUS for transmission over UDP to the authentication server. With EAP, public-key encryption is used, whereby a shared secret key known only to the user and the authentication server is created. The wireless user and the base station can also generate additional keys to perform the link-level encryption of data sent over the wireless link, which makes it much more secure than the one explained for 802.11a,b.

10.8 Firewalls and Packet Filtering

As the name suggests, a *firewall* protects data housed and maintained in a network from the outside world. A firewall is a security mechanism for networks and can be a software program or a hardware device that controls the incoming and outgoing network traffic based on an applied rule set. A firewall can be installed either on an edge router of a network, or on a server between hosts of a certain network and the outside world. The security issues faced by a smaller network like the one used at home are similar to larger networks. A firewall is used to protect the network and servers such as Web servers from unwanted Web sites and potential hackers. A firewall can control the flow of packets by one of the following two methods:

1. *Packet filtering.* A firewall can filter packets that pass through. If packets can get through the filter, they reach their destinations; otherwise, they are discarded. A firewall can be programmed to throw away certain packets addressed to a particular destination IP address or a TCP port number. This condition is especially useful if a particular host does not want to respond to any access from an external source. A firewall can also filter packets based on the source IP address. This filtering is helpful when a host has to be protected from any unwanted external packets. The filtering can additionally be at the application layer as discussed in the next section.

2. *Denial of service.* This method was explained earlier. The compelling feature of this method is that it controls the number of packets entering a network.

In residential networks, a firewall can be placed on the link between a network router and the Internet or between a host and a router. The objective of such a configuration is to monitor and filter packets coming from unknown sources or unauthorized users. Consequently, hackers do not have access to penetrate through a system if a firewall protects the system. For a large company with many small networks, the firewall is placed on every connection attached to the Internet. Companies can set rules about how their networks or particular systems need to work in order to maintain security. Companies can also set rules on how a system can connect to Web sites. These precautionary rules are followed in order to attain the advantage of having a firewall. Hence, the firewall can control how a network works with an Internet connection. A firewall can also be used to control data traffic.

Software firewall programs can be installed in home computers by using an Internet connection with these so-called gateways, and the computer with such software can access Web servers only through this software firewall. But hardware firewalls are more secure than software firewalls. Moreover, hardware firewalls are not expensive. Some firewalls also offer virus protection. The biggest security advantage of installing a firewall in a business network is to protect it from any outsider logging in to the network under protection. Firewalls are preferred for use in almost all network security infrastructures, as they allow the implementation of a security policy in one centralized place rather than end to end. Sometimes, a firewall is put where a large amount of data flow is normally expected.

10.8.1   Packet Filtering

Packet filtering is performed by a firewall to control and secure network access. A packet filter monitors outgoing and incoming packets and allows them to pass or be dropped based on the prevailing rules of the firewall. The rules can be based on several attributes such as source IP address, source port, destination IP address, destination port, time-to-live (TTL) value (explained in Chapter 5), and applications such as Web or FTP. We can thus classify packet filtering rules into two main groups: (1) network/transport-layer packet filtering and (2) application-layer packet filtering, both of which are discussed next.

Network/Transport-Layer Packet Filtering

Network/transport-layer packet filters bring security to a networking device by not permitting packets to pass through the firewall unless they match the established rule set based on certain criteria of network layer, transport layer, or both inserted in the firewall. The firewall administrator may define the rules. The rules are associated with any or a combination of the following parameters:

- *Source* or *destination IP address*
- *Source* or *destination port number*
- *Protocol type* indicated in headers: TCP, UDP, ICMP, OSPF, and so on
- *TCP flags* such as SYN or ACK
- *ICMP message type* and *TTL of expired ICMP message*

A packet received at a firewall is first matched with one of the predefined rules and policies defined in the preceding attribute list. Once matched, the packet is either accepted or denied. There can be a variety of different security policy sets that can be arranged in a firewall. For example, a LAN with an edge router having a firewall can be set up to block all ICMP messages with expired TTL values leaving the LAN. This action is normally taken to disallow outsiders to trace-route or map the LAN.

As another example, a packet filter can be set up to check the source and destination IP addresses of an incoming packet. If both IP addresses match with the rule, the packet is treated as secure and verified. Since basing the policy on only IP addresses provides no protection against packets that have had their source addresses spoofed, the filter may add a second layer of security by applying the protocol type rule and checks source and destination protocols, such as TCP or UDP. Nevertheless, a packet filter can verify source and destination port numbers as well. The rules of packet filtering at the network and transport layers are either *stateless* or *stateful*:

- *Stateless packet filtering* in firewalls is unable to memorize already used packets. This feature of firewalls brings less security but better speed of the filtering function as less time is required to process a packet. Typically, stateless packet filtering is used when there is no session such as a TCP session.

- *Stateful packet filtering* in firewalls uses the state information of a packet flow for making decisions on the security. Stateful packet filters can memorize the results of previously used packet attributes, such as source and destination IP addresses.

Application-Layer Packet Filtering

Application-layer packet filters provide security by determining whether a process or application should accept any given connection. Such filters make policy decisions based on application data. An application-layer firewall operates much like a network/transport-layer packet filter but applies filtering rules based on process instead of IP address or port number. Prompts are primarily used to define rules for processes that have not yet received a connection. The threats to a computer or a server can be stopped through inspecting the payload of packets and blocking the inappropriate packets of a connection. These additional inspection criteria on top of network- or transport-layer filtering can add extra delay to the forwarding of packets.

An application-layer firewall is server program and supplied with the application-layer packet filtering through which all application data are inspected, and then passed or blocked. There can be multiple different-purpose application server programs installed on the same host. Application-layer firewalls, known as socket firewalls, carry out the security task of application servers by hooking into socket gateways to filter the connections between the application layer and the lower layer protocols (network or transport). Also, application firewalls further filter connections by inspecting the process ID of packets against a prevailing rule set for the local process involved in the packet transmission.

Example.   Figure 10.8 shows a local area network supported by two firewalls. The first firewall, F1, has been installed on the edge router R1, and the second firewall, F2, operates on the FTP server. Firewall F1 contains a network/transport-layer

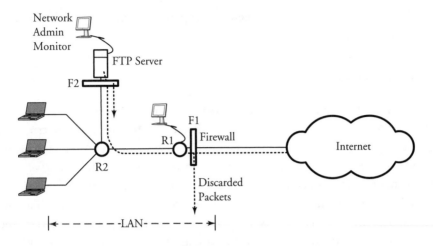

Figure 10.8 A simple configuration of a secured network using a firewall

packet filter. The packet filter is configured to block all FTP connections except those that originate from the IP address of the FTP server and those that are destined to reach the FTP server from outside the LAN. The packet filter in firewall F1 allows all such connections to communicate with the FTP server once the IP address and port number of packets match with the prevailing policy rules. Packets passing R1 are once again inspected in the FTP server through an application layer packet filter of F2. This packet filter is running in the FTP server and listens for incoming FTP socket and prompts the user for a user ID and password. When the user provides this information, the FTP server inspects it to see if the particular user is allowed to reach the FTP server. If permission to access the FTP is secured, the connection can be established, otherwise the connection is denied.

10.8.2 Proxy Server

A *proxy server*, or *proxy*, is dedicated security server software running on a general-purpose machine, and it acts as a firewall or an authorizing server for an application server, primarily Web servers. A proxy server acts as an intermediary for requests from clients seeking resources from other servers. For example, a client wanting to download a file from a Web server first connects to the proxy server requesting a Web page service. The proxy server, which is attached to the Web server, then evaluates the request and authorizes the request for connection to the Web server if the query passes the security. However, a proxy server can be used as an authorizing firewall "proxy" to intermediate between a client/server pair, a pair of networks, a pair of user clients, and so on.

10.9 Summary

Network security is one of the top-priority issues in computer and communication networks. Security issues have been pushed to the forefront of concern for end users, administrators, and equipment suppliers. Networking attacks can be classified as *DNS hacking, routing table poisoning, packet mistreatment,* and *denial of service.* Three major solutions for computer networking security are *cryptographic techniques, authentication techniques* (verification), and *digital signature techniques.* The main tool that network security experts use to encrypt a message is a *key,* and the fundamental operation often used to encrypt a message is the Exclusive-OR operation.

Two secret- or symmetric-key encryption protocols are the *Data Encryption Standard* (DES) and the *Advanced Encryption Standard* (AES). In both methods, a secret key is shared between a transmitter and its receiver by assigning it to both the transmitter point and the receiver point. Public-key cryptography is more effective; a sender/receiver pair use different keys for encryption and decryption, and each party can publish its public (encryption) key so that anyone can use it to encrypt a message for that party. Two public-key protocols are the *Rivest, Shamir, and Adleman* (RSA) protocol and the *Diffie-Hellman key-exchange* protocol.

A receiver can use *message authentication* methods to be assured that the incoming message is from its purported sender. Cryptographic hash functions are used in message authentication codes. Such codes can be generalized to produce a digital signature that guarantees a document's *authenticity.* The *Secure Hash Algorithm* (SHA) has been proposed as part of the digital signature standard.

The IP security (IPsec) protocol requires both the sender and receiver to exchange public encryption keys. IPsec has two encryption modes: tunnel and transport. The tunnel mode encrypts the header and the payload of each packet, and the transport mode encrypts the payload. IPsec can encrypt data between router and router, security device and router, PC and router, and PC and server. Another security mechanism is a firewall, which is placed on the link between a network router and the Internet or between a user and a router. The objective of such a configuration is to filter packets coming from unknown sources.

Finally, at the end of this chapter, *firewalls* and packet filtering were presented. A firewall protects data housed and maintained in a network from the outside world. A firewall is a security mechanism for networks and can be a software program or a hardware device that controls the incoming and outgoing network traffic based on an applied rule set. *Packet filtering* is performed by the firewall to control network access. A packet filter monitors outgoing and incoming packets and allows them to pass or be dropped based on a prevailing rule of the firewall. We classified packet-filtering rules into two main groups, network/transport-layer packet filtering and application-layer packet filtering.

Part II of the book follows. Chapter 11, as the first chapter in Part II, presents analytical methods for delay estimations of single queues of packets and networks of queues.

10.10   Exercises

1. Assume that in round 4 of a DES process for a message, $L_4 = $ 4de5635d (in hex), $R_4 = $ 3412a90e (in hex) and $k_5 = $ be1142 7e6ac2 (in hex).

   (a) Find R_5.

   (b) Find L_5.

2. Use DES to encrypt a 64-bit message, including all 1s with a 56-bit secret key consisting of 0101...01. Assuming a 1-bit rotation in the key process, find the outputs of the first round.

3. Check your system to find out about its encryption utility. If a DES algorithm is used:

   (a) Use an experiment to measure the speed of encryption and decryption.

   (b) Repeat part (a), using different keys.

4. Write a computer program to find the ciphertext for a message, using DES to encrypt a 64-bit message, including all 0s with a 56-bit secret key consisting of 1010...10. Assume a 1-bit rotation in the key process.

5. In the RSA encryption algorithm, show how either of Equations (10.6) or (10.7) is concluded from the other one.

6. For an RSA encryption of a 4-bit message 1010, we choose $a = 5$, $b = 11$, and $x = 3$. Find the public and the private keys for this security action, and show the ciphertext.

7. Apply RSA and do the following.

   (a) Encrypt $a = 5$, $b = 11$, $x = 7$, and $m = 13$.

   (b) Find the corresponding y.

   (c) Decrypt the ciphertext.

8. Consider that user 1 and user 2 implement RSA public-key cryptography for their communications. Now assume that user 3 has found out about one of the prime numbers, a and b, for determining the public-key pairs of users 1 and 2.

   (a) Discuss whether user 3 can use this information to break user 1's code.

   (b) Is it possible for users 1 and 2 to create a different communication session that is secured against intrusion by user 3?

   (c) If your answer to part (b) is yes, is your suggested method practical?

9. Normally the speed of the RSA encryption algorithm is much lower than secret-key encryption algorithms. To solve this issue, we can combine RSA with a secret-key encryption algorithm, such as AES. Assume that user 1 chooses an AES key of 256 bits and encrypts this key with the user 2's RSA public key and also encrypts the message with the AES secret key.

   (a) Prove that this AES key is too small to encrypt securely with RSA.

   (b) Provide an example of a public key that can be recovered by an attacker.

10. Consider again the combination of the two encryption methods discussed in the previous exercise. What solutions would be feasible to overcome the mentioned vulnerability of this method?

11. In the Diffie-Hellman key-exchange protocol, prove that the two keys k_1 and k_2 are equal.

12. Consider that user 1 and user 2 implement the Diffie-Hellman key-exchange protocol for their communications. Suppose that both users agree on the prime number, $a = 2$, and the generator, $g = 3$, for their secured communications.

    (a) Choose a random integer such as x_1, and demonstrate how user 1 computes its secret key, k_1.

    (b) Choose a random integer such as x_2, and demonstrate how user 2 computes its secret key, k_2.

    (c) Repeat part (b) but this time assume that users 1 and 2 agree that user 2 can violate the protocol using a different prime number, $b = 4$, as long as this pime number is also known to user 1. Comment on how these two users can create a secure communication.

13. Consider Figure 10.5 in which the message authentication for message m traversing from one endpoint to another is shown.

    (a) Make any necessary modifications in this figure to illustrate the implementation of confidentiality for users 1 and 2 attached to endpoints of this connection using an authentication key, k, and a symmetric key, a.

(b) Expand part (a) to a scenario in which user 1 has established two simultaneous but separate communication sessions with user 2, one for video streaming and the other one for data. Comment on whether any additional key is necessary for this networking configuration.

10.11 Computer Simulation Project

1. *Network Layer and Transport Layer Packet Filtering in Firewalls.* Use a simulation tool and set up a network of five routers. Connect one of the routers to a LAN consisting of a local router equipped with a firewall, and the local router thereby connects to a server with IP address 133.1.1.1 and port number 80. At the other side of the network, attach two hosts with IP addresses of 151.1.1.1 and 152.1.1.1, respectively, trying to connect to the server. The firewall has a filtering policy that requires the local router to block the following packet flows:

   (a) Any TCP or SYN segments except the ones with destination port 80.
   (b) Any packets except the ones having a destination IP address of 133.1.1.1.
   (c) All packets from a client 152.1.1.1 must be kept out (blocked).

   Run the simulation and generate various types of traffic to the server and show the correctness of your simulation by capturing and examining sample packets.

2. *Application Layer Packet Filtering in Firewalls.* Use a simulation tool and set up a network to simulate the operation of packet filtering at the application layer in firewalls. Your simulation must include the following features:

   (a) The firewall is set up to allow only HTTP request messages to a specific server.
   (b) An outside intruder attempts to send packets with a forged internal address.
   (c) All packets from a given remote server must be kept out.

   Run the simulation and show the correctness of your simulation by capturing and examining sample packets.

ADVANCED CONCEPTS

CHAPTER 11

Network Queues and Delay Analysis

Queueing models offer qualitative insights into the performance of communication networks and quantitative estimations of average packet delay. In many networking instances, a single buffer forms a *queue* of packets. A single queue of packets is a notion of packet accumulation at a certain router or even at an entire network. In the context of data communication, a *queueing buffer* is a physical system that stores incoming packets, and a *server* can be viewed as a switch or a similar mechanism to process and route packets to the desired ports or destinations. A *queueing system* generally consists of a queueing buffer of various sizes and one or more identical servers. This chapter focuses on delay analysis of single queueing units and queueing networks, including feedback. The following topics are covered:

- *Little's theorem*
- *Birth-and-death process*
- *Queueing disciplines*
- *Markovian FIFO queueing systems*
- *Non-Markovian and self-similar models*
- *Networks of queues*

The chapter starts by analyzing a basic theorem and a basic but popular process: Little's theorem and the birth-and-death process, respectively. Next, various scenarios of queueing disciplines are presented: finite versus infinite queueing capacity, one server versus several servers, and Markovian versus non-Markovian systems. Non-Markovian models are essential, as many network applications such as Ethernet, WWW, and multimedia traffic cannot be modeled by Markovian patterns.

Networks of queues rely on two important and fundamental theorems: *Burke's theorem* and *Jackson's theorem*. Burke's theorem presents solutions to a network of several queues. Jackson's theorem is used when a packet visits a particular queue more than once. In such conditions, the network typically contains *loops* or *feedback*.

11.1 Little's Theorem

The fundamental concept of packet queueing is based on *Little's theorem*, or *Little's formula*. This formula states that for networks reaching steady state, the average number of packets in a system is equal to the product of the average arrival rate, λ, and the average time spent in the queueing system. For example, consider the communication system shown in Figure 11.1. Assume that the system starts with empty state at time $t = 0$. Let A_i and D_i be the ith arriving packet and ith departing packet, respectively, and let $A(t)$ and $D(t)$ be the total number of arriving packets and the total number of departing packets, respectively, up to a given time t.

Thus, the total time a packet i spends in the system is expressed by $T_i = D_i - A_i$, and the total number of accumulated packets in the system at time t is described by $K(t) = A(t) - D(t)$. The cumulative timing chart of packets in a first-come, first-served service discipline is shown in Figure 11.2. The total time that all packets spend in the system can be expressed by $\sum_{i=1}^{A(t)} T_i$. Thus, the average number of packets in the system, K_a, can be obtained by

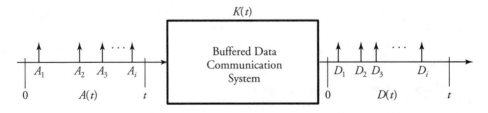

Figure 11.1   Overview of a buffered communication system with arriving and departing packets

Number of Packets

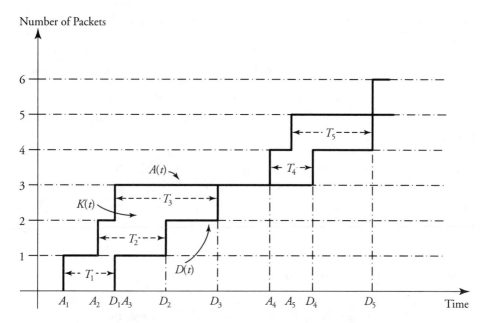

Figure 11.2 Accumulation of packets in a queueing system

$$K_a = \frac{1}{t} \sum_{i=1}^{A(t)} T_i. \tag{11.1}$$

Similarly, the average time a packet spends in the system, T_a, can be represented by

$$T_a = \frac{1}{A(t)} \sum_{i=1}^{A(t)} T_i. \tag{11.2}$$

Also, the average number of arriving packets per second is given by λ as

$$\lambda = \frac{A(t)}{t}. \tag{11.3}$$

By combining Equations (11.1), (11.2), and (11.3), we obtain

$$K_a = \lambda T_a. \tag{11.4}$$

This important result leads to a final form: Little's formula. This formula makes the assumption that t is large enough and that K_a and T_a therefore converge to their expected values of corresponding random processes $E[K(t)]$ and $E[T]$, respectively. Thus:

$$E[K(t)] = \lambda E[T]. \qquad (11.5)$$

Little's formula holds for most service disciplines with an arbitrary number of servers. Therefore, the assumption of first-come, first-served service discipline is not necessary.

Example.   Consider a data-communication system with three transmission lines; packets arrive at three different nodes with arrival rates $\lambda_1 = 200$ packets/sec, $\lambda_2 = 300$ packets/sec, and $\lambda_3 = 10$ packets/sec, respectively. Assume that an average of 50,000 same-size packets float in this system. Find the average delay per packet in the system.

Solution.   This delay is derived by

$$T_a = \frac{K_a}{\lambda_1 + \lambda_2 + \lambda_3} = \frac{50,000}{200 + 300 + 10} = 98.04 \text{ s}.$$

This is a simple application of Little's formula in a communication system.

11.2   Birth-and-Death Process

If a packet arrives at or leaves from a queueing node of a computer network, the state of the node's buffer changes, and thus the state of the queue changes as well. In such cases, as discussed in Appendix C, if the system can be expressed by a *Markov process*, the activity of the process—in terms of the number of packets—can be depicted by a state machine known as the *Markov chain*. A particular instance of a Markov chain is the *birth-and-death process*.

In a *birth-and-death process*, any given state i can connect only to state $i - 1$ with rate μ_i or to state $i + 1$ with rate λ_i, as shown in Figure 11.3. In general, if $A(t)$ and $D(t)$ are the total number of arriving packets and the total number of departing packets, respectively, up to given time t, the total number of packets in the system at time t is described by $K(t) = A(t) - D(t)$. With this analysis, $A(t)$ is the total number of *births*, and $D(t)$ is the total number of *deaths*. Therefore, $K(t)$ can be viewed as a birth-and-death process representing the cumulative number of packets in a first-come first-served service discipline.

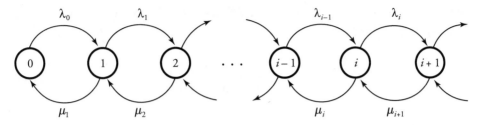

Figure 11.3   A general birth-and-death process and its transitions

Let p_i be the probability that the chain is in state i. The balance equation for the steady-state probability at state 0 denoted by p_0 is related to the one for state 1 denoted by p_1 as

$$\lambda_0 p_0 = \mu_1 p_1. \tag{11.6}$$

Similarly, for state 1, the balance equation is

$$\lambda_0 p_0 + \mu_2 p_2 = \lambda_1 p_1 + \mu_1 p_1, \tag{11.7}$$

and by using Equation (11.6), we derive the balance equation of state 1 as $\lambda_1 p_1 - \mu_2 p_2 = 0$. This development can continue up to state $i - 1$, where the balance equation can be derived as

$$\lambda_{i-1} p_{i-1} - \mu_i p_i = 0. \tag{11.8}$$

We define $\rho_i = \dfrac{\lambda_{i-1}}{\mu_i}$ as *state i utilization*. Thus, we can express the balance Equation (11.8) by a generic form as

$$p_i = \rho_i p_{i-1}. \tag{11.9}$$

If we apply Equation (11.9) for every state, starting with $p_1 = \rho_1 p_0$ up to $p_i = \rho_i p_{i-1}$ and combine all the equations, we obtain a generic equation

$$p_i = (\rho_1 \rho_2 \cdots \rho_i) p_0. \tag{11.10}$$

Since the sum of all the probabilities is always equal to 1, as $\sum_{i=0}^{\infty} p_i = \sum_{i=0}^{\infty}(\rho_1 \rho_2 \cdots \rho_i p_0) = 1$, p_i in Equation (11.10) can also be obtained from

$$p_i = \frac{\rho_1 \rho_2 \cdots \rho_i}{\sum_{j=0}^{\infty}(\rho_1 \rho_2 \cdots \rho_j)}. \tag{11.11}$$

The significance of this result is that a state probability p_i is expressed in terms of state utilizations, $\rho_1, \rho_2, \cdots, \rho_i$ only.

11.3 Queueing Disciplines

Queueing systems are widely described by *Kendal's notations* as *A/B/m/K*, where *A* denotes the distribution of the interarrival times; *B*, the distribution of the service times; *m*, the number of servers; and *K*, the total capacity of the system. If a system reaches its full capacity, the arriving packet number $K+1$ is blocked. *A* and *B* are normally represented by the following symbols:

M	Exponential distribution
E_k	Erlang distribution with k phases
H_k	Hyperexponential distribution with k phases
D	Deterministic distribution
G	General distribution
GI	General distribution with independent interarrival times
MMPP	Markov-modulated Poisson process
BMAP	Batch Markovian arrival process

In a queueing system, packets arrive at the buffer and are stored there. If other packets are waiting for service in the queue, the incoming packet is stored as long as all other packets are ahead of it. Thus, a server state can be either *idle* or *busy*. When a currently in-service packet departs from the system, one of the stored packets is selected for service according to the *scheduling* discipline. A commonly used arriving process assumes that the sequence of interarrival times is *independent and identically distributed* (IID).

Queueing systems can be classified as follows:

- *First in, first out* (FIFO). Packets are served in the order they arrive.
- *Last come, first served* (LCFS). Packets are served in reverse order of their arrival.

- *Random service.* Packets are selected at random for service.

- *Priority service.* The selection of a packet in the queue depends on priorities that are locally or permanently assigned to the packet.

- *Preemption.* The packet currently being serviced can be interrupted and preempted if a packet in the queue has a higher priority.

- *Round robin.* If the time allowed for the service of a packet is through and the process is not finished, the packet returns to the queue, and the action is repeated until the job service is completed.

- *Service sharing.* Servers can share their power with one another to provide services to the packets requiring more processing time.

This chapter focuses on FIFO models to show how the fundamental queueing in computer networks works. Chapter 13 looks at applications of more advanced queueing models, such as priority, preemption, and round-robin queues.

11.4   Markovian FIFO Queueing Systems

In *Markovian* queueing systems, both arrival and service behaviors are based on Markovian-model queueing disciplines: $M/M/1$, $M/M/1/b$, $M/M/a$, $M/M/a/a$, and $M/M/\infty$.

11.4.1   M/M/1 Queueing Systems

Figure 11.4 shows a simple queueing system representing an $M/M/1$ model. In this model, packets with rate λ per seconed arrive at a queueing line with a total capacity of $K(t)$. The queuing line receives and stores packets. With the $M/M/1$ model, it is in fact assumed that the queueing line and therefore its system can accommodate an unlimited number of packets. When the server is prepared for service, packets from the queue enter the server one by one for receiving service at service rate μ per seconed.

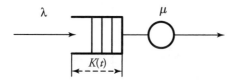

Figure 11.4   A simple queue/server model

Packet Arrival and Service Model

In an *M/M/*1 model, the *packet arrival* distribution is Poisson (see Appendix C) with rate λ, and thus the interarrival time distribution is exponential with mean time $1/\lambda$. Similarly, the service rate distribution is Poisson with rate μ, or the service time distribution is exponential with mean time $1/\mu$. Note that the interarrival time and the service time are independent. Figure 11.5 shows an example in which five packets, whose arrival and departures are denoted by A_1 through A_5 and D_1 through D_5, respectively, arrive at random and require service times S_1 through S_5, respectively. In this situation, queueing occurs while packets A_3 and A_4 wait in the buffer until the server becomes available. The probability that one packet arrives in an interval τ but no packet departs from the system is obtained using the Poisson formula:

$$P[1 \text{ packet arrives, 0 packets depart}] = \frac{\lambda\tau e^{-\lambda\tau}}{1!}$$

$$= \lambda\tau(1 - \frac{\lambda\tau}{1!} + \frac{(\lambda\tau)^2}{2!} - \cdots)$$

$$= \lambda\tau + (-\frac{(\lambda\tau)^2}{1!} + \frac{(\lambda\tau)^3}{2!} - \cdots)$$

$$\approx \lambda\tau. \tag{11.12}$$

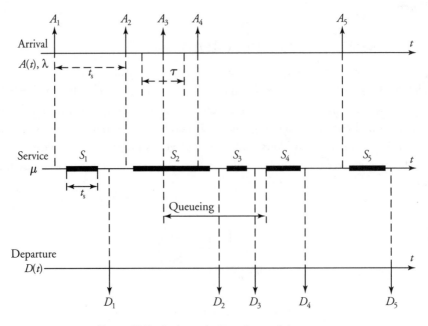

Figure 11.5 Packet arrival, service, and departure

Equation (11.12) assumes that interval τ becomes very small and that therefore, all terms except the first one can be ignored. The same analysis can be derived for the case in which no packets arrive in an interval τ, but one packet departs from the system. Because one packet is serviced in an interval τ, we can use rate μ instead of λ in Equation (11.12). Thus:

$$P[\text{0 packets arrive, 1 packet departs}] = \mu\tau\frac{e^{-\mu\tau}}{1!}$$

$$= \mu\tau\,(1 - \frac{\mu\tau}{1!} + \frac{(\mu\tau)^2}{2!} - \cdots)$$

$$= \mu\tau + (-\frac{(\mu\tau)^2}{1!} + \frac{(\mu\tau)^3}{2!} - \cdots)$$

$$\approx \mu\tau. \tag{11.13}$$

The last situation occurs when no change in the number of packets in the system is made. This means that there can be one arriving packet and one departing packet, or there can be no arriving packet and no departing packet. In either case, the probability can be derived by using Equations (11.12) and (11.13):

$$P\,[\text{no changes in the number of packets}] \approx 1- (\lambda\tau + \mu\tau). \tag{11.14}$$

This analysis of the process is illustrated in Figure 11.6. In this process, a chain starts from a given state i, implying i packets in the system.

Number of Packets in the System

Properties obtained from Equations (11.12), (11.13), and (11.14) lead to the derivation of the number of packets in an *M/M/*1 system: $K(t)$. The fact is that $K(t)$ follows a birth-and-death process, and its Markov chain follows exactly as the generic one shown in Figure 11.3 but with equal rates as modified in Figure 11.7. The main property of the exponential random variable implies that the interarrival time is independent of the present and past status of $K(t)$. Thus, if the system has $K(t) > 0$ packets, the interdeparture time distribution is also

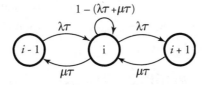

Figure 11.6   Packet arrival and departure

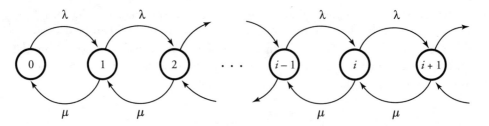

Figure 11.7 $M/M/1$ queueing behavior and its transitions

an exponential random variable. This also implies that the past history of the system is irrelevant for the probabilities of future states, and thus the process follows the property of a Markov chain. Note that $M/M/1$ is a simple case of a birth-death process with:

$$\lambda_0 = \lambda_1 = \lambda_2 = \cdots = \lambda \tag{11.15}$$

and

$$\mu_0 = \mu_1 = \mu_2 = \cdots = \mu. \tag{11.16}$$

We define $\rho = \dfrac{\lambda}{\mu}$ as the system *utilization*. The preceding Markov chain has the state-transition rate diagram shown in Figure 11.7, and its global balance equations for the steady-state probabilities can be set by using the birth-and-death process results, simplified as

$$p_i = (\rho\rho \cdots \rho)p_0 = \rho^i p_0. \tag{11.17}$$

Since the sum of all probabilities is always 1, we can write

$$\sum_{i=0}^{\infty} p_i = \sum_{i=0}^{\infty} \rho^i p_0 = 1. \tag{11.18}$$

A stable situation exists when the arrival rate is less than the service rate, or $\rho = \lambda/\mu < 1$, in which case $K(t)$ does not increase in value without bound, and therefore $\sum_{i=0}^{\infty} \rho^i \to \dfrac{1}{1-\rho}$. This fact simplifies Equation (11.17) for the derivation of the number of packets in the system:

$$p_i = P[K(t) = i] = (1 - \rho)\rho^i \quad i = 1, 2, \ldots. \tag{11.19}$$

The condition $\rho = \lambda/\mu < 1$ must be met if the system is designed to be stable; otherwise, packets arrive at the system more quickly than they can be processed. It is apparent that if the packet-arrival rate exceeds the processing-capacity rate of servers, the number of packets in the queue grows without bound, leading to an unstable situation. Note that the distribution of $K(t)$ follows a *geometric distribution*.

Mean Delay and Mean Number of Packets in System

The result derived from Equation (11.19) can be used to calculate the mean (average) delay a packet spends in a queue or the entire system, and the mean number of packets in a system (length of a queue). The mean number of packets in the system is, in fact, the expected value of $K(t)$:

$$E[K(t)] = \sum_{i=0}^{\infty} i p_i = \sum_{i=0}^{\infty} i(1-\rho)\rho^i = (1-\rho)\sum_{i=0}^{\infty} i\rho^i = \frac{\rho}{1-\rho}. \quad (11.20)$$

where, in the last part of Equation (11.20), we took advantage of the series property of $\sum_{i=0}^{\infty} i\rho^i = \rho/(1-\rho)^2$ that can be found in any basic calculus reference. Little's formula can now be used to derive the mean packet delay in the system:

$$E[T] = \frac{1}{\lambda}E[K(t)] = \frac{1}{\lambda}\frac{\rho}{1-\rho} = \frac{1}{\mu-\lambda}. \quad (11.21)$$

We can now show the mean waiting time of a packet in the queue, $E[T_q]$, in terms of $E[T]$ and the mean processing time of a packet in the server, $E[T_s]$:

$$E[T_q] = E[T] - E[T_s]. \quad (11.22)$$

The mean processing time of a packet in the server is in fact $E[T_s] = \frac{1}{\mu}$, therefore:

$$E[T_q] = \frac{1}{\lambda}\frac{\rho}{1-\rho} - \frac{1}{\mu} = \frac{\rho}{\mu-\lambda}. \quad (11.23)$$

Similarly, Little's formula to find the mean number of packets in the queue can be obtained as $E[K_q(t)] = \lambda E[T_q] = \frac{\rho^2}{1-\rho}$. Interestingly, all of the preceding factors are a function of λ or μ or both only. In other words, the value of arrival and/or service rates in any single-queue system determines the average number of packets and average delay in the system.

Example. A router modelled by an *M/M/*1 queueing system receives packets at rate $\lambda = 0.25$ million packets per second and services them at rate $\mu = 0.33$ million packets per second. Find the utilization, average number of packets, and average packet delay in the router.

Solution. The utilization is $\rho = \lambda/\mu = 0.75$. Equation (11.20) gives us the average number of packets in the router to be $\rho/(1-\rho) = 3$. The average packet delay in the router is obtained by using Equation (11.21) and it turns out to be $E[T] = 1/(\mu-\lambda) = 12.5$ microseconds.

11.4.2   Systems with Limited Queueing Space: *M/M/*1/*b*

In a queue with exponential interarrival times and exponential service times, a single server and a maximum of b packets can be held in the system. Once such a system exceeds its capacity, arriving packet numbered $b + 1$ is turned away from the system, since there is no room for it. Figure 11.8 shows the state-transition diagram for the *M/M/*1/*b* system. This diagram is a Markov chain and is very similar to the one illustrated in Figure 11.7, but the chain for the *M/M/*1/*b* system stops at the maximum capacity of b. Thus, the global balance equations use the same results presented in Equation (11.18), where the sum of all probabilities is always 1 and thus

$$\sum_{i=0}^{b} p_i = \sum_{i=0}^{b} \rho^i p_0 = 1. \tag{11.24}$$

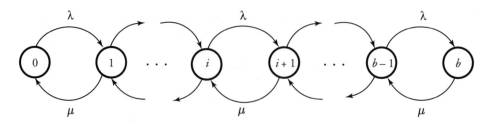

Figure 11.8   State-transition diagram for *M/M/*1/*b* system

A stable situation exists when the arrival rate is less than the service rate, or $\rho = \lambda/\mu < 1$, in which case $K(t)$ does not increase in value without bound and therefore $\sum_{i=0}^{b} \rho^i \rightarrow \dfrac{1 - \rho^{b+1}}{1 - \rho}$. This fact simplifies Equation (11.17) for deriving the number of packets in the system, which is a continuous-time Markov chain taking on values from the set $\{0, 1, \cdots, b\}$:

$$p_i = P[K(t) = i] = \begin{cases} \rho^i \dfrac{1 - \rho}{1 - \rho^{b+1}} & \text{if } \rho \neq 1 \text{ and } i = 1, 2, \cdots b \\ \dfrac{1}{1 + b} & \text{if } \rho = 1 \end{cases} \qquad (11.25)$$

Note that the number of packets in the system is derived in two parts, depending on whether the utilization is maximized ($\rho = 1$) or not.

Mean Number of Packets

The mean number of packets in the system, $E[K(t)]$, can be expressed by Formula C.20 in Appendix C:

$$E[K(t)] = \sum_{i=0}^{b} i\, P[K(t) = i] = \begin{cases} \dfrac{\rho}{1 - \rho} - \dfrac{(b+1)\rho^{b+1}}{1 - \rho^{b+1}} & \text{if } \rho \neq 1 \\ \dfrac{b}{2} & \text{if } \rho = 1 \end{cases} \qquad (11.26)$$

Clearly, results of the mean number of packets in the *M/M/1* and *M/M/1/b* systems are fundamentally different, owing to the difference in capacities available in these two systems.

11.4.3 *M/M/a* Queueing Systems

Some stochastic systems are modeled by *M/M/a*, where a servers instead of one can be used to enhance system performance, as shown in Figure 11.9. The service rate in each server may be different from or equal to that in the others, as rates μ_1 through μ_a are indicated as service rates of the corresponding servers. The advantage of this discipline over systems with one server is its parallel-serving feature. A packet can be partitioned into $i < a$ different tasks and served in parallel in i different servers concurrently.

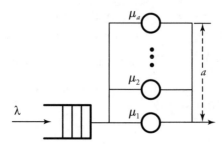

Figure 11.9 Queueing model of $M/M/a$ systems

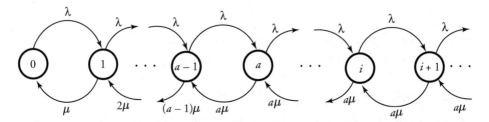

Figure 11.10 State-transition diagram for $M/M/a$ systems

The resulting system can be modeled by a continuous-time Markov chain, as shown in Figure 11.10. The maximum number of servers is denoted by a. As long as the number of packets in the queue is less than a, the service rate is proportionally changing ($i\mu$) with the number of waiting packets while the arrival rate remains constant. However, when the number of packets in the queue reaches a, the service rate stays constant at its maximum of $a\mu$.

Example.   Figure 11.11 shows a statistical comparison between $M/M/1$ and $M/M/3$ systems, each with seven packets. In the $M/M/1$ system, the third packet, S_3, starts to accumulate in the queue. The queueing trend continues, as shown by gray, if the service rate stays low. On the contrary, in the $M/M/3$ system, packets are distributed over the three servers on arrival, and queueing has not happened.

Balance Equations for $i \leq a$

The steady-state probabilities for the $M/M/a$ system can be obtained by using the birth-and-death process. Balance equations for i servers being busy when $i \leq a$ begin with p_i:

$$p_i = \left(\frac{\lambda}{i\mu} p_{i-1} \right) \quad i = 1, \dots, a. \tag{11.27}$$

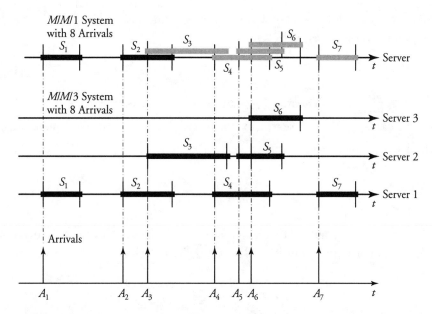

Figure 11.11 Comparison of $M/M/1$ and $M/M/3$ systems, each with seven packets

Recall that $\rho_i = \dfrac{\lambda}{i\mu}$ is the utilization and that $p_i = (\rho_1 \rho_2 \cdots \rho_{i-1} \rho_i) p_0$. Thus, p_i can be rewritten as

$$p_i = \left(\frac{\lambda}{\mu} \frac{\lambda}{2\mu} \cdots \frac{\lambda}{(i-1)\mu} \frac{\lambda}{i\mu} \right) p_0 = \frac{\left(\frac{\lambda}{\mu} \right)^i}{i!} p_0 = \left(\frac{\rho_1^i}{i!} \right) p_0. \quad (11.28)$$

It is easy to realize the probability that all servers are in use. Substitute $i = a$ in Equation (11.28):

$$p_a = \left(\frac{\rho_1^a}{a!} \right) p_0 = \frac{\left(\frac{\lambda}{\mu} \right)^a}{a!} p_0. \quad (11.29)$$

Balance Equations for $i \geq a$

To determine the balance equations for $i \geq a$, we again use the birth-and-death process. The second part of the transition diagram, starting from state a, is formulated over states $i = a, a + 1, a + 2, \cdots$. Using the same formula as obtained for the $M/M/1$ case, p_i for this case is set up by

$$p_i = \rho^{i-a} p_a. \tag{11.30}$$

where $\rho = \dfrac{\lambda}{a\mu}$. In this equation, p_a can be substituted by the value obtained last from the case of $i \le a$, presented in Equation (11.29). Therefore, by replacing p_a with $\dfrac{\rho_1^a}{a!} p_a$, we obtain

$$p_i = \frac{\rho^{i-a} \rho_1^a}{a!} p_0. \tag{11.31}$$

Equations (11.28) and (11.31) together cover all the cases in the state diagram. Since the sum of all probabilities is always 1, $\sum_{i=0}^{\infty} p_i = 1$:

$$\sum_{i=0}^{a-1} \frac{\rho_1^i}{i!} p_0 + \frac{\rho_1^a}{a!} \sum_{i=a}^{\infty} \rho^{i-a} p_0 = 1. \tag{11.32}$$

To have a stable system, we want $\rho < 1$, which causes $\sum_{i=a}^{\infty} \rho^{i-a}$ to converge to $\dfrac{1}{1-\rho}$. With this simplification, we can compute the probability of the first state from Equation 11.32:

$$p_0 = \frac{1}{\sum_{i=0}^{a-1} \dfrac{\rho_1^i}{i!} + \dfrac{\rho_1^a}{a!} \dfrac{1}{1-\rho}}. \tag{11.33}$$

Similar to previous cases, knowing p_0 is essential, as we can derive p_i from Equation (11.31).

In an $M/M/a$ system, we can use the *Erlang-C formula* to compute the blocking probability. This formula calculates the probability that an arriving packet finds all servers busy. This probability is the same as the probability that the waiting time for the packet in the queue is greater than zero, or the probability that the number of packets in the queueing system is greater than or equal to a, $P[K(t) \ge a]$:

$$\text{Erlang-C Blocking Prob.:} P[K(t) \ge a] = \sum_{i=a}^{\infty} p_i = \frac{p_a}{1-\rho}. \tag{11.34}$$

As with the $M/M/1$ queueing system, we can now estimate all the parameters for the $M/M/a$ discipline. The mean number of packets in the queue is

$$E[K_q(t)] = \sum_{i=a}^{\infty}(i-a)p_i = \sum_{i=a}^{\infty}(i-a)\rho^{i-a}p_a = p_a \sum_{i-a=0}^{\infty}(i-a)\rho^{i-a} = \frac{p_a\rho}{(1-\rho)^2}. \quad (11.35)$$

Accordingly, the mean packet delay in the queue is obtained using Little's formula as

$$E[T_q] = \frac{1}{\lambda}E[K_q(t)] = \frac{p_a}{a\mu(1-\rho)^2}. \quad (11.36)$$

Obviously, the total mean packet delay in a system includes the service time of server and is

$$E[T] = E[T_q] + E[T_s] = \frac{p_a}{a\mu(1-\rho)^2} + \frac{1}{\mu}. \quad (11.37)$$

The mean number of packets in the system is therefore derived from Little's formula:

$$E[K(t)] = \sum_{i=0}^{b} i\,P[K(t) = i] = \begin{cases} \dfrac{\rho}{1-\rho} - \dfrac{(b+1)\rho^{b+1}}{1-\rho^{b+1}} \\ \text{if } \rho \neq 1 \\ \dfrac{b}{2} \\ \text{if } \rho = 1 \end{cases}. \quad (11.38)$$

Example. A communication node receives packets at $\lambda = 1/2$ packet per nanosecond, and the switching server processes packets at the rate of one packet per nanosecond. Calculate the queueing delay and the total node's delay, and then compare the results for using queueing disciplines $M/M/1$ and $M/M/3$ with equal service powers as shown in Figure 11.12.

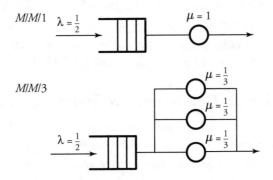

Figure 11.12 Two queueing disciplines with equal service powers

Solution.   With an $M/M/1$ discipline, $\rho = \lambda/\mu = 0.5$. So the mean queueing delay is

$$E[T_q] = \frac{\rho/\mu}{1 - \rho} = 1 \text{ nsec.} \tag{11.39}$$

and the total node's delay is

$$E[T] = \frac{1/\mu}{1 - \rho} = 2 \text{ nsec} \tag{11.40}$$

For the $M/M/3$ discipline, $a = 3$ servers are used; thus, $\rho_1 = \lambda/\mu = 1.5$, and $\rho = \lambda/a\mu = 0.5$. Thus:

$$p_0 = \frac{1}{\sum_{i=0}^{2} \dfrac{\rho_1^i}{i!} + \dfrac{\rho_1^3}{3!} \dfrac{1}{1 - \rho}}. \tag{11.41}$$

Since $p_a = \dfrac{\rho_1^a}{a!} p_0 = 0.12$, the queueing delay is

$$E[T_q] = p_a \frac{1}{a\mu(1 - \rho)^2} = 0.48 \text{ nsec,} \tag{11.42}$$

and the total mean node's delay is

$$E[T] = E[T_q] + E[T_s] = 0.48 + \frac{1}{\mu} = 3.48 \text{ nsec.} \tag{11.43}$$

This useful example expresses an important conclusion: *Increasing the number of servers lowers the queueing delay but increases the total system delay.* In summary, compared with the $M/M/a$ system ($a > 1$), the $M/M/1$ system has a smaller total delay but a larger queueing delay. However, note that the preceding statement should be made with an important condition; that is, the total service rates of a servers in the $M/M/a$ model must be equal to the service rate of the $M/M/1$ model.

11.4.4   Models for Delay-Sensitive Traffic: $M/M/a/a$

Some network nodes can be built with no buffering elements. One application of such systems is for cases in which *delay-sensitive traffic*, such as voice, needs a queueless service. These types of nodes can be shown by queueless models. One example of such models is the $M/M/a/a$ queueing system, which has a servers but no queueing

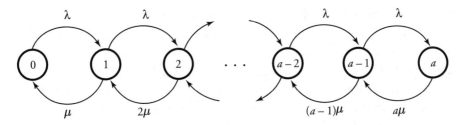

Figure 11.13   State-transition diagram for $M/M/a/a$ systems

line. If all servers are busy, an arriving packet is turned away, resulting in the transition-rate diagram shown in Figure 11.13. This transition rate partially resembles that for an $M/M/a$ system. Thus, we use the previously obtained Equation (11.28) for the probability that the system is in state $i \in \{0, \cdots, a\}$:

$$p_i = \left(\frac{\rho_1^i}{i!} \right) p_0. \tag{11.44}$$

Combining Equation (11.44) and the fact that $\sum_{i=0}^{a} p_i = 1$ gives us

$$p_0 = \frac{1}{\sum_{i=0}^{a} \frac{\rho_1^i}{i!}}. \tag{11.45}$$

Erlang-B Blocking Probability

In an $M/M/a/a$ system, we can compute the blocking probability, this time using the *Erlang-B formula*. This formula calculates the probability that an arriving packet finds all servers busy while there is no waiting line for packets. The probability that all servers in a system are busy is referred to as the Erlang-B formula, using Equation (11.44) with $i = a$:

Erlang-B Blocking Probability: $P[K(t) = a] = p_a = \dfrac{\rho_1^a}{a!} p_0 = \dfrac{\rho_1^a}{a! \left(\sum_{i=0}^{a} \frac{\rho_1^i}{i!} \right)}. \tag{11.46}$

This very important formula presents the blocking probability in a system where there are a resources (servers) and all resources are busy under the utilization $\rho_1 = \lambda/\mu$. In such a case, a new incoming packet is turned away or blocked from service. Appendix D of this book presents a numerical compilation of the Erlang-B formula based on Equation (11.46). This table can be used for a variety of different applications. One of the applications will be presented in Chapter 18 for estimation on blocking probabilities given the number of phone channels.

In such systems, it would also be interesting to find the average number of packets in the system, since no queueing line exists. Let λ, λ_p, and $\lambda_b = p_a\lambda$ represent the arrival rate, the packet-passing rate, and the blocking rate, respectively. Therefore, $\lambda = \lambda_p + \lambda_b$. The packet-passing rate can then be rewritten as $\lambda_p = \lambda(1 - p_a)$. The average number of packets in the system, since no queueing line exists, from Little's formula:

$$E[K(t)] = \lambda_p E[T_s] = \lambda(1 - p_a)\frac{1}{\mu} \tag{11.47}$$

Example. When a mobile user in a wireless network moves to a new region, a handoff process between the two regions is required. If all the new region's channels are used, the handoff call is terminated or blocked. For real-time communications, this scenario is modeled by an $M/M/a/a$ system, where $a = c_i$ is the number of handoff servers of traffic type i. Assume that c_i=10, 50, and 100; mean service time $1/\mu_i = 30$ ms; and handoff request rate $\lambda_i = 0 \cdots 10,000$. Sketch a set of plots showing the performance of the handoff process.

Solution. The calculation effort is left to readers. Instead, the results of the computations in Figure 11.14 are given. The plots in this figure depict the results of an $M/M/a/a$ model for the wireless handoff. Equation (11.46) can be used to compute the handoff blocking probability.

11.4.5 $M/M/\infty$ Queueing Systems

In many high-speed network nodes, higher cost can be tolerated in exchange for better communication quality. One method of improving the quality of handling packets is to consider a large number of servers at a node. If we let a approach a real large number approximated to infinity, an $M/M/a/a$ system becomes an $M/M/\infty$ system. As a result, the transition-rate diagram can continue to ∞, as shown in Figure 11.15. To find steady-state probabilities, p_i, for this queueing system, we use Equation (11.46) of the $M/M/a/a$ system and let a be a number i varying up to ∞ :

$$p_i = \frac{\rho_1^i}{i!\left(\sum_{j=0}^{a}\frac{\rho_1^j}{j!}\right)} \tag{11.48}$$

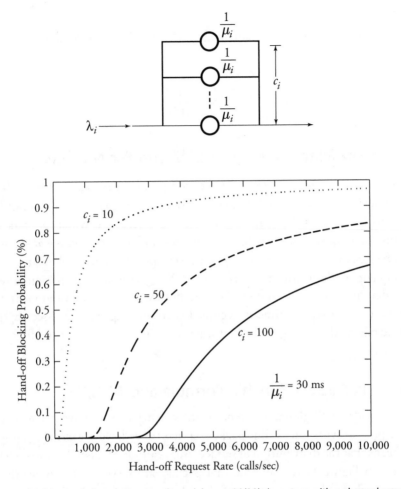

Figure 11.14   A wireless data network model as an $M/M/a/a$ system with c_i channel servers

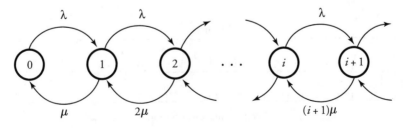

Figure 11.15   State-transition diagram for $M/M/\infty$ system

In the denominator of this equation, $\sum_{j=0}^{i} \frac{\rho_1^j}{j!}$ tends to converge to e^{ρ_1} when i approaches infinity:

$$p_i = \frac{\rho_1^i}{i!\, e^{\rho_1}}. \qquad (11.49)$$

11.5 Non-Markovian and Self-Similar Models

Another class of queueing systems is either completely or partially *non-Markovian*. Partial non-Markovian means that either arrival or service behavior is not based on Markovian models. We first consider a single server in which packets arrive according to a Poisson process, but the service-time distribution is *non-Poisson* or *non-Markovian* as *general distribution*. One example of a non-Markovian system is *M/G/*1 queues with priorities. Another is *M/D/*1, where the distribution of service time is deterministic, not random. Yet another example is reservation systems in which part of the service time is occupied with sending packets—serving packets—and part with sending control information or making reservations for sending the packets.

11.5.1 Pollaczek-Khinchin Formula and M/G/1

Let us consider a single-server scenario in which packets arrive according to a Poisson process with rate λ, but packet service times have a *general distribution*. This means that the distribution of service times cannot necessarily be exponential, as shown in Figure 11.16. Suppose that packets are served in the order they are received, with T_{si} the service time of the ith packet. In our analysis, we assume that random variables T_{s1}, T_{s2}, $\cdots$ are identically distributed, mutually independent,

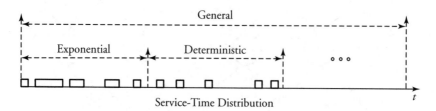

Figure 11.16 A general distribution of service times

and independent of the interarrival times. Let T_{qi} be the queueing time of the ith packet. Then:

$$T_{qi} = \pi_i + \sum_{j=i-K_{qi}}^{i-1} T_{sj}, \qquad (11.50)$$

where K_{qi} is the number of packets found by the ith packet waiting in the queue on arrival, and π_i is the partial service time seen by the ith packet if a given packet j is already being served when packet i arrives. If no packet is in service, π_i is zero. In order to understand the averages of the mentioned times, we take expectations of two sides in Equation (11.50):

$$E[T_{qi}] = E[\pi_i] + E[\sum_{j=i-N_i}^{i-1} T_{sj}] = E[\pi_i] + E[\sum_{j=i-K_{qi}}^{i-1} E[T_{sj} \mid K_{qi}]]. \quad (11.51)$$

With the independence induction of the random variables K_{qi} and T_{qj}, we have

$$E[T_{qi}] = E[\pi_i] + E[T_{si}]E[K_{qi}]. \qquad (11.52)$$

It is clear that we can apply the average service time as $E[T_{si}] = \dfrac{1}{\mu}$ in Equation (11.52). Also, by forcing Little's formula, where $E[K_{qi}] = \lambda E[T_{qi}]$, Equation (11.52) becomes

$$E[T_{qi}] = E[\pi_i] + \frac{1}{\mu}\lambda E[T_{qi}] = E[\pi_i] + \rho E[T_{qi}], \qquad (11.53)$$

where $\rho = \lambda/\mu$ is the utilization. Thus,

$$E[T_{qi}] = \frac{E[\pi_i]}{1-\rho}. \qquad (11.54)$$

Figure 11.17 shows an example of mean π_i representing the remaining time for the completion of an in-service packet as a function of time. If a new service of T_{si} seconds begins, π_i starts at value T_{si} and decays linearly at 45 degrees for T_{si} seconds. Thus, the mean π_i in the interval $[0, t]$ with n triangles is equal to the area of all triangles $\left(\sum_{i=1}^{n} \frac{1}{2} T_{si}^2\right)$ divided by total time (t)

$$E[\pi_i] = \frac{1}{t}\sum_{i=1}^{n} \frac{1}{2} T_{si}^2 = \frac{1}{2}\frac{n}{t}\frac{\sum_{i=1}^{n} T_{si}^2}{n}. \qquad (11.55)$$

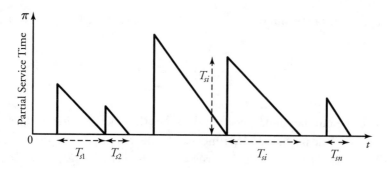

Figure 11.17   Mean partial service time

If n and t are large enough, $\frac{n}{t}$ becomes λ, and $\sum_{i=1}^{n} T_{si}^2/n$ becomes $E[T_{si}^2]$, the second moment of service time. Then, Equation (11.55) can be rewritten as

$$E[\pi_i] = \frac{1}{2}\lambda E[T_{si}^2].\qquad(11.56)$$

Combining Equations (11.55) and (11.54) forms the *Pollaczek-Khinchin* (P-K) formula:

$$E[T_{qi}] = \frac{\lambda E[T_{si}^2]}{2(1-\rho)}.\qquad(11.57)$$

Clearly, the total queueing time and service time is $E[T_{qi}] + E[T_{si}]$. By inducing Little's formula, the expected number of packets in the queue, $E[K_{qi}]$, and the expected number of packets in the system, $E[K_i]$, we get

$$E[K_{qi}] = \frac{\lambda^2 E[T_{si}^2]}{2(1-\rho)}\qquad(11.58)$$

and

$$E[K_i] = \rho + \frac{\lambda^2 E[T_{si}^2]}{2(1-\rho)}.\qquad(11.59)$$

These results of the Pollaczek-Khinchin theorem express the behavior of a general distribution of service time modeled as *M/G/*1. For example, if an *M/M/*1 system needs to be expressed by these results, and since service times are exponentially distributed, we have $E[T_{si}^2] = 2/\mu^2$, and the Pollaczek-Khinchin formula reduces to

$$E[T_{qi}] = \frac{\rho}{\mu(1-\rho)}.\qquad(11.60)$$

Note that the queueing metrics as the expected value of queueing delay obtained in Equation (11.60) is still a function of the system utilization. However, the notion of service rate μ has shown up in the equation and is a natural behavior of the non-Markovian service model.

11.5.2   M/D/1 Models

In an *M/D/*1 model, the *packet arrival* distribution is Poisson with rate λ, and thus the interarrival time distribution is exponential with mean time $1/\lambda$. as explained in the preceding cases. However, the service time distribution is deterministic or constant. An example of constant distribution of service time in a computer network is when equal-sized packets, as described in Chapter 1, arrive at routers for service. When service times are constant (identical) for all packets, we have $E[T_{si}^2] = 1/\mu^2$. Then:

$$E[T_{qi}] = \frac{\rho}{2\mu(1 - \rho)}. \tag{11.61}$$

Note that the value of $E[T_{qi}]$ for an *M/D/*1 queue is the lower bound to the corresponding value for an *M/G/*1 model of the same λ and μ. This is true because the *M/D/*1 case yields the minimum possible value of $E[T_{si}^2]$. It is also worth noting that $E[T_{qi}]$ in an *M/M/*1 queue is twice as much as the one in an *M/D/*1 queue. The reason is that the mean service time is the same in the two cases, and for small ρs, most of the waiting occurs in the service unit, whereas for large ρs, most of the waiting occurs within the queue.

11.5.3   Self-Similarity and Batch-Arrival Models

The case of video streaming traffic, which obeys a model in the form of *batch arrival*, not Poisson, is analyzed in Chapter 20, so our analysis on non-Poisson arrival models is presented there. Here, we give some descriptive and intuitive examples of such models, which give rise to *self-similar* traffic.

Non-Markovian arrival models, or basically *non-Poisson arrival models*, have a number of important networking applications. The notion of self-similarity, for example, applies to WAN and LAN traffic. One example of such arrival situations is self-similarity traffic owing to the *World Wide Web* (WWW). The self-similarity in such traffic can be expressed based on the underlying distributions of WWW document sizes, the effects of caching and user preference in file transfer, and even user think time. Another example of self-similar traffic is video streaming mixed up with regular random traffic backgrounds. In such a case, batches of video packets are generated and are directed into a pool of mixed traffic in the Internet.

Traffic patterns indicate significant burstiness, or variations on a wide range of time scales. Bursty traffic can be described statistically by using *self-similarity patterns*. In a self-similar process, the distribution of a packet, frame, or object remains unchanged when viewed at varying scales. This type of traffic pattern has observable bursts and thus exhibits long-range dependence. The dependency means that all values at all times are typically correlated with the ones at all future instants. The long-range dependence in network traffic shows that packet loss and delay behavior are different from the ones in traditional network models using Poisson models.

11.6   Networks of Queues

Networks of queueing nodes can be modeled and their behavior, including feedback, studied. Two important and fundamental theorems are *Burke's theorem* and *Jackson's theorem*. Burke's theorem presents solutions to a network of several queues. Jackson's theorem is relevant when a packet visits a particular queue more than once.

11.6.1   Burke's Theorem

When a number of queueing nodes are connected, they all may be either in series or in parallel. In such circumstances, the entire system requires a careful and justified procedure for modeling. *Burke's theorem* presents solutions to a network of m queues through two models: m queueing nodes in series (cascaded) and m queueing nodes in parallel. Each node can be modeled by the $M/M/1$ queue or any queuing model in the steady state with an arrival rate such as the Poisson process with arrival rate λ. Then, the departure process is similarly at rate λ. Note that in any case of Burke's model, at any time t, the number of packets in queuing nodes is independent of the departure process prior to time t. The two Burke's models, cascaded and parallel, are described next.

Burke's Theorem on Cascaded Nodes

One common case of queueing networks is cascaded queueing nodes, as shown in Figure 11.18. In this network, the departure of a packet from a queueing node i is the arrival for node $i + 1$. The utilization for any node i is $\rho_i = \lambda/\mu_i$, where λ and μ_i are the arrival rate and service rate of that node, respectively.

The packet-movement activity of this network is modeled by an m-dimensional Markov chain. For simplicity, consider a two-node network of nodes 1 and 2. Figure 11.19 shows a two-dimensional Markov chain for this simplified network.

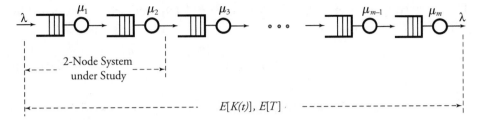

Figure 11.18   Burke's theorem applied on m cascaded queues

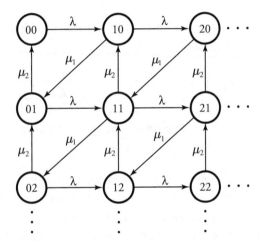

Figure 11.19   Two-dimensional Markov chain of the first 2-node system in Figure 11.18

The chain starts at state 00 identifying the empty-of-packets states of the nodes. When the first packet arrives at rate λ, the chain goes to state 10. State 10 represents the state of node 1 having one packet and node 2 having no packets. At this point, the chain can return to state 01 if node 1 processes this packet at rate μ_1, and sends the packet to node 2. If the packet is sent out of the second node at service rate μ_2, the chain returns to state 00, showing the empty status of the system. The Markov chain can be interpreted similarly for a larger number of packets.

In our system with m nodes, assume an $M/M/1$ discipline for every node; the probability that k packets are in the system, $P[K(t) = k]$, is:

$$P[K(t) = k] = P[K_1(t) = k_1] \times P[K_2(t) = k_2] \times \cdots \times P[K_m(t) = k_m]$$

$$= \prod_{i=1}^{m} (1 - \rho_i)\rho_i^{k_i}. \tag{11.62}$$

The expected number of packets in each node, $E[K_i(t)]$, can easily be estimated by using the $M/M/1$ property of each node:

$$E[K_i(t)] = \frac{\rho_i}{1 - \rho_i}. \tag{11.63}$$

Therefore, the expected number of packets in the entire system is derived by

$$E[K(t)] = \sum_{i=1}^{m} E[K_i(t)] = \sum_{i=1}^{m} \frac{\rho_i}{1 - \rho_i}. \tag{11.64}$$

We can now use Little's formula to estimate the total queueing delay that a packet should expect in the entire system:

$$E[T] = \frac{1}{\lambda} \sum_{i=1}^{m} E[K_i(t)] = \frac{1}{\lambda} \sum_{i=1}^{m} \frac{\rho_i}{1 - \rho_i}. \tag{11.65}$$

This last important result can help estimate the speed of a particular system modeled by a series of queueing nodes.

Example.   Figure 11.20 shows four queueing nodes. There are two external sources at rates $\lambda_1 = 2$ million packets per second and $\lambda_2 = 0.5$ million packets per second. Assume that all service rates are identical and equal to $\mu_1 = \mu_2 = \mu_3 = \mu_4 = 2.2$ million packets per second. Find the average delay on a packet passing through nodes 1, 2, and 4.

Solution.   The figure shows the utilizations as

$$\rho_1 = \frac{\lambda_1}{\mu_1}, \rho_2 = \frac{0.7\lambda_1}{\mu_2},$$

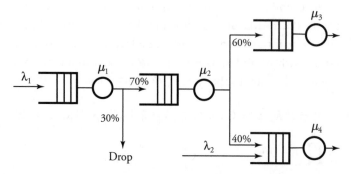

Figure 11.20   A four-queueing-node system solved using Burke's theorem

and

$$\rho_4 = \frac{0.4(0.7)\lambda_1 + \lambda_2}{\mu_4} = \frac{0.28\lambda_1 + \lambda_2}{\mu_4}.$$

The expected numbers of packets in nodes 1, 2, and 4 are, respectively:

$$E[K_1(t)] = \frac{\rho_1}{1 - \rho_1} = \frac{\lambda_1}{\mu_1 - \lambda_1}, E[K_2(t)] = \frac{\rho_2}{1 - \rho_2} = \frac{0.7\lambda_1}{\mu_2 - 0.7\lambda_1},$$

and

$$E[K_4(t)] = \frac{\rho_4}{1 - \rho_4} = \frac{0.28\lambda_1 + \lambda_2}{\mu_4 - 0.28\lambda_1 - \lambda_2}.$$

The expected overall delay, then, is

$$E[T] = \frac{E[K_1(t)]}{\lambda_1} + \frac{E[K_2(t)]}{0.7\lambda_1} + \frac{E[K_4(t)]}{0.28\lambda_1 + \lambda_2}.$$

Burke's Theorem on Parallel Nodes

We can now easily apply Burke's theorem in cases of in-parallel queueing nodes, as shown in Figure 11.21. Suppose that the incoming traffic with rate λ is distributed over m parallel queueing nodes with probabilities P_1 through P_m, respectively. Also assume that the queuing nodes' service rates are μ_1 through μ_m, respectively. In this system, the utilization for any node i is expressed by

$$\rho_i = \frac{P_i \lambda}{\mu_i}. \tag{11.66}$$

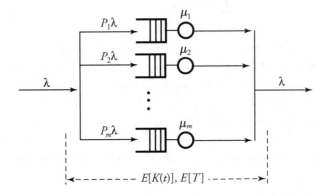

Figure 11.21   Application of Burke's theorem on parallel nodes

Assuming that each node is represented by an $M/M/1$ queueing model, we calculate the expected number of packets in the queue of a given node i by

$$E[K_i(t)] = \frac{\rho_i}{1 - \rho_i}. \tag{11.67}$$

But the main difference between a cascaded queueing system and a parallel queueing system starts here, at the analysis on average delay. In the parallel system, the overall average number of packets, $\sum_{i=1}^{m} E[K_i(t)]$, is an irrelevant metric. The new argument is that a packet has a random chance of P_i to choose only one of the m nodes (node i) and thus is not exposed to all m nodes. Consequently, we must calculate the average number of queued packets that a new arriving packet faces in a branch i. This average turns out to have a perfect stochastic pattern and is obtained by $E[K(t)]$:

$$E[K(t)] = E[E[K_i(t)]] = \sum_{i=1}^{m} P_i E[K_i(t)] = \sum_{i=1}^{m} P_i \left(\frac{\rho_i}{1 - \rho_i} \right). \tag{11.68}$$

Using Little's formula, we can first estimate the delay incurred in branch i:

$$E[T_i] = \frac{E[K_i(t)]}{P_i \lambda}. \tag{11.69}$$

Now, the total queueing delay that a packet should expect in the entire system, $E[T]$, is the average delay over all m parallel branches. This delay is, in fact, a stochastic mean delay of all parallel branches, as follows:

$$E[T] = E[E[T_i]] = \sum_{i=1}^{m} P_i E[T_i] = \sum_{i=1}^{m} P_i \frac{E[K_i(t)]}{P_i \lambda}$$

$$= \frac{1}{\lambda} \sum_{i=1}^{m} \frac{\rho_i}{1 - \rho_i}. \tag{11.70}$$

Clearly, $E[T]$ can help us estimate the speed of a particular m parallel-node system. An important note here is that Equations (11.64) and (11.68) may look the same. But the fact is that since the utilization in the case of cascaded nodes, $\rho_i = \lambda/\mu_i$, and the one for parallel nodes, $\rho_i = P_i \lambda_i / \mu_i$, are different, the results of $E[K(t)]$ in these cases too are different. We can argue identically on $E[T]$ for the two cases. Although Equations (11.65) and (11.70) are similar, we should expect the overall delay in the parallel-node case to be far less than the one for the in-series case, owing to the same reason.

11.6.2   Jackson's Theorem

One of the most frequently applied theorems in analyzing a network of queues is known as *Jackson's theorem*, which has several segments and phases. Here, we emphasize the most applicable phase, known as "open networks of queues." The essence of Jackson's theorem is applied to situations in which a packet visits a particular queue more than once. In such conditions, the network typically contains *loops*, or *feedbacks*. With Jackson's theorem, by having the utilization of the system, we can derive the probability that k packets are in the system, $P[K(t) = k]$, knowing that the system follows a rule such the $M/M/1$ queueing model.

Modeling Feedback in Networks

Figure 11.22 shows a basic cascaded queueing network, including a simple $M/M/1$ queueing element with a server in which simple feedback is implemented. Packets arrive at the left at rate α, passing through a queue and server with service rate μ, and are partially fed back to the system at rate α_1. Thus, this queueing architecture allows packets to visit the queue more than once by circulating them back to the system. This system is a model of many practical networking systems. One good example is switching systems that multicast packets step by step, using a recycling technique discussed in later chapters. In Figure 11.22, if the probability that a packet is fed back to the input is P, it is obvious that the total arrival rate to the queue, or λ, is

$$\lambda = \alpha + p\lambda. \qquad (11.71)$$

Equation (11.71) demonstrates that the equivalent of the system surrounded by the dashed line can be configured as shown in Figure 11.22. Since $\alpha_1 = p\lambda$, we can combine this equation and Equation (11.71) and derive a relationship between λ and α as

$$\lambda = \frac{\alpha}{1 - p}. \qquad (11.72)$$

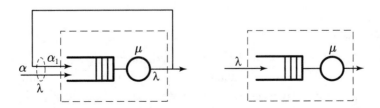

Figure 11.22   A feedback system and its simplified equivalent

The utilization of the simplified system denoted by $\rho = \dfrac{\lambda}{\mu}$ is, clearly:

$$\rho = \frac{\alpha}{\mu(1-p)}. \tag{11.73}$$

By having the utilization of the system, we can derive the probability that k packets are in the system, $P[K(t) = k]$, knowing that the system follows the $M/M/1$ rule:

$$P[K(t) = k] = (1-\rho)\rho^k = \frac{\mu(1-p) - \alpha}{\mu(1-p)} \left(\frac{\alpha}{\mu(1-p)} \right)^k. \tag{11.74}$$

The expected number of packets in the system, $E[K(t)]$, can be derived by using the $M/M/1$ property:

$$E[K(t)] = \frac{\rho}{1-\rho} = \frac{\alpha}{\mu(1-p) - \alpha}. \tag{11.75}$$

Using Little's formula, we can now estimate the total queueing and service delay that a packet should expect. Let $E[T_u]$ be the expected delay for the equivalent unit shown in Figure 11.22 with lump sum arrival rate λ. Let $E[T_f]$ be the expected delay for the system with arrival rate α:

$$E[T_u] = \frac{E[K(t)]}{\lambda} = \frac{\alpha}{\lambda(\mu(1-p) - \alpha)} \tag{11.76}$$

and

$$E[T_f] = \frac{E[K(t)]}{\alpha} = \frac{1}{\mu(1-p) - \alpha}. \tag{11.77}$$

Note that we should always see the inequity $E[T_u] < E[T_f]$, as expected.

Open Networks

Figure 11.23 shows a generic model of Jackson's theorem when the system is open. In this figure, unit i of an m-unit system is modeled with an arrival rate sum of λ_i and a service rate μ_i. Unit i may receive an independent external traffic of α_i. The unit can receive feedback and feed-forward traffic from $i - 1$ other units. At the output of this

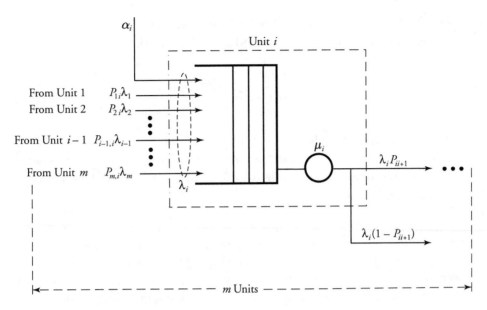

Figure 11.23   Generalization of a node model for Jackson's theorem

unit, the traffic may proceed forward with probability P_{ii+1} or may leave the system with probability $1 - P_{ii+1}$. The total arrival rate, λ_i, is then

$$\lambda_i = \alpha_i + \sum_{j=1}^{m} P_{ji}\lambda_j. \tag{11.78}$$

The instantaneous total number of packets in all m nodes, $\mathbf{K(t)}$, is a vector consisting of the number of packets in every individual node and is expressed by

$$\mathbf{K(t)} = \{K_1(t), K_2(t), \cdots, K_m(t)\}. \tag{11.79}$$

The probability that k packets are in the system is the joint probabilities of numbers of packets in m units:

$$P[K(t) = k] = \prod_{i=1}^{m} P[K_i(t) = k_i]. \tag{11.80}$$

The expected number of packets in all units is obtained by

$$E[K(t)] = E[K_1(t)] + E[K_2(t)] + \cdots + E[K_m(t)]. \tag{11.81}$$

Finally, the most significant factor used in evaluating a system of queueing nodes, total delay measured at stage i, is calculated by applying Little's formula:

$$E[T] = \frac{\sum_{i=1}^{m} E[K_i(t)]}{\alpha_i}. \tag{11.82}$$

We assume that α_i is the only input to the entire system. In practice, there may be other inputs to the system, in which case the total delay can be obtained by using *superposition*. Equations (11.80) through (11.82) are the essence of Jackson's theorem on open queueing networks.

Example.   Figure 11.24 shows a cascade of two $M/M/1$ nodes in which packets arrive at rate $\alpha = 10,000$ packets per second. Service rates of both nodes are $\mu_1 = \mu_2 = 200,000$ packets per second. At the output of node 1, packets exit with a probability of $p = 0.10$; otherwise, they are driven into node 2 and then fed back to node 1. Find the estimated delay incurred on a packet, including the delay from circulations.

Solution.   We first calculate the arrival rates to two nodes, λ_1 and λ_2:

$$\lambda_1 = \lambda_2 + \alpha$$

and

$$\lambda_2 = (1 - p)\lambda_1.$$

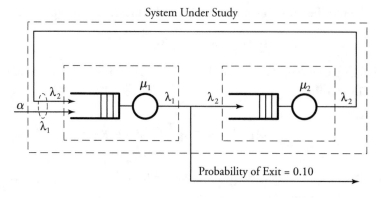

Figure 11.24 Two communication nodes with feedback

By applying the values of $\alpha = 10,000$ and $p = 0.10$, this set of equations results in $\lambda_1 = 100,000$ and $\lambda_2 = 90,000$. The utilization for each system can now be derived as $\rho_1 = \lambda_1/\mu_1 = 0.5$ and $\rho_2 = \lambda_2/\mu_2 = 0.45$. According to $M/M/1$ discipline results obtained in the previous section, the average number of packets in each system is

$$E[K_1(t)] = \frac{\rho_1}{1 - \rho_1} = 1$$

and

$$E[K_2(t)] = \frac{\rho_2}{1 - \rho_2} = 0.82.$$

The delay is

$$E[T_{u1}] = \frac{E[K_1(t)]}{\lambda_1} = 0.01 \text{ ms},$$

$$E[T_{u2}] = \frac{E[K_2(t)]}{\lambda_2} = 0.009 \text{ ms},$$

and

$$E[T_f] = \frac{E[K_1(t)] + E[K_2(t)]}{\alpha} = 0.18 \text{ ms}.$$

11.7 Summary

This chapter presented the mathematical foundation for basic analysis of computer networks developing packet queues, using Markovian and non-Markovian cases. Single queues are the simplest models for the analysis of a single node in a communication network. *Little's theorem* relates the average number of packets and the average time per packet in the system to the arrival rate.

Birth-and-death processes can help identify the activity within a packet queue. Queueing node models in several scenarios were presented: finite versus infinite queueing capacity, one server versus several servers, and Markovian versus non-Markovian systems. The non-Markovian models are further classified into systems with non-Markovian services and systems with non-Markovian traffic arrivals. In a non-Markovian service model, we assume independent interarrivals and service times, which leads to the $M/G/1$ system.

Burke's theorem is the fundamental tool for analyzing networks of packet queues. By Burke's theorem, we can present solutions to a network of several queues. We applied Burke's theorem to in-series queueing nodes and in-parallel queueing nodes. *Jackson's theorem* provides a practical solution to situations in which a packet visits a particular queue more than once through *loops* or *feedback*. Open Jackson networks have a product-form solution for the joint queue length distribution in the steady state. We can derive several performance measures of interest, because nodes can be treated independently. Jackson networks with no external arrivals or departures forming a closed network also have a product-form solution for the steady-state joint queue length distribution.

The next two chapters present the architectures of switches and routers and their internal parts. The structure of routing devices in Chapter 12 requires some analytical approaches that understanding some parts of the current chapter would help. The extended topics of routing devices are presented in Chapter 13.

11.8   Exercises

1. Each buffered output line of a data demultiplexer receives a block of packets every 20 μs and keeps them in the buffer. A sequencer checks each block for any packet misordering and corrects it, if necessary. It takes 10 μs to check for any packet misordering at each block and 30 μs to make the right sequence if there is any packet misordering. Suppose that a buffer is initially empty and that the numbers of misorderings in the first 15 blocks are 2, 4, 0, 0, 1, 4, 3, 5, 2, 4, 0, 2, 5, 2, 1.

   (a) Illustrate a plot of queueing behavior for the number of packet blocks in a demultiplexer's output line as a function of time.

   (b) Find the mean number of packet blocks in an output line's queue.

   (c) Determine the percentage of the time that a buffer is not empty.

2. A buffered router presented by an $M/M/1$ model receives Markovian traffic with a mean packet-arrival rate of λ=40 packets/s and an overall utilization of $\rho = 0.9$.

   (a) Calculate the average number of packets in the queueing system.

   (b) Determine the average time a packet remains in the queueing system.

   (c) Sketch the Markov chain of the node's process.

3. For an $M/M/1$ system with service rate μ, the distribution of service time is exponential and is equal to $e^{-\mu t}$. In other words, by letting T be a random variable to represent the time until the next packet departure, $P[T > t] = e^{-\mu t}$. Now, consider an $M/M/a$ system with i servers busy at a time, equal service rate μ per server, and a similar definition of random variable T.

   (a) Show T in terms of $T_1, T_2, \ldots$, where T_i is a random variable representing the time until the next packet departure in server i.

   (b) Find the distribution of service time, $P[T > t]$.

4. Consider a network node represented by an $M/M/1$ model.

   (a) Find the probability that the number of packets in the node is less than a given number k, $P[K(t) < k]$. This is normally used to estimate the threshold time of the network node to reach a certain load.

   (b) If we require that $P[K(t) < 20] = 0.9904$, determine the switching service rate if the arrival rate to this node is 300 packets per second.

5. For an $M/M/1$ queueing system:

   (a) Find $P[K(t) \geq k]$, where k is a constant number.

   (b) Determine the maximum allowable arrival rate in a system with service rate μ, if $P[K(t) \geq 60] = 0.01$ is required.

6. Consider a network node modeled by an $M/M/1$ queue in which a packet's willingness to join the queue is impacted by the queue size. A packet that finds $i \in \{0, 1, \cdots\}$ other packets in the system joins the queue with probability $\frac{1}{i+1}$ and otherwise leaves immediately. If the arrival rate is λ and the mean service rate is μ:

   (a) Sketch the state-transition diagram for this system.

   (b) Develop and solve the balance equations for the equilibrium probabilities p_i.

   (c) Show that a steady-state distribution exists.

   (d) Find the utilization of the server.

   (e) Find the throughput, the average number of packets in the system.

   (f) Find the average response time for a packet that decides to join.

7. In an $M/M/2$ communication node, packets arrive according to a Poisson process of rate 18 per second. The system has two parallel crossbar switches, and each switch spends an exponentially distributed amount of time with mean 100 ms to process a packet.

   (a) Find the probability that an arriving packet must wait to be processed.

   (b) Find the mean number of packets in the system

   (c) Find the mean time a packet spends in the system.

   (d) Find the probability that more than 50 packets are in the system.

8. Consider a high-speed node of a data network having parallel-plane switching fabrics, in which six packets can be processed at a time without any prior waiting time ($M/M/6/6$). Assume that the arrival rate is 100 packets/sec and that the mean service rate is 20 packets/sec.

   (a) What is the probability of blocking a packet?
   (b) How many more switches are required to reduce the blocking probability to 50 percent more?

9. When a wireless user moves to a new cell, a handoff request for a new channel is needed. A handoff can be modeled with traffic type i assumption. When all the channels are used or none are available, the handoff call has to be terminated or blocked in the new base station. Classify the traffic into k types. Each call uses only one channel, and each channel uses only one radio channel. The handoff process at the new base station is modeled using an $M/M/c/c$ system: random interarrival call time, exponential holding time of a channel, c channels, and c handoff calls. Let λ_i be the handoff request rate for traffic type $i \in \{0, 1, ..., k\}$, and let $1/\mu_i$ be the mean channel-exchange time for traffic type i. When j channels are busy, handoff calls depart at rate $j\mu_i$. When all c_i channels are in use, the channel-exchange rate is $c_i\mu_i$. In this case, any new arriving handoff calls are blocked.

   (a) Show a continuous-time Markov chain for the model.
   (b) Derive a set of global balance equations.
   (c) If P_0 is the probability that no channel exchange is requested for traffic type i, find P_j, the probability that j channel exchanges are requested for traffic type i.
   (d) Find the handoff blocking probability, P_{c_i}.

10. Continuing the previous exercise, we want to obtain some statistical performance-evaluation results for the handoff.

    (a) Assume that the total available numbers of channels (c_i) are 10, 50, and 100, respectively; plot the handoff blocking probability with a choice of three mean holding times of 10 ms, 20 ms, and 30 ms.
    (b) Discuss the results obtained in the plots.

11. Consider a router containing four networked queueing nodes, each represented by an $M/M/1$ model, as shown in Figure 11.25. Any percentage number shown on each branch expresses the share of the branch from the traffic coming to

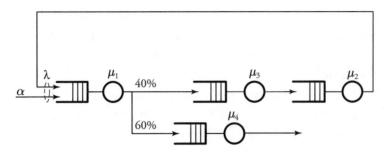

Figure 11.25   Exercise 11 network example

its branching point. The arrival rate to the system is $\alpha = 20$ packets per ms. The service rates in these nodes are $\mu_1 = 100$, $\mu_2 = 100$, $\mu_3 = 20$, and $\mu_4 = 30$ packets per ms, respectively.

(a) Find the arrival rate to each of the four queueing units.

(b) Find the average number of packets in each unit.

(c) Find the average delay for a packet from its arrival to the system until it exits the system.

12. Figure 11.26 shows a network of two routers modeled by two $M/M/1$ systems. The arrival rate to this network is α. Outgoing packets are distributed over the outgoing link and feedback paths with the probabilities indicated on the figure. The arrival rate to the system is $\alpha = 200$ packets per second, and the service rates are $\mu_1 = 4$ and $\mu_2 = 3$ packets per ms.

(a) Find the arrival rate to each of the two queueing units.

(b) Find the average number of packets in each queueing unit.

(c) Find the average total delay experienced by a packet from entering until exiting the network.

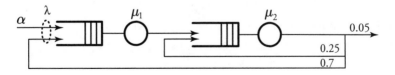

Figure 11.26   Exercise 12 network example

13. A network of four switching nodes is modeled by four *M/M/*1 systems, as shown in Figure 11.27. The arrival rate to the network is $\alpha = 100$ packets per second. The outgoing packets get distributed over the outgoing link and feedback paths with probabilities given on the figure.

    (a) Find the arrival rate to each of the four queueing units.
    (b) Find the average number of packets in each unit.
    (c) Find the average system delay for a packet.

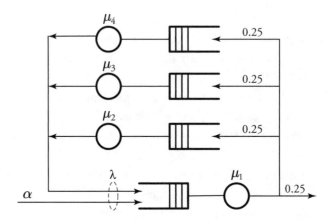

Figure 11.27   Exercise 13 network example

14. A network of six switching nodes is modeled by six *M/M/*1 systems, as shown in Figure 11.28. Each of the five parallel nodes receives a fair share of traffic. The arrival rate to the system is $\alpha = 200$ packets per second, the service rate for the single node is $\mu_0 = 100$ packets per ms, and the service rate for each of the five parallel nodes is $\mu_i = 10$ packets per ms.

    (a) Find the arrival rate to each of the six queueing units.
    (b) Find the average number of packets in each unit.
    (c) Find the average system delay for a packet.

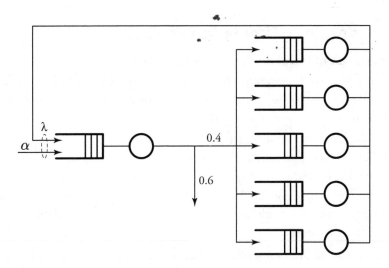

Figure 11.28   Exercise 14 network example

15. A network of four routers is modeled by four $M/M/1$ systems, as shown in Figure 11.29. Outgoing packets get distributed over the outgoing link and feedback paths with the probabilities indicated on the figure. The arrival rate to the system is $\alpha = 800$ packets per second, and the service rates are $\mu_1 = 10$, $\mu_2 = 12$, $\mu_3 = 14$, and $\mu_4 = 16$ packets per ms.

   (a) Find the arrival rate to each of the four queueing units.

   (b) Find the average number of packets in each unit.

   (c) Find the average system delay for a packet.

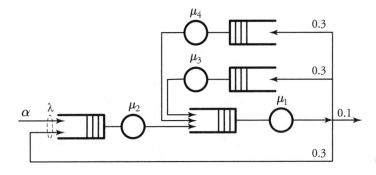

Figure 11.29   Exercise 15 network example

11.9   Computer Simulation Project

1. *Simulation of a Queue/Server System.* Either use a network simulation tool or write a computer program from scratch to simulate an input buffer of a router. Consider the capacity of the buffer to be $K = 64$ buffer slots; and each buffer slot can fit in only a packet of size 1,000 bytes.

   (a) Construct and simulate 1 bit of memory.
   (b) Extend your program to construct 1,000 bytes of memory.
   (c) Further extend your program to simulate all 64 buffer slots.
   (d) Dynamically assign packets of different sizes every 1 ms, and send out the packet every t seconds. Measure the performance metrics of this buffer given different values of t.

2. *Simulation of Queueing Networks.* Use a network simulation tool and extend the simulation in project 1 to two connected buffers: one with $K_1 = 64$ buffer slots and the other one with $K_2 = 128$ buffer slots. Each slot can fit only in a packet of size 1,000 bytes. Dynamically assign packets of different sizes every 1 ms, and send out the packet every t_1 seconds from the first buffer and every t_2 seconds from the second buffer: packet of size 1,000 bytes.

   (a) Construct and simulate each of the two buffers individually.
   (b) Integrate these two buffers and measure the performance metrics such as average packet delay and average queueing length of both buffers together, given different values of t_1 and t_2.

CHAPTER 12

Advanced Router and Switch Architectures

The obvious compelling reason why we need to profoundly know about the internal structure of advanced routers and switches is that the Internet, and especially its backbone, consist of structured advanced and high-speed switches and routers. In this chapter, we proceed to learn the architectures of advanced switches and routers. Recall that Chapter 2 presented an overview of switching and routing devices. This chapter presents in greater detail how the components of such devices are integrated with each other. We especially analyze several core switching segments of these devices and introduce several topologies. This chapter explores the following topics:

- *Overview of router architecture*
- *Input port processor* (IPP)
- *Output port processor* (OPP)
- *Central controller*
- *Switch fabrics*
- *Multicasting packets in routers*

This chapter begins with an overview of the typical advanced router architecture. A general block diagram of routers is discussed in this section. The *input port processor* (IPP) as the first main building block of routers is presented next. We will see how significant the role of IPPs in processing of packets is. Next, the *output port processor* (OPP) as the interfacing processor to output links is described. For both IPP and OPP, the *quality-of-service* (QoS) provisioning unit will be independently presented in the following chapter, Chapter 13.

The *central controller,* discussed next, is the brain of a router or a switch and controls the functionality of switch fabrics, IPP, and OPP. Central controllers are also in charge of congestion control, which is one of the most crucial operations in computer networks.

A considerably large portion of this chapter is dedicated to *switch fabrics.* A switch fabric is the core switching engine in routing and switching devices. First, switch fabrics' classification and characteristics are presented. Then, certain industry commonly used types of nonblocking switch fabrics such as *crossbar* and *Clos* topologies and their building blocks are presented. *Concentration-based* and *expansion-based* switches—two special-purpose switch fabrics—are investigated next. A quite different approach for switching in *time domain* uses shared memory, without using any switch elements. Switch fabric techniques that offer better performance include the use of buffering, combined networks, and parallel-plane switching fabrics.

At the end of this chapter, we extend the topic of Chapter 6 and learn the packet multicasting techniques, this time at the router and switch fabric level. The reader will learn here how a packet becomes copied at the lowest hardware level.

12.1   Overview of Router Architecture

Routers are the building blocks of wide area networks. Figure 12.1 shows an abstract model of a router as a layer 3 device. Packets arrive at n input ports and are routed out from n output ports. The system consists of five main parts:

- *Network interface card* (NIC). NICs are physical link interfaces to the body of a router.

- *Input port processor* (IPP). An IPP is a processing unit in a router that is responsible for receiving, buffering, and interpreting packets arriving from outside. An IPP also finds the best route for a packet according to its routing table.

- *Output port processor* (OPP). An OPP is a processing unit in a router that receives already processed packets and forwards them to output ports.

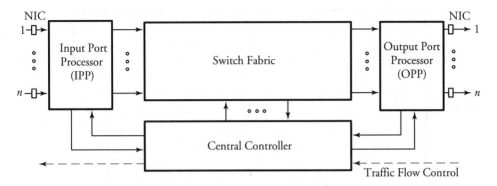

Figure 12.1   Overview of a typical router

- *Central controller.* The central controller is the control heart of a router and authorizes the operation of switch fabric, coordinates functions of the IPP and OPP, and processes the traffic flow control for a router.

- *Switch fabric.* A switch fabric is a network of switching elements to interconnect input ports to output ports of a router.

Since we already studied the functionality of NICs in Chapters 2 and 3, we begin our discussion immediately with the IPP in the next section.

12.2   Input Port Processor (IPP)

Input and *output port processors*, as interfaces to the switch fabric, are commercially implemented together in *router line cards*, which contain some of the tasks of the physical and data link layers. The functionality of the data link layer is implemented in network interface cards (NICs) in a separate chip in the IPP, which also provides a buffer to match the speed between the input and the switch fabric. Switch performance is limited by processing capability, storage elements, and bus bandwidth. The processing capability dictates the maximum rate of the switch. Owing to the speed mismatch between the rate at which a packet arrives on the switch and the processing speed of the switch fabric, input packet rate dictates the amount of required buffering storage. The bus bandwidth determines the time taken for a packet to be transferred between the input and output ports.

An *input port processor* (IPP) typically consists of several main modules, as shown in Figure 12.2. These modules are the *packet parser, packet partitioner, input buffer, multicast scheduler, routing table, forwarding table* and *packet encapsulator*, and a separate

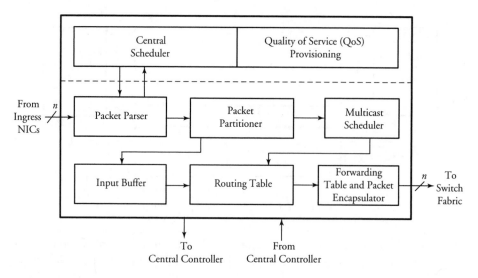

Figure 12.2 Overview of a typical input port processor (IPP) in switches and routers

central scheduler and *quality of service* (QoS) unit. The central scheduler and QoS units are quality-based supervising components in the IPP and are presented separately in Chapter 13. The remaining components of the IPP are described in the following sections.

12.2.1 Packet Parser

A *packet parser* is a packet analyzer or examiner that parses packet headers in order to decide how packets should be processed. The process of examining, identifying, and extracting certain fields of packet headers is called *parsing*. Packet parsing is one way of packet classification required for identifying flows, and implementing quality of service (QoS) goals. The challenge for any switch or router equipped with a parser receiving numerous packets per second is to swiftly analyze them and extract certain fields of their headers used in forwarding decisions of the router.

Packet parsing is a main bottleneck in high-speed networks due to the varieties of lengths, formats, and complexities of packet headers. Guiding packet inspection can be implemented deeper in security policies or even with end-to-end communication protocols. For example, consider arriving packets with multiple headers, each packet carrying information about protocols, such as HTTP, and VLANs in addition to other headers. The process of parsing packets may vary depending on the type of parsing. For example, a router may first examine the destination IP address of an incoming packet to decide where to send the packet next, while a firewall compares several packet fields against its internal list to decide whether to drop a packet. The general step-by-step packet parser algorithm in a typical router is as follows:

Begin Packet Parsing Algorithm

1. **Set** $i = 1$
2. **For** header of packet i:
   - Identify the type of each header
   - Identify the locations of header fields
   - Indicate the length of the current header
   - Indicate the next header
3. Extract the next-header field and use it for forwarding table lookup.
4. **If** the payload field is reached, stop the process.
   Else $i=i+1$, and **Go to** step 2 ■

Parsing a packet requires identifying packet headers "in sequence" before extracting and processing specific fields. Each header of a packet typically contains a "pointer field" to express the next header attached the current header. Thus, in step 2 of the packet parsing algorithm a parser identifies the first header by identifying the type and locations of the first header fields, and by indicating header's length and the next header field. Typically, the type of the first header in an incoming packet is standard such as an Ethernet header and thus is known by the parser. One of the observations to make in this step is that a parser must run at least identically to the link rate in order to support continuous and seamless back-to-back packets entering the IPP.

Also note that some protocol headers do not have any next-header field. Thus they require a look-up table or reading the entire header to reach to the next header. Step 3 of the algorithm extracts the pointer to the next header, which is typically shown in protocols as the *next-header field*. For example, when a parser inspects the first header of a packet, which is the link layer header, it finds a field identifying that the next header is the IPv6 header. Or when the parser further inspects the IPv6 header, it finds the next header to be the UDP header. Clearly, by extracting these fields, a router can use them in its look-up table for decision making.

12.2.2   Packet Partitioner

The *packet partitioner* converts packets to smaller sizes, called *packet parts*. The motivation for partitioning packets inside a switching device is that large packets may not fit in the buffer slots of the device. Packet partitioning is an internal process in

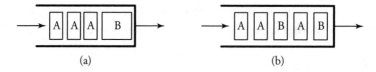

Figure 12.3   Packet buffering: (a) without partitioning, (b) with partitioning

a device and is not subject to standardization. It is extremely important not to be confused here that by packet parts as a result of packet partitioning, we refer only to the parts of packets used inside a router, and that these packet "parts" are different from packet "fragments" occurring at end hosts identified in IP headers. Recall also a similar application of the packet partitioning process that occurs in typical LANs, in which large packets must be partitioned into smaller frames.

Thus, large packets in a router or switch must be partitioned into smaller parts and then buffered at the input port interface of a router, as buffer slots are usually only 512 bytes long. These smaller packet parts are then reassembled at the output port processor (OPP) after processing them in the switching fabric. Figure 12.3 shows a simple packet partitioning at the input buffer side of a router where a larger packet B has been partitioned into two parts. It is always desirable to find the optimum packet size that minimizes the delay.

12.2.3   Input Buffer

An *input buffer* is a large storage system in a switching or routing device that holds incoming packets temporarily until the device becomes ready to process the packets. Input buffers are memory units in nature. To increase memory performance, queue sizes are fixed to reduce control logic. Since packets can arrive and leave the network in different order, a memory monitor is also necessary to keep track of which locations in memory are free for use. Borrowing a concept from operating system principles, a free-memory list serves as a memory manager implemented by a stack of pointers. Input buffers are tightly related to the *central scheduler* and *quality of service* (QoS) unit by which the disciplines of packet buffering are determined. As a result of this relationship, the detailed buffering disciplines are described in Chapter 13 where scheduling and QoS of routers are explained in detail.

12.2.4   Routing Table (IPv4 and IPv6)

The *routing table* is a look-up table containing all available destination addresses and the corresponding switch output port. An external algorithm fills this routing look-up table. Thus, the purpose of the routing table is to look up an entry corresponding to the destination address of the incoming packet and to provide the output network port. As soon as a routing decision is made, all the information should be saved in the routing table. When a packet enters an IPP, the destination port of the switch fabric and therefore the router should be determined and selected based on the destination address of the incoming packet. This destination port is a physical port and needs to be appended to the incoming packet as part of the internal switch header. When a packet carrying a destination address arrives from a given link i, its destination address is used to identify the corresponding output port j.

Figure 12.4 shows an example of routing tables at routers R1 and R2. Each routing table has two entry parts: entries for IPv4 flows and entries for IPv6 flows. Each entry is identified by an *entry number,* which is merely used to indicate the sequential organization of the table's contents. Assume that host 2 with IPv4 address 182.15.0.7 is the destination of a packet arriving at input port 1 of R1 from host 1. The routing table of R1 stores the best-possible path for each destination. Assume that in a given time, this destination is found to have the best match with entry row 5. The routing table then indicates that output port 2 of R1 is the right output to go to. The table makes the routing decision based on the estimated cost of the link, which is also

R1 Routing Table			
IPv4			
Entry Number	Destination IP Address	Port Number	Estimated Cost
4	143.28.3.0/21	1	32
5	182.15.0.0/22	2	56
6	155.76.2.0/22	2	56
7	131.46.0.0/24	1	32
IPv6			
Entry Number	Destination IP Address	Port Number	Estimated Cost
24	1001:AA1A:11/80	3	5
25	FF2:48:0:D3/60	3	5
26	1001:DB8:8:D3/60	3	5
27	33:CC:99:43:D3/71	4	44

R2 Routing Table			
IPv4			
Entry Number	Destination IP Address	Port Number	Estimated Cost
41	135.18.5.0/21	1	3
42	182.15.0.0/22	2	0
43	197.76.2.0/23	1	3
44	171.55.0.0/21	1	3
IPv6			
Entry Number	Destination IP Address	Port Number	Estimated Cost
114	1001:AA1A:11/80	3	44
115	FF2:48:0:D3/60	3	44
116	1001:DB8:8:D3/60	3	44
117	BB30:5:5:91:D3/51	3	44

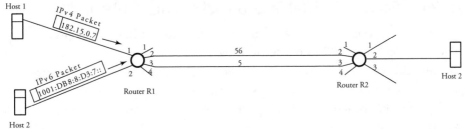

Figure 12.4   Routing tables at routers

stated to be 56 in the corresponding entry. The cost of each link, as described in Chapter 5, is a measure of the load on each link. When the packet arrives at router R2, this switch performs the same procedure to find host 2.

In this figure, we notice that a packet with destination IPv6 address 1001:DB8:8:D3:7:: is arriving at port 2 of R1. Assume for the same given time as the one for previous packet, this destination is found to have the best match in entry row 26. The routing table then indicates that output port 3 of R1 is the right output and with the estimated link cost of 5 in the corresponding entry. We notice the interesting situation that router R2 tries to isolate IPv4 traffic from IPv6 traffic by assigning output ports 1 and 2 to IPv4 flows and port 3 to IPv6 flows.

12.2.5 Multicast Scheduler

A *multicast scheduler* is necessary for copying packets when multiple copies of a packet are expected to be made on a switching node. The process of multicast scheduling is implemented primarily by using a memory module for storage. The actual packet copying according to *multicast techniques and protocols* is implemented in the switch fabric of a router, described in the corresponding section of this chapter. Note that multicast techniques and protocols were described in a greater detail in Chapter 6.

From the scheduling standpoint, the copying function can easily be achieved by appending a counter field to memory locations to signify the needed number of copies of that location. The memory module is used to store packets and then duplicate multicast packets by holding them in memory until all instances of the multicast packet have exited IPP. Writing to memory takes two passes for a multicast packet and only one pass for a unicast packet. In order to keep track of how many copies a multicast packet needs, the packet counter in the memory module must be augmented after the multicast packet has been written to memory. Each entry in the memory module consists of a valid bit, a counter value, and memory data.

12.2.6 Forwarding Table and Packet Encapsulator

A *forwarding table* is a database local to the router and is different from the routing table. In order for an IPP to be able to forward packets to the switch fabric, a forwarding table must hold a list of switch fabric output ports. The *packet encapsulator* performs the forwarding table lookups and encapsulates an incoming packet into a local header that contains the appropriate switch fabric output port number. This local header will be removed from the packet in the OPP. The *serial-to-parallel multiplexing* unit converts an incoming serial bytestream into a fully parallel data stream.

This unit also processes the incoming IP header to determine whether the packet is unicast or multicast and extracts the type-of-service field. Once the full packet is received, it is stored in memory. The packet encapsulation unit formats the incoming packet with a header before forwarding the packet to the crossbar.

12.3   Output Port Processor (OPP)

Implementing *output port processors* in switches includes parallel-to-serial multiplexing, and the main buffer, local packet resequencer, global packet resequencer, error checker, and packet reassembler, as shown in Figure 12.5. Similar to an IPP, an OPP also contributes to congestion control. *Parallel-to-serial multiplexing* converts the parallel-packet format into serial-packet format.

12.3.1   Output Buffer

The *output buffer* unit serves as the OPP central shift register. The purpose of this buffer is to control the rate of the outgoing packets, which impacts the quality of service. After collecting signals serially from the switch fabric, the buffer forwards packets to resequencers. The queue runs on a clock driven by the link interface between the switch and an external link. This buffer must have features that support real-time and non-real-time data.

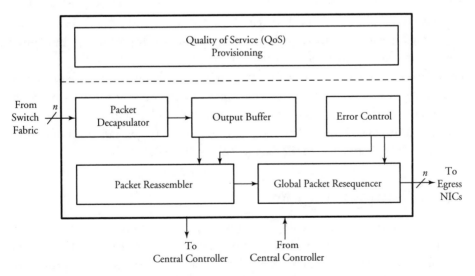

Figure 12.5   Overview of a typical output port processor (OPP) in switches and routers

12.3.2　Reassembler and Resequencer

The output port processor receives a stream of packet parts and has to identify and sort out all the related ones. The OPP reassembles them into a single packet, based on the information obtained from the relevant local header field. For this process, the OPP must be able to handle the arrival of individual packet parts at any time and in any order. Packet parts may arrive out of order for many reasons. Misordered packets can occur because individual packet parts, composed of a fairly large number of interconnections with different delay times, are independently routed through the switch fabric.

A *packet reassembler* unit is used to combine parts of IP packets. Once again, recall that packet partitioning is a different process than the packet fragmentation happening at end hosts identified in IP headers. This unit resequences received packet fragments before transmitting them to outside the OPP, updates the total-length field of the IP header, and decapsulates all the local headers. The resequencer's internal buffer stores misordered parts until a complete sequence of packets is formed and obtained. The in-sequence packet parts are reassembled and transmitted out. A *global packet resequencer* uses this same procedure to enforce another reordering, this time on sequences, not packet parts, of packets that belong to a single user or source.

12.3.3　Error Control

When a user sends a packet or a frame, a *cyclic redundancy check* (CRC) field is appended to the packet. The CRC is generated from an algorithm and is based on the data being carried in the packet. The CRC algorithms divide the message by another fixed-binary number in a polynomial form, producing a *checksum* as the remainder. The message receiver can perform the same division and compare the remainder with the received checksum. The *error checker* applies a series of error-checking processes on packets to ensure that no errors are in the packets and creates a stream of bits of a given length, called frames. A frame produces a *checksum bit*, called a frame check sequence, which is attached to the data when transmitted.

12.4　Central Controller

The *central controller* of a switching or routing device makes decisions leading to the transmission of packets to the requested output(s) of the device. The detail of the controller is illustrated in Figure 12.6. The central controller receives encapsulated packets from the IPP, but only the local headers of packets, made in the IPP, are

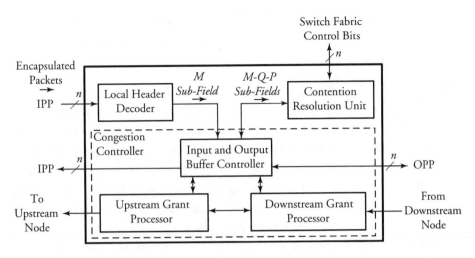

Figure 12.6   Overview of a typical central controller in a switch or router

processed in the central controller. In the central controller, the first unit is the *local header decoder* that reads the local output port addresses of the switch fabric from the encapsulated packets. Remember from the IPP discussion that such local output port addresses are assigned to packets for internal routing purposes only.

For each arriving packet, the header decoder reads and converts the local address to a bit vector, called the M sub-field, and appends it to its packet. The M sub-field is a bit vector indicating the information pertaining to the replication of a packet for multicasting purposes so that each bit of "1" in the M sub-field represents a request for the copy of that packet made for the corresponding switch fabric output. For example, the M sub-field = 0010 means the case is unicast, and the packet needs to be sent to the third output of the device; or the M sub-field = 1010 means the case is multicast and the packet needs to be copied and sent to the first and the third output of the device. Each packet with the inclusion of the M sub-field is then sent to the *input and output buffer controller* and thereby to the *contention resolution unit* for arbitration with other packets, discussed next.

12.4.1   Contention Resolution Unit

We learned in the preceding section that each encapsulated packet with the inclusion of the M sub-field arrives at the *input and output buffer controller*. In order for packets requesting the same output port of the switch fabric to be able to arbitrate for a desired output port, the input and output buffer controller attaches two additional sub-fields, the Q and P sub-fields. Once these two sub-fields are added to the local header of a packet, the packet with M-Q-P is sent to the *contention resolution unit*. These two new sub-fields are:

- Q sub-field. This sub-field is a bit vector indicating the global quality of service (QoS) assigned to a packet. This QoS value is assigned by various entities such as an Internet service provider or by various authorized servers. This sub-field is used as one of the factors of priority by the central controller to decide which packet must win a contention based on a higher Q sub-field.

- P sub-field. This sub-field is a bit vector indicating similar information as the Q sub-field but the value of P sub-field is created locally in the device based on the priority assigned to a packet when a packet loses a contention. Thus, any time a packet loses a contention, its P sub-field becomes incremented, and thereby the losing packet has a higher priority in the next round of contention.

The packet with the M-Q-P field request vector enters the *contention resolution unit*. The contention resolution unit consists of an array of *arbitration elements*. There the packet uses the Q-P part of the M-Q-P field to compete with other packets. Each packet in one column of an arbitration array contends with other packets on a shared bus to access the switch fabric output associated with that column. After a packet wins the contention, its identity (buffer index number) is transmitted to an OPP. This identity and the buffer-control bit explained earlier are also transferred to the switching fabric, signaling it to release the packet. This mechanism ensures that a losing packet in the competition remains in the buffer. The buffer-control unit then raises the priority of the losing packet by 1 so that it can participate in the next round of contention with a higher chance of winning. This process is repeated until, eventually, the packet wins.

Example. Suppose two packets A and B each arrives from one of the inputs of a crossbar switch fabric, and each has an M-Q-P field set for contending to exit an output. Assume the M sub-fields of both packets are identical and each is 00001000. In this case, there should be a contention between the two packets. The Q-P sub-fields for packets A and B are 00110111,0000 and 00110100,1000 respectively. Determine which packet wins the contention.

Solution. As the M sub-fields of both packets are identical, this clearly indicates that the fifth output port of the device is requested by each packet. Therefore, the winning packet between the two, determined based on the Q-P sub-fields, leaves the switch fabric and the losing packet contends later with other packets to exit the router. In spite of the fact that the P sub-field of packet B (1000) is larger than the one for packet A (0000), in this case, packet A wins the contention since its Q sub-field (000110111) is larger than the one for packet B (00110100). Starting from the most significant bit, packet A wins the contention on its seventh bit of the contention resolution process.

12.4.2   Congestion Controller

The *congestion controller* module shields the switching node from any disorders in the traffic flow. Congestion can be controlled in several ways. Sending a reverse-warning packet to the upstream node to avoid exceeding traffic flow is one common technology installed in the structure of advanced switching systems. Realistically, spacing between incoming packets is irregular. This irregularity may cause congestion in many cases. Congestion control was explained in Chapters 5 and 8.

The identities of winning packets in the contention resolution process are transmitted to the switch fabric if traffic flow control signals from downstream neighboring nodes are active. The *upstream grant processor* in turn generates a corresponding set of traffic flow control signals, which are sent to the upstream neighboring nodes. This signal is an indication that the switch is prepared to receive a packet on the upstream node. This way, network congestion comes under control.

12.5   Switch Fabric

The switching function in switches and routers takes place in the *switch fabric*. In the switch fabric of a router, packets are routed from input ports to the desired output ports. A packet can also be multicast to more than one output. Finally, in the output port processors, packets are buffered and resequenced in order to avoid packet misordering. In addition, a number of other important processes and functions take place in each of the mentioned blocks. The switching structure depends on the needs of network operation, available technology, and the required capacity.

A switch fabric can be either a one-piece switch or an interconnected network of smaller switching units. Several factors can be used to characterize switching systems: buffering, complexity, capability of multipoint connections, speed, performance, cost, reliability, fault tolerance, and scalability. Here, we focus on the topology of the interconnection switching systems to form a switch fabric. The key factors for classifying switching fabrics are

- *Single path* versus *multiple paths*. A single-path fabric has exactly one route between each input port and output port. However, this property can be a source of traffic congestion and traffic blocking. In a multipath network, any connection can be established through more than one path.

- *Single stage* versus *multiple stages*. In a single-stage network, a connection is established through one stage of switching; in a multistage network, a packet must pass through several switching stages. In a multistage network, the number of stages often grows with increasing network size.

- *Blocking* versus *nonblocking*. A switch fabric is said to be blocking if an input port cannot be connected to an unused output port. Otherwise, the switching network is nonblocking.

- *Buffered* or *unbuffered*. Buffers may be used to reduce traffic congestion.

- To regulate the flow of packets and prevent buffer overflow, *flow control* can be provided between stages in a multistage network.

- *Discard* versus *deflection*. At each stage of a switching network, a conflict may arise if several packets request the same output. In networks without flow control, arriving packets that cannot be buffered can be either *discarded* or *deflected*. Or, these two methods can be combined in a switch.

- *Multicast capability* versus *unicast capability only*. Modern switch fabrics are expected to have the capability of *multicasting*—copying to any subset of the outputs—along with *broadcasting*.

12.5.1 Complexity of Switch Fabrics

The topic of switch fabrics entails a number of definitions and symbols. Consider a fabric with n inputs and m outputs. This switch fabric is referred to as an $n \times m$ network. A useful measure for approximating the cost of a network is to consider the number of crosspoints and links. In practice, the number of crosspoints has greater impact on the cost of the switching network. Thus, *complexity* refers to the total number of crosspoints used in a switching network. It is important to note that the integrated circuit pin constraints also influence implementation of large-scale networks, especially those with parallel data paths. Practically, a switching network or portions of a network can be placed entirely on a single integrated circuit package. In such cases, the area occupied by the circuits becomes an important complexity measure.

12.5.2 Crossbar Switch Fabrics

Crossbar switches are the building blocks of switch fabrics. A crossbar switch with n inputs and n outputs is shown by $X_{n,n}$. Figure 12.7 shows an $X_{4,4}$, or a 4×4 crossbar switch fabric. In a crossbar, every input can be uniquely connected to any output through a *crosspoint*. A crosspoint is the smallest unit of the switching function and can be built using a variety of electronic or digital elements, such as photodiodes, transistors, and AND gates.

Crossbar switches are considered strictly (wide-sense) nonblocking, as a dedicated crosspoint exists for every connection. This is clearly an attractive feature of a crossbar. The blocking, however, may occur when multiple packets are sent to the same output simultaneously. If a particular output port of the crossbar is idle, the desired connection can always be established by selecting the particular crosspoint dedicated to the particular input/output pair.

Crossbar switches are conceptually simple in structure and ideal from the non-blocking standpoint. Their two potential problems are output port contention and

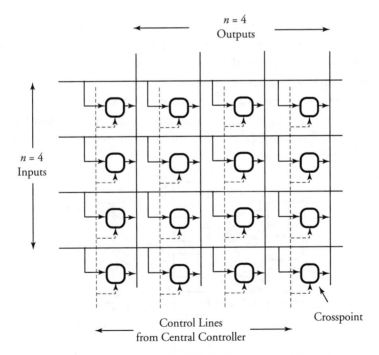

Figure 12.7 A crossbar switch fabric with $n = 4$ inputs/outputs

hardware complexity when the switch is scaled up. The hardware complexity of a crossbar switch lies in the complexity of its crosspoints. For an $n \times n$ crossbar, the complexity rises in a quadratic fashion and is equal to n^2 crosspoints. By some clever design work, the complexity can be reduced at the price of bringing certain blocking into the switching. One possible clever design is *Clos switch fabric* that is described in the next section.

12.5.3 Clos Switch Fabrics

A three-stage *Clos switch fabric* is constructed by three stages of crossbar switches. Figure 12.8 shows a Clos switch fabric with $n = 8$ inputs, $d = 2$, and $k = 5$. Each box in this figure represents a *switch element* made up of a crossbar switch Let d and k be integers to represent the dimension of each first stage switch elements as $d \times k$, and also each last stage switch element as $k \times d$. The three-stage Clos switch fabric shown by $C^3_{n,d,k}$ is defined by

$$C^3_{n,d,k} = X_{d,k} X_{n/d,n/d} X_{k,d}. \tag{12.1}$$

where $X_{d,k}$, $X_{n/d,n/d}$, and $X_{k,d}$ are, respectively, $d \times k$, $n/d \times n/d$, and $k \times d$, crossbars. In any three-stage Clos switch fabric, if the number of middle-stage crossbar switch elements k is greater than or equal to $2d - 1$, the fabric is strictly nonblocking. The proof of this claim can be derived by first observing that a connection through the three-stage switch requires a middle-stage switch element having an idle link from the first stage and an idle link to the third stage, as shown in Figure 12.9. In $C^3_{n,d,k}$, we search for a route realizing a connection request from input x to output y.

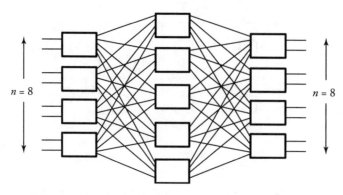

Figure 12.8   A Clos network with $n = 8$ inputs, $d = 2$, and $k = 5$

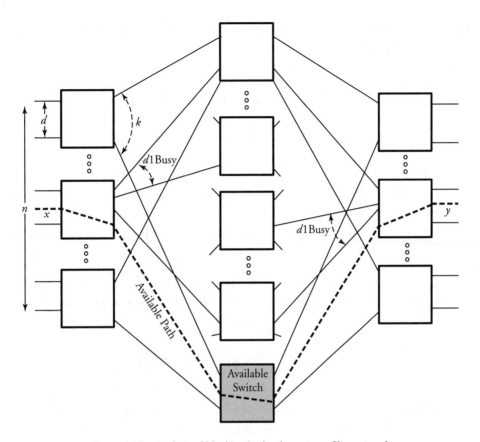

Figure 12.9   Analysis of blocking in the three-stage Clos network

Thus, the number of outputs of the stage 1 switch elements containing input x that are busy is at most $d - 1$. This means that there are at most $d - 1$ middle-stage switch elements that are not accessible from x. Similarly, there are at most $d - 1$ middle-stage switch elements that are not accessible from y.

Clearly, there are at most $2d - 2$ middle-stage switches that are either not accessible from x or not accessible from y. Hence, the worst-case situation for blocking is that these two sets of middle-stage switch elements are unavailable for connection request (x, y). However, if one additional free middle-stage switch element exists as shaded in the figure, that element can be used to set up the connection (x, y). Hence if $k = (d - 1) + (d - 1) + 1 = 2d - 1$, the switch is strictly nonblocking. More generally, at least one middle-stage switch that is accessible from both sides of a state that blocks connection request (x, y) can be found if $k \geq 2d - 1$. The complexity of the three-stage Clos network is

$$X_c = dk\left(\frac{n}{d}\right) + k\left(\frac{n}{d}\right)^2 + dk\left(\frac{n}{d}\right)$$

$$= 2kn + k\left(\frac{n}{d}\right)^2. \tag{12.2}$$

In order to find the complexity of the Clos network under nonblocking conditions, we can substitute $k = 2d - 1$ in Equation (12.2). Thus, the complexity of a nonblocking network, $X_c^{n.b.}$, becomes

$$X_c^{n.b.} = (2d - 1)\left[2n + \left(\frac{n}{d}\right)^2\right]. \tag{12.3}$$

It is always useful to optimize the complexity of switching networks, especially for the nonblocking Clos networks, in which finding the best d would be beneficial. To achieve this goal, we can optimize the network by

$$\frac{\partial X_c^{n.b.}}{\partial d} = \frac{\partial}{\partial d}\left((2d - 1)\left[2n + \left(\frac{n}{d}\right)^2\right]\right) = 0. \tag{12.4}$$

This procedure releases $d = \sqrt{n/2}$, which is the absolute minimized value of d. The optimized crosspoint count under this optimization, therefore, is

$$X_{c,opt}^{n.b.} = 4n(\sqrt{2n} - 1). \tag{12.5}$$

However, the number of crosspoints for large three-stage switches is still quite prohibitive. Large switching systems typically use more than three stages to provide greater reductions in crosspoints. Three-stage Clos networks can be enhanced by substituting another three-stage Clos network for the middle-stage crossbars, resulting in a five-stage Clos network. We can continue in this fashion to construct networks with many stages.

Estimation of Blocking per Input/Output Pair

To estimate the internal blocking probability of a Clos network, consider $d \times k$ switch elements in the first stage. Figure 12.10 shows a probability graph of a three-stage network. All possible internal paths for an input/output connection pair are shown.

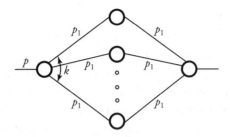

Figure 12.10   A blocking model for a Clos switching network

For the middle-stage crossbars, the blocking-probability estimation for n parallel links, each with probability p, is generally $B = p^n$; for a series of n links, the blocking probability is generally $B = 1 - (1 - p)^n$ according to Lee's formula presented in Chapter 5. To apply this rule, let p_1 be the probability that an internal link is busy, as shown in the figure, and thus $1 - p_1$ is the probability that a link is idle. Then, B, the internal blocking probability of the switching network, or the probability that all paths are busy, is

$$B = [1 - (1 - p_1)^2]^k. \tag{12.6}$$

We want the traffic load to balance at both sides of each node. Specifically, at the first node, we want the external and internal traffic to be equal, such that $kp_1 = dp$ or $p_1 = p(d/k)$. Using this and Equation (12.6) leads to B in terms of p:

$$B = \left[1 - (1 - p(d/k))^2\right]^k. \tag{12.7}$$

Example.   For a Clos network with $k = 8$, $d = 8$, and $p = 0.8$, find the internal blocking probability.

Solution.   Obviously, $k/d = 1$, and therefore the internal blocking probability $B = (1 - (1 - 0.8)^2)^8 = 0.72$.

Example.   For the Clos network presented in the previous example, if we add up to 100 percent more crossbar switches into the middle stage of the network, how much reduction in internal blocking probability do we obtain?

Solution.   Since $k = 16$, $d = 8$, and $p = 0.8$, then $k/d = 2$, and thus $B = ((1 - (1 - 0.8 \times 1/2)^2)^{16} = 0.0008$. The impact is remarkable, as the internal blocking probability is reduced 900 times.

Five-Stage Clos Networks

Figure 12.11 shows a five-stage Clos network obtained by replacing every middle-stage switch element in a three-stage Clos network. This structure provides less complexity, as the complexity of each middle three-stage network has been reduced as was explained for a three-stage network. Note that this statement can be true only if a five-stage switch is strictly nonblocking, where $k_1 \geq 2d_1 - 1$ and also $k_2 \geq 2d_2 - 1$. This type of design is especially useful for large-scale switching systems, in which a substantial reduction in the overall complexity of a network is targeted. The blocking probability of a five-stage network is modeled in Figure 12.12 and is determined as follows:

$$B = \{1 - (1 - p_1)^2[1 - (1 - (1 - p_2)^2)^{k_2}]\}^{k_1}. \qquad (12.8)$$

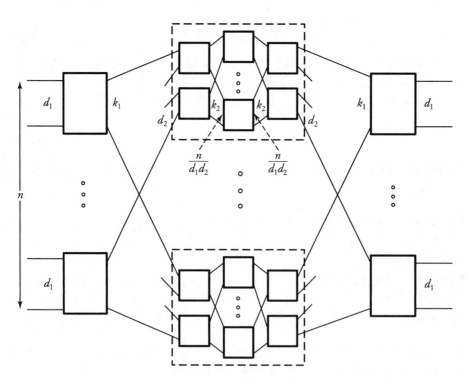

Figure 12.11 Constructing a five-stage Clos network by using three-stage networks to reduce blocking probability

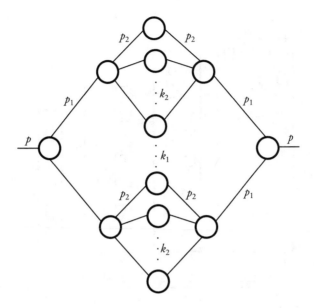

Figure 12.12   A blocking model for the five-stage Clos network

12.5.4   Concentration and Expansion Switch Fabrics

This section introduces switching fabrics that either expand or concentrate incoming traffic. In a concentration-based switch fabrics, the number of output ports is less than the number of input ports. In an expansion-based switch fabrics, the number of output ports is more than the number of input ports. In the following two sections, we explore two of such switch fabrics.

Knockout Concentration Switch Fabric

One of the simplest concentration switch fabrics is called a *knockout switch fabric*, shown in Figure 12.13. The knockout switch is inherently a blocking network and is constructed with interconnected crossbars with less complexity than a crossbar switch of the same size. The knockout switch is a good substitution for a crossbar switch when the likelihood is small that many inputs will need to send packets to the same output simultaneously.

The idea of this switch is based on the concept of knocking a possible k packets out of n active inputs if the number of switch outputs is m, where $m < n$. To implement this mechanism, consider the example illustrated in Figure 12.13, where $n = 8$ and $m = 4$. Assume that all of the eight inputs have packets to transmit to outputs;

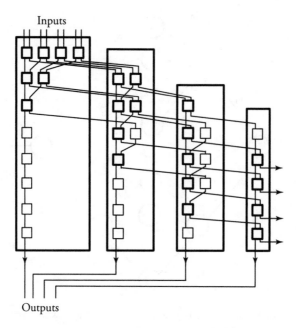

Figure 12.13   The knockout switch fabric

obviously, the system would need to discard a minimum of four packets. The switching network consists of a number of 2 × 2 switch elements and delay elements.

The switch elements act as concentrators, ensuring fairness to all entering packets. The eight incoming packets from eight switch inputs compete in the first four switch elements. A packet that wins the competition, based on a random selection in a switch element, stays in the same column of switches and continues to reach its desired output. Otherwise, a losing packet is knocked out to the next column of switch elements for the next round of competition. Thus, the first-round losers in this process go straight to the second column and play off against one another and at later stages, face the second- and the third-round losing packets from the first column.

Note that the system needs to ensure that no input port is singled out for bad treatment every time the output is overloaded. This fairness task is implemented by playing packets against one another in a form of a knockout column-by-column scenario to select m winners. In the second column, two packets, including those losing packets, are competing in a similar fashion to reach their desired outputs, and so on. Finally, all the losing packets are dropped, and eventually, we select up to $m = 4$ packets, dropping all the rest. Note that this process requires timing synchronization if all the incoming packets are to experience the same switching delay. To ensure packet time synchronization, the delay elements present units of delay to packets, as shown in the figure by additional delay units.

Expansion Switch Fabrics

An *expansion switch fabric* with n_1 inputs and n_2 outputs, where $n_1 < n_2$, can scale up the number of receivers from n_1 to n_2. A three-stage expansion switch fabric is shown in Figure 12.14. This fabric is constructed with three types of crossbars of sizes $d_1 \times m, \frac{n_1}{d_1} \times \frac{n_2}{d_2}$, and $m \times d_2$, respectively. An expansion network is a generalization of the three-stage Clos network and is useful in applications in which an incoming traffic is to be sent to multiple outputs. Such fabrics are also called *distribution fabrics*. Considering the previous network dimensions, the complexity of a three-stage expansion network, X_e, is derived by

$$X_e = d_1 m \frac{n}{d_1} + \frac{n_1 n_2}{d_1 d_2} m + d_2 m \frac{n_2}{d_2}. \tag{12.9}$$

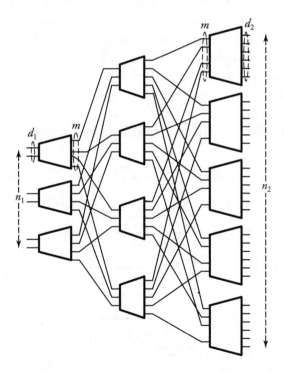

Figure 12.14   A three-stage expansion switching network

An expansion switch fabric is nonblocking if $m \geq (d_1 - 1)n_2/d_2 + d_2$. We can prove this claim by assuming that if a given connection goes to two or more outputs of the same third-stage switch, the connection branches in the third-stage switch supply all the outputs. Suppose that we want to add a new end point to an existing connection from an input x to an idle output y. If an output is in the same third-stage switch as y, we can add the necessary branch at that point. Note that $d_2 - 1$ middle-stage switches are inaccessible from y, and at most $(d_1 - 1)n_2/d_2$ are inaccessible from x. Since m is greater than the sum of these two values, at least one middle-stage switch must be accessible to both x and y. A similar argument applies if we wish to create a new connection from an idle input x to an idle input y.

Example.   Suppose that $n_1 = n_2 = 256, d_1 = 16,$ and $d_2 = 64$. From the preceding theorem, if $m \geq 1024 + 64 = 1,088$, the switch fabric becomes nonblocking.

12.5.5   Shared-Memory Switch Fabrics

A totally different approach for switching can be achieved in time domain and without using any switch elements: the *shared-memory switch fabric*. As shown in Figure 12.15, the distinctive feature of this switch fabric is the use of a high-speed $n : 1$, time-division multiplexer (TDM) with a bit rate n times as large as the rate on each individual input/output line. TDMs were introduced in Chapter 2. Assume packet a at input i needs to be switched on output j and that packet b at input j is supposed to be switched on output i. First, the multiplexer creates an n-channel-long frame from the n inputs. Each frame created at the output of the multiplexer is stored

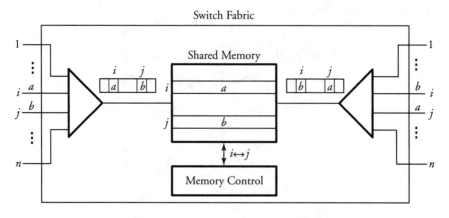

Figure 12.15   Shared-memory switch fabric

in *shared memory* in the same order as the frame's channels. Thus, *a* is written at location *i*, and *b* is written at location *j* of memory.

To implement the switching action between the two channels *i* and *j*, the *memory control* exchanges the reading order of the two memory locations *i* and *j*. This way, the new frame made out of memory contains packet *a* placed in channel *j* and packet *b* placed in channel *i*. This frame is scanned by a demultiplexer for output ports. If the memory partition for an output is empty, the corresponding minislot remains unfilled. It is a matter of implementation whether frame size in shared memory should be rigid or flexible. Clearly, variable-size frames require more sophisticated hardware to manage, but the packet-loss rate improves, since memory does not suffer from overflow until all memory slots are occupied. See Chapter 2 for more on multiplexers handling variable-size frames.

12.5.6 Performance Improvement in Switch Fabrics

Several practical methods can be used to improve the performance of switch fabrics. The enhancement of switch performance is typically related to speed, throughput, and therefore the possibility of blocking. Some possible methods for enhancing performance in switch fabrics are as follows:

- *Redundancy through parallel-plane switch fabrics.* This technique forms parallel planes of switch fabrics to process slices of a packet in parallel.

- *Redundancy through buffering in switch fabrics.* The use of buffers in switch fabrics reduces traffic congestion and thus increases system throughput. With the use of buffers in a switch, packets are not discarded when they request the same switch output but instead are kept in buffers for a later contention resolution.

- *Combined switch fabrics.* Combined switch fabrics consist of several cascaded switch fabrics, providing extra stages and producing extra paths, although a combined network can also be designed for other purposes, such as multicasting.

- *Randomizing traffic.* This technique is used to distribute traffic evenly across the switching network to prevent local congestion.

- *Recirculation of traffic.* A packet that is not successfully delivered to a given port can be recirculated. Such packets contend for delivery—possibly with higher priorities—in the next cycle.

- *Increase speed-up factor.* This *speed advantage* in a switching system refers to the ratio of the internal link speed to the external link speed.

The use of buffering, combined networks, or parallel-plane switch fabrics results in increased system complexity and cost but also better performance. In the following two sections, we take a closer look at the first two techniques: *redundancy through parallel-plane switch fabrics* and *redundancy through buffering in switch fabrics*.

Redundancy Through Parallel-Plane Switch Fabrics

One possible way to improve the performance and speed of switch fabrics, especially to reduce the blocking probability, is to arrange parallel planes, or slices, of the switch fabrics, as shown in Figure 12.16. A parallel-plane switch fabric is constructed by m planes of switch fabrics in which $m - 1$ of the planes are redundant so that each additional (redundant) plane can be used if the main plane fails to operate. The planes are connected to input and output ports through time-division demultiplexers and multiplexers, respectively. These multiplexers were explained in detail in Chapter 2. A second benefit of the parallel-plane switch fabric is apparent when multicasting occurs in the switch. When a multicast packet arrives at a switch fabric, the multiplexer can make as many copies of the packet as needed, and let each plane of the switch route a copy of the packet; thus the overall speed of the router can be enhanced.

The *Cantor switch fabric*, shown by K_m, is a widely used example of parallel-plane switch fabrics. The Cantor switch fabric is strictly nonblocking as long as each plane is strictly nonblocking. The complexity of a Cantor switch fabric is estimated as:

$$X_m = mX_{plane} + 2n \times m. \qquad (12.10)$$

where X_{plane} is the complexity of each plane, and the complexity of each multiplexer is assumed to be m representing approximately m logic gates.

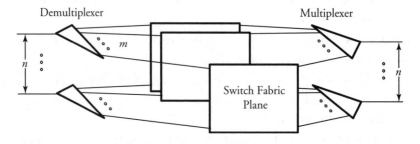

Figure 12.16   A Cantor switch fabric with m parallel switching planes for better reliability

Example.   For $n = 64$, compare the complexity of the following three switch fabrics: a crossbar, a nonblocking and optimized Clos, and a three-plane Cantor made of the same crossbars.

Solution.   If $n = 64$, the complexity for the crossbar is $n^2 = 4{,}096$. For the nonblocking and optimized Clos switch fabric, the complexity is $4n(\sqrt{2n} - 1) = 2{,}640$, (see Section 12.5.3). For the three-plane Cantor switch fabric, the complexity is $X_3 = mX_{plane} + 2n \times m = 3 \times 2640 + 64 \times 3 = 8{,}304$.

In parallel-plane switch fabrics, the chip pin constraint limits the number of signals that can enter or leave a physical component. The integrated circuit pin constraints also influence implementation so that such systems are best designed with each data path passing through physically separate components. Such *bit-sliced organization* causes complexity to grow in proportion to the data path width.

Redundancy on Stages and Through Buffering in Switch Fabrics

For our case study on a switching fabric, we choose an expandable switch fabric constructed with identical building-block modules called the *multipath buffered crossbar* (MBC) switch fabric. Conventional $n \times n$ crossbars are vulnerable to faults. Unlike a conventional crossbar, MBC is a crossbar with n rows and k columns. Each row contains an input bus and an output bus. A packet being transferred from input i to output a is sent by input port processor i on input bus i to one of the k columns. The packet then passes along this column to the output bus in row a. The crosspoints that make up the MBC switch fabric include mechanisms that allow the inputs to contend for access to the various columns. The crosspoint buffers in one row act as a distributed output buffer for the corresponding output port. As shown in Figure 12.17, every crosspoint has two different *switches* and a buffer.

Consider a case of point-to-point connection from input i to output a. The packet is first randomly sent to a crosspoint at one of the k *shared data buses*, say, column $(j - 2)$. In case the crosspoint on this bus is not available for any reason, another crosspoint selected at random is examined, and so on. The reason for randomizing the initial location is to distribute the traffic as evenly as possible. When a functioning crosspoint (crosspoint 3) at column j is selected, the packet can be sent to a second crosspoint (crosspoint 4) at this column unless the selected crosspoint is found to be faulty or its buffer is full. The packet is buffered in crosspoint 4 and can be sent out after a contention-resolution process in its row.

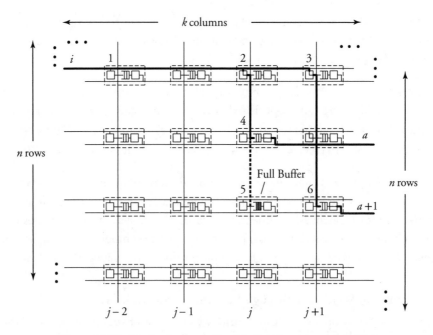

Figure 12.17   Routing in the multipath buffered crossbar switch fabric

The availability of each crosspoint at a given crosspoint (i, j) is dynamically reported to the input ports by a flag $g_{i,j}$. If more than one input port requests a given column, based on a contention-resolution process, only one of them can use the column. Packets in the other input ports receive higher priorities to examine other columns. Obviously, the more the packet receives priority increments, the sooner it is granted one free column, which it selects randomly. Once it gets accepted by one of the β buffers of a second crosspoint, the packet contends to get access to its corresponding output. The losers of the contention resolution get higher priorities for the next contention cycle until they are successfully transmitted. In Figure 12.17, the connections $i \to a$ and $i \to a + 1$ are made possible through nodes $\{2, 4\}$ and nodes $\{3, 6\}$, respectively.

The queueing model for this system is shown in Figure 12.18. Packets enter the network from n *input port buffers* and pass through any of the k crosspoints belonging to the same row as the input. These crosspoints do not contribute in any queueing operation and act only as ordinary connectors. Each packet exiting these nodes can confront n crosspoint buffers of length β that are situated on one of the k-specified columns. A packet selects a buffer on the basis of the desired address. In this system architecture, each crossbar row contains k buffers, constructing a related group of

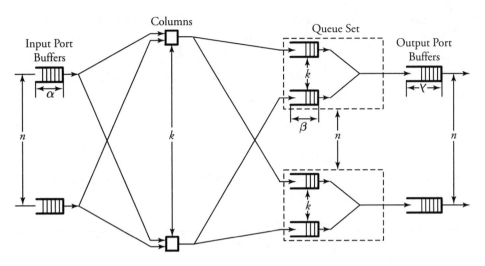

Figure 12.18   Queueing model for multipath buffered crossbar

buffers called a *queue set*, as seen in the figure. The winning packet of each set is then permitted to enter the corresponding *output port buffer*.

Note that the state of a buffer within each queue set is dependent on the state of all other buffers in that queue set. There are no *grant flows* between the output port buffers and the crosspoint buffers, and the admission of a packet by a queue set is made possible by granting the *flag* acknowledgments to the input port buffers. It should also be noted that the analysis that follows assumes that all crosspoints are functional. Let $z_k^\beta(s)$ be the number of ways to distribute s packets among k distinct buffers within a queue set, under the restriction that each buffer may contain at most β packets. Note that, here, we are not concerned about the number of combinations of different packets in the queue. Therefore, $z_k^\beta(s)$ can be recursively computed by

$$z_k^\beta(s) = \begin{cases} 1 & \text{if } (k = 1 \wedge s \le \beta) \vee (s = 0) \\ 0 & \text{if } s > k\beta \\ \sum 0 \le i \le \min\{\beta, s\} \; z_{k-1}^\beta(s - i) & \text{if } 0 < s \le k\beta. \end{cases} \tag{12.11}$$

Let $X_k^\beta(r, s)$ be the probability that a given crosspoint buffer has r packets when the entire queue set contains s packets. Then

$$X_k^\beta(r, s) = \frac{z_{k-1}^\beta(s - r)}{z_k^\beta(s)}. \tag{12.12}$$

To further extend this analysis, an expression for the flow control between a crosspoint queue set and the input buffers is required. A second crosspoint generates a final flag acknowledgment, Ψ, after having completed a three-step process. The probability that a packet is available to enter the network, a, is the same probability that the input port buffer is not empty and is given by

$$a = 1 - \pi_i(0). \tag{12.13}$$

Let ψ be the probability that a packet contending for access to a column wins the contention. Note that the probability that any given input attempts to contend for any given column is a/k. Hence,

$$\psi = \sum_{0 \leq c \leq n-1} \frac{1}{c+1} \binom{n-1}{c} (a/k)^c (1 - a/k)^{(n-1)-c}, \tag{12.14}$$

where $\binom{n-1}{c}$ is a *binomial* coefficient indicating the number of different combinations of $n-1$ possible existing contenders on one of the k columns, taken c contenders at a time. Now, the probability that a packet forwarded by input port buffer i is admitted, Ψ, is given by:

$$\Psi = \psi \sum_{0 \leq s \leq b} \pi_x(s)[1 - X_k^\beta(\beta, s)]. \tag{12.15}$$

We use Ψ later to derive the probability that an input port buffer contains exactly a certain number of packets. The expression for Ψ facilitates the determination of the state of the input port buffers. The input port queue can be modeled as a $(2\alpha + 1)$-state *Markov chain* (see Figure 12.19). The transition rates are determined by the offered load ρ and the crosspoint queue-set grant probability Ψ. Let f be the probability that a packet has fanout 2 (a *bipoint connection*). In this model, a bipoint connection, which is a two-copying packet-recirculation task, is treated as two independent *point-to-point* connections. The upper row of the Markov chain depicts the state of the queue when a packet needs no additional copy. However, if the packet has fanout 2, it proceeds to the second copy of the packet on the upper row once the operation for its first copy in the lower row of the chain is completed.

The state of the queue can be changed from 0 to 1 with transition probability $\rho\bar{f}$ if the packet has fanout 1, or it can enter state $1'$ with transition probability ρf if the

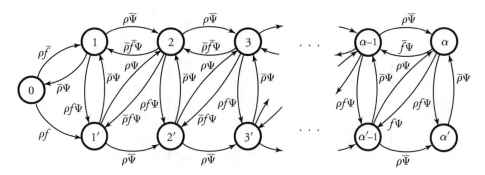

Figure 12.19   Markov chain model of the queue at the input port buffer

packet has fanout 2. On the arrival of a fanout-2 packet at the head of queue, a state in the upper chain is changed to a lower one with probability of $\rho f \Psi$ if a new packet arrives at the queue, or $\bar{\rho} f \Psi$ if no new packet arrives. Similarly, any of the lower chain states can be changed with probabilities $\rho \Psi$ or $\bar{\rho} \Psi$ to an upper one as soon as the first copy of a fanout-2 packet is completed. These transition probabilities are free of f, since only the first copy has been completed at this point.

12.6   Multicasting Packets in Routers

Multicasting techniques can also be used at the router level. To implement a multi-cast connection, a binary tree is normally constructed with the source switch port at the root and the destination switch ports at the leaves. Internal nodes act as relay points that receive packets and make copies. Figure 12.20 shows an overview of a multicasting process in router.

The main task of multicasting in routers is either "IPP centric" or "switch fabric centric." The IPP centric method reduces the hardware complexity in the switch fab-ric controller; however, it requires two switch fabrics. As shown in Figure 12.20 (a), the first switch fabric, called the *copy switch fabric,* makes all the necessary copies of a packet irrespective of their destination port addresses. This task is followed by the *broadcast translated circuit* (BTC). The BTC receives all the copies of a packet and assigns the appropriate output port address to each copy of the packet. Copies of the packet are then sent over to the second switch fabric called the *routing switch fabric,* in which each copy of a packet is routed to the appropriate output port of the switch fabric. In the IPP centric method, all necessary copies of a packet irrespective of their destination port addresses are made in the IPP and routed to the appropriate output

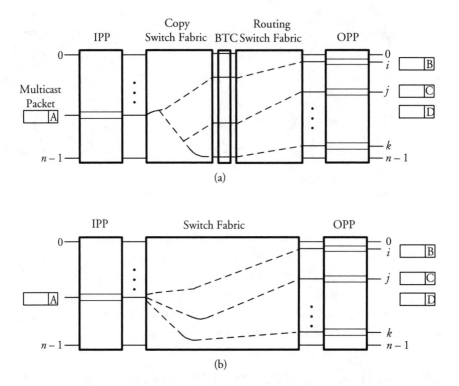

Figure 12.20   Two methods of a multicast process in a router

port of the switch fabric as shown in Figure 12.20 (b). This method causes some delay while the IPP makes all the copies.

A number of such multicast methods are used. One is a *tree-based multicast algorithm* using a separate copy network. The *Boolean splitting multicast algorithm* is used for multistage switches. The third technique is the *packet recirculation multicast algorithm*. The fourth is multicasting in *three-dimensional switches*.

12.6.1   Tree-Based Multicast Algorithm

The *tree-based multicast algorithm* is based on a tree-shape construction of multicast operation in a switch fabric. Imagine that a multicast tree algorithm must be applied on a multistage switch fabric. Multicasting is implemented as a tree structure. A source generates a packet and sends it out to the first stage crossbar switch. The packet may have a field that specifies how many copies of this packet are to be made. All copies may be destined for other crossbars, in which more copies of the packet are made, and some packets may move to their destinations.

For implementing a tree-based multicast algorithm, the copying tasks in multi-stage switch fabrics typically involve a copy switch fabric and a routing switch fabric as explained in the previous section. The following algorithm presents the multicast steps within a copy switch fabric with n inputs constructed with d input switch elements at the first stage:

Begin Tree-Based Multicast Algorithm

Define

```
k = Required number of last stages in which multicasting takes
    place,  k = [log_d n]
j  = Stage number, j ∈ {1, 2, ..., r}
F  = Global number of copies, F ∈ {1, 2, ..., n}
F_j = Number of copies remaining before the packet arrives at stage j
f_j = Local number of copies made at stage j
```

Initialize

$$F_0 = F$$

$$f_0 = 1$$

For Stages $1 \leq j \leq k \Rightarrow$

$$F_j = \left\lceil \frac{F_{j-1}}{f_{j-1}} \right\rceil$$

$$f_j = \left\lceil \frac{F_j}{d^{k-j}} \right\rceil . \quad \blacksquare$$

In the copy switch fabric, packets are replicated as designated by the initial *global number of copies*, F, given in the routing-control field of the packet header. The global number of copies refers to the total number of packet copies requested. Let F_j be the remaining number of copies of a packet when it arrives at stage j, and let f_j be the number of copies made locally at stage j. First, the algorithm initializes F_0 to F and f_0 to 1. The copying method is such that the replication of the packets takes place stage by stage within the network in order to distribute the traffic as evenly as possible. The routing is either a point-to-point or multipoint connection.

Consider a switch fabric with the last k stages dedicated to multicast function. The operation $F_j = \left\lceil \dfrac{F_{j-1}}{f_{j-1}} \right\rceil$ computes a new number of copies for a packet at stage j, with the local number of copies $f_{j-1} = \left\lceil \dfrac{F_j}{d^{k-j}} \right\rceil$. The algorithm is set up to generate the final number of copies that appear on the outputs to be the smallest multiple of 2 greater than or equal to F.

This technique reduces the hardware complexity in the controller. If the final number of copies that appear in the outputs is more than requested, the unnecessary packet copies can be easily thrown away.

Example. Find all numbers of copies in every stage of a three-stage Clos switch fabric shown in in Figure 12.21 in which the global number of copies of an incoming packet is indicated to be $F = 3$ and copies of the packet are to be routed to output port numbers 3, 5, and 7.

Solution. The switch fabric has $k = [\log_d n] = 3$ stages. The algorithm is initialized on $F_0 = 3$ and $f_0 = 1$. For stage $j = 1$ of the copy switch fabric, we have $F_1 = 3$ and the local number of copies $f_1 = 1$, so the packet gets distributed. At stage $j = 2$, $F_2 = \lceil F_1/f_1 \rceil = 3$, and $f_2 = \lceil F_2/d^{k-j} \rceil = 2$; thus, two copies are made at this stage and guided to two crossbars at the last stage ($j = 3$). At the third stage, $F_3 = \lceil F_2/f_2 \rceil = 2$, and the local number of copies $f_3 = \lceil F_3/d^{k-j} \rceil = 2$. Therefore, for each of these switches, two copies of the packet are made. Note that the sum of these copies (4) has exceeded the requested global number of copies (3), so the one additional copy is thrown away in the figure. The end result is a tree-shape routing. As we notice here, the three copies of the packets are made but they are not at the right output. These three copies are then guided to output ports 3, 5, and 7 as requested through BTCs and the routing switch fabric.

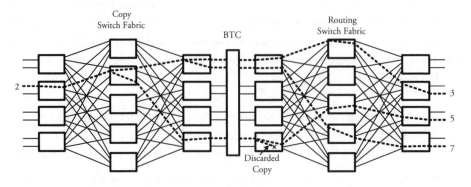

Figure 12.21　Tree-based multicasting and separate routing

12.6.2   Packet Recirculation Multicast Algorithm

Packet recirculation (recycling) is another feasible method for constructing large switching fabrics for broadband switching applications. To implement a multicast connection, a binary tree is constructed with the source port at its root and the destination switch port at its leaves. This technique can be used for almost all kinds of space-division switch fabrics.

If a switch fabric is constructed by a multistage interconnected network, internal crossbars can act as relay points to accept packets and recycle them back into the switch fabric after packet relabeling. New labels carry the information about the destination pair, identifying the next two switch ports to which they are to be sent. Figure 12.22 illustrates the recirculation technique. All the hardware blocks shown on the left side of the switch fabric belong to IPP. A *multicast table* provides an output port/IP address pair. This pair is added to the packet header; thus, two additional bits indicate whether the pair is to be recirculated again. An *IPP buffer* holds packets received from the input link and forwards them to the switching network. An *OPP buffer* holds packets waiting to be transmitted on outgoing links. A *recirculation* buffer provides buffering to the packets that need to be recycled.

Packet recirculation and copying within the switch fabric is straightforward. Figure 12.23 illustrates packet recirculation and copying. Suppose that a is a source that generates packets to be delivered to output ports b, c, d, and e and that x and y are relay points. Suppose that a packet entering at input port a must have several copies. For such a packet, there may be entries of the type (x, j) and (e, k) in the multicast table. This can be interpreted as making two copies of the packet: one to be *recirculated* back to port x on address j; the other one, to port e with address k. The multicast table entry at x may now have entries (b, n) and (y, m), as seen. Typically, each packet header has 2 bits to indicate whether a packet needs to be recirculated.

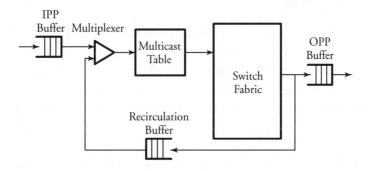

Figure 12.22   Recirculation multicasting

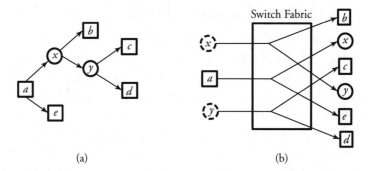

Figure 12.23   Within the switch fabric of routers: (a) packet recirculation and (b) copying

In summary, an end point that is added needs to have a parent. A good candidate is the one that does not have heavy recirculation traffic. Like the parent of the new end point, the intermediate point also is new, so it has to be put into the multicast table entry of another node, which becomes the grandparent of the new end point, whose child will now become a sibling of the new end point.

To remove a connection, we can consider two cases. We should determine whether the output to be removed has no grandparent but its sibling has children; in that case, we replace the parent's multicast table entry with the sibling's children. If the output to be removed has no grandparent and its sibling has no children, we simply drop the output to be removed from its parent's multicast table entry, and the connection reverts to a simple point-to-point connection. Note that since packets must be resequenced when they exit from the system, the resequencing buffer at the output port processor (OPP) of a router must be dimensioned to delay packets long enough so that slow packets have a chance to catch up with fast packets.

12.7   Summary

This chapter presented the internal design of advanced routers and switches. We learned that a typical router has n input ports and n output ports. The system consists of five main parts: a *network interface card* (NIC), which was mainly described in Chapter 3; *input port processors* (IPPs) that are responsible for receiving, buffering, and interpreting packets arriving from outside; *output port processors* (OPPs) that receive already processed packets and forward them to output ports of the router to exit; a *switch fabric* to interconnect input ports to output ports of a router; and a *central controller* that authorizes the operation of the switch fabric, coordinates functions of IPPs and OPPs, and processes the traffic flow control for a router.

Switch fabrics are the core segments of switching devices and routers. A *crossbar* is a nonblocking switch fabric and can be used as the building block of other switch fabrics. A crossbar requires n^2 crosspoints. *Clos switch* fabrics is also nonblocking switches constructed with crossbars. A $C_{n,d,k}^3$ Clos network is strictly nonblocking if $k \geq 2d - 1$. *Concentration-based* and *expansion-based* switching networks are two special-purpose switch fabrics.

In a different approach for switching, *time domain*, a memory controlled by another memory, without using any crossbar, performs the task of switching. Finally, for redundancy purposes, we learned that various techniques such as deploying buffers in the structure of switches offered better performance. The case study presented a switch fabric constructed with a crossbar and buffers in its structure.

Having analyzed architectures of routers and switches, we will proceed to present two remaining components of routers, *schedulers* and *quality of service* (QoS) in the next chapter.

12.8   Exercises

1. Consider another type of switch fabric called an Omega switch fabric indicated by $\Omega_{n,d}$. This switch fabric is the same as a Clos switch fabric but all stages of interconnections are identical and the fabric is limited to $\log_d n$ stages where n is the number of input/output ports and d is the size of building block crossbars. Consider the following two switch fabrics: $\Omega_{16,2}$ and $\Omega_{16,4}$:

    (a) Sketch the networks with the minimum number of stages that provide all possible input/output connections.

    (b) Compare the two networks in terms of complexity and speed.

2. Using Lee's blocking-probability estimation method discussed in Chapter 5, derive an expression for the internal blocking of a multipath buffered crossbar with 10 inputs and 20 outputs.

3. Design an $n = 8$ port three-stage Clos switching network.

    (a) Find d and k that meet the minimum nonblocking condition, and sketch the network.

    (b) To design a nonblocking Clos network, the network is nonblocking as long as $k = 2d - 1$. Why would anyone want to design a network with $k > 2d - 1$?

4. Compare the complexity of large-scale three-stage and five-stage Clos switching systems, where the number of ports varies from 1,000 ports to 2,000 ports.

5. For any nonblocking switching network, Lee's method can still estimate some blocking. Justify this contradiction.

6. There are two ways to design a three-stage Clos network with six inputs and six outputs yielding the "minimum" nonblocking operation.
   (a) Select dimensions for both types of crossbars used in either of the two types of networks, and sketch the networks.
   (b) Show a Lee's model for both networks, and find the total blocking probability for any of the networks.
   (c) Which choice is better? (Compare them from all possible aspects.)

7. To design a five-stage Clos network with $n = 8$ and $d = 2$ yielding "minimum" nonblocking operation:
   (a) Select dimensions for all three types of crossbars—no complexity optimizations needed—and sketch the network.
   (b) Show a Lee's model.
   (c) Assuming the probability that any link in the networks is busy is $p = 0.2$, find the total blocking probability for the network.

8. To increase the speed and reliability of the five-stage Clos network $C^5_{8,2,3}$ using $C^3_{4,2,3}$, we form three multiplexed parallel planes, each of which contains this network.
   (a) Sketch the overview of the network.
   (b) Show a Lee's model.
   (c) Assuming the probability that any link in the networks including multiplexing links is busy is $p = 0.2$, find the total blocking probability for the network.

9. To design a five-stage Clos switching network with n inputs and n outputs:
   (a) Give dimensions for all five types of crossbars to yield nonblocking operation.
   (b) Select dimensions for all five types of crossbars to yield nonblocking operation and minimum crosspoint count. (No optimization is needed.)

10. Design a shared-memory switching system that supports up to 16 links and uses a multiplexer, RAM, and a demultiplexer. The multiplexer output carries 16 channels, each as wide as a segment (transport layer packet fragment). Each segment is as large as 512 bytes, including the segment header for local routing. A total of 0.4 μs forms a frame at each multiplexer. RAM is organized in 32-bit words with 2 ns write-in time, 2 ns read-out time, and 1 ns access time (controller process) per word.
   (a) Find the minimum required size of RAM.
   (b) Find the size of a RAM address.

(c) Find the maximum bit rate that can be supported at the output of RAM.

(d) Find the speed of this switch, which is the segment-processing rate per second per switch port.

11. Consider an advanced router of size 8×8 ports whose switch fabric is a crossbar. Suppose two packets A and B each arriving from one of the inputs of the crossbar and each having a combined Q-P sub-fields contend to exit an output. The winning packet leaves the crossbar and the losing packet contends later with another packet to exit the router. The Q-P sub-fields for packet A and packet B are 10110101,0000 and 10101111,0001, respectively.

(a) Determine the winning packet in the contention.

(b) Specify the bit on which the contention process determines the winning packet.

(c) Show the new Q-P sub-fields bits of the losing packet.

12. Assume an advanced router with congestion control capability labeled R2 is placed in the following broadband network for communications of two hosts H1 and H2. Router R2 receives grant value G_d from downstream router R3 and transmits grant G_u to upstream router R1.

(a) Which entity among H1, R1, R2, R3, and H2 ultimately needs to adjust its transmitting traffic as a result of a change in G_d?

(b) Which two factors among other factors substantially impact the value of G_d? Underline the correct ones: [number of packets transmitted to R3], [link-speed/bandwidth between R2 and R3], or [type of network security protocol]

13. We want to show the copying mechanism in an expansion switch fabric of a router with 8 inputs and 16 outputs whose global number of copies is $F = 7$.

(a) Show the detail of stage-by-stage copying using the algorithm.

(b) Sketch the detail of stage-by-stage copying to make copies of a packet for ports 0, 2, 3, 7, 10, 12, and 13.

14. We want to show the copying mechanism in a Clos switch fabric of a router shown by $C_{8,2,3}^3$ whose global number of copies is $F = 5$.

(a) Show the detail of stage-by-stage copying using the algorithm.

(b) Sketch the detail of stage-by-stage copying to make copies of a packet for ports 0, 2, 4, 5, and 7.

15. Consider a switch fabric of 4×4 crossbars. Design the multicasting portion of its input port processor. Present all the hardware details.

16. Suppose the switch fabric with a redundancy feature and with n inputs and m planes presented in Figure 12.16 is used in a router. We would like to analyze the use of planes for multicasting purposes in this switch. Let ρ be the average offered load per switch input, and assume that a multicast packet arriving at a particular input port and requesting F copies of a packet can be copied over the parallel planes.

   (a) Develop an algorithm that presents the steps of multicasting in this switch fabric in which each plane of the switch has a different priority to be used for routing. Specifically, differentiate the algorithm for cases when $F \leq m$ and $F > m$.

   (b) When $F > m$, find the blocking probability, $P_b(i)$, for an input number i out of n.

12.9   Computer Simulation Project

1. **Simulation of a Crossbar Switch Fabric.** Write a computer program to simulate a 2×2 crossbar switch.

   (a) Assign each packet a switch-output destination at random.

   (b) Construct and simulate a single crosspoint. Clearly demonstrate how it switches on and off, using a central crossbar controller.

   (c) Extend your program to construct a four-crosspoint crossbar.

2. **Simulation of a Buffered Crossbar Switch Fabric.** Carry the program you developed for a single buffer in Chapter 11 (computer simulation project) and extend the preceding 2×2 crossbar switch to a switch with a simple buffered input port. Each of the two inputs of the switch has a buffer with $k = 64$ buffer slots, and each slot can fit only in a packet of size 1,000 bytes. Dynamically assign packets of different size every 1 ms, and send out a packet to the switch every t seconds from the buffer.

   (a) Assign each packet a switch-output destination at random.

   (b) Construct, simulate, and test each of the two buffers individually.

   (c) Integrate these two buffers with the switch, and measure the performance metrics of both buffers together, given different values of t.

   (d) Measure average delay for a packet.

CHAPTER 13

Quality of Service and Scheduling in Routers

Recall from Chapter 12 that the main portion of the input port processor (IPP) and output port processor (OPP) in advanced routers was *quality of service* (QoS). QoS together with the *packet scheduling* used in IPPs were left to be covered completely in this chapter. Therefore, this chapter extends the discussion on the architectures of switches and routers presented in Chapter 12 and explores all angles of QoS and packet scheduling methods included in advanced switches and routers. Numerous methods of providing QoS and implementing packet scheduling at routers are presented in this chapter, including the material that appears under the following main topics:

- *Overview of quality of service* (QoS)
- *Integrated services QoS*
- *Differentiated services QoS*
- *Resource allocation*
- *Packet scheduling*

Two broad approaches to QoS are *integrated services* and *differentiated services*. Integrated services provide QoS to individual applications and flow records.

485

Providing QoS requires certain features to be maintained in switching nodes. QoS protocols govern several quality-based functions such as traffic shaping, reservation control, and resource and bandwidth allocations. Traffic shaping regulates the spacing between incoming packets. Other advanced QoS protocols covered are admission control and RSVP.

The differentiated services provide QoS support to a broad class of applications. The basics of resource allocation for packet-switched networks are reviewed, as is resource allocation for all possible layers of the protocol stack. Resource-allocation algorithms can be used to avoid possible congestion.

Packet scheduling is the last topic of this chapter. Perhaps packet scheduling is one of the most important functions of a router as packets are scheduled to be serviced in various buffers with each buffer holding a different priority policy.

13.1   Overview of Quality of Service (QoS)

Communication networks face a variety of quality-of-service demands. The main motivation for a QoS unit in a data network port processor is to control access to available bandwidth and to regulate traffic. Traffic regulation is always necessary in WANs in order to avoid congestion. A network must be designed to support both real-time and non-real-time applications. Voice and video transmissions over IP must be able to request a higher degree of assurance from the network. A network that can provide these various levels of services requires a more complex structure.

The provision of QoS to a network either does or does not come with a guarantee. Nonguaranteed QoS is typically based on the *best-effort model*, whereby a network provides no guarantees on the delivery of packets but makes its best effort to do so. In a non-real-time application, a network can use the retransmit strategy for successful data delivery. However, in a real-time application, such as voice or video networking where timely delivery of packets is required, the application requires a low-latency communication. Consequently, the network must be able to handle packets of such applications more carefully.

Approaches to providing quality support can be further divided into *integrated services* and *differentiated services*. The details of these two approaches are discussed in Sections 13.2 and 13.3, respectively.

13.2   Integrated Services QoS

The *integrated services approach*, consisting of two service classes, defines both the service class and mechanisms that need to be used in routers to provide the services associated with the class. The first service class, the *guaranteed service class*, is defined for applications that cannot tolerate a delay beyond a particular value. This type of service class can be used for real-time applications, such as voice or video communications. The second, the *controlled-load service class*, is used for applications that can tolerate some delay and loss. Controlled-load service is designed such that applications run very well when the network is not heavily loaded or congested. These two service classes cover the wide range of applications on the Internet.

A network needs to obtain as much information as possible about the flow of traffic to provide optimum services to the flow. This is true especially when real-time services to an application are requested. Any application request to a network has to first specify the type of service required, such as controlled load or guaranteed service. An application that requires guaranteed service also needs to specify the maximum delay that it can tolerate. Once the delay factor is known to a service provider, the QoS unit of the node must determine the necessary processes to be applied on incoming flows. Figure 13.1 shows four common categories of processes providing scheduling and quality of service housed in the input port processor (IPP) of a routing device as follows.

1. *Traffic shaping* regulates turbulent traffic.

2. *Admission control* governs whether the network, given information about an application's flow, can admit or reject the flow.

3. *Resource allocation* lets network users reserve bandwidth on neighboring routers.

4. *Packet scheduling* sets the timetable for the transmission of packet flows. Any involved router needs to queue and transmit packets for each flow appropriately.

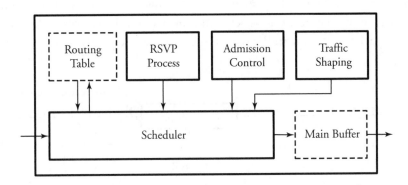

Figure 13.1 Overview of combined QoS and scheduling model in an integrated services model of an IPP

The widespread deployment of the integrated services approach has been deterred owing to scalability issues. As the network size increases, routers need to handle larger routing tables and switch larger numbers of bits per second. In such situations, routers need to refresh information periodically. Routers also have to be able to make admission-control decisions and queue each incoming flow. This action leads to scalability concerns, especially when networks scale larger.

13.2.1   Traffic Shaping

Realistically, spacing between incoming packets has an irregular pattern, which in many cases causes congestion. The goal of *traffic shaping* in a communication network is to control access to available bandwidth to regulate incoming data to avoid congestion, and to control the delay incurred by packets (see Figure 13.2). Turbulent packets at rate λ and with irregular arrival patterns are regulated in a traffic shaper over equal-sized $1/g$ intervals.

If a policy dictates that the packet rate cannot exceed a specified rate even though the network node's access rates might be higher, a mechanism is needed to smooth out the rate of traffic flow. If different traffic rates are applied to a network node, the traffic flow needs to be regulated. (Monitoring the traffic flow is called *traffic policing*.) Traffic shaping also prevents packet loss by preventing the sudden increased usage of system bandwidth. The stochastic model of a traffic shaper consists of a system that converts any form of traffic to a deterministic one. Two of the most popular traffic-shaping algorithms are *leaky bucket* and *token bucket*.

Leaky-Bucket Traffic Shaping

This algorithm converts any turbulent incoming traffic into a smooth, regular stream of packets. Figure 13.3 shows how this algorithm works. A leaky-bucket interface is connected between a packet transmitter and the network. No matter at what rate packets enter the traffic shaper, the outflow is regulated at a constant rate,

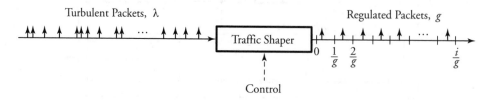

Figure 13.2   Traffic shaping to regulate any incoming turbulent traffic

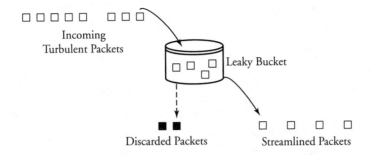

Figure 13.3 The leaky-bucket traffic-shaping algorithm

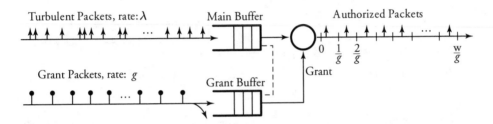

Figure 13.4 Queueing model of leaky-bucket traffic-shaping algorithm

much like the flow of water from a leaky bucket. The implementation of a leaky-bucket algorithm is not difficult.

At the heart of this scheme is a finite queue. When a packet arrives, the interface decides whether that packet should be queued or discarded, depending on the capacity of the buffer. The number of packets that leave the interface depends on the protocol. The packet-departure rate expresses the specified behavior of traffic and makes the incoming bursts conform to this behavior. Incoming packets are discarded once the bucket becomes full.

This method directly restricts the maximum size of a burst coming into the system. Packets are transmitted as either fixed-size packets or variable-size packets. In the fixed-size packet environment, a packet is transmitted at each clock tick. In the variable-size packet environment, a fixed-sized block of a packet is transmitted. Thus, this algorithm is used for networks with variable-length packets and also equal-sized packet protocols.

The leaky-bucket scheme is modeled by two main buffers, as shown in Figure 13.4. One buffer forms a queue of incoming packets, and the other one receives authorizations. The leaky-bucket traffic-shaper algorithm is summarized as follows.

Begin Leaky-Bucket Algorithm

Define:

λ = rate at which packets with irregular rate arrive at the *main buffer*

g = rate at which authorization grants arrive at the grant *buffer*

w = size of the grant buffer and can be dynamically adjusted

1. Every $1/g$ seconds, a grant arrives.

2. Over each period of i/g seconds, i grants can be assigned to the first i incoming packets, where $i \leq w$.

3. Packets exit from the queue one at a time every $1/g$ seconds, totaling i/g seconds.

4. If more than w packets are in the main buffer, only the first w packets are assigned grants, and the rest remain in the main queue to be examined in the next $1/g$ interval.

5. If no grant is in the grant buffer, packets start to be queued. ∎

With this model, w is the bucket size. The bucket in this case is the size of the window that the grant buffer opens to allow w packets from the main buffer to pass. This window size can be adjusted, depending on the rate of traffic. If w is too small, the highly turbulent traffic is delayed by waiting for grants to become available. If w is too large, long turbulent streams of packets are allowed into the network. Consequently, with the leaky-bucket scheme, it would be best for a node to dynamically change the window size (bucket size) as needed. The dynamic change of grant rates in high-speed networks may, however, cause additional delay through the required feedback mechanism.

Figure 13.5 shows the Markov chain state diagram (see Section C.5) depicting the activity of grant generation in time. At the main buffer, the mean time between two consecutive packets is $1/\lambda$. In step 1 of the algorithm, at the grant buffer, a grant arrives at rate g. Hence, every $1/g$ seconds, a grant is issued to the main buffer on times $0, 1/g, 2/g, \ldots$. In step 2, over each period of i/g seconds, i grants can be assigned to the first i incoming packets where each packet is assigned a grant. If the grant buffer contains w grants, it discards any new arriving grants. A state $i \in \{0, 1, \cdots w\}$ of the Markov chain refers to the situation in which i grants are allocated to i packets in the main buffer, and thus $w - i$ grants are left available. In this case, the i packets with allocated grants are released one at a time every $1/g$ seconds. When the packet flow is slow, the grant queue reaches its full capacity, and thus grants $(w + 1)$ and beyond are discarded.

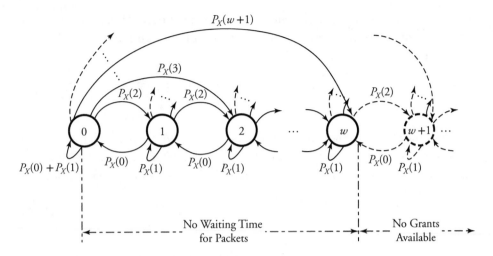

Figure 13.5   State diagram modeling the leaky-bucket traffic-shaping algorithm

We define the following main variables for delay analysis:

- $P_X(x)$ = The probability of x packet arrivals in $1/g$ seconds
- P_i = The probability that i grants have already been allocated to i packets in the main buffer or that the Markov chain is in state i
- P_{ji} = The transition probability from any state j to a state i on the Markov chain

As shown in Figure 13.5, assuming the grant buffer is full, the chain starts at state 0, implying that w grants are available in the grant buffer and that no packet is in the main buffer. In this state, the first arriving packet to the main buffer with probability $P_X(1)$ gets a grant while a new grant arrives in the same period. This creates no changes in the state of the chain. Therefore, the transition probability at state 0 has two components, as follows:

$$P_{00} = P_X(0) + P_X(1). \tag{13.1}$$

This means that P_{00} is equal to the probability that no packet or only one packet arrives ($P_X(0) + P_X(1)$). As long as $i \geq 1$, state 0 can be connected to any state $i \leq w$, inducing the property of the queueing system in Figure 13.5 by

$$P_{0i} = P_X(i+1) \quad \text{for } i \geq 1. \tag{13.2}$$

For example, two new packets arriving during a period $1/g$ with probability $P_X(2)$ change state 0 to state 1 so that one of the two packets is allocated a grant, and thus the chain moves to state 1 from state 0, and the second packet is allocated the new arriving grant during that period of time. The remaining transition probabilities are derived from

$$P_{ji} = \begin{cases} P_X(i-j+1) & for\ 1 \leq j \leq i+1 \\ 0 & for\ j > i+1 \end{cases}. \tag{13.3}$$

Now, the global balance equations can be formed. We are particularly interested in the probability of any state i denoted by P_i. The probability that the chain is in state 0, P_0, implying that no grant has arrived, is the sum of incoming transitions:

$$P_0 = P_X(0)P_1 + [P_X(0) + P_X(1)]P_0. \tag{13.4}$$

For P_1, we can write

$$P_1 = P_X(2)P_0 + P_X(1)P_1 + P_X(0)P_2. \tag{13.5}$$

For all other states, the probability of the state can be derived from the following generic expression:

$$P_i = \sum_{i+1}^{j=0} P_X(i-j+1)P_j \quad for\ i \geq 1. \tag{13.6}$$

The set of equations generated from Equation (13.6) can be recursively solved. Knowing the probability of each state at this point, we can use Little's formula (see Section 11.1) to estimate the average waiting period to obtain a grant for a packet, $E[T_q]$, using the average number of unauthorized packets in the main buffer, $E[K_q(t)]$, as follows:

$$E[K_q(t)] = \sum_{i=w+1}^{\infty} (i-w)P_i,$$

$$E[T_q] = \frac{\sum_{i=w+1}^{\infty} (i-w)P_i}{g}. \tag{13.7}$$

It is also interesting to note that the state of the Markov chain can turn into "queueing of packets" at any time, as shown by dashed lines in Figure 13.5. For example at state 0, if more than $w+1$ packets arrive during $1/g$, the state of the chain can change to any state after w, depending on the number of arriving packets during $1/g$. If this happens, the system still assigns $w+1$ grants to the first $w+1$ packets and assigns no grant to the remaining packets. The remaining packets stay pending to receive grants.

Example.   The probability that x packets arrive in $1/g$ seconds is obtained by

$$P_X(x) = \frac{(\frac{\lambda}{g})^x e^{-\frac{\lambda}{g}}}{x!}.$$

Find the probability that the system has not issued any grants.

Solution.   We give the first final result, which starts at P_0, and leave the rest of this recursive effort to the reader. The final form of P_0, using Equation (13.4) and $P_X(x)$, starts at:

$$P_0 = \frac{g - \lambda}{gP_X(0)},$$

where this equation can be rearranged to $g = \lambda/(1 - P_0 P_X(0))$. We can then state that the system is considered stable if $\lambda < g$ or $P_0 P_X(0) > 1$.

Token-Bucket Traffic Shaping

Traffic flow for most applications varies, with traffic bursts occurring occasionally. Hence, the bandwidth varies with time for these applications. However, the network must be informed about the bandwidth variation of the flow in order to perform admission control and to operate more efficiently. Two parameters—the *token arrival rate*, v, and the *bucket depth*, b—together describe the operation of the token-bucket traffic shaper. The token rate, v, is normally set to the average traffic rate of the source. The bucket depth, b, is a measure of the maximum amount of traffic that a sender can send in a burst.

With the *token-bucket traffic-shaping* algorithm, traffic flow is shaped efficiently as shown in Figure 13.6. The token-bucket shaper consists of a buffer, similar to a water bucket, that accepts fixed-size *tokens* of data generated by a token generator at a constant rate every clock cycle. Packets with any unpredictable rate must pass through this token-bucket unit. According to this protocol, a sufficient number of tokens are attached to each incoming packet, depending on its size, to enter the network. If the bucket is full of tokens, additional tokens are discarded. If the bucket is empty, incoming packets are delayed (buffered) until a sufficient number of tokens is generated. If the packet size is too big, such that there are not enough tokens to accommodate it, a delay of input packets is carried over.

The best operation of this algorithm occurs when the number of tokens is larger than the number of incoming packet sizes. This is not a big flaw, as tokens are periodically generated. The output rate of packets attached to tokens obeys the clock,

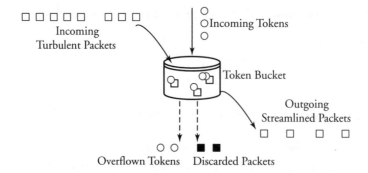

Figure 13.6   The token-bucket traffic-shaping method

and so the corresponding flow becomes a regulated traffic stream. Thus, by changing the clock frequency and varying the token-generation rate, we can adjust the input traffic to an expected rate.

Comparison of Leaky-Bucket and Token-Bucket Approaches

Both algorithms have their pros and cons. The token-bucket algorithm enforces a more flexible output pattern at the average rate, no matter how irregular the incoming traffic is. The leaky-bucket method enforces a more rigid pattern. Consequently, the token bucket is known as a more flexible traffic-shaping method but has greater system complexity. The token-bucket approach has an internal clock that generates tokens with respect to the clock rate. A queueing regulator then attaches incoming packets to tokens as packets arrive, detaches tokens as packets exit, and, finally, discards the tokens. This process adds considerable complexity to the system. In the leaky-bucket approach, no virtual tokens are seen, greatly increasing the speed of operation and enhancing the performance of the communication node. Our primary goal of coming up with a high-speed switching network would thus be easily attained.

13.2.2 Admission Control

The *admission-control* process decides whether to accept traffic flow by looking at two factors:

1. r_s = type of service requested
2. t_s = required bandwidth information about the flow

For controlled-load services, no additional parameters are required. However, for guaranteed services, the maximum amount of delay must also be specified. In any router or host capable of admission control, if currently available resources can provide service to the flow without affecting the service to other, already admitted flows, the flow is admitted. Otherwise, the flow is rejected permanently. Any admission-control scheme must be aided by a policing scheme. Once a flow is admitted, the policing scheme must make sure that the flow conforms to the specified t_s. If not, packets from these flows become obvious candidates for packet drops during a congestion event. A good admission-control scheme is vital to avoid congestion.

13.2.3   Resource Reservation Protocol (RSVP)

The *Resource Reservation Protocol* (RSVP) is typically used to provide real-time services over a connectionless network. RSVP is a soft-state protocol so that it can handle link failure efficiently. The protocol adopts a receiver-oriented approach to resource reservation. This process is required to provide the desired QoS for an application. RSVP supports both unicast and multicast flows. Unlike connection-oriented resource set-up mechanisms, RSVP can adapt to router failures by using an alternative path.

In order for a receiver to make a reservation at intermediate routers, the sender initially sends the t_s message, which passes through each intermediate router before reaching the receiver. This way, the receiver becomes aware of the information on the flow and the path and makes a reservation at each router. This message is sent periodically to maintain the reservation. The router can accept or deny the reservation, based on its available resources. Also, the t_s message is periodically refreshed to adapt to link failures. When a particular link fails, the receiver receives this message over a different path. The receiver can then use this new path to establish a new reservation; consequently, the network operation continues as usual.

Reservation messages from multiple receivers can be merged if their delay requirements are similar. If a receiver needs to receive messages from multiple senders, it requests a reservation meeting the total of t_s requirements of all senders. Thus, RSVP uses a receiver-oriented approach to request resources to meet the QoS requirements of various applications.

13.3   Differentiated Services QoS

The *differentiated services* (DS), or DiffServ, approach provides a simpler and more scalable QoS. DS minimizes the amount of storage needed in a router by processing traffic flows in an aggregate manner, moving all the complex procedures from the core to the edge of the network. A *traffic conditioner* is one of the main features

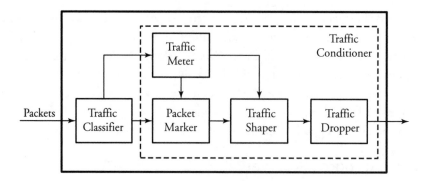

Figure 13.7 Overview of DiffServ operation

of a DiffServ node to protect the DiffServ domain. As shown in Figure 13.7, the traffic conditioner includes four major components: meter, marker, shaper, and dropper. A *meter* measures the traffic to make sure that packets do not exceed their traffic profiles. A *marker* marks or unmarks packets in order to keep track of their situations in the DS node. A *shaper* delays any packet that is not compliant with the traffic profile. Finally, a *dropper* discards any packet that violates its traffic profile.

When users request a certain type of service, a service provider must satisfy the user's need. In order to allocate and control the available bandwidth within the DS domain, a bandwidth broker is needed to manage the traffic. The *bandwidth broker* operates in its own DS domain and maintains contact with other bandwidth brokers at neighboring domains. This is a way to confirm that a packet's requested service is valid throughout all domains within the routing path of the packet.

In order to process traffic flows in an aggregate manner, a packet must go through a *service-level agreement* (SLA) that includes a traffic-conditioning agreement (TCA). An SLA indicates the type of forwarding service, and a TCA presents all the detailed parameters that a customer receives. An SLA can be either static or dynamic. A static SLA is a long-term agreement, and a dynamic SLA uses the bandwidth broker that allows users to make changes more frequently. A user preferring packet-dependent quality of service can simply mark different values in the *type of service* (ToS) field at either the host or its access router. Routers in the DS model then detect the value in the DS field in *per-hop behaviors* (PHBs). The quality of service can then be performed in accordance with the PHB.

In order to establish a traffic-policing scheme, a service provider uses a *traffic classifier* and a *traffic conditioner* at the domain's edge router when packets enter the service provider's network. The traffic classifier routes packets to specific outputs, based on the values found inside multiple fields of a packet header. The traffic conditioner detects and responds if any packet has violated any of the rules specified in the TCA. The DiffServ field value is set at the network boundaries. A DiffServ router uses the traffic classifier to select packets and then uses buffer management and a scheduling mechanism to deliver the specific PHB. The 8-bit DiffServ field is intended to replace the IPv4 ToS field and the IPv6 traffic class field. Six bits are used as a *differentiated services code point* (DSCP) to specify its PHB. The last 2 bits are unused and are ignored by the DS node.

13.3.1   Per-Hop Behavior (PHB)

We define two PHBs: *expedited forwarding* and *ensured forwarding*. As for DiffServ domains, the expedited-forwarding PHB provides low-loss, low-latency, low-jitter, ensured-bandwidth, and end-to-end services. Low latency and ensured bandwidth can be provided with a few configurations on the DiffServ node. Both the aggregate arrival rate for expedited-forwarding PHB packets and the aggregate arrival rate should be less than the aggregate minimum departure rate.

Several types of queue-scheduling mechanisms may be used to implement expedited-forwarding PHB. Ensured-forwarding PHB delivers packets with high assurance and high throughput, as long as the aggregate traffic does not exceed the TCA. However, users are allowed to violate the TCA, but the traffic beyond the TCA is not given high assurance. Unlike the expedited-forwarding PHB, the ensured-forwarding PHB does not provide low-latency and low-jitter application. The ensured-forwarding PHB group can be classified into three service types: good, average, and poor. Three possible drop-precedence values are then assigned to packets within each class, determining the priority of the corresponding packet.

13.4   Resource Allocation

Scheduling algorithms provide QoS guarantees to traffic flows by controlling the flow of transmission, but sufficient buffer space has to be allocated to hold incoming packets, especially in high-speed networks. Some form of protection mechanism has to be implemented to provide flow isolation for preventing ill-behaving flows from occupying the entire queueing buffer. In addition, the mechanism must make packet-discard decisions on the basis of the network congestion level. Thus, buffer management is required to provide rate guarantees for a network.

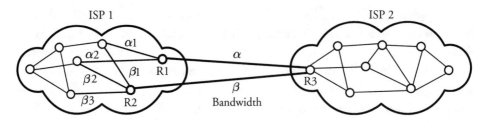

Figure 13.8 The need for network resource allocation when outgoing link capacity (α) is less than the sum of incoming ($\alpha 1 + \alpha 2$) traffic at a router

Issues that involve *resource allocation* for packet-switched networks are fundamentally different from shared-access networks, such as Ethernet, where end hosts are able to directly observe the traffic on the shared medium. End hosts can thus tailor the rate at which they generate and send traffic, based on the traffic on the medium.

Consider the traffic-congestion case shown in Figure 13.8, where two links with a total traffic volume of $\alpha 1 + \alpha 2$ are connected to router R1 with an immediate outgoing link capacity α, where $\alpha < \alpha 1 + \alpha 2$. When it reaches the router, the sum of traffic encounters a low speed at the outgoing gate of the router. Router R1 starts to build up unserved packets and eventually enters a state of congestion. Situations like this, in which traffic from several sources has to be combined onto a common low-speed link, are frequent on the Internet but are unusual in shared-access networks.

If the same situation occurs on router R2, where $\beta < \beta 1 + \beta 2 + \beta 3$, the frequency of severe congestion in edge routers of the ISP 1 network is possible. This situation is by all means undesired from the standpoint of network management. Another important situation shown in Figure 13.8 is that router R3, located in a different domain, must be able to handle a great volume of traffic totaled at $\alpha + \beta$. This situation should convince a network manager that the type of router must depend on the location of the router in the network. The type of router in a specific location of the network must be determined after thorough study, simulation, and taking all the necessary network design factors into consideration.

13.4.1 Management of Resources

Connection-oriented networks have a method of congestion control that leads to an underutilization of network resources. In the virtual-circuit approach, end hosts send a connection set-up message, which traverses the network and reserves buffers at each router for the connection. If adequate resources are not available at each router along the path of the connection, the connection is denied. The resources reserved for one connection cannot be used by another connection, leading to an underutilization of buffers at routers.

Service models of resource allocation are of two basic types:

1. *Best effort*. A network provides no guarantee to end hosts on the type of service to be delivered.
2. *QoS*. An end host may request a QoS connection. The host chooses from a set of QoS classes that the network supports.

In connectionless networks, datagrams are switched independently, and datagrams flowing through a router are called connectionless flows. The router maintains the state of each flow to make necessary informed decisions. For example, in Figure 13.8, either router R2 or the source host attached to this router can initiate a flow record. In some cases, the router observes the source/destination address combination for a packet and classifies packets into different flows. In some other cases, before a flow begins, the source sends some information to identify a connectionless flow originating from the host.

13.4.2 Classification of Resource-Allocation Schemes

Resource-allocation schemes can be classified as router based versus host based, fixed versus adaptive, and window based versus rate based.

Router Based Versus Host Based

Resource allocation can be classified according to whether a router or a host sets up required resources. In a *router-based scheme*, routers have primary responsibility for congestion control. A router selectively forwards packets or drops them, if required, to manage the allocation of existing resources.

A router also sends information to end hosts on the amount of traffic it can generate and send. In a *host-based scheme*, end hosts have primary responsibility for congestion control. Hosts observe the traffic conditions, such as throughput, delay, and packet losses, and adjust the rate at which they generate and send packets accordingly. In most networks, resource-allocation schemes may place a certain level of responsibility on both routers and end hosts.

Fixed Versus Adaptive

In *fixed reservation schemes*, end hosts request resources at the router level before a flow begins. The router then allocates enough resources, such as bandwidth and buffer space, for the flow, based on its available resources. A router also ensures that the new reservation does not affect the quality of service provided to the existing reservations. If resources are unavailable, the router rejects the request from the end host. In an *adaptive reservation scheme*, end hosts send packets without reserving resources at the router and then adjust their sending rates, based on observable traffic conditions or the response from the router.

The observable traffic conditions are the amount of packet loss, delay, or other metrics. A router may also send messages to end hosts to slow down their sending rate. *Fixed reservation schemes* are router based, as the router is responsible for allocating sufficient resources for the flow. Thus, routers have primary responsibility for allocating and managing resources. Adaptive reservation schemes can be either router based or host based. If end hosts adjust rates of transmitted packets based on observable traffic conditions, the scheme is typically host based.

Window Based Versus Rate Based

In *window-based resource allocation*, a receiver chooses a window size. This window size is dependent on the buffer space available to the receiver. The receiver then sends this window size to the sender. The sender transmits packets in accordance with the window size advertised by the receiver. In *rate-based resource allocation*, a receiver specifies a maximum rate of bits per second (b/s) it can handle. A sender sends traffic in compliance with the rate advertised by the receiver. The reservation-based allocation scheme might also involve reservations in b/s. In this case, routers along the path of a flow can handle traffic up to the advertised rate.

13.4.3 Fairness in Resource Allocation

The effectiveness of a resource-allocation scheme can be evaluated by considering two primary metrics: throughput and delay. Throughput has to be as large as possible; delay for a flow should normally be minimal. When the number of packets admitted into the network increases, the throughput tends to improve. But when the number of packets increases, the capacity of links is saturated, and thus the delay also increases, because a larger number of packets are buffered at the intermediate routers, resulting in increased delay.

A more effective method of evaluating the effectiveness of a resource-allocation scheme is to consider the ratio of throughput to delay, or *power*. As the number of admitted packets into a network builds up, the ratio of the throughput to delay increases. This is true until the network load threshold for low delay is reached. Beyond this limit, the network is overloaded, and the power drops rapidly.

A resource-allocation scheme must also be fair. This implies that each equivalent traffic flow through the network receives an equal share of the bandwidth. However, disregarding the flow throughput (flow rate) itself is not fair. Raj Jain proposes a *fairness index* for n flows f_1, f_2, $\cdots$, f_n as

$$\sigma = \frac{\left(\sum_{i=1}^{n} f_i\right)^2}{n \sum_{i=1}^{n} f_i^2}.$$ (13.8)

The fairness index σ is always between 0 and 1 to represent the lowest and the best fairness. With reservation-based resource-allocation schemes, it is always possible for certain traffic, such as voice, to achieve a greater share of the available bandwidth by reservation. This may lead to unfairness in resource allocation. A fair resource-allocation scheme may not always be the most effective method of resource allocation.

13.5   Packet Scheduling

RSVP enables network users to reserve resources at the routers. Once the resources have been reserved, a *packet-scheduling* mechanism has to be in place to provide the requested QoS. Packet scheduling involves managing packets in queues to provide the QoS associated with the packet, as shown in Figure 13.9. A *packet classifier* is the heart of scheduling scheme and performs on the basis of the header information in the packet. Packet classifying involves identifying each packet with its reservation and ensuring that the packet is handled correctly.

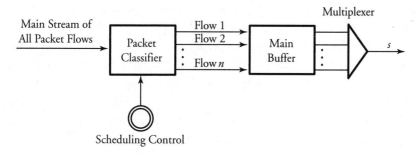

Figure 13.9   Overview of a packet scheduler

Packets are classified according to the following parameters:

- Source/destination IP address
- Source/destination port
- Packet flow priority
- Protocol type
- Delay sensitivity

Based on that information, packets can be classified into those requiring guaranteed services and those requiring controlled-load services. Designing optimal queueing mechanisms for each of these categories is important in providing the requested QoS. For provision of a guaranteed service, *weighted fair queueing* is normally used. This type of queueing is very effective. For controlled-load services, simpler queueing mechanisms can be used.

Packet scheduling is necessary for handling various types of packets, especially when *real-time packets* and *non-real-time packets* are aggregated. Real-time packets include all delay-sensitive traffic, such as video and audio data, which have a low delay requirement. Non-real-time packets include normal data packets, which do not have a delay requirement. Packet scheduling has a great impact on the QoS guarantees a network can provide. If a router processes packets in the order in which they arrive, an aggressive sender can occupy most of the router's queueing capacity and thus reduce the quality of service. Scheduling ensures fairness to different types of packets and provides QoS.

13.5.1   First-In, First-Out Scheduler

Figure 13.10 shows a simple scheduling scheme: *first in, first out* (FIFO). With this scheme, incoming packets are served in the order in which they arrive. Although FIFO is very simple from the standpoint of management, a pure FIFO scheduling scheme provides no fair treatment to packets. In fact, with FIFO scheduling, a higher-speed user can take up more space in the buffer and consume more than its fair share of bandwidth. FIFO is simple to implement from the hardware standpoint and is still the most commonly implemented scheduling policy, owing to its simplicity. With smart buffer-management schemes, it is possible to control bandwidth sharing among different classes and traffic. The delay bound of this scheduler, T_q, is calculated based on the queueing buffer size, as follows:

$$T_q \leq \frac{K}{s}, \tag{13.9}$$

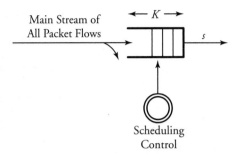

Figure 13.10   A typical FIFO queueing scheduler

where K is the maximum buffer size, and s is the outgoing link speed. Certain control algorithms, such as RSVP, can be used to reserve the appropriate link capacity for a particular traffic flow. However, when high-speed links are active, tight delay bounds are required by real-time applications.

13.5.2   Priority Queueing Scheduler

The *priority queueing* (PQ) scheduler combines the simplicity of FIFO schedulers with the ability to provide service classes. With various priority queueing, packets are classified on the priority of service indicated in the packet headers. Figure 13.11 shows a simple model of this scheduler. Lower-priority queues are serviced only after all packets from the higher-priority queues are serviced. Only a queue with the highest priority has a delay bound similar to that with FIFO. Lower-priority queues have a delay bound that includes the delays incurred by higher-priority queues. As a result, queues with lower priorities are subject to bandwidth starvation if the traffic rates for higher-priority queues are not controlled.

   In this scheduling scheme, packets in lower-priority queues are serviced after all the packets from higher-priority queues are transmitted. In other words, those queues with lower priorities are subject to severely limited bandwidth if traffic rates for the higher-priority queues are not controlled.

   Priority queueing schedulers are either *nonpreemptive* or *preemptive*. In order to analyze these two disciplines, we need to define a few common terms. For a queue with flow i (class i queue), let λ_i, μ_i, and $\rho_i = \lambda_i/\mu_i$ be the arrival rate, mean service rate, and mean offered load (utilization), respectively. We also express a lower value of i for a higher-priority class.

Nonpreemptive Priority Schemes

A *nonpreemptive priority* queueing is a scheme in which the process of lower-priority packets cannot be interrupted under any condition. Every time an in-service packet

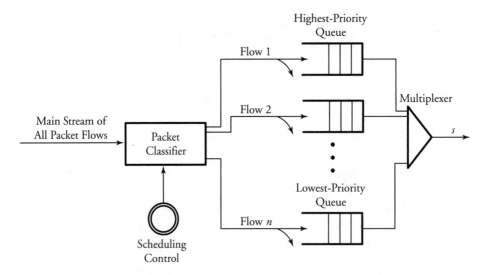

Figure 13.11   A typical priority queueing scheduler

terminates from its queue, the waiting packet from the highest-priority queue enters service. This fact makes the system simple from the implementation standpoint. Let $E[T_i]$ be the mean waiting time for a packet in a flow i (class i) queue where we have a total of n classes in the scheduler. This total queuing delay has four components, as follows:

1. The mean queueing time for any flow i packet until any in-service flow j ($i > j$) packet terminates. We denote this time by $E[T_{q,i}]_1$.

2. The mean queueing time until a packet from a flow i or lower (higher-priority) waiting ahead is serviced. We denote this time by $E[T_{q,i}]_2$.

3. The mean queueing time until a newly arrived higher-priority packet is served while a flow i packet is waiting. We denote this time by $E[T_{q,i}]_3$.

4. The scheduling service time denoted by $1/\mu_i$ due to multiplexing.

The mean queueing times for a flow i, collectively indicated by $E[T_{q,i}]$, can be derived through the sum of all of the first three preceding components:

$$E[T_{q,i}] = E[T_{q,i}]_1 + E[T_{q,i}]_2 + E[T_{q,i}]_3, \qquad (13.10)$$

and thus, the total mean waiting time for a flow i, indicated by $E[T_i]$, is the sum of all the four components, $E[T_i] = E[T_{q,i}] + 1/\mu_i$. Recall that the two parts of expression $E[T_i]$ correspond to Equation (11.22).

The first component of the mean queueing time $E[T_{q,i}]$ is $E[T_{q,i}]_1$. This component is computed using the mean of residual service time for any flow j $(1 \le j \le n)$ currently in service, r_j, and the probability of choosing flow j according to the general rule of expected value (mean) discussed in Appendix C, P_j:

$$E[T_{q,i}]_1 = \sum_{j=1}^{n} r_j P_j, \tag{13.11}$$

The second component of the mean queueing time for a flow i, shown by $E[T_{q,j}]_2$, is the mean time until a packet from a flow i or higher-priority waiting ahead is serviced. Note that a higher-priority flow refers to a flow with a lower value of i, and includes any packet already in the queueing line i. Using Burke's formula, which resulted in Equation (11.68), $E[T_{q,j}]_2$ can be developed as

$$E[T_{q,i}]_2 = \sum_{j=1}^{i} E[T_{q,j}]P_j. \tag{13.12}$$

where $E[T_{q,j}]$ is the mean queueing time for flow i caused by flow j. Similarly, the third component of the mean queueing time, $E[T_{q,i}]_3$, can be derived by

$$E[T_{q,i}]_3 = \sum_{j=1}^{i-1} E[T_{q,i}]P_j = E[T_{q,i}] \sum_{j=1}^{i-1} P_j. \tag{13.13}$$

For this queueing delay component, any packet arriving at queueing line i is stored after the current packet i and that is why $1 \le j \le i-1$ in Equation (13.13). By incorporating Equations (13.11), (13.12), and (13.13) into Equation (13.10), we obtain

$$E[T_{q,i}] = \sum_{j=1}^{n} r_j P_j + \sum_{j=1}^{i} E[T_{q,j}]P_j + E[T_{q,i}] \sum_{j=1}^{i-1} P_j, \tag{13.14}$$

Solving Equation (13.14) recursively (the detail of this recursive solution is not shown here) leads to the total mean queueing time for flow i packets:

$$E[T_{q,i}] = \left(\sum_{j=1}^{n} r_j P_j \right) \Big/ \left(1 - \sum_{j=1}^{i-1} P_j \right) \left(1 - \sum_{j=1}^{i} P_j \right). \tag{13.15}$$

Therefore, the total mean waiting time for flow i, indicated by $E[T_i]$, can be obtained by the inclusion of the mean service time, $1/\mu_i$, in $E[T_i] = E[T_{q,i}] + 1/\mu_i$, as discussed above:

$$E[T_i] = \left(\sum_{j=1}^{n} r_j P_j \right) \Big/ \left(1 - \sum_{j=1}^{i-1} P_j \right) \left(1 - \sum_{j=1}^{i} P_j \right) + \frac{1}{\mu_i}. \tag{13.16}$$

Note that the total mean waiting time of flow i includes the total delay for a packet passing the queuing portion of the scheduler and the server with service time $1/\mu_i$ —in this case, the server is the multiplexer.

Preemptive Priority Schemes

A *preemptive priority* queueing is a scheme in which service in a lower-priority packet can be interrupted by an incoming higher-priority packet. Let $E[T_i]$ be the mean waiting time for a packet in a flow i (class i) queue. Figure 13.12 shows an example in which a class i packet has been interrupted three times by higher-priority packets. This total queuing delay has four components. The first three are identical to those for the nonpreemptive case except we must have $1 \le j \le i$ for W_x instead of $1 \le j \le n$. The fourth component, θ_i, is the total mean completion time for the current class i packet when it is preempted in the server by higher-priority packets (classes $i-1$ to 1). Therefore, by including θ_i, which does include the service time $1/\mu_i$, in Equation (13.6), we calculate the total system delay for a packet passing queue i and the server as

$$E[T_i] = E[T_{q,i}] + \theta_i. \tag{13.17}$$

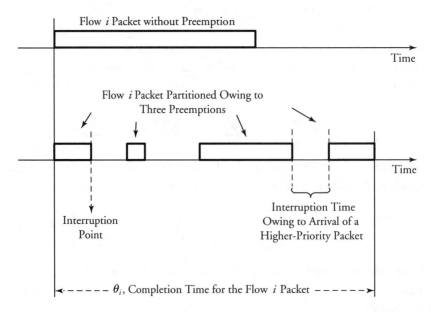

Figure 13.12 Preemptive priority queueing where a flow i packet has been interrupted three times by higher-priority packets

During θ_i, as many as $\lambda_j \theta_i$ new higher-priority packets of class j arrive, where $j \in \{1, 2, \cdots i-1\}$. Each of these packets delays the completion of our current class i packet for $1/\mu_j$. Therefore, θ_i, which also includes the service time of the class i packet, as seen in Figure 13.12, can be clearly realized as

$$\theta_i = \frac{1}{\mu_i} + \sum_{j=1}^{i-1} \frac{1}{\mu_j}(\lambda_j \theta_i). \tag{13.18}$$

From Equation (13.18), we can compute θ_i as

$$\theta_i = \frac{1}{\mu_i \left(1 - \sum_{j=1}^{i-1} \rho_j\right)}. \tag{13.19}$$

If we substitute θ_i of Equation (13.19) in Equation (13.17), we obtain the total system delay for a packet passing queue i and the server:

$$E[T_i] = E[T_{q,i}] + \frac{1}{\mu_i}(1 - \sum_{j=1}^{i-1} \rho_j), \tag{13.20}$$

where $E[T_{q,i}]$ is the same as the one computed for the nonpreemptive case in Equation (13.15).

13.5.3 Fair Queueing Scheduler

The *fair queueing* (FQ) scheduler is designed to better and more fairly treat servicing packets. Consider multiple queues with different priorities. The fair queueing scheduler shown in Figure 13.13 eliminates the process of packet priority sorting. This improves the performance and speed of the scheduler significantly. As a result, each flow i is assigned a separate queue i. Thus, each flow i is guaranteed a minimum fair share of s/n bits per second on the output, where s is the transmission bandwidth, and n is the number of flows (or number of queues). In practice, since all the inputs (flows) may not necessarily have packets at the same time, the individual queue's bandwidth share is typically higher than s/n.

Assume that a_j is the arriving time of packet j of a flow. Let s_j and e_j be the starting and ending times, respectively, for transmission of the packet. Then, c_j, as the virtual clock count needed to transmit the packet, can be obtained from $c_j = e_j - s_j$, since $s_j = \max(e_{j-1}, a_j)$. This simply means that the starting point for transmission of packet j should be either immediate at its arrival time (a_j), or delayed until its previous packet $j-1$ is transmitted completely (e_{j-1}). Then:

$$c_j = e_j - \max(e_{j-1}, a_j). \tag{13.21}$$

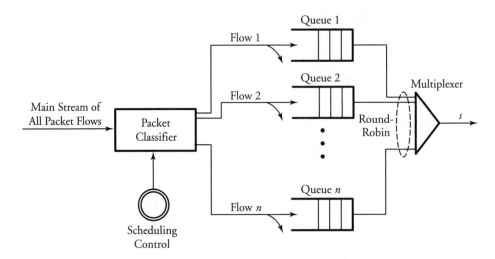

Figure 13.13   Overview of fair queueing scheduler

We can calculate c_j for every flow and use it as a timestamp. A timestamp is used for maintaining the order of packet transmissions. For example, the timestamp is each time the next packet is to be transmitted. In such a case, any packet with the lowest timestamp finishes the transmission before all others.

13.5.4 Weighted Fair Queueing Scheduler

The *weighted fair queueing* (WFQ) scheduler is an improvement over the fair queueing scheduler. Consider the weighted fair queueing scheme shown in Figure 13.14. For an n-queue system, queue $i \in \{1 \cdots n\}$ is assigned a weight w_i. The outgoing link capacity s is shared among the flows with respect to their allocated weights. Thus, each flow i is guaranteed to have a service rate of at least

$$r_i = \left(\frac{w_i}{\sum_{j=1}^{n} w_j} \right) s. \tag{13.22}$$

Given a certain available bandwidth, if a queue is empty at a given time, the unused portion of its bandwidth is shared among the other active queues according to their respective weights. WFQ provides a significantly effective solution for servicing real-time packets and non-real-time packets, owing to its fairness and ability to satisfy real-time constraints. Each weight, w_i, specifies the fraction of the total output port bandwidth dedicated to flow i. Assigning a higher weight to the real-time queues reduces delay for the real-time packets, so real-time guarantees can be ensured. These weights can be tuned to specific traffic requirements, based on empirical results. As

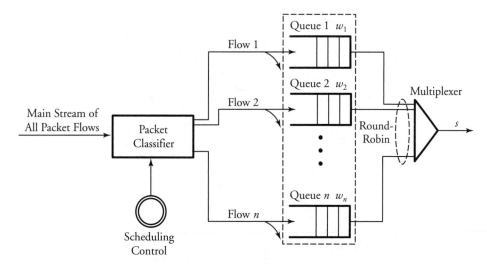

Figure 13.14   Overview of weighted fair queueing scheduler

mentioned, any unused bandwidth from inactive queues can be distributed among the active queues with respect to their allocated weights, again with the same fair share of

$$r_i = \left(\frac{w_i}{\sum_{j \in b(t)} w_j} \right) s, \qquad (13.23)$$

where $b(t)$ is a set of active queues at any time t. The delay bound in this scheme is independent of the maximum number of connections n, which is why WFQ is considered one of the best queueing schemes for providing tight delay bounds. As a trade-off to the effectiveness of this scheme, the implementation of a complete weighted fair queueing scheduler scheme is quite complex.

A version of this scheduler, the so-called *weighted round-robin* (WRR) scheduler, was proposed for asynchronous transfer mode. In WRR, each flow is served in a round-robin fashion with respect to a weight assigned for each flow i, without considering packet length. This is very similar to the deficit round-robin scheduler discussed next for fixed-size packets. Since the system deals only with same-size packets, it is very efficient and fast. The service received by an active flow during its round of service is proportional to its fair share of the bandwidth specified by the weight for each flow.

Example.   Figure 13.15 (a) shows a set of four flows—A, B, C, and D—to be processed at one of the outputs of a router. Each packet's arrival time and label are indicated. The direction of expected packets to the entrance of the scheduler is shown

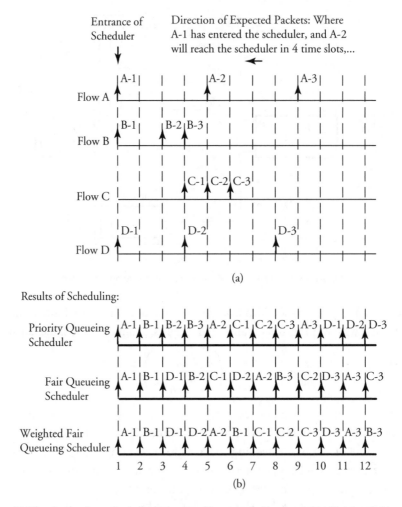

Figure 13.15 Comparison of priority queueing, fair queueing, and weighted fair queueing on the processing of four flows A, B, C, and D: (a) a model of packet arrival expectation and (b) the result of scheduling

in the figure from right to left. For example, as shown, packet A-1 has already entered the scheduler, while packet A-2 is expected to arrive at the scheduler in four time slots, and so on. We would like to compare three schedulers: priority queueing, fair queueing, and weighted fair queueing. All schedulers scan the flows, starting from flow A. With the priority queueing scheduler, priorities decrease from flow A to flow D. With the fair queueing scheduler, if the arrival times of two packets are the same, the smaller flow number is selected. Finally, using the weighted fair queueing scheduler, we assumed that flows A, B, C, and D are given 20 percent, 10 percent, 40 percent, and 30 percent of the output capacity, respectively. Sketch the results of packet scheduling.

Solution.   Figure 13.15 (b) shows the results of packet scheduling. When the priority queueing scheduler is used, the multiplexer scans packet A-1 from line A and then B-1 from line B. After it stays in these two scanning time slots, the multiplexer finds that packet B-2 has now entered the scheduler and since the scheduler operates based on "priority," it then scans B-2 as well instead of advancing to line C. With the same argument, packet B-3 is also scanned next. Now, the multiplexer needs to advance to line C, but it then again finds that A-2 has already reached the scheduler to be scanned and thus A-3 is scanned next. This time the scanner of the multiplexer can move down to line C and starts to explore any arriving packets and so on. The fair priority queueing scheduler operates similarly to the priority scheduler does but it makes sure to give a fair amount of time (in this case 25 percent) to stay for scanning on each line. And in turn, the weighted fair queueing scheduler operates similarly to the fair queueing scheduler does but each line has its own dedicated amount of time in terms of percentage. For example, three packets on line D, which has a weight of 30 percent, can be scanned compared to the one packet on line B, which has a weight of 10 percent.

13.5.5   Deficit Round-Robin Scheduler

In weighted fair queueing, the dependency on a sorting operation that grows with the number of flows is a concern for scalability as speed increases. In the *deficit round-robin* (DRR) scheduler, each flow i is allocated a weight of w_i bits in each round of service, and w_m is defined as the minimum bit-allocation value among all flows. Thus, we have $w_m = \min\{w_i\}$. In every cycle time, active flows are placed in an active list and serviced in round-robin order. If a packet cannot be completely serviced in a round of service without exceeding w_i, the packet is kept active until the next service round, and the unused portion of w_i is added to the next round. If a flow becomes inactive, the deficit does not accumulate until the next round of service and is eventually dropped from the node.

Although DRR is fair in terms of throughput, it lacks any reasonable delay bound. Another major disadvantage of this technique is that the delay bound for a flow with a small share of bandwidth can be very large. For example, consider a situation in which all flows are active. A low-weighted flow located at the end of the active list has to wait for all the other flows to be serviced before its turn, even if it is transmitting a minimum-sized packet.

13.5.6 Earliest Deadline First Scheduler

The *earliest deadline first* (EDF) scheduler computes the departure deadline for incoming packets and forms a *sorted deadline list* of packets to ensure the required transmission rate and maximum delay guarantees. The key lies in the assignment of the deadline so that the server provides a delay bound for those packets specified in the list. Thus, the deadline for a packet can be defined as

$$D = t_a + T_s, \tag{13.24}$$

where t_a is the expected arrival time of a packet at the server, and T_s is the delay guarantee of the server associated with the queue that the packet arrives from.

13.6 Summary

Methods of providing QoS are divided into two broad categories: *integrated services* and *differentiated services*. Integrated services provide QoS to individual applications and flow records. QoS protocols in this category include traffic shaping and packet scheduling. Traffic shaping regulates the spacing between incoming packets. Two traffic-shaping algorithms are *leaky bucket* and *token bucket*. In a leaky-bucket traffic shaper, traffic is regulated at a constant rate, much like the flow of water from a leaky bucket. In the token-bucket algorithm, enough tokens are assigned to each incoming packet. If the bucket becomes empty, packets stay in the buffer until the required number of tokens is generated.

The differentiated services (DiffServ) approach is based on providing QoS support to a broad class of applications. The *traffic conditioner*, one of the main features of a DiffServ node, protects the DiffServ domain. The traffic conditioner includes four major components: *meter*, *marker*, *shaper*, and *dropper*.

Resource allocation in networks can be classified by various approaches: fixed versus adaptive, router based versus host based, window based versus rate based. Finally a few methods of resource control were presented.

Packet scheduling involves managing packets in queues, and includes several scheduling techniques: *FIFO*, *priority queueing*, *fair queueing*, and *weighted fair queueing* (WFQ). WFQ is an improvement over fair queueing, in which each flow i is assigned a weight w_i. Another version of WFQ is *deficit round-robin*, in which each flow i is allocated b_i bits in each round of service.

The next chapter presents some special-purpose routing situations starting with the topic of *tunneling*. Another major topic is how two branches of a geographically separated organization can create a secure route by tunneling and establishing a virtual private network (VPN). Other, related topics covered are *multiprotocol label switching* (MPLS) and point-to-point communications.

13.7   Exercises

1. In a leaky-bucket traffic-shaping scheme, $w = 4$ grants are initially allocated to a session. The count is restored back to 4 every $4/g$ seconds. Assume a Poisson arrival of packets to the system.
   (a) Develop the first five balance equations for the corresponding Markovian process.
   (b) Sketch a Markov chain representing the number of grants allocated to packets, and indicate as many transition values as you have computed.

2. A small router is equipped with the leaky-bucket traffic-shaping scheme; the capacity of the grant buffer is set on window size $w = 2$. Packet arrival during $1/g$ is uniformly distributed, with four possibilities of $k = 0, 1, 2,$ and 3 packets. Consider only non-queueing states with the assumption of $P_0 = 0.008$.
   (a) Find the probability that k packets arrive during $1/g$, denoted by $P_X(k)$.
   (b) Find the four probabilities that 0, 1, 2, and 3 grants are allocated to arriving packets.
   (c) Find all the transition probabilities for three states 0, 1, and 2.
   (d) Sketch a Markov chain representing the number of grants left in the grant buffer for the first three states.

3. A router attached to a mail server is responsible only for receiving and smoothing e-mail. The router is equipped with the leaky-bucket traffic-shaping scheme, whereby the capacity of the grant buffer is set on window size $w = 4$. Packets arrive at $\lambda = 20$ packets per second, and grants arrive at $g = 30$ packets per second. Packet arrival during $1/g$ is distributed according to Poisson. Consider only non-queueing states with the assumption of $P_0 = 0.007$.
   (a) Find the probability that k packets arrive during $1/g$, denoted by $P_X(k)$.
   (b) Find the four probabilities that 0, 1, 2, and 3 grants are allocated to arriving packets.
   (c) Find all the transition probabilities for four states 0, 1, 2, and 3.
   (d) Sketch a Markov chain representing the number of grants allocated to packets for the first four states.

4. Consider a token-bucket traffic shaper. Let the bucket size be b bits and the token arrival rate be v b/s; let the maximum output data rate be z b/s.

   (a) Derive an equation for T_b, the time consumed for a flow to be transmitted at the maximum rate.

   (b) Find T_b when the bucket size is $b = 0.5$ Mb, $v = 10$ Mb/s, and $z = 100$ Mb/s.

5. Does priority queueing change the packet transmission orders if the following service is used?

   (a) Nonpreemptive service

   (b) Preemptive service

6. We want to understand the fairness index of resource allocations. Suppose that a congestion-control scheme can face five possible flows with the following throughput rates: $B_1 = 1$Gb/s, $B_2 = 1$Gb/s, $B_3 = 1$Gb/s, $B_4 = 1.2$Gb/s, and $B_5 = 16$Gb/s.

   (a) Calculate the fairness index for this scheme for B_1, B_2, and B_3.

   (b) What useful information does the result of part (a) provide?

   (c) Now, consider all five flows, and calculate the fairness index for this scheme.

   (d) What would the result of part (c) mean to each flow?

7. Derive an expression for a priority scheduler to present the mean residual service time, r_i, used in Equation (13.11). (*Hint:* Use μ_i.)

8. Assume that all components of a three-flow ($n = 3$) priority scheduler are identical: $\lambda_i = \lambda = 0.2$ ms, $\mu_i = \mu = 1$ ms, and $r_i = r = 0.5$ ms. Find the total system delay for a packet passing each of the three queues 1, 2, and 3 and the server denoted by $E[T_1]$, $E[T_2]$, and $E[T_3]$, respectively. Do the following:

   (a) Use a nonpreemptive priority scheduler for the task.

   (b) Use a preemptive priority scheduler for the task.

   (c) Comment on the results obtained in parts (a) and (b).

9. We want to compare the impact of an increased number of inputs on total delay in priority schedulers. Assume that all components of a three-flow ($n = 3$) and a four-flow ($n = 4$) priority scheduler are identical: $\lambda_i = \lambda = 0.2$ ms, $\mu_i = \mu = 1$ ms, and $r_i = r = 0.5$ ms. Find the total system delay for a packet passing queue 3 denoted by $E[T_3]$. Do the following:

   (a) Use a nonpreemptive priority scheduler for the task.

   (b) Use a preemptive priority scheduler for the task.

   (c) Justify the results obtained in parts (a) and (b).

10. Suppose that four flows are processed in a router that accepts only equal-size packets. Packets in these flows arrive at the following virtual clock times:

   Flow 1: 4, 5, 6, 7, 9
   Flow 2: 1, 6, 9, 12, 14
   Flow 3: 1, 4, 8, 10, 12
   Flow 4: 2, 4, 5, 6, 12

   (a) For each packet, give the virtual clock count at which it is transmitted, using fair queueing. If the arrival times of two packets are the same, the smaller flow number is selected.

   (b) Now consider weighted fair queueing, whereby flows 1, 2, 3, and 4 are given 10 percent, 20 percent, 30 percent, and 40 percent of the output capacity, respectively. For each packet, give the virtual clock count at which it is transmitted.

11. Consider the router's IPP and OPP discussed in Chapter 12 Explain where and how fair queueing can be implemented.

12. We define the timing parameters s_i, f_i, and a_i for a weighted fair queueing scheduler similar to what we did for the fair queueing scheduler. Derive a relationship among these parameters, taking into consideration the weight of each flow (packet), w_i.

13. In a nonpreemptive priority queueing scheme, a low-priority flow is guaranteed to receive 10 percent of the total bit rate s of the transmission link.

   (a) How much better does this low-priority flow perform?

   (b) What would be the impact on the performance of the high-priority flows?

14. Does priority queueing change the order of packets if any of the following types of priority schedulers is used?

   (a) Nonpreemptive

   (b) Preemptive

15. Use the algorithm language presented in various parts of this book (using the terms **Define, Begin, For, If, Otherwise, Receive, Move, ...**) and develop simple algorithms to show the functionality of the following schedulers. Suppose there are n different flows, and you can make any reasonable assumption.

   (a) Preemptive priority scheduler

   (b) Fair queueing scheduler

16. Each output port processor unit of a router has four inputs designated to four different flows. The unit receives packets in the following order during a period

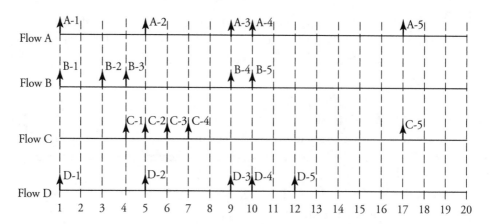

Figure 13.16 Exercise 17 comparison of priority queueing, fair queueing, and weighted fair queueing on processing of four flows

in which the output port is busy but all queues are empty. Give the order in which the packets are transmitted.

> Flow: 1, 1, 1, 1, 1, 1, 2, 2, 3, 3, 3, 4
> Packet: 1, 2, 3, 4, 5, 6, 7, 8, 9, 10, 11, 12
> Packet size: 110, 110, 110, 100, 100, 100, 100, 200, 200, 240, 240, 240

(a) Assume a fair queueing scheduler.

(b) Assume a weighted fair-queueing scheduler with flow $i \in \{1, 2, 3, 4\}$ having weights $w_i \in \{10\%, 20\%, 30\%, 40\%\}$ of the output capacity, respectively.

17. In Figure 13.16, flows A, B, C, and D are processed at one of the outputs of a router. For each packet, the time it arrives and its label are indicated in the figure. Specify the order of packets transmitted at this output, using the following three schedulers. All schedulers scan the flows, starting from flow A.

(a) *Priority queueing.* Priorities decrease from line A to line D.

(b) *Fair queueing.* If the arrival times of two packets are the same, the smaller flow number is selected.

(c) *Weighted fair queueing,* where flows A, B, C, and D are given 10 percent, 20 percent, 30 percent, and 40 percent, respectively, of the output capacity.

18. Figure 13.17 shows four flows (A, B, C, and D) to be processed at one of the outputs of a router. For each packet, the time it arrives and its label are indicated in the figure. Specify the order of packets transmitted at this output, using the following three schedulers. All schedulers scan the flows, starting from flow A.

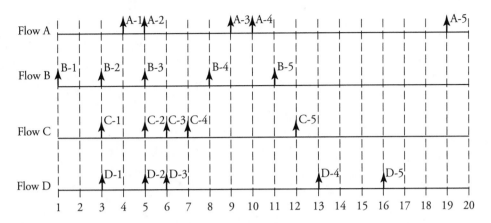

Figure 13.17   Exercise 18 comparison of priority queueing, fair queueing, and weighted fair queueing on processing of four flows

(a) *Priority queueing.* Priorities decrease from line A to line D.
(b) *Fair queueing.* If the arrival times of two packets are the same, the smaller flow number is selected.
(c) *Weighted fair queueing,* where flows A, B, C, and D are given 30 percent, 10 percent, 40 percent, and 20 percent, respectively, of the output capacity.

13.8   Computer Simulation Project

1. ***Simulation of Weighted-Fair Queueing Scheduler.*** Use a simulation tool to simulate the implementation of the weighted fair queueing scheduler of Figure 13.14. The scheduler is set to process four flows A, B, C, and D to be processed using the weighted fair queueing scheme. In the weighted fair queueing scheduler, we assumed flows A, B, C, and D are given 20 percent, 10 percent, 40 percent, and 30 percent of the output capacity, respectively. Establish a packet classifier that can receive packets and encapsulate a field representing a priority according to the preceding weights. Sketch the results of the packet scheduling through statistics of packets processed in each queueing line.

CHAPTER 14

Tunneling, VPNs, and MPLS Networks

Returning to layers 3 and 4 of the protocol reference model, this chapter introduces some special-purpose networking features, in particular, how networks can be *tunneled*. In networking, tunneling is the act of encapsulating a packet from one protocol into another one. Among application-specific communication networks, *virtual private networks* (VPNs) and *multiprotocol label switching* (MPLS) networks are two important and popular tunnel-based ones discussed in this chapter. These two network infrastructures can also be tied together for certain applications. The main topics covered in of this chapter are

- *Tunneling*
- *Virtual private networks* (VPNs)
- *Multiprotocol label switching* (MPLS)

The chapter starts with a description of *tunneling* in a network, a fundamental topic on which the subsequent sections of this chapter are based. Tunneling is the act of encapsulating a packet into another packet. One of the applications of tunneling discussed in this chapter is the establishment of paths for IPv6 flows tunneled into networks that support IPv4.

A VPN is a networking infrastructure whereby a private network makes use of the public network. A VPN maintains privacy by using tunneling protocols and security procedures. The two types of VPNs, each determined by its method of tunneling, are *remote access* and *site to site*.

Multiprotocol label switching (MPLS) networks are a good example of VPNs. In MPLS, multiple labels can be combined in a packet to form a header for efficient tunneling. The *Label Distribution Protocol* (LDP) is a set of rules by which routers exchange information effectively. MPLS uses *traffic engineering* for efficient link bandwidth assignments. Such networks operate by establishing a secure *tunnel* over a public network. Finally, we look at *overlay networks*. An overlay network is a computer network that creates a virtual topology on top of the physical topology of the public network.

14.1   Tunneling

Tunneling in a network is the act of encapsulating a packet into another packet. Encapsulating a packet can be done by inserting the entire packet, including headers and payload, into the payload of another packet so that the encapsulated packet appears as data. Tunneling can also be formed at network- and transport-layer protocols, where equal layers are involved, such as IP-in-IP tunnels. One can easily see from our previous understanding of the five-layer protocol stack that a packet with a link-layer header, network-layer header, and transport-layer header is indeed a result of three packet encapsulation acts in which (1) the payload has been encapsulated in the transport-layer "segment," (2) the result has been in turn encapsulated in the network-layer "datagram," and finally (3) that result has been encapsulated in the link-layer "frame."

A *tunnel* is a virtual path that corresponds to the tunneling act. In computer networking, a tunnel resembles a telephone line in a public switched telephone network. As an example of tunneling, consider the two hosts, host 1 and host 2, shown in Figure 14.1. We want to connect these two hosts through the Internet by using a tunnel. Assume that the router adjacent to host 1 prepares packets with IP1 and UDP1 headers (the link-layer header is not shown for simplicity) and payload1. In this figure, IP1 implies the source and destination addresses are host 1 and host 2, respectively.

When the packet reaches the beginning of the tunnel, R3 encapsulates the packet into a new packet with IP2 addressing. IP2 implies the source and destination addresses inside the tunnel are R3 to R6, respectively. IP1, UDP1, and payload1 collectively shown by payload2 are considered as the payload of the new packet. Note

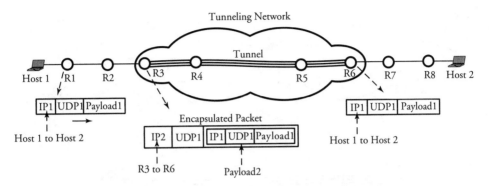

Figure 14.1 A customized protocol packet tunneling through the Internet

that in this example, we assume that there is no change required on the transport-layer header, and thus, UDP1 can also be used for the encapsulating packet. However, the transport-layer header could also be encapsulated and thus the newly created packet could use its own transport protocol.

14.1.1 Point-to-Point Protocol (PPP)

Tunneling can also be implemented by using special-purpose protocols. A tunnel is a relatively inexpensive connection, since it typically uses the Internet as its primary form of communication. Besides the Internet protocols, tunneling requires two types of protocols:

1. *Carrier protocols*, through which information travels over the public network
2. *Encapsulating protocols*, through which data is wrapped, encapsulated, and secured

The basic notion in tunneling is packet encapsulation from one protocol into another one. Thus, a tunnel can also be defined as an encapsulating protocol for protocols at the lower layers. Tunneling protocols, such as the *Point-to-Point Protocol* (PPP) or the *Point-to-Point Tunneling Protocol* (PPTP), are encapsulating protocols that allow an organization to establish secure connections from one point to another while using public resources. A PPP connection is a serial connection between a user and an Internet service provider.

Example. In Figure 14.2, a UDP tunnel connection is established while another virtual PPP connection exists. In this networking scenario, a host with IP address

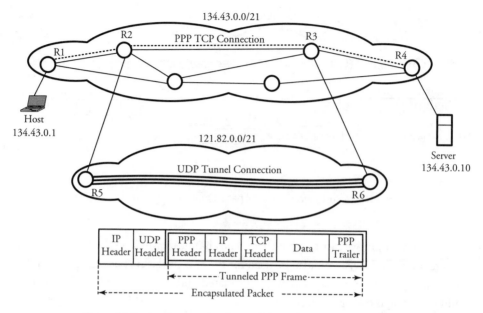

Figure 14.2   A point-to-point protocol (PPP) UDP tunnel connection

134.43.0.1 has made a TCP connection through R1, R2, R3, and R4 to a server with IP address 134.43.0.10. This TCP connection is privileged by PPP encapsulation over network 134.43.0.0/21. Due to the expected high traffic flows between R2 and R3, the network administrator has constructed connections to a separate network of 121.82.0.0/21 as a possible tunneling option. Router R2 has been configured to divert traffic to R5 to establish a UDP tunnel through the separate network of 121.82.0.0/21. This tunnel is established at an interface layer in a UDP transport-layer protocol as it appears from the frame format in the figure. The encapsulated packets formed at R5 are shown in the figure. Once the encapsulated packets reach R6, they are sent to R3 for decapsulation and continue on their original path to the server.

14.1.2   IPv6 Tunneling and Dual-Stack Lite

As IPv4 and IPv6 networks are not directly interoperable. Tunneling techniques can facilitate the transitioning of the Internet from the IPv4 infrastructure to the successor addressing and routing system of Internet Protocol version 6 (IPv6). Figure 14.3 illustrates tunneling that can solve the problem of routing between IPv4 and IPv6 environments. Assume that host 1 located in a network supported by IPv4 connects to host 2 in the same network. This connection creates IPv4 packets as shown in the

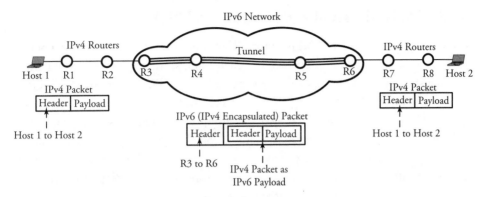

Figure 14.3 A tunneling of IPv4 packets through an IPv4 network

figure. In the meantime, suppose the network management team in this area of the ISP has configured the network so that the IPv4 flows must pass over an intermediating network supported by IPv6, forming a tunnel as shown in the figure. The basic idea behind tunneling here is that two IPv4 routers R2 and R7 want to interoperate using IPv6 packets (datagrams) but are connected to each other by intermediating IPv6 routers. Routers R3 and R6 act as IPv4 to IPv6 converting (or vice versa) routers, forming a tunnel.

With tunneling, the first router on the sending side of the tunnel, R3, takes the entire IPv4 packet and inserts it in the payload field of an IPv6 datagram. The IPv6 packet (datagram) is then addressed to the end point at the receiving side of the tunnel, R6, and transmitted to the first router in the tunnel. Inside the IPv4 network, IPv4 routers forward such IPv6 packets among themselves, just as they would any other IPv6 packet, but they are not aware of the encapsulated IPv4 packet inserted into the IPv6 packet. The IPv6 to IPv4 router at the end of the tunnel, R6, eventually receives the IPv6 packet, extracts the IPv4 packet, and then routes it as it would if it had received the IPv4 packet to the destination, host 2.

Dual-Stack Lite Protocol

*Dual-stack lit*e is the standard for transitioning from the IPv4 to IPv6 approach. Any networking device, including any router or server equipped with the dual-stack lite protocol, has a complete IPv4 and IPv6 implementation. A dual-stack lite device is capable of transmitting and receiving both IPv4 and IPv6 packets. Such devices hold both IPv4 and IPv6 addresses, and are able to indicate to a Domain Name System (DNS) server whether they require an IPv4 or IPv6 address in exchange for a name or URL.

14.2 Virtual Private Networks (VPNs)

A virtual private network (VPN) is a virtually created private network across a public network. A private network normally has clients and servers owned by its organization that share information specifically with each other. The servers are assured that they are the only ones using the private network, and that information sent among them and its users can be viewed only by the group authorized to use that private network. A VPN, then, can be viewed as a simulation of a private network over a public network. The line between the private network and the public network is typically drawn at a gateway router to which a firewall is also attached to keep intruders from the public network away from the private network.

With the globalization of businesses, many corporations have facilities across the world and deploy VPNs to maintain fast, secure, and reliable communications across their branches. A VPN for a corporation enables a host in the corporation to communicate across shared or public networks as if it were directly connected to the private network, while benefiting from the functionality, security, and management policies of the private network. This is done by establishing a secure virtual point-to-point connection through the use of dedicated or predefined connections. In order to create a VPN for an individual or a corporation, the implementation of the following two fundamental functions is required:

1. *Packet encapsulation and tunneling*

2. *Network security*

Packet encapsulation and tunneling were explained in the preceding section. One of the amazing implications of VPNs is that a packet that uses a protocol or IP address not supported by the ISP of the user's public network can be placed inside another IP packet and sent safely over the Internet. This is done through packet encapsulation. VPNs can put a packet that uses a nonroutable IP address, normally blocked by an ISP, inside a packet with a different destination IP address to extend a private network over the Internet. Such encapsulation functions of packets result in a tunnel. VPNs typically rely on tunneling to create a private network that reaches across a public network. Employees of a corporation who are located outside an corporation's main building can use point-to-point connections to create tunnels through the Internet. Since tunneling connections normally run over the Internet, they need to be secure.

The *network security* of a connection is normally provided through public-key encryption, authentication, and IPsec (explained in Chapter 10). Note that most layer 1 and layer 2 VPNs do not require encryption. For example, Ethernet virtual

LANs (VLANs) used to separate projects or customers in large corporations do not need encryption.

Users can connect to the Internet and their business offices using home Internet access facilities by using a VPN. The principle of using VPNs for services is based on private routing through forwarding packets in such a way that the result becomes a virtual private domain within a real physical network. This can be implemented through a pair of edge routers at which the end points are connected. If routing traffic between more than one VPN is desired, dynamic routing information received from other edge routers should be used.

VPNs are deployed with privacy through the use of a tunneling protocol and security procedures. Figure 14.4 shows two organizations, 1 and 2, connected through their corresponding internal nodes and the public border routers R1 and R3, forming a tunnel in the public network. The public network can be as large as a combined series of wide area networks in the Internet. Such a structure gives both private organizations the same capabilities they have on their own networks but at much lower cost. They can do this by using the shared public infrastructure. Creating a VPN benefits an organization by providing

- Extended geographical communication
- Reduced operational cost
- Enhanced organizational management
- Enhanced network management with simplified local area networks
- Improved productivity and globalization

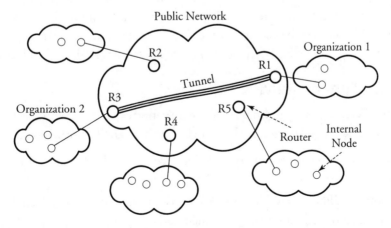

Figure 14.4   Two organizations connected through a tunnel using public facilities

But since each user has no control over wires and routers, one of the issues with the Internet is still its lack of security, especially when a tunnel is exposed to the public. Thus, VPNs remain susceptible to security issues when they try to connect between two private networks using a public resource. The challenge in making a practical VPN, therefore, is finding the best security for it. Before discussing VPN security, we focus on types of VPNs. There are two types of VPNs each determined by its method of tunneling, *remote-access* and *site-to-site*. We will explain these two approaches in the next two sections.

14.2.1   Remote-Access VPN

A *remote-access* VPN is a user-to-LAN connection that an organization uses to connect its users to a private network from various remote locations. Large remote-access VPNs are normally outsourced to an Internet service provider to set up a *network-access server*. Other users, working off campus, can then reach the network-access server and use the VPN software to access the corporate network. Remote-access VPNs allow encrypted connections between an organization's private network and remote users through a third-party service provider.

The three types of business services leading to VPNs in the marketplace are: Layer 3 VPNs, Layer 2 VPNs, and enhanced Internet access. Various packet encapsulations could be used on the local access. The simplest approach is to use the same DHCP-based IP over Ethernet (IPoE) addressing and encapsulation between the user and the network edge router.

Tunneling in a remote-access VPN uses mainly the *Point-to-Point Protocol* (PPP). PPP is the carrier for other Internet protocols when communicating over the network between a host computer and a remote point. Besides IPsec, other types of protocols associated with PPP are L2F, PPTP, and L2TP. The *Layer 2 Forwarding* (L2F) protocol uses the authentication scheme supported by PPP. The *Point-to-Point Tunneling Protocol* (PPTP) supports 40-bit and 128-bit encryption and uses the authentication scheme supported by PPP. The *Layer 2 Tunneling Protocol* (L2TP) combines features of both PPTP and L2F.

14.2.2   Site-to-Site VPN

By using effective security techniques, an organization can connect multiple fixed sites over a public network. *Site-to-site* VPNs can be classified as either intranets or extranets.

- *Intranet* VPNs connect an organization's remote-site LANs into a single private network.

- *Extranet* VPNs allow two organizations to work in a shared environment through a tunnel built to connect their LANs.

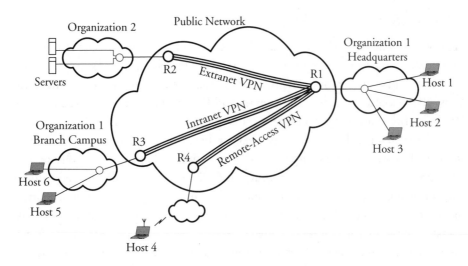

Figure 14.5 Three types of VPNs to and from an organization's headquarters

Figure 14.5 shows the three types of VPNs discussed so far. Organization 1's main campus and its branch campus are connected through an intranet VPN tunnel. For example, host 1 can securely create an intranet VPN through R1 and R3 to be connected to host 6. Organization 1's headquarters can also be connected to organization 2 through an extranet VPN tunnel requiring a different level of security to be applied on the VPN tunnel. For example, host 2 in organization 1 can securely create an extranet VPN through R1 and R2 to be connected to servers of organization 2. The employees of organization 1 located in remote areas can additionally access their corporation through a remote-access VPN. For example, host 4 belonging to organization 1 can securely create a remote-access VPN through R4 and R1 to be connected to host 3. Each remote-access member must communicate in a secure medium. The main benefit of using a VPN is *scalability* with a reasonable cost. However, the physical and virtual distances of two communicating organizations have a great impact on the overall cost of building a VPN.

In a site-to-site VPN, *Generic Routing Encapsulation* (GRE) is normally the encapsulating protocol. GRE provides the framework for the encapsulation over an IP-based protocol. IPsec in tunnel mode is sometimes used as the encapsulating protocol. IPsec works well on both remote-access and site-to-site VPNs but must be supported at both tunnel interfaces. The *Layer 2 Tunneling Protocol* (L2TP) can be used in site-to-site VPNs. L2TP fully supports IPsec features and can be used as a tunneling protocol for remote-access VPNs.

14.2.3   Security in VPNs

Without using dedicated hardware, a VPN uses virtual connections routed through the Internet from the company's private network to the remote site. Companies can create their own VPNs to accommodate the needs of remote employees and distant offices. This section looks at methods for keeping VPN connections secure. A well-protected VPN uses firewalls, encryption systems, IPsec features, and an authentication server.

A firewall provides an effective barrier between a private network and the Internet. Firewalls can be set up to restrict the number of open ports and to monitor what types of packets are passed through and which protocols are allowed through. The authentication server performs authentication, authorization, and accounting for more secure access in a remote-access environment. When a request to establish a session comes in, the request is loaded onto this server. The server then checks who the sender is (authentication), what it is allowed to do (authorization), and what it actually does (accounting and bills).

14.3   Multiprotocol Label Switching (MPLS)

Multiprotocol label switching (MPLS) is another example of tunneling. MPLS is a technology used as part of backbone networks of the Internet to allow multiple protocols to be carried over a converged routing infrastructure faster. This technology provides fast forwarding rates between the routers. In any MPLS network, the routers at the edge of the network are the most complex ones. In edge routers, user services such as policies, rate limiters, logical circuits, and address assignment are created. In a certain connection between a pair of users, edge routers keep a clean separation between a complex edge and create services while routers in the middle mainly do basic packet forwarding by switching MPLS packets from one interface to the other.

MPLS improves the overall performance and delay characteristics of the Internet. MPLS transmission is a special case of tunneling and is an efficient routing mechanism. Its connection-oriented forwarding mechanism, together with layer 2 label-based lookups, enables *traffic engineering* to implement peer-to-peer VPNs effectively. This technology adds new capabilities to IP-based networks:

- Connection-oriented QoS support
- Traffic engineering
- VPN support
- Multiprotocol support

Traditional IP routing has several limitations, ranging from scalability issues to poor support for traffic engineering. The IP backbone also integrates poorly with layer 2 in large service provider networks. For example, a VPN must use a service provider's IP network and build a private network and run its own traffic shielded from prying eyes. In this case, VPN membership may not be well engineered in ordinary IP networks and can therefore result in an inefficient establishment of tunnels.

MPLS adds some traditional layer 2 capabilities and services, such as traffic engineering, to the IP layer. The separation of the MPLS control and forwarding components has led to multilayer, multiprotocol interoperability between layer 2 and layer 3 protocols. MPLS uses a small label or stack of labels appended to packets and typically makes efficient routing decisions. Another benefit is flexibility in merging IP-based networks with fast-switching capabilities.

MPLS network architectures also support other applications, such as IP multicast routing and QoS extensions. The power of MPLS lies in the number of applications made possible with simple label switching, ranging from traffic engineering to peer-to-peer VPNs. One of the major advantages of MPLS is integration of the routing and switching layers. The development of the label-switched protocol running over all the existing layer 2 and layer 3 architectures is a major networking development.

14.3.1 Labels and Label Switch Routers (LSRs)

In MPLS networks, any IP packet entering the MPLS network is encapsulated by a simple header called a *label*. The entire routing is therefore based on the assignment of labels to packets. The compelling point of MPLS is that this simple label is processed for routing instead of the IP header at all times in the network. Note that labels have only local significance. This fact removes a considerable amount of the network-management burden.

An MPLS network consists of nodes called *label switch routers* (LSRs). An LSR switches label packets according to its particular *forwarding tables*. The content of a forwarding table consist of labels to be assigned to a flow of traffic. An LSR has two distinct functional components: a control component and a forwarding component. The control component uses routing protocols, such as OSPF and the *Border Gateway Protocol* (BGP) presented in Chapter 5. The control component also facilitates the exchange of information with other LSRs to build and maintain the forwarding table. Figure 14.6 (a) illustrates an abstract model of a regular router. As we remember from Chapter 12, a typical router mainly consists of an input port processor (IPP), an output port processor (OPP), switch fabric, and a controller. Figure 14.6 (b) shows a model of a label switch router. As we notice, an LSR has a separate forwarding table to

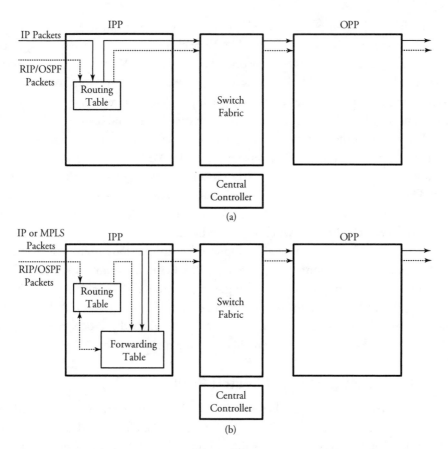

Figure 14.6 Abstract model of (a) a regular router compared with the one for (b) a label switch router (LSR)

store labels. The forwarding table interacts with the routing table in order to arrange the conversion of IP address to labels or vice versa.

Figure 14.7 shows a basic comparison of IP and MPLS. In Figure 14.7 (a), a typical IP network is shown where a source host, as host 1, connects to a destination host, as host 2. The generated IP packets enter a wide-area IP network at edge router R1 and pass over the network using all the relative routing protocols we learned in Chapter 5, and eventually reach edge router R2 from which they exit. In Figure 14.7 (b), an MPLS-enabled network is contrasted with the IP network; any IP packet entering the MPLS network is encapsulated by a label. The entire routing is therefore based on the assignment of labels to packets. We will see in the next sections how this technique would substantially reduce the time for packet processing and routing.

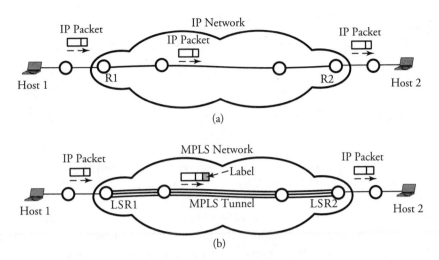

Figure 14.7   Basic operations of MPLS compared with IP: (a) host-to-host communication using IP, and (b) host-to-host communication tunneling into MPLS

Assigning labels to each packet makes a label-swapping scheme perform the routing process efficiently and quickly. In Figure 14.7 (b), the edge LSRs of the MPLS network are ingress LSR1 and egress LSR2. It can be seen that a label is indeed a header processed by an LSR to forward packets. The header format depends on the network characteristics. LSRs read only labels and do not engage in the network-layer packet headers. One key to the scalability of MPLS is that labels have only local significance between two devices that communicate. When a packet arrives, the forwarding component uses the label of the packet as an index to search the forwarding table for a match. The forwarding component then directs the packet from the input interface to the output interface through the switching fabric.

14.3.2   Label Binding and Switching

Figure 14.8 shows the label-switching paradigm in an MPLS network. Suppose the edge device, LSR1, is an *ingress* LSR of an MPLS network. LSR1 performs the initial packet processing and classification and assigns the first label, label 5, on an arriving packet with a destination IP address of 185.2.1.1. Notice that, before the arrival of the packet and as part of the network routing configuration, label 5 had been requested to LSR2 by LSR1 for assignment to any packet whose destination address is 185.2.1.1, and hence both engaging LSRs have agreed on the label for that route. Such an advance mutual agreement between two adjacent LSRs on a certain label to be used for a route is called *label binding*. Thus, in this case, LSR1 knows immediately that

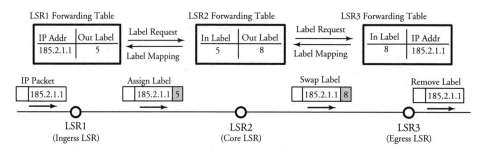

Figure 14.8   Multiple layer 2 switching example in MPLS

when a packet with destination IP address 185.2.1.1 arrives, it must assign label 5 to the packet without any further action. The reader can see how wonderfully the routing becomes simple in an MPLS domain. An ingress LSR always creates the first label.

The *core* LSR, shown by LSR2, swaps the label of the incoming labeled packet with a corresponding next-hop label found in its forwarding table. The label swapping from 5 to 8 takes place in the core LSR2. Finally, at the other end of the network, another edge router, the *egress* LSR, indicated by LSR3, is an outbound edge router and pops the label from the packet.

Label Switched Paths (LSPs) and FECs

Figure 14.9 illustrates an MPLS network with six edge LSRs known as ingress or egress LSRs, indicated by LSR1 through LSR6, and one core LSR labeled as LSR7. Once an IP packet enters an MPLS domain, the ingress LSR processes its header information and maps that packet to a *forward equivalence class* (FEC). Any traffic is thus grouped into FECs. An FEC indeed implies that a group of IP packets are forwarded in the same manner—for example, over the same path or with the same forwarding treatment. A packet can be mapped to a particular FEC, based on the following criteria:

- Source and/or destination IP address or IP network addresses
- TCP/UDP port numbers
- Class of service
- Applications

At this point, a *label switched path* (LSP) through the network must be defined, and the QoS parameters along that path must be established. An LSP resembles a tunnel. In this figure, two LSPs are identified: LSP1 defined over a path from ingress LSR1, core LSR7, and egress LSR3. Similarly, another LSP has been identified by LSP2 and defined over a path from ingress LSR5, core LSR7 and egress LSR3.

Merging LSPs

One of the most compelling features of MPLS technology is LSP merging. Two or more LSPs can be merged as long as their destination egress LSR is identical. Referring to Figure 14.9, LSP1 and LSP2 are merged at LSR7 as both LSPs have the same egress LSR, which is LSR3. Merging LSPs has a great impact on increasing the speed of the routing process due to dealing with one label for all flows of packets.

Packet forwarding at the core LSR is based on a label-swapping mechanism. Once a core LSR receives a labeled packet, it reads the label as an index to search in the *incoming label map table* for the corresponding next-hop label. The label in the MPLS header is swapped with the out label and sent on the next hop. This method of packet forwarding simplifies the routing process by replacing the longest-prefix match of IP routing with simple short-label exact-match forwarding. The real benefit of this method is that instead of processing IP headers for forwarding packets, routers process a short label. Once a packet arrives at the egress LSR, its MPLS header is decapsulated, and the stripped packet is routed to its destination.

In summary, an MPLS domain has three label manipulation instructions: An *ingress* LSR creates a new label and pushes it to the label stack of a packet, a *core* LSR swaps the incoming label with a corresponding next-hop label found in the forwarding table, and an *egress* LSR (outbound edge router) pops a label from the label stack. Only the label at the top of the stack determines the forwarding decision. The egress LSR strips the label, reads the IP packet header, and forwards the packet to its final destination.

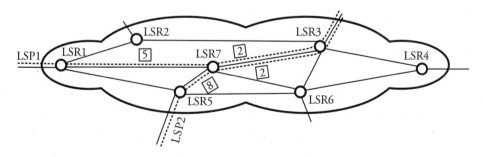

Figure 14.9   A label switched path (LSP) acts as a tunnel between each pair of ingress and egress LSRs

14.3.3   Routing in MPLS Domains

Routing in MPLS domains requires two preparatory actions: link status updates and LSP constructions. Each LSR needs to be updated on available bandwidth and cost of its attached links. As we learned in Chapter 5, knowing link costs helps a router develop its cost and routing tables; this is also the case in MPLS networks. MPLS additionally requires having the available bandwidth information of its links. With these two pieces of information about links, each ingress LSR can construct the best label switched paths (LSPs) to all egress LSRs of the network. An LSP is intuitively treated as a tunnel, and a constructed LSP's information remains in the forwarding table of the ingress LSR for routing. LSPs must be updated once in a while and as soon as a significant change of information occurs on links' status.

The creation of the two preparatory attributes, link status updates and LSPs at ingress, egress, and eventually core LSRs, prepares the network for routing. Routing in MPLS networks is based on the *Label Distribution Protocol* (LDP) and also traffic engineering, which are explained in the next sections.

Label Distribution Protocol (LDP)

The *Label Distribution Protocol* (LDP) is a set of rules by which an LSR informs another LSR of an FEC. LDP enables two LSRs to understand each other's MPLS capabilities. LSP schemes are either *downstream on demand* or *downstream unsolicited*. With the downstream-on-demand scheme, an upstream node explicitly requests a label from a downstream node, and the downstream node forms the requested label. With the downstream-unsolicited scheme, a downstream node advertises a label mapping without receiving any advance requests. Both types of LDPs can be used in explicit and hop-by-hop routing; however, a simple LDP can function using the routing protocol, such as OSPF, to design routes, since hop-by-hop routing does not follow the traffic engineering.

Begin Algorithm to Construct Forwarding Table Using LDP

1. **Ingress LSR:** Extract the final IP address of the destination from the incoming packet.
2. **Ingress LSR:** Form FECs to the destination egress LSR.
3. **Ingress LSR:** Identify the best LSP to the destination egress LSR.
4. **Label Binding:** Each LSR requests a label from its next attached LSR on each LSP.
5. **Ingress LSR:** Form the forwarding table.   ∎

The QoS parameters define how many resources are to be used for the path and what queueing and discarding policy are to be used. For these functions, two protocols are used to exchange necessary information among routers: An intradomain routing protocol, such as OSPF, is used to exchange routing information, and the *Label Distribution Protocol* (LDP) assigns labels. At the end of the process, the router appends an appropriate label for FEC purposes and forwards the packet through.

Example.   Figure 14.10 shows an example of an MPLS network as part of a broadband network architecture connected to IPv6 network 3 with an IP address block of 3:1:AA:0:1::/81. There are two other IPv6 networks 1 and 2 with address blocks 2::D8:0:1:1/95 and 1::30:1C:1/78, respectively. All links provide a minimum of 20Gb/s of bandwidth. A packet with the final destination address 3:1:AA:0:1:: arrives at ingress LSR1. Tables 14.1, 14.2, and 14.3 show a forwarding table for ingress LSR1, core LSR4, and egress LSR6, respectively, assuming that the best path from LSR1 to network 2, which is the first destination of the packet, is found to be LSR1-LSR4-LSR6.

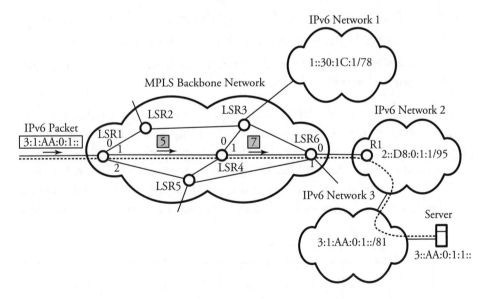

Figure 14.10   Routing in an MPLS backbone network

Table 14.1   Forwarding table for ingress LSR1 in Figure 14.10

Next Destination	Out Label	Output Port	Final Destination	FEC	LSP	BW	Backup LSP
2::D8:0:1:1/95	5	1	3:1:AA:0:1::	FEC1	<LSR1,4,6>	20Gb/s	<LSR1,5,6>

Table 14.2 Forwarding table for core LSR4 in Figure 14.10

In Label	Out Label	Output Port	Next Destination	FEC	LSP
5	7	1	2::D8:0:1:1/95	FEC1	<LSR1,4,6>

Table 14.3 Forwarding table for egress LSR6 in Figure 14.10

In Label	Next Destination	Output Port
7	2::D8:0:1:1/95	0

14.3.4 MPLS Packet Format

Figure 14.11 shows the MPLS header encapsulation for an IP packet. An MPLS label is a 32-bit field consisting of several fields as follows:

- *Label value* is a 20-bit field label and is significant only locally.
- *Exp* is a 3-bit field reserved for future experimental use such as QoS priority.
- *S* is set to 1 for the last entry in the stack and to 0 for all other entries.
- *Time to live* is an 8-bit field used to encode a hop-count value to prevent packets from looping forever in the network.

MPLS uses *label stacking* to become capable of multilevel hierarchical routing. A label enables the network to perform faster by using smaller forwarding tables, a property that ensures a convenient scalability of the network.

It should be noted that multiple labels may be attached to a packet, forming a stack of labels. Label stacking enables multilevel hierarchical routing. For example, BGP labels are used for higher-level hierarchical packet forwarding from one BGP

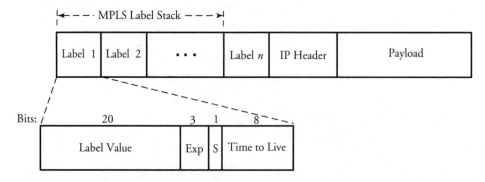

Figure 14.11 MPLS header encapsulation for an IP packet

speaker to the other, whereas *Interior Gateway Protocol* (IGP) labels are used for packet forwarding within an autonomous system. Only the label at the top of the stack determines the forwarding decision.

14.3.5   Multi-Tunnel Routing

As mentioned earlier, labels have only local significance. This fact removes a considerable amount of the network-management burden. An MPLS packet may carry as many labels as required by a source. The process of labeled packets can always be performed based on the top label. The feature of label stacking allows the aggregation of LSPs into a single LSP for a portion of the route, creating an MPLS *tunnel*. Figure 14.12 shows an IP packet moving through an MPLS domain. When the labeled packet reaches the ingress LSR, each incoming IP packet is analyzed and classified into different FECs. This traffic-classification scheme provides the capability to partition the traffic for service differentiation.

Route selection can be done either hop by hop or by *explicit routing*. With hop-by-hop routing, each LSR can independently choose the next hop for each FEC. Hop-by-hop routing does not support traffic engineering, owing to limited available resources. Explicit routing can provide all the benefits of traffic engineering. With explicit routing, a single LSR determines the LSP for a given FEC. For explicit routing, LSRs in the LSP are identified, whereas in hop-by-hop routing, only some of the LSRs in an LSP are specified.

With the introduction of constraint-based routing, FEC can segregate the traffic into different levels of QoS, each with different service constraints, to support a variety of services, such as latency-based voice traffic and security-based VPN. At the beginning of the tunnel, an LSR assigns the same label to packets from a number of LSPs by pushing the label onto each packet's stack. At the other side of the tunnel, another LSR pops the top element from the label stack, revealing the inner label.

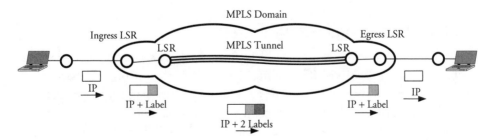

Figure 14.12   An IP packet labeled in an MPLS domain and tunneled to reach the other end of the domain

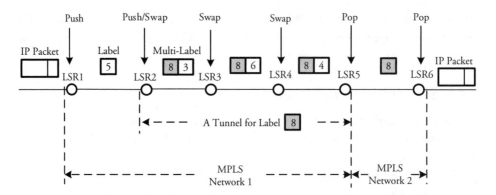

Figure 14.13 Illustration of label stack where multiple labels are carried by a packet

Example. Figure 14.13 shows two MPLS networks, network 1 and network 2, that are adjacent to each other. An IP packet enters at the ingress LSR of network 1, LSR1. This network "pushes" label 5 to this packet. Suppose there is a tunnel formed within network 1 to carry a label, in this case label 8, to be used in network 2. This is a popular technique for sorting certain flows of traffic. Thus, at the beginning of the tunnel in network 1, label 5 is swapped with another label, in this case label 3, and label 8, to be used in network 2, is also pushed into this packet. Remember, once again tunnel created in network 1 benefits the transmission of the IP packet with two labels such that the entire IP packet along with label 8 are encapsulated into the MPLS packet with label 3 housed at the head of the packet. When this multi-label packet reaches LSR3, only the label at the head of the packet, label 3, is swapped with another one, in this case label 6. This trend continues similarly until the packet reaches the end of tunnel at LSR5 where label 4, which belongs to network 1, is popped out of the packet, and the packet having the reserved label 8 is released to network 2. This figure also shows that the packet is stripped completely of all labels at the end of network 2 and continues its journey in the IP domain.

14.3.6 Traffic Engineering

High-quality connections can be expensive in an Internet service provider domain. *Traffic engineering* enables an ISP to route high-quality traffic to offer the best service to users in terms of throughput and delay. This way, traffic engineering reduces the cost of a network connection. Traffic engineering replaces the need to manually configure network devices to set up explicit routes. In MPLS, traffic engineering is an automated scheme for control signaling and link bandwidth assignment and has a dynamic adaptation mechanism.

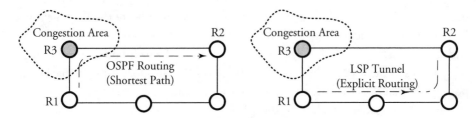

Figure 14.14 A traffic engineering scenario

Traffic engineering can be either *traffic oriented* or *resource oriented*. Traffic-oriented traffic engineering relates to the optimization of such traffic performance parameters as the minimization of packet loss and delay and quick fault recovery when a node or a link fails. The resource-oriented technique engages in the optimization of network resource utilization.

Example. Figure 14.14 shows an example of traffic engineering in MPLS. Assume that router R1 has a packet to send to R2. With the OSPF-based routing policy, routes can be set up through the shortest path, regardless of whether node R3 is experiencing congestion. In contrast, with the MPLS-based routing policy, an LSP can be set up explicitly to avoid the congested node R3. In this case, if a constraint-based routing algorithm is used, an LSP avoiding the congested node R3 is set up dynamically, even though the routing path is longer. This path-management capability is very appealing for traffic engineering.

14.3.7 MPLS-Based VPNs

Routine operations of virtual private networks require the use of both wide-area intradomain routing and interdomain routing schemes. A VPN's request to form a tunnel can be processed at the edge routers. For example, the multiprotocol-based Border Gateway Protocol (BGP) makes it easier for an MPLS-based VPN to manage VPN sites and VPN membership, mainly owing to the traffic engineering feature of MPLS. In an MPLS network, VPNs can be deployed by delivering the service using MPLS-aware subscriber equipment on the same infrastructure used for deploying Internet services.

An MPLS network domain acts as a backbone network between VPN users. Also, core LSRs act as *providing routers*, and edge routers act as *customer edge routers*. Customer edge routers distribute VPN information through MPLS-BGP to other providing routers. In order to forward an IP packet encapsulated for VPN through an MPLS backbone, the top label of the MPLS label stack is used to indicate the outgoing interface, and the second-level label is used to indicate the BGP next hop. When it receives a normal encapsulated IP packet from a router, an ingress customer edge router performs an "IP longest match" and finds the next hop corresponding to the packet's home VPN. The second-to-last MPLS router forwards the packet and pops the top label so that the customer edge router can forward the packet, based on the second-level label, which gives the VPN.

14.4 Summary

Our discussion of *tunneling* issues began with *virtual private networks* (VPNs), which are virtually used by a private-sector entity over a public network. Tunneling is an encapsulation of a packet data segment to move from one protocol to another protocol at the same or higher layer. An organization using a VPN uses a service provider's IP network and builds a private network and runs its own traffic.

Tunneling has two forms: *remote-access* tunneling, which is a user-to-LAN connection, and *site-to-site* tunneling, whereby an organization can connect multiple fixed sites over a public network. Employees who are located beyond their main campus can use *point-to-point* (PPP) connections to create tunnels through the Internet into the organization's resources. Both PPTP and L2TP depend on PPP to frame tunneled packets.

Multiprotocol label switching (MPLS) improves the overall performance of traditional IP routing, especially for the establishment of more effective VPNs. In MPLS, multiple labels can be combined in a packet to form a header used by an LSR for efficient tunneling. The *Label Distribution Protocol* (LDP) is a set of rules by which an LSR informs another LSR. The MPLS *traffic engineering* feature is an automated scheme for a control-signaling process and link-bandwidth assignment to improve the quality of network management.

The next chapter starts a new topic. We are ready to study the basics of optical switching networks and other optical networking topics. An optical network is the backbone of high-speed networking and is presented in the next chapter.

14.5 Exercises

1. Suppose a user client equipped with VPN1 functionality tries to reach a server with the IPv6 address 1001:DB8:8:D3:7:: while this IP address has been blocked by its ISP. VPN1 provides the client with a virtual address 4444:D33:8:43:4:: that is allowed by the ISP.

(a) Show the encapsulation of packets the user requires to successfully reach the destination.

(b) Now suppose packets of this connection have no choice but to cross over another ISP in which the 4444:D33:8:43:4:: address is also blocked. The client is then required to use VPN2 with address 1111:CC:C:23:2:: to pass through the intermediating ISP. Show the hierarchy of packet encapsulations for the user to successfully reach the destination.

(c) Show the network security setup of this connection.

2. Label routing in MPLS networks is similar to VPN tunneling. Compare these two schemes in terms of

(a) Traffic engineering capability

(b) Security

3. Consider a path consisting of six serially connected nodes in a network. Compute the number of two-hop-long tunnels existing on this path.

4. A label in an MPLS network is 20 bits long.

(a) How many different labels can be generated per LSR?

(b) Show that the label field is sufficient to run an MPLS network.

5. Traffic engineering in MPLS networks can be done in the following two locations. Compare the advantages of each approach.

(a) Egress nodes estimate routing to and from all ingress nodes.

(b) A preassigned router estimates routing and propagates to all LSRs.

6. Consider the MPLS network shown in Figure 14.10 and assume that the LSP from LSR1 to LSR6 through LSR4 is no longer preferred due to traffic congestion. The results of a traffic engineering analysis performed based on the available bandwidth require the adoption of other LSPs for routing. The observation from the traffic engineering analysis is as follows: The available bandwidth on any of the links LSR5 to LSR4, LSR4 to LSR3, and LSR5 to LSR6 is 800Mb/s, while the bandwidth on any other non-congested link is 340Mb/s.

(a) Show an updated forwarding table for LSR1.

(b) Show an updated forwarding table for LSR4.

(c) Show an updated forwarding table for LSR6.

7. In a four-node fully connected MPLS network, the four LSRs (LSR1, LSR2, LSR3, and LSR4) are located at four different corners of a square. Assume all links are bidirectional so that traffic can enter the network from any LSR in the network.

(a) For this part, assume the traffic can only enter the network from ingress LSR1. How many different labels at least are needed for binding at LSR1? Consider the length constraint on any path to be a maximum of two hops.

(b) For this part, assume the traffic can only enter the network from ingress LSR2. How many different labels at least are needed for binding at LSR1? Consider the length constraint on any path to be a maximum of two hops.

(c) For this part, assume the traffic can only enter the network from ingress LSR1 and LSR2. How many different labels at least are needed for binding at LSR1? Consider the length constraint on any path to be a maximum of two hops.

(d) How many different FECs can exist in the network?

8. Consider the MPLS/IP networks shown in Figure 14.15 in which all packets arriving at the ingress LSR1 and LSR2 are destined for either IP network 192.18.23.3/24 or IP network 192.17.24.3/25. The number next to each circle represents the associated LSR's port number and the number on each link represents the cost of the link reported by OSPF protocol. Links are unidirectional and from the traffic engineering standpoint all links provide sufficient bandwidth. Design a detailed forwarding table.

(a) Ingress LSR1

(b) Core LSR3 in which Labels 31 through 39 are available for binding

(c) Core LSR4 in which Labels 41 through 49 are available for binding

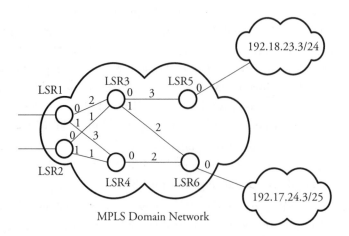

Figure 14.15   A case of routing from an MPLS network to IP networks in exercise 7

   (d) Egress LSR5 in which Labels 51 through 59 are available for binding
   (e) Egress LSR6 in which Labels 61 through 69 are available for binding
9. Consider the MPLS/IP networks shown in Figure 14.16. All packets arriving at ingress LSR1 are destined for IP network 192.3.18.4/21 while all packets arriving at ingress LSR2 are destined for IP network 174.4.11.5/24. The number next to each circle represents the associated LSR's port number and the number on each link represents the cost of the link reported by the OSPF protocol. Links are unidirectional and from the traffic engineering standpoint, all links provide sufficient bandwidth. Design a detailed forwarding table applicable for any of the following LSRs. Each LSR can produce a two-digit label starting with a number equivalent to its own number (for example, LSR2 produces labels 20 through 29):
   (a) Ingress LSR1
   (b) Ingress LSR2
   (c) Core LSR3
   (d) Egress LSR5

14.6   Computer Simulation Project

1. *Simulation of Label Binding and LSPs in an MPLS Network.* Use a network simulator and simulate the label binding function and construction of LSPs in the network presented in Figure 14.15 The label binding must be arranged in

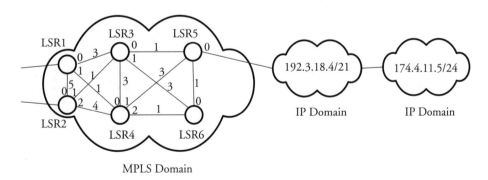

Figure 14.16   A case of routing from an MPLS network to an IP network through another IP network in exercise 8

such a way that, for example, LSR1 and LSR3 agree on a label that takes packets over the constructed LSP to one of the IP destinations defined over the best LSP.

(a) Capture labels of packets traversing the network at each instance of time, and show your results of label binding in a table for the ingress LSR1.

(b) Change the costs indicated on the links, and see what impact on results the simulator reports as a result of various link costs.

CHAPTER 15

All-Optical Networks, WDM, and GMPLS

Optical communication technology uses principles of light transmission in a glass medium, which can carry more information over longer distances than electrical signals can carry in a copper or coaxial medium. All-optical networks have been developed to meet two main objectives: reaching higher data transmission bandwidths and reducing the overall cost of backbone networks. This chapter focuses on principles of optical networks, wavelength-division multiplexing (WDM), and switching used in optical computer networks. Following are the major topics covered:

- *Overview of optical networks*
- *Basic optical networking devices*
- *Large-scale optical switches*
- *Structure of optical cross connects* (OXCs)
- *Routing in all-optical networks*
- *Wavelength allocation in networks*
- *Case study: an all-optical switch*

This chapter starts with an overview of optical networks and the evolution of the application of photonics in communication systems. *Generalized multiprotocol label switching* (GMPLS) technology, a viable choice of operational protocol for all-optical networks, is also described. We will see how a number of optical routing devices are interconnected by *optical links* (OLs).

Next, basic optical devices utilized in optical networks are covered. Some basic optical devices are *optical filters, wavelength-division multiplexers* (WDMs), *optical switches, optical buffers,* and *delay lines.* Optical switches are given special attention, as they are the core engines of all-optical networks. The topic of optical devices is followed by descriptions of detailed large-scale optical switches and thereby *optical cross connects* (OXCs).

Routing and wavelength allocation on optical networks are two critical topics that are presented next. Optical networks use light wavelengths as units of transmission, and thus we have a detailed description of how routing with wavelengths is carried out. Finally, a case study at the end of the chapter describes an optical switch with a *spherical switching network* (SSN) topology.

15.1   Overview of Optical Networks

One of the main concerns with the operation of the Internet is the tremendous demand for higher bandwidth. *Optical communication technology* and in particular *optical networks* have the potential for meeting the emerging needs of obtaining information at much faster yet more reliable rates, mainly due to their potentially limitless capabilities, huge bandwidth availability, low signal distortion, low power requirement, and low cost.

Optical networks have been developed as an outgrowth of *photonics.* The concept of the photonics medium is represented by the generation, transmission, switching, amplification, and sensing of light. Most applications of optical networks are in the range of the visible and near infrared light. The field of photonics is indeed attributed to the invention of semiconductor light emitters and lasers through which engineers found out later that photonic devices and links could be used for communication systems leading to the era of *optical networking.*

Optical networks can provide larger bandwidth than regular electronic networks can due to the much higher carrier frequency of the optical signal. In spite of the benefits that photonic systems present to optical networks, however, photonic logic devices are much less developed than electronic devices. Photonic logic devices consume a larger amount of power, and require substantially larger volume and size, which results in their being poorly integrated. The potential higher speed in a photonic device for faster data bit-rate transmission compared to an electronic device made photonic devices remarkable choices for communications systems and networking. Optical communication systems have been developed to meet two main objectives: reaching higher data transmission bandwidths and reducing the overall cost of data communication. The invention of optical communications started with fiber optic links.

15.1.1   Fiber Optic Links

Optical communication technology uses principles of light transmission in a glass medium. This type of medium was later extended to glass-type transmission cable leading to creation of *fiber optic links* (FOLs), generally known as *optical links* (OLs). Fiber optic links can carry more information over longer distances than electrical signals over a copper or coaxial medium. Most applications in optical networks are in the range of the visible and near infrared light that can travel through optical links. Fiber optic links can transmit digitized light signals over long distances because of the purity of glass fiber combined with improved electronics technology. With some acceptable transmission loss, low interference, and high-bandwidth potential, a fiber optic link is literally an ideal transmission medium.

Optical communication systems may sometimes be combined with electrical components. In such systems, electrical data bits are converted into light, using a certain *wavelength*; when the transmission is completed, the optical signal is converted back to an electrical signal, which is then passed to higher layers that manage switching, restoration, and grooming. Major advantages of partial optical networks are gained by incorporating some electronic switching functions.

15.1.2   SONET/SDH Standards

Synchronous Optical Networking (SONET) and *Synchronous Digital Hierarchy* (SDH) are the two standards that present the transfer of multiple digital bitstreams synchronously over optical fiber using lasers or highly coherent light from light-emitting diodes (LEDs). Optical networks provide routing and restoration of data at the wavelength level. The challenges of optical networks are network management in the presence of different wavelengths and keeping the cost down to be able to add new services. An optical network's agility gives it the speed and intelligence required for efficient routing, thereby improving network management and faster connections and network restorations. For an optical system with many channels on a single fiber, a small fiber cut can potentially initiate multiple failures, causing many independent systems to fail.

Several standards apply in the optical communication environment. The widely used SONET standard provides the transport infrastructure for worldwide telecommunications and defines interface standards at the physical layer of the protocol stack. SONET also defines a hierarchy of interface rates that allow data streams at different rates to be wavelength multiplexed. SONET establishes *optical carrier* (OC) levels ranging from level 1 at 51.8Mb/s (OC-1) to level 768 at approximately 39.95Gb/s (OC-768). Communication carriers throughout the world use this technology to interconnect their existing digital carriers and fiber optic systems.

In optical networks, client layers and optical layers are managed separately, with no direct interaction between the clients and optical-layer equipment. A centralized network-management system provides optical-layer connections. However, distributed control protocols are used to handle network protection and restoration. Because of the centralized management scheme for connection provisioning, a network may not be reliable. From a control and management perspective, there is a great deal of interest in obtaining a closer interaction between the network layer and the optical layer.

Two popular models are the *overlay model* and the *peer model*. In the overlay model, the optical layer and the network (IP) layer have their own independent control planes. Here, the client layer interacts with the optical layer through a *user-to-network interface* (UNI), and optical-layer elements talk to each other through a *network-to-network interface* (NNI). In an overlay model, the optical network topology is hidden from the client layer through UNI. In the peer model, the network layer and the optical layer run the same control-plane software. Routers have full topology awareness of the optical layer. But the peer model is complicated because the optical layer imposes significantly different constraints from those on the IP layer. This elegant model has a closer coupling between the IP layer and the optical layer.

15.1.3 Generalized MPLS (GMPLS) Protocol

All-optical networks can be managed through different protocols. One of the most effective protocols is *generalized multiprotocol label switching* (GMPLS). GMPLS technology is based on the similar concept of MPLS, covered in Chapter 14. In MPLS, labels are assigned over a link, but in GMPLS, wavelengths are assigned over optical links. GMPLS was invented shortly after the advent of MPLS and is a protocol suite used to manage certain interfaces and switching technologies in an optical environment.

Optical Cross Connects (OXCs) and Generalized Labels

Figure 15.1 shows an optical networking scenario with various components that are discussed in this and the following sections. The all-optical network shown as the backbone structure of the Internet in this figure consists of major optical nodes, typically called *optical cross connects* (OXCs), interconnected with physical optical links (OLs). OXCs at either end of a fiber have to agree on which frequency to use. GMPLS provides the necessary bridges between the IP and optical layers to deliver effective traffic-engineering features. The control plane of GMPLS supports all the required traffic-engineering functions while simplify the integration of OXCs. GMPLS can automatically and dynamically configure any kind of network elements and links such as SONET/SDH and provides virtual links or tunnels through the optical network to connect nodes located at the edge of the network.

We learned in Chapter 14 how a label can be used for routing. In contrast to MPLS, in an optical network the idea of a label can be generalized to be anything that is sufficient to identify a traffic flow. GMPLS defines several forms of labels called *generalized labels*. For example, a wavelength on an optical fiber can be allocated to a requested flow. GMPLS is based on labels that can represent either a single fiber in a bundle, a single waveband within a fiber, a single wavelength within a fiber, or a set of time slots within a wavelength (or fiber). Similar to what we had in MPLS label stacking, GMPLS labels only contain information about a single level of hierarchy. The hierarchy in GMPLS is defined as fiber, wavelength, time slot, or packet based.

These labels comprise specific indicators that represent wavelengths, fiber bundles, or fiber ports and are distributed to OXCs. There is a means for identifying explicit

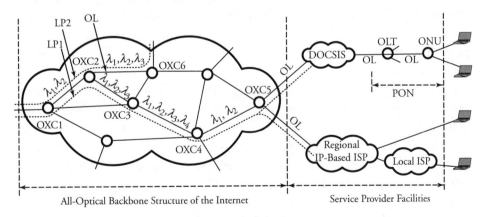

Figure 15.1   Overview of an optical network consisting of an all-optical backbone of the Internet and the service provider facilities

data channels allowing the control message to be associated with a particular data flow, whether it is a wavelength, fiber, or fiber bundle. From a control plane perspective, an OXC bases its functions on a table that maintains relations between an incoming label or a port and an outgoing label or a port. Note that in the case of GMPLS, the forwarding table is called a *cross connect table* and this table is not a software entity but is implemented in the structure of the optical switching fabric. It is easy to realize that in GMPLS there are no equivalent concepts of label merging or label push and pop operations. Label swapping can be treated as wavelength conversion.

Lightpaths (LPs)

A point-to-point connection from an ingress optical cross connect (OXC) to an egress OXC may consists of several "logical" paths called *lightpaths* (LPs). An LP can be thought of as a *generalized label switched path* (G-LSP), which is equivalent to an LSP in MPLS networks studied in Chapter 14. In GMPLS, the LPs can be established bidirectionally, and conveniently the traffic-engineering requirements for bidirectional LPs are the same in both directions through only one signaling message, resulting in reduced latency-related setup time. In optical networks, an OXC carries out wavelength assignments and sets up LPs using their local control interfaces to the other switching devices.

Reconsider Figure 15.1 where the all-optical backbone structure of the Internet shows a number of lightpaths. A lightpath is associated with a set of different wavelengths and since it may be defined over multiple optical links, it can be set up by assigning a dedicated wavelength to each of its optical link segments. LP2, for example, is defined by assigning the available wavelength λ_1 identified as available over the optical link between OXC1 and OXC2, and λ_3 identified as available over the optical link between OXC2 and OXC6. In the upcoming sections, we will present more detail about such a wavelength assignment, which may require wavelength conversion as well.

As GMPLS provides traffic engineering, it allows an ingress OXC to specify the route that a lightpath takes by using "explicit routing." An explicit route is determined by the ingress as a sequence of hops and wavelengths that must be used to reach the egress OXC. As an example of lightpath assignment, consider lightpath LP1 shown in Figure 15.1 established as a logical path over optical cross connects OXC1, OXC2, OXC3, OXC4, and OXC5, and lightpath LP2 as a logical path established over optical cross connects OXC1, OXC2, and OXC6. The two lightpaths have an overlap of routing over the connection from OXC1 to OXC2. The data can be sent over the lightpath once it is set up at the ingress optical cross connect.

In GMPLS, optical link bundling is also possible. In order for the adjacent optical links to be bundled, they must be on the same GMPLS domain and with same traffic-engineering requirements.

Traffic Grooming

In all-optical networks, the bandwidth demanded by traffic typically is lower than the capacity of optical links, and the number of available wavelengths per fiber is limited and costly. Hence, it is not wise to exclusively assign lightpaths to each demand. To increase the throughput of an all-optical network given the limited number of wavelengths per OL, signals can be multiplexed typically at ingress OXCs. This operation is referred to as *traffic grooming*. Traffic-grooming capability is ensured on edge OXCs by operating on a two-layer model: the first layer is an underlying pure wavelength routed all-optical network, and the second layer is an "optoelectronic" time-division multiplexing (TDM) layer built over the first layer. In the all-optical network layer, when a lightpath connects two OXCs, these OXCs seem adjacent for the upper layer. This way the TDM layer can perform multiplexing of different traffic streams into a single wavelength-based lightpath.

15.1.4   Passive Optical Networks (PONs)

A *passive optical network* (PON) is another type of optical network primarily designed for data distribution in residential areas. Figure 15.1 shows a service provider facility portion of the Internet including a PON setup. As seen in this figure, a PON is a point-to-multipoint fiber-based access network. Point-to-multipoint in this context refers to broadcasting downstream signals to all premises sharing multiple fibers. The advantage of using a PON is reduction in the number of fibers and the volume of central office equipment required compared with point-to-point architectures. A typical PON consists of a central office node, which is a switching node called an *optical line terminal* (OLT), the optical fibers and splitters, and a number of user nodes called optical network units (ONUs). ONUs are strictly layer 2 devices and are not assigned IP addresses.

PONs have been developed for premises in which unpowered optical splitters are used where a single optical fiber can supply multiple premises. A PON's downstream broadcasting signals must be supplied with a multiple access protocol. The multiple access protocol of choice is typically *time-division multiple access* (TDMA). As explained in Chapter 3, TDMA divides a given frequency spectrum into multiple channels in the frequency domain. Each user is then allocated one channel for the "entire" duration of its usage. Each user is allowed to transmit only within specified time intervals so that when a user transmits, it occupies the entire frequency bandwidth. The separation among users is performed in the time domain. These time slots are nonoverlapping.

Ethernet PON (EPON) and Interaction with DOCSIS

Ethernet passive optical network (EPON) technology is standardized under IEEE 802.3ah. EPON is a technology for full-service voice, data, and video networks that uses Ethernet frames. Because of the tremendous demand on carriers for bandwidth in the access network, the two access technologies, EPON and cable TV services, can be combined, as seen in Figure 15.1. The resulting technology is *DOCSIS provisioning of EPON* (DPoE), through which EPON operates for DOCSIS. Recall from Chapter 4 that cable TV companies use the *Data over Cable Service Interface Specification* (DOCSIS) protocol, which is a standard specifying cable data network architecture and its technology.

DOCSIS provides a mature cable service based on centralized back-office automation, and EPON provides a reliable transport between the DPoE system and a number of optical network units (ONUs). The passive interconnection structure of EPoN helps reduce the cost of operational expenditures, as it requires no electrical power outside of EPON nodes. An EPON to DOCSIS connectivity requires some intermediating middleware to convert control signaling between the two systems. In most areas, the DPoE network deploys a similar layering model used successfully in the cable operator domain and stacks the service and management layers on top of EPON.

At the physical layer of DPoE, the IEEE Std 802.3 standard is used. Beside the typical physical functions, this layer represents the total attenuation introduced by all passive elements of the fiber plant, including optical fiber itself and optical devices. At the link layer, the data exchanged in EPON between an optical line terminal (OLT) and an ONU is transmitted through Ethernet media access control (MAC) frames. One fundamental difference between the frames in this case and a regular MAC frame is that EPON frames do not support any frame fragmentations. Consequently, the smallest exchangeable and available unit of data between peer stations over the PON medium is applied as a rule of frame size. The practical EPON frame size in this case is typically 1600 bytes. The MAC-based control signaling in EPON is encapsulated into standard Ethernet frames and transmitted with the highest priority.

At the service layer, the DPoE network covers the connectivity for residential and commercial users. In the DPoE network, any service is mapped to an EPON *logical link*. A logical link is identified by a *logical link identifie*r (LLID), which represents independent bandwidth enforcement policies and QoS guarantees. An ONU can support more than one LLID, differentiating logical separation among services such that a service type is represented by a single LLID.

Telephony over a PON (TPON)

PON technology used for telephony is known as *telephony over passive optical network* (TPON). Telephony data in TPON is initiated from a single exchange station and broadcast as a stream of time-division multiplexed (TDM) data frames in the downstream direction over an optical fiber network, then to optical network units (ONUs), and typically terminated in customer premises.

15.2 Basic Optical Networking Devices

An optical network comprises optical devices interconnected by optical links (OLs). Other basic elements on optical networks are tunable lasers, optical buffers or delay elements, optical amplifiers, optical filters, wavelength-division multiplexers, and optical switches.

15.2.1 Tunable Lasers

Tunable lasers can continuously change their emission wavelengths, or colors, in a given spectral range. These changes work in collaboration with optical switches to select a particular wavelength for connection establishment. A *tunable dispersion compensator* is used to compensate for fiber-dispersion losses over the length of the fiber.

15.2.2 Optical Buffers or Delay Elements

Buffering in optical nodes also faces serious limits forced by optical-technology shortcomings. *Optical buffers*, or *optical delay elements*, can be implemented by using a certain length of fiber to delay signals. No practical optical memory is available with the current technology.

15.2.3 Optical Amplifiers

Often in non-all-optical networks, a signal may not be able to remain in optical form and may have to be regenerated, requiring the *amplification* of the signal or the conversion of the signal from optical to electronic. The fact is that the regeneration of optical signals is very costly compared to optical amplification, since the process of signal regeneration requires several steps including optical to electrical to optical conversion with electrical signal processing. The use of *optical amplifiers* enables the achievement of large-distance communication without the need of a regenerator. A major milestone in the evolution of optical fiber transmission systems was *Erbium-doped fiber amplifiers* (EDFAs), or simply, optical amplifiers. An optical amplifier can amplify signals at many wavelengths simultaneously.

15.2.4 Optical Filters

Signal filtering is often needed in optical networks. An *optical filter* equalizes the gain of transmission systems and filters the noise or any unwanted wavelengths. In Figure 15.2 (a), an optical cable carries four wavelengths, λ_1, λ_2, λ_3, and λ_4, and is connected to a filter. This particular filter is designed to allow only λ_1 to pass and to filter λ_2, λ_3, and λ_4.

The design of an optical filter has a number of challenging factors. *Insertion loss* is one and is the loss of power at a filter. A low insertion loss is one of the specifications for a good optical filter. The state of polarization of the input signals should not affect the loss.

Keeping the temperature at the desired level in optical systems, especially on filters, is another factor. Temperature variation should not affect the passband of a filter. As a result, wavelength spacing between adjacent channels on transmission systems should be large enough that the wavelength shift does not affect the entire operation. The passband of filters in an optical system can be narrower if a number of filters are cascaded. The objective of cascading a broad passband is that each filter causes only a small change in the operating wavelengths.

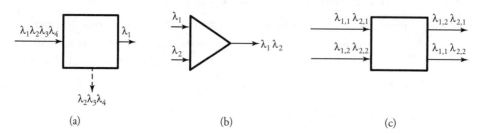

Figure 15.2 Basic communication devices for optical networks: (a) optical filter; (b) wavelength-division multiplexer; (c) optical switch

15.2.5 Wavelength-Division Multiplexer (WDM)

Wavelength-division multiplexer (WDM) is fundamentally the same as frequency-division multiplexing (FDM) described in Chapter 2. In fact, in optical networks, FDM is called WDM, where WDM is basically a multiplexing method of different wavelengths instead of frequencies. A wavelength-division multiplexer mixes all incoming signals with different wavelengths and sends them to a common output port as shown in Figure 15.2 (b). When a WDM is placed in a multiplexing system as depicted in Figure 15.3, *n* optical fibers come together at an optical multiplexer, each with its energy present at a different wavelength. The *n* optic lines are combined onto a single shared link for transmission to a distant destination.

At the demultiplexer, each frame, including *n* channels, is split up over as many optical fibers as there were on the input side. At each output of the demultiplexer, a tuned filter refines the desired signal at the tuned wavelength, and thus all other wavelengths are bypassed. A demultiplexer does the opposite operation, separating the wavelengths and dispatching them onto output ports. On the common link, each channel carries information at light speed with minimal loss. This multiplexing mechanism provides much higher available transmission capacity in communication networks.

The main issue of WDM compared with FDM is that an optical system using a diffraction grating is completely passive and thus highly reliable. With the higher-speed variations of WDM, the number of channels is very large, and the wavelengths are as close as 0.1 nm. Such systems are referred to as DWDM (dense WDM).

Example. Consider a practical multiplexing system with 100 channels, each at rate 10Gb/s. Compute the number of full-length movies per second that can be transferred with this WDM system.

Solution. The total bit rate of this WDM is 100 × 10, or 1,000 Gb/s. Since a movie (MPEG-2 technology) requires 32Gb/s bandwidth, the system can carry approximately 31 full-length movies per second.

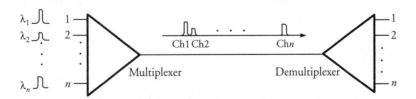

Figure 15.3 A wavelength-division multiplexer (WDM) with *n* inputs

15.2.6 Optical Switches

An *optical switch* is the heart of switching and routing operation in an optical network. The objective in using optical switches rather than semiconductor switches is to increase the speed and volume of traffic switching in a core node of a computer communication network. We will see in the next sections of this chapter how a larger-scale optical switch can act as an *optical cross connect* (OXC) to accept various wavelengths on network input ports, and route them to appropriate output ports. An optical switch performs one or more of the following three main functions:

1. Routes all wavelengths of an incoming port to a different outgoing port
2. Switches specific wavelengths from an incoming port to multiple outgoing ports
3. Takes incoming wavelengths and converts them to another wavelength on the outgoing port

Figure 15.2 (c) shows a simple 2×2 optical switch. A signal with wavelength i arriving at input j of the switch denoted by $\lambda_{i,j}$ can be switched on any of the two output ports. In this figure, $\lambda_{1,1}$ and $\lambda_{2,1}$ arrive on the first input port of the switch; $\lambda_{1,1}$ can be switched on output port 2, and $\lambda_{2,1}$ can be forwarded on output port 1. This basic optical switch is a switch element in larger-scale switch architectures. The basic switch can be made using various technologies. Such switch elements are broadly classified as either *non-electro-optical* or *electro-optical*.

Classification of Switch Elements

Non-electro-optical switches have simple structures. For example, a *mechanical optical switch* uses mirrors at a switch's input and output ports. A switch can be controlled by moving the mirrors and directing a light beam to a desired direction, and eventually to the desired output port. The advantages of mechanical switches are low insertion, low crosstalk, and low cost. However, they have low speed. Another example is the *thermo-optic switch*, which is built on a waveguide. In this type of switch, a change of temperature in the thermo-optic structure of the waveguide can change the refractive index of the material, thereby allowing a switching function to be formed. Although similar to mechanical switches, thermo-optic switches operate at low speeds, but their crosstalk is lower.

Figure 15.4 shows a typical 2×2 *electro-optic switch*, which uses a *directional coupler*. A 2×2 directional coupler is an integrated waveguide that can combine or split signals at its output ports. A coupler is the building block of filters, multiplexers, and switches and is known as a *star coupler*. A star coupler operates by changing the

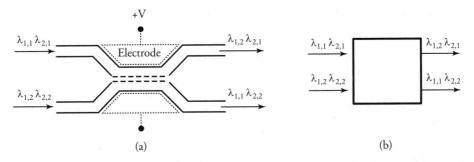

Figure 15.4   Smallest optical switch constructed with a directional coupler: (a) architecture; (b) symbol

refractive index of the material placed in the coupling region. The switching function can be achieved by applying an appropriate voltage across the two electrodes.

The switching function is achieved by taking a fraction, Φ, of the power from input port 1 and placing it on output port 1, with the remaining fraction $1 - \Phi$ of the power on output port 2. Similarly, a fraction $1 - \Phi$ of the power from input port 2 is placed on output port 1, with the remaining power fraction Φ on output port 2. The advantages of this switch are its speed and a modest level of integration to larger modules. However, the high cost of its production is a disadvantage of this switch over the other switch types.

Contention Resolution

Designing large-scale switching devices is one of the main challenges in optical networks. Ideally all the functions inside an optical node should be performed in the optical domain. However, packet contention in switches can be processed only in electronic devices. Several technological factors bring restrictions to the design of an optical switch.

The expansion of a fixed-size switch to higher scales is also a noticeable challenge. Electronic switches have much better flexibility of integration than do optical devices. Some performance factors other than switching speed should be considered in order to prove the suitability of a switch for optical networks. As do regular switches, optical switches face the challenge of *contention resolution* within their structures. Contention resolution may require one or more of the following three operations:

1. *Optical buffering.* Although buffering is a challenge in an optical environment, optical buffers are implemented using fixed-length delay fibers.

2. *Deflection routing.* If two or more lightpaths need to use the same output link, only one is routed along the desired output link; the others are deflected onto

undesired paths directed to the destination through a longer route but with higher priorities.

3. *Wavelength conversion.* By changing wavelengths, signals can be shuffled and forwarded onto other channels.

Another important factor in optical switches is *insertion loss*, which is the fraction of power lost in the forward direction. This factor should be kept as small as possible in optical switches. Sometimes, the dynamic range of the signals must be increased in switches just because the level of loss may not be acceptable for the corresponding particular connection.

The factor of *crosstalk* in switches must be minimized. Crosstalk is the ratio of output power from a desired input to the output power from all other inputs. At issue is the amount of energy passing through from adjacent channels. This energy can corrupt system performance. The cost of optical devices, especially WDMs, is high compared to that of electronic modules. The production of all-fiber devices can also be a way to reduce the cost.

15.3   Large-Scale Optical Switches

Large-scale optical switches can be achieved either by implementing large-scale star coupler optical switches or by cascading 2 × 2 optical switches or even 1 × 2 multi-plexers. However, the implementation of star couplers larger than 2 × 2 is expensive, owing to difficulties in the manufacturing process. Cascading small optical switches is a practical method to expand an optical switch. This method of switch expansion can make a desired-size optical switch quickly and at lower cost. However, some factors affect the overall performance and cost of an integrated switch, such as the following:

- *Path loss.* Large-scale switches have different combinations of switch elements; therefore, a signal may experience different amounts of loss on different paths. Hence, the number of switch elements cascaded on a certain path might affect the overall performance of the switch.

- *Number of crossovers.* Large optical switches can be manufactured on a single substrate by integrating multiple switch elements. In an integrated optical system, a connection between two switch elements is achieved by one layer of a waveguide. When paths of two waveguides cross each other, the level of cross-talk increases on both paths. As a result, the number of crossovers in an optical switch must be minimized.

- *Blocking.* A switch is *wide-sense nonblocking* if any input port can be connected to any unused output port without requiring a path to be rerouted; it is *rearrangably nonblocking* if, for connecting any input port to an unused output port, a rearrangement of other paths is required.

There are several proposed topologies for large-scale switching networks. Two of the more practical ones are *crossbar* and the *Spanke-Beneš network* architectures.

15.3.1   Crossbar Optical Switches

The architecture of a *crossbar* optical switch is not quite the same as the crossbar presented in Chapter 12, as indicated in Figure 15.5. A crossbar optical switch is wide-sense nonblocking. The fundamental difference in the architecture of the optical crossbar and traditional crossbars is the existence of different and variable-length paths from any input to any output. This feature was created in the structure of the optical crossbar to minimize the crossover of interconnections. A crossbar optical switch is made up of 2×2 optical switches. Denoting the number of switches a signal faces to reach an output port from an input port by ℓ, the bounds for ℓ can be derived from the figure as

$$1 \le \ell \le 2n - 1, \tag{15.1}$$

where n is the number of inputs or outputs of the crossbar. In an $n \times n$ crossbar, the number of required 2×2 switches is n^2. The 16 2×2 switches in the Figure 15.5 crossbar are structured in an appropriate way. The main issue with the crossbar structure is its cost, which is a function of n^2. But a great advantage of such an architecture is that the switch can be manufactured without any crossovers.

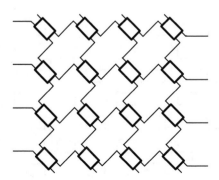

Figure 15.5   A 4 x 4 wide-sense nonblocking crossbar optical switch without waveguide crossovers, using basic 2 x 2 switch elements

15.3.2 Spanke-Beneš Optical Switch

Figure 15.6 shows a rearrangeably nonblocking switch called a *Spanke-Beneš optical switch*. This switch is designed with identical 2×2 optical switch elements, and there are no crossover paths. This optical switch is also known as *n*-stage planar architecture. Denoting the number of 2×2 optical switch elements a signal faces to reach an output port from an input port by ℓ, and assuming there are *n* optical switch elements in each row, we can derive the bounds for ℓ by

$$\frac{n}{2} \leq \ell \leq n. \tag{15.2}$$

This inequity can be verified from Figure 15.6, which shows multiple paths between each input/output pair. Thus, the longest possible path in the network of the switch is *n*, and the shortest possible path is *n*/2. This arrangement is made to achieve a moderately low blocking. Thus, there are *n* stages (columns) and $\frac{n(n-1)}{2}$ switch elements in an $n \times n$ optical switch.

15.4 Structure of Optical Cross Connects (OXCs)

An *optical cross connect* (OXC), also known as the *wavelength router*, is a major device in optical networks that directs and routes an input wavelength to a specified output port. Each optical cross connect in a network is thus considered a node. OXCs are made of various components and they are classified as either *broadcast nodes* or *wavelength routing nodes*.

In a broadcast node, a wavelength is broadcast by a passive device to all nodes. The passive device can be an *optical star coupler*. A coupler combines all incoming signals and delivers a fraction of the power from each signal onto each output port.

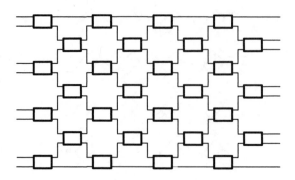

Figure 15.6 An 8 x 8 Spanke-Beneš optical switch with rearrangeably nonblocking structure without requiring any interconnection crossover

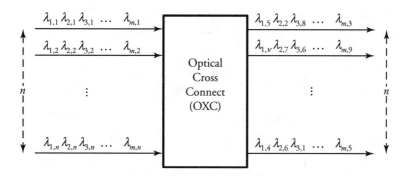

Figure 15.7   Overview of an optical cross connect (OXC)

A *tunable optical filter* can then select the desired wavelength for reception. Broadcast nodes are simple and suitable for use in access networks, mainly LANs. The number of optical links connected to a broadcast node is limited, since the wavelengths cannot be reused in the network.

Wavelength routing nodes are more practical. Figure 15.7 shows an overview of an $n \times n$ wavelength routing node in which full connectivity is ensured between n inputs and n outputs, using m wavelengths per input. In general, a signal with wavelength i arriving at input j of the optical cross connect denoted by $\lambda_{i,j}$ can be switched on any of the n output ports. For example, a light with wavelength $\lambda_{3,2}$ among all wavelengths $\{ \lambda_{1,2}, \lambda_{2,2}, \lambda_{3,2}, \cdots , \lambda_{m,2} \}$ arrives on the second input port of the optical cross connect. This wavelength can be switched on any of the outputs and, possibly, with a different wavelength, as $\lambda_{4,7}$.

15.4.1   Structure of Wavelength Routing Nodes

Wavelength routing optical cross connects (OXCs) are of two types. The first type can switch an input only to an output using the same wavelength. Figure 15.8 gives an overview of this OXC. Consider this OXC with n inputs and n outputs, where each input i can bring up to m wavelengths as $\{ \lambda_{1,i}, \lambda_{2,i}, \lambda_{3,i}, \ldots , \lambda_{m,i} \}$. In this case, any wavelength $\lambda_{k,i}$ can be switched on output j with wavelength $\lambda_{k,j}$. This way, in each round of switching, all wavelengths at the input ports with the same wavelengths can be switched to desired output ports taking place in the same corresponding channels. As shown in Figure 15.8, the OXC consists of n input WDMs, m optical switches of size $n \times n$, and n output WDMs.

The second type of OXC requires *wavelength-conversion* capabilities, as illustrated in Figure 15.9. Consider this OXC with n inputs and n outputs with up to m wavelengths per input. With this OXC, a wavelength $\lambda_{k,i}$ at input i can be

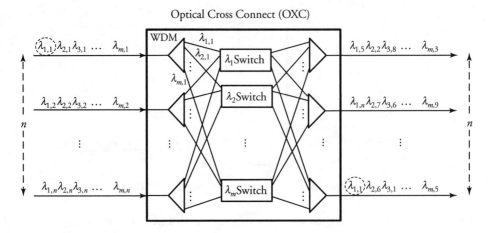

Figure 15.8 An all-optical optical cross connect that replaces wavelength channels

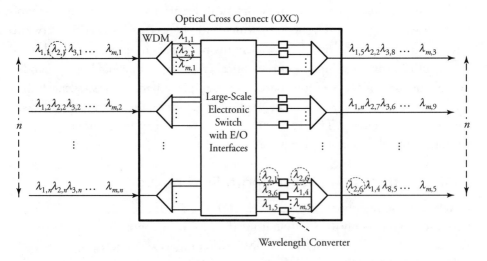

Wavelength Converter

Figure 15.9 An optical cross connect that is able to replace wavelength channels and convert wavelengths

switched on output port j; in addition, the kth wavelength can be converted to the gth, to be shown by $\lambda_{g,j}$. This way, in each round of switching, any wavelength at the input port with the same wavelengths can be switched on any output port, using any available wavelength. In Figure 15.9, $\lambda_{2,1}$ from input 1 is switched to $\lambda_{2,6}$ on the nth output.

In general, wavelengths may need to be converted in a network for the following reasons:

- The wavelength of a signal entering the network may not be appropriate at a node.
- A node may realize the availability of different and better wavelengths on the network links.

Depending on whether a wavelength converter converts a fixed- or variable-input wavelength to a fixed- or variable-output wavelength, there are different categories for wavelength converters, such as fixed-input fixed-output, fixed-input variable-output, variable-input fixed-output, and variable-input variable-output.

Semi-Optical Cross Connects

Depending on the type of switch fabric used in the structure of an optical cross connect, we can further classify optical cross connects into two main groups:

1. Optical cross connect with *all-optical switches*, in which signals traverse the network entirely in the optical domain.
2. Optical cross connect with *optically opaque optical switches*, in which some forms of optoelectronic processing take place within multiplexing elements.

All-optical switches are the ones we have studied so far. In such switches, the optical signal need not be converted to electrical, and switching is handled in the optical domain. All-optical domains have an advantage of large-capacity switching capabilities. In the optically opaque, generally called semi-optical switches, an optical signal is converted to electrical, and then the appropriate switching takes place. It is obviously a case with an electrical switch core followed up with optical interfaces.

In an optical switch, switching and wavelength conversion take place partially or entirely in the optical domain. An optically opaque optical switch uses an optoelectronic conversion mechanism. This architecture requires other interfaces, such as optical-to-electrical (O/E) converters or electrical-to-optical (E/O) converters as shown in Figure 15.9. The electronic segments are used around the optical switch matrix.

15.5   Routing in All-Optical Networks

Routing in all-optical networks is based on establishment of lightpaths (LPs). Any two LPs traversing the same fiber optical link (OL) cannot share the same wavelength on that link. That is, each wavelength on a given OL is not a sharable resource between LPs. When there are more than one feasible wavelength between a source OXC and a destination OXC, then a wavelength assignment algorithm is required to select a wavelength for a given lightpath. Similar to IP networks, routing in all-optical networks can be classified as unicast routing, more professionally called *wavelength routing* and *broadcasting*, and which is explained next.

15.5.1 Wavelength Routing Versus Broadcasting

Figure 15.10 (a) illustrates a network that uses wavelength routing nodes. These types of nodes are capable of reusing wavelengths and handling many simultaneous lightpaths with the same wavelength in the network. The routing is based on unicast point-to-point routing wavelengths. In this figure, the two lightpaths— OXC1-OXC2-OXC3-OXC4 and OXC6-OXC2-OXC5—do not use any shared optical link and can therefore be assigned the same wavelength. If two or more lightpaths share part of their common paths over an optical link, they must therefore use a different wavelength.

Figure 15.10 (b) shows an optical network with a broadcasting node. A broadcasting node combines all incoming signals and delivers a fraction of the power from each signal to each output port, creating a broadcast function of wavelengths. A *tunable optical filter* can then select the desired wavelength for reception. To route from OXC1 to OXC4 and OXC5, the information is broadcast at OXC2, so that one copy of the information is directed to destination OXC5 and the other copy of the information is headed to destination OXC4. Similarly, to broadcast information from OXC6 to destinations OXC4 and OXC5, the information is broadcast at OXC2.

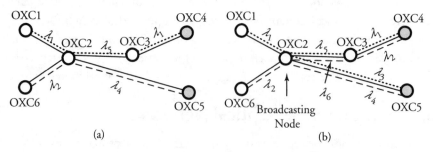

Figure 15.10 An optical network with OXC2 acting as (a) a wavelength routing node and (b) a broadcasting node

15.5.2   Blocking Estimation over Lightpaths

When lightpaths are formed in an all-optical network and taken down dynamically, routing and wavelength assignment decisions must be made as connection requests are initiated to the network. When there are insufficient network resources to set up a lightpath, the requested connection is blocked. Any connection may also be blocked if there is no wavelength available on all the OLs along the chosen route.

To gain insight into how a lightpath (LP) can be blocked, first note that not only does the overlap between LPs impact the wavelength-conversion gain, so too does the number of nodes. Figure 15.11 illustrates a lightpath (LP) including r optical links (OLs) connecting $r + 1$ optical cross connects, OXC0 through OXCr, where each OL includes n wavelengths. Assume that for each lightpath, a route through the network is specified. Let the probability that a wavelength is used on an optical link (OL) and thus is not available be p. If the network provides n wavelengths on every OL and an LP is constructed by r OLs, the probability that an OL is not available denoted by B_{OL} is actually the probability that all wavelengths on the OL are taken and/or unavailable and can be derived by

$$B_{OL} = p^{n}. \tag{15.3}$$

Note that for B_{OL}, we use Lee's method of the parallel link rule developed in Chapter 5. The probability that a given wavelength is free on any given link is $(1 - p)$. The probability that a lightpath request is blocked, or in other words, the probably that a lightpath is not available denoted by B_{LP} can be developed using Lee's method rule of series links explained in Chapter 5 as

$$B_{LP} = 1 - (1 - B_{OL})^{r} = 1 - (1 - p^{n})^{r}, \tag{15.4}$$

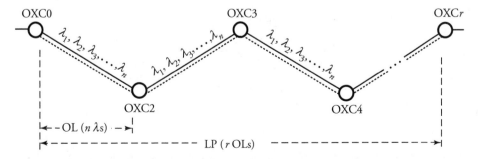

Figure 15.11   Illustration of lightpath (LP) including r optical links (OLs) where each OL includes n wavelengths

if the number of available wavelengths on each OL can be different from the ones on any other optical links so that for optical links $1, 2, \cdots, r$ the number of available wavelengths can be $n_1, n_2, \cdots, n_r$ respectively. Consequently, Equation (15.4) can be generalized to

$$B_{LP} = 1 - \prod_{i=1}^{r} \left(1 - B_{OL}^i\right) = 1 - \prod_{i=1}^{r} \left(1 - p^{n_i}\right). \tag{15.5}$$

Back to special case in Equation (15.3), nevertheless, we can also estimate the possibility that all wavelengths of all optical links are taken leading to the total blocking of a light path (LP) as

$$B_{LPT} = (p^n)^r. \tag{15.6}$$

Example. Consider the 5-node optical network shown in Figure 15.12. Suppose for any optical link (OL), the probability that a wavelength is used on the OL is $p = 0.2$. All the available wavelengths on each OL are shown on the figure. Find individual probability that the corresponding lightpath over any of the three routes from OXC1 to OXC3, from OXC3 to OXC4, or from OXC1 to OXC4 is not available.

Solution. From OXC1 to OXC3, we have $n = 2$ available wavelengths on each of the two OLs ($r = 2$), OL1 and OL2, and thus $B_{OL1} = p^n = 0.2^2 = 0.04$. The blocking probability for OXC1 to OXC3 can therefore be estimated as $B_{LP1} = 1 - (1 - 0.2^2)^2 = 0.078$. From OXC3 to OXC4, $n = 3$, and thus $B_{OL2} = p^n = 0.2^3 = 0.008 = B_{LP2}$. From OXC1 to OXC4, we use Equation (15.5) and the result is $B_{LP} = 1 - (1 - 0.2^2)^2(1 - 0.2^3) = 0.085$.

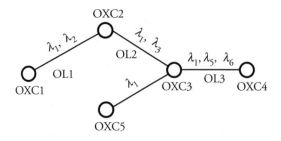

Figure 15.12   An example of wavelength assignment on optical links (OLs)

15.6   Wavelength Allocation in Networks

Similar to nonoptical networks, optical networks consist of a number of routing nodes connected by communication links. In optical networks, nodes may have optical multiplexing, switching, and routing components, and links are typically optical fibers. In the early generations of optical fibers, transmission of signals was degraded on short distances mainly because of lack of amplification. In later versions of optical-fiber systems, the loss of signals was significantly reduced through carefully designed amplifiers. In the latest generations of optical communication systems, the overall cost has been lowered, the effect of dispersion has been eliminated, the data bit rate has been enhanced up to beyond tens of gigabits per second, and WDM technology has been used for multiplexing purposes.

All-optical networks can be designed to carry data using any wavelength regardless of the protocol and framing structure. All-optical networks were encouraged by the development of ultralong-haul fibers mounted on a single physical fiber. By transmitting each signal at a different frequency, network providers could send many signals on one fiber, just as though each signal were traveling on its own fiber. All-optical networks handle the intermediate data at the optical level. This efficient functioning of the network provides a number of advantages in handling data, including reduced overall cost and increased system bandwidth.

A lightpath carries not only the direct traffic between the nodes it interconnects but also traffic from nodes upstream of the source to downstream of the destination. Thus, a lightpath can reduce the number of allocated wavelengths and improve the network throughput. In practice, a large number of lightpaths may be set up on the network in order to embed a virtual topology.

Consider an all-optical network in which each optical link (OL) in the network can carry a maximum of λ_n wavelengths. Because of the maximum wavelength capacity, a network may not be able to handle all lightpath (LP) requests, and thus some requests may be blocked. To keep lightpaths separated on the same optical link, they should be allocated different wavelengths. For example, consider the all-optical network shown in Figure 15.13, with five lightpaths, LP1 through LP5.

A lightpath with wavelength λ_i at any OXC's input can be converted to any available wavelength $\lambda_j \in \{\lambda_1, \cdots, \lambda_n\}$ on the OXC's output link. Based on our earlier discussion, wavelength allocations for this case can be arranged as follows: LP1 is assigned λ_2, LP2 is assigned λ_1, LP3 is assigned λ_2, LP4 is assigned λ_3, and LP5 is assigned λ_4.

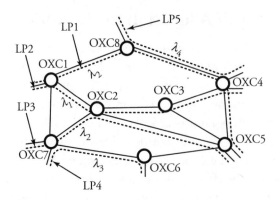

Figure 15.13   Allocation of wavelengths in an all-optical network

The concept of wavelength allocation can be analyzed in two ways. One way is to assume that the probability of a wavelength being used on a link is independent of the use of the same wavelength on all other links of the lightpath. Although this method is not practical, the analysis provides a quick approximation on how effective the assignment of wavelengths is. The second method removes the assumption of independence.

15.6.1   Wavelength Allocation Without Dependency

The wavelength-allocation algorithm assigns an arbitrary wavelength on every link segment of a lightpath when one such wavelength is free on every segment. In this section, we assume that the probability of a wavelength being used on a link is independent of the use of the same wavelength on all other links (segments) of the lightpath. Consider a single link in which n wavelengths are available. For each lightpath request, the first available wavelength is assigned. The wavelength-request arrival is assumed to be Poisson with the rate that leads to a utilization ρ. Then, the blocking probability on this link follows the Erlang-B formula expressed by Equation (11.46) and numerically presented in Appendix D:

$$P(n) = \frac{\rho^n}{n! \left(\sum_{i=0}^n \frac{\rho^i}{i!} \right)}. \tag{15.7}$$

This formula calculates the probability that an arriving request finds no available wavelength while there is no waiting line for the request. For gaining the highest efficiency on assigning wavelengths to requests, wavelengths must be reused effectively. If lightpaths overlap, the *wavelength-conversion gain* would be low.

The wavelength allocation with dependency is much more complicated. Next, we try to present a simplified analysis for this case.

15.6.2 Wavelength Allocation with Dependency

In practice, the allocation of a free wavelength to a lightpath on its every link is dependent on the use of other wavelengths on the same link. Let $P(\ell_i | \hat{\ell}_{i-1})$ be the probability that a wavelength is used on link i, given that the wavelength is not used on link $i - 1$. Also, let $P(\ell_i | \ell_{i-1})$ be the probability that a wavelength is used on link i, given that the wavelength is used on link $i - 1$. Then, if we substitute $P(\ell_i | \hat{\ell}_{i-1})$ for p in Equation (15.4), B_{LP} can be reexpressed for the dependency condition as

$$B_{LP} = 1 - \left[1 - \left(P(\ell_i | \hat{\ell}_{i-1}) \right)^n \right]^r. \tag{15.8}$$

We can now estimate the delay over a lightpath on link i, j from node i to node j. Assume that transmission times are exponentially distributed with mean time $1/\mu$, and Poisson arrival distribution with mean arrival rate Λ. Let $s_{i,j}$ be the loading value on link i, j, or the number of source/destination pairs whose traffic is routed across link i, j. Then, we can obtain the average delay on link i, j by using Equation (11.21):

$$E[T] = \frac{1}{\mu - s_{i,j}\Lambda}. \tag{15.9}$$

If a path in a network has a total of m nodes, the average queueing delay incurred through all nodes over all source/destination pairs is expressed by

$$E[T_m] = \frac{m - 1}{\mu - s_{i,j}\Lambda}. \tag{15.10}$$

15.7 Case Study: An All-Optical Switch

As a case study on optical switches, we consider the *spherical switching network* (SSN). The SSN is a regular mesh network that can be realized as a collection of horizontal, vertical, and diagonal rings, as shown in Figure 15.14. Rings appear in bidirectional pairs that can form cyclical entities and create full regularity in the structure of

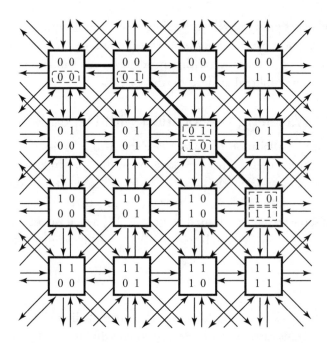

Figure 15.14 A 16-port proposed spherical switching network. Each square represents a 9 × 9 switch element with eight pairs of internal links (shown) and one pair of external links (not shown). An example of self-routing is from switch element 0000 to 1011.

the network. The spherical network uses a simple self-routing scheme. Furthermore, the availability of a large number of interconnections among switch elements and the special arrangement of interconnections potentially reduce the number of deflections compared to existing deflection-routing networks. The network is constructed with *fixed-size* switch elements, regardless of the size of the network. Each switch element consists of a 9 × 9 crossbar. Although not indicated in the figure, one of the nine pairs of links is external and carries the external traffic; the other eight pairs are internal.

Contention resolution in each switch element is based on the deflection of losing lightpaths on undesired internal links and with increments in their priority fields. With the *torus*-shaped topology embedded in the network, when more than one lightpath requests the same outgoing link at each switch element, only one of them is forwarded on the preferred link; the others are deflected onto other links. By maintaining this rule in the system, once a lightpath is admitted to a network, it is not discarded when congestion occurs. Instead, the lightpath receives an increment in its priority field and is misrouted temporarily but will reach its destination. It might be possible at each point in the network to find more than one shortest path to a destination.

15.7.1 Self-Routing in SSN

The routing in the spherical network is self-routing and is fairly simple. Any switch element is given an index number. For example, the indices in a 16-port network are [00 − 00] through [11 − 11], as in Figure 15.14. Depending on whether the flowing traffic is directed toward decreasing index or increasing index, the self-routing is performed by decremental or incremental addressing, respectively. Clearly, the network has four routing cases: straight horizontal, straight vertical, straight diagonal, and a combination of diagonal/horizontal routing or diagonal/vertical.

In each case, there are a certain number of *shortest paths* through which a lightpath is channeled to its destination by taking a corresponding direction. In the first case, depending on whether the index number of the source is greater or smaller than the index number of the destination, the value of the second two index bits of the source address is decreased or increased hop by hop, respectively, until the address of a source and a destination becomes identical where the routing is completed.

In the second case, the process is identical to the horizontal case but in a vertical direction, and index decrement or increment is done on the value of the first two index bits of the source address. In case 3, the routing process is accomplished when the values of both the first and second two index bits of the source address simultaneously receive increment or decrement, as described in cases 1 and 2. Case 4 can be a combination of either the first and third cases or the second and third cases. In case 4, there might be more than one preferred path.

The preceding routing rules use the preferred directions to route each lightpath to its destination along a shortest path. Contention resolution in each switch element is based on deflection of a losing lightpath onto an undesired output if all preferred outputs are not available and giving an increment to the priority field of the lightpath.

15.7.2 Wavelength Assignment in SSN

SSN can be used to construct an all-optical switch core. Suppose that any optical signal is assigned a unique wavelength. To use the fiber bandwidth efficiently, 72 nonoverlapping optical wavelengths corresponding to 8 + 1 pairs of links at each switch element can be arranged. Each node is connected into eight other nodes through eight pairs of internal optical links plus a pair of external links. There are nine groups of wavelengths: $\Lambda(1)$, through $\Lambda(9)$. Each of the following nine groups of wavelengths, $\Lambda(i)$ while $0 \leq i \leq 9$, includes eight nonoverlapping optical wavelengths:

$$\Lambda(i) = \left\{ \lambda_{i,1}, \lambda_{i,2}, \lambda_{i,3}, \lambda_{i,4}, \lambda_{i,5}, \lambda_{i,6}, \lambda_{i,7}, \lambda_{i,8} \right\} \text{ for } 0 \leq i \leq 9$$

Wavelength groups $\Lambda(1)$ through $\Lambda(8)$ are assigned to the eight pairs of internal links, and $\Lambda(9)$ is assigned to the external links. At each incoming fiber link, there are at most eight lightpaths multiplexed into one fiber. All lightpaths are destined to different addresses. When lightpaths arrive at a node, they are demultiplexed, and the node makes the routing decision for each lightpath. After a next hop for each incoming lightpath is decided, the wavelength of that lightpath is converted to one of the available wavelengths by a wavelength converter and is then transmitted to the next switch element.

15.8 Summary

This chapter focused on optical communication networks, beginning with an overview of optical networks. We learned that all-optical networks can be managed through different protocols but one of the most promising network management protocols is *generalized multiprotocol label switching* (GMPLS). In GMPLS technology, wavelengths are assigned over optical links. We then learned about the concept of lightpaths (LPs), which are similar to what we defined as label switched paths (LSPs) in MPLS.

We then presented basic definitions and a review of optical devices such as *optical filters, wavelength-division multiplexers* (WDMs), *optical switches, optical buffers,* and *optical delay lines.* We learned that due to some restrictions presented by optical technology, optical switches could not be scaled up very much. The high cost of large-scale optical switches constructed by a one-segment optical switch was one of the restrictive factors. Therefore, several topologies of large-scale switching networks use simple switch elements, such as *crossbar* and *Spanke-Beneš network* architectures.

Optical networks constructed with optical devices provide routing and restoration of data at the wavelength level. Two popular models for managing the network (IP) layer and the optical layer are the *overlay model* and the *peer model.* In the overlay model, the optical layer and IP layer each have their own independent control planes.

We also described routing and wavelength allocations in all-optical networks. *Wavelength reuse and allocation* in optical networks is a key topic. Because of the maximum capacity on the number of wavelengths that can be carried on a link, a network may not be able to handle all lightpath requests; consequently, some requests may be blocked. To keep lightpaths separated on the same link, they should be allocated different wavelengths. Wavelength allocation can be analyzed in two ways. One way is to assume that the probability of a wavelength being used on a link is independent of the use of the same wavelength on all other links of the lightpath. The other method does not make any assumption of independence.

An all-optical switching network called a *spherical switching network* (SSN) was presented as a case study. Routing in that network is self-routing and is fairly simple. Any switch element is given an index number. Depending on whether the flowing traffic is directed toward decreasing index or toward increasing index, the self-routing is performed by decremental or incremental addressing, respectively.

The next chapter presents cloud computing and network virtualization. Cloud computing is an important networking mechanism that has substantial potential for the creation of data centers, file sharing, and massive data storage efficiently.

15.9   Exercises

1. Consider a crossbar switching network similar to the one shown in Figure 15.5 but of size 8×8. Suppose that the crosstalk suppression of each 2×2 switch element is 40 dB.

   (a) Calculate the maximum and minimum overall crosstalk suppressions for the crossbar switch.

   (b) Calculate the average of overall crosstalk suppressions, using all possible existing paths.

2. Consider the Spanke-Beneš network shown in Figure 15.6. Suppose that the crosstalk suppression of each 2×2 switch element is 40 dB. Calculate the overall crosstalk suppressions, using all possible existing paths.

3. To design an 8×8 optical cross connect, we are comparing three different structures, each using, respectively, a crossbar switching network, a Spanke-Beneš network, and an 8×8 directional coupler.

   (a) Which structure offers the best overall crosstalk suppression?

   (b) Which structure has the lowest overall average switching delay?

4. Consider a ring optical backbone network consisting of eight 2×2 switching nodes labeled 1 through 8. Nodes are interconnected with two fiber-optic rings carrying traffic in opposite directions. Three wavelengths, λ_1, λ_2, and λ_3, are available on each link.

   (a) A SONET network consisting of duplex lightpaths 2-4, 4-7, and 3-6 is constructed over this backbone. For convenience, assume that both halves of the duplex SONET network are identical in terms of wavelengths. Find the minimum number of wavelengths to construct the SONET network.

   (b) Now, assume that another SONET network, consisting of duplex lightpaths 2-5, 5-6, and 2-8 is constructed over this backbone. Using the same assumptions as in part (a), find the minimum number of wavelengths to construct this SONET network.

(c) Both SONET networks are supposed to be constructed over this backbone network simultaneously. Find the minimum number of wavelengths to construct the two SONET networks.

5. Suppose that four wavelengths exist on each single link of a three-link path. For each lightpath request, the first available wavelength is assigned. The wavelength request arrival is assumed to be Poisson, with a rate that leads to 80 percent utilization. For each lightpath, the probability that a wavelength is used on a link is 20 percent. Assume that a lightpath request chooses a route with two links.

(a) Find the blocking probability on this link.

(b) Find the probability that a given wavelength is not free on at least one of existing two links of a route.

(c) Find the probability that a lightpath request is blocked.

6. Consider an optical network with n nodes. Let $L_{i,j}$ be an arriving Poisson traffic rate on link i,j in lightpaths per second, and let $1/\mu_{i,j}$ be the mean time of exponentially distributed lightpath transmission on link i,j.

(a) Find the average queueing delay on link i,j.

(b) Let $s_{i,j}$ be the number of source/destination pairs whose traffic is routed over link i,j. In this case, find the average queueing delay on link i,j.

(c) Find the average queueing delay for a lightpath, given all source/destination pairs.

7. Suppose an all-optical network provides n wavelengths on every optical link (OL) and an OL request chooses a lightpath (LP) with r optical links. Find the probability that a given wavelength is not free on at least one of existing r OLs of an LP.

8. Consider the all-optical network shown in Figure 15.15. Suppose we want to establish lightpath LP1 on the indicated optical cross connects: OXC1-OXC2-OXC3-OXC4-OXC5 on which IP traffic arriving at ingress OXC1 can pass through the network and finally leave from egress OXC5. All available wavelengths on each optical link (OL) of LP1 are shown on the corresponding OL. On any OL, each available wavelength is statistically known to be taken with a chance of $p = 20\%$. Assume that all links are unidirectional, and the number next to each circle (OXC) represents the associated OXC's port number.

(a) Find B_{OL}, the probability that the OL connecting OXC1 and OXC2 gets blocked. Do the same calculation for the other segments of LP1.

(b) Find B_{LP}, the probability that LP1 gets blocked.

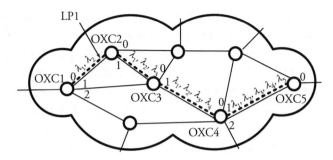

Figure 15.15   Exercise 8: routing in an all-optical network

9. Consider the two lightpaths (LPs) of the optical network indicated in Figure 15.1. Suppose that the optical cross connects involved in these two lightpaths have two restrictions: first, they can only use wavelengths within the λ_1 through λ_6 range, and second, their input wavelengths cannot be the same as their output wavelengths.

   (a) Propose a complete wavelength assignment for implementation in the mentioned optical cross connects so that the two incoming traffic flows modulated on λ_1 and λ_2 can be transmitted over the necessary segments of the two lightpaths and exit the network with the indicated wavelengths.

   (b) Find the lightpath blocking probability, B_{LP}, for each LP used for network resource management by ISP server. Assume the blocking probability for a wavelength is 0.3.

15.10   Computer Simulation Project

1. ***Simulation of an Optical Network.*** Study the interoperability between the IP and optical networks using the *generalized multiprotocol label switching* (GMPLS) technology. Use a network simulator to simulate the wavelength binding function in a GMPLS network size of your choice. In the constructed network, each node is in fact an optical cross connect (OXC) but you can use all the techniques learned about label switching in the previous chapter to create a negotiating protocol between each pair of nodes interconnected by an optical link. You are limited to a maximum of five different wavelengths that can be available for assignment on each optical link (OL). For the sake of simulation only, assume a packet or any type of connection request to be a notion of lightpath. Your simulation must show time-stamped packet movement originating

at an IP source passing through the GMPLS optical network and sinking at the egress optical cross connect. Traversal movements between the GMPLS nodes are made possible by wavelengths, but your simulation assigns a number (such as a label) to an IP packet as a token of wavelength assignment. Your simulation must have a predetermined wavelength assignment table stored in a database at the ingress optical cross connect quite similar to the label assignment mechanism in MPLS.

(a) Capture wavelengths assigned to packets traversing the network at each instance of time on an optical link, and show your results of wavelength binding in a table for the ingress optical cross connect.

(b) Increase the queries to the GMPLS network by either increasing the packet flow rate or by increasing the number of various destination nodes, and see the impact on the rate of blocking on queries due to the limited number of resources (5 wavelengths per OL).

CHAPTER 16

Cloud Computing and Network Virtualization

Cloud computing has emerged as a widely accepted computing paradigm. It arose from the demand for shared computing resources, establishing a pay-as-you-go business model for computing and information technology services. Without *virtualization* as a part of the structure of the cloud, it is hard to imagine that cloud computing could have become a new computing paradigm. Virtualization encompasses the administration of *virtual machines* (VMs) and possibly *virtual networks* (VNs) to achieve optimum utilization of cloud resources. This chapter focuses on the fundamentals of cloud computing and describes the following major topics:

- *Cloud computing and data centers*
- *Data center networks* (DCNs)
- *Network virtualization*
- *Overlay networks*

We start the chapter by exploring some basic topics of cloud computing including data center structures and virtual machines (VMs), and see how a cloud computing enterprise is formed. We then extend our discussion of data centers to the interconnection of data center servers, and focus on the design of *data center networks* (DCNs) that interconnect cloud servers to outside world. These topics build on the knowledge gained from various previous chapters. We also explore three well-known topological schemes of DCNs and their routing.

We then move on to the topic of *network virtualization*. We explain the need for virtualization in networks, and describe the components of such networks. This chapter concludes with a description of a type of virtualized network called an *overlay network*. An overlay network creates a virtual topology on top of the physical topology. This type of network has a number of applications in the new Internet structure.

16.1   Cloud Computing and Data Centers

A *cloud computing* or a *cloud-based* system is a network-based computing system in which clients use a shared pool of configurable computing resources. Cloud-based systems provide services from large *data centers* (DCs). Such services have radically changed the way in which computer services are built, managed, and delivered. The term *cloud computing* implies a variety of computing concepts that involve a large number of servers connected to a network, typically to the Internet. The driving forces behind the birth of cloud computing were

- The possibility of creating overcapacity at large corporate data centers
- The decrease in the cost of storage
- The ubiquity of broadband and wireless networking
- Significant improvements in networking technologies

Cloud computing, on the other hand, is equivalent to "distributed computing over a network" that runs programs or applications on numerous connected host servers at the same time. A host server in a data center is typically called a *blade*. A blade includes a CPU, memory, and disk storage. Blades are normally stacked in racks, with each rack having an average of 30 blades. These racks of host blades are also known as *server racks*.

A key factor for the success of cloud computing is the inclusion of *virtualization* in its structure. Cloud computing is a method of providing computing services from a large, highly "virtualized" data center to many independent users utilizing shared applications. In data centers, the services are provided by "physical" servers and "virtual" servers. A virtual server is a machine that emulates a server through software running on one or more real servers. Such virtual servers do not physically exist and can therefore be moved around and scaled up or down without affecting the end user.

From the application point of view, cloud computing is an on-demand, self-service, and metered service at various quality levels. Cloud data centers provide a variety of computing resources, attributes, and services such as database storage, computing, e-mail, voice, multimedia, and enterprise applications. As well as providing applications, data centers can be classified into two main types according to their functions. One type provides online services to customers, such as search engines, while the second type offers resources to users on a pay-as-you-go basis, such as storage service centers. From the application standpoint, cloud computing provides numerous benefits, including the following:

- *Infrastructure-less*. Cloud computing enables companies and applications, which are system infrastructure dependent, to be infrastructure-less and use network-based computing.

- *Flexibility*. Cloud computing enables utilizing resources of all kinds: CPU, storage, server capacity, load balancing, and databases. Cloud can be scaled up or down in capacity and functionalities.

- *Availability*. Services or data in the form of both hardware and software are available to the general public and businesses from anywhere. Cloud services are built on clusters of servers and off-the-shelf components plus open source software combined with in-house applications and/or system software.

- *Use of platforms*. Clients can use more efficient computing platforms instead of their own desktops or laptops.

- *Commodified and on-demand*. Clients pay for services as needed; thus, the cloud is a utility computing model similar to traditional utilities.

- *Availability of an application programing interface (API)*. An API specifies how underlying software components should interact with each other. This enables users of the cloud to have "no-need-to-know" about the underlying details of the infrastructure.

There are two main types of cloud. The first is the *public cloud,* in which resources are dynamically available for on-demand and self-service use by the public through Web applications and open APIs. The second type is the *private cloud,* which is simply the on-site cloud of a corporation. A cloud can also be a *hybrid cloud* consisting of some portion of computing resources located on-site (on the premises) and some located off-site (in the public cloud). We can also have a *community cloud* that is formed when several organizations with similar requirements share a common infrastructure.

Figure 16.1 shows an overview of a cloud computing system connected to the Internet. The system consists of two distinct parts: a *data center* (DC) and a *data center network* (DCN). A data center consists of a collection of massive server racks called a "server farm." Depending on the function of a data center, the server racks can also include a storage system to store public or private data. Cloud computing utilizes data centers to play the pivotal role of leasing computing, applications, and storage resources to users. Data centers are driven by large-scale computing services such as Web searching, online offices, online social networking, infrastructure outsourcing, and computations.

Any data center has its own DCN that interconnects its host machines (servers) with each other, and also connects the data center itself to the Internet. Thus, a DCN is an essential segment of a cloud computing system through which data centers can reliably communicate with the public network, such as the Internet.

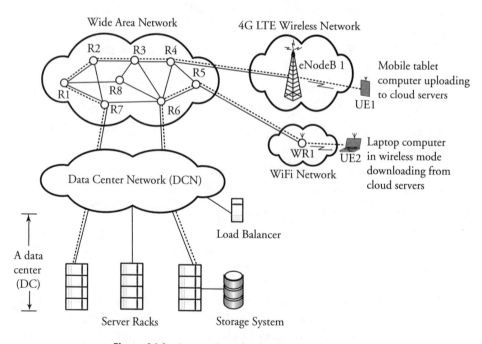

Figure 16.1   An overview of a cloud computing system

DCNs play an extremely important role in the performance of cloud computing, as determining the speed of data transfer and balancing the load on servers are done by DCNs.

As seen in in Figure 16.1, a *load balancer*, which is essentially a server, monitors the traffic coming into the data center and distributes the incoming traffic load evenly over the servers and storage systems. This task requires the load balancer to have a good knowledge of the location and functionality of the data center components. This figure illustrates two examples of data center usage. In the first example, a mobile tablet computer, UE1, is uploading files to a storage facility in the data center through the base station eNodeB 1 of a 4G LTE network, the Internet routers R4, R3, R2, R1, R7, and the DCN. In the second example, a laptop computer, UE2, in wireless mode and located in a WiFi network, is downloading a certain application from the data center through the DCN, the Internet routers R6, R5, and its own WiFi private router WR1.

16.1.1 Platforms and APIs

In general, a *platform* is a base technology on which other technologies or processes are built. In the context of cloud computing, a platform is a collection of integrated hardware, software, and Internet infrastructure that is used as base to provide an on-demand service. In Chapter 9, we learned that an *application programming interface* (API) is a set of programs and software tools that specifies how an application running on a host must request the network to transfer a piece of data to a destination application running on another host in the network.

Knowing that a platform can be a collection of numerous pieces of integrated hardware and software, we realize that an ordinary Internet user may only want to know how a communication transaction, such as sending e-mail or performing a Web search, can be carried out, and does not want to be concerned with the details of the underlying platform. In this sense, an API is treated as a simple *graphical user interface* (GUI, discussed in Chapter 6) that hides the complexity and details of the underlying infrastructure from users. An API can be utilized to ease the operation of programming GUI components.

16.1.2 Cloud Computing Service Models

The cloud computing environment provides services that customers can use remotely and online. The advantage of such a service model is that any software or hardware service can be rented by a customer remotely while the cloud management upgrades it frequently. The most common models of services and service developments in cloud computing are *software as a service* (SaaS), *infrastructure as a service* (IaaS), and *platform as a service* (PaaS). We next focus briefly on each of these service types.

In Chapter 20, we present a few detailed examples of cloud computing applications. We introduce distributed *cloud-based multimedia,* defined as a cloud computing infrastructure that can provide a variety of multimedia services including voice, video, and data services. Examples of cloud-based multimedia services can also include *distributed media mini-clouds, cloud-based interactive voice response* (IVR), and *audio and video conferencing.*

Software as a Service (SaaS)

Software as a service (SaaS), sometimes referred to as "on-demand software," is a software delivery model in cloud computing by which software and associated data are centrally hosted in the cloud. SaaS is a highly scalable software delivery methodology that provides licensed access to software and its functions remotely as a Web-based service. SaaS is usually billed based on usage and is a multitenant environment. With SaaS, the need to install and run an application on a user's own computer is removed and no software maintenance and support are needed.

SaaS has become a common delivery model for many business applications, such as management software, computer-aided design (CAD) software, development software, accounting, collaborative customer relationship management, management information systems (MIS), enterprise resource planning, invoicing, and human resource management. In many enterprise software companies, SaaS has been incorporated into their marketing strategy. One of the main reasons for doing so is the potential to reduce IT support costs by outsourcing hardware and software maintenance and support to the SaaS provider.

Infrastructure as a Service (IaaS)

Infrastructure as a service (IaaS) is the delivery of technology infrastructure as an on-demand service. With the IaaS service model, an organization can outsource the use of any equipment needed to support operations such as storage, hardware, servers, and networking components. The service provider owns the equipment and is responsible for running and maintaining it, and a client typically pays on a per-use basis. Thus, IaaS is billed to the client based on usage in a virtualized environment. IaaS is not a managed hosting. Traditional managed hosting is a form of Web hosting where a user chooses to lease an entire server housed in an off-site data center.

Platform as a Service (PaaS)

Platform as a service (PaaS) is a service model that provides a computing platform and a solution stack as a service. PaaS is a method of renting hardware, operating systems, storage, and network capacity online. This service delivery model allows the customer to rent virtualized servers and associated services for running existing applications or developing and testing new ones. With PaaS, geographically distributed development software teams can collaborate on software development projects, and thus expenses can be minimized by the unification of programming development efforts. In this service model, applications must typically be developed with a particular platform in mind.

16.1.3 Data Centers

A *data center* consists of numerous server racks and database units, and depending on the application, a data center can provide a variety of different computing, storage, or other services. Cloud-based companies have built massive *data centers*, each containing hundreds of thousands of hosts and database units. The advent of data centers enables the proliferation of numerous cloud applications such as data search, e-mail, social networking, Internet gaming, video streaming, and e-commerce.

Beside servers, another important element of a data center is the cloud *storage system*. A cloud storage system is a large-scale data storage system that can be used remotely and temporarily cached on desktop computers, mobile phones, or other Internet-linked devices from outside the data center.

Several design principles should be considered when the design of a data center is planned. The first principle is *reliability*. Individuals, enterprises, service providers, and content providers rely heavily on data in their selected data centers to run their businesses. *Load balancing* is another principle to keep in mind. Any data center runs a huge variety of applications and services, and thus an effective routing protocol should guarantee the performance of each application. This can be done by utilizing the link capacity appropriately. A load balancer in a data center distributes the traffic among the links inside the data center as evenly as possible. Last but not least, *energy consumption control* is an important design factor. It is now well known that data centers consume substantial energy. Energy-efficient methods include deployment of low-consumption hardware and software on servers and effective link and switch utilization at the routing phase by switching off inactive links and switches.

One of the challenges a data center faces is the *cost* of running a center and its maintenance. The cost of a large data center is significant and typically attributable to the hosts. Servers acting as hosts need to be increased in number day by day, and need to be replaced by newer and faster machines every few years. Networking devices are not big contributors to the cost of running a data center; however, effective networking is key to reducing the cost, as the network interface between a data center and outside users plays an important role in speedy access to data.

Other factors contributing to the cost of data centers are power supplies and cooling systems. One persistent issue with data centers is the power consumption of the servers. Sophisticated methods and policies must be adopted to prevent high power consumption in a data center. Normally, a dynamic adjustment on active links and switches to satisfy changing traffic loads is helpful in reducing power consumption.

Big Data

As the global Internet generates data at an increasing speed, the end result is *big data*, which presents a management challenge for Internet service providers and cloud-computing storage administrators. Data is explosively generated daily and pours into the Internet continuously from individuals and organizations. Peer-to-peer (P2P) networking and content delivery networks (CDNs) for uploading and downloading content substantially contribute to the formation of big data. The architecture and management of data centers and data center networks are other factors that play a critical role in managing big data. The issue of big data requires sophisticated estimation and control of the data volume exchanged at each cloud or large server system. In this chapter, we set aside the concept of big data and focus on the efficient architectures of data centers and DCNs.

16.1.4 Virtualization in Data Centers

Virtualization in data centers, and generally in cloud computing, is the act of creating a virtual, rather than an actual, version of a computing component, such as an operating system, a server, or a storage device. One can see that the virtualization of a system is the act of decoupling an infrastructure service from the system's physical components. Virtualization in a more general interpretation has impacted most aspects of our life. Our method of online shopping, education, or games and entertainment are all partially or fully virtual.

The very first component that was virtualized was the memory unit of a computer in the mid 1970s. Since then, an enormous amount of effort has been spent on virtualizing any system or resource possible. Migration of compact discs (CDs) or a personal hard disk to virtual cloud-based storage is an example. We can think of several key reasons behind the need for virtualizing our resources. The three most important reasons are:

1. *Sharing of resources.* When a resource, such as a server, is too large for a user or a network entity, the resource can be partitioned into multiple virtual pieces, each having similar properties as the original resource. This way a large-scale resource can be shared virtually among multiple users or entities. For example, a host can be virtually partitioned to multiple virtual machines for multiple users.

2. *Aggregation of resources.* There are other circumstances under which a resource might be too small for a user or a network entity. In such cases, a larger resource can be virtually engineered to fill the need. For example, numerous inexpensive disks can be aggregated to make up a large reliable storage system.

3. *Resource management.* The implementation of virtualization on resources or devices makes the management of devices and their networking easier because they can be managed using software.

There are, however, other compelling reasons to implement virtualization in various parts of the Internet. On some occasions, for example, sharing a resource among users requires that they be isolated from each other. Users of one virtual component are isolated securely from monitoring activities of other users. This may have not been possible in traditional shared-resource systems. Furthermore, due to the fast pace of changes in resource allocations and sometimes even in the nature of the resources themselves, virtual resources and virtual resource allocations are more conveniently for implemented in a network than physical resource allocations.

Virtual Machines (VMs)

The provision of several attributes and services in a large enterprise cloud service system requires a significant number of servers, networking devices, and storage resources. This is only achievable through extensive use of resource virtualization. A *virtual machine* (VM), as a result, is a simulation of a computing machine, such as a desktop, laptop, or server, decoupled from hardware and providing an execution environment to clients by using well-defined protocols. Multiple VMs can run on a single physical machine. In contrast, multiple physical machines can form a single VM. Figure 16.2 illustrates a representation of virtual machines for both applications: multiple physical servers (machines) forming a virtual machine and a physical server (machine) being configured as multiple virtual machines VM1 through VM4.

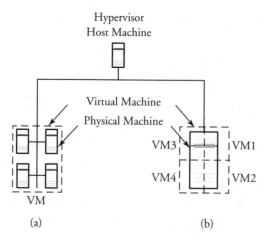

Figure 16.2   Representation of virtual machines: (a) multiple physical servers (machines) form a virtual machine, and (b) a physical server (machine) configured as multiple virtual machines

Server virtualization was first implemented by IBM Corporation in the 1960s using mainframes. Machine virtualization enables new architectures for computer hosting and provides the following fundamental benefits:

- *Effective use of a machine.* Multiple independent users can share computing and infrastructure facilities.

- *Lower system maintenance cost.* The maintenance cost of servers can be reduced as each machine can be utilized close to its optimal capacity, avoiding any unnecessary unused active machines.

- *Rapid and dynamic provisioning of new features.* Clearly, the agility of creating multiple VMs in a physical machine allows new features to be added to a system rapidly and more effectively.

- *Load balancing at and beyond data centers.* The computing load can be distributed evenly in or beyond a data center.

The load-balancing feature in large-scale data centers is probably the best benefit of using VMs. If a company has multiple data centers located in different geographic areas of a networking domain, the load balancing can be extended over multiple physical locations. In this case, the company has an option to move its VMs anywhere in its data centers. But this process comes with a challenge: figuring out a way to allow network administrators to move VMs across physical hosts without having to stop and reconfigure them individually. We will learn in later sections that virtualization should also be extended over network components in order to overcome such a challenge.

In the meantime, virtualization of machines generates several other networking challenges at both layer 2 (the data link layer) and layer 3 (the network layer). Switches and routers deployed in creating a cloud computing infrastructure must overcome these challenges. One challenge attracting researchers' attention is the impact of virtualization on transport layer protocols. Virtualization dramatically deteriorates the performance of transport layer protocols to the point that throughput of both TCP and UDP becomes unstable. The end-to-end delay of packets is large even if the network load is light. The basic reason for the unstable throughput and large delay is simply the larger than normal latency of scheduling hypervisors.

One solution to overcome the negative impact of the large scheduling latency at the receiver and sender side of TCP is to deploy a device within the driver domain to generate acknowledgments (ACKs) on behalf of the receiving VM. This way, the sender can receive feedback faster. Another solution is to offload the congestion control functionality of TCP to the driver domain. The driver domain then handles the congestion control instead of the VMs and thus VMs flood packets to the driver domain. In this case, a larger queueing buffer is needed in the driver domain accommodate the TCP segments (packets) from VMs of the same physical host. This is due to the increased number of connections on the same host.

Hypervisor

A *hypervisor* is a monitoring and managing mechanism in virtual machines. It consists of software, hardware, or firmware (software/hardware) that creates and runs virtual machines. A real computer (machine) on which a hypervisor is running one or more virtual machines is defined as *host machine,* as seen in Figure 16.2, while each virtual machine is called a *guest machine.* The hypervisor provides the guest operating systems with a virtual operating platform and administers the execution of the guest operating systems. Multiple instances of operating systems in the real machine may share the virtualized hardware resources using the hypervisor.

On top of its regular tasks, a hypervisor should be able to intermediate between its machine and the outside world during certain device failures. For example, a hypervisor must be capable of isolating network applications from awareness of changes in the physical machine state, such as failure of a NIC port. In some instances, a certain outside controller is needed to enable hypervisors to troubleshoot and potentially isolate and mitigate certain internal errors.

16.2 Data Center Networks (DCNs)

Data center networks (DCNs) are networks that connect data center machines to the Internet. The geographically distributed nature of data centers in the cloud has posed challenges in the design and deployment of DCNs. Data center applications are both data and communication intensive. For example, a simple Web search request may touch thousands of servers as it is executed and then process petabytes of data on thousands of machines.

Figure 16.3 shows an abstract model of a DCN that acts as the communication component of data servers. Typical DCNs are currently based on routers and layer 2 and 3 switches connected in a certain topology. The servers of each rack are directly interconnected using one tier of *top-of-rack* (ToR) or *edge switches* that are layer 2 type switches. Each host (server) in a server rack has a network interface card (NIC) that connects it to its ToR switch while each host is also assigned its own data-center internal IP address.

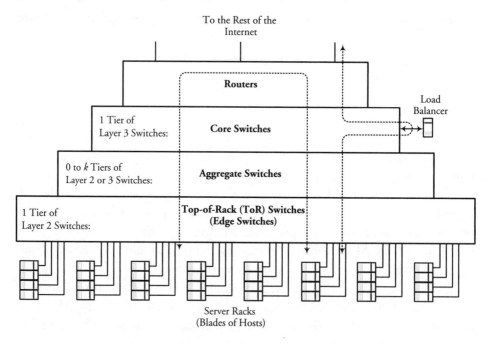

Figure 16.3 An overview of a data center network as the communication component of data servers

Edge switches are in turn connected through 0 to k tiers of layer 2 or 3 type *aggregate switches*. The notion of 0 and k tiers here means that there may not be a need for aggregate switches in small-size data centers, while in larger-size data centers there could be a need for several levels of aggregate switches. The number of tiers, k, depends on the complexity and number of server racks. However, depending on the size of the data centers or other design factors, adding more layers of switching to, or removing some layers from the typical switching architecture is possible. Finally, aggregate switches are interconnected to layer 3 type *core switches*. Considering such a hierarchical architecture in a data center network, scaling up a data center to a substantially larger number of hosts is made possible.

As shown in the figure, two types of traffic flows are supported by a DCN: traffic flow between clients residing outside of the data center and the data center hosts (servers), and traffic flow among data center hosts. Thus, the border *routers* sitting on top of core switches handle connections between the data center servers to the clients residing in the rest of the Internet.

Switches in DCNs frequently use Ethernet copper or fiber cabling. The operational structure of data centers and their networks allows any two servers within a rack or even outside a rack to communicate with each other. This feature is especially needed when a certain function in one server has to be completed, confirmed, or updated by another server. The need for the creation of link or device *redundancy* in the structure of DCNs is also inevitable since cloud applications must continually provide applications with high availability.

16.2.1   Load Balancer

Load balancers (LBs) are adopted in data centers to balance traffic flow among servers. A large data center offers many types of real-time applications concurrently to numerous clients. Imagine that numerous clients from outside a data center request a variety different applications. This would require the data center to find the right resource within its facility quickly and communicate back to the source swiftly and appropriately. A prevalent solution to overcome the traffic load volatility is the deployment of a load balancer. A load balancer distributes requests from clients over the hosts of a data center as evenly as possible. In other words, a load balancer decides which server must carry out the task of an individual request.

One basic method of load balancing is to select a path to the host that handles the application for each incoming request in a random manner if more than one of the same resource exists in the data center. A load balancer looks at the destination host IP address and port number of an incoming packet to decide which path to select to a specific host in the data center. If the destination host cannot find an answer or for any reason cannot respond to the query, it forwards the query to another host in the server racks. Once the host executes the query, it returns its response to the load balancer. The load balancer then communicates with the external client who originally made the query.

In designing DCNs, it makes sense to incorporate *network address translation* (NAT) into the load-balancing operation, as the load-balancing server is indeed an interface between the data center and the outside world. We learned in Chapter 5 that NAT has the benefit of hiding the internal network structure for security reasons, and it prevents clients from directly associating with data center resources. Thus, in most optimal design cases, load balancers also translate the public IP address to the private IP address of a particular host and vice versa.

Larger data centers must have several load balancers, each one dedicated to specific application(s). Note that load balancing can, on the other hand, lead to congestion when large flows are present and a limited number of load-balancing machines are operable. There are several methods in which load balancing can be implemented in data center networks. Two of the most common methods are the *round robin* and *least-connect* algorithms.

Round Robin Algorithm

In the *round robin algorithm*, a load balancer does not collect and save the present state of the servers. Once a request for a certain type of application is received by the load balancer, it immediately distributes the incoming request to all the servers in the data center network. The algorithm assigns the request to servers one by one and in a round robin fashion until a free eligible server for the requested application is found. In this method, if all the eligible servers are found to be busy, then the load balancer returns to the first server to restart a second round of checking until a free server is identified to carry out the request.

Round robin load balancing does not require any communication among servers; the load balancer makes decisions on its own without taking into consideration the current state of the servers. The round robin algorithm is generally used in smaller data centers and for applications such as HTTP requests.

Least-Connect Algorithm

The *least-connect algorithm* presents an alternative approach to load balancing in data centers. In this method, the load balancer performs the traffic load distribution based on its knowledge of the number of active connections to each server in a data center.

The load balancer must monitor the number of open connections to its servers, and then choose servers with the least number of active connections as eligible ones. A load balancer contains all the states of data center servers including their general load, average daily load, and current traffic being handled. Using this information, a load balancer can identify the right server to carry out the requested task without any need for a search. The least-connect algorithm is more complicated than the round robin algorithm, but it is more efficient in large-scale data centers.

16.2.2   Traffic Engineering

Traffic engineering (TE) in a network is a method of optimizing the performance of a network by dynamically monitoring, analyzing, predicting, and regulating the behavior of packets and frame flows over that network. Traffic engineering has been sufficiently investigated for IP and MPLS-based networks. Because of the unique features of high-volume traffic, the use of traffic engineering in data centers is inevitable.

The type of unique traffic pattern requiring certain security in data centers makes the engineering of traffic challenging. The traffic pattern in data centers can be predicted only in a very short period of time and thus the TE should be performed in a fine-grained manner. When host-to-host communication is a targeted task in a data center, supporting its required bandwidth is important. For example, a situation in which an Internet search engine runs on thousands of hosts spread across multiple server racks and requires significant bandwidth between pairs of server hosts may result in exhaustive bandwidth consumption and therefore poor performance.

Since the number of core switches or routers is far smaller than that of the data center servers, core switches or routers as root nodes become the bottleneck of a DCN. The magnitude of this issue becomes more apparent when taking into account distributed algorithms that shuffle the virtual machine workload from one switch to another across different edge switches. *Efficient scheduling* technique is another solution for TE where global knowledge of active flows is employed to distribute the large flows on different paths.

16.2.3   DCN Architectures

The main role of a data center network (DCN) is to interconnect a large number of servers with significant aggregate bandwidth requirements. The largest portion of the cost incurred to set up a networking infrastructure for a data center is attributed to switches and routers, load balancers, and data center links. Among the items in this list, switches and routers are the most expensive ones. Smart design of the networking portion of cloud computing therefore plays an important role in reducing network cost. Three networking structures used in DCNs are:

1. *Server-routed networking* scheme

2. *Switch-routed networking* scheme

3. *Fully-connected optical networking* scheme

Server-Routed Networking Scheme

In the *server-routed networking* scheme, servers or server racks in data centers act as end hosts and also as relay nodes. In this scheme, servers are configured with multiple ports, and switches connect an identical number of server racks. In the server-routed networking scheme, there is no aggregate switch tier in the DCN structure.

The network routing configuration in the server-routed networking scheme has a recursively defined structure. In this algorithm, we assume m server racks, each having k servers, and each server rack being connected to a ToR switch; as result there are m k-port ToR layer 2 switches. Two servers are neighbors if they connect to the same ToR switch. In this algorithm, any server in a server rack SRi has an address $a_i a_{i-1} \ldots a_0$ where $a_j \in [0, k - 1]$, and $j \in [0, k]$. Two servers in a server rack are neighbors if their address arrays differ in one digit. The routing is based on a path by "correcting" one digit at one hop from the source sever to the destination server. We assume there are n tiers of switching.

Example.   Show the structure of a server-routed networking scheme of a cloud computing center where $k = 4$, and then indicate the path of routing from server SE00 in server rack SR00 to server SE01 in server rack SR02.

Solution.   Figure 16.4 shows the structure of the network when $k = 4$ resulting in a ToR switch having 4 ports. There are several paths connecting the two servers. Two such paths can be either: SE00 (in SR00) – S10 – SE00 (in SR02) – S02 – SE01; or the other path: SE00 (SR00) – S00 – SE01 (in SR00) – S11 – SE01 (in SR02).

Switch-Routed Networking Scheme

In *switch-routed networking*, the interconnection topology among the switches is regular. Figure 16.5 shows a data center network using three layers of switches called *core switches, aggregate switches,* and *edge switches.* Edge switches directly connect to end servers at server racks, and core switches directly connect to the Internet. The aggregate switches are the middle layer switches.

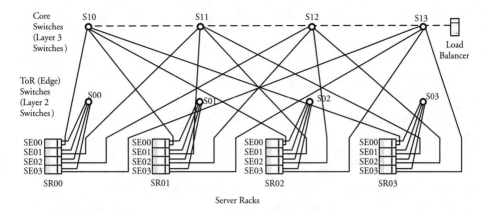

Figure 16.4   A data center network using the server-routed networking scheme with two layers of switching

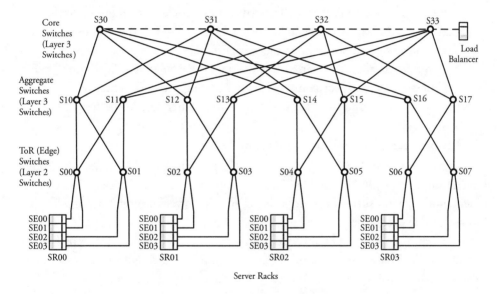

Figure 16.5   A data center network using the switch-routed networking scheme

Each server has its actual MAC address and physical identification number (PIN). The information of a sever is encoded into its PIN in the form of 6-field MAC address L6-L5-L4-L3-L2-L1 as follows:

- L1 (16 bits): represents the ID of the virtual machine (VM) on a physical machine.

- L2 (8 bits): represents the edge switch port number the host is connected to.

- L3 (8 bits): represents the position of the edge switch column in L1.
- L4 (16 bits): reflects the ID number of the aggregate switch block. An aggregate switch block refers to a block of aggregate switches (such as S10 and S11) that are connected to a server rack such as SR00. In a sense, L4 represents the server rack number.
- L5 and L6 are reserved for network expansion.

For example, a PIN of 00:00:01:00:01:198 means the hundred and ninety-ninth (L1=198) virtual machine in a server host connected to the second (L2=01) port of the edge switch, where the edge switch is located in the first (L3=00) switching column in the second (L4=01) aggregate switch block, which is the second server rack (SR01).

Routing from outside of the DCN to the data center using *switch-routed networking* topology starts with core switches forwarding a packet based on its destination PIN address so that the core switch inspects L4 bits of a new arriving packet to make a decision on an output port. When the packet reaches an aggregate switch, it checks its PIN to find out the L2 bits in order to extract the edge switch port number. The PIN address is also used for communications among the data center hosts, from a host to a core switch and from the core switch to another host in the center.

Fully Connected Optical Networking Scheme

A *fully connected optical networking scheme* deploys all-optical switches in the core switching tier of DCNs. In high-speed communication applications, nonoptical switching schemes suffer from deficiencies such as lower throughput, high latency, and high power consumption. The inclusion of an all-optical switching scheme as the core switching engine of a DCNs that is directly attached to the ToR switching tier is an alternative solution to the deficiencies of general DCNs. Figure 16.6 shows a data center network using a fully connected optical networking scheme.

16.2.4 Multicast Methods

Multicasting at layer 3 benefits the DCN by reducing network traffic and releasing the sender from repeated transmission tasks. Multicasting in DCNs, especially in DCNs of those cloud centers serving public services, becomes a challenging task since multicasting requires an increased bandwidth capacity of DCNs and a lowered cost per virtual machine hour. Multicasting in data networks is attributed to group communications in both online applications and back-end infrastructural computation in data centers, as discussed in Chapter 6. For example, search queries can be

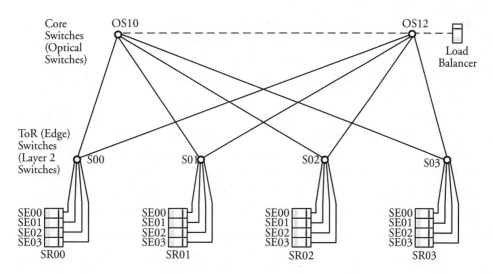

Figure 16.6   A data center network using fully connected optical networking scheme

multicast to multiple indexing servers to find answers quickly. Another example is to multicast executable binaries to a group of servers participating in cooperative computations for a faster result.

Multicasting in DCNs differs from multicasting in the Internet, as DCNs typically comprise layer 2 or 3 switches in their structures while the wide-area segment of the Internet deploys routers. Layer 2 or 3 switches are not as powerful and reliable as the Internet routers. Several multicast algorithms have been examined for use in data centers, among which PIM is the most widely used one. In sparse mode *protocol-independent multicast* (PIM), studied in Chapter 6, hosts independently send group join/leave requests to a rendezvous point or the source node, and a multicasting tree is formed by the reverse unicast routing in the intermediate nodes. The *explicit multi-unicast* (Xcast) protocol is an alternative for multicasting that provides reception addresses of all destinations with each packet. With the Xcast model, the hosts participating in the multicast function are identified ahead of time, so that multicast trees can be generated and given proper resource allocation by network elements in advance of actual data traffic.

16.3   Network Virtualization

Network virtualization is the act of decoupling networking services from network infrastructures. The virtualization in the Internet is derived from various computer networking technologies. At this point, it is interesting to note that computer networking as a whole must also be virtualized to operate more effectively. Network virtualization offers a powerful approach to the paradigm of "shared network infrastructure." Migration toward virtual local area networks (VLANs) studied in Chapter 4, and virtual private networks (VPNs) studied in Chapter 14 are two examples.

The important role that networking plays in cloud computing calls for an improved, combined control and optimization of networking and computing resources in a cloud environment. This control and optimization is especially needed in the convergence of networking and cloud computing where the TCP/IP architecture by itself is an insufficient networking protocol model. Two other issues that advanced converged networking and cloud computing must overcome are:

- The general delay in computer networks
- The lack of seamless connections often experienced in wireless networks

Network virtualization enables network operators to compose and operate multiple independent and application-specific virtual networks that share a common physical infrastructure. To achieve this capability, the virtualization mechanism must guarantee isolation between coexisting virtual networks. In a virtual network, a service is described in a data structure, and exists entirely in a software abstraction layer, reproducing the service on any physical resource running the virtualization software. The configuration attributes of the service can be found in software with API interfaces, thereby unlocking the full potential of networking devices.

16.3.1   Network Virtualization Components

Machine virtualization and network virtualization have similarities and differences. In machine virtualization, the familiar attributes of a physical machine are decoupled and reproduced in virtualization software called a *hypervisor*. The hypervisor can create virtual components such as a virtual CPU (VCPU) and virtual RAM (VRAM). The attributes of virtualization can be easily assembled in any arbitrary combination producing a unique virtual machine in a short period of time.

The same method of decoupling possible in machine virtualization can also be implemented in network virtualization. However, network virtualization does not have the same capabilities as machine virtualization does, such as computing. Additionally, there is no mobility in networks and thus the network configuration is anchored to hardware and its state is spread across a number of networking devices.

Virtual machines often require network connectivity to other virtual machines as well as to the outside world. The connectivity to other virtual machines requires security and load balancing. Virtual machines are fully decoupled from physical machines by machine virtualization. However, the virtual network is not fully decoupled from the physical network. Therefore, the configuration of a virtual network must be carefully engineered across many networking physical and virtual devices in layers 1, 2, and 3 of the protocol stack as well as layer 4 and 5 entities.

In network virtualization, certain networking services and features, such as routing, should be decoupled from the physical network and moved into a virtualization software layer for the express purpose of automation. Once a virtual network is decoupled from a physical network to its ultimate potential, the physical network configuration is simplified to provide packet forwarding service from one hypervisor to the next. The implementation details of physical packet forwarding are separated from the virtual network while both the virtual and physical network can evolve independently.

In a virtual network, the network virtualization software produces *virtual links*, *virtual switches* (vSwitches), *virtual NICs* (VNICs), *virtual routers* (vRouters), *virtual load balancers* (VLBs), and *logical firewalls*. We can also define virtual network topology such as an *overlay network*. The network configuration can be implemented at the software layer. For example, the physical network provides basic packet forwarding while software at the virtual switch layer provides the complete virtual network feature. The concept of network virtualization, can be thought of as a virtual network that operates using software that is built on certain physical network devices. One obvious benefit of building a virtual network is that it is inherently able to synchronize with the agility of virtual machines associated with the network.

Virtual Links

We now move on to a discussion on the concept of resource virtualization starting with *link virtualization*. Consider multiple hosts connected by a shared physical link. The link can then be viewed as a multichannel medium for each host to transmit its data through a channel. From the connectivity viewpoint, this channelization mechanism arranged over a physical link can be prevalently referred to as a "virtual link" over a physical link.

Virtual NICs

A *network interface card* (NIC), described in Chapters 2 and 3, is attached to any host or networking device. A NIC processes link layer (layer 2) protocol functions such as the ones for the Ethernet and WiFi protocols. In Chapter 4, we learned that the interconnections and networking at layer 2 are typically made possible by using bridges or layer 2 switches. Layer 2 switches are in turn connected to layer 3 switches in order to be connected to the rest of the Internet. This networking policy can also be generalized the same way in data centers. Each top-of-rack (ToR) layer 2 switch or an aggregate switch in a data center uses a NIC for its connection.

The need for a *virtual NIC* (VNIC) becomes apparent when a virtual machine in a data center moves from one subnet to another. In this case, the IP address of the virtual machine must change while its MAC address (IEEE 802 address) remains unchanged. Thus, when a virtual machine's network connection crosses multiple layer 2 networks, the virtual machine needs to be given a new IP address. Any host or networking device uses at least one NIC for communication. When more than one virtual machine is active on the system, each virtual machine needs its own virtual NIC.

Figure 16.7 shows an overview of virtual machines (VMs) inside a physical machine managed by a hypervisor. The figure also shows that any VM is also associated with a VNIC housed in the physical machine. The switching and communication among VNICs are carried out by a *virtual Ethernet port aggregator* (VEPA), specified by the IEEE 802.1Qbg standard. As an alternative architecture, VNICs can also be housed in the physical NIC of the machine; however, this alternative approach would require significant software overhead, and VNICs may not be easily manageable externally.

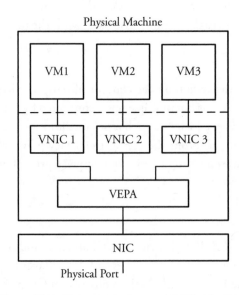

Figure 16.7   Network interface card (NIC) virtualization

Virtual Switches (vSwitches)

We can now discuss *virtual switches* (vSwitches). In networking scenarios with a large number of hosts requiring connections to an outside system, the number of hosts is normally larger than the number of ports in a layer 2 switch. Figure 16.8 shows an example in which a physical Ethernet (layer 2) switch has the capability to act as three vSwitches. The first network component to which a virtual switch is attached is the virtual switch software. In light of this fact, as we described in Chapter 4, several tiers of layer 2 and 3 switches have to be deployed. A certain software standard such as IEEE 802.1BR, called the *bridge port extension* (BPE) standard, can be used in physical switches to extend the number of ports to multiple virtual ports, resulting in a vSwitch as shown in Figure 16.8.

A virtual switch does more than just forward frames; it can intelligently direct communication on the network by inspecting frames before passing them on. Virtual switching functions can be embedded right into their virtualization software, but a virtual switch can also be included in a machine attached to the physical switch as part of its firmware. Virtual switches can also perform the task of moving VMs across physical hosts; otherwise, the task would be time consuming and can potentially expose the network to security breaches. With intelligent software embedded in virtual switches, the integrity of a VM's profile including its network and security settings can potentially be ensured.

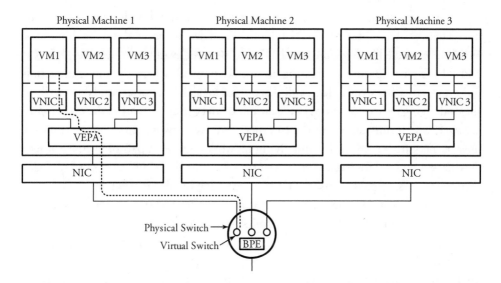

Figure 16.8   An overview of virtual switches (vSwitches) connecting a virtual machine to a system outside its physical machine

Virtual LANs (VLANs) in Cloud Computing

In Chapter 4, we learned that a *virtual local area network* (VLAN) methodology allows a single physical LAN to be partitioned into several seemingly and virtually separate LANs. A VLAN is a group of hosts with a common set of requirements communicating as if they were attached to the same domain regardless of their physical locations. Each virtual LAN is assigned an identifier and frames can only be forwarded from one segment to another if both segments have the same identifier. With respect to cloud computing, we can extend the VLAN discussion and understand that multiple VMs in a single physical machine may belong to different clients and thus need to be in different virtual LANs (VLANs). Hence, each of these VLANs may span several data centers interconnected via layer 3 networking components.

16.4   Overlay Networks

An *overlay network* is an application-specific virtual network built on top of a physical network. In other words, an overlay network creates a virtual topology on top of the physical topology. This type of network is created to protect the existing network structure from new protocols whose testing phases require Internet use. Such networks protect packets under test while isolating them from the main networking infrastructure in a test bed.

Figure 16.9 shows an overlay network configured over a wide area network for host 1 in LAN 1 and host 2 in LAN 4. Nodes in an overlay network can be thought of as being connected by logical links. In Figure 16.9, for example, routers R4, R5, R6, and R1 are participating in creating an overlay network where the interconnection links are realized as overlay logical links. Such a logical link corresponds to a path in the underlying network. An obvious example of an overlay network is the *peer-to-peer network*, which runs on top of the Internet. Overlay networks have no control over how packets are routed in the underlying network between a pair of overlay source/destination nodes. However, these networks can control a sequence of overlay nodes through a message-passing function before reaching the destination.

An overlay network might be needed in a communication system for various reasons. Using an overlay network permits routing messages to destinations when the IP address is not known in advance. Sometimes, an overlay network is proposed as a method to improve Internet routing as implemented in order to achieve higher-quality streaming media. Sometimes, for the implementation of such techniques as

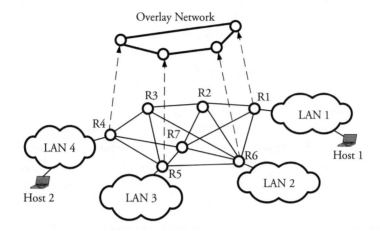

Figure 16.9 An overlay network for connections between two LANs associated with routers R1 and R4

DiffServ and IP multicast, modification of all routers in the network is required. In such cases, an overlay network can be deployed on end hosts running the overlay protocol software, without cooperation from Internet service providers.

Overlay networks are *self-organized*. When a node fails, the overlay network algorithm should provide solutions that let the network recover and re-create an appropriate network structure. A fundamental difference between an overlay network and an unstructured network is that an overlay's look-up routing information is based on identifiers derived from the content of moving frames.

16.5 Summary

This chapter focused on *cloud computing* and its related networking topologies. Cloud computing is a network-based computing system by which a client outside the data center can use a shared pool of configurable computing resources located in the data center. We started the chapter by exploring basic topics of cloud computing including data center structures and virtual machines (VMs), and learned how a cloud computing enterprise is formed.

We covered several important topics under data center networks (DCNs). One of the challenging tasks faced by of data centers concerns routing techniques. A DCN is designed based on routers and layer 2 and 3 switches connected in a certain topology. At the lowest level of a DCN, servers in each rack are directly interconnected using one tier of *top-of-rack* (ToR) or *edge switches,* which are layer 2 type switches. Edge switches are in turn connected through layer 2 or 3 type *aggregate switches.* Finally, aggregate switches are interconnected to layer 3 type *core switches.* Such a hierarchical architecture in a data center network makes it possible to scale up to a substantially larger number of hosts.

Three typical networking structures of DCNs were presented: the server-routed networking scheme, switch-routed networking scheme, and fully connected opti-cal networking scheme. Among these three schemes, the fully connected structure was considered a possibility for future optical DCNs. We discussed the applications and challenges of data center routing from different aspects, including basic routing schemes, traffic engineering, and multicasting issues.

This chapter presented several key topics of virtualization technologies, among which the development of *network virtualization* was of particular interest. *Overlay networks* create a virtual topology on top of an existing physical topology on a public network. Overlay networks are *self-organized*; thus, if a node fails, the overlay net-work algorithm can provide solutions that let the network re-create an appropriate network structure.

In Chapter 17, we explore *software-defined networking* (SDN) as a networking paradigm by which a central software program known as "controller" determines and controls the overall network instead of individual switches. We consider SDN as a network management tool in situations such as the ones in data center networks in cloud computing environments.

16.6 Exercises

1. Design the networking segment of a cloud center using a *switch-routed* DCN. The cloud data center has 32 main hosts, and each host has 8 virtual machines.

   (a) Show an overview of the DCN.

   (b) Give the PID number of the fifth VM of the sixth host.

2. Consider a data center network topology similar to the one shown in Figure 16.4. The data rate at a network interface card (NIC) of any server host is 1Gb/s, which constitutes the data rate between a server and a ToR switch.

   (a) Estimate the data rate between any pair of ToR switch and aggregate switch.

   (b) Estimate the data rate between any pair of aggregate switch and core switch.

   (c) Estimate the data rate between any pair of core switch and border router.

3. Consider a data center network topology using the fully connected optical networking scheme. The data center consists of racks of 40 servers. The data center require 800 such servers. The data rate at the network interface card (NIC) of any server host is 1Gb/s.
   (a) Find the sizes of ToR switches and optical switches.
   (b) Estimate the data rate between any pair of ToR switch and optical switch.
   (c) Estimate the data rate between any pair of optical switch and the link connected to outside world through an optical switch.

4. For the data center network topology shown in Figure 16.3
   (a) Show a Lee's model.
   (b) Assuming the probability that any link in the network is busy is P, find the total blocking probability for the network.

5. For the data center network topology shown in Figure 16.4
   (a) Show a Lee's model.
   (b) Assuming the probability that any link in the network is busy is P, find the total blocking probability for the network.

6. For the data center network topology shown in Figure 16.5
   (a) Show a Lee's model.
   (b) Assuming the probability that any link in the network is busy is P, find the total blocking probability for the network.

7. Develop a routing algorithm for *server-routed* DCNs of a cloud computing data center. The network routing algorithm in the server-centric networking scheme has a recursively defined structure. In this algorithm, we assume n tiers of switching (normally $n = 2$), m server racks each having k servers, and each server rack being connected to a ToR switch, as result there are m k-port ToR layer 2 switches. Your work must present an algorithm in terms of m, n, and k. Use any algorithmic clauses such as **for, if, otherwise,** and so on, and develop:
   (a) Routing from outside the DCN to a server.
   (b) Routing internally from a server in server rack to another server in a different server rack.

8. Develop a routing algorithm for *switch-routed* DCNs following the instructions given in exercise 7.

9. Consider an overlay network that consists of five connected nodes. Compare two methods for a peer-to-peer connection on top of the Internet, using

   (a) A ring topology
   (b) A star topology

10. Suppose that two peers are connected to a four-node overlay network interconnected with a ring topology, as shown in Figure 16.9. There are 200 requests per second arriving at one of the peers, and the average service rate is 230 requests per second. Assuming that the time required for establishing a connection is 10 ms, that the time to finish the service as soon as the connection is established is 120 ms, and that there is an equal chance that the peer is connected or not connected

    (a) Find the average service time of the peer.
    (b) Find the total utilization of the peer.

11. We would like to compare the virtual NIC (VNIC) presented in this chapter with other design possibilities.

    (a) Present a physical machine having four VMs but the VNICs are housed separately in the physical NIC.
    (b) Compare the performance of your design with the one presented in this chapter.

12. Suppose a client host tries to detect the number of servers in a cloud computing data center. The client observes that the IP protocol stamps a certain sequence ID number (SIN) on each IP packet. The SIN of the first packet generated by a server is a random number starting from 6000, and SINs of the next packets are sequentially assigned. Assume all IP packets constructed by servers behind NAT are sent to the outside world beyond the data center. Recall that NAT in a data center is incorporated in the load balancer.

    (a) Assuming you can sniff all packets transmitted by NAT to the outside, present an algorithm that detects the number of unique servers behind the NAT/load balancer.
    (b) Reconsider the conditions presented in part (a), this time considering that the SINs are not sequentially assigned.
    (c) If the number of servers is substantially large, which is the case in practice, comment on how efficient your algorithm executes the objectives of the algorithm.

16.7   Computer Simulation Projects

1. *Simulation of a Load Balancer in a Data Center of a Cloud Network.* Set up a network simulation tool to implement a small-scale data center network. Include four server racks each having three servers. Consider a separate server to essentially function as a load balancer for the data center network that consists of four edge switches and two core switches both connected to a router and the load balancer. On the cloud server side, each server displays to the load balancer its window size and the maximum number of packets it can receive. On the client's side, the requests are simply forwarded to the load balancer. Then, the load balancer estimates the availability factor among various server nodes in the server farm and buffer capacity and routes the packets accordingly. Thus the load balancer distributes the load entering the network based on the server's buffer size. Packets used here are of various types of your choice including FTP–TCP, UDP, and so on. Various network topologies are created to understand load sharing in distributed networks. Use the *round robin algorithm* for the load balancer.

   (a) Insert a targeted application or file that a client wants to reach and download in one of the 16 servers of your choice. Measure the round-trip time (RTT) of a successful query plus its response.

   (b) Insert a targeted application or file that a client wants to reach and download in 3 of the 16 servers of your choice. Measure the RTT of a successful query plus its response.

2. *Simulation of an Overlay Network.* Use a network simulation tool to simulate the seven-node network presented in Figure 16.9. Then add a sub-program to simulate the operation of overlay networks.

   (a) First simulate packet transfer through using UDP for the original network from R1 to R4 without the construction of the overlay network.

   (b) Compare the results of part (a) to the case, using the overlay network shown in the figure.

CHAPTER **17**

Software-Defined Networking (SDN) and Beyond

The focus of this chapter is primarily on advanced network control methods. The motivation for yet other networking control methodologies is the rise of significant competition in communication services where large-scale organizations on the public Internet have spurred service providers to look for ways to disrupt the status quo through a dependable approach.

We start the chapter with a different paradigm in the management of networks. In previous chapters, we learned how complex the traffic management of traditional networks could be. Traditional networks are structured with special-purpose devices running distributed protocols for topology discovery, routing, traffic monitoring, quality of service, and access control. Growth in the infrastructure and applications of the Internet causes profound changes in the technology ecosystems of Internet-related industries. *Software-defined networking* (SDN) is a networking paradigm by which a central software program known as a "controller" (or SDN controller) determines and controls the overall network behavior, resulting in potential improvement in network performance.

This chapter focuses on the fundamentals of software-defined networking and a few other alternative, innovative networking features, and provides details of related concepts at the network level. Major topics covered in this chapter are the following:

- *Software-defined networking* (SDN)
- *SDN-based network model*
- *Small-size SDN architectures*
- *SDN architectures for clouds*
- *Network functions virtualization* (NFV)
- *Information-Centric Networking* (ICN)
- *Network emulators for advanced networks*

First, we explore some basic ideas of SDN. We then study some of the standards of SDN-based network models such as *OpenFlow*, which is a standard communication interface protocol defined between the control functions and forwarding functions of an SDN-enabled network. We also cover the interaction of SDN with cloud data centers and learn how an SDN-based cloud data center can be constructed and run.

Another important topic is *network functions virtualization* (NFV), an alternative to SDN. Some similarities and differences between NFV and SDN are provided. The discussion of SDN and NFV ends with a case study on *Information-Centric Networking* (ICN), which is another technique to manage routing in a network by using object names instead of IP addresses.

This chapter concludes with a section that presents network emulators with a focus on the Mininet emulator and Wireshark. These tools are effective in the presentation of a simulated, advanced, controlled network like SDN.

17.1   Software-Defined Networking (SDN)

Computer and communication networks have grown in size and complexity. Perhaps the most salient factor determining the success of the underlying network growth is performance. Network engineers want to expand the Internet, but they are well aware that this expansion must be accompanied by good network performance. Parameters closely tied to the underlying network that affect network performance are bit rate, packet loss, and latency. *Software-defined networking* (SDN) has been introduced to offer a solution that enables better network performance. SDN is based on three innovative ideas:

1. Separation of the control and data planes
2. Programmability of the control plane
3. Standardization of *application programming interfaces* (APIs)

In the next several sections, we discuss these innovative ideas. We show how these ideas can result in a system that is capable of running a computer network independent of brand, underlying operating system, or embedded policies of routing and switching devices. Note that implementing sophisticated policies individually in a networking device would lead to high network delay and lower quality of service. This is a network shortcoming that SDN strives to overcome.

17.1.1   Separation of Control and Data Planes

In a computer network, the transmission of data is handled by certain dedicated devices such as switches and routers of various brands that forward packets between servers and other connected devices. However, the governing functional rules of all such devices can be classified and mapped into three basic categories called "planes." These three planes are:

1. The *control plane* carries signaling traffic and is responsible for tasks such as setting up routing, routing packets from once device to another, access control, quality of service, and so on. OSPF, introduced in Chapter 5, is a functional example of the control plane. Functions of the control plane also include system configuration and management.

2. The *data plane* is responsible for switching data in the form of packets once routes are determined by the control plane. An example of the data plane function is switching of packets on output ports of a router.

3. The *management plane* is responsible for administration of a network and enforces the policies in a network. For example, SNMP, protocol introduced in Chapter 9, is included in the management plane and can be used to monitor a device's operation and its performance. The management plane is normally considered as a subset of the control plane.

All three planes are implemented through the combination of software and hardware, often called *firmware*. A networking device requires the interaction of both the data and control planes, so these two planes are substantially integrated. In fact, a networking device has such a tightly integrated control and data plane that a network operator needs to separately configure every protocol on each individual device. Implementing all sophisticated policies individually at a device would lead to high network delay and also lower quality of service. The tightly integrated control and data planes in conventional networks creates a very time-consuming task for a network device specifically, and causes a bottleneck for the Internet in general.

In traditional networking, each networking device needs to find the least-cost paths using layer 3 routing protocols, such as *Open Shortest Path First* (OSPF), or layer 2 forwarding protocols such as *Spanning Tree Protocol* (STP), as described in previous chapters. To carry out such tasks, every device is required to propagate control query messages, receive responses, and implement essential operations based on responses. Furthermore, a network manager must keep track of traffic statistics and the state of various networking devices via network management.

Another challenge faced by network operators of traditional networking is the need for implementation of increasingly sophisticated policies while there is a limited and highly constrained set of low-level networking device configuration commands. Network operators additionally need to implement complex policies and tasks with a highly constrained set of low-level device configuration commands in link interfaces. As a result, the Internet with its traditional structure can cause considerable *network latency*. Implementing all sophisticated policies individually at any device would lead to high network latency or delay and also lower quality of service.

Frequent network misconfiguration is yet another challenge. The state of a network can change continually, and thus network operators must reconfigure the network in response to changing network conditions. This may require manual adjustments in which operators may need to use external tools to dynamically reconfigure network devices when certain events occur. Routers are then equipped with engines to react to continually changing network conditions. This method may not be sophisticated enough to prevent misconfiguration.

Software-defined networking (SDN) offers a solution to the above network challenges by separating the data plane and control plane. SDN removes the control plane from network hardware and implements it in centralized "software" instead. By separating the network control plane (acting as the brain) and its data plane (acting as muscle), a centralized view of the distributed network for more efficient orchestration and automation of network services is provided. This way, the control plane prepares routing or forwarding tables for networking devices, and the data plane implements forwarding packets in networking devices using the forwarding tables prepared by the control plane. This key innovation of SDN results in switches to implement data plane logic that is greatly simplified and reduces the complexity and cost of the switches significantly. Figure 17.1 shows an abstract model of a network deploying an SDN controller compared with conventional networking.

The logically "centralized" SDN controller manages the packet processing functionality of switches and routers. In the early years of Internet development, centralization was considered an ineffective method of management due to reliability, but it is now considered effective for good reason. Since the SDN controller handles all the routing decisions in its network, the concept of "router" can simply be replaced by "switches." As a result, we can use switching nodes in an SDN such as switches S1 through S7 as shown in Figure 17.1 (b).

The control plane can be run in software on a standard server, and thus the creation of new virtualized controllers becomes feasible, and custom services are created more easily. The centralized control method can dynamically administer a network, and handle state changes much faster than distributed protocols can. When a network experiences state change or a policy change, the change is propagated much faster than in a distributed system. To overcome the old issue of reliability in the centralized control method, SDN suggests multiple standby controllers can be used to take over tasks of the failed main controller.

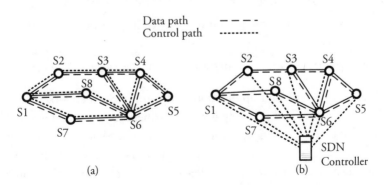

Figure 17.1 Comparison of (a) conventional networking with (b) software-defined networking

17.1.2 Programmability of the Control Plane

Moving the control plane to software allows for dynamic access to network resources and administration. This technique presents evolving a vertically integrated network model to a more horizontal and open model. A network administrator can then use programs to shape traffic from a centralized control console without having to touch individual devices. The administrator can change any network switch's rules when necessary, and prioritize or block specific types of packets with a very granular level of control all through programing tools.

A network control plane is used to find and configure the required resources in SDN, and map the applications to these resources. An application must request and receive a service from its associated network, and interact with some sort of a network control plane. Network devices such as switches and routers become simple packet forwarding devices in SDN. They only focus on the data plane, while the brain is implemented in the SDN controller that focuses on the control plane. In summary, an SDN controller must be responsible for the following:

- Computing the least-cost path for every device in the network
- Updating low-level network device flow-table entries according to network policy
- Translating the network policy to actual packet forwarding rules
- Establishing a connection to each networking device
- Updating packet forwarding rules in networking devices
- Reacting to arriving packet-in events and device-join events
- Installing relevant forwarding rules in a device with packet-in events
- Establishing a new connection with the specific device for any device-join event
- Shutting down links or a switch after directing traffic along other paths to conserve energy
- Performing load balancing, especially in locations close to data centers

With SDN, systems and applications can program a network to control the underlying data plane, and precisely define treatment for packets down to the flow level. This enables networking operations with minimized delay through "programming" the network, rather than manual configuration via low-level interfaces. With the convenience of a centralized controller in SDN, a programmable control plane allows the network to be partitioned into several virtual networks, each having different policies and yet housed on a shared hardware infrastructure. This is possible by defining and creating a standard *application programming interface* (API), which is described next.

17.1.3 Standardization of Application Programming Interfaces (APIs)

The decoupling of the data and control planes in SDN leads to other outstanding properties. One of the most important ones is that the components of the data and control planes can evolve independently when we define a standard *application programming interface* (API) between the two planes. In order to meet application performance objectives, it is necessary to ensure that the underlying network is aware of the application requirements and provides the necessary services.

SDN enables rapid introduction of new network functions at software rather than hardware speed, and can integrate with technology processes in an enterprise network through standard programmable service-oriented APIs. SDN provides a new horizon for applications to interact with networks. Certain APIs in this sense can help direct the configuration of networks and help with plans to optimize the operations of networks.

17.2 SDN-Based Network Model

An SDN-enabled network model is illustrated in Figure 17.2. As shown in this figure, the SDN is modeled by three main segments: the *data plane*, the *control plane*, and *applications*. The control plane communicates with the data plane including all the physical and virtual infrastructure devices through the *southbound API*, and communicates with the network applications segment through the *northbound API*. In addition, *eastbound* and *westbound* APIs have been defined to enable other SDN controllers from neighboring domains or even in the same domain to communicate with each other.

The southbound API is mainly *OpenFlow*, a standard managed by the *Open Networking Foundation* (ONF). A number of other southbound APIs have also been developed. It is also a possibility that a number of network management protocols such as the Simple Network Management Protocol (SNMP), covered in Chapter 9, can also be potential southbound APIs.

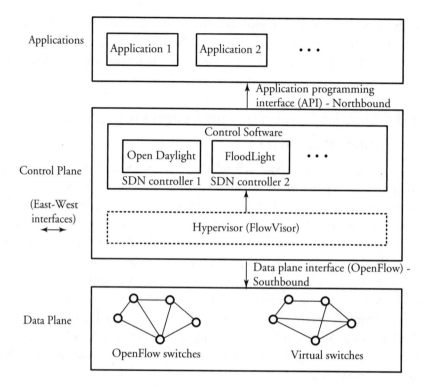

Figure 17.2   SDN-enabled network model

17.2.1   Control Plane

The control plane consists of a *hypervisor* as defined in Chapter 16, and a number of control software modules. The hypervisor in the SDN environment is called *FlowVisor*. FlowVisor performs similarly to a proxy between the data plane and the central controller software. There are various controller software modules, each created for a certain objective such as *OpenDaylight* and *Floodlight*.

OpenDaylight Controller

The *OpenDaylight* project is an industry coalition open source project hosted by the Linux Foundation. OpenDaylight delivers a common open source framework and platform for SDN. The first release from the OpenDaylight project is called *Hydrogen* and includes an open controller, a virtual overlay network, protocol plug-ins, and switch device enhancements. The OpenDaylight framework is Java based and supports applications that run in the same address space as the controller application.

At the heart of this controller is a module called the *service abstraction layer* (SAL) that maps internal and external service queries to the appropriate southbound plug-in. Depending on the capabilities of a plug-in, SAL offers basic service abstractions over which higher-level services are built. An example of this service is the packet handling service, which allows an application to register interest for forwarding or receiving certain packet types without knowing the methods or capabilities of the individual plug-in that generate these packets.

Topology abstraction and discovery are other services of OpenDaylight. The OpenDaylight controller can also introduce powerful and effective networking functions such as *virtualization management* for building and tracking overlay networks. In a later section of this chapter, we discuss *network functions virtualization* (NFV), a complementary-to-SDN method of network control, that can also be supported by the OpenDaylight controller.

Floodlight Controller

Floodlight is another controller that provides basic features such as routing, topology discovery, security, or even firewall rules. It provides the means to control or direct the network that lies beneath. Floodlight is a contribution from the open source community and is an Apache-licensed, and Java-based OpenFlow controller. It is supported by a community of developers including Big Switch Networks project developers. The architecture of the Floodlight controller includes management modules for (1) topology, (2) MAC and IP tracking devices, (3) path computation, and (4) Web access. Furthermore, this controller has OpenFlow counters and a state storage.

17.2.2 Data Plane Interface (OpenFlow Protocol)

OpenFlow is a standard communication interface protocol defined between the control plane and data plane of an SDN-enabled network. OpenFlow protocol is one of the most compelling features of SDN and is essentially responsible for the communication between the data plane inside switches and the control plane in an external controller using a secure channel. It allows direct access to the data plane of networking devices, and makes forwarding decisions by analyzing the first packet of every flow based on rules that are predefined.

The motivation for creating the OpenFlow protocol is indeed the lack of an open interface to the data (forwarding) plane. OpenFlow moves network control out of proprietary network switches and routers and moves it instead into control software that is open source and locally managed. OpenFlow creates a flow of packets over the network of switches to be determined by software running on multiple routers. The separation of the control plane from the data plane discussed earlier as the key advantage of SDN falls on the shoulders of OpenFlow.

OpenFlow Switches

The *OpenFlow switch* is a kind of switch capable of implementing the OpenFlow protocol. A variety of different networking device manufacturers are currently producing this kind of switch. In an SDN-enabled network, the network is implemented through the use of OpenFlow switches. The OpenFlow controller is in charge of managing the OpenFlow switches. OpenFlow is mainly utilized between a switch and the SDN controller on a secure channel. In summary, an SDN controller establishes a connection to each OpenFlow-capable device, and updates packet forwarding rules residing in devices of the data plane through rules and guidelines provided by the controller.

The OpenFlow protocol can generate three types of messages: controller-to-switch messages, switch-to-controller messages, and mixed messages. Controller-to-switch messages are generated and sent by the controller to switches to

- Specify or modify flow tables.
- Request specific information on switch capabilities.
- Retrieve information on a certain flow from the switch.
- Return a packet to a switch for processing after a new flow is defined.

Switch-to-controller messages are sent by the switch to the controller to

- Transmit to the controller a packet that does not match a flow.
- Inform the controller that a flow has been discarded due to the expiration of its timer.
- Inform the controller of an error in a switch or a change in a port.

Mixed messages are sent by the switch or the controller and are of three types:

- *Hello messages.* These are startup messages exchanged between the controller and switch.
- *Echo messages.* These messages are used to verify the liveliness of a controller-to-switch connection.
- *Experimenter messages.* These messages provide a path for future extensions to OpenFlow technology.

The controller-to-switch messages are very common. For example, when an OpenFlow switch is not able to route a packet, the switch buffers the packet, and then it sends the header of the packet along with a buffer ID to the SDN controller. This information can be carried by a *packet-in message*. Then the controller can process the message to discover the network routing solution. The controller can consult an external resource or even another SDN controller in such circumstances. When the routing solution is obtained and finalized, the controller uses a *packet-out message* containing the finalized routing solution and the buffer ID of the switch from which the packet-in message came, and forwards it to the switch. The switch tries to route the packet again, this time using a revised instruction.

Flow Table

Now, we would like to correlate the OpenFlow protocol to the mechanism by which packets flow in an SDN-based network. In practice, a flow of traffic consists of a sequence of packets released from a source. For example, the downloading a large file from a data center performed by a host would create a large "flow" of packets coming from the same source forwarded to the same destination. In such instances, any decision that is made for the first packet of the flow at the controller must be copied for the remaining subsequent packets of the flow. This method of packet handling is called flow-based routing and generally reduces the network latency. A flow can be identified by any mask implemented on packet headers and the input port from which the packet was received.

As shown in Figure 17.3, the input port processor (IPP) of an OpenFlow switch has a number of *flow tables*, table 0 through table *n*, each containing flow entries. The SDN controller creates flow tables consisting of all the necessary rules and guidelines, called "match action rules," for devices in the data plane. The flow tables are conveyed to devices for implementation by OpenFlow protocol. Remember, devices such as switches should not do anything but implement what is indicated in the flow tables.

Each incoming packet is first provided an OpenFlow channel to reach the flow tables. The packet status is then evaluated in flow table 0. This table tries to see if there is a match with an arriving packet. When a match is found, the flow *counter* is incremented and the specified set of instructions is carried out. A match field contains either a specific value against which the corresponding parameter in the incoming packet is compared or a value indicating that the entry is not included in this flow's parameter set. At this point, if a perfect match is found the packet is sent to the *execute action set*. Otherwise, the packet is forwarded to the next table in sequence for the

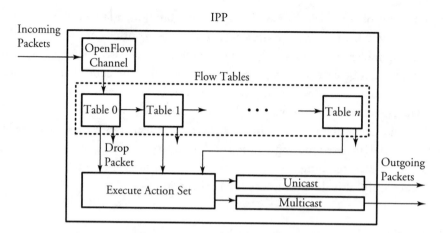

Figure 17.3   Input port processor (IPP) of an OpenFlow switch

same process as performed in table 0. The end result is an accumulation of matches carried with the packet to be executed in the execute action set. The packet is eventually sent out through either unicast or multicast depending on the desired mode of the packet. If a multicast is desired, the necessary copies of the packet are produced and transmitted. A packet can be dropped out of the switch if it is absolutely a wrong packet in the switch or there is no queueing space for it.

In case a packet arrives that does not match any flow table entry, a new flow must be created. In this case, a switch may have been configured to either drop packets or send them to the controller. The controller then defines a new flow for the packets and creates one or more flow table entries. It then sends the newly created entries to the switch to be added to the flow tables. Finally, the packets are sent back to the switch to be processed as determined by the new flow entries.

Details of Matching Fields

There are several *matching fields* against which a packet of a flow can be examined to determine an action. The matching fields are generally partitioned into layer 2 fields, layer 3 fields, layer 4 fields, and an MPLS field. The layer 2 fields are input port, source MAC address, destination MAC address, Ethernet frame type, VLAN ID, and VLAN priority. The layer 3 fields are IP type of service, IP protocol, IP (including IPv6) source address, and IP (including IPv6) destination address. The layer 4 fields are TCP/UDP source port number, and TCP/UDP destination port number. The MPLS field includes MPLS labels.

Example. Table 17.1 shows a typical flow table matching field with some examples of flow entries made by the SDN controller delivered to a switch. In the first row entry, the SDN controller tells the switch that if a packet arrives at port 1 of the switch, the switch needs to (1) send the packet to output port 2, (2) send a copy of it to the controller (for a certain reason), and (3) give a priority of 100 to this task. In the second row entry of this table, the SDN controller tells the switch if a packet with destination address 10.1.2.1 arrives, the switch needs to (1) reassign the destination address to 129.4.4.1 for NAT purposes as the switch may act as the NAT device, (2) send the packet to output port 6, and (3) give a priority of 300 to this task. Finally in the third row entry, we see that the SDN controller specifies to the switch that if a packet arrives at port 5 of the switch, the switch is required to set up output ports 2, 6, 7, and 11 to receive a copy of this packet, as the packet needs to be multicast to these output ports. According to the priority values indicated in the table, the switch routes the packets as shown in the entries of this table. Notice that for one of the entries in the table, the counter field is incremented, as a match is assumed to have been found.

In this example, note that there are two other fields in the flow table: timer and counter. Each flow entry has an idle timeout and a hard timeout associated with it. The idle timeout is the number of seconds after which the flow is removed from the flow table due to a situation under which a switch cannot find a reasonable action for the flow. The hard timeout is the number of seconds after which the incoming flow is removed from the flow table as well as the switch, regardless. In the example, we show only one type of timer for simplicity.

Table 17.1 An example of a flow table matching field and switch action

Matching Field	Switch Action	Priority Given by Switch	Timer (sec)	Counter
Input port = 1	1. Send it to output port = 2	100	300	0
	2. Encapsulate and send to controller as well			
Dest. IP address = 10.1.2.1	1. Reassign dest. IP address to 129.4.4.1 (NAT)	300	X	0
	2. Send to output port = 6			
Input port = 5	Set up output ports = 2, 6, 7, 11 (multicast)	200	X	0
Input port = 3	Drop the entire flow	0	X	0
VLAN ID = 10	Send it to output port = 8	400	4000	1

17.3   Small-Size SDN Architectures

Figure 17.4 shows a campus deploying SDN. Suppose the campus deployment spans building 1 and building 2 where an SDN controller controls the networking functions of the campus. Each building is equipped with OpenFlow switches for packet forwarding. The OpenFlow switch S4 is connected to the Internet. Normally, a modern campus network policy requires every unregistered host to undergo an authentication process through an authentication Web portal to be scanned for possible vulnerabilities. If no vulnerability is found, the host can be granted access to the internal network and the Internet.

Campus network operators rely on *virtual LAN* (VLAN) technology, through which unregistered and registered hosts are first completely separated by different VLAN domains. Once the authentication scanning is completed, hosts are moved back and forth in the different VLAN domains. This is followed by switches having to constantly download the up-to-date VLAN configuration from a central VLAN management controller. Building 2 has an *authentication Web portal* (AWP), an intrusion detection (ID) system, and a scanner.

17.3.1   Scalability of SDN

SDN has been developed based on the perception of centralization of network control. This would lead to concerns about to what extent SDN is scalable and resilient. A central controller cannot be scaled as the network grows. We notice that the Internet grows in time and thus the number of networking devices, traffic flows, and the amount of bandwidth increase. This growth in the resources of the SDN-based

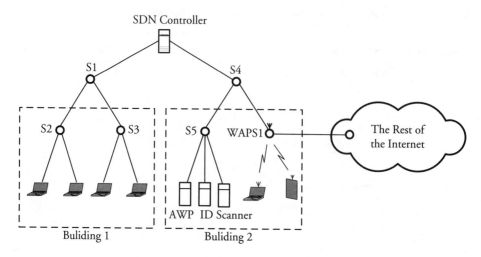

Figure 17.4   An SDN-based small-size network

infrastructure could fail to handle networking flows when the provision of service guarantees is required.

17.3.2   Multicasting in SDN-Based Networks

Multicasting in an SDN-based network becomes effectively simpler than in a regular network. With SDN, the action segment of the flow table indicates the ports to which an incoming packet needs to be copied. Thus the switch does not need to do any assessment of multicast tree assignment, which is a tedious task for a device.

17.4   SDN Architectures for Clouds

The emergence of SDN allows closely integrated application provisioning in cloud computing centers with the network through programmable interfaces and automation. Network engineers can present architecture and implementation of an SDN controller platform that supports a service-level model for application networking in clouds.

Enterprise information technology (IT) environments must be highly responsive to support rapidly changing business requirements. Cloud computing platforms offer an IT model that enables enterprises to procure computing resources on an as-needed basis, as explained in Chapter 16. Cloud architectures delegate management of the infrastructure to the cloud service provider. Clouds can offer services beyond basic virtual servers, storage volumes, and network connectivity.

Cloud centers can offer a *virtual private cloud* (VPC), allowing a user to organize its cloud servers into different subnets while having access to control rules for traffic that may pass between them. Clouds can even offer virtual private network (VPN) services to connect cloud instances to the user's portion of the data center.

17.4.1   Software-Defined Compute and Storage

The idea of software-defined networking leads logically to thinking about the evolution of other software-defined functions. New resources such as *software-defined compute* or *software-defined storage* can also be developed along with a software-defined network. In a combined software-defined compute and storage, most elements of the cloud infrastructure such as networking, storage, CPU, and security are virtualized and delivered as a service. These elements are controlled by one or more central software-defined controllers. Software-defined storage separates the control plane from the data plane of a storage system and thus leverages heterogeneous storage resources dynamically to respond to events such as changing demand. Software-defined compute establishes abstraction of heterogeneous computing resources in terms of both capacity and capability.

A great networking infrastructure would then be equipped with a "software-defined environment" that brings together software-defined compute, storage, and networking. The integration of these three elements unifies the control planes of individual software-defined components. Unified control planes can create incredibly programmable infrastructures for dynamic optimization of communication systems in response to changing users' requirements.

17.4.2 Application Delivery in Data Centers by SDN

SDN-based architectures can also be expanded to network applications involving the delivery of policies on application traffic flows. Delivering massive numbers of complicated applications from private data centers has increasingly become a challenge. The root of the challenge is that any *application service* may need to be replicated over multiple hosts while the *service to applications* must be partitioned to provide better performance. A service is partitioned into several pieces, with each hosted on a different group of servers.

Another challenge is that the majority of services require multiple TCP segments in which each segment can be served by multiple destinations by replication or partitioning. This is true, yet accessing the service itself requires traversing through a sequence of middle devices to provide security. This means that a client-to-server connection associated with a cloud data center can no longer be an end-to-end connection, as we described in Chapter 8. In such cases, the *application service providers* (ASPs) housed in proximity to data centers need to implement complex *application policy routing* (APR) policies inside their data centers.

Example.   Consider a user at a wireless client computer UE1 attached to WiFi node WR1 trying to play an online game. This client requires computing and storage facilities using cloud services from multiple cloud computing providers distributed throughout a nation. What is the solution to the routing challenges in cloud computing if ISPs do not allow dynamic routing over the servers of the data center?

Solution.   In this case, the application layer must be flexible to include an application "delivery layer" including ASP policies allowing ISPs to disperse ASP policies into their application layer protocols and implement them in SDN controllers. ISPs can then offer application delivery services to ASPs as well as clients. As illustrated in Figure 17.5, a data center has an ASP controller that manages the organization of application policies. The ASP controller is directly connected to the ISP's SDN controller and interacts with the SDN controller through specific software made for each type of application. Thus, a client wanting to use a certain application needs to

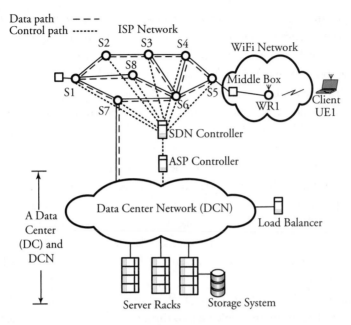

Figure 17.5 Interaction of an SDN controller and an application service provider (ASP) controller for a data center

be connected to one of the application middle boxes available in the ISP that contains the required software for the application. This can be arranged by the SDN controller and, as shown in the figure, the middle box is connected through switch S5. Note that the application software for its associated application requires some extensions to the southbound interface, OpenFlow. In this setup, SDN controllers orchestrate complete control over their network resources, while ASP controllers have complete control over their encrypted application data.

17.5 Network Functions Virtualization (NFV)

Internet service providers (ISPs) employ numerous and varied proprietary hardware appliances. When an ISP plans to launch a new network service, it faces challenges in interfacing these appliances with each other, and also in finding the space and power to accommodate them. Furthermore, when hardware-based appliances reach end of life, they require that the procure design, integrate, and deploy cycle be repeated with minimal revenue benefit.

Given our discussion about SDN, *network functions virtualization* (NFV) is an alternative and to some extent complementary-to-SDN networking approach that aims to address these problems, especially for building networks with complex applications. The solution that NFV offers can be viewed as leveraging standard Internet technology to consolidate numerous network equipment types into an industry standard. High-volume servers, switches, routers, and storage could be located in data centers, in end-user premises, or in any data plane using distributed virtualized functions.

NFV virtualizes the entire class of network node functions, from routing to billing, into building blocks that may be connected or chained together to create communication services. Although there is a virtualization component in the nature of NFV, this method of networking relies solely on traditional server virtualization techniques, as explained in Chapter 16. Examples of virtualized functions in NFV include virtualized load balancers, virtualized firewalls, and virtualized intrusion detection devices.

The objective of NFV is to increase the flexibility of network services deployment. When network functions are implemented through software, any specific hardware-based devices can be avoided. The idea behind NFV is that each network element has a set of various functions that can be potentially inserted into external elements that can later be managed individually. This method of network management opens a wide range of possibilities. One of the immediate benefits is easier migration from IPv4 to IPv6, as separation between IPv4 and IPv6 brings the option of separation in the decisions that need to be made in different routing instances.

17.5.1 Abstract Model of NFV

The operation of NFV in networks can be realized in several ways. The virtualization component of NFV leads us to first think of virtual machines (VMs), presented in Chapter 16, as a vital entity in constructing NFV-based networks. We know that virtual machines provide tremendous advantages with respect to network management, and hence they act as a primary vehicle for NFV. It is logical to think of NFV as a naturally reliable technology that can be used in cloud computing and data centers. Figure 17.6 shows an overview of NFV operation. Any NFV-enabled networking system consists of three main segments:

- *Virtualized network functions* (VNFs). The reliance of NFV on virtualization is primarily defined by *virtualized network functions* (VNFs). Instead of creating custom hardware appliances for each network function, a VNF allows one or more virtual machines to run different software and processes on top of

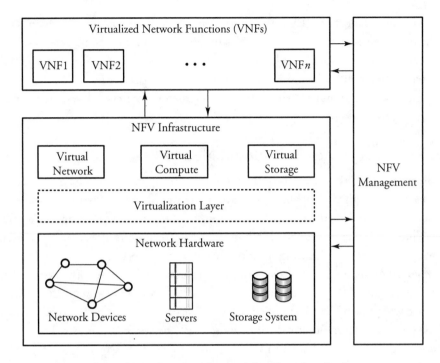

Figure 17.6   Overview of network functions virtualization

industry standard high-volume servers, switches, and storage in a cloud computing infrastructure.

- NFV *infrastructure.* This segment includes hardware components such as network devices, servers, and storage systems supplying a virtualization layer that
acts as an interface between VNFs and the hardware.

- NFV *management.* This part is an orchestrator that includes the tasks of performance measurements, event correlation, event termination, global resource management, resource requests and policy management, the overall coordination
and adaptation of configuration and events, and reporting between functions.

VNFs can be deployed to protect a network without the typical cost and complexity of obtaining and installing physical units. NFV focuses on optimizing network services, and decouples the network functions, such as DNS and caching, from
proprietary hardware appliances. This technique enables network functions to run
in software, which may be located in data centers, in network nodes, or even in a
virtual machine. Furthermore, it accelerates service innovation and provisioning,
particularly within Internet service provider environments.

One useful aspect of NFV is the *network orchestration layer* process, which is part of the management function that enables highly reliable and scalable services. NFV requires that the network be able to monitor virtualized network functions (VNFs) and repair them in real-time fashion if necessary. Importantly, the orchestration layer must be able to manage the virtualized segments of a network regardless of the underlying technology.

17.5.2 Distributed NFV-Based Networks

As the purpose of NFV was primarily to improve the operation of data centers, NFV has been built with the capability of supporting distributed networking resources. Typically, virtualized functions are housed in a location where they are most effective. Thus, an ISP can precisely distribute virtualized functions over the network by identifying the best performing spots on the network for NFV.

Figure 17.7 shows host-to-host communication using NFV. A networking operation that includes NFV can be modeled with hosts connected through a network of VNFs in which each VNF is supplied by a wireline or wireless infrastructure network. Thus, one can imagine that each host in an NFV network is connected to a VNF by a virtual NIC, as explained in Chapter 16. In this figure, host A has a physical connection to host B through infrastructure networks 1, 2, and 3 while the connection is set up logically through a number of VNFs shown as VNFs 1, 8, 6, and 5.

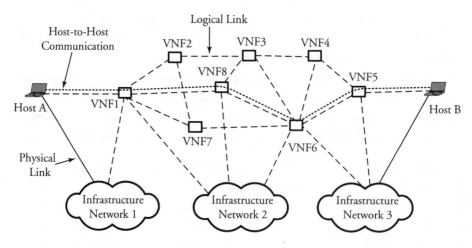

Figure 17.7 A communication model for networking using VNFs

Note that each VNF is associated with an infrastructure network. For example, VNF1 can be a virtual function that acts as a firewall.

NFV builds on some SDN and cloud data center features, including virtualization, data center, SDN control-data plane separation, and SDN controllers.

17.5.3   Virtualized Services

Network services and functions have evolved into *virtualized services, service chaining*, and *platform virtualization*. Virtualized functions can be found in all parts of the Internet, at customer premises connected to the network infrastructure and at data centers. *Virtualized services* primarily imply services implemented in (1) a machine with multiple operating systems, (2) hypervisors, and (3) a distributed fashion. From a different angle, we can see that the virtualization of network services presents some reliability concerns. Specifically, the existence of hypervisors, explained in Chapter 16, and the possibility of multiple virtualized services on the same physical hardware can lead to contention for physical resources in a network. This in turn causes a potential performance degradation experienced by individual services. A solution to this issue was mentioned when we described NFV management in the previous section. The NFV orchestration layer must be vigilant for such degradation to enable hypervisors to troubleshoot and potentially isolate and mitigate the error.

17.6   Information-Centric Networking (ICN)

Information-Centric Networking (ICN) is a method of networking that considers pieces of information, called *named objects*, as the main entities of a networking architecture rather than identifying them via a node to host the information. The motivation for yet another control paradigm in networking is that the vast majority of the Internet traffic consists of content or information dissemination that is addressed to more than one recipient. ICN requires finding and forwarding information to users instead of connecting a known host to download the information.

One of the most common events an Internet user faces is the change of object's URL over time. Most objects' URLs are actually object locators. This means when a DNS resolution is completed for an object, the IP address of the Web server that is serving requests by resolving the URL is exhibited to a requester. Hence, the name-object binding can easily break when an object is moved to another location, the site changes domain, or the site for some reason is unavailable. ICN overcomes this issue with a unique approach for naming objects with its service model that decouples consumers from producers.

Application programming interfaces (APIs) in ICN models are different from the typical APIs in TCP/IP. A typical API in TCP/IP is meant to establish a communication channel between two end hosts, while an API in ICN is meant to activate applications to request an object from a network without knowing the object's location. As we will learn in the following sections, ICN APIs are based on "publishing" objects at some network points and then "getting" the objects from those points.

17.6.1 Named Objects

ICN is based on "named objects" or simple objects such as Web pages, photos, songs, videos, documents, or any other pieces of information. Information-Centric Networking can be compared to regular networking, which is host-centric and in which communication is based on "named hosts," such as Web servers, laptops, mobile handsets, and other devices. Although in ICN, we use information, content, data, and also object interchangeably, one of the variants of ICN is *Content-Centric Networking* (CCN). In CCN, content as interchanged objects is specifically the focus of networking. In ICN, any type of object that can typically be stored in and accessed via computing devices is independent of location. An object is also identified uniquely regardless of its location and regardless of how it is created and communicated.

17.6.2 ICN Routing and Network Management

As an average Internet user has his or her social network profile to post content, the Internet must act as a distributed system for reading information from and writing information to, as well as be accessible from many different devices. ICN allows the shift from a location-based network to an information-based network. In such a case, the TCP/IP system may not be suitable for one-to-many communications. With ICN, information or content becomes independent of the devices in which it is stored. This in turn enables application-independent information or content caching in the network. In terms of network security in ICN, there must be a trust on a copy of information coming from an untrusted device. Any host must be able to verify the integrity of the information, which means a naming scheme must require cryptographic binding.

The real motivation for ICN is that the IP model is designed to establish a connection between two IP addresses so that a user can access content. It would seem that the server that holds the information is mainly irrelevant, as the same information may reside on various servers and the user may want to obtain the information from the best available server. ICN generally assumes that users, content, and hosts are untrustworthy. In ICN, a network is configured to create "name resolution" and routing based on object names. The name resolution can be viewed as a variant of the Domain Name System (DNS), and routing based on object names can also be viewed as a variant of IP routing. In this configuration, packets are routed to the location of the resolution records or to a copy of the object.

The main goal of ICN is to achieve a smart distributed system containing objects by creating a platform similar to peer-to-peer (P2P) overlays. Figure 17.8 illustrates an overview of ICN in which objects are made available to "receivers" by "senders" through publishing the objects. The role of networks is to support application-independent client requests and to locate any source holding a copy of the desired object. Any copies of a named object are equivalent, such that any server holding a copy of the named object can make it available to a requester. Figure 17.8 shows a scenario in which a host is querying object A from the Internet among a number of servers connected together virtually (logically). The figure shows the network of servers without illustrating the connecting routers. Among servers SE11 through SE17 of autonomous system 1, assume an untrusted copy of a requested object exists in SE13, and among servers SE21 through SE26 of autonomous system 2, a trusted copy of object A is located in SE23.

When it comes to routing in ICN, the routing of object *requests* requires a *name resolution node* that holds bindings from object names to topology-based locators. This process then points to corresponding storage locations in the network. Any request message is routed to the responsible name resolution node in which the object name is turned into one or more source addresses. The request message is then routed to the source address followed by routing the data from the source to the requester.

There are a number of methods of routing in ICN. In the following sections, we describe three ICN methods, object-routed networking, Content-Centric Networking (CCN), and rendezvous-based networking.

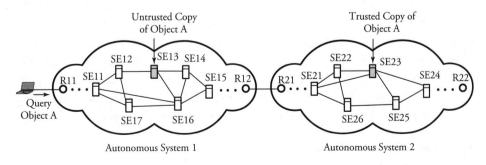

Figure 17.8   Overview of Information-Centric Networking (ICN)

Object-Routed Networking

In *object-routed networking*, shown in Figure 17.9 (a), object names are published by sources of named objects to certain servers called "data finders" on a network. This way, servers that are allowed to perform the task of data finding register as data finders. Find packets are then forwarded to an appropriate data finder from a requesting host, for example, through routers R1, R2, R3, R4, and R5. Data finders form a network through which requested data can be found and sent back as a response to the requester of an object. The response may not necessarily be routed to the requester through the same path on which the data was requested, and indeed tends to be forwarded over a more direct route, as seen in the figure through routers R5, R8, R2, and R1. The requesting host at this point can directly request the targeted object as it has learned the address of the server holding the desired object (SE1).

Object names in this method of ICN can be from a flat name space in the form $a{:}b$, where a is a globally unique field containing the cryptographic hash of the publisher's public key, and b is a unique object label. As a identifies the *publisher* of an object, republishing the same content by a different host implies a different name for the same content that results in a complication in benefiting from all available object copies.

Content-Centric Networking (CCN)

Content-Centric Networking (CCN) is another method of ICN shown in Figure 17.9 (b). In CCN, named objects are published at routers, and routing protocols are employed to distribute the information about the location of named objects. CCN requires a hierarchical naming system. This system must include data security in the form of public key cryptography to the hierarchy, including a certificate chain based on the naming hierarchy. Request packets from a requester in search of a named object are routed over CCN-based routers. A CCN-based router is a router that has an index of object locations and maintains a *pending interest table* (PIT) for outstanding requests.

The PIT segment of CCN-based routers can also cache named objects on the response path. Caching in this context means that the router does not have to find the same object name for another requester once the request has recently been processed. Object names in CCN can be from a hierarchical name space through name-prefix aggregation. The hierarchical name space has a root in a prefix unique to each publisher. The publisher prefix provides requesters with the ability to construct nonexisting names for objects. Remember that object names are also used for the purpose of routing.

Rendezvous-Based Networking

Rendezvous-based networking is another ICN method shown in Figure 17.9 (c). It requires the publication of and subscription to objects by users at a rendezvous point of a network—a server/router combination that matches publications and subscriptions

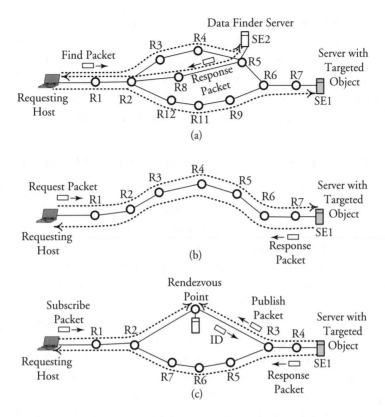

Figure 17.9 Three approaches of Information-Centric Networking: (a) object-routed networking, (b) Content-Centric Networking (CCN), and (c) rendezvous-based networking

to resolve requests for objects. For example, a requesting host sends a subscribe packet through its router R1 to the rendezvous point of its network requesting a subscription to an object on a server as SE1. SE1 originally creates a publish packet that specifies the object identifier and the rendezvous identifier, which together identify the named object, and sends it to the rendezvous point through router R4. The rendezvous point then includes the identification of the requesting host in a reply packet named ID and sends it back to SE1. As the ID includes the information about the requesting host furnished in the subscription step, the source of the targeted object, SE1, is now able to forward the object to the requesting host through any available network path such as the one shown in the figure over routers R4, R3, R5, R6, R7, R2, and R1.

17.6.3 ICN Security

As ICN requires unique names for individual objects irrespective of objects' locations, it is important to establish a verifiable binding between any object and its name.

There are a number of ways to manage name integrity. One way is self-certification through binding the hash (see Chapter 10 for a definition of hash) of the content closely to the object's name and by embedding the hash of the content in the name. An alternative approach may be obtained through embedding the public key of the publisher in the name and signing the hash of the content with the corresponding secret key. Self-certifying an object renders it unreadable by a human.

17.7   Network Emulators for Advanced Networks

Network emulation is an exact, or close to exact, reproduction of an existing or planned network using software, hardware, or both. Network emulation is different from the well-known technique of "network simulation" in which simplified mathematical models of data sources, channels, and protocols are applied for simulation. A *network emulator* is hardware or software or both that duplicates the functions of one network in another network that is different from the first one, so that the emulated behavior closely resembles the behavior of the real network.

A number of emulators are available to reproduce advanced network controls for SDN, NFV, and ICN. One of the promising emulators is Mininet, which is described in the next section. Before we introduce the details of the Mininet emulator, we emphasize that it is necessary to know how to use a packet analyzer in network emulation. An effective packet analyzer is Wireshark, which can also be used for network troubleshooting, analysis, and communications protocol development. Wireshark uses a toolkit to implement its user interface, and "pcap" software to capture packets. Wireshark is incorporated into Mininet.

17.7.1   Mininet

Mininet is one of the SDN *emulators*. It uses simulated hosts, switches, routers, and links on a single Linux kernel. Besides such simulated devices, it is also equipped with lightweight virtualization to make a single system look like a complete network. With Mininet, one can use SSH protocol and send packets through what seems like a real Ethernet interface, with any typical given link speed and delay. Packets are processed by an emulated Ethernet switch or router and queueing packets can be analyzed.

Prompts and Commands

Mininet commands are preceded by a `mininet>` prompt. To use virtualization in Mininet , tools like VMware or VirtualBox must be installed. When Mininet runs on VirtualBox, for example, a prompt such as `mininet@mininet -vm:-$` is created.

Since Mininet is an emulator, any real-time program including Web servers, TCP window monitoring programs, or Wireshark can run on it. Software-defined network (SDN) designs that are developed in Mininet can be transferred to hardware OpenFlow switches for packet forwarding. Servers in Mininet, can create virtual machines (VMs), and thus this emulator can be used in cloud computing. Any Mininet topology can be connected to an SDN controller like OpenDaylight or Floodlight and the default port is 6633.

Table 17.2 presents a set of some useful Mininet commands and their descriptions. These commands can be applied anytime that the Mininet emulator is running to get the status of the simulation.

Table 17.2   A handy set of useful Mininet commands and descriptions

Mininet Command	Description
mininet> nodes	Displays all of the elements (nodes) in the network. Nodes starting with "h" are hosts and nodes starting with "s" are switches.
mininet> net	Displays the list of links in the network, specifically shows a list of switches, and for each switch, a list of hosts and switches connected to that switch, and network interfaces on each host and switch.
mininet> h1 ping -c 5 h2	Generates traffic run on individual hosts (an alternative to ping is iperf). This example sends 5 ping packets to host h2 from h1.
mininet> pingall	Sends a ping from any host to other hosts.
mininet> iperf	Shows TCP bandwidth between hosts.
mininet> h1 iperf -s &	Runs iperf, first starting the iperf server on one host, running the command in the background, and then starting the iperf client on another host. This example runs an iperf server on h1 and an iperf client on h2 mininet> h2 iperf -c h1)
mininet> h1 kill 'ps | grep iperf | cut -f2 -d" "'	Kills the iperf server on h1 when the task is finished. Note that when running ping or iperf, an SDN controller must run on the local machine, otherwise no traffic is sent to the switches, as there are no OpenFlow rules in the switches. A process can also be killed by: h1 ps -a | grep iperf | kill "pid_iperf".
mininet> h1 ifconfig -a	Gives the host's h1-eth0.
mininet> dump	Provides information about all nodes including switches and hosts listed, and addresses of host and switch interfaces.
mininet> h1 ps -a	Prints the process list from a host process.
mininet> exit	Exits from Mininet.

Constructing Networks and Default Topologies

Complex topologies can be created by Mininet using scripts written in Python. Custom topologies such as larger Internet-like topologies or a data center can be simulated with this emulator. However, Mininet has a few very useful script templates that are available as default packages. These script templates include *minimal, single, reversed, linear,* and *tree* topologies.

A *minimal* topology has been created based on an SDN controller c0 controlling switch s1, where this switch is connected to hosts h1 and h2, as seen in Figure 17.10 (a). To see the simulated detail of the minimal topology, while we are on a single virtual machine (the prompt is `mininet@mininet –vm:-$`), type `sudo mn --topo minimal`. At this point, the network has been automatically constructed and we can go back to Mininet and obtain a simulated visualization of this topology by entering `mininet> net`. Steps 1, 2, 3, and 4 provide us with the topology detail as shown in the following output. For example, at step 1, controller c0 is created; at step 2, `h1 h1-eth0:s1-eth1` tells us that host h1 at its interface eth0 is connected to switch s1 at its interface eth1; at step 3, `h2 h2-eth0:s1-eth2` shows that host h2 at interface eth0 is connected to switch s1 at interface eth2; and finally, at step 4, `s1 lo: s1-eth1:h1-eth0 s1-eth2: h2-eth0` shows the summary of the switch s1 links to h1 and h2.

```
mininet@mininet –vm:-$ sudo mn --topo minimal
mininet> net
1. c0
2. h1 h1-eth0:s1-eth1
3. h2 h2-eth0:s1-eth2
4. s1 lo: s1-eth1:h1-eth0 s1-eth2:h2-eth0
```

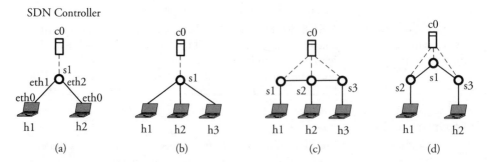

Figure 17.10   Available default SDN topologies in the Mininet emulator where an SDN controller controls four different topologies: (a) minimal, (b) single, (c) linear, and (d) tree

A *single* topology is similar to a minimal topology but the number of hosts specified must be more than two as seen in Figure 17.10 (b). The summary of creating this topology in a virtual machine as seen in a Mininet window is as follows:

```
mininet@mininet -vm:-$ sudo mn --topo single,3
mininet> net
1. c0
2. h1 h1-eth0:s1-eth1
3. h2 h2-eth0:s1-eth2
4. h3 h3-eth0:s1-eth3
5. s1 lo: s1-eth1:h1-eth0 s1-eth2:h2-eth0 s1-eth3:h3-eth0
```

A *reverse* topology is similar to the single topology but the order of links and therefore hosts is reversed (not shown in the figure). In a *linear* topology an SDN controller, c0, controls cascaded switches as shown in Figure 17.10 (c) where three switches s1, s2, and s3 are connected to hosts h1, h2, and h3, respectively. The summary of creating this topology in a virtual machine as seen in a Mininet window is as follows:

```
mininet@mininet -vm:-$ sudo mn --topo linear,3
mininet> net
1. c0
2. h1 h1-eth0:s1-eth1
3. h2 h2-eth0:s2-eth1
4. h3 h3-eth0:s3-eth1
5. s1 lo: s1-eth1:h1-eth0 s1-eth2:s2-eth2
6. s2 lo: s2-eth1:h2-eth0 s2-eth2:s1-eth2 s2-eth3:s3-eth2
7. s3 lo: s3-eth1:h3-eth0 s3-eth2:s2-eth3
```

A *tree* topology is similar to a single topology, but there is a hierarchy of switches, in which the number of levels in the hierarchy can be determined as desired. Figure 17.10 (d) illustrates a two-level hierarchy in a tree topology.

17.8 Summary

The primary focus of this chapter was software-defined networking (SDN). We learned that the key innovations of SDN are the separation of the control and data planes, programmability of the control plane, and standardization of APIs. This allows a large number of networking devices to be flexibly and effectively orchestrated through software.

We covered the important topic of OpenFlow. OpenFlow was defined by the Open Networking Forum for use as the standard interface protocol between the control plane and the data plane. We learned that message exchange between these planes is performed over a secure channel and provides a number of information pieces such as delivery of flow tables to switches for operation of SDN.

We also described the SDN-based controller framework for cloud networking. We introduced a network service model that enables users to construct and manage logical applications in clouds. *Application service providers* (ASPs) residing in proximity to data centers implement complex *application policy routing* (APR) policies inside their data centers.

We also studied *network functions virtualization* (NFV), which is a complementary networking approach to SDN. *Virtualized network functions* (VNFs) are a main component of any NFV-enabled networking system. A VNF allows one or more virtual machines to run different software and processes on top of industry standard devices.

Next, a very efficient networking method called *Information-Centric Networking* (ICN) was introduced. With ICN, *named objects* are the target and focus of requesting hosts and network operation. This can be compared with traditional networking, in which the locations of objects, such as IP addresses, are the focus of network operation. Three methods of routing in ICN were presented.

The chapter concluded with a discussion of advanced network control and management. We presented network emulators, focusing primarily on the Mininet emulator and Wireshark.

In Chapter 18 and the two chapters that follow, we explore voice over IP and multimedia networking. We consider these topics together with cloud computing in the structure of multimedia networking in Chapter 20.

17.9 Exercises

1. Consider the application of SDN in MPLS networks.
   (a) Show the role of an SDN controller for "traffic engineering."
   (b) Explain how label assignment management can be done.

2. Assume an SDN controller uses as its central processor a CPU having the clock rate c. Let each clock cycle handle one binary bit. The SDN controller gives services to n switches. Suppose the average packet size in the network is 500 bytes, and each hour the controller sends an average of 200 kilobytes of updated routing information to a switch and receives an average of 10 kilobytes of routing-related information from a switch.
   (a) Develop an expression for the total required bandwidth of the SDN controller.
   (b) Obtain the number of packets per second the SDN controller generates.

(c) Do a search and find out about the fastest available CPU in terms of clock rate. Use the actual speed of the CPU for the central processor of the SDN and obtain a numerical figure for the total required bandwidth of the SDN controller.

3. Consider the SDN controller presented in exercise 2. If the number of switches, n, increases as the network expands, estimate to what limit n can increase given the maximum CPU speed found in part (c) of exercise 2.

4. We want to design an SDN-based campus for 12 buildings, where each building is supplied with a switch and has two offices, each requiring WiFi access. The campus has a Web server, an e-mail server, and three other servers connected through routers to the campus gateway router. Assume that each networking device in the campus requires two updates per hour released from the SDN controller. The average size of an update is 2KB.

(a) Show an overview of the campus networking.
(b) Estimate the total amount of management data that needs to be exchanged per day in the campus.

5. Consider a fully connected computer network consisting five routers, with four routers located at edge and the fifth one located in the center. Assume that one of the edge routers becomes highly congested to the extent that it does not respond to its outside world. Assume a mean distance between each pair of routers of 0.3 km; links are of the 1Gb/s type, and the propagation speed is 200 m/μs.

(a) Calculate the mean total time for routers in the network to send OSPF packets of 1,000 bytes to one another and settle the network on the congestion event.
(b) If the network is changed to an SDN-controlled type, recalculate the mean total time for the controller to send control packets of 1,000 bytes to all routers and settle the network on the congestion event.

6. Think about the challenges that Information-Centric Networking (ICN) can possibly face. Develop your opinion on the following networking factors:

(a) *Scalability*. Can name resolution be extended to construct a global name resolution? If so, how about the practicality of routing?
(b) *Resource management and cache storage*. Specifically, analyze challenges on the efficiency of ICN protocol for collaboration between caches for network administrators.
(c) *Congestion control*. Comment on how a network with ICN capability must overcome the issue of controlling the rate of information delivery.

7. Rethink the current cloud model in light of Information-Centric Networking (ICN). ICN requires storage and computing facilities distributed over the Internet at a very fine granularity level.

   (a) Does leveraging current cloud computing based on server farms sitting at the edge of the network provide an insufficient level of flexibility when ICN is used to find an object?

   (b) Does serving ICN requests from the edge of the network in lieu of clouds result in acceptable performance?

17.10 Computer Simulation Projects

1. **Simulation of Flow Tables.** Use a simulation tool to simulate the implementation of OpenFlow forwarding tables based on the following parameters: match fields, priority, counters, timeouts, cookies (data value chosen by the controller for filtering flow statistics, flow modifications, and flow timeouts). Create four different such tables and let each table have a different criteria set.

   (a) Run the simulation such that an arriving packet is examined to match it against a table's criteria. Plan to compile all the results.

   (b) Try to improve your results by suggesting other parameters to be added to the flow tables. In particular, try to see if you can improve the performance of the router in terms of latency that is high due to the hypervisor interface.

2. **Simulation of the OpenFlow Protocol for a Small Network.** Use the Mininet emulator to simulate a small SDN-based network with three OpenFlow switches fully connected together. Use benchmarking utilities like cbench and iperf and then implement the northbound and southbound APIs for different standards such as OpenFlow and OpenDaylight for implementing an application. Do the following:

   (a) Test multicasting traffic controlled at the SDN controller.

   (b) Test the policy management capability by embedding in your simulation that it is the policy of the network that the load will be distributed over the switches evenly at all times.

   (c) Express your expectation of the results if the network was a traditional one instead of an SDN-based network.

3. ***Simulation of a Hierarchical SDN-Controlled Cloud Computing DCN Network.*** Use the Mininet emulator to simulate a small SDN-based and *switch-routed* type data center network (DCN) as shown in Figure 16.5. The DCN consists of three layers of switches called *core switches, aggregate switches*, and *edge switches*. Edge switches directly connect to end servers at server racks, and core switches directly connect to the Internet. The aggregate switches are the middle layer switches. Do the following:

(a) First, take advantage of the Mininet default tree template and show a simple three-layer switching arrangement irrespective of the *switch-routed* type data center network (DCN) architecture where each edge switch supplies only one host.

(b) Modify the Mininet default tree template result in part (a) and show the simulation of the *switch-routed* type data center network (DCN) architecture.

CHAPTER 18

Voice over IP (VoIP) Signaling

The communication industry has spent considerable effort in designing the IP-based media exchange mechanism, *voice over IP* (VoIP), which can deliver voice-band telephony with an acceptable quality. The Internet offers phone services that are less expensive and that have numerous additional features such as videoconferencing, online directory services, and Web incorporation. *Multimedia networking* is another innovative development in the Internet. With multimedia networking, the Internet can be used to transport phone calls, audio, and video content distribution. This chapter highlights the following topics:

- *Public Switched Telephone Network* (PSTN)
- *Overview of voice over IP* (VoIP)
- *H.323 protocol*
- *Session Initiation Protocol* (SIP)
- *Softswitch methods and MGCP*
- *VoIP and multimedia internetworking*

We begin by reviewing the basics of the *public switched telephone network* (PSTN). PSTN is the backbone of today's "traditional" voice communication and phone system and consists of numerous switching centers that allow telephone subscribers around the world to communicate with each other.

We then present an overview of the signaling in "packet-based" voice communication and the phone system known as *voice over IP* (VoIP). The signaling of two VoIP protocols are the topics of the next sections: the *H.323 series of protocols* and *Session Initiation Protocol* (SIP). We explain session signaling and numbering for these and other related protocols.

At the end of the chapter, we introduce situations in which a combination such protocols must be implemented to establish a call between users. This section is titled VoIP and Multimedia Internetworking and describes how various types of multimedia or VoIP environments are integrated for communications.

18.1   Public Switched Telephone Networks (PSTN)

The *Public Switched Telephone Network* (PSTN) includes two communication networking structures to provide telephone call services: *circuit-switched networks* in which a circuit is predetermined for each voice session, and the *Signaling System 7* (SS7) *network* for call control signaling. As a result of such structures, two separate transmission paths are used when a telephone call needs to be established: one for call control "signaling" established over the SS7 network; and the other one for media exchange or voice established over circuit-switched networks. Besides ordinary telecommunication services, the SS7 network provides special services such as caller ID, toll-free calling, and call screening. SS7 can also become compatible with voice over IP (VoIP) carriers. Before we get into any details of this topic, let us review some basic definitions of components of the PSTN:

- *Service switching point* (SSP). The SSP is the main switching node of the PSTN. Any phone set is directly attached to its corresponding SSP. When a phone number is dialed by a subscriber, SSP is the node through which a circuit to the destination SSP is initiated.

- *Signal transfer point* (STP). The STP acts as a router and transfers signaling messages from one STP to another once released from the first switching node.

- *Service control point* (SCP). The SCP is a node of the SS7 network that carries out advanced services. For example, when a toll-free 800 number is requested, the SCP finds the location address of the destination SSP to which the call should actually be sent.

- *Line.* A connection between a phone and its attached SSP is called a telephone *line.*
- *Link.* A connection between each of the two main nodes of an SS7 network that carries signaling messages is referred to as a *link.*
- *Trunk.* A connection between each of the two main nodes of circuit-switched networks such as SSPs is referred to as a *trunk.* A trunk carries voice and not signaling packets.

Figure 18.1 shows the networking overview of the PSTN including an SS7 network and a circuit-switched network. The SS7 network handles telephone network signaling and is separate from the portion of the circuit-switched network that handles media and voice communications. One can imagine the SS7 network and the circuit-switched network as two separate but fully connected networks.

As seen in the figure, each telephone set is connected to a *signal transfer point* (SSP) through a phone *line.* Each SSP also acts as a point of call signaling origination and termination and therefore functions as the first signaling point for the SS7 network. Each *signal transfer point* (STP) acts as a router and transfers signaling messages from one STP to another once released from the first SSP. Each SSP is typically associated with two STPs, and thus the failure of a single STP does not result in a total loss of signaling capability between different endpoints. Another signaling node in the SS7

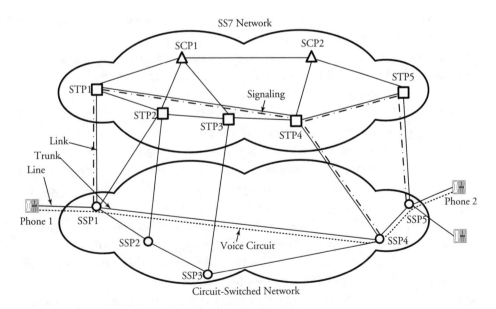

Figure 18.1 A call establishment in the PSTN and the interaction between the SS7 network and circuit-switched networks

network is the service control point (SCP) in which advanced services are provided. For example, if a toll-free 800 number is requested, the SCP entity contains translation information between the dialed 800 number and the location to which the call should actually be sent.

Figure 18.1 also shows an example of a call establishment. Suppose the user of phone 1 wants to contact the user of phone 2. Phone 1 then forwards the dialed number to its attached node, SSP1. SSP1 sends a request message to one of its attached STPs, in this case STP1, to find a route to the destination SSP associated with the dialed number, in this case SSP5. STP1 processes the message very similarly to what a regular router does, and finds the shortest path to the destination's STP for the dialed call. STP1 first checks the destination address of the message, and then checks its routing table to figure out to which STP the message should be sent to next. The path as shown in the figure is found to be STP1-STP4-STP5.

Upon the determination of the signaling route by the SS7 network, each corresponding SSP of an STP is informed of the selection. In this case, SSP4 and SSP5 are informed to prepare for establishment of a circuit. At this point, the circuit-switched network establishes the circuit initiated from phone 1 to phone 2 over SSP1-SSP4-SSP5 and the voice conversation can be sent over an available channel of this circuit.

18.1.1   SS7 Network

The *Signaling System 7* (SS7) network defines its own protocol stack. The *message transfer part* (MTP) forms layers 1, 2, and 3 of the SS7 protocol, known as MTP1, MTP2, and MTP3, and they are responsible for getting a particular message from a source to a destination. MTP1 acts as the physical layer and handles issues related to the signals on signaling links. MTP2 acts as the link layer and transfers messages on a given link from one node to another. Signaling messages are packaged at MTP2 for transmission on a given signaling link. MTP3 acts as the network layer and determines a path over the SS7 network to forward signaling messages of a call.

Above the MTP layers are two other protocol layers, the *ISDN user part* (ISUP) and the *signaling connection control part* (SCCP). The ISUP is used to provide services for *Integrated Services Digital Network* (ISDN) applications and is responsible for setting up or terminating phone calls. The ISUP acts as a connection-oriented protocol such as the transport protocol. SCCP provides an addressing mechanism to enable signaling between each two connected entities. One of most important roles of the SCCP is to provide *global translation title* (GTT) services. GTT messages are sent from an STP to an SCP to query the addressing information about toll-free 800 numbers. On top of the SCCP, the *transaction capabilities application part* (TCAP) coordinates applications between remote sites. The last layer in an SS7 network, application layer, has limited operation and functionality compared to IP networks.

Message Signal Unit (MSU) and ISUP MSUs

The term *message signal unit* (MSU) refers to packet type data acting as a signaling message for routing in SS7 networks. Any of the SS7 protocol layers can have its own MSU. Our focus in this section is the ISUP-based MSU, which is strictly meant for finding a route in the SS7 network. Therefore, when we use the term MSU, we refer to an ISUP-based MSU. The MSU has different formats depending on the country in which it is used, while all countries can configure any type of such MSUs through international signaling gateways for ISUP. One of the popular MSU formats used for ISUP applications has a variable length but maximum length of 279 bytes. Each MSU contains different fields, among which the following fields carry the most important data as follows:

- *Point code* (PC), 24 bits. Any networking device in the PSTN, such as SSP, STP, or SCP, is identified by a unique identifier called a *point code* (PC). A point code can be an *origination point code* (OPC) to indicate the originating device address, or a *destination point code* (DPC) to indicate the destination device address.
- *Signaling link selection* (SLS), 5 bits. SLS indicates a particular link to be used.
- *Circuit identification code* (CIC), 14 bits. Each channel on a trunk is identified by a CIC value.

One can easily realize that an OPC and a DPC act similar to source and destination IP addresses, respectively, for routing in the SS7 network. Note that the conversation takes a different path than the signaling. In order to differentiate many simultaneous calls between any two involved SSPs, the CIC field of a message indicates a specific trunk between the switches. Also, a given circuit between two SSPs is uniquely identified by the combination of the OPC, DPC, and CIC fields.

Phone Call Process and a Signaling Session

Depending on the operation of the SS7 network, MSUs are created in different types for different purposes. The most commonly used MSUs are: IAM, *initial address message;* ACM, *address release message;* CPM, *call progress message;* ANM, *answer message;* RLM, *release message;* and RCM, *release complete message.*

Figure 18.2 shows a detailed exchange of different MSUs between phone 1 and phone 2 for a call establishment and release shown in Figure 18.1. A call begins with a user picking up phone 1 and receiving a dial tone from its attached switching point, SSP1, followed by dialing the number of phone 2. At the receipt of the phone number, SSP1 sends an IAM message to its attached STP1 to find a path to the destination phone 2. This message contains information such as called and calling numbers, the transmission rate requirement, and the type of caller. STP1 finds the shortest path of STP1-STP4-STP5 to the destination's STP, which is STP5 and forwards the IAM message to STP4 and eventually SSP5.

On the same path but in the opposite direction, an ACM is returned indicating that the call path is confirmed. Right after the completion of the ACM process, a one-way ring-back tone is sent from the destination switch, SSP5, to the originating

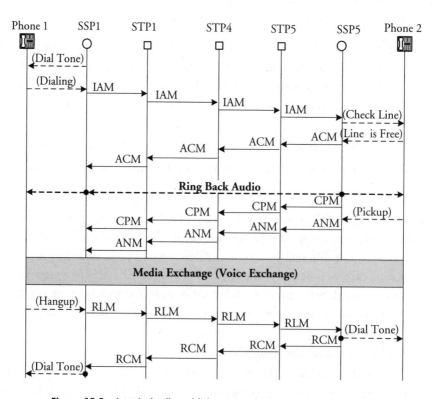

Figure 18.2 A typical call establishment and release process in an ISUP

switch, SSP1. After the release of the tone, there might be an optional call progress message, CPM, providing additional information about handling the call. Once the callee picks up the handset and answers, an answer message (ANM) is returned. The purpose of the ANM is to open a bidirectional *media exchange* or voice exchange channel over the transmission trunk and to instigate the call charge that begins when the call is answered. At this point, the conversation can begin between the two parties. During the conversation, any of the two parties can hang up and end the conversation, resulting in the generation of an RLM to be sent to the other end. The party who receives an RLM confirms with a confirmation message RCM.

18.1.2   Circuit-Switched Networks

The actual voice during a telephone call, or any other kind of *media exchange* session, is carried over *circuit-switched networks*. As we discussed in the previous section, when a phone number is dialed by a subscriber, a *service switching point* (SSP) is the first level switching node initially responding to the call. In a circuit-switched network, there can be five different hierarchical SSPs. The first level SSP is called central office 5 (CO5). Depending on the distance of the phone call to its destination, the connection can be established requiring the engagement of CO5 or higher layer switching nodes CO4 through CO1.

Besides the five switching levels, there are local switching nodes for campus level applications called *private branch exchange* (PBX). PBXs can be small-capacity such as the ones that can handle 30 to 40 calls and known as *key systems*, or large-capacity such as the ones that can give services to 20,000 phone calls. As mentioned in the previous chapter, a connection between each two SSPs or a PBX and SSP in a circuit-switched network is referred to as a *trunk*. Trunks can be of different types such as T1 (1.544 Mb/s) or E1 (2.048 Mb/s). By the telecommunication standard, each phone connection uses 4KHz bandwidth from voice or any audio spectrum, and a T1 line carries 23 multiplexed such phone spectra, each belonging to a pair of phone conversations.

Phone Network Design and Erlang-B Blocking Estimation

In Section 11.4.4, we learned how a system with a resources and no queueing line can be blocked using the Erlang-B formula. In this section, we recall the Erlang-B formula derived by Equation (11.46). This equation provides us with blocking probability, p_a given that a is the number of resources, and the utilization $\rho_1 = \lambda/\mu$. We can use this very important formula to estimate call blocking in circuit-switched networks. In such a case, a new incoming voice call is turned away or blocked from service if all channels on a trunk are taken. Appendix D of this book presents a numerical compilation of the Erlang-B formula based on Equation (11.46). This table can be used for the estimation of blocking probabilities given the number of phone channels, where number of channels is a, the blocking probability of the system is p_a, and system utilization is ρ_1.

Begin Steps to Design a Campus Phone Network

1. Choose the switching node type, examples:
   - Key system for up to 40 phones.
   - PBX for up to 20,000 phones.

2. Identify the required campus blocking probability, P_a, based on the traffic non-blocking need of the campus. The standard for voice systems is: $0.01 < P_a < 0.05$.

3. Find the number of channels, a, from the Erlang-B table using P_a and P_1, for which λ and μ are used to obtain utilization $\rho_1 = \lambda/\mu$.

4. Choose a trunk type. Examples: T1 (23 voice channels), E1 (30 voice channels), or another type.

5. Find the number of trunks. Examples: If T1 trunks are used, the number of trunks is $\lceil \frac{a}{23} \rceil$; and if E1 trunks are used, the number of trunks is $\lceil \frac{a}{30} \rceil$. ∎

Example. Design a phone network for a company consisting of a headquarters campus and a branch building. The entire company can sustain a blocking probability of 0.05. The headquarters needs a total of 3500 phones while the branch requires 35 phones. Each telephone in the entire company uses phone lines an average of 6 minutes per hour during the day with an average call arrival rate of 0.2 per hour. All trunks must be T1. Show an overview of the design of this phone network.

Solution. Figure 18.3 shows the design result for this company. In step 1, we choose a PBX node for the headquarters and a key system for the branch according to the number of existing phones in each campus. In step 2, we calculate that the entire company can sustain a blocking probability of $p_a = 0.05 = 5\%$. In step 3, we have $m = 3500$ phones in the headquarters generating calls with an average of 0.2 calls per hour resulting in a total average arrival rate of $\lambda = 3500 \times 0.2 = 700$ calls per hour. Also, since each phone is in use an average of 6 minutes per hour, the service rate becomes $m = 1/(6 \text{ min per hour}) = 10$ calls per hour, and therefore $\rho_1 = \lambda/\mu = 700/10 = 70$.

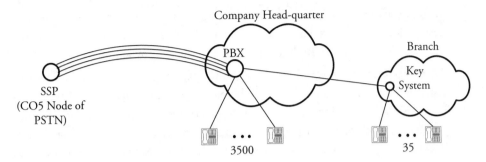

Figure 18.3 Overview of a phone network design for a company requiring 3,500 phones at its headquarters and 35 phones at its branch building

Since we have p_a and ρ_1, we can now use the Erlang-B table in Appendix D and find the number required channels on trunks as $a = 76$. Using a similar approach, the utilization and the number of channels can be found for the branch to be, respectively, $\rho_1 = 0.6$ and $a = 3$. Since all trunks must be T1, between the key system to the PBX in step 5 we need to dedicate a full T1 line even though we have an average of 3 channels active. From the PBX to the CO5 node of the PSTN, we have to induce the requirement of $76 + 3 = 79$ as the total average active channels. Therefore, we need a total of $\lceil 79/23 \rceil = 4$ T1 trunks as indicated in the figure.

18.2 Overview of Voice over IP (VoIP)

Unlike traditional voice networks such as the PSTN discussed in the previous section, *voice over IP* (VoIP) technology or IP-telephony uses packet-switched networks. Network resources of a packet-switched network are shared between voice and data traffic. In traditional voice networks, the network resources dedicated to an active connection between two phones remain unavailable to others when the phone users are in silent mode. But silent mode in an active VoIP connection means the users do not send packets and thus the unused network resources can be utilized by other users. This results in substantial bandwidth savings and efficient use of the available network resources compared to PSTN. A VoIP network operates through two different sets of protocols as follows:

1. *Signaling protocols.* Signaling protocols handle call setups and are controlled by the signaling servers. Once a connection is set through signaling protocols,

media exchange protocols transfer voice, video, or data in real-time fashion to destinations. Media exchange protocols typically run over the UDP scheme because TCP has a very high overhead due to the acknowledgments.

2. *Media exchange protocols.* After the signaling phase for call setup is completed, voice or any other media can start to be processed and exchanged. This process includes the conversion of voice to binary, compression of data, and creation of packets to be sent over packet-switched networks. At a receiver, the data is decoded and converted back to analog form. Media exchange protocols build some reliability into the UDP scheme.Chapter 19 discusses the details of the voice and media exchange processes and introduces several theories and algorithms for processing of voice, video, and data.

Figure 18.4 illustrates an overview of VoIP networking. Basic components of a VoIP telephone system include: *VoIP telephones, multimedia terminals* such as host computers with the appropriate software (any host computer or a VoIP telephone can be used to make calls over IP networks), the Internet backbone including its voice-enabled (shown by "v") *media gateway* (MG) router, and *signaling servers.* An MG router acts as a gateway to the domain in which the user is present. The signaling servers in each domain are analogous to the CPU in a computer and they are responsible for the coordination between VoIP phones and call setup.

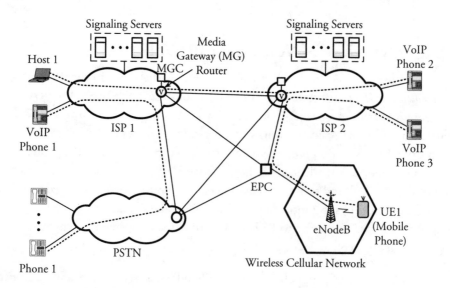

Figure 18.4   Overview of a voice over IP (VoIP) communication

Recall from the discussion of the Internet applications in Chapter 9 that a connection between each pair of VoIP phones may require a *Domain Name System* (DNS) server that maps a domain name to an IP address in the *user information database* (UID). The user information database contains information about users such as preferences and the services to which it has subscribed. The database also stores information on the related IP addresses. Each user is normally configured with more than one DNS server.

In Figure 18.4, several examples of VoIP connections are presented. In the first example, host 1 is placing a call from the Internet service provider 1 (ISP 1) through its media gateway to VoIP phone 2 housed in ISP 2. In the second example, VoIP phone 1 is placing a call to a traditional phone (phone 1) residing in the PSTN. We should remember here that the connection between these two phones requires a substantial protocol conversion by the intermediating MG. Finally, in the third example, VoIP phone 3 housed in ISP 2 has dialed a mobile phone, UE1, residing in an LTE wireless cellular network. The call has been established through a number of interfacing devices contained in the *evolved packet core* (EPC) and thereby an eNodeB base station as explained in Chapter 7.

The IP telephone system must be able to handle signaling for call setup, conversion of phone numbers to IP addresses, and proper call termination. Signaling is required for call setup, call management, and call termination. In any standard telephone call, the signaling process involves:

1. Identifying user's location given a phone number.

2. Finding a route between a calling and a called party.

3. Handling the issue of call forwarding and other call features

IP telephone systems can employ either a distributed or centralized signaling scheme. The distributed approach enables two VoIP telephones to communicate using a client/server model as most Internet applications do. The distributed approach works well with voice over IP networks within a single company. The centralized approach utilizes the conventional model and can provide some level of guarantee. There are several different approaches for the signaling protocols among which the following protocols are well known:

- *H.323 series of protocols*
- *Session Initiation Protocol* (SIP).
- *Softswitch methods and MGCP*

The H.323 series of protocols is the first topic of discussion, as it was implemented in the Internet before SIP. SIP is a newer protocol and has several trade-offs compared with H.323.

18.3   H.323 Protocol

The H.323 protocol is implemented in layer 5 of the TCP/IP protocol model and it runs over either TCP or UDP or a combination of both. The protocol consists of a group of protocols that interact to provide a decent telephone communication. It provides phone number to IP address mapping and handles the digitized audio streaming in IP telephony and provides signaling functions for call setup and call management. This protocol supports simultaneous voice and data transmission. It can transmit binary messages that are encoded using basic encoding rules. From the security standpoint, the H.323 scheme provides a unique framework for security, user authentication, and authorization. It also supports conference calls and multipoint connections. With the H.323 protocol, services like accounting and call forwarding are easily supported.

18.3.1   Main Components of H.323 Protocol

Figure 18.5 shows an overview of the H.323 protocol connections. The H.323 scheme defines the following components:

1. *Terminal.* A terminal is a multimedia end-user device that supports at least one audio coder/decoder (codec), and is designed to support video and data traffic in addition to providing support for IP telephony.

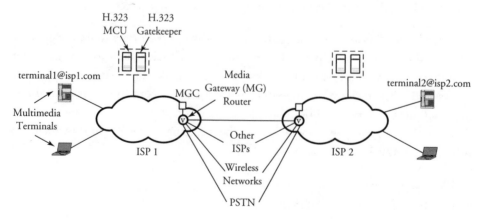

Figure 18.5   Overview of H.323 protocol setup

2. *Gatekeeper* (GK). A gatekeeper provides address translation and authorizes access to the network domain it belongs to. The gatekeeper also communicates with all end points such as the gateways and terminals, and manages quality of service.

3. *Multipoint control unit* (MCU). This unit provides multipoint services such as conference calls.

Beside the preceding components, the *media gateway* (MG) router with its attached *media gateway controller* (MGC) are also present in ISPs for providing protocol message translation services between the H.323-enabled IP network and other types of communication networks. H.323 enables the exchange of media streams between H.323 endpoints. An H.323 endpoint can be a multimedia terminal, an MG, or an MCU. A gatekeeper can send signals to other gatekeepers of different domains to access users of those domains.

18.3.2   H.323 Protocol Organization

Figure 18.6 shows the placement of H.323 protocols in the five-layer TCP/IP model. The application layer as the fifth layer of this stack handles media exchange and control. The *media exchange* segment of this protocol is represented by several protocols such as the Real-time Transport Protocol (RTP), which runs over UDP handling packetized voice and video. There is an extension to RTP called the Real-time Transport Control Protocol (RTCP). The next two chapters will discuss the nature of real-time protocols in detail.

The *control* segment of the protocol structure is responsible for the management of calls. The actual signaling messages exchanged between H.323 entities are specified in the H.225.0 and H.245 protocols. H.225.0 is partially used for *registration*,

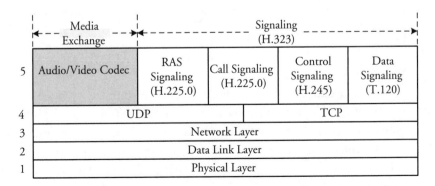

Figure 18.6   Placement of the H.323 protocol in the five-layer protocol stack model

admission, and status (RAS) *signaling* between endpoints and gatekeepers. With the RAS protocol, an endpoint can register with a gatekeeper, and a gatekeeper allows an endpoint to access its network resources. RAS protocol is carried over UDP.

Another portion of H.225.0 is used for *call signaling* and mainly for establishment and termination of connections between endpoints. Call signaling is carried over either UDP or TCP. Since the establishment of a TCP connection takes a longer time for call setup, H.323 version 4 specifies a mechanism whereby both TCP and UDP can be used simultaneously. In such a case, a UDP and a TCP connection are established simultaneously but the TCP connection is used if no response has been received from the UDP request and vice versa.

The *control signaling* portion of H.323 is mandated by H.245 protocol. This protocol applies media type or bit rate limits if there is any restriction at the receiving media. H.245 operates by the establishment of one or more logical channels between endpoints. H.323 can also support the transmission data. T.120 is the protocol that provides services for data transmission using TCP connections.

Example. Reconsider VoIP phone with an assigned e-mail address of terminal1@isp1.com shown in Figure 18.5 to be an endpoint that starts to establish a call to the terminal2@isp2.com endpoint housed in ISP 2. First, terminal1 uses RAS signaling to obtain permission from a gatekeeper. It then uses call signaling to establish communication with terminal2to set up the call. Finally, terminal1 applies H.245 control signaling to negotiate media parameters with terminal2 and sets up the transfer of media.

H.323 messages are transmitted on various types of channels where a channel is a reference to a socket address (an IP address and port number). For example, if a given endpoint uses a particular IP address and port number to receive RAS messages, then any message that arrives at that IP address and port in fact arrives on the channel of the endpoint's RAS.

DNS Server and Addressing

As most networking entities, every unit in the H.323 network has a unique network IP address. With H.323 protocol, a *Domain Name System* (DNS) server is also an active cooperative server to map a domain name to an IP address the same way as discussed in Chapter 5. If this server is available, any IP address may be specified in the server in the form of a Uniform Resource Locator (URL) based on RFC 1738 and RFC 2396 recommendations. As an example, ras://GateKeeper1@isp1.com would be a valid URL for a gatekeeper existing in Internet service provider 1 (ISP 1). Other units such as terminals, gateways, and MCUs each should have a domain name in common with their corresponding gatekeeper. In this example, "ras" is the application layer protocol defined for H.323, discussed next.

Any URL has a port number. A default port number 1719 should be used for RAS when its port number is not specified. Other examples are UDP discovery port number 1718, the gatekeeper UDP registration and status port number 1719, and the call-signaling TCP or UDP port number 1720. Other port numbers for signaling transactions or even for media exchanges are assigned dynamically.

18.3.3   RAS Signaling

Registration, admission, and status (RAS) is an optional signaling protocol by which a gatekeeper controls all the endpoints within its network. Any endpoint has an option to use the services of a gatekeeper, or all the functions that a gatekeeper provides must be provided within that endpoint. RAS signaling involves nine processes: (1) *gatekeeper discovery*, (2) *endpoint registration*, (3) *admission*, (4) *bandwidth modification*, (5) *status*, (6) *disengage*, (7) *resource availability*, (8) *service control*, and (9) *request in progress*. These processes are described next, in the same order.

Gatekeeper Discovery

Any endpoint has an option to register with a gatekeeper of the network it belongs to through either a configuration process or an automatic discovery process. In a network, there might be several gatekeepers. The gatekeeper discovery function enables an endpoint to determine which gatekeeper is available. An endpoint attempts to find its gatekeeper by sending a gatekeeper request (GRQ) message. Normally, this message is multicast to all gatekeepers with the multicast address 224.0.1.41 at port 1718. Any gatekeeper that is available and willing to control the endpoint to be the gatekeeper for a given endpoint may respond with a gatekeeper confirmation (GCF) message. In case a gatekeeper is not available due to various reasons such as lack of resources, it responds with a gatekeeper reject (GRJ) message. An example of the gatekeeper discovery function is illustrated in Figure 18.7. In this figure, an endpoint terminal multicasts the GRQ message to the three existing gatekeepers 1, 2, and 3. Gatekeeper 2 announces its unavailability by responding with a GRJ message, while gatekeepers 1 and 3 respond with an availability confirmation message of GCF. In this case, the task of selecting a gatekeeper between the two is left to the terminal.

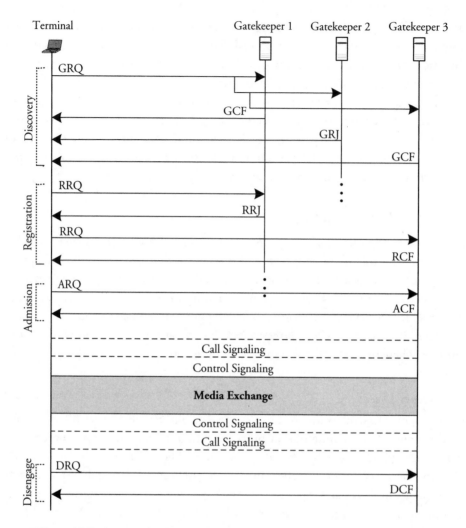

Figure 18.7   An example of H.323 gatekeeper discovery, registration, and admission

Endpoint Registration

Once the gatekeeper discovery procedure is completed, an endpoint joins a gate-keeper through an *endpoint registration* process starting with the issuance of a registration request (RRQ) message. The port number to be used for the message is still the RAS signaling port of 1719. The gatekeeper can choose to reject a registration by responding with a registration reject (RRJ) message. For example, if the endpoint requests a name that is already in use within the network, the registration is voided.

Otherwise, the gatekeeper responds with a registration confirmation (RCF) message. Any registration has a limited lifetime up to 136 years, equivalent to hexadecimal FFFFFFFF seconds. The registration can be cancelled by the endpoint through sending an unregistration request (URQ) message to be confirmed by the gatekeeper through sending an unregistration confirmation (UCF) message. If an endpoint tries to cancel a registration while still carrying a call, the registration request is rejected through the release of an unregistration reject (URJ) message. An example of an endpoint registration with a gatekeeper is illustrated in Figure 18.7.

Admission

Once an endpoint is registered with a gatekeeper, it can then enter the *admission* process by sending an admission request (ARQ) message to the gatekeeper. The ARQ message indicates parameters such as whether the type of call is two-party or multi-party, the endpoint identifier, a unique string as call identifier, a call reference value, and other party aliases and signaling addresses. A gatekeeper may choose to deny a particular admission request by responding with an admission reject (ARJ) message. Possible reasons in this case include lack of available bandwidth, or an endpoint not being registered. An example of an endpoint admission is illustrated in Figure 18.7.

In normal circumstances, a gatekeeper indicates the admission by responding to the endpoint with an admission confirm (ACF) message consisting of the same parameters that are included in the admission request message. This message also specifies the amount of bandwidth required in units of 100b/s. A gatekeeper may not guarantee the requested bandwidth, but once it agrees on a certain bandwidth, the admitted bandwidth is reserved for the call. For example, when a three-party conference call takes place, with each party sending voice at 64kb/s, then the bandwidth required is 192kb/s; therefore, the value carried in the bandwidth parameter is 1,920. If the gatekeeper specifies a lower value than that requested in the ARQ for the bandwidth, the endpoint must stay within the imposed bandwidth. The actual media call can be either through the gatekeeper or directory to the other party. This situation is also indicated in the ARQ message.

Bandwidth Modification

An endpoint can modify its bandwidth through the *bandwidth modification* process. If the bandwidth modification does not exceed the limit specified by the gatekeeper, it does not require the approval of the gatekeeper; otherwise, a modification in bandwidth must be requested by sending a bandwidth request (BRQ) message. The gatekeeper can in turn either approve the new bandwidth with a bandwidth confirm (BCF) message or disapprove the request with a bandwidth reject (BRJ) message. Under severe bit-rate demand in a network during the time that network resource utilization approaches its capacity, a request to reduce bandwidth can also be made by the associated gatekeeper. In this case, the endpoint must agree with the request and respond with a BCF message.

Status

The *status* mode allows a gatekeeper to be informed whether an endpoint is still functional or active. A gatekeeper polls an endpoint by sending an information request (IRQ) message to the endpoint. The endpoint in turn sends an information request response (IRR) message to deliver information to its associated gatekeeper about its functionality status and its one or more current active calls. The information consists of the call identifier, the call reference value, the call type (two-party or multiparty), the bandwidth, RTP session, and so on.

Disengage

Once a call or media transmission ends, each endpoint must enter a *disengage* process by sending a disengage request (DRQ) massage to its associated gatekeeper. This message must contain a disengage reason. The associated gatekeeper then responds either with a disengage confirm (DCF) message or with a disengage reject (DRJ) message. A gatekeeper could also decide to terminate a call, in which case the gatekeeper sends a DRQ message to the endpoint. The endpoint must stop transmitting media and must bring the session to a close using H.245 control messages and call-signaling messages.

Resource Availability

The *resource availability* is a process that informs the level of call capacity. A gateway can send a resource available indicate (RAI) message to inform the gatekeeper of the currently available call capacity and bandwidth for each protocol supported by the gateway. The gatekeeper acknowledges the gateway with a resource available confirm (RAC) message.

Service Control

The purpose of the *service control* process is to enable some advanced features. Any network entity can initiate this process by sending a service control indication (SCI) message and by receiving a service control response (SCR) message. These messages can also be used to implement the specific capability of certain vendor brand equipment.

Request in Progress

The *request in progress* is a process defined by H.225.0. By creation of the request in progress (RIP) message, an entity informs that the response to a given request may take longer than expected. In such a case, the entity indicates an expected delay before it expects to send a response to the original request.

18.3.4   Call Signaling

Call signaling is a set of signaling rules used to enable the establishment of calls among endpoints. Call signaling is supported by the H.225.0 protocol set. These signaling rules use messages defined in Q.931 for the support of call-signaling functions. A majority of the call signaling messages require a number of parameters to accompany the message such as the call identifier, the call type, and information about the originating endpoint. The most important call-signaling messages are:

- Setup. Once an endpoint has been granted admission from a gatekeeper, the Setup message must be sent to establish a call. The Setup message contains several parameters such as a call reference and the user-to-user information element.

- Call Proceeding. This message is optional and sent to indicate that the Setup message has been received.

- Alerting. This message is sent to alert a called party of the upcoming connection establishment.

- Progress. This message can be sent by a called gateway router to indicate that a call is in progress.

- Connect. The Connect message is sent by a called endpoint to a calling endpoint to indicate that the called party has accepted the call.

- Release Complete. This message terminates a call. The entity that releases the call should provide the other user with a reason for the release.

- Facility. The Facility message is used to redirect a call. For example, consider a case when a Setup message is sent to an endpoint and the endpoint's gatekeeper indicates to the endpoint that it wants to intervene. Thus, the user who receives this message releases the call and attempts to set up the call again via the called gatekeeper.

It is important to note that the call signaling and the control signaling are closely tied together. Once a Setup message is released, H.323 protocol requires that H.245 messages be exchanged without enforcing that the exchange of these messages must occur at any particular point within the call signaling. When a call is set up, there can be four main different scenarios:

Mode 1: Terminal-only-routed signaling

Mode 2: Observing-gatekeeper-routed signaling

Mode 3: Partial-gatekeeper-routed signaling

Mode 4: Gatekeeper-routed signaling

In *terminal-only-routed signaling*, gatekeepers are not present in a call establishment process and only endpoints establish call signaling directly. To gain insight into this mode, imagine that a calling terminal initiates a Setup message. The called terminal replies with an optional Call Proceeding message followed by a Connect message. Once the media exchange process is over, the calling terminal (or called terminal) releases the connection by a Release Complete message. This mode is fairly simple at the cost of no security and no reliability.

In a call establishment using *observing-gatekeeper–routed signaling* the two endpoints establish a call, however in the presence of gatekeepers. In this case, once the endpoints such as terminals are registered with their gatekeepers, they are granted admission from their gatekeepers through ARQ and ACF massages. Gatekeepers after this point are observing the connection and stay on but do not directly play any role. Then, the calling terminal sends the Setup message. The called terminal in turn sends a Call Proceeding message to the calling terminal that the Setup has been received successfully. The called terminal is now allowed to establish a call by sending a Connect message. Once the media exchange process is over, the calling terminal (or called terminal) can release the connection by a Release Complete message. Notice that in this mode, since gatekeepers are present even though they are not involved, each endpoint must notify the gatekeeper of its disengagement by exchanging DRQ and DCF messages. However, a given endpoint can choose to send call signaling directly to the other endpoint, bypassing gatekeepers.

Partial-gatekeeper-routed signaling shown in Figure 18.8 is the third mode of call signaling. The compelling part of this mode is that the call signaling is routed via only one of the gatekeepers rather than directly from endpoint to endpoint and thus ensures the reliability of the call establishment to some extent. As seen in the figure, the gatekeeper of the terminal 1 VoIP phone as the calling endpoint chooses to route the call

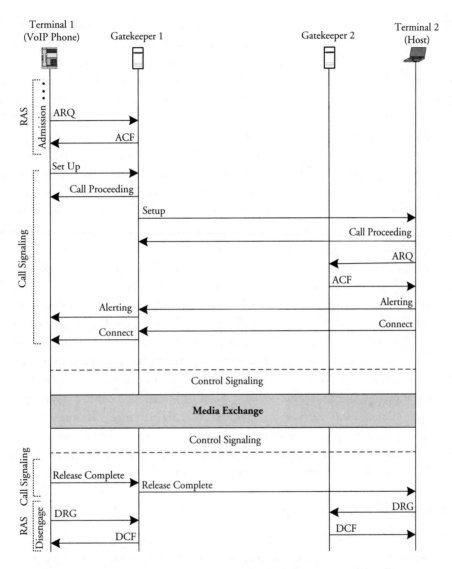

Figure 18.8   An example of a call using partial-gatekeeper-routed signaling
in the presence of gatekeepers

signaling using the ACF message. This message indicates that call signaling should be
sent to the gatekeeper by including its call-signaling address in the ACF. Then, terminal 1 exchanges a Setup message and Call Proceeding message with the gatekeeper.
The calling gatekeeper in turn exchanges a Setup message and Call Proceeding message with the host terminal 2 as the called endpoint using the call-signaling address of

that terminal. At this point, terminal 2 responds with a Call Proceeding message and an ARQ to its gatekeeper and receives an ACF message presenting direct call signaling. Note that ARQ and ACF messages are not required if the terminal has a pre-granted admission. The called terminal now propagates an Alerting message to the gatekeeper of terminal 1, which is forwarded to terminal 2. Similarly, terminal 2 propagates a Connect message to the gatekeeper of terminal 1, which is forwarded to terminal 1. This procedure prepares the media exchange process.

In a fourth scenario, the gatekeeper of the called terminal wishes to be in the path of call-signaling messages. Similar to the previous cases, the gatekeeper of the calling terminal sends a Setup message, and the called terminal makes a request for permission from its own gatekeeper to control the call, but here, since the gatekeeper is the controlling entity, it rejects the request by issuing an ARJ message. Consequently, the called terminal sends a Facility message to the gatekeeper of the calling endpoint and indicates that the reason for the Facility message is that the call is to be routed to the gatekeeper so that the calling gatekeeper knows where to send the call signaling. Note that ARQ/ACF messages are not required if the terminal has a pre-granted admission. The gatekeeper of the calling terminal attempts to establish the call to the gatekeeper of the called terminal by sending a Setup message. The gatekeeper of the called terminal in turn returns a Call Proceeding message, and then forwards the Setup message to the called terminal. The called terminal similarly returns a Call Proceeding message leading to a propagation of the Connect message from one end to another through gatekeepers, and preparation of media exchange. At the end of media exchange, a Release Complete message is passed on the same way as the Connect message but in the opposite direction. Note that, at the end of each connection, the terminals must disengage from the network using the DRQ and DCF messages, which are not shown in the figure.

18.3.5   Control Signaling

Control signaling is a set of rules called the H.245 protocol that is used to establish and control media exchange. It ensures media formats, bandwidth requirements, and multiplexing multiple media streams. In this section, some important aspects of this signaling set are described such as *capabilities exchange*, *master/slave assignment*, and *media exchange establishment control*.

Capabilities Exchange

The first step of control signaling is called *capabilities exchange*, performed in the form of message exchanging. A message queries on various parameters such as whether the receiver is capable of receiving video, and if yes, in which format. Upon informing the capabilities from one endpoint, other endpoints must limit their transmission to what the endpoint has indicated it can handle. A calling endpoint releases its capabilities in a terminal capability set request (TCS-Req) message indicating a sequence number, the types of audio/video formats that the endpoint can send and receive, and what media can be handled simultaneously. A TCS-Req message, however, can indicate all capabilities or confirmation about specific capabilities. This message is in fact a request and requires a confirmation response of a terminal capability set acknowledgment (TCS-Ack) message containing a sequence number that matches the sequence number received in the original request. If there is no capabilities match, the called endpoint responds with a terminal capability set reject (TCS-Rej) message. Figure 18.9 shows an example of this process.

Master/Slave Assignment

The *master/slave assignment* is a method through which the system decides who the controlling entity should be when a call dispute occurs. This assignment is especially important in multiparty communications such as conference calling. According to H.323 protocol, any endpoint has a terminal type and any terminal type has a value. In a multiparty communication, whichever endpoint has the largest value of terminal type becomes the master. For example, an MCU that supports audio, video, and data conferencing has a terminal type value of 190. Besides the terminal type value, any endpoint is assigned a random number between 1 and 16,777,215 where this number is used to determine the master if two endpoints have the same terminal value. The assignment of master in a communication session starts with each endpoint sending the master/slave assignment (MSA) message. This message contains the terminal type value and its random number. Once an MSA message is received at an endpoint, the endpoint compares the terminal type value with its own value and makes the decision as to who the master is. It then returns a master/slave assignment acknowledgment (MSA-Ack) message. This message delivers the ranking view of the endpoint as to whether it is a master or slave. Figure 18.9 also shows an example of the master/slave process.

Media Exchange Establishment Control

H.245 protocol handles *media exchange establishment control*, a necessary control signaling immediately before and after a media exchange. This signaling requires the construction of logical channels between endpoints before media can be exchanged. A logical channel is a combination of IP address and port number. Media streaming

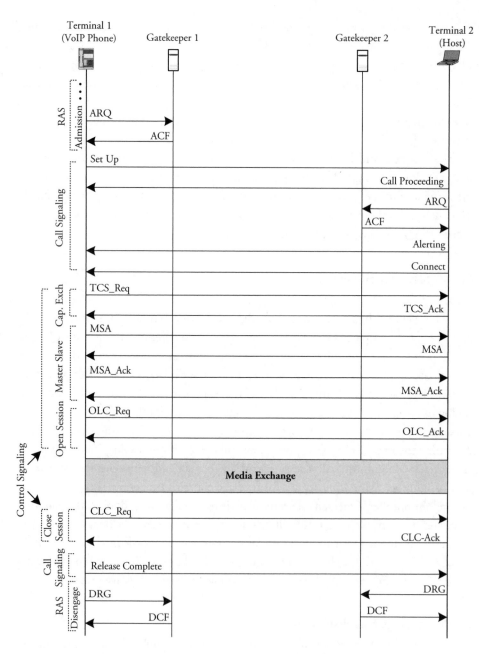

Figure 18.9   An example of a call establishment with all signaling components

can be carried in a unidirectional mode or bidirectional mode. In any unidirectional session with n endpoints, n unidirectional logical channels should be opened. Although, a unidirectional session between each two endpoints can itself consist of multiple logical channels. Each involved endpoint sends an open logical channel request (OLC-Req) message to others containing the information such as the type of data to be sent, an RTP session ID, and an RTP payload type. If the receiving endpoint is prepared for the media, it responds with an open logical channel acknowledgment (OLC-ACK) message containing information such as the same logical channel number as received and a transport address to which the media stream should be sent. An endpoint has an option to deny a request for variety of reasons such as inability to handle the suggested media format. In this case, it responds with an open logical channel reject (OLC-Rej) message.

When an endpoint wishes to transmit media and meanwhile expects to receive media, such as a typical voice conversation, then a bidirectional logical channel is required. In this case, each endpoint needs to establish a logical channel from its own direction each using an OLC-Req message. This message also contains reverse logical channel parameters that represent information such as the type of media that the endpoint can receive. Upon receipt of OLC-ACK, the calling endpoint responds with an open logical channel confirm (OLC-Con) message to indicate that the bidirectional setup is fine. Once the media exchange is over, a close logical channel request (CLC-Req) message should be sent from either endpoint, which is confirmed by the other endpoint using a close logical channel acknowledgment (CLC-Ack). Upon closure of all logical channels in a session, the session must be terminated by both endpoints each sending an end session (END-Ses) message. Figure 18.9 shows an example of a media stream establishment as a media exchange process.

18.3.6 Conference Calling with H.323 Protocol

In any session with the engagement of multiple endpoints, multiple logical channels should be opened. In a conference call, we need to establish a session engaging several parties even in a bidirectional mode. There are two ways to establish a conference call: *MCU conference calling* and *MC-endpoint conference calling*.

In MCU conference calling, endpoints are connected to the conference through the establishment of a call with the multipoint controller unit (MCU). In this case, the media itself could be routed either through the MCU or by multicasting directly among endpoints. The MCU determines the conference mode and accommodates unicast or multicast addresses for each session.

MC-endpoint conference calling is demanded in the middle of a two-party calling session when a need for a multiparty calling session is requested. In such a case, one of the endpoints or its gatekeeper with multipoint controller (MC) capability must take control of the conference calling. A two-party calling session can be converted to the multiparty calling session by sending a Setup message from one of the active endpoints to the joining one. The Setup message must contain a unique conference ID (CID) number. If the joining endpoint wishes to accept the conference call, it returns a connect message containing the value of the CID and followed by capability exchange and master/slave assignment steps. The calling endpoint becomes the master and the called endpoint becomes the slave. Subsequently, the master decides to invite other endpoints to join the conference by sending a Setup message to other endpoints with the CID value of the conference, If any of the other endpoints decides to join the conference, it must use the same CID in its connect message. After performing capability exchange and master/slave assignment between the master endpoint and any of the joining endpoints, the MC of the calling endpoint broadcasts a multipoint conference message to all of the participating endpoints.

18.4 Session Initiation Protocol (SIP)

The *Session Initiation Protocol* (SIP) is one of the most powerful VoIP and multimedia signaling protocols. Compared with the H.323 protocol, SIP is easier to implement so that the engaging devices can be set up faster. SIP can perform both unicast and multicast sessions for conference calls, and it also supports user mobility for wireless applications. SIP provides many pieces of information in its messages by offering numerous intelligent features to subscribers while the control of those features is also placed in the hands of users. SIP is designed in such a way that the media exchange session could be executed using any protocol, while generally the *Real-time Transport Protocol* (RTP), explained in Chapter 20, is fairly common.

SIP is based on the client/server protocol. A response to a SIP message could include a piece of text, an HTML document, or an image. One of the main advantages of SIP is that a SIP address is of type *Uniform Resource Locator* (URL), and thus it can easily be included in the Web content for applications performed by click-to-call. SIP is well suited to be easily integrated with existing traditional telephone networking technology and IP-based technology and can always leverage applications of both technologies in the creation of new services.

SIP is part of the multimedia data and control architecture and is used with other related multimedia protocols such as the *Session Description Protocol* (SDP), the *Real-time Streaming Protocol* (RTSP), and the *Session Announcement Protocol* (SAP). These protocols are discussed in Chapter 20. SDP is responsible for formatting the description of media information such as the RTP payload type, addresses, and ports. SIP and SDP collaborate with each other for the transmission of session information.

SIP carries the messaging mechanisms for the establishment of a media exchange session, and SDP carries a structured language for describing the sessions.

18.4.1   Main Components of SIP

SIP is indeed a client/server protocol. With SIP, a call is requested from a client, also known as user agent, that is an application program. A server is another application program that responds to the client's requests. VoIP calls using SIP are initiated at a user agent and terminated at a server. A user agent may be found within its device. User devices could be a VoIP telephone, a laptop computer, or any multimedia handheld communication device. The devices in which servers may operate could be the same as the ones used for user agents. Figure 18.10 shows an overview of the Session Initiation Protocol. A VoIP device performs as both a client for initiating call requests, and as a server to receive and respond to requests. In practical terms, any SIP device is able to initiate and receive calls. This enables SIP technology to be used for peer-to-peer communication. As seen in the figure, SIP consists of the following four servers that make up the signaling system:

1. *Proxy server.* The proxy server forwards requests from a user agent to a different location and handles authorizations by checking if the caller is authorized to make a particular call. This server's functionalities are similar to the ones of proxy servers used for Web access. Once a user agent makes a request to the proxy, the proxy either handles the request itself or forwards it on to other

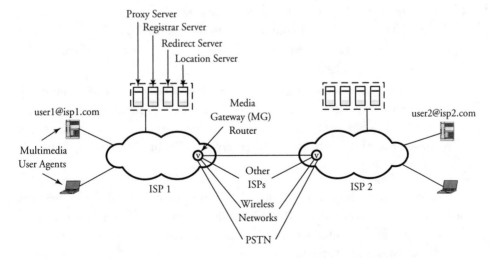

Figure 18.10   Overview of Session Initiation Protocol (SIP) setup

servers. A proxy program is an entity that can act as both a server and a client. For example, in Figure 18.10, user agent 1 located in the ISP 1 domain and identified by user1@isp1.com can make a request to be connected to user agent 2 located in the ISP 2 domain and identified by user2@isp2.com. In this case, the proxy server checks the authorizations of user agent 1 and user agent 2. Also, when a particular user agent is registered at several locations, a proxy server can fork requests by requesting from several registered locations.

2. *Registrar server.* The registrar server is responsible for registering user agents with their available addresses. The server also frequently updates the user information database that the location server consults. The requests for registration must be authenticated before the registration is granted. The feature of using a registrar server gives SIP a great leverage to support mobility. In a scenario where a user has two VoIP user agents, the user could issue a request from the user agent 1 terminal to the appropriate registrar server, enabling all calls to be routed to this terminal. When the user logs off from user agent 1 and activates the user agent terminal 2 from a different location, the second terminal can perform a new registration, enabling the user to be reached at a new terminal and all users' calls to be routed to the second terminal.

3. *Redirect server.* The redirect server performs call forwarding. It provides alternate paths for a user agent. This server admits requests, maps the destination address to other new addresses, and reports new addresses to the user agent that initiates the request. Once the originating user agent receives the redirect report, it can send its requests directly to the addresses returned by the server. For example, the request from user1@isp1.com wanting to contact user2@isp1.com is sent to a redirect server where the server finds out that user 2 temporarily resides in ISP 2 as identified by user2@isp2.com.

4. *Location server.* The location server is responsible for address resolution for proxy and redirect servers. It interacts with the databases of proxy and redirect servers during a call setup. A location server accepts requests and contacts the user. A response from the user to the location server results in a response on behalf of the user.

Besides the preceding components, the *media gateway* (MG) router with its attached *media gateway controller* (MGC) are also present in ISPs for providing protocol message translation services between the SIP-enabled IP network and other types of communication networks.

18.4.2   SIP Messages

SIP has a particular syntax that looks similar to the Hypertext Transfer Protocol (HTTP). This similarity supports programs for parsing of HTTP that can be easily adapted for use with SIP. Although the method of syntaxing consumes more bandwidth compared to binary encoding, this method has the advantage that system testing and error finding can be performed faster. Having a syntax also enables handling of messages and control of VoIP sessions more effectively. SIP messages are classified into three categories:

1. *Request messages* sent from a user agent to a server. The most common request messages are Register, Invite, ACK, Options, Bye, Cancel, Info, Subscribe, and Notify.

2. *Response messages* sent from a server to a user agent. The most common request messages are Trying, Ringing, Call Is Being Forwarded, Session Progress, OK, Moved Temporarily, Moved Permanently, Bad Request, Unauthorized, Payment Required, Forbidden, Not Found, Proxy Authorization Request, Request Timeout, Gone, Temporarily Not Available, Busy Here, Server, Internal Error, Bad Gateway, Message Too Large, Busy Anywhere, Decline, and Does Not Exist Anywhere.

3. *Feature messages*. The most common feature messages are Subscribe, Notify, Options, Message, Prefer, and Cancel.

In the upcoming sections, we present examples of some of these messages. All request and response messages are transmitted to particular addresses.

Interchanging Phone Numbers, IP Addresses, and URIs

A SIP address is known as a SIP *Uniform Resource Indicator* (URI). An address, like any e-mail address, takes the form of user@server. An e-mail address and a SIP address are similar. For example, an e-mail address uses a "mailto:" *Uniform Resource Locator* (URL) address such as mailto:user1@isp1.com, and similarly a SIP URI uses "sip:" as in sip:user1@isp1.com. SIP also allows the user portion of the SIP address to be a telephone number. For example, a SIP address can be sip:4082261180@isp1.com, which shows the telephone number at a certain service provider, or it can be in the form of an address combination such as: sip:4082261180@isp1.com;user1@isp2.com.

When IP addresses are used for establishing a connection, the task of locating users in an integrated network consisting of different networks is complex. It is also necessary to find an optimal route to the user after the user is located. The location servers use a protocol called Telephony Routing over IP (TRIP) to locate a user in an integrated network. TRIP advertises routes and exchanges routing information. It also classifies the globe into different domains called IP Telephony Administrative Domains (ITADs). Location servers exchange information about routes with signaling gateways connecting to a different ITAD.

SIP Message Structure

A SIP message consists of three parts: a *start line* indicating the category of a header and version of SIP, a *message header* containing routing information and indicating whether the message is a request or response type, and a *message body* that contains information about the session or information to be presented to the user. The header of SIP messages can also be expressed by SIP syntax. A number of different message headers have been considered for SIP to provide further information about the message or enable the method of handling of the message. A certain type of header specifies the application of the header to each request or response.

A message header normally contains typical fields such as From, To, Via, and CallID. The Via field contains information such as the path taken by the request so far, requiring that the calling user agent include its own address in this field and specifying the transport protocol being used (in this case UDP). For example, in from:sip:user1@isp1.com the "from" field shows the address of the originating user, and the "to" field indicates the recipient of a request. These two fields are identical if a user wants to register itself such as in: from:sip:user1@isp1.com and to:sip:user1@isp1.com. A CallID field is a number that uniquely identifies a specific invitation to a session. Besides these typical fields, there are some other fields that are used in certain application-specific headers. For example, the Subject field in a request message provides a topic description of the session. Another example is the Priority field, which is used to express the urgency of the request. SIP also has an entity header that indicates the type and format of information included in the message body.

Example. Assume user1@isp1.com is sending an OK message to user2@isp2.com. The message header starts with a start line consisting of the SIP version (2.0), status code (200), and the message name of status 200 (OK). The message header contains the following information: the first line of the message, such as Via: (showing the path taken in ISP 1); From: (stating the sender); To: (indicating the receiver); CallID: (presenting a unique number of 1234 assigned to the session); CSeq: (showing the this OK message is a response to the Invite message); and Subject: (indicating a subject for this message).

```
SIP/2.0 200 OK
Via: Station2.isp1.com
From: sip:user1@isp1.com
To: sip:user2@isp2.com
CallID: 1234@station2.isp1.com
CSeq: 1 Invite
Subject: OK message structure
This line is the body of the message.
```

18.4.3   SIP Protocol Organization

Figure 18.11 shows the placement of SIP in the five-layer TCP/IP model. The application layer as the fifth layer of this stack is divided into media exchange and control. The media exchange segment of this protocol structure is represented by the *Real-time Transport Protocol* (RTP) running over UDP handling packetized voice and video. There is an extension to RTP called *Real-time Transport Control Protocol* (RTCP). Next two chapters discuss the nature of real-time protocols in detail. The control segment of the protocol structure is responsible for the management of calls and it is divided into the following three categories:

1. Registration process

2. Call establishment process

3. Features and extensions

All of these processes are handled by the UDP transport layer. SIP can also support the transmission of data using TCP connections. The first action in making a call through SIP is for a user agent to register with the network under an operation called the *registration process,* discussed next.

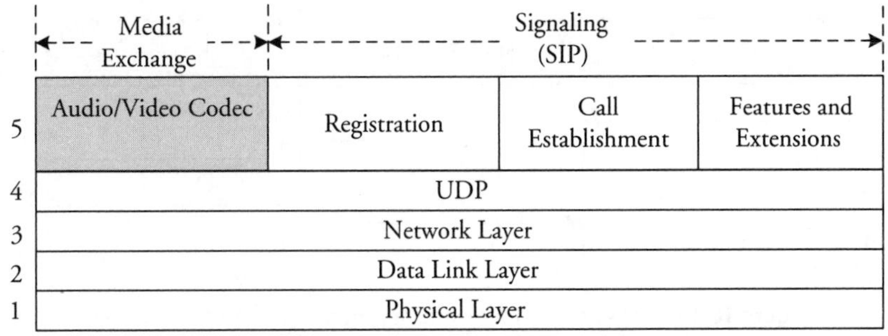

Figure 18.11   Placement of SIP in the five-layer protocol stack model

18.4.4   Registration Process

Figure 18.12 shows an example of a SIP session between user agent 1 and user agent 2 with e-mail addresses user1@isp1.com and user2@isp2.com, respectively. In this example, user 1 equipped with user agent 1 places a call to contact user 2 containing user agent 2. Users exchange messages through servers.

The first step in establishing a call is the execution of the registration process. This process starts with a user agent sending a Register message. This message requests the registrar server with an address at which the called user can be found for a call session. The header of this message contains some general fields such as from, to, via, and call-id as defined before. Register messages for an individual user agent should use the same value of call-id. To guarantee that any user agent chooses a different call-id and

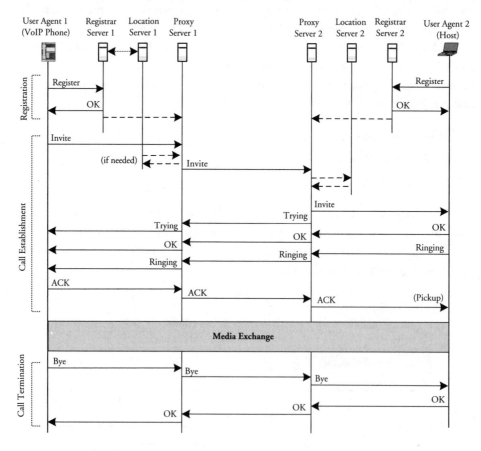

Figure 18.12   SIP signaling for a basic registration process followed by
call establishment, media exchange, and call termination

to make it host specific, the recommended syntax for the call-id is local-id@host. For example, a local-id of 354843 can be used for a call-id of 354843@isp1.com. There are some specific header fields for this message such as an expire header field that indicates how long (in hours) the registration should last.

In Figure 18.12, user agents 1 and 2 use the same procedure to complete their registrations. User agent 1 sends a Register message to the registrar server. The body of such messages has a null content since a Register message is not used to describe a session of any kind. If the local-id of user agent 1 is assumed to be 354843, the header of this message must insert the from, to, and call-id fields, respectively, as: from:sip:user1@isp1.com, to:sip:user1@isp1.com, and call-id:354843@isp1.com. Notice that the from and to fields are the same since user agent 1 is trying to register itself.

The response to the Register request is indicated by an OK message. This message acknowledges the registration and it uses the same call-id as the Register message uses. However, the registrar server may reduce the requested duration of registration by responding with a different number than requested in the expire field. By default, a registration may be active for up to approximately 136 years.

A given user agent belonging to a user can have multiple registrations at a single server from different locations. In such situations, calls to the user may be sent to all registered destinations. This allows a one-number service where the user publishes just a single number, so when that number is called, all the user's phones or terminals ring.

18.4.5   Call Establishment

Figure 18.12 also shows an overview of SIP signaling of a basic call establishment. Before a call can be established, the calling user agent first communicates with its DNS server to map the domain name or SIP UID to an IP address. The DNS server then communicates with the proxy server of the called user agent. At this point, the calling user agent has resolved the name of called user agent into an IP address through the DNS query and response. A basic call establishment engages the following two processes:

1. Call origination process
2. Call termination process

A call origination process is a process that initiates a call session. The process starts with a calling user agent sending an Invite message to a called user through a proxy server. This message in fact invites the called party to start a mutually participated session. The header of this message contains some general fields such as from, to, via, and call-id as defined before. The Invite message is addressed to the proxy server at to:sip:proxy@isp1.com using the "to" field in the message's header. There are also some specific header fields for this message such as a subject field that indicates a suggested reason for initiating a session. Another header field, which is optional, is scheduled call, in which case a busy called terminal can tell the calling user agent that the called user agent expects to be available at a certain time. This feature can further program a session to be automatically initiated at a certain time.

As seen in Figure 18.12, the called party user2@isp2.com is sent an Invite message to initiate a session. Once user agent 2 receives its connection query, the Trying signal is propagated to user agent 1 from the proxy server indicating that the call is being routed. This signal is also used to keep track of the call process. A Ringing message is transmitted from user agent 2 all the way back to user agent 1. When user agent 2 accepts the call, an OK signal is issued back to user agent 1 to indicate that the called party has accepted the call. This last signal is acknowledged by an ACK message without any response. The called party picks up the call and the two users communicate directly through a media exchange using a real-time protocol.

At the end of the conversation, the Bye message is used for session termination. This message is basically used to end a call by any of the engaging parties. The Bye message has many of the same header fields as the original Invite message. Upon the receipt of a Bye message, the recipient(s) of the message should immediately stop transmitting all active media. Figure 18.12 shows the call termination process of two parties using the appropriate termination messages. Notice that there is also another message indicated by Cancel that can be used to cancel a pending request such as an Invite request.

18.4.6   Features and Extensions

There are a number of extensions to SIP that makes it attractive from the consumer standpoint. Some of the extensions are in fact enhancements to its capability and others are the same capabilities of digital telephone systems. In this section, we review some of the important features of SIP.

Call Forwarding

Figure 18.13 shows an overview of the call forwarding feature of SIP. Assume that user agent 1 starts to establish a call through the proxy server to user agent 2.

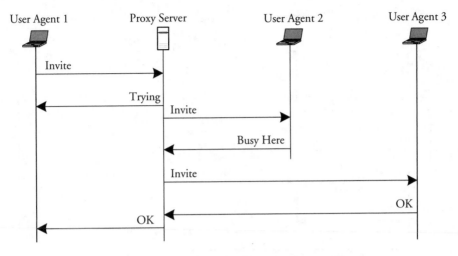

Figure 18.13   SIP signaling for basic call forwarding

This requires an exchange of Invite messages as described before. However, user agent 2 has set up the system in such a way that its calls are forwarded to user agent 3 with a busy-call status; in such a case, a Busy Here message is returned to the proxy. The proxy server then sends user agent 3 an Invite message while the "to" header field of this message still points to user agent 2. This scenario is completed with the transmission of an OK message from user agent 3 to user agent 1.

Call on Hold

Figure 18.14 depicts a SIP signaling scenario that performs the *call-on-hold* feature. In this figure, user agent 1 calls user agent 2 and the media exchange in the form of a live conversation session is established. After a while, user agent 1 places user agent 2 on hold to establish another call to user agent 3 by sending user agent 2 an Update message followed by an OK message confirmation. Upon the receipt of this message, user agents 1 and 2 should stop receiving audio from each other, entering an on-hold session. User agent 1 at this point can initiate a new session with user agent 3. Once the connection with user agent 3 is complete, user agent 1 should send another Update message back to user agent 2 to resume the on-hold connection with user agent 2.

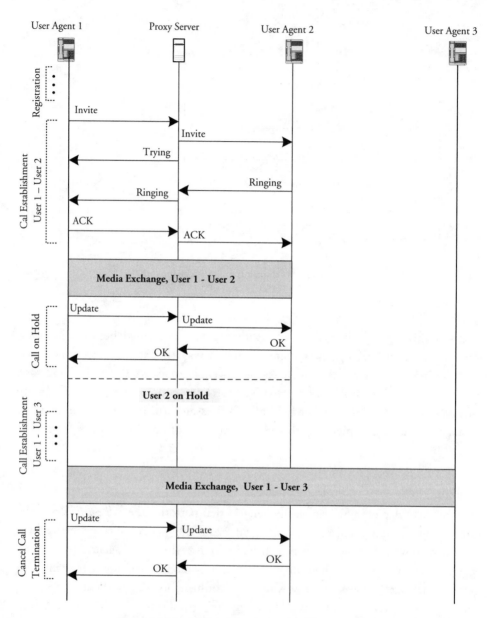

Figure 18.14   SIP signaling for the call-on-hold feature

Other Features

Other Features in SIP provide with several message types featuring situations such as the temporary move of a user or the subscription of a user to a message. A complete list of Other Feature messages is as follows:

- Moved Temporarily message. The role of a redirect server is to respond to a request with an alternative address and redirect the request. Assume a scenario in which user1@isp1.com wishing to establish a call session with user2@isp1.com has to send an Invite message to the redirect.isp1.com server. The redirect server responds with a Moved Temporarily message containing the address that user agent 1 should try as an alternative. User agent 1 then acknowledges the new address of user agent 2 by sending and ACK message to the redirect server. Now, user agent 1 is all set to send a new Invite message to user agent 2 using its new address.

- Options message. The Option message is used to learn about the parameters such as type of supported media used by the called party. The Options message requests a server to determine whether a called user agent can support a particular type of media

- Info message. The Info message is used to transfer information during an ongoing session. The message operates in cases such as transferring account balance information. An example of an application for this message is when a prepaid user is informed in the middle of a call that the paid account is nearing zero. In this case, the account balance notification could be delivered in text format in a message body.

- Subscribe and Notify messages. The Subscribe message is sent by a user agent to subscribe to certain events and the Notify message is delivered to a user agent to inform of the occurrence of a subscribed event. When any of the two messages is sent, the other side must acknowledge the receipt of the notification by sending an OK message. These messages can be used when a user wants to know about the price of certain goods or stocks and he or she needs to be notified of the price.

- Message. Message is used for instant messaging purposes and typically requires the exchange of a short data, image, or video clip between two or more participants. Each instant message is stand-alone and is handled through a message called Message. Such messages normally are different from e-mails. This message carries a request with the actual message in the message body. A Message can be sent during an existing session. The response to a Message is an OK message.

- Refer message. A Refer message enables a user to have the receiver contact a third user. This application is what we know as a call transfer. For example, user agent 1 is talking on the VoIP phone to user agent 2, and suddenly user agent 1 realizes that user agent 2 needs to talk to user agent 3. User agent 1 can make this happen by sending user agent 2 a Refer message including user agent 3's contact details. Upon the receipt of the Refer message, user agent 2 sends an

Invite message to user agent 3 followed by receiving an OK message. Now, user agent 2 acknowledges user agent 3 by sending it an ACK message, and indicates user agent 2 by sending a Notify message. A Notify message is then recognized by user agent 1 through an OK message. User agents 1 and 2 can always terminate the dialog through the use of the Bye message.

18.5   Softswitch Methods and MGCP

So far in this chapter, we have learned that in SIP and the H.323 protocol, the VoIP signaling can take a different path from the media exchange path. The media exchange might be placed directly between endpoints, while the signaling part might pass through gatekeepers or a proxy server. The idea behind the separation of signaling and media exchange is similar to the one in traditional phone networks with the Signaling System 7 (SS7) architecture. However, the separation of media exchange and call signaling in VoIP systems starts to occur through the immediate entity connected to a user such as a gateway.

We can now consider a different VoIP architecture in which media exchange and call signaling can be completely separate. This would enable the media exchange to take place as close as possible to the traffic source while centralizing the call signaling. The benefit of centralizing call control signals is attributed to the fact that the deployment of new features to the system can be done more quickly, as it requires modifications only in the call-control nodes rather than at every node in the network. The two most commonly used protocols in this category are the Media Gateway Control Protocol (MGCP) and MEGACO/H.248, also known as MEGACO or H.248. When one of these protocols is integrated into VoIP protocols such as SIP, the result is known as the softswitch architecture. The name *softswitch* is formed based on the use of software for switching compared to traditional circuit switching. In a softswitch architecture, the devices that handle signaling are known as *call agents* or *media gateway controllers* (MGCs), while the devices that handle the media exchange are known as *media gateways* (MGs). With the softswitch technology, the operations of MGs, which require signal processing, and MGCs can be completely separated.

The Media Gateway Control Protocol (MGCP) is a VoIP signaling protocol in which call agents control the operation of media gateways (MGs). An MG supports the establishment and termination of connection commands from an MGC. The role of MGCP is to address the communication between an MGC and an MG and does not offer communication from one MGC to another. MGCP defines an endpoint as a device that can be either a source or a sink of media, each including an interface to connection lines.

18.6 VoIP and Multimedia Internetworking

Let us conclude our discussion on VoIP by expanding the multimedia architecture to internetworking among various media protocols. One of the real challenges in multimedia internetworking is how traditional telephone networks and the Internet must be connected together. In order to interconnect these two types of networks, we need a protocol to make a traditional phone communicate with an IP phone. The main challenge in such communications is how VoIP networks can emulate SS7 signaling. The *Signaling Transport* (sigtran) group of the *Internet Engineering Task Force* (IETF) has made an effort to address issues related to the signaling performance of internetworking IP networks and the PSTN. The key operation behind the sigtran effort is aimed at the reliable transfer of signaling information through certain adaptation layers. There are two distinct situations that might occur: two SS7 phones use VoIP networks to communicate, and an SS7 phone and a VoIP phone use VoIP networks to communicate.

18.6.1 SIP to H.323 Internetworking

Figure 18.15 shows a possible communication scenario between user agent 1 using a VoIP phone supported by SIP in ISP 1 and terminal 1 using a computer host supported by the H.323 protocol in ISP 2. The detailed signaling for communication between host 1 supported by the SIP protocol and host 2 supported by H.323 is depicted in Figure 18.16. As usual, the SIP user agent starts the communication by sending an Invite message to be received by the MGC. The Invite message is then translated by the MGC to its H.323 equivalent, the Setup message. As seen in the figure, a series of messages similar to the ones explained earlier are exchanged following the Setup message that result in the issuance of the Ringing message.

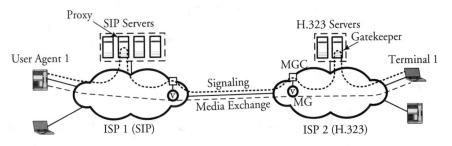

Figure 18.15 Communication between user agent 1 (VoIP phone) residing in ISP 1 supported by SIP protocol and terminal 1 (computer host) housed in ISP 2 supported by H.323

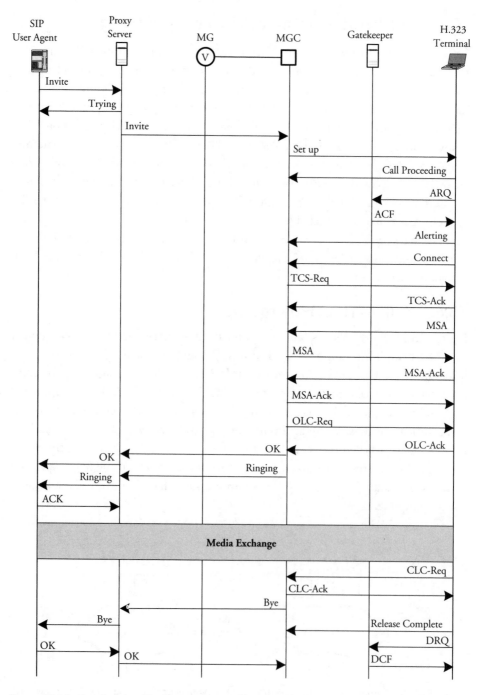

Figure 18.16 Detail of signaling for communication between host 1 supported by SIP protocol and host 2 supported by H.323

18.6.2   SIP to PSTN Internetworking

We now proceed to outline an interesting communication situation between a VoIP entity and a non-VoIP entity. As an example, consider a laptop host as a VoIP device trying to connect to a traditional phone as shown in Figure 18.17. In this

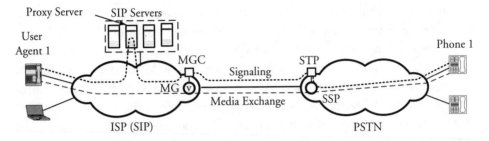

Figure 18.17   Communications between a SIP VoIP phone (user agent 1) and a traditional phone (phone 1)

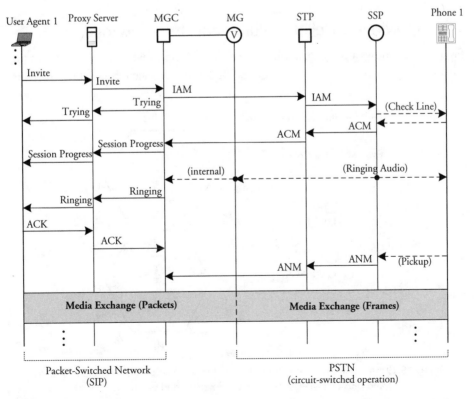

Figure 18.18   Signaling between a SIP host (user agent 1) and a traditional phone (phone 1)

communication scenario, user agent 1 residing in an ISP supported by SIP is contacting phone 1, which is a traditional phone attached to the PSTN.

Figure 18.18 shows the required signaling to establish a connection between user agent 1 supported by SIP and phone 1 attached to the PSTN. A call starts with sending an Invite message to the proxy server, and thereby to the MGC. At this point the message needs to be routed to the PSTN network. This can be done by translating the Invite message to its equivalent IAM message and sending it to the STP. Recall that the STP is the signaling component of the PSTN. The IAM message is then forwarded to the SSP. Once the phone line is checked and it is free, an ACM message is sent back as a response. Similarly, the ACM message is translated in the MGC to its SIP equivalent of Session Progress. When the PSTN issues the ringing audio to phone 1, the audio itself needs to be translated to a packet-type message. This process happens in the combined MG and MGC as seen in the figure, and the result of this translation is the issuance of a Ringing message to user agent 1. The timing diagram illustrates that at this point the ACK message sent naturally from user agent 1 and the ANM message sent from phone 1 are both terminated in the MGC without any further action.

18.6.3   Wireless Cellular Multimedia Internetworking

Figure 18.19 shows a possible communication scenario in wireless LTE cellular networks between two user equipment units, UE1 and UE2, each housed in a different

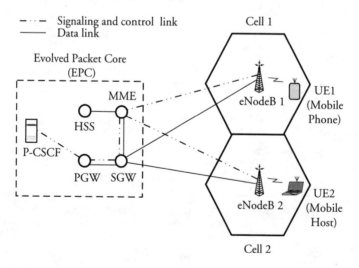

Figure 18.19   An example of communications between two mobile user equipment units, UE1 and UE2, in a wireless cellular network supported by LTE technology.

cell. In Chapter 7, we learned how two mobile units in an LTE cellular network can establish a connection. The dominant VoIP and multimedia protocol in LTE is SIP. Thus, we should expect the SIP messages to be encapsulated while moving in the LTE networks. In the example presented in the figure, UE1 is a mobile phone and UE2 is a mobile host. Consider a scenario in which UE1 is entering a voice over IP session with UE2.

Figure 18.20 illustrates a timing diagram for the communication between UE1 and UE2. These two UEs must first register with their base stations, eNodeB 1 and eNodeB 2, respectively, as we discussed in Chapter 7 and seen in the timing diagram. Once a UE is registered with its base station, it can freely dial a phone number or enter a media exchange session. UE1 needs to send an Invite message to eNodeB 1. The first LTE device to process signaling messages is the *Mobility Management Entity* (MME). MME ensures that UE1 is registered with cell 1 without any issues and lets the two gateway routers, *Serving Gateway* (SGW) and *Packet Data Network Gateway* (PGW) route the Invite message to the *Proxy-Call Session Control Function* (P-CSCF) server. The P-CSCF server acts as a SIP proxy server for LTE sessions and is used to process SIP signaling messages. After SIP authorization

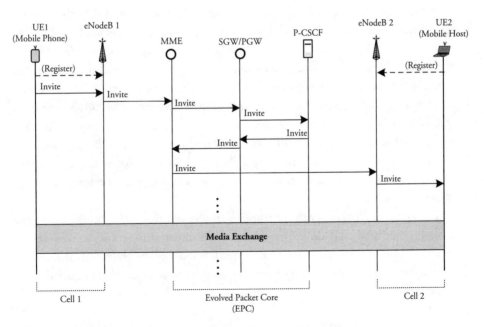

Figure 18.20   The signaling of communications between
UE1 and UE2 in an LTE wireless cellular network

of the Invite message, this server forwards the message back to the MME, and thereby the MME sends it to the destination UE2 via base station eNodeB 2. The remaining portion of the SIP process is not shown in the timing diagram but we can realize that the next step would be a Trying message, and so on, as we learned in other SIP scenarios.

18.7   Summary

A study of VoIP signaling protocols was the objective of this chapter. We saw that the networking hardware devices required for deployment packet-switched networks for voice exchange were less expensive than those required for use in the public-switched telephone network (PSTN).

We started the chapter with a discussion on how sampled and digitized voice is treated in networks and reviewed the fundamentals of the traditional PSTN. We learned that the PSTN has two distinct segments: *circuit-switched networks,* in which a circuit is predetermined for each voice session; and the *Signaling System 7 (SS7) network* for call control signaling. As a result of such structures, two separate transmission paths are used when a telephone call needs to be established: one for call control "signaling" to be established over the SS7 network, and the other one for media exchange or voice to be established over circuit-switched networks.

We then investigated two main VoIP signaling session protocols, the *H.323 series of protocols* and the *Session Initiation Protocol* (SIP), and showed how calling and numbering for these protocols could be achieved. The signaling in H.323 uses both UDP and TCP and is partitioned into *call setup, initial communication capability, audio/video communication establishment, communications,* and *call termination.* SIP identifies user location signals, call setup, call termination, and busy signals. User agents assist in initiating or terminating a phone call in VoIP networks. User agents can be implemented in a standard telephone or in a laptop with a microphone that runs some software.

We also had opportunity to see some examples of internetworking among the PSTN, H.323, and SIP domains. One of the most important factors in the internetworking of multimedia is the need for a center that can administer the "translation" of messages received from one protocol to their equivalent at the destination protocol. This is carried out by the Media Gateway Controller (MGC).

We continue our VoIP and multimedia discussions in the next two chapters. We allocate these chapters to the process and compression of media exchange followed by distributed multimedia networking.

18.8   Exercises

1. Sketch a block diagram that represents the functionality for each of the following PSTN devices: STPs and SCPs.

2. The signaling links among SSPs, STPs, and SCPs in SS7 networks are classified into six groups of A, B, C, D, E, and F. Do some research and answer the following questions:
    (a) Give the purpose of each link group.
    (b) Sketch an example of a simple SS7 network consisting of all types of link groups.

3. Besides the MSU in SS7 networks, there are two other types of signaling units (SUs): *fill-in signal unit* (FISU) and *link status signal unit* (LSSU). Do some research to learn more about these SUs with the ANSI standard and
    (a) Give the applications of each unit.
    (b) Sketch the detailed structure of each unit and present the purpose of the following fields in each unit: FLAG, BSN, BIB, FSN, FIB, and LI.

4. Consider a circuit-switched network consisting of four SSPs with the following point codes: SSP 1 (1-1-1), SSP 2 (1-1-2), SSP 3 (1-2-1), and SSP 4 (1-3-1). The SSPs are connected through their associated trunks with the following available trunks: (SSP 1 to SSP 2), (SSP 1 to SSP 3), (SSP 2 to SSP 4), (SSP 3 to SSP 4), and (SSP 4 to SSP 3). Assume that SSP1 is the origination of all calls and SSP2, SSP3, and SSP4 are destinations. Also assume that each SSP only has CIC = 1, 2, or 3 values available for use.
    (a) List all possible circuits.
    (b) For each segment of a circuit obtained in part (a), give the circuit identity (CIC/DPC).

5. Consider five serially connected nodes: SSP1-SSP2-SSP3-SSP4-SSP5 in a PSTN. Each frame on a trunk connecting a pair of SSPs carries 30 channels which are occupied at all times.
    (a) Find the minimum number of CIC values required at each instance of time between each two consecutive nodes.
    (b) Find the maximum number of CIC values required at each instance of time between each two consecutive nodes.
    (c) How many different telephone calls can be established between SSP1 and SSP5 at each instance of time?
    (d) Repeat parts (a), (b), and (c) and now assume that between each two nodes there are two identical trunks.

6. Consider a two-stage multiplexing system in which four TDMs each with 22 inputs and each input having utilization of 10% are time-multiplexed on a four-input TDM. The desired blocking probability for this system is $p_a = 4\%$. Using the Erlang-B table in Appendix D.

   (a) Find the offered load from each first-stage TDM to the second-stage TDM.
   (b) Find the required number of voice channels in each first-stage TDM.
   (c) Find the required number of voice channels for the system.

7. Knowing that the number of channels in an E1 line is 32 (30 voice + 2 control), calculate the following for an E1 line:

   (a) Frame length in bits
   (b) Frame bit rate
   (c) Frame time

8. Design a digital telephony system for a company having three campuses: a head-quarters and two remote branches A and B connected directly to the headquarters campus. The entire company allows a blocking probability of 5% and all phone calls on any phone line arrive at rate 0.2 per hour. The headquarters campus is connected to the PSTN through a CO switch and needs 4,000 phones, each requiring an average holding time of 3 minutes per hour. Branches A and B need 1,000 and 10 phones, requiring average holding times of 3.6 minutes per hour and 9 minutes per hour, respectively.

   (a) For each of the three campuses, find out what kind of switch should be ordered.
   (b) For each of the three campuses, calculate an optimal number of T1 lines needed.
   (c) For each of the three campuses, find the total trunk bandwidth.
   (d) Sketch an overview of the company network.

9. Design a digital telephony system for a company having three campuses: a head-quarters and two remote branches A and B where the headquarters campus is connected to branch A and branch B is connected to branch A. The entire company allows a blocking probability of 5% and all phone calls on any phone line arrive at rate 0.2 per hour. The headquarters campus is connected to the PSTN through a CO switch and needs 5,000 phones, each requiring an average holding time of 3 minutes per hour. Branches A and B need 1,000 and 10 phones, requiring average holding times of 3.6 minutes per hour and 9 minutes per hour, respectively.

   (a) For each of the three campuses, find out what kind of switch should be ordered.

(b) For each of the three campuses, calculate an optimal number of T1 lines needed.

(c) For each of the three campuses, find the total trunk bandwidth.

(d) Sketch an overview of the company network.

10. In a network using the H.323 protocol with one gatekeeper, a conference call between two terminals 1 and 2 must be established. Terminal 2 has a multi-point controller (MC) and becomes the master in a master/slave process. After a while, terminal 3 belonging to another Internet service provider (ISP) with gatekeeper 3 is invited by terminal 2 and successfully joins the multimedia session. Terminal 2 remains the master in all master/slave processes. Show a timing diagram for the exchange of RAS (show only Registration, Admission, and Disengage steps of RAS), call signaling, and control signaling messages (capability exchange, master/slave, and media exchange control) in this connection.

11. Show a detailed timing diagram for a conference call among terminal 1, terminal 2, and terminal 3 all belonging to the same H.323-based ISP. For this scenario, terminal 1 connects to terminal 2 first, then terminal 2 invites terminal 3 through a multipoint control unit (MCU). At the end, terminal 3 leaves first and then terminal 2 hangs up. Assume there is only one gatekeeper in this ISP and also mode 2 of H.323 is used at all times. Ignore all RAS processes for this timing.

12. Show a detailed timing diagram for a conference call among user agent 1, user agent 2, and user agent 3 each belonging to a separate SIP-based ISP. For this scenario, user agent 1 connects to user agent 2 first, then user agent 2 invites user 3. At the end, first user agent 3 leaves and then hangs up.

13. A connection between two user agents 1 and 2, belonging to two different VoIP networks each using SIP must be established. Show a timing diagram for the exchange of messages for the following series of events in order of time:

- At time t1: user agent 1 registers with its proxy server.
- At time t2: user agent 2 registers with its proxy server.
- At time t3: user agent 1 tries to connect to user agent 2 and later it succeeds.
- At time t4: user agent 2 terminates the media session.
- At time t5: however, user agent 2 informs user agent 1 using an Options message that short contacts would be fine.
- At time t6: user agent 1 tries to subscribe with user agent 2 on a certain short event and later it succeeds.
- At time t7: user agent 1 receives its first subscription information from user agent 2.
- At time t8: user agent 2 cancels the subscription.

14. A conference call between two user agents, 1 and 2, belonging to two different ISPs each using SIP must be established. After a while, user agent 3, belonging to a third ISP using SIP, is invited by user agent 2 and successfully joins the media exchange session. Ignoring the registration process, show a timing diagram for the exchange of messages until user agent 1 completes the call termination.

15. A connection between two user agents, 1 and 2, belonging to two different VoIP networks each using SIP must be established. Show a timing diagram for the exchange of messages for the following series of events in order of time:

   • At time t1: user agent 1 registers with its proxy server.
   • At time t2: user agent 2 registers with its proxy server.
   • At time t3: user agent 1 tries to connect to user agent 2 and later it succeeds.
   • At time t4: user agent 2 terminates the media session.
   • At time t5: user agent 2 informs user 1 that it needs to contact another user (this user should not be shown in your chart).
   • At time t6: user agent 2 cancels its request of the third-party contact.
   • At time t7: user agent 2 hangs up.
   • At time t8: user agent 2 contacts phone 1 located in the PSTN.
   • At time t9: user agent 2 is informed that phone 1 is busy.

16. Show a timing diagram for a situation in which phone 1 attached to the PSTN uses a prepaid calling card through which VoIP services for a long distance call to phone 2 can be obtained. Phone 1 dials the desired number using the prepaid access code, thereby the significant part of the connection is made through the VoIP process over the Internet resulting in a PSTN-Internet-PSTN connection. This is an interesting situation in which two non-VoIP phones each naturally connected to the PSTN establish a connection partially through the Internet, in this case using SIP. A call starts with sending IAM to switch from the switch to a gateway router. At this point the message needs to be routed in the SIP environment to the other side of the network. This can be done by sending an Invite message that encapsulates the IAM to the gateway router at the other side via a proxy server. The gateway router at the other side decapsulates the message and sends a raw IAM to the called party via its switch. The same process occurs in the opposite direction for the reply message of the ACM. At this point the called party generates a ringing audio in the opposite direction; however, once this audio reaches SIP, it is temporarily converted to a Ringing message. Next, an ANM is sent from a called party to the calling party indicating that it is ready

for the communications. For this, SIP must encapsulate the ANM into an OK message. At this point, the speech or media can be transported.

17. Consider two digital telephone sets located in two different areas of the PSTN with two different ISPs. Phone 1 is attached to central office SSP 1 and tries to make a call to phone 2 attached to SSP 2. The PSTN company of the caller uses VoIP technology of the H.323 protocol type. Ignoring the registration process,

    (a) Show a timing diagram for the exchange of RAS (Admission and Disengage processes only), call signaling, and control signaling messages in this connection.

    (b) Indicate the portions of this diagram that use UDP, TCP, or circuit switching.

18. Show a detailed timing diagram for a connection between two digital phones in the PSTN through the H.323-based Internet requiring two gatekeepers. This is an example of using a VoIP-based prepaid calling card.

18.9   Computer Simulation Projects

1. *A Hands-on Experimental Simulation of SIP-Based Voice over IP (VoIP).* The objective of this project is to learn the implementation of voice over IP (VoIP) using SIP connections through a hands-on experiment over WiFi networks. The learning process is carried out by utilizing a proxy server and a few VoIP user agents as clients. For this project, use three laptop computers, one as the SIP proxy server and two as user agents (VoIP clients).

    A. Preparing the proxy server: (1) Install Linux on the laptop that you want to act as the SIP proxy server. (2) Download and install the proxy server software. (3) Download VoIP software on the proxy server laptop. As an example, consider the Asterisk software used for telephone systems that allows attached telephones to make calls to one another. One of the important features of Asterisk is its support of SIP. (4) Set up a WiFi network. (5) Configure SIP. For example, in the Asterisk software:

    ```
    port = 5060;
    bindaddr = 169.254.x.x;
    allow = ulaw; Allow
    ```

    SIP servers use `port` 5060 UDP. The term `bindaddr` is the IP address of the server. This address can be found by entering the `ifconfig` command in the terminal window. The term `allow` states which codecs are allowed. Now we create two new user agents by adding the following lines:

```
username=2000                    username=2010

type=friend                      type=friend

secret=password                  secret=password

host=dynamic                     host=dynamic

context=from-sip                 context=from-si
```

The term `secret` can be anything of your choice, and 2000 and 2010 are the contexts that act as phone numbers for the two user agents. The term `user-name` is the name that is displayed on the soft phone when you are connected to the server. The term `type` is used to authenticate incoming calls, `peer` for outgoing calls, and `friend` for both. In our example we have a `friend` extension to make a call. The word `secret` is the password used to authenticate. In this case, we have used `password`. We have put `host=dynamic` meaning that the telephone will be able to connect from any IP address. We can limit this user to access with only one IP address or a domain name. If we put `host=static` it would not be necessary for the user to register itself with the password provided in `secret`. Finally, `context=from-sip` shows the context where the instructions for this extension will be executed.

Preparing the SIP user agents: (1) You need to have the Windows OS platform on each of the user agents (clients). (2) Download and install client VoIP software such as X-Lite on the two laptop computers that act as client computers. (3) Connect the clients to the WiFi network by assigning IP addresses manually to the wireless adaptor of the laptops in the range 169.254.x.x with subnet mask 255.255.0.0.

(a) Demonstrate how the two SIP user agent clients are configured on the two laptop computers and how they register with the proxy server. Also, show how a call will be made between them via the server. The extensions are set as follows:

```
from-sip]

exten => 2000, 1, Dial(SIP/2000,20)

exten => 2000, 2, Hangup

exten => 2010, 1, Dial(SIP/2010,20)

exten => 2010, 2, Hangup
```

Note that 2000 or 2010 act as phone numbers assigned to the two SIP clients. Dial refers to the dialing mode and Hangup means the phone is hung up. (SIP/2000,20) means that we are using the SIP protocol for calling 2000 and 20 refers to the duration of time in seconds.

(b) Configure the VoIP software at the two clients by incorporating into the software the necessary parameters such as: Protocol (enter SIP), Display Name (choose 2000 and 2010 for your two SIP phones), User Name (enter a unique numeric value; a good example would be 2000 for the first phone and 2010 for the second), Password (any password), Domain (the IP address of your domain server).

(c) Capture snapshots of all activity in this experiment using Wireshark or similar software. Initially, connect only the server and one of the clients, and then see and record the stack overflow in the features, packets involved, ports connected, and any notable processes.

CHAPTER 19

Media Exchange and Voice/Video Compression

This chapter looks at the advanced topic of data, voice, and video exchange and compression. This important topic requires a thorough understanding of the process of preparing compressed voice and video. A raw piece of information, whether voice or video, must be converted to digital form and then compressed to save link bandwidth. This chapter discusses methods of preparing digital voice and video for multimedia networks, including the analysis of information sources, source coding, and limits of data compression. Typical voice and video streaming compression techniques, such as JPEG, MPEG, and MP3, are explained. The major topics of this chapter are

- *Overview of data compression*
- *Digital voice and compression*
- *Still images and JPEG compression*
- *Moving images and MPEG compression*
- *Compression methods with loss*
- *Compression methods without loss*
- *Scanned document compression*

Our discussion starts with an overview of data preparation and compression, focusing on voice, image, and moving-image data. Considerable effort is required to turn analog voice into digital form. This process of converting from raw voice to compressed binary form involves sampling, quantization, and encoding.

We then take a quick look at some practical compression methods with and without loss. We review the compression schemes that are used after the binary voice or image is prepared. We discuss both JPEG and MPEG compression techniques for still images and moving images, respectively. Still images or moving images might contain redundant or repeated elements that can be eliminated and codes substituted for the future decoding process. We also summarize Shannon's limits of compression with loss. At the end of the discussion on compression, we review lossless compression techniques such as *Huffman encoding* and *run-length encoding*. The chapter ends with a special topic on scanned document compression where we learn how a document's content containing a picture or text can be compressed for transmission.

19.1   Overview of Data Compression

The benefits of data compression in high-speed networks are obvious. Following are those that are especially important for the compressed version of data.

- Less transmission power is required.
- Less communication bandwidth is required.
- System efficiency is increased.

There are, however, certain trade-offs with data compression. For example, the encoding and decoding processes of data compression increase the cost, complexity, and delay of data transmission. Both of the two processes of data compression are required for producing multimedia networking information: *compression with loss* and *compression without loss*.

In the first category of data compression, some less valuable or almost similar data must be eliminated permanently. The most notable case of compression with loss is the process of signal sampling. An example of this category is the process of voice sampling, which is discussed in Section 19.2. In data compression without data loss, the compressed data can be recovered and converted back to its original form when received. This method of compression is typically applied to digital bits after sampling.

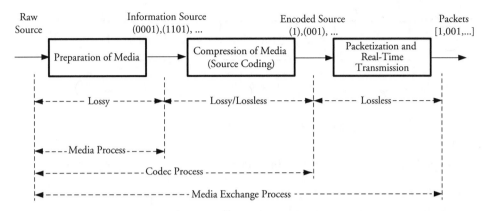

Figure 19.1 Overview of information process and compression in multimedia networks

Figure 19.1 shows the basic information process in high-speed communication systems. Any type of *raw source* data is converted to digital form through a *preparation of media* process. The outcome, which is referred to as the *information source,* is the generation of digital words. Digital words are then encoded in the *compression of media process* (*source coding*), which results in a compressed form of the data called the *encoded source*. Finally, the encoded source undergoes the process of packetization and real-time transmission to become a packetized source to be routed in the Internet.

19.2 Digital Voice and Compression

Our discussion starts with voice as a simple real-time signal. We first review the fundamentals of voice digitization and sampling. Figure 19.2 shows the process of preparing digital voice. Raw natural voice is first sampled in a *sampling* stage. Values of voice samples must be adjusted through a *quantization* phase for optimal usage of the communication medium. Finally, the resulting values are digitally encoded in an *encoding* stage. The following two sections describe the details of these processes.

19.2.1 Sampling

In the process of digitizing a signal, analog signals first go through a *sampling* process, as shown in Figure 19.2. The sampling function is required in the process of converting an analog signal to digital bits. However, acquiring samples from an analog signal and eliminating the unsampled portions of the signal may result in some permanent loss of information. In other words, the sampling resembles an *information-compression* process with loss.

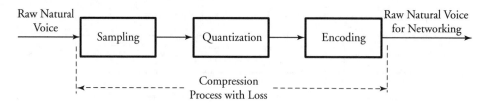

Figure 19.2 Overview of digital voice process

Sampling techniques are of several types:

- *Pulse amplitude modulation* (PAM), which translates sampled values to pulses with corresponding amplitudes
- *Pulse width modulation* (PWM), which translates sampled values to pulses with corresponding widths
- *Pulse position modulation* (PPM), which translates sampled values to identical pulses but with corresponding positions to sampling points

PAM is a practical and commonly used sampling method; PPM is the best modulation technique but is expensive. PWM is normally used in analog remote-control systems. The sampling rate in any of these schemes should obey the *Nyquist theorem*, according to which at least two samples on all components of the spectrum are needed in order to reconstruct a spectrum:

$$f_S \geq 2f_H, \tag{19.1}$$

where f_H is the highest-frequency component of a signal, and f_S is the sampling rate.

19.2.2 Quantization and Encoding

Samples are real numbers—decimal-point values and integer values—and, thus, up to infinite bits are required for transmission of a raw sample. The transmission of infinite bits occupies infinite bandwidth and is not practical for implementation. In practice, sampled values are rounded off to available quantized levels. However, rounding off the values loses data and generates *distortion*. A measure is needed to analyze this distortion. The distortion measure should show how far apart a signal denoted by $x(t)$ is to its reproduced version, denoted by $\hat{x}(t)$. The distortion measure of a single source is the difference between source sample X_i and its corresponding quantized value $\hat{X}_i$, denoted by $d(X, \hat{X})$, and is widely known as *squared-error distortion*:

$$d(X, \hat{X}) = (x - \hat{x})^2. \qquad (19.2)$$

Note that $\hat{X}_i$ is noninvertible since lost information cannot be recovered. The distortion measure of n samples is based on the values of source samples obtained at the sampler output. As a result, the collection of n samples forms a random process:

$$X_n = \{X_1, X_2, \ldots, X_n\}. \qquad (19.3)$$

Similarly, the reconstructed signal at the receiver can be viewed as a random process:

$$\hat{X}_n = \{\hat{X}_1, \hat{X}_2, \ldots, \hat{X}_n\}. \qquad (19.4)$$

The distortion between these two sequences is the average between their components:

$$d(X_n, \hat{X}_n) = \frac{1}{n} \sum_{i=1}^{n} d(X_i, \hat{X}_i). \qquad (19.5)$$

Note that $d(X_n, \hat{X}_n)$ itself is a random variable, since it takes on random numbers. Thus, the total distortion between the two sequences is defined as the expected value of $d(X_n, \hat{X}_n)$:

$$D = E[d(X_n, \hat{X}_n)] = E\left[\frac{1}{n} \sum_{i=1}^{n} d(X_i, \hat{X}_i) \right] \qquad (19.6)$$

$$= \frac{1}{n} E[d(X_1, \hat{X}_1) + d(X_2, \hat{X}_2) + \cdots + d(X_n, \hat{X}_n)].$$

If all samples are expected to have approximately the same distortion denoted by $d(X, \hat{X})$, $d(X_1, \hat{X}_1) = d(X_2, \hat{X}_2) = \ldots = d(X_n, \hat{X}_n) = d(X, \hat{X})$. By using squared-error distortion, we obtain the total distortion:

$$D = \frac{1}{n}(n E[d(X, \hat{X})]) = E[d(X, \hat{X})] = E[(X - \hat{X})^2]. \qquad (19.7)$$

Let R be the minimum number of bits required to reproduce a source and guarantee that the distortion be less than a certain distortion bound D_b. Clearly, if D decreases, R must increase. If X is represented by R bits, the total number of different values X_i takes is 2^R. Each single-source output is quantized into N levels. Each level $1, 2, \ldots, N$ is encoded into a binary sequence. Let $\mathfrak{R}$ be the set of real numbers $\mathfrak{R}_1, \ldots, \mathfrak{R}_k, \ldots, \mathfrak{R}_N$, and let $\hat{X}_k$ be the quantized value belonging to subset $\mathfrak{R}_k$. Note that $\hat{X}_k$ is a quantized version of X_k. Apparently, $R = \log_2 N$ bits are required to encode N quantized levels. Figure 19.3 shows a model of N-level quantization: For the subsets $\mathfrak{R}_1 = [-\infty, a_1]$, $\mathfrak{R}_2 = [a_1, a_2], \ldots, \mathfrak{R}_8 = [a_{N-1}, \infty]$, the quantized values are $\hat{X}_1, \hat{X}_2, \ldots, \hat{X}_n$, respectively. We can use the definition of expected value to obtain D, as follows:

$$D = \int_{-\infty}^{+\infty} (x - \hat{x})^2 f_X(x) dx = \sum_{i=1}^{N} \int_{\mathfrak{R}_i} (x - \hat{x})^2 f_X(x) dx. \qquad (19.8)$$

Typically, a distortion bound denoted by D_b is defined by designers to ensure that $D \le D_b$.

Example.   Consider that each sample of a sampled source is a Gaussian random variable with a given probability distribution function $f_X(x) = 0.02 e^{-\frac{1}{800} x^2}$. We want eight levels of quantization over the regions $\{a_1 = -60, a_2 = -40, \ldots, a_7 = 60\}$ and $\{\hat{x}_1 = -70, \hat{x}_2 = -50, \ldots, \hat{x}_8 = 70\}$. Assuming that the distortion bound for this signal is $D_b = 16.6$, find out how far the real distortion, D, is to D_b.

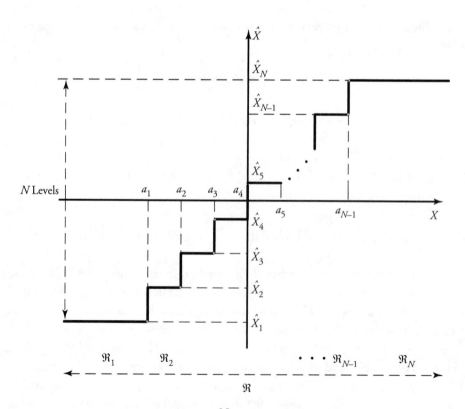

Figure 19.3 N-level quantization

Solution.   Since $N = 8$, the number of bits required per sample is $R = \log_2 8 = 3$. Using this, D can be developed further:

$$D = \sum_{i=1}^{8} \int_{\Re_i} (X - \hat{X})^2 f_X(x)dx$$

$$= \int_{-\infty}^{a_1} (x - \hat{x})^2 (0.02 e^{-\frac{1}{800}x^2})dx + \sum_{i=2}^{7} \int_{a_{i-1}}^{a_7} (x - \hat{x})^2 (0.02 e^{-\frac{1}{800}x^2})dx$$

$$+ \int_{a_7}^{\infty} (x - \hat{x}_8)^2 (0.02 e^{-\frac{1}{800}x^2})dx = 33.3.$$

We note here that the total distortion as a result of eight-level quantization is 33.3, which is considerably greater than the given distortion bound of 16.6.

The conclusion in the example implies that the quantization chosen for that source may not be optimal. A possible reason may be inappropriate choices of $(a_1, \ldots, a_7)$ and/or $(\hat{x}_1, \ldots, \hat{x}_8)$. This in turn means that R is not optimal.

Optimal Quantizers

Let Δ be the length of each region equal to $a_{i+1} - a_i$. Thus, regions can be restated as $(-\infty, a_1) \cdots (a_{N-1}, +\infty)$. Clearly, the limits of the upper region can also be shown by $(a_1 + (N - 2)\Delta, +\infty)$. Then, the total distortion can be rewritten as

$$D = \int_{-\infty}^{a_1} (x - \hat{x})^2 f_X(x)dx + \sum_{i=1}^{N-2} \int_{a_1+(i-1)\Delta}^{a_1+i\Delta} (x - \hat{x}_{i+1})^2 f_X(x)dx$$

$$+ \int_{a_1+(N-2)\Delta}^{\infty} (x - \hat{x}_N)^2 f_X(x)dx.$$

(19.9)

For D to be optimized, we must have $\frac{\partial D}{\partial a_1} = 0$ and $\frac{\partial D}{\partial \Delta} = 0$; and by solving these two partial differential equations and given the following arrangements when N is odd or even:

$$a_i = -a_{N-i} = -\left(\frac{N}{2} - i\right)\Delta \quad 1 \leq i \leq \frac{N}{2}$$

(19.10)

and

$$\hat{x}_i = -\hat{x}_{N+1-i} = -\left(\frac{N}{2} - i + \frac{1}{2}\right)\Delta.$$

(19.11)

Table 19.1 Optimal uniform quantizer for a
Gaussian source

No. of Quantization Levels, N	$\dfrac{\Delta_{opt}}{\sqrt{V[X]}}$	$\dfrac{D_{opt}}{V[X]}$
1	-	1.000
2	1.596	0.364
3	1.224	0.190
4	0.996	0.119
5	0.843	0.082
6	0.733	0.061
7	0.651	0.047
8	0.586	0.037
9	0.534	0.031
10	0.491	0.026
11	0.455	0.022
12	0.424	0.019
13	0.398	0.016
14	0.374	0.014
15	0.353	0.013
17	0.319	0.010
18	0.304	0.009
19	0.291	0.008
20	0.279	0.008

The optimal values, Δ_{opt} and D_{opt} can be obtained as a result of solving the two differential equations. The optimal values, Δ_{opt} and D_{opt}, are numerically presented in Table 19.1 assuming that the source has Gaussian distribution. Note that in this table $V[X]$ is the variance of the random variable representing the Gaussian source explained. Appendix C reviews fundamentals of probability theory and random variables including variance and the Gaussian random variable.

Example.   Suppose we a have a Gaussian media source in a multimedia network whose variance $V[X] = 400$. The source is quantized to $N = 8$ levels. Find the optimal values Δ_{opt} and D_{opt} for this quantization process and compare with the non-optimal values obtained in the previous example.

Solution.   Given $N = 8$, Table 19.1 provides us with $\Delta_{opt}/\sqrt{V[X]} = 0.586$ and $D_{opt}/V[X] = 0.037$. Knowing $V[X] = 400$, the optimal values are obtained as $\Delta_{opt} = 11.72$ and $D_{opt} = 14.80$. The result of distortion in optimal quantization shows that the optimal quantization helped reduce the distortion to 14.80 compared to $D = 33.3$ calculated in the previous example. We can also find out how improved our new level values are in the case of optimization by using Equations (19.10) and (19.11). For example, $a_1 = -a_7 = -(\frac{8}{2} - 1)11.72 = -35.16$ and $\hat{x}_1 = -\hat{x}_8 = -\left(\frac{8}{2} - 1 + \frac{1}{2}\right) 11.72 = -41.02$ are clearly different compared to the ones we obtained in the previous example.

Once samples are quantized, they are naturally encoded with binary bits. For example, if there are a total of 7 possible samples, each sample requires a 3-bit encoding, or if a total of 11 possible samples, each sample requires 4-bit, and so on.

19.3   Still Images and JPEG Compression

This section investigates algorithms that prepare and compress still and moving images. The compression of such data substantially affects the utilization of bandwidth over the multimedia and IP networking infrastructures. We begin with a single visual image, such as a photograph, and then look at video, a motion image. *Joint Photographic Experts Group* (JPEG) is a key compression standard for still images. It is used for gray-scale and quality color images. Similar to voice compression, JPEG is a lossy process. An image obtained after the decompression at a receiving end may not be the same as the original.

Figure 19.4 gives an overview of a typical JPEG process, which consists of three processes: *discrete cosine transform* (DCT), *quantization*, and *compression*, or encoding. The DCT process is complex and converts a snapshot of a real image into a matrix of corresponding values. The quantization phase converts the values

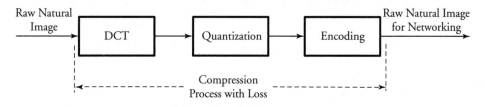

Figure 19.4   A typical JPEG process for production and compression of still images

generated by DCT to simple numbers in order to occupy less bandwidth. As usual, all quantizing processes are lossy. The compression process makes the quantized values as compact as possible. The compression phase is normally lossless and uses standard compression techniques. Before describing these three blocks, we need to consider the nature of a digital image.

19.3.1   Raw-Image Sampling and DCT

As with a voice signal, we first need samples of a raw image: a *picture*. Pictures are of two types: *photographs*, which contain no digital data, and *images*, which contain digital data suitable for computer networks. An image is made up of $m \times n$ blocks of picture units, or *pixels*, as shown in Figure 19.5. For fax transmissions, images are made up of 0s and 1s to represent black and white pixels, respectively. A *monochrome image*, or *black-and-white image*, is made up of various shades of gray, and thus each pixel must be able to represent a different shade. Typically, a pixel in a monochrome image consists of 8 bits to represent $2^8 = 256$ shades of gray, ranging from white to black, as shown in Figure 19.6.

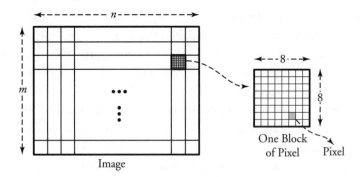

Figure 19.5   A digital still image

		Red	Green	Blue
White	0000,0000	0000,0000	0000,0000	0000,0000
	0000,0001	0000,0001	0000,0001	0000,0001
	⋮	⋮	⋮	⋮
Black	1111,1111	1111,1111	1111,1111	1111,1111
	(a)		(b)	

Figure 19.6   A still image in bits: (a) monochrome codes for a still image;
(b) color codes for a still image

JPEG Files

Color images are based on the fact that any color can be represented to the human eye by using a particular combination of the base colors red, green, and blue (RGB). Computer monitor screens, digital camera images, or any other still color images are formed by varying the intensity of these three base colors at the pixel level, resulting in the creation of virtually any corresponding color from the real raw image. Each intensity created on any of the three pixels is represented by 8 bits, as shown in Figure 19.6. The intensities of each 3-unit pixel are adjusted, affecting the value of the 8-bit word to produce the desired color. Thus, each pixel can be represented by using 24 bits, allowing 2^{24} different colors. However, the human eye cannot distinguish all colors among the 2^{24} possible colors. The number of pixels in a typical image varies with the image size.

Example. A JPEG-based computer screen can consist of $1,024 \times 1,280$ 3-color pixel bundles. Consequently, this computer image requires $(1,024 \times 1,280) \times 24 = 31,457,280$ bits. If a video consists of 30 images per second, a 943Mb/s bandwidth is required.

GIF Files

JPEG is designed to work with full-color images up to 2^{24} colors. The *Graphics Interchange Format* (GIF) is an image file format that reduces the number of colors to 256. This reduction in the number of possible colors is a trade-off between the quality of the image and the transmission bandwidth. GIF stores up to $2^8 =$ 256 colors in a table and covers the range of colors in an image as closely as possible. Therefore, 8 bits are used to represent a single pixel. GIF uses a variation of Lempel-Ziv encoding (discussed later in this chapter) for compression of an image. This technology is used for images whose color detailing is not important, such as cartoons and charts.

DCT Process

The *discrete cosine transform* (DCT) is a lossy compression process that begins by dividing a raw image into a series of standard $N \times N$ *pixel* blocks. For now, consider a monochrome block of pixels. With a standard size of $N = 8$, N is the number of pixels per row or column of each block. Let x, y be the position of a particular pixel in a block where $0 \leq x \leq N - 1$ and $0 \leq y \leq N - 1$. Hence, a gray scale of a given pixel x, y can get an integer value in $\{0, 1, 2, \ldots, 255\}$. For an $N \times N$ pixel block, the DCT process is summarized in two steps:

1. Form a $P[x][y]$ matrix to represent the collection of light-intensity values taken from various points of a real raw image.
2. Convert the values of the $P[x][y]$ matrix to a matrix with normalized and reduced values denoted by $T[i][j]$ obtained as follows.

The objective of matrix $T[i][j]$ is to create as many 0s as possible instead of small numbers in the $P[x][y]$ matrix in order to reduce the overall bandwidth required to transmit the image. Similarly, matrix $T[i][j]$ is a two-dimensional array with N rows and N columns, where $0 \leq i \leq N - 1$ and $0 \leq j \leq N - 1$. The elements of $T[i][j]$ are known as *spatial frequencies* and are obtained from

$$T[i][j] = \frac{2}{N} C(i) C(j) \sum_{x=0}^{N-1} \sum_{y=0}^{N-1} P[x][y] \cos\left(\frac{\pi i (2x + 1)}{2N}\right) \cos\left(\frac{\pi j (2y + 1)}{2N}\right), \quad (19.12)$$

where

$$C(i) = \begin{cases} \frac{1}{\sqrt{2}} & \text{for } i = 0 \\ 1 & \text{otherwise} \end{cases}$$

$$C(j) = \begin{cases} \frac{1}{\sqrt{2}} & \text{for } j = 0 \\ 1 & \text{otherwise} \end{cases}$$

Example. An 8×8 matrix $P[x][y]$ for an image is formed as shown in Figure 19.7(a). The $P[x][y]$ matrix is converted to matrix $T[i][j]$ as shown in Figure 19.7(b) by using Equation (19.12). This example clearly shows that a matrix as $P[x][y]$ consisting of 64 values can be converted to $T[i][j]$ with 9 values and 55 zeros. It is easy to figure out the advantages of this conversion. The 55 zeros can be compressed, conveniently resulting in significant reduction of transmission bandwidth.

The spatial frequencies depend directly on how much the pixel values change as functions of their positions in a pixel block. Equation (19.12) is set up such that the generated matrix $T[i][j]$ contains many 0s, and the values of the matrix elements generally become smaller as they get farther away from the upper-left position in the

$$
\begin{bmatrix}
22 & 31 & 41 & 50 & 60 & 69 & 80 & 91 \\
29 & 42 & 52 & 59 & 71 & 80 & 90 & 101 \\
40 & 51 & 59 & 70 & 82 & 92 & 100 & 110 \\
51 & 62 & 70 & 82 & 89 & 101 & 109 & 119 \\
60 & 70 & 82 & 93 & 100 & 109 & 120 & 130 \\
70 & 82 & 90 & 100 & 110 & 121 & 130 & 139 \\
79 & 91 & 100 & 110 & 120 & 130 & 140 & 150 \\
91 & 99 & 110 & 120 & 130 & 140 & 150 & 160
\end{bmatrix}
\qquad
\begin{bmatrix}
716 & -179 & 0 & -19 & 0 & -6 & 0 & -1 \\
-179 & 1 & 0 & 0 & 0 & 0 & 0 & 0 \\
0 & 0 & 0 & 0 & 0 & 0 & 0 & 0 \\
-19 & 0 & 0 & 0 & 0 & 0 & 0 & 0 \\
0 & 0 & 0 & 0 & 0 & 0 & 0 & 0 \\
-6 & 0 & 0 & 0 & 0 & 0 & 0 & 0 \\
0 & 0 & 0 & 0 & 0 & 0 & 0 & 0 \\
-1 & 0 & 0 & 0 & 0 & 0 & 0 & 0
\end{bmatrix}
$$

(a)   (b)

Figure 19.7   Matrix examples: (a) P[x][y]; (b) T[i][j]

matrix. The values of $T[i][j]$ elements at the receiver can be converted back to matrix $P[x][y]$ by using the following function:

$$
P[x][y] = \frac{2}{N} C(i)C(j) \sum_{i=0}^{N-1} \sum_{j=0}^{N-1} T[i][j] \cos\left(\frac{\pi i(2i+1)}{2N}\right) \cos\left(\frac{\pi j(2j+1)}{2N}\right). \quad (19.13)
$$

Note that as values become farther away from the upper-left position in $P[x][y]$, they correspond to a fine detail in the image.

19.3.2   Quantization

To further scale down the values of $T[i][j]$ with fewer distinct numbers and more consistent patterns to get better bandwidth advantages, this matrix is *quantized* to another matrix, denoted by $Q[i][j]$. To generate this matrix, the elements of matrix $T[i][j]$ are divided by a standard number and then rounded off to their nearest integer. Dividing $T[i][j]$ elements by the same constant number results in too much loss. The values of elements in the upper-left portions of the matrix must be preserved as much as possible, because such values correspond to less subtle features of the image. In contrast, values of elements in the lower-right portion correspond to the highest details of an image. To preserve as much information as possible, the elements of $T[i][j]$ are divided by the elements of an $N \times N$ matrix denoted by $D[i][j]$, in which the values of elements increase from the upper-left portion to the lower-right portion

$$
Q[i][j] = \frac{T[i][j]}{D[i][j]}.
$$

This way, once the division is complete, the important values of the upper-left corner of $Q[i][j]$ are intensified further.

Example.   Consider again the 8×8 matrix $P[x][y]$ already converted to matrix $T[i][j]$ shown in Figure 19.7. Figure 19.8(a) shows a divisor matrix $D[i][j]$. Figure 19.8(b) shows the corresponding matrix $Q[i][j]$ resulting from the quantization process. Note particularly that big values, such as -179 have become smaller and that some such values, as -1 in the upper-right corner turn into 0, making it easier for compression.

We notice here that the process of quantization, as discussed at the beginning of this chapter, is not quite reversible. This means that the values of $Q[i][j]$ cannot be exactly converted back to $T[i][j]$, owing mainly to rounding the values after dividing them by $D[i][j]$. For this reason, the quantization phase is a lossy process.

19.3.3   Encoding

In the last phase of the JPEG process, encoding finally completes the task of compression. In the quantization phase, a matrix with numerous 0s is produced. Consider the example shown in Figure 19.8(b). The **Q** matrix in this example has produced 57 zeros from the original raw image. A practical approach to compressing this matrix is to use run-length coding (explained in Section 19.6). If run-length coding is used, scanning matrix $Q[i][j]$ row by row may result in several phrases.

A logical way to scan this matrix is in the order illustrated by the arrows in Figure 19.8(b). This method is attractive because the larger values in the matrix tend

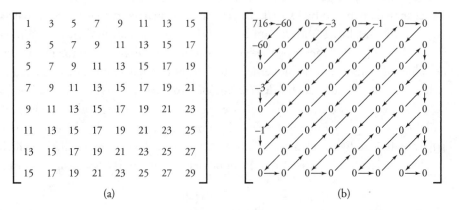

Figure 19.8   (a) Divisor matrix $D[i][j]$ and the quantization of a still image to produce; (b) matrix $Q[i][j]$ and the order of matrix elements for transmission

to collect in the upper-left corner of the matrix, and the elements representing larger values tend to be gathered together in that area of the matrix. Thus, we can induce a better rule: Scanning should always start from the upper-left corner element of the matrix. This way, we get much longer runs for each phrase and a much lower number of phrases in the run-length coding.

Once the run-length coding is processed, JPEG uses some type of Huffman coding or arithmetic coding for the nonzero values. Note here that, so far, only a block of 8 × 8 pixels has been processed. An image consists of numerous such blocks. Therefore, the speed of processing and transmission is a factor in the quality of image transfer.

19.4 Moving Images and MPEG Compression

A *motion image*, or video is a rapid display of still images. Moving from one image to another must be fast enough to fool the human eye. There are different standards on the number of still images comprising a video clip. One common standard produces a motion image by displaying still images at a rate of 30 frames per second. The common standard that defines video compression is *Moving Picture Experts Group* (MPEG), which has several branch standards:

- MPEG-1, primarily for video compression
- MPEG-2, for multimedia entertainment and *high-definition television* (HDTV) and the satellite broadcasting industry
- MPEG-4, for object-oriented video compression and videoconferencing over low-bandwidth channels
- MPEG-7, for a broad range of demands requiring large bandwidths providing multimedia tools
- MPEG-21 for interaction among the various MPEG groups

Logically, using JPEG compression for each still picture does not provide sufficient compression for video as it occupies a large bandwidth. MPEG deploys additional compression. Normally, the difference between two consecutive frames is small. With MPEG, a base frame is sent first, and successive frames are encoded by computing the differences. The receiver can reconstruct frames based on the first base frame and the submitted differences. However, frames of a completely new scene in a video may not be compressed this way, as the difference between the two scenes is substantial. Depending on the relative position of a frame in a sequence, it can be compressed through one of the following types of frames:

- *Interimage* (I) frames. An I frame is treated as a JPEG still image and compressed using DCT.
- *Predictive* (P) frames. These frames are produced by computing differences between a current and a previous I or P frame.
- *Bidirectional* (B) frames. A B frame is similar to a P frame, but the B frame considers differences between previous, current, and future frames.

Figure 19.9 illustrates a typical grouping of frames, with I, P, and B frames forming a sequence. In any frame sequence, I frames appear periodically as the base of the scene. Normally, there is a P frame between each two groups of B frames.

19.4.1 MP3 and Streaming Audio

Section 19.2 explained how an audible sound or a human voice ranging between 20Hz and 20KHz can be converted into digital bits and eventually into packets for networking. A signal is processed in three stages of sampling, quantizing, and encoding; one example of such as a process is called *pulse code modulation* (PCM). A variety of methods for compressing such encoded products at the output of PCM are available. However, Huffman compression of the processed signal may not be sufficient for transmission over IP networks.

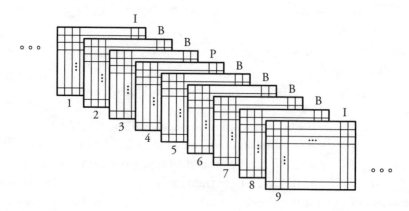

Figure 19.9 Snapshot of moving frames in MPEG compression including I, P, and B frames

The MPEG-1 layer 3 (MP3) technology compresses audio for networking and producing CD-quality sound. The sampling part of PCM is performed at a rate of 44.1KHz to cover the maximum of 20KHz of audible signals. Using the commonly used 16-bit encoding for each sample, the maximum total bits required for audio is $16 \times 44.1 = 700$ kilobits and 1.4 megabits for two channels if the sound is processed in a stereo fashion. For example a 60-minute CD (3,600 seconds) requires about $1.4 \times 3,600 = 5,040$ megabits, or 630 megabytes. This amount may be acceptable for recording on a CD but is considered extremely large for networking, and thus a carefully designed compression technique is needed.

MP3 combines the advantages of MPEG with "three" layers of audio compression. MP3 removes from a piece of sound all portions that an average ear may not be able to hear, such as weak background sounds. In any audio streaming, MP3 specifies what humans are not able to hear, removes those components, and digitizes the remaining. By filtering some part of an audio signal, the quality of compressed MP3 is obviously degraded to lower than the original one. Nonetheless, the compression achievement of this technology is remarkable.

19.5   Compression Methods with Loss

Hartley, Nyquist, and Shannon are the founders of *information theory*, which has resulted in the mathematical modeling of information sources. Consider a communication system in which a source signal is processed to produce sequences of n words (samples), as shown in Figure 19.10. These sequences of samples can be compressed in the *source encoder* unit to save transmission link bandwidth. An information source (in our case, encoded samples) can be modeled by a *random process* $X_n = (X_1, \dots, X_n)$, where X_i is a random variable taking on values from a set of values as $\{a_1, \dots, a_N\}$, called *sample space*. We use this model in our analysis to show the information process in high-speed networks.

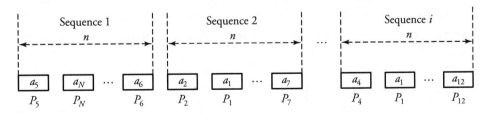

Figure 19.10   A model of data sequences

19.5.1   Basics of Information Theory

The challenge of data compression is to find the output that conveys the most information. Consider a single source with random variable X, choosing values in $\{a_1, \ldots a_N\}$. If a_i is the most likely output and a_j is the least likely output, clearly, a_j conveys the most information and a_i conveys the least information. This observation can be rephrased as an important conclusion: *The measure of information for an output is a decreasing and continuous function of the probability of source output.* To formulate this statement, let P_{k_1} and P_{k_2} be the probabilities of an information source's outputs a_{k_1} and a_{k_2}, respectively. Let $I(P_{k_1})$ and $I(P_{k_2})$ be the information content of a_{k_1} and a_{k_2}, respectively. The following five facts apply:

1. $I(P_k)$ depends on P_k.
2. $I(P_k)$ is a continuous function of P_k.
3. $I(P_k)$ is a decreasing function of P_k.
4. $P_k = P_{k_1} \times P_{k_2}$ (the probability of two outputs happening in the same time).
5. $I(P_k) = I(P_{k_1}) + I(P_{k_2})$ (the sum of two pieces of information).

These facts lead to an important conclusion that can relate the probability of certain data to its information content:

$$I(P_k) = -\log_2 P_k = \log_2 \left(\frac{1}{P_k}\right). \tag{19.14}$$

The log function has a base 2, an indication of incorporating the binary concept of digital data.

19.5.2   Entropy of Information

In general, *entropy* is a measure of uncertainty. Consider an information source producing random numbers, X, from a possible collection of $\{a_1, \ldots, a_N\}$ with corresponding probabilities of $\{P_1, \ldots, P_N\}$ and information content of $\{I(P_1), \ldots, I(P_N)\}$, respectively. In particular, the entropy, $H(x)$, is defined as the average information content of a source:

$$H_X(x) = \sum_{k=1}^{N} P_k I(P_k)$$

$$= \sum_{k=1}^{N} -P_k \log_2 P_k = \sum_{k=1}^{N} P_k \log_2 \left(\frac{1}{P_k}\right). \tag{19.15}$$

Example. A source with bandwidth 8KHz is sampled at the Nyquist rate. If the result is modeled using any value from $\{-2, -1, 0, 1, 2\}$ and corresponding probabilities $\{0.05, 0.05, 0.08, 0.30, 0.52\}$, find the entropy.

Solution.

$$H_X(x) = -\sum_{k=1}^{5} P_k \log_2 P_k = 1.74 \text{b/sample}.$$

The information rate in samples/sec $= 8,000 \times 2 = 16,000$, and the rate of information produced by the source $= 16,000 \times 1.74 = 27,840$ bits.

Joint Entropy

The joint entropy of two discrete random variables X and Y is defined by

$$H_{X, Y}(x, y) = -\sum_{x, y} P_{X, Y}(x, y) \log_2 P_{X, Y}(x, y), \tag{19.16}$$

where $P_{X, Y}(x, y) = \text{Prob}[X = x$ and at the same time $Y = y]$ and is called the *joint probability mass function* of two random variables. In general, for a random process $X_n = (X_1, \ldots, X_n)$ with n random variables:

$$H_{Xn}(x_n) = -\sum_{X_1, \ldots, X_n} P_{X_1, \ldots, X_n}(x_1, \ldots, x_n) \log_2 P_{X_1, \ldots, X_n}(x_1, \ldots, x_n), \tag{19.17}$$

where $P_{X_1, \ldots, X_n}(x_1, \ldots, x_n)$ is the joint probability mass function (J-PMF) of the random process X_n. For more information on J-PMF, see Appendix C.

19.5.3 Shannon's Coding Theorem

This theorem limits the rate of data compression. Consider again Figure 19.10, which shows a discrete source modeled by a random process that generates sequences of length n using values in set $\{a_1, \ldots, a_N\}$ with probabilities $\{P_1, \ldots, P_N\}$, respectively. If n is large enough, the number of times a value a_i is repeated in a given sequence $= nP_i$, and the number of values in a typical sequence is therefore $n(P_1 + \cdots + P_N)$.

We define the *typical sequence* as one in which any value a_i is repeated nP_i times. Accordingly, the probability that a_i is repeated nP_i times is obviously $P_i P_i \cdots P_i = P_i^{nP_i}$, resulting in a more general statement: The probability of a typical sequence is the probability $[(a_1$ is repeated $np_1)] \times$ the probability $[(a_2$ is repeated $np_2] \times \ldots$. This can be shown by $P_1^{np_1} P_2^{np_2} \cdots P_N^{np_N}$, or

$$\text{Prob (A Typical Sequence)} = \prod_{i=1}^{N} P_i^{nP_i}. \qquad (19.18)$$

Knowing $P_i^{nP_i} = 2^{nP_i \log_2 P_i}$, we can obtain the probability of a typical sequence P_t as follows:

$$P_t = \prod_{i=1}^{N} 2^{nP_i \, \log_2 \ P_i}$$

$$= 2^{(nP_1 \, \log_2 \ P_1 + \cdots nP_N \, \log_2 \ P_N)}$$

$$= 2^{n(P_1 \, \log_2 \ P_1 + \cdots P_N \log_2 \ P_N)}$$

$$= 2^{n(\sum_{i=1}^{N} P_i \log_2 \ P_i)}. \qquad (19.19)$$

This last expression results in the well-known Shannon's theorem, which expresses the probability that a typical sequence of length n with entropy $H_X(x)$ is equal to

$$P_t = 2^{-nH_X(x)}. \qquad (19.20)$$

Example. Assume that a sequence size of 200 of an information source chooses values from the set $\{a_1, \dots, a_5\}$ with corresponding probabilities $\{0.05, 0.05, 0.08, 0.30, 0.52\}$. Find the probability of a typical sequence.

Solution. In the previous example, we calculated the entropy to be $H_X(x) = 1.74$ for the same situation. With $n = 200$, $N = 5$, the probability of a typical sequence is the probability of a sequence in which a_1, a_2, a_3, a_4, and a_5 are repeated, respectively, $200 \times 0.05 = 10$ times, 10 times, 16 times, 60 times, and 104 times. Thus, the probability of a typical sequence is $P_t = 2^{-nH_X(x)} = 2^{-200(1.74)}$.

The fundamental Shannon's theorem leads to an important conclusion. As the probability of a typical sequence is $2^{-nH_X(x)}$ and the sum of probabilities of all typical sequences is 1, the number of typical sequences is obtained by $= \dfrac{1}{2^{-nH_X(x)}} = 2^{nH(x)}$. Knowing that the total number of all sequences, including typical and nontypical ones, is N^n, it is sufficient, in all practical cases when n is large enough, to transmit only the set of typical sequences rather than the set of all sequences. This is the essence of data compression: The total number of bits required to represent $2^{nH_X(x)}$ sequences is $nH_X(x)$ bits, and the average number of bits for each source $= H_X(x)$.

Example.   Following the previous example, in which the sequence size for an information source is 200, find the ratio of the number of typical sequences to the number of all types of sequences.

Solution.   We had $n = 200$ and $N = 5$; thus, the number of typical sequences is $2^{nH(x)} = 2^{200 \times 1.74}$, and the total number of all sequences is 5^{200}. The ratio in this case is almost zero, which may cause a significant loss of data if it is compressed, based on Shannon's theorem. It is worth mentioning that the number of bits required to represent $2^{nH_X(x)}$ sequences is $nH_X(x) = 104$ bits.

19.5.4   Compression Ratio and Code Efficiency

Let $\bar{R}$ be the average length of codes, ℓ_i be the length of code word i, and P_i be the probability of code word i:

$$\bar{R} = \sum_{i=0}^{N} P_i \ell_i. \tag{19.21}$$

A *compression ratio* is defined as

$$C_r = \frac{\bar{R}}{\bar{R}_x}, \tag{19.22}$$

where $\bar{R}_x$ is the length of a source output before coding. It can also be shown that

$$H_X(x) \leq \bar{R} < H_X(x) + 1. \tag{19.23}$$

Code efficiency is a measure for understanding how close code lengths are to the corresponding decoded data and is defined by

$$\eta_{code} = \frac{H_X}{(x)} \bar{R}. \tag{19.24}$$

When data is compressed, part of the data may need to be removed in the process.

19.6   Compression Methods without Loss

Some types of data, including text, image, and video, might contain redundant or repeated elements. If so, those elements can be eliminated and some sort of codes substituted for future decoding. In this section, we focus on techniques that do not incur any loss during compression:

- Arithmetic encoding
- Run-length encoding
- Huffman encoding
- Lempel-Ziv encoding

Here, we ignore arithmetic encoding and consider only the last three encoding techniques.

19.6.1   Run-Length Encoding

One of the simplest data-compression techniques is *run-length encoding*. This technique is fairly effective for compression of plaintext and numbers, especially for facsimile systems. With run-length code, repeated letters can be replaced by a run length, beginning with C_c to express the compression letter count.

Example.   Assume a compression system that represents b as a blank. Find the compressed version of the following sentence:

THISSSSSS b IS b b b b AN b EXAMPLE b OF b RUN-LENGTH b CODE

Solution.   According to the conventions stated, the compressed version of that sentence turns into: THIS C_c 6 S b IS C_c b 4AN b EXAMPLE b OF b RUN-LENGTH b CODE. It is obvious that the longer the text sequence, the smaller the compression

Table 19.2   Statistics obtained for run-length compression of a 1,000-character piece of text

Number of Repeated Characters	Average Length of Repeated Characters	Compression Ratio C_r
10	4	0.99
10	10	0.93
20	4	0.98
20	10	0.85
30	4	0.97
30	10	0.79

ratio becomes, as shown in Table 19.2. The statistics obtained in this table are based on a 1,000-character piece of text.

19.6.2 Huffman Encoding

Huffman encoding is an efficient frequency-dependent coding technique. With this algorithm, source values with smaller probabilities appear to be encoded by a longer word. This technique reduces the total number of bits, leading to an efficient compression of data. The algorithm that implements such a technique is as follows.

Begin Huffman Encoding Algorithm

1. **Initialize.**

   Sort the information source outputs (samples) in decreasing order of their probabilities.

2. **Create a Huffman diagram**

3. **Merge** the two least probable samples into a single sample whose probability is the sum of two samples' probabilities.

4. **Update sorting** the information source outputs (samples) in decreasing order of their probabilities.

5. **If** the number of remaining samples is two, **go** to the next step; ... **otherwise, go** to step 1.

6. **Assign** 0 and 1 as codes on the diagram where each two samples merge.

7. Obtain the code for a sample by tracing the available 0s and 1s assigned in step 4 from the path connecting the rightmost of the diagram to the corresponding sample. ■

Example. Design a Huffman encoder for an information source generating outputs (samples) $\{a_1, a_2, a_3, a_4, a_5\}$ and with probabilities $\{0.05, 0.05, 0.08, 0.30, 0.52\}$.

Solution. Following the algorithm, in the initialization phase, the five samples are sorted as shown in Figure 19.11. In step 1, the merging action starts from samples a_4 and a_5, and in steps 2, and 3, the remaining list is updated to four sorted outputs with probabilities $\{0.08, 0.10, 0.30, 0.52\}$, and the merging continues to the last sample. In steps 4 and 5, the 0s and 1s are assigned as seen, an the information related to $\{a_1, a_2, a_3, a_4, a_5\}$ is compressed to $\{0, 10, 111, 1100, 1101\}$, respectively. For example, the compressed code obtained for sample a_5 is the four logic bits 1101 traced from the rightmost of the chart to a_5 as seen in the figure.

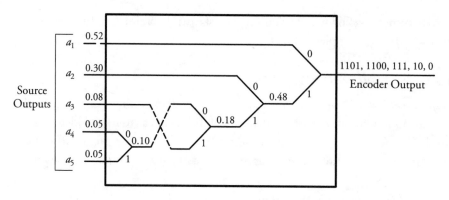

Figure 19.11   Huffman encoding

19.6.3   Lempel-Ziv Encoding

Lempel-Ziv codes are independent of the source statistics. This coding technique is normally used for UNIX compressed files. The algorithm that converts a string of logical bits into a Lempel-Ziv code is summarized as follows.

Begin Lempel-Ziv Encoding Algorithm

1. Identify phrases of the smallest length that have not appeared so far for any sequence of information source output (sample). (Note that all phrases are different, and lengths of words grow as the encoding process proceeds)

2. Phrases are encoded using code words of equal length, then:
   - k_1 = the number of bits needed to describe the code word
   - k_2 = the number of phrases such that $k_1 = \log_2 k_2$ (round up if needed).

3. A code is the location of the prefix to the phrases.

4. A code is followed by the last bit of parser output to double-check the last bit. ∎

Example.   For the following string of bits, find the encoded Lempel-Ziv words:

$$11110111011000001010010001111010101100$$

Solution.   Implementing step 1 on the string, there are 14 phrases, as follows:

$$1-11-10-111-0-110-00-001-01-0010-0011-1101-010-1100$$

Table 19.3 An example of the Lempel-Ziv coding process

Parser Output	Location	Encoded Outputs
1	0001	00001
11	0010	00011
10	0011	00010
111	0100	00101
0	0101	00001
110	0110	00100
00	0111	01010
001	1000	01111
01	1001	01011
0010	1001	10000
0011	1011	10001
1101	1101	01101
010	1101	10010
1100	1110	01100

Thus, $k_2 = 14$ and $k_1 = \log_2 14_2 = 4$, and thus the encoded words must have 4 bits (step 3) plus an additional bit (step 4). Table 19.3 shows the encoded outputs as steps 3 and 4 are applied on the parser output.

19.7 Scanned Document Compression

As a case study, consider the process of a paper document to be scanned and transmitted through e-mail or FTP. The scanned document process is similar to the process of old-time *facsimile* (fax) technology. In this process, a picture as the content of a paper document is scanned and then compressed in two steps: run-length encoding and then Huffman encoding. First, the transmission of the digital line scan is replaced by the transmission of a quantity count of each of the successive runs of black or white elements.

Consider a document of standard size 8.5 inches by 11 inches. The picture is first partitioned into *pixels*. If the desired resolution is 200 × 200 pixels per square inch, the total number of pixels per picture is exactly $200^2 \times (8.5 \times 11) = 37,400,000$

Table 19.4 Statistics on frequency of occurrences for strings obtained afterrun-length coding for a black-and-white document

Number of Repeated Pixels $(C_c X)$	Huffman Code for White Pixels	Huffman Code for Black Pixels
C_c1	000111	010
C_c2	0011	01
C_c10	00011	1000011
C_c50	00111001	000001101111

pixels. As mentioned earlier, processing a picture document requires both run-length coding and Huffman coding. Since black and white always alternate, no special characters are needed to specify that a run is black or white. Thus, the encoded data stream is a string of numbers indicating the lengths of the alternating black and white runs. The algorithm for the first phase is as follows.

Scanned Document Compression Process Algorithm

1. **Identify** the first row out of the n-row document.
2. At any row i, start at the first pixel of the row.
   - **if** the pixel is black, assign code 1;
   - **if** the pixel is white, assign code 0.
3. At any step of counting j,
   - **let** X_j be the number of consecutive 0s before a 1 appears,
     - **assign** code $C_c X_j 0$ to the string of 0s;
     - **assign** code $C_c X_j 1$ to the string of 1s. ■

At this point, the document is converted into a number of $C_c X_j 0$s and $C_c X_j 0$s. In phase 2 of coding, we need the statistics on the frequencies of a certain run-length code in order to compress it further, using the Huffman algorithm. Table 19.4 shows practical statistics for a black-and-white document.

19.8 Summary

A number of algorithms effectively compress voice, still images, and moving images. We started with how sampled and digitized voice are treated in networks. A raw voice signal is converted to a binary-encoded form through three phases of sampling, quantizing, and encoding. In this process, sampling and quantization both present some sort of loss. Compression schemes used for the preparation of an image include *Joint Photographic Experts Group* (JPEG), a compression standard for still images. JPEG consists of three processes: *discrete cosine transform* (DCT), *quantization*, and *compression*. In particular, DCT converts a snapshot of a real image into a matrix of corresponding values, and the quantization phase converts the values generated by DCT to simple numbers.

A *motion image*, or video, is the rapid display of still images that fool the human eye. Standards differ on the number of still images that make a video clip. The common standard that defines video compression is *Moving Picture Experts Group* (MPEG). MPEG-1 layer 3 (MP3) is a technology for compressing audio for networking and producing CD-quality sound.

Compression has limits, as presented by Shannon. Shannon's theorem expresses the probability of a typical sequence of length n with entropy $H_X(x)$ to be equal to $2^{-nH_X(x)}$. Although some compression processes entail loss of data, others do not, such as Huffman or run-length encoding techniques.

The next chapter looks at distributed and cloud-based multimedia networking. This topic is the concluding concept in voice and video over IP and includes a distributed method of streaming objects in the Internet.

19.9   Exercises

1. A sinusoidal audio signal $g(t)$ with period 10 ms is to be sampled by a sampler $s(t)$ with period $T_s = 1$ ms and pulse width $\tau = 0.5$ ms. The maximum voltages for both signals are 1 volt. Let the sampled signal be $g_s(t)$; compute and sketch $g(t)$, $s(t)$, $g_s(t)$, $G(f)$, $S(f)$, and $G_s(f)$ (the range of nT_s in $s(t)$ is $[-2T_s, +2T_s]$).

2. Consider a sinusoidal audio signal $g(t)$ with period 10 ms to be sampled for media exchange purposes. The sampler has a period $T_s = 1$ ms and a pulse width $\tau = 0.25$ ms. The maximum voltages for both sampled and sampler signals are 1 volt.

   (a) Sketch the detail of a sampled signal for one period using the sampling technique.

   (b) Assume that the real value taken from a sample for quantization is its starting value. We would like to see the difference in the quality of sampling if the real value taken from a sample is based on its ending value. Show your result in terms of the percentage of the difference with respect to the starting value of a sample for the third, sixth, and the ninth samples.

3. Consider a pulse signal $g(t)$ being 1 volt in intervals: ... [−4 and −2], [−1 and +1], [+2 and +4] −1 ms. This signal is to be sampled by an impulse sampler $s(t)$ being generated at ... , −3, 0, +3, ... ms, with pulse width $\tau = 0.5$. Compute and sketch all the processes from analog signal $g(t)$ to sampled version $g_s(t)$ in both time and frequency domains.

4. Assume that a normal distributed source with zero mean and variance of 2 is to be transmitted via a channel that can provide a transmission capacity of 4 bits/ each source output.

   (a) Find the distortion bound defined by $D_b = V[X]2^{-2R}$.

   (b) What is the required transmission capacity per source output if the maximum tolerable distortion is 0.05?

5. Let $X(t)$ denote a normal (Gaussian) source with $V[X] = 10$, for which a 12-level optimal uniform quantizer is to be designed.

   (a) Find optimal quantization intervals (Δ).

   (b) Find optimal quantization boundaries (a_i).

   (c) Find optimal quantization levels ($\hat{x}_i$).

   (d) Find the optimal total resulting distortion.

   (e) Compare the optimal total resulting distortion with the result obtained from the distortion bound defined by $D_b = V[X]2^{-2R}$.

6. Consider the same information source discussed in exercise 4. This time, apply a 16-level optimal uniform quantizer.

   (a) Find optimal quantization boundaries (a_i).

   (b) Find optimal quantization intervals (Δ).

   (c) Find optimal quantization levels ($\hat{x}_i$).

   (d) Find the optimal total resulting distortion.

7. To encode two random signals X and Y that are uniformly distributed on the region between two squares, let the marginal PDF of random variables be

$$f_X(x) = \begin{cases} 0.25 & -2 \leq X < -1 \\ 0.25 & -1 \leq X < 0 \\ 0.25 & 0 \leq X < +1 \\ 0.25 & +1 \leq X < +2 \end{cases}$$

and

$$f_Y(y) = \begin{cases} 0.3 & -2 \le Y < -1 \\ 0.1 & -1 \le Y < 0 \\ 0.4 & 0 \le Y < +1 \\ 0.2 & +1 \le Y < +2 \end{cases}.$$

Assume that each of the random variables X and Y is quantized using four-level uniform quantizers.

(a) Calculate the joint probability $P_{XY}(x, y)$.

(b) Find quantization levels x_1 through x_4 if $\Delta = 1$.

(c) Without using the optimal quantization table, find the resulting total distortion.

(d) Find the resulting number of bits per (X, Y) pair.

8. The sampling rate of a certain CD player is 80,000, and samples are quantized using a 16 bit/sample quantizer. Determine the resulting number of bits for a piece of music with a duration of 60 minutes.

9. The PDF of a source is defined by $f_X(x) = 2\Lambda(x)$. This source is quantized using a four-level uniform quantizer described as follows:

$$\hat{x} = \begin{cases} +1.5 & 1 < x \le 2 \\ +0.5 & 0 < x \le 1 \\ -0.5 & -1 < x \le 0 \\ -1.5 & -2 < x \le -1 \end{cases}.$$

Find the PDF of the random variable representing the quantization error $X - \hat{x}$.

10. Using logic gates, design a PCM encoder using 3-bit gray codes.

11. To preserve as much information as possible, the JPEG elements of $T[i][j]$ are divided by the elements of an $N \times N$ matrix denoted by $D[i][j]$, in which the values of elements increase from the upper-left portion to the lower-right portion. Consider matrices $T[i][j]$ and $D[i][j]$ in Figure 19.12.

(a) Find the quantized matrix $Q[i][j]$.

(b) Obtain a run-length compression on $Q[i][j]$.

12. Find the differential entropy of the continuous random variable X with a PDF defined by

$$f_X(x) = \begin{cases} x + 1 & -1 \le x \le 0 \\ -x + 1 & 0 < x \le 1 \\ 0 & \text{else} \end{cases}.$$

$$\begin{bmatrix} 1 & 3 & 5 & 7 & 9 & 11 & 13 & 15 \\ 3 & 5 & 7 & 9 & 11 & 13 & 15 & 17 \\ 5 & 7 & 9 & 11 & 13 & 15 & 17 & 19 \\ 7 & 9 & 11 & 13 & 15 & 17 & 19 & 21 \\ 9 & 11 & 13 & 15 & 17 & 19 & 21 & 23 \\ 11 & 13 & 15 & 17 & 19 & 21 & 23 & 25 \\ 13 & 15 & 17 & 19 & 21 & 23 & 25 & 27 \\ 15 & 17 & 19 & 21 & 23 & 25 & 27 & 29 \end{bmatrix} \qquad \begin{bmatrix} 513 & -138 & 0 & -17 & 0 & -6 & 0 & -1 \\ -138 & 1 & 0 & 6 & 0 & 0 & 0 & 0 \\ 0 & 0 & 0 & 0 & 0 & 0 & 0 & 0 \\ -17 & 6 & 0 & 0 & 0 & 0 & 0 & 0 \\ 0 & 0 & 0 & 0 & 0 & 0 & 0 & 0 \\ -6 & 0 & 0 & 0 & 0 & 0 & 0 & 0 \\ 0 & 0 & 0 & 0 & 0 & 0 & 0 & 0 \\ -1 & 0 & 0 & 0 & 0 & 0 & 0 & 0 \end{bmatrix}$$

(a)   (b)

Figure 19.12 Exercise 11 matrices for applying (a) divisor matrix $D[i][j]$ on (b) matrix $T[i][j]$ to produce an efficient quantization of a JPEG image to produce matrix $Q[i][j]$

13. A source has an alphabet $\{a_1, a_2, a_3, a_4, a_5\}$ with corresponding probabilities $\{0.23, 0.30, 0.07, 0.28, 0.12\}$.

   (a) Find the entropy of this source.

   (b) Compare this entropy with that of a uniformly distributed source with the same sample space.

14. We define two random variables X and Y for two random voice signals in a multimedia network, both taking on values in sample space $\{1, 2, 3\}$. The joint probability mass function (J-PMF), $P_{X,Y}(x, y)$, is given as follows:

$$\begin{cases} P_{X,Y}(1, 1) = P(X = 1, Y = 1) = 0.1 \\ P_{X,Y}(1, 2) = P(X = 1, Y = 2) = 0.2 \\ P_{X,Y}(2, 1) = P(X = 2, Y = 1) = 0.1 \\ P_{X,Y}(1, 3) = P(X = 1, Y = 3) = 0.4 \\ P_{X,Y}(2, 3) = P(X = 2, Y = 3) = 0.2 \end{cases}$$

   (a) Find the two marginal entropies, $H(X)$ and $H(Y)$.

   (b) Conceptually, what is the meaning of the marginal entropy?

   (c) Find the joint entropy of the two signals, $H(X, Y)$.

   (d) Conceptually, what is the meaning of the joint entropy?

15. We define two random variables X and Y for two random voice signals in a multimedia network.

   (a) Find the conditional entropy, $H(X|Y)$, in terms of joint and marginal entropies.

   (b) Conceptually, what is the meaning of the joint entropy?

16. Consider the process of a source with a bandwidth $W = 50\text{Hz}$ sampled at the Nyquist rate. The resulting sample outputs take values in the set of sample space $\{a_0, a_1, a_2, a_3, a_4, a_5, a_6\}$ with corresponding probabilities $\{0.06, 0.09, 0.10, 0.15, 0.05, 0.20, 0.35\}$ and are transmitted in sequences of length 10.

    (a) Which output conveys the most information?

    (b) What is the information content of outputs a_1 and a_5 together?

    (c) Find the least-probable sequence and its probability, and comment on whether it is a typical sequence.

    (d) Find the entropy of the source in bits/sample and bits/second.

    (e) Calculate the number of nontypical sequences.

17. A source with the output sample space $\{a_1, a_2, a_3, a_4\}$ and corresponding probabilities $\{0.15, 0.20, 0.30, 0.35\}$ produces sequences of length 100.

    (a) What is the approximate number of typical sequences in the source output?

    (b) What is the ratio of typical sequences to nontypical sequences?

    (c) What is the probability of a typical sequence?

    (d) What is the number of bits required to represent only typical sequences?

    (e) What is the most probable sequence, and what is its probability?

18. For a source with a sample space $\{a_0, a_1, a_2, a_3, a_4, a_5, a_6\}$ and with corresponding probabilities $\{0.55, 0.10, 0.05, 0.14, 0.06, 0.08, 0.02\}$

    (a) Design a Huffman encoder.

    (b) Find the code efficiency.

19. A voice information source can be modeled as a band-limited process with a bandwidth of 4,000 Hz. This process is sampled at the Nyquist rate. In order to provide a guard band to this source, 200 Hz is added to the bandwidth for which a Nyquist rate is not needed. It is observed that the resulting samples take values in the set $\{-3, -2, -1, 0, 2, 3, 5\}$, with probabilities $\{0.05, 0.1, 0.1, 0.15, 0.05, 0.25, 0.3\}$.

    (a) What is the entropy of the discrete time source in bits/output?

    (b) What is the entropy in b/s?

    (c) Design a Huffman encoder.

    (d) Find the compression ratio and code efficiency for part (c).

20. Design a Lempel-Ziv encoder for the following source sequence:

$$0101000010001111100101010111101001 0101010$$

21. Design a Lempel-Ziv encoder for the following source sequence:

    111110001010101011101111100010101010001111010100001

19.10   Computer Simulation Project

1. *Computational Simulation of a JPEG Compression Processor.* Using a
   computer program, implement Equation (19.15) to obtain a $T[i][j]$ matrix for a
   JPEG compression process. Make any reasonable assumption or image size for
   your computational experiment.

CHAPTER 20

Distributed and Cloud-Based Multimedia Networking

The discussion in the previous chapter on compressed voice and video sets the stage for the discussion in this chapter on *multimedia networking*. Internet phone services have numerous features, such as videoconferencing, online directory services, and Web incorporation. Multimedia networking is one of the most effective Internet developments. In addition to data, the Internet is used to transport phone calls, audio, and video in a distributed fashion. Video streaming presents a real challenge to network designers. A video in a single server can be streamed from a video server to a client at the client's request. High-bit-rate video streaming must sometimes pass through many Internet service providers (ISPs), leading to the likelihood of significant delay and loss in the video. One practical solution to this challenge is to utilize *content distribution networks* (CDNs) as a means of distributing stored multimedia content. This chapter looks at the transportation of real-time data and protocols used in voice telephony, video streaming, and multimedia networking, covering the following major topics:

- *Real-time media exchange protocols*
- *Distributed multimedia networking*

- *Cloud-based multimedia networking*
- *Self-similarity and non-Markovian streaming analysis*

This chapter focuses on transport mechanisms for the delivery of media streams with the highest possible quality. After reviewing how sampled and digitized streams of voice are treated in networks, we present *real-time media exchange protocols*, by which a sender sends a stream of data at a constant rate. The most widely applied such protocols are the *Real-time Transport Protocol* (RTP) *Real-time Transport Control Protocol* (RTCP), *Real Time Streaming Protocol* (RTSP), *HTTP-based streaming*, and *Stream Control Transmission Protocol* (SCTP).

The details of distributed and cloud-based multimedia networking are the next topics of discussion. We start by presenting a well-known scheme called *content distribution networks* (CDNs), which can bring multimedia content to users more efficiently. We then proceed to a description of *Internet Protocol television* (IPTV), a system through which television services are delivered using packet-switched networks or the Internet. *Video on demand* (VoD), a unique feature of IPTV, allows users to select and view movies or programs over the Internet whenever they choose. Online gaming as another example of distributed multimedia networking is also covered in this section of the chapter.

Next, cloud-based multimedia networking is introduced. This type of networking consists of distributed and networked services for voice, video, and data. For example, voice over IP (VoIP), video streaming, or *interactive voice response* (IVR), which allows human voice and computer interaction, can be distributed in various clouds of services.

The chapter ends with a detailed model and analysis of source streaming and modeling traffic patterns in source streaming using *self-similarity* patterns.

20.1   Real-Time Media Exchange Protocols

In real-time applications, a *stream* of data must ideally be sent at a constant rate. Streaming a video file or an object can be categorized in one of the following forms:

- *Prerecorded media streaming*
- *Live media streaming*

In *prerecorded media streaming*, such as the ones seen on YouTube, the media contents are stored on servers. One can think in terms of streaming a stored music concert or a movie to be watched online. A user can search for a content file, such as a video file, by sending a request to the servers to view the contents. Therefore, in prerecorded media streaming, a user begins the content file playout shortly after the arrival of the media file content from the server, and while the content plays out at the user side, the user receives the later parts of the content from the server. This way, the user does not need to download the entire file at once.

Live media streaming allows a user to receive a *live* audio/video or data program streamed from one location to another location(s) such as when television programs are broadcast over the Internet. Because live media streaming is by nature any a live event transmission, delay is the main factor that degrades the quality of broadcasting.

Depending on whether the streaming is prerecorded or live, media streaming is delivered to the appropriate application on the destination system using one of the following widely applied real-time media exchange protocols:

- *Real-time Transport Protocol* (RTP)
- *Real-time Transport Control Protocol* (RTCP)
- *Real Time Streaming Protocol* (RTSP)
- *Stream Control Transmission Protocol* (SCTP)
- *HTTP-Based Streaming*

A real-time media exchange protocol is set up on top of either UDP or TCP as appropriate and suitable for the objective of the streaming. Although a TCP transport method guarantees no packet loss in a streaming session, the developing packet delay in TCP connections that results from the connection-oriented nature of TCP may not be a suitable method of transport for all kinds of streaming applications. Furthermore, real-time applications may use multicasting for data delivery. As an end-to-end protocol, TCP is not suited for multicast distribution and some real-time applications cannot afford such delays. These protocols are described in the next sections.

20.1.1   Real-Time Transport Protocol (RTP)

The *Real-time Transport Protocol* (RTP) provides basic functionality to real-time applications and includes some specific functions to each application. RTP typically runs on top of the transport protocol UDP. As noted in Chapter 8, UDP is used as a connectionless transport protocol. UDP is also used for functions such as datagram (packet) reordering.

RTP provides application-level framing of real-time data by adding application-layer headers to datagrams. The application breaks the data into smaller units, called *application data units* (ADUs). Lower layers in the protocol stack, such as the transport layer, preserve the structure of the ADU. The size of ADU is usually determined by the type of codec as described in the preceding chapter, or by the amount of tolerable delay for the application. However, large ADUs span multiple packets, and hence the loss of a packet containing a partial ADU causes the entire ADU to be discarded.

Real-time applications, such as voice and video, can tolerate a certain amount of packet loss and do not always require data retransmission. The mechanism RTP uses typically informs a source about the quality of delivery. The source then adapts its sending rate accordingly. If the rate of packet loss is very high, the source might switch to a lower-quality transmission, thereby placing less traffic load on the network. A real-time application can also provide the data required for retransmission. Thus, recent data can be sent instead of retransmitted old data. This approach is more practical in voice and video applications. If a portion of an ADU is lost, the application is unable to process the data, and the entire ADU would have to be retransmitted.

Real-Time Session

The TCP/IP models divide the network functions, based on a layered architecture. Each layer performs distinct functions, and the data flows sequentially between layers. The layered architecture may restrict the implementation of certain functions out of the layered order. RTP is used to transfer data among *sessions* in real time. A session is a logical connection between an active client and an active server and is defined by the following entities:

- *RTP port number*, which represents the destination port address of the RTP session. Since RTP runs over UDP, the destination port address is available on the UDP header.
- *IP address* of the RTP entity, which involves an RTP session. This address can be either a unicast or a multicast address.

RTP uses two relays for data transmission. A *relay* is an intermediate system that acts as both a sender and a receiver. Suppose that two systems are separated by a firewall that prevents them from direct communication. A relay in this context is used to handle data flow between the two systems. A relay can also be used to convert the data format from a system into a form that the other system can process easily. Relays are of two types: *mixer* and *translator*.

A *mixer relay* is an RTP relay that combines the data from two or more RTP entities into a single stream of data. A mixer can either retain or change the data format. The mixer provides timing information for the combined stream of data and acts as the source of timing synchronization. Mixers can be used to combine audio streams in real-time applications and can be used to service systems that may not be able to handle multiple RTP streams.

The *translator* is a device that generates one or more RTP packets for each incoming RTP packet. The format of the outgoing packet may be different from that of the incoming packet. A *translator relay* can be used in video applications in which a high-quality video signal is converted to a lower-quality signal in order to service receivers that support a lower data rate. Such a relay can also be used to transfer packets between RTP entities separated by an application-level firewall. Translators can sometimes be used to transfer an incoming multicast packet to multiple destinations.

RTP Packet Header

RTP contains a fixed header and an application-specific, variable-length header field. Figure 20.1 shows the RTP header format. Overall, the main part of an RTP header includes 12 bytes and is appended to a packet being prepared for multimedia application. The RTP header fields are:

- *Version* (V), a 2-bit field indicating the protocol version.

- *Padding* (P), a 1-bit field that indicates the existence of a padding field at the end of the payload. Padding is required in applications in which the payload is supposed to be a multiple of a certain predefined length.

- *Extension* (X), a 1-bit field indicating the use of an extension header for RTP.

- *Contributing source count* (CC), a 4-bit field that indicates the number of contributing source identifiers.

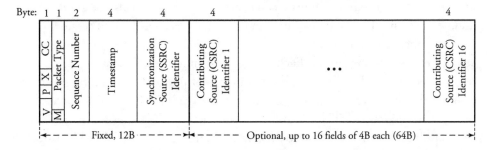

Figure 20.1   Packet header format for the Real-time Transport Protocol (RTP)

- *Marker* (M), a 1-bit field indicating boundaries in a stream of data traffic. For video applications, this field can be used to indicate the end of a frame.

- *Payload type*, a 7-bit field specifying the type of RTP payload. This field also contains information on the use of compression or encryption.

- *Sequence number*, a 16-bit field that a sender uses to identify a particular packet within a sequence of packets.

- *Timestamp*, a 32-bit field enabling the receiver to recover timing information. This field indicates the timestamp of when the first byte of data in the payload was generated.

- *Synchronization source* (SSRC) *identifier,* a randomly generated field used to identify the RTP source in an RTP session.

- *Contributing source* (CSRC) *identifier,* an optional field in the header to indicate the contributing sources for the data. There can be up to 16 contributing sources, CSRC_1 through CSRC_16.

RTP does not guarantee the delivery of a particular packet, but the presence of the *sequence number* field makes it possible to detect missing packets. The sequence number in the RTP header is used by a receiver to detect packet loss and to restore packet sequence. The initial value of this sequence number is selected at random to make network attacks on encryption more difficult. Note that RTP does not deploy any action on packet loss, and indeed leaves this task to the application layer to take appropriate action. In video streaming, for example, video applications may execute the last known packet in place of a missing packet.

During an RTP session, there may be a situation in which multiple sources of a media stream are present. In such situations, the SSRC field is a randomly generated value used to uniquely identify the contributing source in an RTP session. SSRC identifies the source of a media stream. If a source chooses the same SSRC as the one chosen by another source, it must change its SSRC. There can also be another situation during an RTP session in which multiple sources contribute to create a single source of media stream. Because of this, CSRC fields enumerate the contributing sources to a streaming media. Each CSRC field indicates the contributing source of a media stream. This field expresses an array of up to 16 contributing sources, numbered 1 to 16. The contributing source count (CC) field identifies the number of contributing sources. The CC content is inserted by mixers, using the SSRCs of the contributing sources. For audio packets, for example, the SSRC field identifies by listing all sources that were mixed together to create a packet.

In the preceding situations of multiple contributing sources, the *timestamp* field also acts independently in each media stream. The timestamp provides a sampling instant of the first byte in the payload. The sampling instant must be derived from a clock that allows synchronization and jitter calculations. A jitter analysis for the RTP sessions is presented in the following section. The clock frequency depends on the format of the payload. For a source with periodically generated RTP packets, the sampling instant is specified using the sampling clock, and not through a reading of the system clock. For example, in a fixed-rate voice transmission, the timestamp clock ticks in each sampling period.

20.1.2 Analysis of Jitter in RTP Traffic

The jitter factor is a measure of the delay experienced by RTP packets in a given session. The average jitter can be estimated at the receiver. Let us define the following parameters at the receiver:

t_i Timestamp of the RTP data packet i indicated by the source.

a_i Arrival time of the RTP data packet i at the receiver.

d_i Measure of difference between the interarrival time of RTP packets at the receiver and the one for packet departure from the source. This value represents the difference in packet spacing at the source and receiver.

$E[i]$ Estimated average jitter until the time of packet i arrival.

The difference interval d_i is given by

$$d_i = (a_i - a_{i-1}) - (t_i - t_{i-1}). \qquad (20.1)$$

The estimated average jitter until the time of packet i arrival is given by

$$E[i] = k(E[i-1] + |d_i|), \qquad (20.2)$$

where k is a normalizing coefficient. The interarrival jitter value indicated in the sender report provides useful information on network conditions to the sender and the receiver. The jitter value can be used as an estimate to calculate the variation of network congestion.

RTP packet-sequence numbers are used to help a receiver sequence packets in order to recover lost packets. When packets arrive out of order at the receiver, the sequence number can be used to assemble data packets. Consider Figure 20.2. When certain packets are lost, the gaps are filled in with previously received data packets.

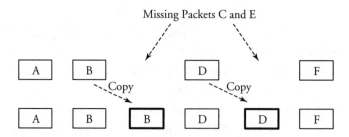

Figure 20.2   Missing voice packets and reconstructing the real-time data stream

As shown in the figure, packet D is replayed twice, since packet C is lost. This mechanism can help reduce the pops and clicks in voice signals owing to lost packets. This reconstructed data stream is sent to the receiver, with the lost packets replaced by previously received packets. This can significantly improve the latency.

20.1.3   Real-Time Transport Control Protocol (RTCP)

The *Real-time Transport Control Protocol* (RTCP) also runs on top of UDP. RTCP performs several functions, using unicasting or multicasting to provide feedback about the data quality to all session members. The session multicast members can thus get an estimate of the performance of other members in the current active session. Senders can send reports about data rates and the quality of data transmission. Receivers can send information about packet-loss rate, jitter variations, and any other problems they might encounter. Feedback from a receiver can also enable a sender to diagnose a fault. A sender can isolate a problem to a single RTP entity or a global problem by looking at the reports from all receivers.

RTCP Packet Type and Format

RTCP transmits control information by combining a number of RTCP packets in a single UDP datagram. The RTCP packet types are *sender reports* (SR), *receiver reports* (RR), *source descriptor* (SDES), *goodbye* (BYE), and *application-specific types*. Figure 20.3 shows the RTCP packet header format. The fields common to all packet types are as follows:

- *Version* (V), a 2-bit field that indicates the current version.
- *Padding* (P), a 1-bit field that indicates the existence of padding bytes at the end of the control data.

Byte: 1   1   2   2   8   4   4   4   4   1   3   2   4   4   4

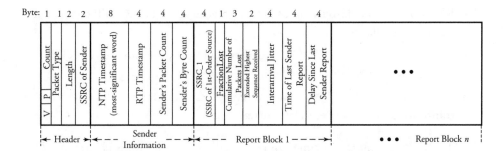

Figure 20.3   Format of the SR packet header in RTCP

- *Count*, a 5-bit field that indicates the number of sender reports and receiver reports or the number of source items in the SDES packet.

- *Packet type*, an 8-bit field that indicates the type of RTCP packet. (Four RTCP packet types were specified earlier.)

- *Length*, a 16-bit field that represents the length of packet in 32-bit words minus 1.

- *Synchronization source* (SSRC) *identifier*, a field common to the SR and RR packet types; it indicates the source of the RTCP packets.

RTCP performs *source identification*. RTCP packets contain some information to identify the source of the control packet. The rate of RTCP packets must also be kept to less than 5 percent of the total session traffic. Thus, this protocol carries out "rate control" of RTCP packets. At the same time, all session members must be able to evaluate the performance of all other session members. As the number of active members in a session increases, the transmission rates of the control packets must be reduced. RTCP is also responsible for *session control* and can provide some session-control information, if necessary.

Figure 20.3 also shows a typical format of a sender report field. The report consists of the common header fields and a block of sender information. The sender report may also contain zero or more receiver report blocks, as shown in the figure. The fields in the sender information block are:

- *Network time protocol* (NTP) *timestamp*, a 64-bit field that indicates when a sender report was sent. The sender can use this field in combination with the timestamp field returned in receiver reports to estimate the round-trip delay to receivers.

- RTP *timestamp*, a 32-bit field used by a receiver to sequence RTP data packets from a particular source.
- *Sender's packet count*, a 32-bit field that represents the number of RTP data packets transmitted by the sender in the current session.
- *Sender's byte count*, a 32-bit field that represents the number of RTP data octets transmitted by the sender in the current session.

The NTP *timestamp* is a timestamp created by a sender for each stream. This timestamp is the a common timebase used for all media transmitted by a sending endpoint. A separate timestamp, called RTP *timestamp*, is also used by RTCP for the sender to synchronize any combination of media streams. For example, if a sender transmits five video streams and all must be synchronized without accompanying audio stream, RTP timestamp synchronizes them collectively. The SR packet includes zeros or more RR blocks. One receiver block is included for each sender from which the member has received data during the session. The RR block includes the following fields:

- SSRC_*i*(*synchronization source i identifier*), a 32-bit field that identifies the source in the report block, where $0 \leq i \leq n$ is the source number assuming there are n sources.
- *Fraction lost*, an 8-bit field indicating the fraction of data packet loss from source SSRC_*i* since the last SR or RR report was sent.
- *Cumulative number of packets lost*, a 24-bit field that represents the total number of RTP data packets lost from the source in the current active session identified by SSRC_*n*.
- *Extended highest sequence number received*, the first 16 least-significant bits, used to indicate the highest sequence number for packets received from source SSRC_*n*. The first 16 most-significant bits indicate the number of times that the sequence number has been wrapped back to zero.
- *Interarrival jitter*, a 32-bit field used to indicate the jitter variations at the receiver for the source SSRC_*i*.
- *Last* SR *timestamp*, a 32-bit field indicating the timestamp for the last SR packet received from the source SSRC_*i*.
- *Delay since last* SR, a 32-bit field indicating the delay between the arrival time of the last SR packet from the source SSRC_*i* and the transmission of the current report block.

Receivers in RTCP can provide feedback about the quality of reception through a receiver report. A receiver that is also a sender during a session also sends the sender reports.

20.1.4   Real Time Streaming Protocol (RTSP)

The *Real Time Streaming Protocol* (RTSP) is another real-time communication protocol designed to control streaming media servers. The protocol is used for establishing and controlling media sessions between clients and video servers. Clients of media servers issue commands, such as play and pause, to facilitate real-time control of media content streamed from a media server. Note that the transmission of streaming media itself is not carried out by the RTSP protocol. A decent setup for a media stream delivery server enables it to use RTSP and the Real-time Transport Protocol (RTP) in conjunction with the Real-time Transport Control Protocol (RTCP). Unlike HTTP, RTSP is stateful where an identifier is assigned as needed to track concurrent sessions. RTSP uses TCP for end-to-end connections, hence it introduces higher network bandwidth usage in exchange for better reliability. The default transport layer port number is 554 for TCP. The majority of RTSP control messages are sent by the client to the server.

20.1.5   Stream Control Transmission Protocol (SCTP)

The *Stream Control Transmission Protocol* (SCTP) provides a general-purpose transport protocol for message-oriented applications. SCTP is a reliable transport protocol for transporting stream traffic, can operate on top of unreliable connectionless networks, and offers acknowledged and nonduplicated transmission data on connectionless networks (datagrams). SCTP has the following features:

- The protocol is error free. A retransmission scheme is applied to compensate for loss or corruption of the datagram, using checksums and sequence numbers.

- It has ordered and unordered delivery modes.

- SCTP has effective methods to avoid flooding congestion and masquerade attacks.

- This protocol is *multipoint* and allows several streams within a connection.

In many ways SCTP outperforms TCP when used in video streaming. In TCP, a stream is a sequence of bytes; in SCTP, a sequence of variable-sized messages. SCTP services are placed at the same layer as TCP or UDP services.

Streaming data is first encapsulated into packets, and each packet carries several correlated chunks of streaming details. If an MPEG movie is displayed live over the Internet, a careful assignment of data per packet is required. An MPEG video consists of frames, each consisting of $n \times m$ pixel blocks, with each pixel block normally an 8×8 matrix of pixels. In this case, each block of pixels can be encapsulated into a chunk of an SCTP packet, where each row of the pixel block is formatted as a packet.

SCTP Packet Structure

Figure 20.4 shows the structure of streaming packets used in SCTP. An SCTP packet is also called a *protocol data unit* (PDU). As soon as the streaming data is ready to be transmitted over IP, an SCTP packet forms the payload of an IP packet. Each packet consists of a *common header* and *chunks*. The streaming data is distributed over packets, and each packet carries correlated "chunks" of streaming data. Multiple chunks representing multiple portions of streaming information are in fact multiplexed into one packet up to the path-maximum packet size.

A chunk header starts with a chunk *type* field used to distinguish data chunks and any other types of control chunks. The *type* field is followed by a *flag* field and a chunk *length* field to indicate the chunk size. A chunk, and therefore a packet, may contain either control information or user data. The common header begins with the *source port number* followed by the *destination port number*. SCTP uses the

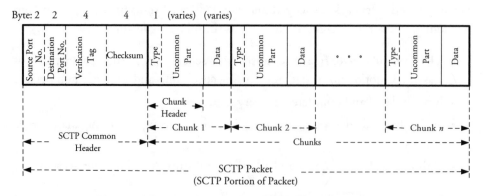

Figure 20.4 The structure of packets in the Stream Control Transmission Protocol (SCTP). Streaming data is encapsulated into packets and each packet carries several correlated chunks of streaming details.

same port concept as TCP or UDP does. A 32-bit *verification tag* field is exchanged between the endpoint servers at startup to verify the two servers involved. Thus, two tag values are used in a connection. The common header consists of 12 bytes. SCTP packets are protected by a 32-bit checksum. The level of protection is more robust than the 16-bit checksum of TCP and UDP.

Chunk Header Format

Each packet has *n* chunks, and each chunk is of two types: a *data chunk* for transmitting actual streaming data and *control chunks* for signaling and control. Figure 20.5 shows the structure of a Type-0 chunk where the Type-0 chunk is a data chunk. Control chunks are of several different types, as follows:

- *INIT*, to initiate an SCTP session between two endpoints
- *INIT-ACK*, to acknowledge the initiation of an SCTP session
- *SELECTIVE ACK*, to be transmitted to a peer endpoint to acknowledge received data chunks
- *HEARTBEAT REQUEST*, to probe the reachability of a particular destination transport address defined in the session
- *HEARTBEAT-ACK,* to respond to the HEARTBEAT REQUEST chunk
- *ABORT,* to close a session
- *OPERATION ERROR*, to notify the other party of a certain error

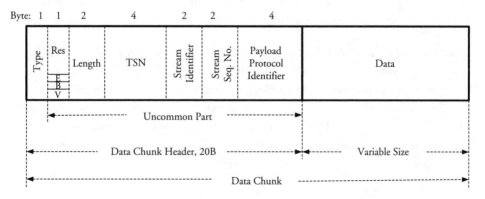

Figure 20.5   An overview of a data chunk (Type-0 chunk)

- *COOKIE-ECHO*, sent by the source to its peer to complete the initialization process
- *COOKIE-ACK*, to acknowledge receipt of a COOKIE chunk
- *SHUTDOWN*, to initiate a graceful close of a session
- *SHUTDOWN-ACK*, to acknowledge receipt of the SHUTDOWN chunk once the shutdown process is completed
- *SHUTDOWN COMPLETE*, to acknowledge receipt of the SHUTDOWN-ACK chunk at the completion of the shutdown process

SCTP Signaling and Comparison with TCP

Figure 20.6 shows a client/server call establishment and call termination for scenarios for both TCP and SCTP cases. A call establishment with TCP is a three-way handshake process, requiring SYN, SYN+ACK, and ACK segments to be exchanged, as we learned in Chapter 8. In contrast, a call establishment with SCTP requires a four-way handshake process starting with transmission of an *INIT* chunk by the client to initiate an SCTP session between the client and server. The server then acknowledges the initiation of the SCTP session by sending the *INIT-ACK* chunk. The client at this point generates a *COOKIE-ECHO* chunk to complete the initialization process, and thereby the server acknowledges the completion of this process by sending a *COOKIE-ACK* chunk.

After this four-way handshake process, data can be transmitted. The connection termination process for TCP and SCTP is also compared in Figure 20.6. As learned for TCP, a call termination is a three-way handshake process, requiring FIN, FIN+ACK, and ACK segments to be exchanged. A call termination with SCTP also requires a three-way handshake process starting with transmission of a SHUTDOWN chunk.

Example.   Suppose we want to stream a compressed video clip using SCTP. Each frame of the video clip contains 1000×1000 pixel blocks (refer to Chapter 19 for a definition of pixel block). A pixel block is compressed to an average of 70 bits and occupies one chunk of an SCTP packet. We also know that a partial row of each image frame fits into one SCTP packet as shown in Figure 20.7, and thus the entire one image frame of the video is carried by as many SCTP packets as the number of frame rows. Estimate the number SCTP packets generated as a result of this video streaming.

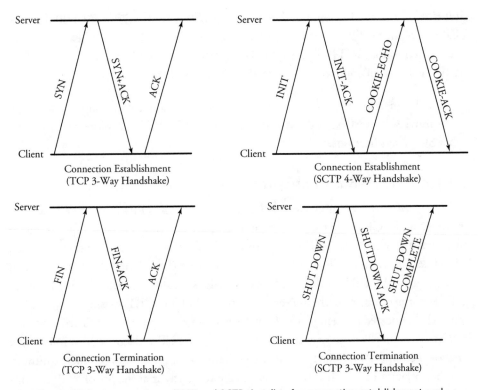

Figure 20.6   A comparison of TCP and SCTP signaling for connection establishment and connection termination

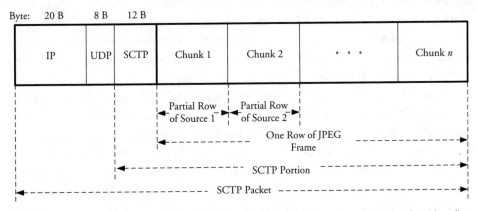

Figure 20.7   An example of an SCTP packet carrying rows of an image frame as part of a video clip

Solution.   The total amount of data in each packet is $1000 \times 70 = 70,000$ bits. The total size of an SCTP packet is therefore 70,000 plus 20 bytes of IP header plus 12 bytes of common SCTP header plus 1000×16 bytes of all chunk headers. This results in a total of approximately 24KB of SCTP packet.

SCTP can easily and effectively be used to broadcast live video clips or full-color video movies. The SCTP exercises at the end of this chapter explore further some other SCTP applications.

20.1.6   HTTP-Based Streaming

HTTP-based streaming uses two well-known protocols: HTTP as the application protocol, and TCP as the transport protocol. In this method of streaming, a content file, such as a video file, is first saved in an HTTP server. The file is then assigned a URL as discussed in Chapter 9. A user can browse the Internet for this file or can directly enter the URL of the file. Once the file is located, the use's browser creates a TCP connection with the server through an HTTP GET message. The server sends the requested content in an HTTP Response message. The user's browser then receives bytes of the content according to the rule of TCP and stores them in its *client application buffer*. The playback of the content can start as soon as the minimum number of bytes has reached the buffer. It is noteworthy that the use of TCP streaming allows the video to pass through firewalls and NATs without any issue.

The packet (segment) delay in TCP connections results from the connection-oriented nature of TCP, especially the TCP's congestion avoidance mechanism. This issue has been resolved to some extent when data storage at the client application buffer is deployed. The HTTP server transmits a content file at a rate by which it knows the file requires to be played out. At the client side, the browser needs to download the content file at a higher rate than the user uses to play out the content, called the display bit rate. In most cases, the hosts' browsers are programmed in such a way so that if the capacity of the client application buffer is larger than the requested content file, then the entire content file is downloaded from the server to the client application buffer after which there is no need for streaming the content file.

If a pause action occurs during a streaming session by a user, the stored data in the client application buffer are not erased from the client application buffer. In such cases, the buffer continues to receive the later pieces of the content file and ultimately becomes full, thereby the *client TCP receive buffer* and the *client TCP send buffer* also become full. The TCP connection can clearly detect this capacity overflow of its buffers and informs the HTTP server to stop transmitting. Another situation that might occur is that the display freezes. This happens if the arrival rate to the client application buffer is less than the client display rate exactly when the client application buffers become empty.

20.2 Distributed Multimedia Networking

We can now proceed to the networking aspects of multimedia. Video streaming presents a significant challenge to network designers. The challenge may appear in a situation in which a video in a single server needs to be streamed from a video server to a client at the client's request, or a television program or an online game is required to be transmitted over the IP infrastructure. The high-bit-rate video streaming must sometimes pass through many Internet service providers, leading to the likelihood of significant delay and loss on the video. This section covers the following solutions to such challenges:

- *Content distribution (delivery) networks* (CDNs)
- *Internet Protocol television* (IPTV) and *video on demand* (VoD)
- *Online gaming*

Note that any of such distributed multimedia networking solutions must use one of the five real-time media exchange protocols described in Section 2.1: RTP, RTCP, RTSP, SCTP, and HTTP-based streaming. In the next sections, the details of the above distributed multimedia networking solutions are presented.

20.2.1 Content Distribution (Delivery) Networks (CDNs)

A *content distribution (or delivery) network* (CDN) is a group of proxy servers located at a certain strategic location around an Internet service provider. CDNs ensure that a download request can always be handled from the nearest server. With CDNs, the content of streaming is geographically brought to a user unable to access the content at the desired data rate in the original location. Therefore, a user deals with *content providers*, such as private TV broadcast companies, not ISPs. The content provider hires a CDN company to deliver its content (streaming video) to the user. This does not mean that a CDN company cannot expose its server to ISPs.

A CDN company has several CDN server centers around the Internet. Each group of servers is installed in proximity to ISP access points. At the request of a user, the content is provided by the closest branch server of the CDN company that can best deliver the content. The CDN company also owns a *content control server*.

The content control server has the updated list of content existing in the CDN servers and their URLs. Once in a while, the list of available content in CDN servers must be updated by the content control server. Once a host requests content such as a video clip, the browser of the host is redirected onto the content control server in order to provide the host the URL of the best CDN location. This URL needs to be resolved later to an IP address by which the host can communicate with the CDN server to stream the content. The following is a four-step video streaming algorithm from a CDN server:

Begin CDN Algorithm

1. **Select content**

   – The client browses and selects the desired content from the Web page of the content owned by a content owner.

   – The content servers redirect the Web page to the content control server of a CDN company who can provide the content.

2. **Obtain URL of CDN server**

   – The content control server returns the URL of the CDN server that contains the desired content to client.

3. **Resolve URL to obtain IP address**

   – The client queries the DNS server or uses another approach to find the IP address of the CDN server containing the desired content.

4. **Stream content**

   – The client uses the IP address and the application software to connect to the CDN server and stream the desired content. ■

Example. Figure 20.8 shows a content streaming session performed by a client. In ISP 1, a movie making company with Web site www.filmmaker.com owns a variety of movies. These movies are leased by a CDN company with the Web site www.cdnco.com for rent on line. The host wishes to watch a movie named movie1.mpg from this company. Therefore, this video file has a reference of www.filmmaker.com/movies/movie1.mpg. The host first browses on the Internet for this movie as indicated in the preceding algorithm and shown in the figure by step 1. The CDN company has a *content control server*. The content control server is a server that has URLs of movies installed on its CDN servers for rent on the Internet. Now, since the CDN company interacting with the movie making company is accessed through www.cdnco.com, it must replace this reference with the one affected by the CDN company's URL domain name as www.cdnco.com/www.filmmaker.

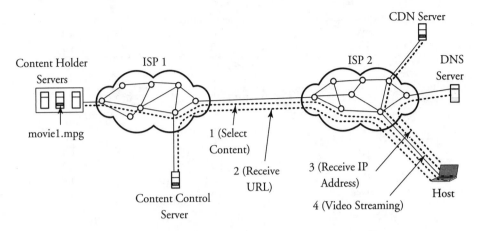

Figure 20.8   An example of video streaming provided to a host in the ISP 2 domain engaging a content control server, Domain Name System (DNS) server, and CDN server

com/movies/movie1.mpg. The client's browser learns now that whenever it selects movie1 at the previous link, it is directed to the CDN's content control server at www.cdnco2.com. The content control server finds the CDN server in the ISP 2 domain near the client with URL www.cdnco2.com and forwards it to the client (step 2). At this point, the host queries the DNS server to find the IP address of the URL. Once the IP address is resolved, the client host can communicate with the CDN server located in a place with minimal congestion, and stream the content using the appropriate software (step 4).

Methods of Resolving a URL

Up to this point, we have learned that in any streaming process, the URL of the targeted CDN server must first be resolved to obtain an IP address before a host can communicate with the CDN server identified by the URL. There are three methods of finding the IP address of the CDN server. As shown in Figure 20.9 (a), the first method requires the host to receive the URL of the CDN server (step 2), and then resolve it separately through the DNS server (steps 3 and 4).

Figure 20.9 (b) depicts the second method of URL resolution. In this method, the content control server contacts the DNS server ahead of time and acquires the potential IP addresses of the CDN servers (dashed lines). Then, the content control server uploads the list of URLs and IP addresses to the host browser (dashed lines). This way, when the host queries for content (step 1), it receives the corresponding URL (step 2), but it does not need to resolve the URL through the DNS server since the host now has a database through which it can resolve the URL by itself (step 3).

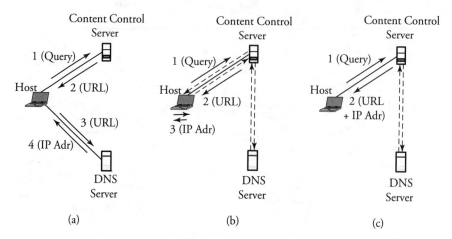

Figure 20.9   Three methods of resolving the URL of the CDN server to obtain the IP address

In Figure 20.9 (c), we see yet another method of URL resolution. In this method, after the host queries the URL of the desired content (step 1), the IP address of the targeted CDN server is integrated into the URL of the CDN server (step 2). Thus, the client in this case must only be instructed through its software as to how this IP address needs to be extracted form the URL. As seen in the figure, in order to implement this third method, the content control server must always get the latest IP address updates from the DNS server from time to time (dashed lines).

Example.   In the third method of resolving a URL, if the URL and IP address of the targeted CDN server having the desired movie named movie1.mpg are http://www.cdnco2.com and 166.1.2.1, respectively, the response of the content control server in step 2 would be a URL that looks like: http://www.cdnco2.com/movie1.mpg/166.1.2.1. The application software loaded in the host for streaming must then be enabled to distinguish and extract the IP address 166.1.2.1 from the URL.

Providing QoS to Streaming

Consider Figure 20.10 illustrating ISPs 1, 2, and 3, in which host 1, host 2, and host 3 all belonging to ISP 3 are using the Internet simultaneously. Host 1 is communicating with a public e-mail server and requires small bandwidth. Host 2 is searching for documents in a public library archive server and requires a non-real-time but modest bandwidth. Host 3 is using a video streaming service from a CDN server and

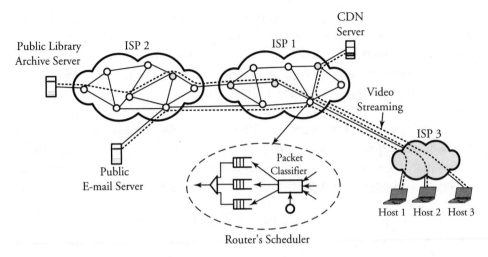

Figure 20.10 Providing QoS at the main router connected to an Internet service provider

requires substantial high-quality bandwidth. Packet flows from these hosts need to be scheduled as shown in the main router between the LAN and ISP 1.

Video streaming, e-mail, and document packets in the best-effort Internet are mixed in the output queue of the main exit router of a domain. Under such circumstances, a burst of packets, primarily from the image file source, could cause IP video streaming packets to be excessively delayed or lost at the router. One solution in this case is to mark each packet as to which class of traffic it belongs to. This can be done by using the type-of-service (ToS) field in IPv4 packets. As seen in the figure, transmitted packets are first classified in terms of their priorities and are queued in a first in, first out (FIFO) order. The priority of an image file can be equal to or less than the one for video streaming, owing to the arrangement of purchased services.

20.2.2 IP Television (IPTV) and VoD

Internet Protocol television (IPTV) is a television content distribution service delivered over the Internet. IPTV is implemented either over multicast services or *video on demand* (VoD) unicast services. IPTV allows its customers who are in various locations geographically to watch a movie together, while also using the Internet for other purposes simultaneously. IPTV requires that video content from each channel turn into a stream of encoded data encapsulated into IP packets. An Internet service provider can deliver TV channels either live or in a stored video format, and bundle it with other Internet services, including VoIP and high-speed Internet access.

Non-VoD IPTV services are characterized by efficient transport of television channels over a packet-switched network using multicast protocols. The multicast function in fact reduces utilization of network links between the video server and the customer as only a single copy of a media stream is sent into the network. The network then replicates the stream to individual subscribers far enough from the source and thus saves bandwidth in the core.

Besides the use of the Internet in IPTV broadcasting systems, there is another fundamental difference between traditional television delivery and IPTV delivery. In traditional TV broadcast systems such as the cable TV system, all TV programs are broadcast simultaneously so that the TV program signals flow downstream and a viewer selects a TV program. In IPTV broadcast systems, only one TV program is sent at a time while the content remains on the ISP's network and only the program the viewer selects is sent to the viewer's receiver. The viewer's receiver is called a *set-top box*. When a viewer chooses a channel, a new stream of IP packets is transmitted from the ISP's server directly to the viewer. Note, however, that in certain circumstances, multicasting in IPTV is also part of the functionality of the system and is not inevitable in cases where multiple users are watching the same channel.

It is worth mentioning at this point that there has been considerable research toward reducing the channel change time by using predictive techniques to pre-stream a few additional channels in cases where excess unused bandwidth exists.

IPTV Architecture

Figure 20.11 shows an overview of an IPTV operation block diagram consisting four main segments: *headend*, *core network*, *access network*, and *home network*.

The *headend* refers to the IPTV broadcasting headquarters of TV signal transmitting and receiving facilities of an ISP. A headend typically consists of TV signal receiving *cloud-based content servers* and their content. This is the primary source for video content in an IPTV network. Functions such as content capturing, encoding, signal conditioning and processing, media preparation, and formatting the data for distribution are done at this segment. In this segment the main video content arrives from various television companies through different communication systems such as satellite microwave, cellular networks, or other IP sources in encrypted, modulated, and aggregated form. This form of data is called *digital video broadcasting* (DVB) and is an internationally accepted open standard. The content servers encode the video stream and encapsulate it into IP packets ready for transmission over the network. The encapsulated IP packets are forwarded over a wide-area, Internet-based broadband network called the *core network* in the IPTV block diagram.

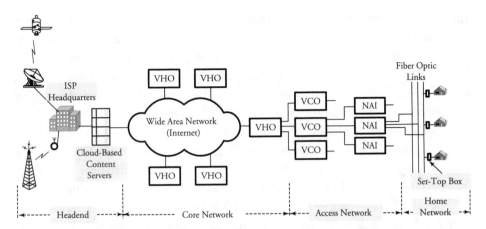

Figure 20.11   Overview of an Internet Protocol television (IPTV) system

The *core network* is the backbone for IPTV broadcasters. It consists of a high–bandwidth, packet-switched wide area network (WAN) equipped with a series of *video hub offices* (VHOs). A VHO transmits (and multicasts when needed) IPTV traffic received from the headend to the access network. It may have certain provisions for insertion of local content and also certain policies for maintaining the bandwidth demands. It is quite understandable that due to the high rate traffic through VHOs, fiber-optic technologies are necessary in the entire wide area network architecture. Given our discussion in Chapter 6 about multicasting, we can now understand that users of IPTV simply form a multicast group according to the TV channels they select. The job of multicast is performed either by routers or designated servers in the network or both. In either way, the multicast must be performed close enough to the users to prevent waste of bandwidth in the network. The multicast protocol in the core network is usually *Protocol-Independent Multicast* (PIM), described in Chapter 6.

The access network, also called the last-mile network, is the interfacing network between the core network and the subscriber home networks. The IPTV packets travel from the access network over this high-bandwidth network using video central offices (VCOs). Each VCO routes data to video network access interfaces (NAIs). NAIs are the interface between the optical fiber technologies of the access network and the existing home facilities such as the copper or cable line technologies used for signal delivery. Some ISPs use a fiber-to-the-home based access network architecture directly making use of fiber technology. In such cases, the TV content packets are first transmitted over active optical fiber networks and then sent over passive optical networks (PONs), which are comparatively inexpensive to implement. A PON is a point-to-multipoint, fiber-based access network as described in Chapter 15. Point-to-multipoint in this context refers to broadcasting downstream signals to all premises sharing multiple fibers. A typical PON consists of a central office node, which is a switching node called an optical line terminal (OLT), the optical fibers and splitters in between, and a number of user nodes called optical network units (ONUs). The advantage of using a PON is the reduction in the number of fibers and the volume of central office equipment required compared with point-to-point architectures. The upstream signals must be combined together using a multiple access protocol. The multiple access protocol of choice is typically time division multiple access (TDMA), explained in Chapter 3.

The home network delivers IPTV packet flows to users. Users can have a variety of receiving devices such as TVs or laptop computers to view a TV program. Depending on the technology used in the home network, a user must have a receiver box, known as a set-top box(STB), to process and decode the received packets to digital TV signals. An STB recognizes IP datagrams and transmits customer channel requests to existing multicast streams and transmits unicast video-on-demand requests using IP technology. An STB may also provide additional functions such as Web browsing, voice and video over IP, and browsing capability through channel guides.

Example.   Figure 20.12 shows an IPTV broadcast for multiple users. Suppose channel 002 generated from server SE02 is broadcast to the first two homes as shown in the figure and also to other users located on a different street not shown in this figure. For this, packets of channel 002 are multicast from SE02 in the wide area network of the core network using PIM protocol. One copy of each packet generated

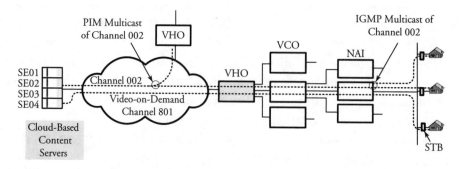

Figure 20.12   An example of an IPTV broadcast: two users are viewing channel 002 while another user is watching a video-on-demand (VoD) movie from channel 801

for this channel is sent directly to the first two homes through the VHO, VCO, and NAI, and a second copy of the each packet is sent out to the corresponding VHO of the other users as partially shown in the figure. The copies of the channel 002 packets reaching the NAI are further multicast (using IGMP, explained in the following paragraph), and each of the first two homes receives a copy of the channel 002 packets. In the meantime, the third user has set up to view a video on demand on channel 801 as shown in the figure. For this, assume the content of the channel 801 movie is housed in server SE04. The STB of this user sets up a "unicast" point-to-point connection to SE04 and streams the movie.

IPTV Protocols

IPTV technology utilizes a number of real-time and multicast protocols. The commonly used streaming protocols in IPTV systems are the *Real-time Transport Protocol* (RTP) for regular TV channel programs, and the *Real Time Streaming Protocol* (RTSP) for on-demand programs, both studied in this chapter. We remember that both of these protocols are considered application layer protocols and reside on top of the UDP transport protocol.

IP multicasting operation near users' premises allows live transmission of video content to be sent to multiple receivers using a single multicast group address. For multicasting in the access network, the *Internet Group Management Protocol* (IGMP) is used for live television broadcasts. In Chapter 6, we learned that IGMP is a *local and membership multicast protocol* primarily designed for joining a host to a multicast group and for simple multicasting in a small network such a local area network. In IPTV, IGMP operates between users' set-top boxes and a local multicast router called a designated router (DR) located in the NAI.

For compression of video, IPTV employs compatible video compression standards including H.263 or H.264 encapsulated in either an MPEG transport stream or RTP packets.

IPTV Packet Format

Figure 20.13 shows an IP datagram (packet) containing audio and video media stream content. Audio and video media streams are packetized in groups with added header data, creating a unique *packetized elementary stream* (PES). PES is defined in the MPEG-2 standard that specifies carrying of elementary streams of an audio or video encoder in packets within the MPEG program stream. The elementary stream

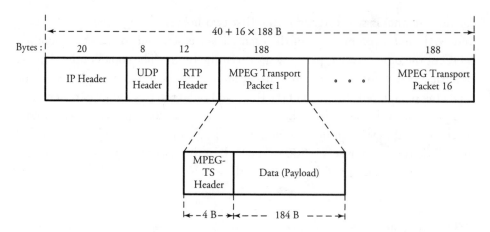

Figure 20.13 IPTV packet header format

is packetized by encapsulating sequential data bytes from the elementary stream inside PES packet headers. Normally, elementary stream data from a video or audio encoder is first converted to PES packets and then encapsulated inside transport stream (TS) packets or program stream (PS) packets.

In IPTV systems, a channel may be composed of several PESs and the main function of the MPEG-transport stream (MPEG-TS) layer is to identify PESs and multiplex them into one program stream. The MPEG-TS packet has a fixed size of 188 bytes including 4 bytes of packet header and 184 bytes of data. Generally, each MPEG transport packet contains data from one PES, and an MPEG-TS contains information from more than one TV program. These MPEG transport packets are encapsulated within an RTP packet having an RTP header, a UDP header at the transport layer, and an IP header forming the IP datagram. Thus, assuming there are a maximum of 16 MPEG transport packets encapsulated in an RTP packet, the total size of the resulting packet is $(20 + 8 + 12) + 188 \times 16$ as indicated in the figure.

Video on Demand (VoD)

Video on demand (VoD) may be provided to users through *unicast* IPTV systems. The unicast service is provided to a user who wishes to view certain content on demand. In unicast IPTV, each transmitting server generates a unique stream to the set-top box of a user. The set-top box in this case can be considered as a client. A unicast VoD service can be provided from a central ISP broadcast center or from a designated content server contracted by the ISP. As a result of this service model, the VoD service architecture consists of either a central server system or several distributed servers.

20.2.3   Online Gaming

Online gaming is branded as part of the broadband service package. Using a quality end-to-end facility, an ISP can differentiate itself from the competition. Traffic congestion is the most important factor in the operation of online gaming. It causes latency and jitter to increase. Jitter has a dramatic impact on online games, which need fast, consistent feedback of players' movements to the servers. Because of this, a well-engineered core gaming server should not be congested, as heavy downloads at the time of online game playing can disrupt a user's gaming session. A solution is to divert all IP traffic going from gaming servers to portions of the broadband network with traffic engineering and QoS capabilities such as MPLS networks. In such circumstances, packets coming from gaming servers and going to users can be marked with a priority value so that dynamic policies can be applied to users who have purchased the gaming service.

20.3   Cloud-Based Multimedia Networking

We learned that cloud computing can fulfill the need for providing data and computing resources on demand by allowing customers to access infrastructure, platforms, and software. As a great number of customers are attached to the Internet through a wireless network, *mobile cloud computing* is presented as an integration of cloud computing and mobile technology. In mobile cloud computing, data storage and processing are accessed from mobile devices to the cloud.

Distributed *cloud-based multimedia* is defined as a cloud computing infrastructure that can provide a variety of multimedia services including voice, video, and data services. Media communication services based on the cloud can range from voice over IP (VoIP) to multimedia communications that satisfy voice, video, and data requirements. Examples of cloud-based multimedia services can also include:

- *Distributed media mini-clouds.* Small-size clouds can form media mini-clouds in a self-organized fashion.
- *Cloud-based interactive voice response* (IVR). This is a distributed IVR system in which IVR is an automated telephony technology that enables a server computer to interact with a human.
- *Audio- and videoconferencing.* An automated call coordinator can be in any location in a distributed call coordinator cloud.

- *Outbound notification.* An outbound notification service delivers information via a variety of media such as phone, text message, e-mail, or Web communication. Messages can be sent from a source in the cloud on a one-by-one basis, or broadcast to numerous recipients.

- *Contact center.* A contact center is a service deployed by companies to coordinate client contact through a variety of media such as telephone, e-mail and online live chat. Contact centers integrate several roles to provide an all-encompassing solution to clients, and also to client contacts. Such centers can be operated in various cloud-based departments responsible for day-to-day communications.

In the following two sections we learn more about the first two services.

20.3.1   Distributed Media Mini-Clouds

Some multimedia networks can be implemented by incorporation of numerous self-organized, small-size media clouds. Small-size clouds are called *media mini-clouds.* Media or multimedia mini-clouds that can serve for any type of media can also include mobility in their architecture. Such a distributed multimedia system typically has a set of integrated multimedia data centers and a wireless base station. A multimedia data center presents multimedia resource information for retrieving requested data from the databases and communicating it to the cloud units. Mini-clouds then forward the requested multimedia information to mobile or stationary users.

Figure 20.14 illustrates a scenario of cloud-based multimedia networking with three small-size media clouds: mini-cloud 1 stores voice and images, mini-cloud 2 stores video, and mini-cloud 3 stores video, images, and data. When various media flows arrive at the backbone network, they form multi-stream multimedia traffic. The process of multiple streams of multimedia traffic brings a challenge to the backbone network from the standpoint of bandwidth provisioning and synchronization among data streams.

Clouds must ensure QoS to users, and have the capability to coordinate with wireless base stations for the allocation of wireless channel resources. Multimedia clouds have real-time multimedia information sources in the form of audio, images, video, data, and any combination of these, referred to as multimedia. The traffic from and to such clouds can be of form: download, upload, or streaming. In multimedia communication, data rate, utilization, delay, maximum jitter, and maximum bit error rate are the main measures of quality. Real-time video streaming may require a high data rate and tolerate moderate delay and jitter while other applications such as interactive

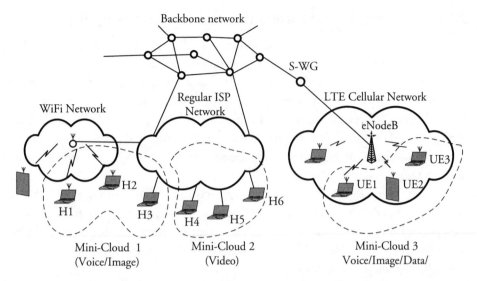

Figure 20.14   Overview of distributed multimedia mini-cloud networking

multimedia cannot tolerate high delay and jitter. Media streams can also be synchronized between two adjacent mini- clouds to create seamless media for a mobile user.

When QoS provisioning is a concern at data centers, especially in locations where virtualized access and retrieval mechanisms are used, the replication of multimedia at a larger number of data centers may be required. As an alternative solution, service virtualization that hides the selection and configuration of the multimedia data center from end users can be applied at data centers. This method may result in creation of a virtual data center or a hierarchy of virtual data centers. Since mobile hosts can also be present in such multimedia environments, the size of mini-clouds can change as hosts leave a cloud or are included in a cloud dynamically. Thus, data center management, synchronization of multimedia streams to users, and coordination among clouds become crucial and challenging in distributed media clouds.

One of the ideal solutions to the challenges of distributed media clouds is the use of software-defined networking (SDN) technology, described in Chapter 17. SDN can be used to separate the control plane from the data plane, which is a tremendous help in managing the functionality of media clouds. For example, the wireless base station, which is an integral part of the control plane and responsible for session setup and teardown, can be completely separated from the media exchange if SDN is used. This means control of the synchronization of multimedia streams becomes independent of session signaling.

20.3.2   Cloud-Based Interactive Voice Response (IVR)

Interactive voice response (IVR) is an automated telephony technology by which a server computer is able to interact with customers through voice or phone keypad tones. One common application of IVR is that a customer can contact a server through a telephone keypad or by speech recognition to acquire a certain service. Typically, the IVR server can respond using dynamically prerecorded audio. Other applications of IVR include voice message to e-mail, automated phone surveys, automated phone questionnaires, automated meter reading, and checking bank accounts through phone systems.

An abstract model of an IVR networking scheme is shown in Figure 20.15. An IVR system interacts with its user according to a predefined instruction. A user can use a phone keypad to interact with the IVR system and instruct it to receive a service according to a menu. The IVR system consists of an IVR *phone unit, voice application servers*, and an *audio file database*.

The IVR phone unit itself consists of a *speech recognition* unit to process incoming speech and respond with voice interaction, a *text-to-speech* unit to convert incoming text to audio, and a *voice interpreter* unit. The voice interpreter unit uses a mark-up digital document standard to specify interactive media and voice dialogs between humans and computers. The commonly used language is *Voice Extensible Markup Language* (VoiceXML or VXML). The function of VoiceXML is analogous to how a Web browser interprets and visually presents the Hypertext Markup

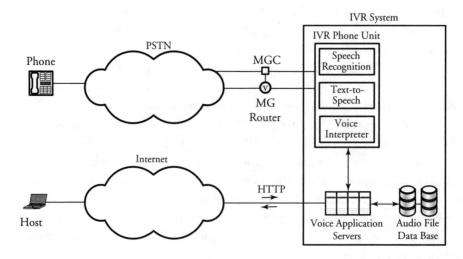

Figure 20.15   An abstract operational model of an interactive voice response (IVR) system

Language (HTML) it receives from a Web server. (HTML is described in Chapter 9.) VoiceXML has enabled hosted IVR services to be deployed on a standards basis, and is used to develop response applications, such as in financial customer service portals. Therefore, we can see that VoiceXML documents are interpreted by a voice browser. VoiceXML also has tags that instruct the voice browser to manage dialog and provide speech recognition and audio playback.

Voice application servers are managed to run various applications pertaining to audio. These servers are attached to a number of preconstructed *audio file database units*. The IVR system can be connected to the PSTN to supply services to phones. In this case, an intervening media gateway (MG) router and an MG controller (MGC) are required. In the meantime, an IVR system can also provide service to the Internet user hosts as shown in the figure. Hosts can browse services using HTTP, while the voice application servers forward the requests to the voice interpreter to translate the request to VXML.

An example of a cloud-based interactive voice response (IVR) system in a distributed environment is shown in Figure 20.16. Compared to a single IVR system, a distributed IVR system is a more cost-effective and intelligent method designed to act

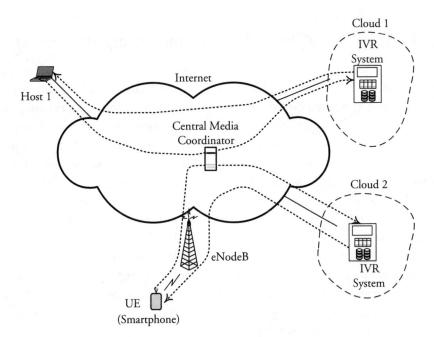

Figure 20.16   An example of a cloud-based interactive voice response system

more efficiently. When the IVR operation is distributed over the Internet, the service to customers is more conveniently rendered according to class of service requested and the location of the customer to the closest IVR system housed in a cloud. When IVR systems are hosted in the external data centers of clouds, the customer may only need the software component or only data connectivity to use an IVR service.

A *central media coordinator* is required to process the initial customers' requests. In Figure 20.16, host 1 sends its inquiry to the central media coordinator, through which the best IVR system for that request is identified to be in cloud 1. A similar process happens for smartphone UE1 attached to base station eNodeB of a cellular network; the best IVR system for this request is identified to be in cloud 2. As seen in the figure, the outbound response from a cloud does not need to be routed back on the same path as the inbound request path.

Remember that, in all distributed and cloud-based networking, virtualization is a key factor for efficiency. As we learned in Chapter 16, clouds enable an infrastructure as a service (IaaS) model with virtualization as the key technology and a platform as a service (PaaS) model, both of which can play a significant role in speed and quality service from clouds to customers. IaaS can especially help in optimizing services such as an announcement player, a voice recorder, and call transfer.

20.4   Self-Similarity and Non-Markovian Streaming

Multimedia applications are delay sensitive and loss tolerant, unlike static-content communications, which are delay and loss intolerant. Distributed multimedia networks must be able to support the exchange of multiple types of information, such as voice, video, and data among users while also satisfying the performance requirements of each individual application. Consequently, the expanding diversity of high-bandwidth communication applications calls for a unified, flexible, and efficient network to prevent any congestion.

A network handling heavy video streaming must reserve some resources based on the source QoS. With reservation techniques, lossless transmission is guaranteed for the entire duration of the block; otherwise, the block is lost. However, sudden changes in the total volume of traffic at a node can impact the performance of streaming transmission. Multimedia networks are expected to support a large number of *bursty sources* with different characteristics. This fact enforces the use of processes other than Poisson for describing network traffic. The aggregated arrivals of packets are assumed to form *stream batches* of packets.

20.4.1 Self-Similarity with Batch Arrival Models

Section 11.5.3 explained that some traffic patterns indicate significant "burstiness," or variations on a wide range of timescales. Bursty traffic, such as a video stream, can be viewed as a *batch* of traffic units and described statistically using *self-similarity patterns*. In self-similar traffic, a certain property of the traffic is preserved with respect to scaling in time such that if the traffic is magnified in part, it resembles the shape of the whole. This model is clearly different from traditional network models using Poisson models. Self-similar traffic can be constructed by multiplexing a large number of ON/OFF sources that have ON and OFF intervals. This mechanism corresponds to a network of streaming servers, each of which is either silent or transferring a video stream at a constant rate. Using this traffic, the distributions of transmission times and quiet times for any particular session are *heavy tailed*, which is an essential characteristic of traffic self-similarity.

The discrete-time representation of a communication system is the natural way to capture its behavior. In most communication systems, the input process to a queue is not *renewal* but correlated. A renewal process is a process in which the interval between consecutive occurrences of a certain event are independently and identically distributed. For example, the Poisson process is a renewal case with an exponential distribution. In a practical environment, the input process of packetized voice, data, or video traffic to a multiplexer does not form a renewal process but is bursty and correlated.

In streaming-traffic analysis, a batch of packets may arrive simultaneously. With the relatively more accurate traffic model being presented here, maximum and average traffic rates over *a number of given intervals* are determined. This method is especially effective for realistic sources, such as compressed streaming video. In such situations, a source can even transmit at its peak rates when sending its large-size frames immediately followed by smaller frames. In the performance analysis, the packet-loss probability and the impact of increase in switching speed to link-speed ratio on the throughput are of particular interest.

In this analysis, consider a small buffered multiplexer or router, as large queuing delays are not expected in a multimedia network with a real-time transmission. A bursty arrival is modeled as a *batch*, or packets with identical interarrivals. This model captures the multi-rate burstiness characteristic of realistic sources. One property of self-similarity is that an object as an image is preserved with respect to scaling in space or time. In this environment, the traffic-relational structure remains unchanged at varying timescales. For any time $t > 0$ and a real number $a > 0$, a self-similar process, $\mathbf{X}(t)$, is a continuous-time stochastic (random) process with parameter $0.5 < H < 1$ if it satisfies

$$\mathbf{X}(t) = \frac{\mathbf{X}(at)}{a^H}, \tag{20.3}$$

where parameter H is known as the *Hurst parameter*, or *self-similarity parameter*. The Hurst parameter is an important factor in bursty traffic, representing a measure of the dependence length in a burst. The closer H is to its maximum, 1, the greater the persistence of long-range dependence.

The expected values of both sides in Equation (20.3) must then be related as

$$E[\mathbf{X}(t)] = \frac{E[\mathbf{X}(at)]}{a^H}. \tag{20.4}$$

This result indicates that a self-similar process when $H = 0.5$ can also be obtained from the *Brownian random process* discussed in Section C.4.2. Based on Equation (C.34), and for any time increment δ, the increment of process, $\mathbf{X}(t + \delta) - \mathbf{X}(t)$, has the following distribution:

$$P[\mathbf{X}(t + \delta) - \mathbf{X}(t) \le x] = \frac{1}{\sqrt{2\pi\delta}} \int_{-\infty}^{x} e^{-y^2/2\delta} dy. \tag{20.5}$$

To better understand the behavior of aggregated batch sequences of traffic, we can also present the self-similar process, $\mathbf{X}(t)$, in terms of a discrete-time version, $\mathbf{X}_{n,m}$, defined at discrete points in time. In this process, $n \in \{1, 2, \cdots\}$ is discrete time and m is the batch size. Thus:

$$\mathbf{X}_{n,m} = \frac{1}{m} \sum_{i=(n-1)m+1}^{nm} \mathbf{X}(i). \tag{20.6}$$

Note that for $\mathbf{X}_{n,m}$, the corresponding aggregated sequence with a level of aggregation m, we divide the original series $\mathbf{X}(t)$ into nonoverlapping blocks of size m and average them over each block where index n labels blocks.

Example. Consider traffic with batch size $m = 4$. Self-similar process averaging is expressed by

$$\mathbf{X}_{n,4} = \frac{1}{4} \left(\mathbf{X}(4n - 3) + \mathbf{X}(4n - 2) + \mathbf{X}(4n - 1) + \mathbf{X}(4n)\right). \tag{20.7}$$

Heavy-Tailed Distributions

Self-similarity implies that traffic has similar statistical properties in a timescale range, such as milliseconds, seconds, minutes, hours, or even days. In a practical situation, in which bursts of streams are multiplexed, the resulting traffic tends to produce a bursty aggregate stream. In other words, the traffic has a long-range dependence characterized by a *heavy-tailed distribution*. A random variable has heavy-tailed distribution if for $0 < \alpha < 2$, its cumulative distribution function (CDF)

$$F_X(x) = P[X \le x] \sim 1 - \frac{1}{x^\alpha} \tag{20.8}$$

as $x \to \infty$. Heavy-tailed distributions are typically used to describe the distributions of burst lengths. A simple example of heavy-tailed distributions is the *Pareto distribution*, which is characterized by the following CDF and probability density function (PDF):

$$\begin{cases} F_X(x) = 1 - \left(\dfrac{k}{x}\right)^\alpha, \\ f_X(x) = \dfrac{\alpha k^\alpha}{x^{\alpha+1}} \end{cases} \tag{20.9}$$

where k is the smallest possible value of the random variable. For this distribution, if $\alpha \le 1$, the distribution has infinite mean and variance; if $\alpha \le 2$, the distribution has infinite variance. To define *heavy tailed*, we can now use a comparison over PDFs of a Pareto distribution and exponential distribution. Making this comparison shows how the tail of the curve in a Pareto distribution takes much longer to decay. A random variable that follows a heavy-tailed distribution may be very large with a probability that cannot be negligible.

20.5 Summary

This chapter explored transport mechanisms for application delivery with the highest possible quality. We focused on media applications, such as streaming audio and video, one-to-many transmission of real-time audio and video, and real-time interactive audio and video.

Senders use various *real-time media exchange protocols* to send a stream of data at a constant rate. One of the protocols for real-time transmission is the *Real-time Transport Protocol* (RTP), which provides application-level framing. Real-time applications, such as voice and video, can tolerate a certain amount of packet loss and do not always require retransmission of data. But if the rate of packet loss is very high, the source might use a lower-quality transmission, thereby placing less load on the network. We also covered other types of real-time media exchange protocols, such as a variation of RTP called *Real-time Transport Control Protocol* (RTCP), and also *Real Time Streaming Protocol* (RTSP), *HTTP-based streaming*, and *Stream Control Transmission Protocol* (SCTP). We noticed the HTTP-based streaming allowed the use of TCP mechanisms which made the streaming more reliable and secure.

A video in a single server can be streamed from a video server to a client for each client request. *Content distribution networks* (CDNs) can be used for streaming data. Video streaming provided to a user in an ISP domain can use Domain Name System (DNS) servers to direct browsers to the correct server. The *Stream Control Transmission Protocol* (SCTP) is a general-purpose transport protocol for transporting stream traffic. SCTP offers acknowledged transmission of datagrams in connectionless networks.

We then proceeded to a description of *Internet Protocol television* (IPTV). IPTV is a system through which television services are delivered using packet-switched networks or the Internet. We learned that with IPTV technology, movies and programs are streamed directly from the source while an ISP coordinates their broadcasting. We saw that most of the Internet Protocol rules could be applied to IPTV. For example, when two or more users are viewing the same TV channel, the IPTV system can multicast the flow of that TV program by treating it as any other Internet traffic flows. *Video on demand* (VoD) is a unique feature of IPTV by which a user can demand to view a movie or program for which a point-to-point connection needs to be set up.

Next, we covered cloud-based multimedia networks. Two examples of such networking schemes were presented. In the first scheme, smaller self-organizing clouds, called mini-clouds, can introduce media services in various locations on the Internet. The second scheme presented cloud-based *interactive voice response* (IVR) systems. IVR can be designed to recognize human voice and respond accordingly. Depending on the level of speech-recognition sophistication, IVRs can recognize names and locations.

Finally, a *non-Markovian analysis of streaming traffic* was presented. A stream of packets generated from a server source can be modeled as a discrete sequence of events and defined as a discrete-time 0-1 valued process called self-similar traffic.

The last two chapters of the book consider two advanced and related subjects: *mobile ad-hoc networks* and *wireless sensor networks*. These two topics are independent of the rest of the book and present networks in which sensors and hosts, free of access to the Internet, form their own network and communicate with each other.

20.6 Exercises

1. We want to transmit a speaker's voice through a digital radio broadcast system that uses 8-bit code PCM (explained in Chapter 19) placed on the Internet.
   (a) How many bits are produced in each second?
   (b) Estimate the size of an encapsulated RTP/IP datagram (the basic transmission unit of data in the Internet) that carries a half second of PCM-encoded audio using UDP.

2. Two voice sources come to one server for live transmission together, using RTP packets. Each source bandwidth has been compressed to 31Kb/s. Assume packets of 1,500 bytes long including all headers.
   (a) Show an overview of the encapsulated RTP/IP datagram, and estimate the size of each packet, utilizing an RTP packet using UDP.
   (b) How many packets are produced each 5 minutes?

3. We have five packets to transmit in real time. The estimated average jitter until the time of the first packet is 0.02 ms. Table 20.1 shows the timestamps of RTP data packets indicated by the source, t_i, and the arrival times of RTP packets at the receiver a_i. Assume that the normalizing coefficient k is 0.2.
   (a) Estimate the average jitter until every packet has arrived.
   (b) What would be possible reason(s) that t_i increases at a different rate from i?

4. SCTP is applied to transmit a color video clip between two points of an IP network requiring 4 minutes of network use. Each image of this video clip consists of $1,024 \times 1,280$ pixel blocks, and the video consists of 30 images per second. The video clip is not compressed but is passed through the quantization process, and each pixel can be a value among a sample space of 77 numbers. One-tenth of each row of a frame (image) is formatted by one chunk.

Table 20.1   Exercise 3 example of source timestamps and receiver arrival times for five packets

i	a_i	t_i
1	43	69
1	45	74
1	47	73
1	49	91
1	51	99

(a) Find the size of each SCTP chunk, including its header.

(b) Find the total size of each SCTP packet, including its header.

(c) Find the total size of bits transmitted, based only on payload packets.

(d) Determine the required bandwidth between these two nodes.

5. Suppose that a live transmission of a compressed color video movie between two points of an IP network requires 2 hours of network use. We want to apply SCTP for this transmission. Each image of this video consists of $1,024 \times 1,280$ pixel blocks, and the video consists of 30 images per second. One option is to encapsulate each block of pixels in a chunk, allowing each row of a frame (image) to be formatted by one packet. Assume that each pixel block is compressed on average to 10 phrases and each phrase requires on average 5 bits.

(a) Find the size of each SCTP chunk, including its header.

(b) Find the total size of each SCTP packet, including its header.

(c) Find the total size of bits transmitted, based only on payload packets.

(d) Determine the required bandwidth between these two nodes.

6. Consider an HTTP-based streaming session and let b be the size of a client's application buffer. Also assume that r_c is the minimum amount of data in bytes that must be buffered before the browser application can start a playout session. Let also r_c and r_s be respectively the display rate at the client side, and server's transmission where both being bit rates are constant.

(a) Under what condition, the playout goes to freeze?

(b) Find the period during which the playout is uninterrupted.

(c) In case $r_s > r_c$, find the time that the client application buffer becomes completely full.

7. Consider an HTTP-based streaming session and let b be the size of a client's application buffer. Also assume that b_m is the minimum amount of data that must be buffered before the browser application can start a playout session. The HTTP server transmits continuously with a constant bit rate r_s for t_n milliseconds and interrupts its transmission for t_i milliseconds at all times. Let also r_c be the constant display bit rate at the client side.

(a) Under what condition, the playout goes to freeze?

(b) Find the period during which the playout is uninterrupted.

(c) In case $r_s > r_c$, find the time that the client application buffer becomes completely full.

8. Assume that a real-time bursty source is modeled using a Brownian motion process $\mathbf{X}(t)$. Let $\mathbf{Z}(t) = \mathbf{X}(t) + 2t$.

   (a) Find the probability distribution function (PDF) of $\mathbf{Z}(t)$.

   (b) Find the joint PDF of $\mathbf{Z}(t)$ and $\mathbf{X}(t+1)$.

9. In Figure 20.17, a remote medical emergency host is streaming the 70-cycle/minute heartbeat of a patient to a hospital, using SCTP. Each heart cycle has six peaks: P, Q, R, S, T, and U. Suppose that all information about each peak is formatted into one chunk of the SCTP data packet. Because of their importance and complexity, each of the Q, R, and S pulses requires four samples; and each of the P, T, and U pulses requires only one sample. Assume that each sample is encoded by 8 bits.

   (a) Determine the required bandwidth between the host and the hospital.

   (b) If multiple patients' samples are included in a packet, find the maximum number of heartbeat cycles that can be formatted into a packet.

   (c) Evaluate the approach presented in part (b), and compare it with the original one.

10. For self-similar traffic, we have seen the relationship between the expected values in Equation (20.4), using the Hurst parameter, H.

   (a) Derive a relationship between the variances of the two sides of Equation (20.3).

   (b) Compare situations in which the Hurst parameter, H, takes values 0.5, 0.8, or 1 in Equation (20.3).

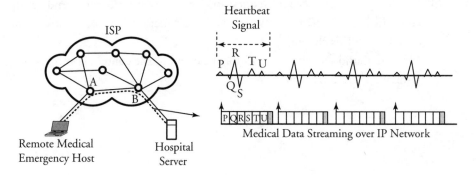

Figure 20.17   Exercise 7 example of a remote medical emergency unit streaming a patient's heartbeat to a hospital. The heartbeat signal is converted to a stream of packets.

11. To better understand the behavior of bursty traffic, such as a video streaming source, assume that the traffic is described by a Pareto distribution with $k = 1$. Plot PDFs of the following two cases of α, and compare them with that of an exponential distribution. Comment on the heavy-tailed phenomenon.

(a) $\alpha = 0.8$
(b) $\alpha = 3.8$

20.7 Computer Simulation Project

1. *Experimental Simulation of a Content Delivery Network* (**CDN**). This project requires four computers, either laptops or PCs, for a client, a content control server, a DNS server, and a CDN (content) server, respectively.

(a) Set up the CDN server. Create three short video clips and name them content 1 through content 3, respectively, and upload them to the CDN server in a known folder.

(b) Set up the DNS server. Find out the IP address of the CDN server. Create a lookup table database in the DNS server that shows five URLs versus five IP addresses where one of the pairs of URL + IP address belongs to the CDN server.

(c) Set up the content control server. Create a lookup table database in the content control server that contains a list of ten hypothetical movies and matches them to their URLs in the CDN server. Make sure three of these entries exhibit the URLs of the ones that exist in the CDN server.

(d) Use the client browser and request one of the existing movies, and set up your client to experimentally simulate the functionality of the streaming explained in this chapter.

(e) Measure round-trip time (RTT) for the client to the content control server, resolving the URL through the DNS server.

CHAPTER 21

Mobile Ad-Hoc Networks

Mobile ad-hoc networks (MANETs) have had a profound impact in the world of computer networks. Characterized by anytime/anywhere, untethered establishment of a wireless network, the MANET infrastructure enables location-independent services. Ad-hoc networks do not need any fixed infrastructure to operate and support dynamic topology scenarios in which no wired infrastructure exists. This chapter covers the following topics on wireless mobile ad-hoc networks:

- *Overview of wireless ad-hoc networks*
- *Routing in ad-hoc networks*
- *Routing protocols for ad-hoc networks*
- *Security of ad-hoc networks*

A mobile user can act as a routing node, and a packet can be routed from a source to its destination without having any static router in the network. Two classes of routing strategies in ad-hoc networks are *table-driven routing protocols* and *source-initiated routing protocols*. Security of ad-hoc networks is a key issue. Ad-hoc networks are, by their nature, vulnerable to attacks. An intruder can easily attack ad-hoc networks by loading available network resources and disturbing the normal operation of routing protocols by modifying packets.

21.1   Overview of Wireless Ad-Hoc Networks

Wireless *mobile ad-hoc network* (MANET) technology is designed for the establishment of a network anywhere and anytime, without any fixed infrastructure to support the mobility of the users in the network. In other words, a wireless ad-hoc network is a collection of mobile nodes with a dynamic network infrastructure forming a temporary network. Such networks have no central server or base station for providing connectivity and all network intelligence must be placed inside the mobile user devices. Figure 21.1 gives an overview of an ad-hoc network, in which wireless mobile hosts A through I have formed a network, with host E being too far to reach.

In this figure, each circle surrounding a node in its center represents the effective wireless range of reachability to other devices for that node. As seen in the figure, there are cases in which two ad-hoc hosts can reach each other, such as hosts C and D, for which a bidirectional arrow represents the bidirectional reachability. There are, however, cases in which one ad-hoc host can reach another one but the other host's effective wireless range is too short, such as the case of host H and I for which a unidirectional arrow is shown.

In such an environment, each mobile host acts as a routing node, and a packet is routed from a source to its destination by incorporating other network nodes. Since the topology of an ad-hoc network can change quickly and unpredictably, the network should be adaptable to changes, such as when a link breaks, a node

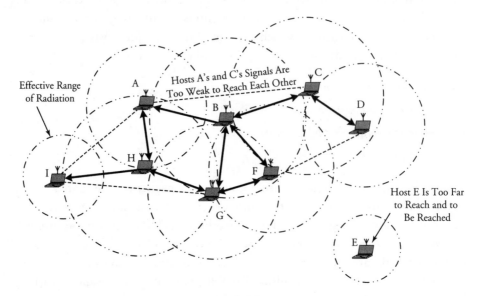

Figure 21.1   Overview of an ad-hoc network including mobile nodes and their effective ranges of radiation

leaves the network, or a new node is attached to the network. Thus, unlike with the intradomain routing algorithm for regular networks, if a node leaves an ad-hoc network, all affected nodes can discover new routes. Ad-hoc networks have several types of applications:

- *Rescue operations*. In an emergency public disaster, such as an earthquake, ad-hoc networks can be set up at a location where no infrastructure is present. Ad-hoc networks can be used to support network connectivity when no fixed network is available.

- *Military*. Ad-hoc networks can be used in a battle zone, for a military command and mobile units.

- *Law enforcement and security operations*. An ad-hoc network can be used in a temporary security operation, acting as a mobile surveillance network.

- *Home networks*. An ad-hoc network can be used to support seamless connectivity among various devices.

- *Conferencing*. Ad-hoc networks can be set up for a presentation. An audience can download a presentation, browse the slides on a portable device, print them on the local printer, or e-mail the presentation to an absent colleague.

Ad-hoc networks must possess several unique features. One is *automatic discovery* of available services. Each time a new service becomes available, an ad-hoc networking device has to configure use of the new service. As an ad-hoc network lacks centralized administration, the network must be able to prevent network collapse when one of the mobile nodes moves out of transmitter range. In general, nodes should be able to enter or leave the network as they wish. Thus, every node acts as both a host and a router, and the network must be intelligent enough to handle network dynamics. This property is called *self-stabilization*.

One of the most common tasks of an ad-hoc network is to multicast a message to many users efficiently. In such an environment, networks are subject to severe blocking. Thus, the performance of an ad-hoc system depends on the stability of the network architecture. The inclusion of all these features in ad-hoc networks requires considerable architecture sophistication.

21.2 Routing in Ad-Hoc Networks

The lack of a backbone infrastructure makes packet routing in ad-hoc networks a challenging task. A routing protocol should be able to automatically recover from any problem in a finite amount of time without human intervention. Conventional routing protocols are designed for nonmoving infrastructures and assume that routes are bidirectional, which is not always the case for ad-hoc networks. Identification of mobile terminals and correct routing of packets to and from each terminal while moving are certainly challenging.

Since the topology of an ad-hoc network is dynamic, reserving resources and sustaining QoS are difficult. In an ad-hoc medium, it may not be possible to communicate bidirectionally, so ad-hoc routing protocols should assume that links are unidirectional. The power of a wireless device is another important factor. The routing protocol also has to support node standby mode. Devices such as laptops are very limited in battery power; hence, the use of standby mode to save power is important.

21.2.1   Classification of Routing Protocols

Ad-hoc routing protocols can be classified into two broad categories:

1. *Centralized versus distributed.* In centralized routing protocols, the routing decision is made at a central node. In distributed routing protocols, the routing decision is made by all the network nodes. Routing protocols in most efficiently designed ad-hoc networks are distributed to increase the reliability of the network. In such cases, nodes can enter or leave the network easily, and each node can make routing decisions, using other collaborative nodes.

2. *Static versus adaptive.* In static routing protocols, a route of a source/destination pair does not change because of any traffic condition or link failure. In adaptive routing protocols, routes may change because of any congestion.

Whether a protocol is centralized, distributed, static, or adaptive, it can generally be categorized as either *table driven* or *source initiated.*

Table-Driven Routing Protocols

Table-driven, or *proactive, routing protocols* find routes to all possible destinations ahead of time. The routes are recorded in the nodes' routing tables and are updated within the predefined intervals. Proactive protocols are faster in decision making but need more time to converge to a steady state, causing problems if the topology of the network continually changes. However, maintaining routes can lead to a large overhead. Table-driven protocols require every node to maintain one or more tables to store updated routing information from every node to all other nodes. Nodes propagate updated tables all over the network such that the routing information in each table corresponds to topological changes in the network.

Source-Initiated Routing Protocols

Source-initiated (or *reactive*) *routing protocols* are on-demand procedures and create routes only when requested to do so by source nodes. A route request initiates a *route-discovery process* in the network and is completed once a route is discovered. If it exists at the time of a request, a route is maintained by a route-maintenance procedure until either the destination node becomes irrelevant to the source or the route is no longer needed. On-demand protocols are more suitable for ad-hoc networks. In most cases, reactive protocols are desired. This means that the network reacts only when needed and does not broadcast information periodically. However, the control overhead of packets is smaller than for proactive protocols.

21.3   Routing Protocols for Ad-Hoc Networks

This section discusses three table-driven protocols and four source-initiated protocols. The table-driven protocols are the *Destination-Sequenced Distance-Vector* (DSDV) protocol, the *Cluster-head Gateway Switch Routing* (CGSR) Protocol, and the *Wireless Routing Protocol* (WRP). The source-initiated protocols are the *Dynamic Source Routing* (DSR) protocol, the *Temporally Ordered Routing Algorithm* (TORA), the *Associativity-Based Routing* (ABR) protocol, and *Ad-hoc On-Demand Distance Vector* (AODV) protocol.

21.3.1   Destination-Sequenced Distance-Vector (DSDV) Protocol

The *Destination-Sequenced Distance-Vector* (DSDV) protocol is a table-driven routing protocol based on the improved version of the classical Bellman-Ford routing algorithm. DSDV is based on the *Routing Information Protocol* (RIP), explained in Chapter 5. With RIP, a node holds a routing table containing all the possible destinations within the network and the number of hops to each destination. DSDV is also based on *distance vector routing,* explained in Chapter 5, and thus uses bidirectional links. A limitation of DSDV is that it provides only one route for a source/destination pair.

Routing Tables

The structure of the routing table for this protocol is simple. Each table entry has a sequence number that is incremented every time a node sends an updated message.

Routing tables are periodically updated when the topology of the network changes and are propagated throughout the network to keep consistent information throughout the network.

Each DSDV node maintains two routing tables: one for forwarding packets and one for advertising incremental routing packets. The routing information sent periodically by a node contains a new sequence number, the destination address, the number of hops to the destination node, and the sequence number of the destination. When the topology of a network changes, a detecting node sends an update packet to its neighboring nodes. On receipt of an update packet from a neighboring node, a node extracts the information from the packet and updates its routing table as follows:

DSDV Packet Process Algorithm

1. **Update route for each node.** Detect the new address and its sequence number received from an update packet:

   If the new incoming sequence number is higher than the sequence number belonging to the existing route, the node chooses the route with the higher sequence number and discards the old sequence number.

   If the new incoming sequence number is identical to the one belonging to the existing route, a route with the least cost is chosen.

   Otherwise go to step 2.

2. All the metrics chosen from the new routing information are incremented.

3. If there are duplicate updated packets, the node considers keeping the one with the least-cost metric and discards the rest. ■

In case of a broken link, a cost of ∞ metric with a new sequence number (incremented) is assigned to it to ensure that the sequence number of that metric is always greater than or equal to the sequence number of that node. Figure 21.2 shows a routing table for node 2, whose neighbors are nodes 1, 3, 4, and 8. The dashed lines indicate no communications between any corresponding pair of nodes. Therefore, node 2 has no information about node 6, 7, and 8.

The large packet overhead of the DSDV protocol impacts the total number of nodes in the ad-hoc network. This fact makes DSDV suitable for small networks. However, in large ad-hoc networks, the mobility rate—and therefore the overall large volume of packet overheads—makes the network unstable to the point that updated packets might not reach nodes on time.

Routing Table for Node 2

Destination	Next Hop	Metric	Dest. Seq. No.
1	1	1	123
2	0	0	516
3	3	1	212
4	4	1	168
5	4	2	372
8	1	∞	432

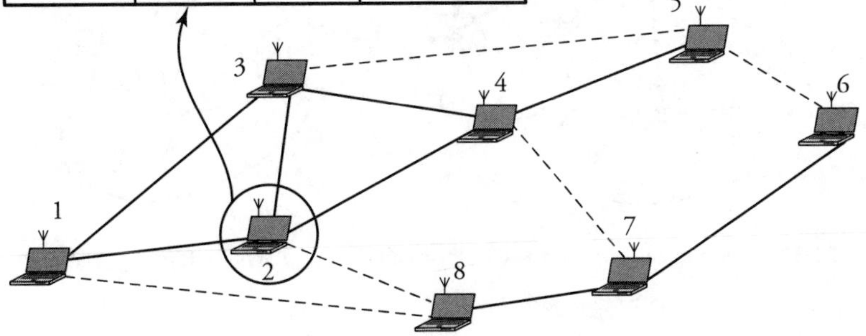

Figure 21.2 DSDV protocol and a routing table

21.3.2 Cluster-Head Gateway Switch Routing (CGSR) Protocol

The *Cluster-head Gateway Switch Routing* (CGSR) Protocol is a table-driven routing protocol. In a clustering system, each predefined number of nodes is formed into a *cluster* controlled by a *cluster head*, which is assigned using a distributed clustering algorithm. However, with the clustering scheme, a cluster head can be replaced frequently by another node for several reasons, such as lower-level energy left in the node or a node moves out of contact.

With this protocol, each node maintains two tables: a *cluster-member table* and a *routing table*. The cluster-member table records the cluster head for each destination node, and the routing table contains the next hop to reach the destination. As with the DSDV protocol, each node updates its cluster-member table on receiving a new update from its neighbors.

Clustering and Routing Algorithms

CGSR routing involves cluster routing, whereby a node is required to find the best route over cluster heads from the cluster-member table. Figure 21.3 shows an example of routing in an area in which six clusters have been formed. A node in cluster A is transmitting a packet to a node in cluster F. Nodes within each cluster route their

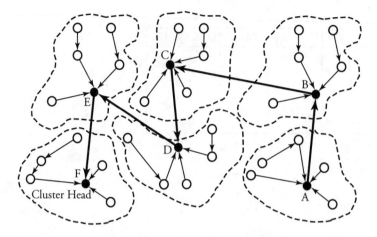

Figure 21.3 Communication with the Cluster-head Gateway Switch Routing (CGSR) Protocol

packets to their own associated clusters. The transmitting node then sends its packet to the next hop, according to the routing table entry associated with that cluster head. The cluster head transmits the packet to another cluster head until the cluster head of the destination node is reached. The routing is made through a series of available cluster heads from A to F. Packets are then transmitted to the destination.

21.3.3   Wireless Routing Protocol (WRP)

The *Wireless Routing Protocol* (WRP) is a table-based protocol maintaining routing information among all nodes in the network. This protocol is based on the distributed Bellman-Ford algorithm. The main advantage of WRP is that it reduces the number of routing loops. With this protocol, each node in a network maintains four tables, as follows:

1. *Distance table*, which holds the destination, next hop, distance, and predecessors of each destination and each neighbor.

2. *Routing table*, which saves the destination address, next hop, distance, predecessor, and a marker for each destination, specifying whether that entry corresponds to a simple path.

3. *Link-cost table*, which provides the link cost to each neighbor and also the number of periodic update periods elapsed since the node received any error-free message from it.

4. *Message transmission-list table*, which records which updates in an update message are to be retransmitted and which neighbors need to acknowledge the

retransmission. The table provides the sequence number of the update message, a retransmission counter, acknowledgments, and a list of updates sent in the update message.

Nodes should either send a message including the update message or a HELLO message to their neighbors. If a node has no message to send, it should send a HELLO message to ensure connectivity. If the sending node is new, it is added to the node's routing table, and the current node sends the new node a copy of its routing table content.

Once it detects a change in a route, a node sends the update message to its neighbors. The neighboring nodes then change their distance entries and look for new possible paths through other nodes. This protocol avoids the count-to-infinity issue present in most ad-hoc network protocols. This issue is resolved by making each node perform consistency checks of predecessor information reported by all its neighbors in order to remove looping and make a faster route convergence in the presence of any link or node failure.

21.3.4 Dynamic Source Routing (DSR) Protocol

The *Dynamic Source Routing* (DSR) protocol is an on-demand, or source-initiated, routing protocol in which a source node finds an unexpired route to a destination to send the packet. DSR quickly adapts to topological changes and is typically used for networks in which mobile nodes move with moderate speed. Overhead is significantly reduced with this protocol, since nodes do not exchange routing table information when there are no changes in the topology. DSR creates multiple paths from a source to a destination, eliminating route discovery when the topology changes. Similar to most ad-hoc networks, DSR has two phases: route discovery and route maintenance.

Route Discovery and Maintenance

Route discovery is initiated when a node wants to send packets to another node and no unexpired route to the destination is in its routing table. In such circumstances, the node first broadcasts a *route-request packet*, including the destination address, source address, and a unique identification number. When it receives a route-request packet, the neighboring node looks at its table; if any route to the requested destination address is already present in the node's route record, the packet is discarded to avoid the looping issue. Otherwise, the node adds its own address to the preassigned field of the route-request packet and forwards it to its neighboring nodes.

When the route-request packet reaches a destination node or another intermediate node that has an unexpired route to the destination, this node generates a *route-reply packet*, which contains a route record of the sequence of nodes taken from the source to this node. Once the source receives all the route-reply packets, it updates its routing table with the best path to the destination and sends its packets through that selected route.

Example.   Figure 21.4 shows an ad-hoc network with eight mobile nodes and a broken link (3-7). Node 1 wants to send a message to the destination, node 8. Node 1 looks at its routing table, finds an expired route to node 8, and then propagates route-request packets to nodes 3 and 2. Node 3 finds no route to the destination and so appends the route record 1-3 to the route-request packet and forwards it to node 4. On receiving this packet, node 7 finds a route to the destination and so stops propagating any route-request packets and instead sends a route-reply packet to the source. The same happens when a route-request packet reaches the destination node 8 with a route record 1-2-4-6. When the source, node 1, compares all the route-reply packets, it concludes that the best route is 1-2-4-6-8 and establishes this path.

Route maintenance in this protocol is fast and simple. In case of a fatal error in the data-link layer, a *route-error packet* is generated from a failing node. When the route-error packet is received, the failing node is removed from its route cache, and all routes containing that node are truncated. Another route-maintenance signal is the acknowledgment packets sent to verify the correct operation of the route links.

21.3.5   Temporally Ordered Routing Algorithm (TORA)

The *Temporally Ordered Routing Algorithm* (TORA) is a source-initiated routing algorithm and, thus, creates multiple routes for any source/destination pair. The advantage of multiple routes to a destination is that route discovery is not required

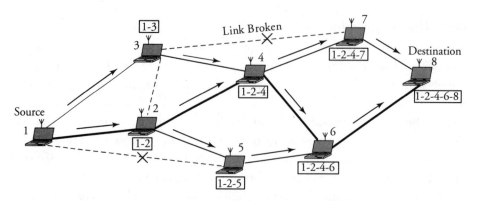

Figure 21.4   Summary of DSR connection setup from node 1 to node 8

for every alteration in the network topology. This feature conserves bandwidth usage and increases adaptability to topological changes by reducing communication overhead.

TORA is based on the following three rules:

1. Route creation/discovery

2. Route maintenance

3. Route erasure

TORA uses three types of packets: *query packets* for route creation, *update packets* for both route creation and maintenance, and *clear packets* for route erasure. With TORA, nodes have to maintain routing information about adjacent nodes. This loop-free protocol is distributed based on the concept of *link reversal.*

Every node maintains a table describing the distance and status of all connected links. When a node has no route to a desired destination, a *route-creation process* starts. A query packet contains the destination ID, and an update packet contains the destination ID and the distance of the node. A receiving node processes a query packet as follows:

- If the receiving node realizes that there are no further downstream links, the query packet is again broadcast. Otherwise, the node discards the query packet.

- If the receiving node realizes that there is at least one downstream link, the node updates its routing table to the new value and broadcasts an update packet.

Once it receives the update packet, a node sets its distance greater than the neighbor from which it received the packet and then rebroadcasts it. The update is eventually received by the source. When it realizes that there is no valid route to the destination, the node adjusts its distance and generates an update packet. TORA performs efficient routing in large networks and in mildly congested networks.

21.3.6   Associativity-Based Routing (ABR) Protocol

Associativity-Based Routing (ABR) is an efficient on-demand, or source-initiated, routing protocol. ABR's is better than WRP's network-change adaptation feature, to the extent that it is almost free of loops and is free of packet duplications. In ABR, the destination node decides the best route, using node *associativity.* ABR is ideal for small networks, as it provides fast route discovery and creates shortest paths through associativity.

In ABR, the movements of nodes are observed by other nodes in the network. Each node keeps track of associativity information by sending messages periodically, identifying itself and updating the *associativity ticks* for its neighbors. If the associativity ticks exceed a maximum, a node has associativity stability with its neighbors. In other words, a low number of associativity ticks shows the node's high mobility, and high associativity indicates a node's sleep mode. The associativity ticks can be reset when a node or its neighbor moves to a new location.

Each point-to-point routing in ABR is connection oriented, with all nodes participating in setting up and computing a route. In a point-to-point route, the source node or any intermediate node decides the details of routes. If the communication must be of broadcast type, the source broadcasts the packet in a *connectionless routing* fashion.

Route discovery is implemented when a node wants to communicate with a destination with no valid route. Route discovery starts with sending a *query packet* and an *await-reply*. The broadcast query packet has the source ID, destination ID, all intermediate nodes' IDs, sequence number, *CRC*, *LIVE* field and a *TYPE* field to identify the type of message. When it receives a query packet, an intermediate node looks at its routing table to see whether it is the intended destination node; otherwise, it appends its ID to the list of all intermediate IDs and rebroadcasts the packet. When it receives all copies of the query packet, the destination node chooses the best route to the source and then sends a *reply packet* including the best route. This way, all nodes become aware of the best route and thereby make other routes to the destination invalid.

ABR is also able to perform *route reconstruction*. This function is needed for partial route discovery or invalid route erasure.

21.3.7   Ad-Hoc On-Demand Distance Vector (AODV) Protocol

The *Ad-Hoc On-Demand Distance Vector* (AODV) routing protocol is an improvement over DSDV and is a source-initiated routing scheme capable of both unicast and multicast routing. AODV establishes a required route only when it is needed, as opposed to maintaining a complete list of routes with DSDV. AODV uses an improved version of the *distance vector* algorithm, explained in Chapter 5, to provide on-demand routing.

AODV offers quick convergence when a network topology changes because of any node movement or link breakage. In such cases, AODV notifies all nodes so that they can invalidate the routes using the lost node or link. This protocol adapts quickly to dynamic link conditions and offers low processing and memory overhead, and low network utilization. Loop-free AODV is self-starting and handles large numbers of mobile nodes. It allows mobile nodes to respond to link breakages and changes in network topology in a timely manner. The algorithm's primary features are as follows:

- It broadcasts packets only when required.
- It distinguishes between local connectivity management and general maintenance.
- It disseminates information about changes in local connectivity to neighboring mobile nodes that need this information.
- Nodes that are not part of active paths neither maintain any routing information nor participate in any periodic routing table exchanges.
- A node does not have to find and maintain a route to another node until the two nodes communicate. Routes are maintained on all nodes on an active path. For example, all transmitting nodes maintain the route to the destination.

AODV can also form multicast trees that connect multicast group members. The trees are composed of group members and the nodes needed to connect them. This is similar to multicast protocols, explained in Chapter 6.

Routing Process

A route is *active* as long as data packets periodically travel from a source to a destination along that path. In other words, an active route from a source to a destination has a valid entry in a routing table. Packets can be forwarded only on active routes. Each mobile node maintains a *routing table entry* for a potential destination. A routing table entry contains

- Active neighbors for a requested route
- Next-hop address
- Destination address
- Number of hops to a destination
- Sequence number for the destination
- Expiration time for the route table entry (timeout)

Each routing table entry maintains the addresses of the active neighbors so that all active source nodes can be notified when a link along the route to the destination breaks. For each valid route, the node also stores a list of precursors that may transmit packets on this route. These precursors receive notifications from the node when it detects the loss of the *next-hop* link.

Any route in the routing table is tagged with the destination's *sequence number*, an increasing number set by a counter and managed by each originating node to ensure the freshness of the reverse route to a source. The sequence number is incremented whenever the source issues a new route-request message. Each node also records information about its neighbors with bidirectional connectivity. The insertion of a sequence number guarantees that no routing loops form even when packets are delivered out of order and under high node mobility. If a new route becomes available to the requested destination, the node compares the destination sequence number of the new incoming route with the one stored in the routing table for the current route. The existing entry is updated by replacing the current entry with the incoming one if one of the following conditions exists:

- The current sequence number in the routing table is marked invalid.
- The new incoming sequence number is greater than the one stored in the table.
- The sequence numbers are the same, and the new hop count is smaller than the one for the current entry.

Once the source stops sending data packets on an established connection, the routes time out and are eventually deleted from the intermediate-node routing tables. At the reverse-path entry of any routing table, a *request-expiration timer* purges the reverse-path routing entries from the nodes that do not lie on the route from the source to the destination. When an entry is used to transmit a packet, the timeout for the entry is reset to the current time plus the active-route timeout. The routing table also stores the *route caching timeout*, which is the time after which the route is considered to be invalid.

Route Discovery and Establishment

Suppose that a source node does not have information about a destination node, perhaps because it is unknown to the source node or a previously valid path to the destination expires or is marked invalid. In such cases, the source node initiates a *route-discovery* process to locate the destination. Route discovery is done by broadcasting a *route request* (RREQ) packet to neighbors, which in turn is forwarded to their neighbors until the destination node is reached. If it receives an already processed RREQ, a node discards the RREQ and does not forward it. Neighboring nodes update their information and set up backward pointers to the source node in their routing tables. Each neighbor either responds to the RREQ by sending back a route-reply RREP to the source or increases the hop count and broadcasts the RREQ to its own neighbors; in this case, the process continues. An RREQ packet contains the following information:

- Source address
- A unique RREQ
- Destination address
- Source sequence number
- Destination sequence number
- Hop count
- Lifetime

When an RREQ packet arrives at an intermediate node on a route, the node first updates the route to the previous hop. The node then checks whether the available route is current and completes this check by comparing the destination sequence number in its own route entry to the destination sequence number in the RREQ packet. If the destination sequence number is greater than the one available in the intermediate node's routing table, the intermediate node must not use its recorded route to respond to the RREQ. In this case, the intermediate node rebroadcasts the RREQ to its neighboring node.

On receipt of an RREQ, an intermediate node maintains the address of each neighbor from which the first copy of the packet is received in their routing tables and establishes a reverse path. Therefore, if additional copies of the same RREQ are received, they are discarded. When the RREQ reaches the destination node, it responds by sending a *route reply* (RREP) packet back to the neighbor from which the RREQ was first received. As the RREP is routed back, nodes along this reverse path set up forward route entries in their routing tables, which indicate the node from which the RREP came.

Any intermediate node checks whether it has received an RREQ with the same source node IP address and RREQ within at least the last path-discovery time. If such an RREQ has been received, the node drops the newly received RREQ. The reverse-route entries are maintained long enough for the RREQ packet to pass through the network and produce a reply to the sender. For the RREQ that is not dropped, the node increments the hop count and then searches for a reverse route to the source. At this point, a routing timer associated with each route times out and deletes the entry if it has not received any RREP or is not used within a specified time. The protocol uses destination sequence numbers to ensure that links are free of loops at all times and thus avoids counting to infinity. The destination address field is incremented every time a source issues a new RREQ.

Example. Figure 21.5 shows the process of signals with AODV from node 1 to node 8. To establish a connection, source node 1 searches in its table for a valid route to destination node 8. In the figure, an RREQ reaches the destination for the first time through path 1-2-4-6-8. The destination then issues an RREP packet to the source. After a while, the destination receives another RREQ, this time through path 1-3-7-8. The destination evaluates this path, and finds that path 1-3-7-8 is better, and then issues a new RREP packet, telling the source to discard the other reply.

As an RREP packet is propagated back to the source, involving nodes set up forward pointers to the destination. At this time, the hop-count field is incremented at each node. Thus, when the RREP packet reaches the source, the hop count represents the distance of the destination from the originator. The source node starts sending the data packets once the first RREP is received. If it receives an RREP representing a better route to the destination, the source node then updates its routing information. This means that, while transmitting, if it receives a better RREP packet containing a greater sequence number or the same sequence number with a smaller hop count, the source may update its routing information for that destination and switch over

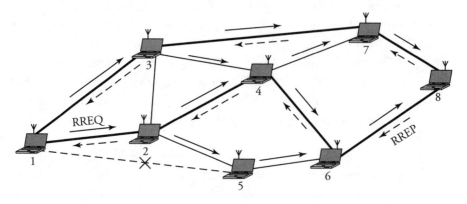

Figure 21.5   AODV communication signaling from node 1 to node 8

to the better path. As a result, a node ignores all less-desired RREPs received while transmitting.

At the reverse-path entry of any routing table, a *request-expiration timer* purges the reverse-path routing entries from the nodes that do not lie on the route from the source to the destination. When an entry is used to transmit a packet, the timeout for the entry is reset to the current time plus the active-route timeout. The routing table also stores the *route caching timeout*, which is the time after which the route is considered invalid. In Figure 21.6, a timeout has occurred. From the source node 1 to the destination node 8, two routes 1-2-4-6-8 and 1-3-7-8, are found. However, the RREP at the intermediate node 7 exceeds the time allowed to be released. In this case, route 1-3-7-8 is purged from the involved routing tables.

Route Maintenance

After a source knows how to establish a path, the network must maintain it. In general, each forwarding node should keep track of its continued connectivity to its active next hops. If a source node moves, it can reinitiate *route discovery* to find a fresh route to the destination. When a node along the route moves, its upstream neighbor identifies the move and propagates a link-failure notification message to each of its upstream neighbors. These nodes forward the link-failure notification to their neighbors, and so on, until the source node is reached. The source node may reinitiate *path discovery* if a route is still desired.

When the local connectivity of a mobile node is required, each mobile node can get information about other nodes in its neighborhood by using local broadcasts known as HELLO messages. A node should use HELLO messages only if it is part of an active route. A node that does not receive a HELLO message from its neighbors

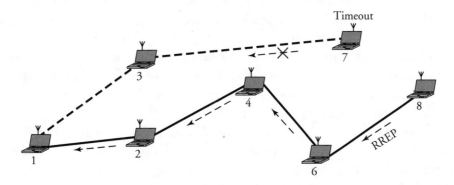

Figure 21.6   Occurrence of a timeout

along an active route sends a link-failure notification message to its upstream node on that route.

When it moves during an active session, a source node can start the route-discovery process again to find a new route to the destination node. If the destination or the intermediate node moves, a special RREP is sent to the affected source nodes. Periodic HELLO messages can normally be used to detect link failures. If a link failure occurs while the route is active, the upstream node of the breakage propagates a *route-error* (RERR) message. An RERR message can be either broadcast or unicast. For each node, if a link to the next hop is undetectable, the node should assume that the link is lost and take the following steps:

1. Make all related existing routes invalid.

2. List all destination nodes that would potentially be affected.

3. Identify all neighboring nodes that may be affected.

4. Send an RERR message to all such neighbors.

As shown in Figure 21.1, some next-hop nodes in a network might be unreachable. In such cases, the upstream node of the unreachable node propagates an unsolicited RREP with a fresh sequence number, and the hop count is set to infinity to all active upstream neighbors. Other nodes listen and pass on this message to their active neighbors until all nodes are notified. AODV finally terminates the unreachable node (broken associated links).

Joining a New Node to a Network

A new node can join an ad-hoc network by transmitting a HELLO message containing its identity and sequence number. When a node receives a HELLO message from a neighbor, the node makes sure that it has an active route to it or, if necessary, creates one. After this update, the current node can begin using this route to forward data packets. In general, nodes in a network may learn about their neighbors when a node receives a normal broadcast message or HELLO message. If the HELLO message is not received from the next hop along an active path, the active neighbors using that next hop are sent notification of a link break.

A node receiving HELLO messages should be part of an active route in order to use them. In every predetermined interval, active nodes in a network check whether they received HELLO messages from their neighbors. If it does not receive any packets within the hello interval, a node broadcasts a HELLO message to all its neighbors. Neighbors that receive this packet update their local connectivity information. Otherwise, if it does not receive any HELLO messages for more than some predetermined time, a node should assume that the link to this neighbor failed.

21.4   Security of Ad-Hoc Networks

Because of dynamic topological changes, ad-hoc networks are vulnerable at the physical link, as they can easily be manipulated. An intruder can easily attack ad-hoc networks by loading available network resources, such as wireless links and energy (battery) levels of other users, and then disturb all users. Attackers can also disturb the normal operation of routing protocols by modifying packets. The intruder may insert spurious information into routing packets, causing erroneous routing table updates and thus misrouting. Some other security vulnerabilities of ad-hoc networks follow.

- *Limited computational capabilities.* Typically, nodes in ad-hoc networks are modular, independent, and limited in computational capability and therefore may become a source of vulnerability when they handle public-key cryptography during normal operation.

- *Limited power supply.* Since a node normally use a battery as a power supply, an intruder can exhaust batteries by creating additional transmissions or excessive computations to be carried out by nodes.

- *Challenging key management.* Dynamic topology and movement of nodes in an ad-hoc network make *key management* difficult if cryptography is used in the routing protocol.

In any network, routing information can give an attacker access to relationships among nodes and their IP addresses. Especially in ad-hoc networks, an attacker may be able to bring the network down.

21.4.1   Types of Attacks

Attacks in ad-hoc networks are either *passive* or *active*. In a passive attack, the normal operation of a routing protocol is not interrupted. Instead, an intruder tries to gather information by listening. Active attacks can sometimes be detectable and thus are less important. In an active attack, an attacker can insert some arbitrary packets of information into the network to disable it or to attract packets destined to other nodes.

Pin Attack

With the *pin*, or *black-hole*, *attack*, a malicious node pretends to have the shortest path to the destination of a packet. Normally, the intruder listens to a path set-up phase and, when he or she learns of a request for a route, sends a reply advertising a shortest route. Then, the intruder can be an official part of the network if the requesting node receives its malicious reply before the reply from a good node, and a forged route is set up. Once it becomes part of the network, the intruder can do anything within the network, such as undertaking a denial-of-service attack.

Location-Disclosure Attack

By learning the locations of intermediate nodes, an intruder can find out the location of a target node. The *location-disclosure attack* is made by an intruder to obtain information about the physical location of nodes in the network or the topology of the network.

Routing Table Overflow

Sometimes, an intruder can create routes whose destinations do not exist. This type of attack, known as *routing table overflow*, overwhelms the usual flow of traffic, as it creates too many dummy active routes. This attack has a profound impact on *proactive* routing protocols, which discover routing information before it is needed, but minimal impact on *reactive routing protocols*, which create a route only when needed.

Energy-Exhaustion Attack

Battery-powered nodes can conserve their power by transmitting only when needed. But an intruder may try to forward unwanted packets or request repeatedly fake or unwanted destinations to use up the energy of nodes' batteries.

21.4.2 Criteria for a Secure Routing Protocol

In order to protect ad-hoc networks from attacks and vulnerability, a routing protocol must possess the following properties:

- *Authenticity*. When a routing table is updated, it must check whether the updates were provided by authenticated nodes and users. The most challenging issue in ad-hoc networks is the lack of a centralized authority to issue and validate certificates of authenticity.

- *Integrity of information.* When a routing table is updated, the information carried to the routing updates must be checked for eligibility. A misleading update may alter the flow of packets in the network.

- *In-order updates.* Ad-hoc routing protocols must contain unique sequence numbers to maintain updates in order. Out-of-order updates may result in the propagation of wrong information.

- *Maximum update time.* Updates in routing tables must be done in the shortest possible time to ensure the credibility of the update information. A timestamp or time-out mechanism can normally be a solution.

- *Authorization.* An unforgeable credential along with the certificate authority issued to a node can determine all the privileges that the node can have.

- *Routing encryption.* Encrypting packets can prevent unauthorized nodes from reading them, and only those routers having the decryption key can access messages.

- *Route discovery.* It should always be possible to find any existing route between two points in a network.

- *Protocol immunization.* A routing protocol should be immune to intruding nodes and be able identify them.

- *Node-privacy location.* The routing protocol must protect the network from spreading the location or other unpublic information of individual nodes.

- *Self-stabilization.* If the self-stabilization of ad-hoc network performs efficiently, it must stabilize the network in the presence of damage continually received from malicious nodes.

- *Low computational load.* Typically, an ad hoc node is limited in power as it uses a battery. As a result, a node should be given the minimal computational load to maintain enough power to avoid any denial-of-service attacks from low available power.

21.5 Summary

A wireless ad-hoc network supports "independent" wireless and mobile communication systems. A mobile user in fact acts as a routing node. Routing protocols can be *centralized versus distributed*, *static versus adaptive*, and *table-driven versus source-initiated routing*.

Table-driven routing protocols find routes to all possible destinations before they are needed. The routes are recorded in nodes' routing tables and are updated within predefined intervals. Examples of such protocols are DSDV, CGSR, and WRP. CGSR has a better converging capability than the others do. Source-initiated routing protocols, such as DSR, ABR, TORA, and AODV, create routes only when they are requested by source nodes. AODV is very popular owing to its ability to stabilize the routing and its better security. Security is a critical issue in ad-hoc networks. Security vulnerability to various types of attacks can be minimized by meeting specific security criteria.

The next chapter explores a special version of an ad-hoc network: a *sensor network* by which sensors instead of switches and routers are networked to construct a powerful sensing system.

21.6 Exercises

1. Compare table-driven and source-initiated routing algorithms in terms of
    (a) Speed of routing table updates
    (b) Point-to-point routing when there is a sudden change in the network topology
2. Suppose that we have the ad-hoc network shown in Figure 21.7. The number on each link indicates the strength of the signal on that link. At time t_1, the threshold value of 2.5 is applied on all links as the minimum good connection. Use the DSDV protocol to
    (a) Show the content of the routing table for each node for $t < t_1$
    (b) Perform the routing algorithm to connect A to F
    (c) Show the content of the routing table for each node in $t \geq t_1$

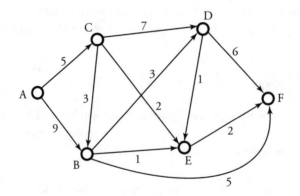

Figure 21.7   Exercises 2 and 3 ad-hoc network

3. With the same conditions stated in exercise 2, use the AODV protocol to
   (a) Show the content of the routing table for each node for $t < t_1$
   (b) Show the details of routing to connect A to F, including the communications with neighboring nodes
   (c) Show all the detailed steps of updating the neighboring nodes for each node in $t \geq t_1$

4. Consider an ad-hoc network consisting of users spread randomly in locations with Poisson distribution, where there are n users per square meter. Each user transmits with 40 percent probability and receives data with 60 percent probability in an assigned time slot. Make an assumption that the path loss exponent is β.
   (a) Find the distribution of interference power received in any randomly selected user.
   (b) Show that if $\beta > 2$, the average interference power is finite.

5. Consider Figure 21.3. We want to make a more detailed assignment to each node for routing from node A to F, using CGSR. Assume that the energy of cluster heads is normalized to $A = 23$, $B = 18$, $C = 15$, $D = 16$, $E = 25$, and $F = 14$. Find the best path from A to F. Assume that cluster heads have bidirectional links.

21.7   Computer Simulation Projects

1. **Simulation of an AODV-based Ad-hoc Network—Project 1.** Consider the ad-hoc network shown in Figure 21.5. We want to implement AODV on this network. We first apply distance vector routing to discover routes on an interconnected network. The primary distance vector routing uses the Bellman-Ford algorithm. Consider the network to be subject to topological changes at any time. You assign these times. Changes include a link failing unexpectedly or a new link being created or added. Let your program discover these changes, automatically update nodes' routing tables, and propagate these changes to the other nodes.

2. **Simulation of an AODV-based Ad-hoc Network—Project 2.** Reconsider the network you analyzed in project 1. We want to test the AODV route-discovery procedure and the ability of AODV to handle link and node failures. At the network level, design a least-cost algorithm that gives the shortest path, taking failing nodes (malicious nodes) into account. If one of the nodes in the

shortest path is a bad one, the next available shortest path must be found in the algorithm. In the algorithm you develop, the failure of a link should not affect the shortest-path determination. If a malicious node is in the network, that node should be discarded, and fresh routes are determined that have shortest path to the destination requested by the source node in the network. Assign faults deterministically, starting from the best path, and determine the shortest paths available. Determine how the best paths vary when the number of failing nodes is assigned randomly. Study how the network topology changes for a given n nodes with k failing nodes in the network. You will see that the total costs of the shortest paths between the sources and the destinations gradually increase with the number of fault nodes in the network if the fault nodes are assigned starting from the best path.

CHAPTER **22**

Wireless Sensor Networks

Self-organizing sensor networks hold the potential to revolutionize many segments of public security, environmental monitoring, and manufacturing. Sensors can be connected to form a network to enhance sensing capability. Like a computer network, a sensor network has a packet with a header flowing in a network of nodes (sensor nodes). This chapter presents the architectures and protocols of such networks, discussing the following topics:

- *Sensor networks and protocol structures*
- *Communication energy model*
- *Clustering protocols*
- *Routing protocols*
- *Case study: simulation of a sensor network*
- *Other related technologies*

We begin with an overview of sensor networks and explain some popular applications. We also provide an overview of a protocol stack for sensor networks and explain how the power factor distinguishes the routing protocols of sensor networks from those of computer networks. The protocol stack combines power efficiency and least-cost-path routing. Networking protocols and power efficiency are integrated through the wireless medium, and cooperative efforts of sensor nodes are promoted.

Clustering protocols in sensor networks specify the topology of the hierarchical network partitioned into nonoverlapping *clusters* of sensor nodes. Typically, a robust clustering technique is essential for self-organizing sensor networks. Two clustering protocols are the *Low-Energy Adaptive Clustering Hierarchy* (LEACH) algorithm and the *Decentralized Energy-Efficient Cluster Propagation* (DEEP) protocol. After well-distributed cluster heads and clusters have been established in a network, energy-conscious routing is essential in order to set communication routes among cluster heads.

This last chapter also offers a detailed numerical case study on the implementation of a clustering protocol, as well as a discussion of *ZigBee technology*, which is based on the IEEE 802.15.4 standard. This technology uses low-power nodes and is a well-known low-power standard.

22.1   Sensor Networks and Protocol Structures

Chemical, biological, or solar sensors can be networked together as a *sensor network* to strengthen the power of sensing. A sensor network is controlled through a software core engine. The network is typically wireless but may also be wired. Sensor networks are designed to be self-configuring such that they can gather information about a large geographical area or about movements of an object for surveillance purposes.

Sensor networks can be used for target tracking, environmental monitoring, system control, and chemical or biological detection. In military applications, sensor networks can enable soldiers to see around corners and to detect chemical and biological weapons long before they get close enough to cause harm. Civilian uses include environmental monitoring, traffic control, and providing health care monitoring for the elderly while allowing them more freedom to move about.

22.1.1   Clustering in Sensor Networks

The region being sensed is normally partitioned into equally loaded *clusters* of sensor nodes, as shown in Figure 22.1. A cluster in a sensor network resembles a domain in a computer network. In other words, nodes are inserted in the vicinity of a certain predefined region, forming a cluster. Different types of sensors can also be deployed in a region. Thus, a sensor network is typically cluster based and has irregular

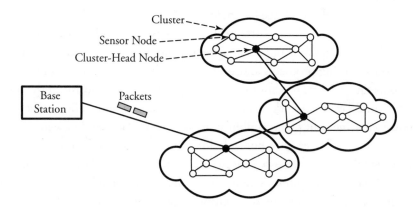

Figure 22.1 A sensor network and its clusters

topology. The most effective routing scheme in sensor networks is normally based on the energy (battery level) of nodes. In such routing schemes, the best path has the highest amount of total energy. The network of such sensing nodes is constructed with identical sensor nodes, regardless of the size of the network. In Figure 22.1, three clusters are interconnected to the main base station, and each cluster contains a *cluster head* responsible for routing data from its corresponding cluster to a *base station*.

Communicating nodes are normally linked by a wireless medium, such as radio. The wireless sensor node is equipped with a limited power source, such as a battery or even a *solar cell*, where there is enough sunlight exposure on the node. However, a solar cell may not be the best choice as a power supply, owing to its weight, volume, and expense. In some application scenarios, sensor-node lifetime depends on the battery lifetime. Removal of dead nodes can cause significant topological changes and may require packet rerouting. As a result, power management is a key issue in system design, node design, and communication protocol development. In summary, efficient energy-conscious clustering and routing algorithms can potentially prolong the network lifetime.

22.1.2 Protocol Stack

The algorithms developed for wireless ad-hoc networks cannot be used for sensor networks, for several reasons. One is that the number of sensor nodes is typically much more than in a typical ad-hoc network, and sensor nodes, unlike ad-hoc nodes, are prone to permanent failure. In addition, sensor nodes normally use broadcast rather than point-to-point communication with its limited power and memory.

Unlike computer networks, sensor nodes do not have global IDs, since a typical packet overhead can be too large for them.

Figure 22.2 shows a protocol architecture for sensor networks. The protocol stack combines power efficiency and least-cost-path routing. This protocol architecture integrates networking protocols and power through the wireless medium and promotes cooperative efforts of sensor nodes. The protocol stack consists of the physical layer, data-link layer, network layer, transport layer, and application layer, backed by a power-management plane, mobility-management plane, and task-management plane. The physical layer is responsible for robust modulation, transmission, and receiving signals. *Media access control* (MAC) at the data-link layer must minimize packet collision with neighboring nodes, as power is a restricted factor. The network layer routes packets provided by the transport layer. The application layer uses software for preparation of data on an event. The power-management plane monitors the sensor's power level among the sensor nodes and manages the amount of power a sensor node has used.

Most of the sensor network routing techniques and sensing tasks require an accurate knowledge of location. Thus, a sensor node commonly has a location-finding system. A mobilizer may sometimes be needed to move sensor nodes to carry out assigned tasks. Sensor network routing protocols must be capable of self-organizing. For these purposes, a series of energy-aware MAC, routing, and clustering protocols have been developed for wireless sensor networks. Most of the energy-aware MAC protocols aim to either *adjust the transmission power* or *keep transceivers off as long as possible*.

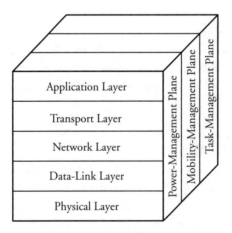

Figure 22.2   Sensor network protocol stack architecture

22.1.3   Sensor Node Structure

Figure 22.3 shows a typical sensor node. A node consists mainly of a sensing unit, a processing unit and memory, a self-power unit, and a wireless transceiver component, as well as a self- and remote-testing unit, a synchronizing and timing unit, a routing table, and security units. Since nodes in a network are not physically accessible once they are deployed in the field, they are not worth being brought under test. An option is an on-board remote self-testing unit for the node on a routine basis.

Each node must determine its location. This task is carried out by a location-finding system based on the *Global Positioning System* (GPS). All the processes within the sensor node are synchronized by a local clocking and synchronizing system. The communication and security protocol units are in fact part of the processing unit. These two units are responsible for computing the best path for networking and security of the data being transmitted. The three main blocks of the sensor node—sensing unit, processing and memory unit, and power unit—are described in more detail in the following subsections.

Sensing Unit

The sensing unit consists of a sensor and an analog-to-digital converter. A smart sensor node consists of a combination of multiple sensors. The analog signals produced by the sensors, based on the observed event, are converted to digital signals by the converter and then fed into the processing unit. The sensing unit collects data externally and interacts with the central processor at the heart of the node.

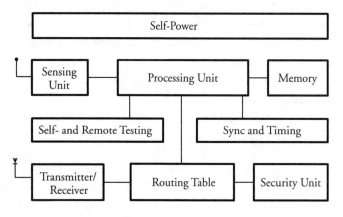

Figure 22.3   A typical wireless sensor node

Processing and Memory Unit

The *processing unit* performs certain computations on the data and, depending on how it is programmed, may send the resulting information out to the network. The processing unit, which is generally associated with memory, manages the procedures that make the sensor node collaborate with the other nodes to carry out the assigned sensing task. The central processor determines what data needs to be analyzed, stored, or compared with the data stored in memory. The streamed data from the sensor input is processed as it arrives. The database in memory stores an indexed data list to be used as a reference to detect an event. Since sensing nodes are typically tiny and many nodes are engaged in a network, the communication structure makes use of a hierarchically arranged self-routing network through cluster heads.

In smart wireless sensor networks, a tiny processor and a tiny database are used in a node. Thousands of such nodes are spread on fields to power up the sensing task, as in the deployment of numerous small intelligent sensor nodes in a battlefield to monitor enemy movements. By inserting self-organizing capability into a sensor network, a smart node can extract data, compare it with the data stored in its memory database, and process it for relevance before relaying it to its central base station.

Power Supply of Sensor Nodes

A sensor node is supposed to be mounted in a small physical unit with a limiting space for the battery. Moreover, the random distribution of sensors makes it impossible to periodically recharge or exchange batteries. In most types of sensor networks, the power unit in a sensor node is the most important unit of the node because the liveliness and existence of a node depend on the energy left in the node, and the routing in the sensor network is based on the algorithm that finds a path with the most energy. Thus, it is essential to use energy-efficient algorithms to prolong the life of a sensor network. The main task of the sensor node is to identify events, to process data, and then to transmit the data. The power of a node is consumed mainly in the transmitter and receiver unit. A sensor node can be supplied by a self-power unit battery, or a solar cell unit if possible.

22.2 Communication Energy Model

IEEE standards 802.11a, b, and g provide a wide range of data rates: 54, 48, 36, 24, 18, 12, 9, and 6 Mb/s. This range reflects the trade-off between the transmission range and data rate intrinsic in a wireless communication channel. An accurate energy model is crucial for the development of energy-efficient clustering and routing protocols. The energy consumption in watts, $E(d)$, as a function of several transceiver variables with the most important variable being the distance, d, is summarized as

$$E(d) = \theta + \eta\omega d^n, \tag{22.1}$$

where θ is the distance-independent term that accounts for the overhead of the radio electronics and digital processing, and $\eta\omega d^n$ is the distance-dependent term, in which η represents the amplifier inefficiency factor, ω is the free-space path loss, d is the distance, and n is the environmental factor. Based on an environmental condition, n can be a number between 2 and 4, and η specifies the inefficiency of the transmitter when generating maximum power ωd^n at the antenna. Clearly, the distance-dependent portion of total energy consumption depends on the real-world transceiver parameters, θ, η, and the path attenuation ωd^n. If the value of θ overshadows $\eta\omega d^n$, the reduction in the transmission distance through the use of multi-hop communication is not effective.

In theory, the maximum efficiency of a power amplifier is 48.4 percent. However, practical implementations show that the power-amplifier efficiency is less than 40 percent. Therefore, θ is calculated assuming that $\eta = 1/0.4 = 2.5$. Using Equation (22.1), we can express the energy consumption of a transmitter and a receiver, E_T and E_R, respectively, by

$$E_T = \theta_T + \eta\omega d^n \tag{22.2}$$

and

$$E_R = \theta_R, \tag{22.3}$$

where θ_T and θ_R are the distance-dependent terms for the transmitter and the receiver, respectively. Although maximum output power and total power consumption are provided in the manufacturer's data sheet, θ can be calculated using the following formula:

$$\theta = \theta_{TX} + \theta_{RX} = (E_T - \eta\omega d^n) + E_R. \tag{22.4}$$

Example.   Table 22.1 shows values of E_T and E_R based on a manufacturer's data sheet and θ and $\eta\omega d^n$ calculated for a selected chipset. Although path-attenuation energy increases exponentially by the transmission distance, the data illustrates that the static power consumption, θ, dominates the path loss. Clearly, this causes total power consumption to remain constant as the transmission distance increases. Standards 802.11a, 802.11b, and 802.11g have multi-rate capabilities. Although,

Table 22.1 Energy consumption parameters

IEEE Standard	Max. Output Power, ωd^n (dBm)	Total Power Consumption (W)	θ (W)	$\eta \times \omega d^n$ (W)
802.11a	+14	1.85 (E_{TX}) 1.20 (E_{RX})	2.987	0.0625
802.11b	+21	1.75 (E_{TX}) 1.29 (E_{RX})	2.727	0.3125
802.11g	+14	1.82 (E_{TX}) 1.40 (E_{RX})	3.157	0.0625

Table 22.2 Expected data rate of IEEE 802.11g technology

Rate (Mb/s)	Maximum Range	Rate (Mb/s)	Maximum Range
1	100.00 m	18	51.00 m
2	76.50 m	24	41.25 m
6	64.50 m	36	36.00 m
9	57.00 m	48	23.10 m
12	54.00 m	54	18.75 m

sensor nodes in general generate data at low rates, they can transmit the information using wireless high-speed modulation and techniques.

Table 22.2 shows the expected data rate for the 802.11g wireless technology. Although exploiting the multi-rate capabilities of wireless standards has never been proposed for sensor networks, this technique can decrease the transmission energy for smaller distances by switching to higher data rates and keeping the transceiver on for a shorter period of time. In this case, the energy in terms of Joule/bit reduces discretely as transmission distance shrinks:

$$E(d) = \frac{1}{R}(\theta + \eta\omega d^n), \tag{22.5}$$

where R is the rate in bits/sec. Figure 22.4 shows energy consumption using 802.11g technology at the constant rate of 1Mb/s and the same technology with the multi-rate extension. Because of large values of θ compared to the maximum output power term, single-rate communication energy consumption remains constant as the transmission distance increases, whereas the communication energy consumption for multi-rate transmission decreases for shorter transmission ranges. However, this scenario does not follow the model of ωd^n. Meanwhile, the multi-rate communication necessitates the presence of a robust rate-selection protocol.

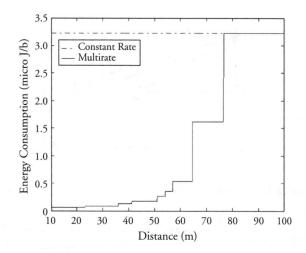

Figure 22.4 Energy consumption versus transmission distance for single-rate and multi-rate communication using 802.11g technology

Multi-Hop Communication Efficiency

Considering the impact of real-world radio parameters and multi-rate communication, we should reevaluate the effectiveness of multi-hop communication. Since a multi-rate communication reduces energy consumption for shorter distances by switching to higher data rates, multi-hop communication can conserve energy. The traditional objective of multi-hop communication is to divide the transmission distance into a number of hops, m, and to relatively conserve energy, considering Equation (22.3), by means of

$$E(d) = m \left(\theta + \omega \left(\frac{d}{m} \right)^n \right). \qquad (22.6)$$

However, if the division of transmission distance happens when the maximum range is less than 18.75 m for standard 802.11g, the data rate remains constant, and total energy consumption is multiplied by the number of hops. Since sensor networks deal with two- or even three-dimensional spaces, multi-hop efficiency depends on the network scale and density.

Example. Figure 22.5 shows an organization in which sensor nodes A, B, C, D, and E are placed d meters apart and tend to send their data packets to the *cluster head* (CH). Note that d is an application-dependent parameter and can be chosen based on the sensor's characteristics. Assume that standard 802.11g technology is used in an environment in which sensors are placed on average no more than 10 meters

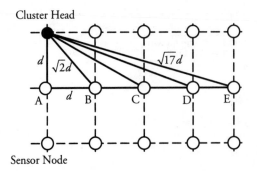

Figure 22.5   Cluster-head distances from sensor nodes A, B, C, D, and E

apart. Compare the nodes' energy consumption, using the 802.11g chart illustrated in Figure 22.4.

Solution.   With the choice of $d = 10$ meters, if node B tries to use node A as a relay node and then sends data to the cluster head, the total energy of the chosen two-hop path (B to A, then A to cluster head) is larger than the direct-transmission energy (B to cluster head). The two-hop transmission energy, $E(d) + E(d)$, compared to direct-transmission energy, $E(\sqrt{2}d)$, according to the 802.11g chart illustrated in Figure 22.4, can be obtained as

$$E(\sqrt{2}d) = 0.0517 < E(d) + E(d) = 0.1034. \qquad (22.7)$$

Similarly, for nodes C and D, there is no multi-hop path that can lead to better energy consumption than the direct communication path:

$$E(\sqrt{5}d) = 0.0581 < E(\sqrt{2}d) + E(d) = 0.1034 \qquad (22.8)$$

and

$$E(\sqrt{10}d) = 0.0775 < E(\sqrt{5}d) + E(d) = 0.1098. \qquad (22.9)$$

But if node E first sends the data to the intermediate node D, total energy consumption will be less than the direct communication path:

$$E(\sqrt{17}d) = E(41.23) = 0.1789 > E(\sqrt{10}d) + E(d) = 0.1292 \qquad (22.10)$$

Node E is 41.23 meters away from the cluster head. This shows that for nodes more than 41.23 meters apart, direct transmission is no longer the best possible communication method.

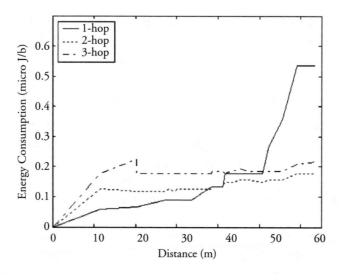

Figure 22.6   Communication energy versus distance from cluster head for 802.11g technology

Example.   Continuing the previous example using 802.11g technology, set up an environment representing one cluster. The dimension of the field is 50 m × 50 m, and 25 nodes are randomly dispersed in the field. Compare the energy consumption of direct and multi-hop communication inside the cluster.

Solution.   At this point, we assume that the cluster head is chosen randomly among the sensors. (The details of cluster-head selection algorithms are explained in Section 22.3.) Figure 22.6 shows the energy consumption of a direct, minimum-energy two-hop and minimum-energy three-hop path, based on the distance between nodes in the cluster and the cluster head. For 802.11g technology, the direct transmission is the optimum choice for ranges less than 37 meters, which is almost the same as the result from analytical calculations (41 m). However, for ranges greater than 37 meters, the minimum-energy two-hop path can lead to significantly lower energy consumption.

22.3   Clustering Protocols

Clustering protocols specify the topology of the hierarchical nonoverlapping *clusters* of sensor nodes. A robust clustering technique is essential for self-organizing sensor networks. An efficient clustering protocol ensures the creation of clusters with almost the same radius and cluster heads that are best positioned in the clusters. Since every node in a clustered network is connected to a cluster head, route discovery among cluster heads is sufficient to establish a feasible route in the network. For a large sensor network, clustering can simplify multi-hop route discovery and limit the number of transmissions compared to a flat, nonclustered network.

22.3.1 Classification of Clustering Protocols

Clustering techniques can be either *centralized* or *decentralized*. Centralized clustering algorithms require each sensor node to send its individual information, such as energy level and geographical position, to the central base station. Based on a predefined algorithm, a base station calculates the number of clusters, their sizes, and the cluster heads' positions and then provides each node with its newly assigned duty.

Given the assumption that sensor networks might consist of thousands of nodes, it is impractical, if not impossible, for a base station to collect information about every node in the network prior to route setup. Therefore, centralized clustering is not an option for large sensor networks. Since a sensor node begins a clustering process without any knowledge about its location relative to the corresponding base station, a clustering algorithm should be able to form clusters without the help of the base station and knowledge of node positioning. Although location-finder devices can also be deployed to perform this task, they are often either costly or add too much overhead on the network.

Decentralized clustering techniques create clusters without the help of any centralized base station. An energy-efficient and hierarchical clustering algorithm can be designed in such a way that each sensor node becomes a cluster head with a probability of p and advertises its candidacy to nodes that are no more than k hops away from the cluster head. Given the limited transmission range of wireless sensor nodes, a hierarchical structure with an arbitrary number of levels has its limitations. As the number of hierarchical levels grows, the distance between upper-level cluster heads may increase to the point that they are no longer able to communicate with one another. The *Low-Energy Adaptive Clustering Hierarchy* (LEACH) algorithm and the *Decentralized Energy-Efficient Cluster Propagation* (DEEP) protocol are two examples of the decentralized clustering protocols and are explained next.

22.3.2 LEACH Clustering Protocol

The *Low-Energy Adaptive Clustering Hierarchy* (LEACH) protocol is a decentralized clustering algorithm that does not offer a complete energy-optimization solution, as it has no strategy for specifying cluster-head positioning and distribution. LEACH is an application-specific protocol architecture that aims to prolong network lifetime by periodic reclustering and change of the network topology.

LEACH is divided into *rounds* consisting of a clustering phase and a steady-state phase for data collection. At the start of each round, a sensor node randomly chooses a number between 0 and 1 and then compares this number to a calculated threshold called $T(n)$. If $T(n)$ is larger than the chosen number, the node becomes a cluster head for the current round. The value $T(n)$ is calculated using the following formula:

$$T(n) = \begin{cases} \dfrac{p}{1 - p(r \bmod(1/p))} & \text{for } n \in G \\ 0 & \text{otherwise} \end{cases}, \qquad (22.11)$$

where p is the ratio of the total number of cluster heads to the total number of nodes, r is the number of rounds, and G is a set of nodes that have not been chosen as cluster heads for the last $1/p$ rounds. For the first round ($r=0$), $T(n)$ is equal to p, and nodes have an equal chance to become cluster heads. As r gets closer to $1/p$, $T(n)$ increases, and nodes that have not been selected as cluster heads in the last $1/p$ rounds have a greater chance to become cluster heads. After $1/p - 1$ rounds, $T(n)$ is equal to 1, meaning that all the remaining nodes have been selected as cluster heads. Thus, after $1/p$ rounds, all the nodes have had a chance to become a cluster head once. Since being the cluster head puts a substantial burden on the sensor nodes, this ensures that the network has no overloaded node that runs out of energy sooner than the others.

After cluster heads are self-selected, they start to advertise their candidacy to the other sensor nodes. When it receives advertisements from more than one cluster-head candidate, a sensor node starts to make a decision about its corresponding cluster head. Each node listens to the advertisement signals and chooses the candidate whose associated signal is received with higher power. This ensures that each sensor node chooses the closest candidate as cluster head. The LEACH algorithm is distributed, as it can be accomplished by local computation and communication at each node, rather than by the transmission of all the nodes' energy levels and geographical position to a centralized point. However, cluster heads are chosen randomly, and there is no optimization in terms of energy consumption.

22.3.3 DEEP Clustering Protocol

The *Decentralized Energy-Efficient Cluster Propagation* (DEEP) protocol establishes clusters with uniformly distributed cluster heads. This protocol balances the load among all the cluster heads by keeping the clusters' radii fairly equal. This protocol is completely decentralized, and there is no need for any location-finder device or hardware. The protocol starts with an initial cluster head. It gradually forms new cluster-head candidates by controlling the relative distance between a pair of cluster heads and the circular radius of each cluster. Owing to the balanced load among cluster heads, periodic reclustering is not necessary, and operational expenses caused by frequent reclustering are therefore eliminated.

An efficient path-selection algorithm for nodes that are placed more than ℓ meters away from a cluster head is necessary in order to find the optimum two-hop or three-hop path. Although direct transmission to a cluster head can eliminate the overhead created by the route set-up packets, its efficiency is questionable, owing to the limited transmission range. In order to avoid the frequent control signal transmission and extra power consumption associated with that, a cluster head can be placed at the center of the cluster, with sensor nodes positioned closer than ℓ meters around it. In this case, cluster members can send the data packets directly to the cluster head without the need for any route set-up protocol, while efficiency has already been achieved through the choice of cluster shape and cluster size.

In order to explain the details of this algorithm, control signals and protocol parameters need to be introduced:

- Control signals: (1) cluster-head declaration signal or (2) cluster-head exploration signal
- Membership search signal with control parameters: declaration range (d_r), exploration range (d_{r1}, d_{r2}), minimum number of members (m_n), E_{rc1}, and E_{rc2}.

Protocol control parameters are application-specific choices and can be defined prior to network deployment. DEEP forms clusters by starting with an initial cluster head that can be chosen prior to network deployment. This initial cluster head starts the cluster set-up phase by propagating cluster-head declaration signals within the range of d_r. This means that the cluster-head candidate chooses an appropriate data rate and signal output power so that it can reach nodes that are less than d_r away from the sender.

At this point, sensor nodes that receive the declaration signal accept the corresponding cluster head as a leader. They can then estimate their relative distance to the candidate by looking at the received signal's energy level. Once they know the relative distance to the cluster head, they can conserve energy by adjusting the transmission speed to the appropriate value and switching to sleep mode. Now, the initial cluster-head candidate propagates the cluster-head exploration signal within the range of d_{r2}, as shown in Figure 22.7. All the sensor nodes in this range can listen to the exploration signal, but only nodes that have never played the role of a cluster head and verify the following inequality are chosen as new candidates:

$$E_{rc1} < E_r < E_{rc2},$$ (22.12)

where E_r is the received signal energy. Note that E_{rc1} and E_{rc2} are fixed protocol parameters that can be precalculated and stored in the sensor-node memory, using the following formula:

$$E_{rc1} = P_{out} - \omega d_{r1}^n$$ (22.13)

and

$$E_{rc2} = P_{out} - \omega d_{r2}^n,$$ (22.14)

where P_{out} is the constant output power of the cluster-head exploration signal, and ω and n are parameters that can be determined based on the environmental conditions of the deployment area. This way, any of these nodes can consider itself a candidate. This ensures that new cluster-head candidates are positioned between d_{r1} and d_{r2}, away from the initial cluster head.

After a new cluster-head candidate is assigned, it sends a declaration signal within the range of d_r to find new cluster members. If two candidates can hear each other's declaration signal, they are too close to each other to be considered cluster-head candidates. Therefore, one of them is eliminated through a negotiation phase. Whenever it receives a declaration signal, a cluster head informs the sender of the message, using an acknowledgment message. A cluster head that receives the acknowledgment sends

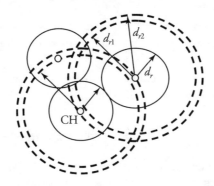

Figure 22.7   Initial cluster head starts the advertisement process. New cluster-head candidates send the exploration signal within the range of d_{r2} to continue the process of cluster establishment.

a dissolution message and informs all nodes within the range of d_r about its elimination. A node that receives a declaration signal from more than one candidate chooses the candidate whose associated signal is received with a higher power.

At this point, all confirmed cluster heads propagate exploration signals and search for new cluster-head candidates. Nodes that have already been chosen as cluster heads or members ignore the cluster-head exploration or declaration signals. Therefore, this advertisement process terminates automatically when all the nodes in the field belong to a cluster. At this point, the algorithm might have produced some clusters with a very small number of members. Therefore, a cluster whose total number of members is smaller than the minimum number of members, m_n, is dissolved, and all its members, including its cluster head, initiate a *membership-search signal*.

After this process is completed, nodes listen to the responses from the local cluster heads and choose the closest cluster head, based on the received signal power. At the end, if the timeout has been reached, a sensor node that has not received any control signal sends a *membership-search signal* and chooses the closest cluster head as leader. The following algorithm summarizes the core segment of the DEEP protocol.

Begin DEEP Clustering Algorithm

1. **Initialize.** The initial cluster head finds cluster members by sending a cluster-head declaration.

2. The initial cluster head finds new cluster-head candidates by sending a cluster-head exploration signal.

3. **Repeat.** Cluster-head candidates that are placed on the (d_{r1}, d_{r1}) ring find cluster members.

4. Nodes that receive more than one cluster-head declaration choose the closest cluster head, based on the received signal energy.

5. Cluster-head candidates that receive a cluster-head declaration signal negotiate with the sender, and one of them gets eliminated.

6. Confirmed cluster heads send cluster-head exploration signals to find new cluster-head candidates.

7. **Finalize.** If the number of members in a cluster is less than m_n, all the members find new clusters by sending the membership-search signal.

8. **If** a node has not received any control signal, it sends the membership-search signal. ∎

DEEP has several advantages over other clustering protocols. With DEEP, a sensor node can either select itself as a cluster head by receiving a cluster-head exploration signal or join a cluster by receiving a cluster-head declaration signal. After the execution of the protocol, all the sensor nodes are covered and belong to only one cluster. This clearly shows that this protocol is completely decentralized. In addition, for the execution of DEEP, there is no need for any location-finder hardware, such as the *Global Positioning System* (GPS) or a position-estimation protocol that puts extra overhead on sensor nodes.

DEEP can control a cluster-head distribution across the sensor network through protocol-execution methodologies. For example, cluster-head candidates should receive the cluster-head exploration signal with a certain amount of energy; if they can hear the declaration signal of each other, one of the candidates is eliminated. Communication cost is low through proper selection of protocol parameters, such as declaration range, exploration range, and minimum number of members.

With DEEP, *intracluster* communication is controlled by cluster heads, and nodes transmit their data directly to cluster heads. Therefore, no additional control signal is associated with route selection and maintenance inside the cluster. Also, owing to the uniform distribution of cluster heads, communication cost of a direct transmission path between a pair of neighboring cluster heads is almost identical across the sensor field. This is one of the most important protocol characteristics contributing to convenient deployment of an *intercluster* routing protocol.

22.3.4   Reclustering

In order to prevent overutilization of some sensor nodes, clustering technique should ensure that the cluster-head responsibility rotates among all sensor nodes. To achieve this, reclustering is performed periodically in LEACH. However, every round of reclustering requires several control-signal exchanges among self-elected cluster heads and sensor nodes. The reclustering process in DEEP is based on one small shift in the initial cluster head. When the current period of cluster setting is finished, the current initial CH chooses the nearest node that has never acted as an initial cluster head. This newly chosen initial cluster head starts the clustering process and creates a totally different cluster-head constellation.

22.4   Routing Protocols

After clusters with well-distributed cluster heads have been established in a network, energy-conscious routing is essential in order to set communication routes among cluster heads in a two-level hierarchical system. Similar to computer networks, routing protocols in sensor networks can be classified as either *intracluster* or *intercluster*. This section looks at both categories.

The fundamental concept behind them is much the same as the concept behind intradomain and interdomain routings (see Chapter 5). Assuming that every node in a cluster can act as a relay node, there could be a large number of possible routes from a source to a sink. Because of the limited transmission range associated with low-power wireless technologies, cluster-head packets cannot reach the base station unless other cluster heads act as relay nodes. Two major approaches can be used for routing and selecting the best path in a sensor network, as follows:

1. *Centralized routing*, whereby the routing decision is made by a single command center

2. *Distributed routing*, whereby the routing decision is made in a distributed fashion by several entities

Distributed routing algorithms are further classified as *proactive* or *reactive*. With proactive routing algorithms, such as link-state routing and distance vector routing, nodes keep a routing table that contains next-hop information to every node in the network. Reactive routing protocols set a route to the desirable destination only when it is needed. Note that none of the ad-hoc network protocols explained earlier consider energy consumption.

Another group of on-demand reactive routing protocols address the exclusive issues of wireless sensor networks. For example, *directed diffusion* introduces a concept of "interest" propagation whenever a node wants to send data or a source needs to ask for it. With this type of protocol, flooding the network with interest signals establishes a path from a sink to every possible source (spanning tree).

22.4.1   Intracluster Routing Protocols

A routing algorithm within a cluster can be either *direct* or *multi-hop*. In a direct routing algorithm, the cluster head as the destination for all cluster nodes is located in the center of the cluster, so all nodes can communicate with the cluster head directly, as shown in Figure 22.8. Note that in this figure, two nodes cannot reach the destination, as they are located far from it. The number shown in each node indicates the level of energy the corresponding node has.

In a multi-hop routing algorithm, a node can face multiple hops in order to reach the destination. If a multi-hop algorithm is used for the centralized clustering procedure, the algorithm aims to choose the appropriate next neighbor for each node, using a central command node. Typically, a central command node collects the information about direct paths' costs and geographical positions of the nodes and finds the best path.

Figure 22.9 shows a routing implementation. Sensor nodes are usually scattered in the field. A packet from a node is routed to a neighboring node that exhibits the highest amount of energy. The energy is an indication of the node's battery level. The number associated with each node indicates a normalized value of the remaining energy in that node. Figure 22.9 shows two paths from a node to a cluster-head node.

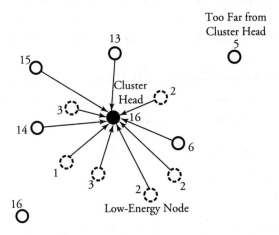

Figure 22.8   Direct routing in a cluster. The number associated with each node indicates a normalized value of the remaining energy in that node.

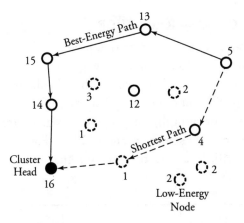

Figure 22.9   Multi-hop routing in a cluster in which the number associated with each node indicates a normalized value of the remaining energy in that node

One path involves the shortest distance in terms of hop counts; the other one uses the highest-energy route. The challenge here is to find the best path that suits the rapid and secure deployment of data.

The least-cost algorithm and the best-energy path can be modeled and compared for a network to provide a behavioral benchmark. The model can determine all possible paths available between a given source and destination. The energy of each node and hence all possible least-cost paths are computed regularly by cluster heads and propagated to all cluster nodes for database updating. During the phase of path finding to a cluster head, the routing algorithm accepts a failing (low-energy) node and finds the least-cost path, taking the failing node into account. The inputs for the routing process then include source node, destination node, failing nodes, and all other nodes.

22.4.2   Intercluster Routing Protocols

Intercluster protocols are not typically different from the multi-hop ones for intradomain cases. Interdomain protocols are available for

- Intercluster energy-conscious routing (ICR)
- Energy-aware routing (EAR)
- Directed diffusion

ICR uses interest flooding similar to directed diffusion and EAR to establish routes between the base station and sensor nodes but differs from EAR and directed diffusion in some aspects.

Intercluster Energy-Conscious Routing (ICR)

ICR is a destination-initiated reactive routing protocol. This means that a destination, a local base station (LBS), initiates an explicit route-discovery phase, which includes the propagation of an *interest* signal that floods throughout the network and establishes energy-efficient routes. Based on the application, which can be either periodic data collection or event driven, the interest signal can include the *type* and the *period* of the desired data shown in Figure 22.10. For an application requiring information from specific locations, the interest signal also includes the position of the required information.

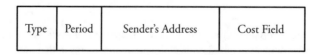

Figure 22.10   Interest-signal structure in a packet

If the LBS requires some periodic data collection, it sets the *period* in which nodes send the specific *type* of information. Monitoring and surveillance applications are examples of the data-collection paradigm. If it requires sensor nodes to detect one specific event, an LBS includes the *type* of the event in the interest signal. Following the route-discovery phase, sensor nodes switch to sleep mode and wait for the specific event. In case of event detection, non-cluster-head nodes send the data directly to the associated cluster head, which uses the previously established route to send the information back to the LBS. In short, ICR occurs in two phases: *route discovery* and *data acquisition*.

As shown in Figure 22.11, in the *route discovery* phase, the local base station initiates route discovery by sending an interest signal within the range of R_i. The value of R_i should be both high enough to keep the cluster-head network connected and low enough to prevent unnecessary energy consumption and interest generation. Owing to even distribution of cluster heads achieved by a clustering protocol, R_i can be chosen slightly bigger than the average distance between a pair of adjacent cluster heads. The LBS should adjust its output power and data rate of the interest signal to limit its transmission range to R_i. Also, the cost field is set to zero before interest propagation starts.

Since the distance between a pair of neighboring cluster heads is approximately the same across the network, the communication energy consumption associated with two distinct adjacent cluster heads is also the same. Therefore, the cost, or weight, of a multi-hop path is defined exclusively by the number of hops. In addition, the remaining energy in the cluster heads along the path affects the route-selection decision. The total-cost function C is defined as

$$C = \alpha h + \beta \sum_i \frac{B_M}{B_{ri}}, \tag{22.15}$$

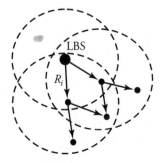

Figure 22.11   LBS starts route discovery by generating interest signals.

where h is the hop number and B_{ri} represents the remaining energy in the battery of node i B_M, shows the maximum battery capacity of a sensor node, and α and β are normalization factors. The second part of the cost field favors the paths that include nodes with higher energy. To update the cost field, each intermediate cluster head calculates the inverse of its remaining battery power plus 1 (increment in the number of hops) and adds the outcome to the existing cost value.

Each intermediate cluster head that receives the interest signal saves the interest in its memory, including the address of the nodes that sent the message. Then the node should update the cost field of the outgoing interest signal and send it within the range of R_i. All the cluster heads within this range around the sender can hear the incoming signal. If it receives an interest signal that currently exists in memory but the sender's address is different, a cluster head compares the cost field of the received signal with the cost field of the previously saved message. If the incoming interest signal includes a cost field smaller than the previously saved message, the node replaces the old interest entry, updates the cost field, and propagates the packet, since the new signal represents a shorter, or more energy-efficient, path. If the new interest signal represents a path with a higher number of hops, the node should destroy the packet.

The *data-acquisition phase* occurs after each cluster head collects the requested information from sensor nodes and compresses it into a packet with fixed length, searches for the neighbor's address in memory, and relays the packet to that neighbor. In order to reduce the diffusion of spare data bits in the network, relay nodes can receive the data packets, each of length L, from N nodes and aggregate them into one single packet of length L. This reduces the number of data bits forwarded by the relay node from NL to L. To enable data aggregation during the data-collection period, cluster heads that are closer to the base station—that is, the cost field of the saved interest message includes fewer hops—should wait for their neighbors to send their data packets and then compress the incoming information with their own data and send the packet with the fixed length to the relay neighbor.

Comparison of ICR and EAR

ICR is different from EAR in two aspects. In EAR, sensor nodes save and propagate most of the incoming interest signals and eliminate only the ones with a very high cost field. However, in ICR, every time that the cost field of the incoming interest message is higher than the previously saved one, the packet gets destroyed. This puts a limit on the generation of interest messages.

In EAR, in order to ensure that the optimal path does not get depleted and that the network degrades evenly, multiple paths are found between a source and a destination. Each node has to wait for all the interest signals to come and then calculates the average cost between itself and the destination. Based on the average cost, each path is assigned a probability of being chosen. Depending on the probability, each time one of the paths is chosen, ICR assumes that data aggregation is executed among cluster heads, and no packet moves along the chosen path independently. This means that during the data-collection period, each cluster head aggregates the data from its N adjacent cluster heads and has to forward only one compressed packet rather than N distinct packets. After the execution of the routing protocol, a spanning tree is established that is rooted in the base station and connects all the cluster heads to the base station. Therefore, only the least-cost, or the optimum, path is a final, established route for each cluster head. This way, the degradation of the optimal path for each packet is prevented.

22.5   Other Related Technologies

Other sensor network based technologies use low-power nodes. The one discussed in this section is the *ZigBee technology*.

22.5.1   ZigBee Technology and IEEE 802.15.4

The *ZigBee technology* is a communication standard that provides a short-range, low-cost networking capability that allows low-cost devices to quickly transmit small amounts of data, such as temperature readings for thermostats, on/off requests for light switches, or keystrokes for a wireless keyboard. Other ZigBee applications are in professional installation kits for lighting controls, heating, ventilation, air conditioning, and security. Even the Bluetooth short-range wireless technology found in laptops and cellphones lacks the affordability, power savings, and mesh-networking capabilities of ZigBee.

ZigBee comes from higher-layer enhancements by a multi-vendor consortium called the ZigBee Alliance. IEEE standard 802.15.4/ZigBee specifies the MAC and physical layers. The 802.15.4 standard specifies 128-bit AES encryption; ZigBee specifies how to handle encryption key exchange. The 802.15.4/ZigBee networks run in the unlicensed frequencies, 900MHz and 2.4GHz band, based on a packet radio standard and support many cordless telephones, allowing data to be sent over distances up to 20 meters.

ZigBee devices, typically battery powered, can transmit information much farther than 20 meters, because each device within listening distance passes the message along to any other device within range. Only the intended device acts on the message. By instructing nodes to wake up only for those split-second intervals when they are needed, ZigBee device batteries might last for years. Although this technology is targeted for manufacturing, health care, shipping, and homeland defense, the ZigBee Alliance is initially keeping its focus small.

22.6 Case Study: Simulation of a Sensor Network

This section presents a case study that shows the implementation of DEEP and ICR for a wireless sensor network spread over an area. The network is used for monitoring and protecting the area. The basic objective is to deploy a large number of low-cost and self-powered sensor nodes, each of which acquires and processes data from a hazardous event and alerts a base station to take necessary action. In this scenario, 3,000 sensor nodes are randomly distributed in a field of 550 m × 550 m. Therefore, the density of sensor nodes is about one per 10 m × 10 m area, which is the maximum detection range for the hazard sensors.

MAC assigns a unique channel for every node and prevents possible collisions. With this assumption, we extracted the MAC layer from our simulations, and data packets were sent directly from the network layer of one node to the network layer of the neighbor. We simulated the DEEP algorithm, using parameters d_r, d_{r1}, d_{r2}, and m, and put the initial cluster head at the center of the field.

22.6.1 Cluster-Head Constellation and Distribution of Load

Figure 22.12 shows the result of the simulation with parameters $d_r = 30$ m, $d_{r2} = 80$ m, $d_{r1} = 78$ m, and $m = 14$. Based on the results obtained from Section 22.2, the distance of 30 meters is an initial choice for d_r. In order to avoid overlapping between clusters, the value of d_{r1} and d_{r2} should be more than twice the value of d_r. Since the average distance between sensor nodes in this application is 10 m, 80 m is a fair choice for d_{r2}. The width of the (d_{r1}, d_{r2}) ring should be large enough to accommodate new cluster-head candidates and small enough to avoid cluster-head candidates that are too close to each other. We chose an initial value of 2 m for the ring width.

In order to balance the load among cluster heads, DEEP controls the cluster-head distribution rather than the number of cluster members. Although cluster heads that manage more members should execute more signal processing for the sake of data aggregation, digital processing consumes much less energy than wireless transmission, and no over utilized cluster head is using this protocol. Figure 22.13 demonstrates the cluster-head distribution achieved using LEACH and DEEP. Because of the random selection of cluster heads in LEACH, some of the cluster

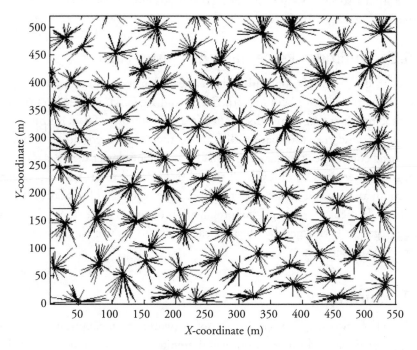

Figure 22.12   Simulation results on distributed clusters whose sensor nodes are directly connected to their associated cluster heads

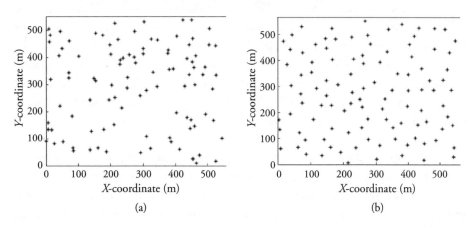

Figure 22.13   Comparison of cluster-head constellations between (a) LEACH and (b) DEEP

heads are too close to each other; others, too far. This type of cluster-head selection causes a lot of burden on some cluster heads and quickly drains their batteries. It can be shown that compared with LEACH, DEEP is capable of minimizing energy consumption associated with reclustering overheads more efficiently by reducing the number of necessary rounds.

22.6.2   Optimum Percentage of Cluster Heads

In order to determine the optimum cluster-head density and compare the performance of the routing protocol in both DEEP and LEACH, we used a 1,600-node network. Nodes were randomly distributed in a field 400 m × 400 m. In this scenario, sensor nodes send the information directly to their associated cluster head. Each cluster head compresses the data and waits for neighbor cluster heads' data packets. Then, the cluster head compresses all the received data packets into a packet with fixed length and sends it to the relay neighbor. The relay neighbor address has been saved in node memory through the propagation of the interest signal. In-network data aggregation performed by cluster heads helps to reduce the amount of data dispersed in the network.

22.7   Summary

This last chapter focused on wireless sensor networks. Some applications of sensor networks are target tracking, environmental monitoring, system control, and chemical or biological detection.

The protocol stack for sensor networks is concerned with the power factor. The sensor network protocol stack combines two features: power efficiency and least-cost-path routing. Thus, the protocol architecture integrates networking protocols and power efficiency through the wireless medium and promotes cooperative efforts among sensor nodes. The protocol stack consists of the physical, data-link, network, transport, and application layers, and the power-management, mobility-management, and task-management planes. The internal structure of an intelligent sensor node consists of three units for sensing, processing, and storage, respectively, and communications capabilities.

An energy model for a transceiver of a node can be developed. The energy consumption, E, for all components of a transceiver in watts can be modeled by $E = \theta + \eta\omega d^n$, where θ is the distance-independent term that accounts for the overhead of the radio electronics and digital processing, and $\eta\omega d^n$ is the distance-dependent term in which η represents the amplifier inefficiency factor, ω is the free-space path loss, and d is the distance.

Two *clustering protocols* in sensor networks are the *Low-Energy Adaptive Clustering Hierarchy* (LEACH) algorithm and the *Decentralized Energy-Efficient Cluster Propagation* (DEEP) protocol. DEEP is based on the idea of controlling the geographical dimensions of clusters and the distribution of cluster heads. Because of the balanced load among cluster heads, there is no need for frequent reclustering, but after current cluster heads are out of energy, the protocol can rotate the cluster-head position among all the sensor nodes. Also, the identical distance between each pair of neighboring cluster heads leads to convenience in route set-up deployment. After establishing well-distributed cluster heads and clusters in a network, energy-conscious routing is essential in order to set communication routes among cluster heads.

We also covered the *ZigBee technology*, which is based on the IEEE 802.15.4 standard, is a related technology that uses low-power nodes. At the end of the chapter, a simulation case study based on DEEP was presented. The simulation showed the locations of cluster heads and their corresponding nodes.

22.8 Exercises

1. Assume that the maximum line of sight for each node in the sensor network shown in Figure 22.9 is exactly 1 mile. The normalized maximum energy at each node is 20. Assume that 1 mile is scaled down to 1 inch on this map, measured between two centers of circles.

   (a) Apply the cost function presented in Equation (22.15) for the best-energy path.

   (b) Apply the cost function for the shortest path shown in the figure.

2. Suppose a sensor network consisting of 40 sensor nodes formed by clusters each contains five sensor nodes. The sensor network is required to be connected to an LTE cellular phone network and thereby to an ultimate host of an ISP.

   (a) Show a networking sketch of this scenario.

   (b) Assume one of the sensors has discovered a reportable and needs to deliver the sensed information to its base station. Give the detail information contained in the IP packet delivered to the host

22.9 Computer Simulation Projects

1. *Simulation of a Sensor Network.* Consider a field of 100×100 square meters, on which 50 sensor nodes are randomly distributed. Apply DEEP, and use a mathematical tool, such as MATLAB to simulate the clustering process

where each cluster contains five sensor nodes. Randomly use one of the four available levels of energy on each node.

(a) Sketch all clusters and the locations of cluster heads.

(b) Show on the same chart how cluster heads are connected to regular nodes.

2. ***Simulation of a Sensor Network.*** Continue the project from project 1, and now assume that an event is detected by a sensor at the closest cluster to one of the field's corners. Sketch the intercluster routing to a base station situated at the opposite corner from the event cluster.

3. ***Simulation of LEACH Sensor Network.*** Repeat project 2 but this time, but use the LEACH protocol instead.

APPENDIX A

Glossary of Acronyms

AAL	*ATM application layer*
ABR	*Associativity-Based Routing*
ACC	*arriving-cell counter*
AE	*arbitration element*
AES	*Advanced Encryption Standard*
AODV	*Ad-Hoc On-Demand Distance Vector*
APR	*application policy routing*
ARP	*Address Resolution Protocol*
ARQ	*automatic repeat request*
ASCII	*American Standard Code for Information Interchange*
ASN.1	*Abstract Syntax Notation One*
ASP	*application service provider*
ATM	*asynchronous transfer mode*
BISDN	*Broadband Integrated Services Digital Network*
BBC	*buffer-control bit circuit*
BCC	*buffer control circuit*
BCN	*broadcast channel numbers*
BER	*bit error rate*
BGMP	*Border Gateway Multicast Protocol*
BGP	*Border Gateway Protocol*
BPDU	*bridge protocol data unit*
BS	*bit slice*
BTC	*broadcast translation circuit*
CBR	*constant bit rate*

CCITT   *Consultative Committee for International Telephony and Telegraphy*
CCN   *Content-Centric Networking*
CD   *column decoder*
CDMA   *code-division multiple access*
CDN   *content distribution network*
CGSR   *Cluster-head Gateway Switch Routing*
CH   *cluster head*
CIDR   *classless interdomain routing*
CMOS   *complementary metal-oxide semiconductor*
CN   *copy network*
CRC   *cyclical redundancy check*
CSMA   *Carrier Sense Multiple Access*
DEEP   *Decentralized Energy-Efficient Cluster Propagation*
DQDB   *distributed queue dual bus*
DNS   *Domain Name System*
DRR   *deficit round robin*
DS   *differentiated service*
DSDV   *Destination-Sequenced Distance Vector*
DSF   *distributed coordination function*
DSSS   *direct-sequence spread spectrum*
DSR   *Dynamic Source Routing*
DVMRP   *Distance Vector Multicast Routing Protocol*
EDF   *earliest deadline first*
FCFS   *first come, first served*
FDM   *frequency-division multiplexing*
FDMA   *frequency-division multiple access*
FEC   *forward equivalence class*
FHSS   *frequency-hopping spread spectrum*
FIFO   *first in first out*
FOL   *fiber optic link*
FTP   *File Transfer Protocol*
GFC   *generic flow control*
GIF   *Graphics Interchange Format*
GPS   *Global Positioning System*
GSS   *grant signal selector*
GUI   *graphical user interface*
HD   *header decoder*
HDTV   *high-definition television*
HEC   *header error control*
HLR   *home location register*
HTTP   *Hhypertext Transfer Protocol*

IaaS	*Infrastructure as a Service*
ICANN	*Internet Corporation for Assigned Names and Numbers*
ICMP	*Internet Control Message Protocol*
IID	*independent and identically distributed*
IGMP	*Internet Group Management Protocol*
IKE	*Internet Key Exchange*
IMSI	*international mobile subscriber identity*
IPP	*input port processor*
IPv6	*Internet Protocol version 6*
IVR	*interactive voice response*
JPEG	*Joint Photographic Experts Group*
L2TP	*Layer 2 Tunneling Protocol*
LACP	*Link Aggregation Control Protocol*
LBC	*local buffer controller*
LDP	*Label Distribution Protocol*
LEACH	*Low-Energy Adaptive Clustering Hierarchy*
LIB	*Label Information Base*
LLC	*Logical Link Control*
LSP	*label switched path*
LSR	*label switch router*
MAC	*message authentication code*
MAC	*media access control*
MBC	*multipath buffered crossbar*
MBGP	*Multiprotocol extensions for BGP*
MIB	*management information base*
MOSPF	*Multicast Open Shortest Path First*
MPEG	*Moving Picture Experts Group*
MPLS	*multiprotocol label switching*
MSC	*mobile switching center*
MSDP	*Multicast Source Discovery Protocol*
MSN	*Manhattan Street Network*
MSS	*maximum segment size*
MUA	*mail user agent*
NDS	*network data slice*
NFV	*network functions virtualization*
NNI	*network-node interface*
NVT	*network virtual terminal*
OC	*optical carrier*
OCC	*output control circuit*
OD	*output port decoder*
OFDM	*orthogonal frequency division multiplexing*

OPP	*output port processor*
OSI	*Open Systems Interconnection*
OSPF	*open shortest path first*
OXC	*optical cross connect*
PAM	*pulse amplitude modulation*
PCF	*point coordination function*
PDF	*probability density function*
PDU	*protocol data unit*
PFC	*priority field circuit*
PIM	*Protocol Independent Multicast*
PIT	*pending interest table*
PHB	*per-hop behavior*
PMF	*probability mass function*
PSTN	*Public Switched Telephone Network*
PPP	*Point-to-Point Protocol*
PPTP	*Point-to-Point Tunneling Protocol*
PPM	*pulse position modulation*
P2P	*peer to peer*
PWM	*pulse width modulation*
QAM	*quadrature amplitude modulation*
QoS	*quality of service*
QPSK	*Quadrature Phase Shift Keying*
PaaS	*Platform as a Service*
PDU	*protocol data unit*
PON	*passive optical network*
POP3	*Post Office Protocol, version 3*
RARP	*Reverse Address Resolution Protocol*
RCB	*receive buffer*
RCYC	*recycling buffer*
RED	*random early detection*
RIP	*Routing Information Protocol*
RN	*routing network*
RNG	*row number generator*
RPC	*request priority circuit*
RPF	*reverse path forwarding*
RSA	*Rivest, Shamir, and Adelman*
RSQ	*resequencing buffer*
RSVP	*Resource Reservation Protocol*
RTCP	*Real-time Transport Control Protocol*
RTP	*Real-time Transport Protocol*
RTSP	*Real Time Streaming Protocol*

RTT	*round-trip time*
RVC	*request vector circuit*
SaaS	*Software as a Service*
SBC	*shared buffer crossbar*
SCP	*secure copy*
SCTP	*Stream Control Transmission Protocol*
SDC	*self-driven crosspoint*
SDH	*Synchronous Digital Hierarchy*
SDN	*Software-Defined Networking*
SHF	*super-high frequency*
SIP	*Session Initiation Protocol*
SMI	*Structure of Management Information*
SMTP	*Simple Mail Transfer Protocol*
SNMP	*Simple Network Management Protocol*
SNR	*signal-to-noise ratio*
SONET	*Synchronous Optical Networking*
SSH	*Secure Shell*
TCP	*Transmission Control Protocol*
TDM	*time-division multiplexing*
TDMA	*time-division multiple access*
ToR	*top-of-rack*
TOS	*type-of-service*
TORA	*Temporally Ordered Routing Algorithm*
TP	*transport protocol*
TRIP	*Telephony Routing over IP*
UDP	*User Datagram Protocol*
UGC	*upstream grant circuit*
UHF	*ultrahigh frequency*
UPnP	*Universal Plug and Play*
UNI	*User Network Interface*
URI	*Universal Resource Identifier*
URL	*Uniform Resource Locator*
VBR	*variable bit rate*
VCI	*virtual circuit identifier*
VHO	*video hub office*
VLAN	*virtual local area network*
VLR	*visited location register*
VLSI	*very large scale integration*
VM	*virtual machine*
VPI	*virtual path identifier*
VPN	*virtual private network*

VXT   *virtual circuit translation table*
WDM   *wavelength-division multiplexing*
WEP   *Wired Equivalent Privacy*
WFQ   *weighted fair queuing*
WiMAX   *Worldwide Interoperability for Microwave Access*
WMN   *wireless mesh networks*
WRP   *Wireless Routing Protocol*
WTG   *waiting time generator*
WWW   *World Wide Web*
XMB   *transmit buffer*

RFCs

Requests for Comments (RFCs) are an informal series of reports about the computer communication protocols, including TCP/IP and other Internet architectures, wireless and mobile networks, and their history. RFCs are loosely coordinated sets of notes but are rich in information. RFCs are generally available online for public access.

Protocol	RFC
AODV	3561
ARP	826, 903, 925, 1027, 1293, 1329, 1433, 1868, 1931, 2390
ARQ	3366
BGP	1092, 1105, 1163, 1265, 1266, 1267, 1364, 1392, 1403, 1565, 1654, 1655, 1665, 1771, 1772, 1745, 1774, 2283, 4271
BOOTP and DHCP	951, 1048, 1084, 1395, 1497, 1531, 1532, 1533, 1534, 1541, 1542, 2131, 2132
CIDR	1322, 1478, 1479, 1517, 1817
CDN	6707, 6770
DHCP	2131, 2132
DHCP-IPv6	3315

DNS	799, 811, 819, 830, 881, 882, 883, 897, 920, 921, 1034, 1035, 1386, 1480, 1535, 1536, 1537, 1591, 1637, 1664, 1706, 1712, 1713, 1982, 2065, 2137, 2317, 2535, 2606, 2671
Dual-Stack Lite IPv6	4213, 6333
Echo	862
E-mail	822
EPP	3730
FTP	114, 133, 141, 163, 171, 172, 238, 242, 250, 256, 264, 269, 281, 291, 354, 385, 412, 414, 418, 430, 438, 448, 463, 468, 478, 486, 505, 506, 542, 553, 624, 630, 640, 691, 765, 913, 959, 1635, 1785, 2228, 2577, 4217
Gopher	1436
GSSAPI	2743, 2744, 2853
H.323	3508, 4123
HTML	1866
HTTP	1945, 2068, 2109, 2616, 6265, 7230, 7231, 7232, 7233, 7234, 7235
ICMP	777, 792, 1016, 1018, 1256, 1788, 2521
IGMP	966, 988, 1054, 1112, 1301, 1458, 1469, 1768, 2236, 2357, 2365, 2502, 2588, 3376, 4541
IKE	2407, 2408, 2409
IMAP	1730, 2177, 3501
IMAP/POP Authorize	2195
IP	760, 781, 791, 815, 1025, 1063, 1071, 1141, 1190, 1191, 1624, 2113
IP Spoofing	1948
IPv6	1365, 1550, 1678, 1680, 1682, 1683, 1686, 1688, 1726, 1752, 1826, 1883, 1884, 1886, 1887, 1955, 2080, 2373, 2452, 2460, 2463, 2465, 2466, 2472, 2492, 2545, 2590, 4291
IPv6 on IPv4	5969

IRC	1459, 2810, 2811, 2812, 2813
IVR	6231
LTE	6653
MD5	1321
MIB, MIME, IMAP	196, 221, 224, 278, 524, 539, 753, 772, 780, 806, 821, 934, 974, 1047, 1081, 1082, 1225, 1460, 1496, 1426, 1427, 1652, 1653, 1711, 1725, 1734, 1740, 1741, 1767, 1869, 1870, 2045, 2046, 2047, 2048, 2177, 2180, 2192, 2193, 2221, 2342, 2359, 2449, 2683, 2503
Mobile IP	2002, 5944
MPLS	3031
Multicast	1584, 1585, 2117, 2362
MIKEY	3830
NAT	1361, 2663, 2694, 3022, 4787
NFS	3530
NTP	1059, 1119, 1305
OSPF	1131, 1245, 1246, 1247, 1370, 1583, 1584, 1585, 1586, 1587, 2178, 2328, 2329, 2370
OSPF over IPv6	2740
P2P	5128, 5694
PIM	2362
POP3	937, 1939
PPP	1661
RADIUS	2865, 2866
RARP	826, 903, 925, 1027, 1293, 1329, 1433, 1868, 1931, 2390
RIP	1131, 1245, 1246, 1247, 1370, 1583, 1584, 1585, 1586, 1587, 1722, 1723, 2082, 2453
RTP	3550

RTSP	2326
SASL	4422
SCTP	2960, 3257, 3284, 3285, 3286, 3309, 3436, 3554, 3708
SDP	2327
SHA-1, 2	4634
SIP	3261, 3311, 3325, 3841, 4353, 4575, 4579, 6065
SDN	3746, 7149
SDP	2327
SMTP	821, 2822, 2822
SNMP, MIB, SMI	1065, 1067, 1098, 1155, 1157, 1212, 1213, 1229, 1231, 1243, 1284, 1351, 1352, 1354, 1389, 1398, 1414, 1441, 1442, 1443, 1444, 1445, 1446, 1447, 1448, 1449, 1450, 1451, 1452, 1461, 1472, 1474, 1537, 1623, 1643, 1650, 1657, 1665, 1666, 1696, 1697, 1724, 1742, 1743, 1748, 1749
SSH	4251
TCP	675, 700, 721, 761, 793, 879, 896, 1078, 1106, 1110, 1144, 1145, 1146, 1263, 1323, 1337, 1379, 1644, 1693, 1901, 1905, 2001, 2018, 2488, 2580
TELNET	137, 340, 393, 426, 435, 452, 466, 495, 513, 529, 562, 595, 596, 599, 669, 679, 701, 702, 703, 728, 764, 782, 818, 854, 855, 1184, 1205, 2355
TFTP	1350, 1782, 1783, 1784
UDP	768
UPnP	3092, 6970
URI	1630, 1737
URL	1630, 1737, 1738, 3986
VPN	2547, 2637, 2685
Web	1945, 2616, 6455
WWW	1614, 1630, 1737, 1738

APPENDIX C

Probabilities and Stochastic Processes

Communication systems, particularly computer networks, often encounter random arrivals of tasks as packets. Such systems require analysis using the theory of probabilities, as seen in various chapters. This appendix reviews principles of probability theory, random variables, and random processes.

C.1 Probability Theory

Let's first consider a random experiment, such as producing random logic 0s and 1s. The *sample space* of the experiment, usually denoted by the symbol S, consists of the set of all possible *outcomes*, indicated by w. In this case, for integers 0 and 1, the sample space is $S = \{0, 1\}$. We define an *event*, A, to be a subset of sample space, which may consist of any number of sample points. Thus, if we define event A = {1}, the event consists of only one point.

The *union* of two events, A and B, covers all outcomes belonging to both events and is shown by A ∪ B. The *intersection* of events A and B refers to all outcomes shared between the two events and is shown by A ∩ B. The *complement* of event A is an event that covers all events but the ones belonging to A and is shown by Ā.

The probability of an event A is shown by $P[A]$ and always $0 \leq P[A] \leq 1$. Also, if A ∩ B = 0, then:

$$P[A \cup B] = P[A] + P[B]. \qquad (C.1)$$

827

In most engineering cases, especially in analyzing random signals and systems, we are often interested in the conditional probability. The probability that event A occurs given that event B has occurred is defined as

$$P[A|B] = \frac{P[A \cap B]}{P[B]}. \qquad (C.2)$$

Two events A and B are independent of each other if

$$P[A \cap B] = P[A]P[B]. \qquad (C.3)$$

C.1.1 Bernoulli and Binomial Sequential Laws

Two fundamental laws of *sequential experiments* are *Bernoulli* and *binomial* trials. A Bernoulli trial is a sequence of repeated independent random experiments whose outcomes are either a success with probability p or a failure with probability $1 - p$. A binomial trial measures k successes, each with probability p in n independent Bernoulli trials. As a result, the probability of having k successes in n trials is

$$P_n(k) = \binom{n}{k} p^k (1 - p)^{n-k}, \qquad (C.4)$$

where $\binom{n}{k} = \dfrac{n!}{k!\,(n - k)!}$.

C.1.2 Counting and Sampling Methods

One can simply observe that the probability of an event A can also be computed through a counting method by:

$$P[A] = \frac{n_A}{n}, \qquad (C.5)$$

where n_A is the number of outcomes in event A, and n is the total number of outcomes in global sample space.

C.2 Random Variables

Sometimes, the behavior of outcomes in a sample space whose values are real numbers must be considered. A *random variable*, $X(w)$, or simply X, is a function that maps each outcome of the sample space to real numbers. In the previous example,

0 and 1 are real numbers, but they could have been interpreted as "success" and "fail" outcomes. In such a case, the random variable maps them into 0 and 1, respectively.

C.2.1   Basic Functions

Random variables are either *discrete* or *continuous*. In either case, the probability that any type random variable, X, takes a value that does not exceed a given number, x, is called the *cumulative distribution function* (CDF) of X. This is a function of x and is usually denoted by $F_X(x)$:

$$F_X(x) = P[X \leq x].\tag{C.6}$$

For a discrete random variable, we define the *probability mass function* (PMF) to be the probability function of the random variable at any given number x. PMF is denoted by

$$P_X(x) = P[X = x].\tag{C.7}$$

It is obvious that for a discrete random variable X, CDF at any given point x is computed by adding all PMF values up to point x :

$$F_X(x) = \sum_{i\,=\,\text{all values upto } x} P_X(i).\tag{C.8}$$

Similarly, we can define the *probability density function* (PDF) for a continuous random variable to be the probability function of X. PDF is denoted by $f_X(x)$. Similarly, CDF and PDF are associated with each other through

$$F_X(x) = \int_{-\infty}^{x} f_X(x)dx.\tag{C.9}$$

C.2.2   Conditional Functions

We can define the conditional CDF of a random variable X as a CDF given that an event A has already occurred. This CDF is obtained naturally by

$$F_X(x|A) = \frac{P\left[(X \leq x) \cap A\right]}{P[A]}.\tag{C.10}$$

Similarly, the conditional PDF can be defined as

$$f_X(x|A) = \frac{d}{dx}F_X(x|A),\tag{C.11}$$

and the conditional PMF can be defined as

$$P_X(x|A) = \frac{[P(X = x) \cap A]}{P[A]}.$$
(C.12)

C.2.3 Popular Random Variables

Three popular discrete random variables are *Bernoulli, binomial,* and *Poisson* random variables. Three popular continuous random variables are *uniform, Gaussian,* and *exponential.* All are briefly reviewed.

Bernoulli Random Variable

A *Bernoulli random variable* X is discrete and is defined over a sample space of the two real numbers as $S_X = \{0, 1\}$, where 0 and 1 represent, respectively, *failure* with probability $1 - p$ and *success* with probability p. Therefore, PMF of this random variable is defined by

$$P_X(x) = \begin{cases} 1 - p & x = 0 \\ p & x = 1 \end{cases}.$$
(C.13)

Binomial Random Variable

A *binomial random variable* X is discrete and is defined over a sample space $S_X = \{0, 1, \ldots, n\}$. This random variable is basically n Bernoulli random variables, and its PMF is obtained from

$$P_X(x) = \binom{n}{x} p^x (1 - p)^{n-x}.$$
(C.14)

Geometric Random Variable

A *geometric random variable* X is discrete and is defined over a sample space $S_X = \{1, 2, \ldots, x\}$. This random variable is defined for counting x Bernoulli random trials in a binomial random variable with only one success at the last trial. Consequently, its PMF is obtained from

$$P_X(x) = p(1 - p)^{x-1}.$$
(C.15)

Poisson Random Variable

A *Poisson random variable* X is discrete and is defined over a sample space $S_X = \{1, 2, \ldots\}$. This random variable is approximated for a binomial random variable when n is large and p is small. With these conditions, its PMF is obtained from Equation (C.14), taking into account the mentioned approximations:

$$P_X(x) = \frac{\alpha^x e^{-\alpha}}{x!}. \qquad (C.16)$$

Uniform Random Variable

A *uniform random variable* X is continuous and is defined over a sample space $S_X = [a, b]$, where a and b are two constant numbers. PDF of a uniform random variable is obtained from

$$f_X(x) = \frac{1}{b - a}. \qquad (C.17)$$

Exponential Random Variable

An *exponential random variable* X is continuous and is defined over a sample space $S_X = [o, \infty)$. PDF of an exponential random variable is expressed by

$$f_X(x) = \begin{cases} \lambda e^{-\lambda x} & x \geq 0 \\ 0 & x < 0. \end{cases} \qquad (C.18)$$

Gaussian (Normal) Random Variable

A *Gaussian (normal) random variable* X is continuous and is defined over a sample space $S_X = [-\infty, +\infty)$. PDF of an exponential random variable is expressed by

$$f_X(x) = \frac{e^{-(x-E[X])^2/2V[X]}}{\sqrt{2\pi V[X]}}, \qquad (C.19)$$

where $E[X]$ and $V[X]$ are the expected value and the variance of the random variable, respectively.

C.2.4   Expected Value and Variance

For a random variable X, the *expected value* or mean, $E[X]$, is defined as the statistical average of all possible values of the random variable. Thus, for a discrete random variable X taking on values from a total of N possible values, the expected value is

$$E[X] = \sum_{\text{all values of } x} x\, P_X(x). \tag{C.20}$$

The concept is identical for a continuous random variable having infinite points:

$$E[X] = \int_{-\infty}^{\infty} x f_X(x)\, dx. \tag{C.21}$$

We can also define the *variance* of a random variable that gives a measure of how values differ:

$$V[X] = E[(X - E[X])^2]. \tag{C.22}$$

C.2.5   A Function of a Random Variable

If $g(X)$ is a function of X, the expected value of $g(X)$ for a discrete random variable can also be defined as follows:

$$E[g(X)] = \sum_{\text{all values of } x} g(X) P_X(x) \tag{C.23}$$

and for a continuous random variable:

$$E[g(X)] = \int_{-\infty}^{\infty} g(X) f_X(x)\, dx. \tag{C.24}$$

The expected value of a random variable by itself may not be useful for the numerical evaluation of the random variable. The reason is that two random variables with an identical expected value can take on values, each from a totally different range of numbers. The variance can be calculated by using either Equation C.23 or C.24, depending on the type of the random variable.

C.3   Multiple Random Variables

We often encounter several random variables that are related somehow. For example, a random signal as noise enters several circuits, and the outputs of these circuits can form *multiple random variables*. Multiple random variables are denoted by a vector $X = \{X_1, X_2, \ldots X_n\}$.

C.3.1   Basic Functions of Two Random Variables

For two random variables X and Y, the *joint cumulative distribution function* denoted by $F_{X,Y}(x, y)$, the *joint probability mass function* denoted by $P_{X,Y}(x, y)$, and the *joint probability density function*, $f_{X,Y}(x, y)$, are, respectively, derived from:

$$F_{X,Y}(x, y) = P[X \leq x, \ Y \leq y], \tag{C.25}$$

$$P_{X,Y}(x, y) = P[X = x, \ Y = y], \tag{C.26}$$

and

$$f_{X,Y}(x, y) = \frac{\partial^2 F_{X,Y}(x, y)}{\partial x \partial y}. \tag{C.27}$$

We can define the *marginal* CDF of the two random variables as

$$F_X(x) = F_{X,Y}(x, \infty).$$

Similarly, the *marginal* PMF of the two discrete random variables is

$$P_X(x) = \sum_{\text{all ys}} P_{X,Y}(x, y),$$

and the *marginal* PDF of the two continuous random variables is

$$f_X(x) = \int_{-\infty}^{\infty} f_{X,Y}(x, y) \, dy.$$

C.3.2   Two Independent Random Variables

Two random variables are considered independent of each other if one of the following corresponding conditions is met:

$$P_{X,Y}(x, y) = P_X(x)P_Y(y), \tag{C.28}$$

$$f_{X,Y}(x, y) = f_X(x)f_Y(y), \qquad\qquad\qquad (C.29)$$

or

$$F_{X,Y}(x, y) = F_X(x)F_Y(y). \qquad\qquad\qquad (C.30)$$

C.4   Stochastic (Random) Processes

A *stochastic (random) process* is a special version of a random variable that is a function of time. When time is countable, a stochastic process is called *discrete time* and denoted by $X(n, w)$, or $X(n)$, or simply $\mathbf{X}_n$, where n is time. Otherwise, a stochastic process is *continuous time* and is denoted by $\mathbf{X}(t)$, where t is time.

C.4.1   IID Random Process

As an example of discrete-time random processes, consider the *independent and identically distributed* (IID) *random process*. This discrete-time random process is denoted by $\mathbf{X}_n$, in which n "independent" discrete random variables have "identical" CDFs. Therefore, the n random variables X_1, occurring at time 1, all the way to X_n, occurring at time n, make up the random process $\mathbf{X}_n = \{X_1, X_2, \dots, X_n\}$.

C.4.2   Brownian Motion Random Process

The *Brownian motion random process*, also called the *Wiener random process*, is an example of continuous-time random processes. A Brownian motion random process, $\mathbf{X}(t)$, begins at the origin, has zero expected value for all time t, but has a variance that increases linearly with time as

$$E[\mathbf{X}(t)] = 0 \qquad\qquad\qquad (C.31)$$

and

$$V[\mathbf{X}(t)] = \alpha t. \qquad\qquad\qquad (C.32)$$

The PDF of a Brownian motion random process can be approximated by the PDF of a Gaussian (normal) random variable presented in Equation (C.19) as

$$f_X(x) = \frac{e^{-x^2/2\alpha t}}{\sqrt{2\pi\alpha t}}, \qquad\qquad\qquad (C.33)$$

where αt is the variance. For any time increment δ, the increment of a Brownian motion random process, $X(t + \delta) - X(t)$, has a distribution defined by

$$P[\mathbf{X}(t + \delta) - \mathbf{X}(t) \leq x] = \frac{1}{\sqrt{2\pi\delta}} \int_{-\infty}^{x} e^{-y^2/2\delta} dy, \qquad (C.34)$$

using a variance equal to $\alpha t = \delta$. This process is used to capture the nature of batch arrival and bursty traffic (see Chapter 20).

C.5   Theory of Markov Chains

A *Markov process*, $\mathbf{X}_n$, is a stochastic process in which the past state has no impact on the future state if the present state is specified. In other words, in a Markov process, any subsequent behavior of a state is independent of its past activity. We use a state machine called a *Markov chain* to express a Markov process. Therefore, a Markov chain depicts the activities of a Markov process, state by state, which is a convenient way to grasp the essence of the process. Figure C.1 shows a simple Markov chain.

A chain can start from a state 0 and move toward an ending state, if there is one. The chain in this figure shows three sample states on a Markov chain: $i - 1$, a past state; i, the present state; and $i + 1$, a future state. These three states are connected through their associated probabilities, shown in the figure. Markov chains are also classified as either *discrete time* or *continuous time*.

C.5.1   Continuous-Time Markov Chains

In a continuous-time Markov chain based on a random process, $\mathbf{X}(t)$, the transition probabilities occur in a very short period of time, δ. Assuming $\alpha_{i,\,i}$ to be the rate at

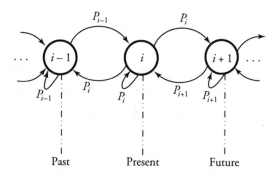

Figure C.1   A simple Markov chain

which the process leaves state i, the probability that the process remains in state i during δ is estimated as

$$P_{i,i} = P[T_i > \delta] = e^{\alpha_{i,i}\delta}$$

$$= 1 - \frac{\alpha_{i,i}\delta}{1!} + \frac{(\alpha_{i,i}\delta)^2}{2!} - \ldots \approx 1 - \alpha_{i,i}\delta. \qquad (C.35)$$

When it leaves state i, the process enters state j with probability $\pi_{i,j}$. Thus, the probability that the process remains in state j during δ is

$$P_{i,j} = (1 - P_{i,i})\pi_{i,j}. \qquad (C.36)$$

Combining Equations (C.35) and (C.36), we derive

$$P_{i,j} = \alpha_{i,i}\delta\pi_{i,j} = \alpha_{i,j}\delta, \qquad (C.37)$$

where $\alpha_{i,j} = \alpha_{i,i}\,\pi_{i,j}$ is the rate at which process $\mathbf{X}(t)$ moves from state i to state j. If we divide Equations (C.35) and (C.37) by δ and take a limit, we get

$$\begin{cases} \lim_{\delta \to 0} \left(\dfrac{P_{i,i} - 1}{\delta} \right) = \alpha_{i,i} \\[2mm] \lim_{\delta \to 0} \left(\dfrac{P_{i,j}}{\delta} \right) = \alpha_{i,j} \end{cases}. \qquad (C.38)$$

To find a state j probability of the process at a given time t denoted by $P_j(t) = P[X(t) = j]$, we can elaborate further:

$$P_j(t + \delta) = P[\mathbf{X}(t + \delta) = j] = \sum_i P[\mathbf{X}(t + \delta) = j | \mathbf{X}(t) = i]\, P[\mathbf{X}(t) = i]$$

$$= \sum_i P_{i,j} P_i(t). \qquad (C.39)$$

By subtracting $P_j(t)$ from both sides of this equation, dividing them by δ, taking a limit of $\delta \to 0$, and applying the Equations in (C.38), we can derive

$$P_j'(t) = \sum_{i \neq j} \alpha_{i,j}\, P_i(t). \qquad (C.40)$$

This is an important result, known as the *Chapman-Kolmogorov equation* on continuous-time Markov chains. This equation clearly deals with the differential operation of a state probability with respect to time t.

APPENDIX D

Erlang-B Blocking Probability Table

In Section 11.4.4 of Chapter 11, we learned how a system with a resources and no queueing line can be blocked using the Erlang-B formula. Resources in communication networks can be channels, servers, or any other factors or entities. As a result of the discussion in this section, we studied the well-known Erlang-B formula derived by Equation (11.46). This equation provided us with blocking probability in any system, p_a, given that there are a resources in the system with system utilization $\rho_1 = \lambda/\mu$. In such systems, traffic arrival rate is λ, and the service rate is μ.

The following table provides a numerically expanded version of the Erlang-B formula using the three varying parameters: number of channels (a), which is shown in the left column; blocking probability of the system (p_a), indicated in the first row; and the system utilization (ρ_1) that varies in the table given the other two parameters.

Appendix D. Erlang-B Blocking Probability Table

Number of Channels (a)	Blocking Probability (p_a)												
	0.01%	0.05%	0.1%	0.5%	0.6%	0.7%	0.8%	0.9%	1.0%	2.0%	3.0%	4.0%	5.0%
1	0.0	0.0	0.0	0.0	0.0	0.0	0.0	0.0	0.0	0.0	0.0	0.0	0.1
2	0.0	0.0	0.0	0.1	0.1	0.1	0.1	0.1	0.2	0.2	0.3	0.3	0.4
3	0.1	0.2	0.2	0.3	0.4	0.4	0.4	0.4	0.5	0.6	0.7	0.8	0.9
4	0.2	0.4	0.4	0.7	0.7	0.8	0.8	0.8	0.9	1.1	1.3	1.4	1.5
5	0.5	0.6	0.8	1.1	1.2	1.2	1.3	1.3	1.4	1.7	1.9	2.1	2.2
6	0.7	1.0	1.1	1.6	1.7	1.8	1.8	1.9	1.9	2.3	2.5	2.8	3.0
7	1.1	1.4	1.6	2.2	2.2	2.3	2.4	2.4	2.5	2.9	3.2	3.5	3.7
8	1.4	1.8	2.1	2.7	2.8	2.9	3.0	3.1	3.1	3.6	4.0	4.3	4.5
9	1.8	2.3	2.6	3.3	3.4	3.5	3.6	3.7	3.8	4.3	4.7	5.1	5.4
10	2.3	2.8	3.1	4.0	4.1	4.2	4.3	4.4	4.5	5.1	5.5	5.9	6.2
11	2.7	3.3	3.7	4.6	4.7	4.9	5.0	5.1	5.2	5.8	6.3	6.7	7.1
12	3.2	3.9	4.2	5.3	5.4	5.6	5.7	5.8	5.9	6.6	7.1	7.6	7.9
13	3.7	4.4	4.8	6.0	6.1	6.3	6.4	6.5	6.6	7.4	8.0	8.4	8.8
14	4.2	5.0	5.4	6.7	6.8	7.0	7.1	7.2	7.4	8.2	8.8	9.3	9.7
15	4.8	5.6	6.1	7.4	7.6	7.7	7.9	8.0	8.1	9.0	9.6	10.2	10.6
16	5.3	6.2	6.7	8.1	8.3	8.5	8.6	8.7	8.9	9.8	10.5	11.1	11.5
17	5.9	6.9	7.4	8.8	9.0	9.2	9.4	9.5	9.7	10.7	11.4	12.0	12.5
18	6.5	7.5	8.0	9.6	9.8	10.0	10.1	10.3	10.4	11.5	12.2	12.9	13.4
19	7.1	8.2	8.7	10.3	10.6	10.7	10.9	11.1	11.2	12.3	13.1	13.8	14.3
20	7.7	8.8	9.4	11.1	11.3	11.5	11.7	11.9	12.0	13.2	14.0	14.7	15.2
21	8.3	9.5	10.1	11.9	12.1	12.3	12.5	12.7	12.8	14.0	14.9	15.6	16.2

N													
22	8.9	10.2	10.8	12.6	12.9	13.1	13.3	13.5	13.7	14.9	15.8	16.5	17.1
23	9.6	10.9	11.5	13.4	13.7	13.9	14.1	14.3	14.5	15.8	16.7	17.4	18.1
24	10.2	11.6	12.2	14.2	14.5	14.7	14.9	15.1	15.3	16.6	17.6	18.4	19.0
25	10.9	12.3	13.0	15.0	15.3	15.5	15.7	15.9	16.1	17.5	18.5	19.3	20.0
26	11.5	13.0	13.7	15.8	16.1	16.3	16.6	16.8	17.0	18.4	19.4	20.2	20.9
27	12.2	13.7	14.4	16.6	16.9	17.2	17.4	17.6	17.8	19.3	20.3	21.2	21.9
28	12.9	14.4	15.2	17.4	17.7	18.0	18.2	18.4	18.6	20.1	21.2	22.1	22.9
29	13.6	15.1	15.9	18.2	18.5	18.8	19.1	19.3	19.5	21.0	22.1	23.0	23.8
30	14.2	15.9	16.7	19.0	19.4	19.6	19.9	20.1	20.3	21.9	23.1	24.0	24.8
31	14.9	16.6	17.4	19.9	20.2	20.5	20.7	21.0	21.2	22.8	24.0	24.9	25.8
32	15.6	17.3	18.2	20.7	21.0	21.3	21.6	21.8	22.0	23.7	24.9	25.9	26.7
33	16.3	18.1	19.0	21.5	21.9	22.2	22.4	22.7	22.9	24.6	25.8	26.8	27.7
34	17.0	18.8	19.7	22.3	22.7	23.0	23.3	23.5	23.8	25.5	26.8	27.8	28.7
35	17.8	19.6	20.5	23.2	23.5	23.8	24.1	24.4	24.6	26.4	27.7	28.8	29.7
36	18.5	20.3	21.3	24.0	24.4	24.7	25.0	25.3	25.5	27.3	28.6	29.7	30.7
37	19.2	21.1	22.1	24.8	25.2	25.6	25.9	26.1	26.4	28.3	29.6	30.7	31.6
38	19.9	21.9	22.9	25.7	26.1	26.4	26.7	27.0	27.3	29.2	30.5	31.6	32.6
39	20.6	22.6	23.7	26.5	26.9	27.3	27.6	27.9	28.1	30.1	31.5	32.6	33.6
40	21.4	23.4	24.4	27.4	27.8	28.1	28.5	28.7	29.0	31.0	32.4	33.6	34.6
41	22.1	24.2	25.2	28.2	28.6	29.0	29.3	29.6	29.9	31.9	33.4	34.5	35.6
42	22.8	25.0	26.0	29.1	29.5	29.9	30.2	30.5	30.8	32.8	34.3	35.5	36.6
43	23.6	25.7	26.8	29.9	30.4	30.7	31.1	31.4	31.7	33.8	35.3	36.5	37.6
44	24.3	26.5	27.6	30.8	31.2	31.6	31.9	32.3	32.5	34.7	36.2	37.5	38.6

(Continued)

Number of Channels (a)	Blocking Probability (p_a)												
	0.01%	0.05%	0.1%	0.5%	0.6%	0.7%	0.8%	0.9%	1.0%	2.0%	3.0%	4.0%	5.0%
45	25.1	27.3	28.4	31.7	32.1	32.5	32.8	33.1	33.4	35.6	37.2	38.4	39.6
46	25.8	28.1	29.3	32.5	33.0	33.4	33.7	34.0	34.3	36.5	38.1	39.4	40.5
47	26.6	28.9	30.1	33.4	33.8	34.2	34.6	34.9	35.2	37.5	39.1	40.4	41.5
48	27.3	29.7	30.9	34.2	34.7	35.1	35.5	35.8	36.1	38.4	40.0	41.4	42.5
49	28.1	30.5	31.7	35.1	35.6	36.0	36.4	36.7	37.0	39.3	41.0	42.3	43.5
50	28.9	31.3	32.5	36.0	36.5	36.9	37.2	37.6	37.9	40.3	41.9	43.3	44.5
51	29.6	32.1	33.3	36.9	37.3	37.8	38.1	38.5	38.8	41.2	42.9	44.3	45.5
52	30.4	32.9	34.2	37.7	38.2	38.6	39.0	39.4	39.7	42.1	43.9	45.3	46.5
53	31.2	33.7	35.0	38.6	39.1	39.5	39.9	40.3	40.6	43.1	44.8	46.3	47.5
54	31.9	34.5	35.8	39.5	40.0	40.4	40.8	41.2	41.5	44.0	45.8	47.2	48.5
55	32.7	35.3	36.6	40.4	40.9	41.3	41.7	42.1	42.4	44.9	46.7	48.2	49.5
56	33.5	36.1	37.5	41.2	41.7	42.2	42.6	43.0	43.3	45.9	47.7	49.2	50.5
57	34.3	36.9	38.3	42.1	42.6	43.1	43.5	43.9	44.2	46.8	48.7	50.2	51.5
58	35.1	37.8	39.1	43.0	43.5	44.0	44.4	44.8	45.1	47.8	49.6	51.2	52.6
59	35.8	38.6	40.0	43.9	44.4	44.9	45.3	45.7	46.0	48.7	50.6	52.2	53.6
60	36.6	39.4	40.8	44.8	45.3	45.8	46.2	46.6	46.9	49.6	51.6	53.2	54.6

Index

4G, 258, 581

A

Abort chunks, 737
ABR (Associative-Based Routing) Protocol, 775–776
Abstract syntax notation one (ASN.1) language, 359
Access networks in IPTV, 747
Access points, 139–140
Accounting, network management for, 358
Accuracy of routing algorithms, 162
ACK frames, 148
ACK/NAK process in DHCP, 169
Acknowledgment (ACK) field, 299, 301, 304, 338
Acknowledgment number field, 299
ACMs (address release messages), 646
Acronyms, 817–822
Active attacks, 783
Ad-hoc networks, 245
    MANETs. *See* Mobile ad-hoc networks
        (MANETs)
    WMN support for, 279
Ad Hoc On-Demand Distance Vector (AODV)
        protocol
    new nodes for, 782–783
    route discovery and establishment in, 778–781
    route maintenance in, 781–782
    routing process in, 778–779
Adaptability of routing algorithms, 162
Adapters for ARP, 132
Adaptive modulation, 284
Adaptive protocols, 768
Adaptive reservation schemes, 500

Additional information field, 329–330
Additive increase, multiplicative decrease (AIMD)
        congestion control, 309–311
Address autoconfiguration procedure, 266–267
Address field, 147
Address family identifier field, 186
Address mapping in DNS, 327–329
Address release messages (ACMs), 646
Address Resolution Protocol (ARP), 39, 130–132
Addresses
    distributed hash table objects, 353
    Internet, 21–22
    IP. *See* IP addresses
    MAC, 21–22, 130–133, 153
    in mobile IP, 260–261
    routing tables. *See* Routing tables
Admission control, 494–495
Admission in RAS signaling, 657
ADSL (asymmetric DSL), 56
ADUs (application data units), 728
Advanced Encryption Standard (AES) protocol,
        379–380
Agent address field, 361
Agents
    mobile IP, 260–261
    network management, 358
    SIP, 671–683
Aggregate switches, 130, 589
Aggregate technique in CIDR, 27
Aggregation, link, 107–109
AIMD (Additive increase, multiplicative decrease)
        congestion control, 309–311